Midterm #1
- Ch 1, 2, 4, 5, 7
- p. 458 - 464 (attachment)

Instructor Praise for *The Personality Puzzle*

"Quite simply, it was an outstanding book and it made teaching personality an enjoyable and intellectually engaging experience."
—*Brent Donnellan, Michigan State University*

"The book as a whole reads like a smart, articulate, experienced personality psychologist thinking about the field. . . . It helps students think about the issues rather than just memorizing underlined concepts without understanding anything. I wish more psychology books were like this one."
—*Phillip R. Shaver, University of California, Davis*

"Students consistently tell me (without my asking) that this is a very readable text and they actually enjoy reading it. In fact, this term many of my students are saying this is the most readable psychology text they've had."
—*Tani McBeth, Portland Community College*

"[M]any of my ex-students have remarked that the Funder text is one of the few psychology textbooks that remain on their bookshelves."
—*Krista Phillips, York University, Toronto, Canada*

"I think this is the best, most readable textbook not just in personality, but in psychology in general. This is such a fun book to read."
—*Shigehiro Oishi, University of Virginia*

Student Praise for *The Personality Puzzle*

"*Personality Puzzle* . . . is the best textbook I have ever read in university (I am only in second year, but I've gone through lots of books already!)! I just cannot seem to put your wonder of a book down."
—*Tammy Fichman, student, York University, Toronto, Canada*

"My husband saw me laughing while reading the book and he asked me to share the cartoons with him. Anytime I shared a cartoon with him I also had to quickly summarize the topic those cartoons were illustrating. The 're-telling' of the context of the cartoon helped me to better learn the concepts in the book."
— *Maria Parra, student, University of California, Los Angeles*

"Without a doubt, it's the best textbook I've ever read. You write in plain English. The examples you've given clearly illustrate all the concepts. You inform the reader of both sides of an issue. . . . And (best of all) you write with an amazing amount of wit."
—*Brian Abend, student, Middlebury College*

"For some reason, at 1:3o in the morning, from the east coast, I'm compelled to inform you that your textbook may be one of the most interesting and informative textbooks I've had the good fortune to read. Aside from capturing a tremendously interesting subject in a very captivating way, reading it is simply entertaining."
—*Nate Birky, student, Lehigh University*

"Your book reads almost like a novel; I sometimes don't want to put it down. I would credit your book partly with my interest in becoming a psychology major."
—*Jonathan Hill, student, University of Virginia*

THE
PERSONALITY PUZZLE

FIFTH EDITION

THE PERSONALITY PUZZLE

FIFTH EDITION

DAVID C. FUNDER

University of California, Riverside

W. W. NORTON & COMPANY
New York · London

W. W. Norton & Company has been independent since its founding in 1923, when William Warder Norton and Mary D. Herter Norton first published lectures delivered at the People's Institute, the adult education division of New York City's Cooper Union. The firm soon expanded its program beyond the Institute, publishing books by celebrated academics from America and abroad. By midcentury, the two major pillars of Norton's publishing program—trade books and college texts—were firmly established. In the 1950s, the Norton family transferred control of the company to its employees, and today—with a staff of four hundred and a comparable number of trade, college, and professional titles published each year—W. W. Norton & Company stands as the largest and oldest publishing house owned wholly by its employees.

Editor: Sheri Snavely
Associate editor: Sarah England
Project editor: Carla L. Talmadge
Production manager: Benjamin Reynolds
Marketing manager: Amber Chow
Editorial assistants: Josh Bisker, Wamiq Jawaid
Managing editor, College: Marian Johnson
Book designer: Judith Abbate
Art directors: Lissi Sigillo, Rubina Yeh
Photo editor: Stephanie Romeo
Media editor: Dan Jost
Ancillaries editor: Matthew A. Freeman
Composition: Dooen Books LLC
Art file adjustment: Jay's Publishers Services
Illustrations: John McAusland
Manufacturing: The Courier Companies—Westford, MA
Cover design: Gearbox

Library of Congress Cataloging-in-Publication Data

Funder, David Charles.
  The personality puzzle / David C. Funder. — 5th ed.
      p. cm.
  Includes bibliographical references and index.
  ISBN 978-0-393-93348-2 (hardcover)
  1. Personality. I. Title.
  BF698.F84 2010
  155.2—dc22
                                   2009043812

W. W. Norton & Company, Inc., 500 Fifth Avenue, New York, NY 10110
      www.wwnorton.com

W. W. Norton & Company Ltd., Castle House, 75/76 Wells Street, London W1T 3QT

2 3 4 5 6 7 8 9 0

For my father

ABOUT THE AUTHOR

DAVID C. FUNDER is Distinguished Professor of Psychology and former chair of the department at the University of California, Riverside. Winner of the 2009 Jack Block Award for Distinguished Research in Personality, he is a former editor of the *Journal of Research in Personality* and a former associate editor of the *Journal of Personality and Social Psychology*. He is best known for his research on personality judgment and has also published research on delay of gratification, attribution theory, the longitudinal course of personality development, and the psychological assessment of situations. He has taught personality psychology to undergraduates at Harvey Mudd College, Harvard University, and the University of Illinois, Urbana-Champaign, and continues to teach the course every year at the University of California, Riverside.

Anybody in science, if there are enough anybodies, can find the answer—it's an Easter-egg hunt. That isn't the idea. The idea is: Can you ask the question in such a way as to facilitate the answer?

—GERALD EDELMAN

Even if, ultimately, everything turns out to be connected to everything else, a research program rooted in that realization might well collapse of its own weight.

—HOWARD GARDNER

The first step is to measure whatever can easily be measured. That's OK as far as it goes. The second step is to pretend that whatever cannot be easily measured isn't very important. That's dangerous. The third step is to pretend that whatever cannot easily be measured doesn't exist. That's suicide.

—DANIEL YANKELOVICH

There once was an entomologist who found a bug he couldn't classify—so he stepped on it.

—ERNEST R. HILGARD

Interpretation is the revenge of the intellect upon art.

—SUSAN SONTAG

CONTENTS IN BRIEF

CONTENTS

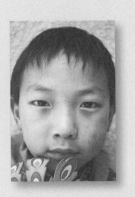

PREFACE

THE WAY A COURSE in personality psychology should be taught—and the way its textbook should be written—depends on its purpose. Therefore, any instructor or author needs to ask at the outset, what do I hope to accomplish? Several different answers are possible, all of them legitimate. Each implies a different approach to teaching and to textbook writing.

The Goals for a Personality Course

First, an instructor might wish to ensure that every student becomes deeply familiar with the classic theories of personality and learns to appreciate the history of, and the intellectual connections between, these theories. Such a course in personality can be an important part of a liberal education and fit easily into a "great books" curriculum. This goal is well served by any of the hefty theoretical tomes that have been on the market for many years. But at the end, students sometimes have little idea of what modern personality psychology is all about.

A second, very different goal is for students to learn the current activities of modern research psychologists and all of the latest findings. The classic theories typically are neglected when this goal is pursued, sometimes on the grounds that all of the old theories are false and only modern empirical research offers anything worth teaching. (I have actually heard psychology professors say this.) Several recent books seem to have been written with this goal in mind.

However, the modern empirical literature is not an infallible source of ultimate truth. Moreover, a textbook or course that focuses exclusively on what modern personality psychologists do is limited to whatever topics current research happens to emphasize. I do not know that any of the answers that psychology has provided are eternal, but some of the questions are—and some of those questions are neglected in modern research.

This book serves both of the goals just listed. It covers the main theories of personality and traces some relevant intellectual history. It also includes

"As a matter of fact, I confess to modest hopes—not wildly unfounded, I trust—that my book may resonate beyond the reaches of academe."

a large amount of current research, including recent work on biology, cross-cultural psychology, and cognitive processes relevant to personality. But the goal that has driven this book, above all other goals, is to convince the reader that personality psychology matters. To the extent that, after reading the final page, the reader walks away believing that personality psychology is intellectually exciting and provides valuable insights into real-life concerns, this book—and, perhaps the personality course of which it may be a part—will have accomplished what it set out to do.

Personality and Life

To convince somebody new to the field that personality psychology matters, an instructor must teach each basic approach in a form that is relevant not just to its historical antecedents or to current research, but to everyday life. That is exactly what I have tried to do in this book. The result is a presentation that strays from the conventional versions of the basic approaches to personality in favor of a new and modern rendition of each.

This strategy is applied most obviously in the chapters on Freud, where I present a psychoanalytic approach that certainly stems from Freud but departs from orthodoxy in numerous ways and in the end, may not really be Freud anymore. Someone who wants to learn in detail what Freud really said should read a different book. But someone who wants to see how some derivations from Freud's basic ideas can be presented in what I think is a fairly convincing contemporary context might find this book illuminating. Parallel comments could be made about the presentations of the other approaches.

The humorist Dave Barry once wrote a history of the United States that he touted as more interesting than any other because, he said, it left out all of the boring parts. While I have not gone that far, I have freed myself of the obligation to cover topics just because they are "there," or are traditional, or are covered in every other book on personality. I also have included quite a bit of material on topics that some other books either underemphasize or neglect entirely. These topics include person perception, biology (including anatomy, physiology, genetics, and evolutionary theory), cross-cultural studies, and personality disorders.

The Organization of This Book

In broad outline, this book follows a traditional organization according to theories, or paradigms (I usually call them "approaches"). It begins with a treatment of research methods, and then considers the basic approaches to personality: trait, biological, psychoanalytic, phenomenological, learning, and cognitive. The learning and cognitive process chapters are contained in a single section, as the latter approach grew directly out of the former and the two approaches overlap in many ways. The cognitive approaches are presented in two chapters, one of which covers processes associated with perception, thought, motivation, and emotion, and the other of which focuses on the psychological structure called the self. The book concludes with an integrative summary of the personality disorders.

Some of my colleagues believe that a paradigmatic organization like this is outdated and should be replaced by a scheme organized around topics such as aggression, or development, or achievement. The components of the traditional paradigms presumably would be scattered across these chapters. The suggested model seems to be social psychology, which in its courses and textbooks almost always follows such a topical organization.

There are several reasons why I believe a topical organization is a mistake for a personality text (and it is interesting to note that some authors who tried this approach abandoned it in later editions). A pragmatic reason is that the basic approaches are complex theoretical systems, and breaking them up across topics seems unlikely to yield a clear understanding of any of them. A more substantive reason is that the topical organization of social psychology represents an intellectual deficit of that field, as compared with personality psychology, rather than any sort of advantage. Social psychology lacks even one organizing theoretical approach with any scope, as far as I am aware; it organizes itself by topic because it must. Personality psychology, by contrast, has at least six approaches, each of which offers an organized way to cover a wide range of data and theory.

A further reason became clearer as I worked on this book. In personality, a "topics" organization and a "basic approaches" organization are not, at a deep level, truly different. A consistent theme throughout this book is that the basic approaches to personality are not different answers to the same question—they are different questions! To make this point another way, each of the basic approaches has a few topics it addresses most centrally and many others it ignores. The basic topics ignored by each approach tend to be central concerns of one or more of the other approaches. As a result, a "basic approaches" organization is a topics organization, to a considerable degree, because each approach focuses on different topics.

Individual differences = the trait approach
Biological influences = the biological approach
Psychodynamics and the unconscious = the psychoanalytic approach
Experience and awareness =
                                    the phenomenological-humanistic approach
                                        (I include cross-cultural psychology here.)
Behavioral change = the learning approach
Perception and thinking = the cognitive process approach

I hope this organizational scheme makes this textbook easy to use. It matches in broad outline the way most personality courses are taught already. Beyond that, it should not be hard for an instructor using this text to find places where she or he wishes to amplify, supplement, or disagree.

I present my own opinions throughout this book, sometimes quite strongly. I have no interest in writing a "plain vanilla" book that plays it safe. But I have tried limit the opinions I express to psychological issues where I have relevant training and experience, where it might make sense to take seriously what I think. On other issues, I have tried to be more circumspect. For example, the debate over abortion is considered in Chapter 14 (in the context of a discussion of individualist versus collectivist values). A student told me that she read that section and couldn't figure out what my own position was. Good.

An instructor who disagrees with some of my opinions on psychological matters—and surely nobody will agree with me on everything—should be able to put together compelling lectures about those disagreements. The result of this intellectual give-and-take between instructor and author could be, for the student, an exciting introduction to a fascinating subject. Such an exchange would also teach the student that the material presented in textbooks is not infallible truth, and deserves to be questioned. This lesson might be one of the most valuable of the student's entire college education.

Changes in the Fifth Edition

The progress of personality psychology is accelerating. An increasing number of students and researchers are attracted to the field, including those originally trained in other subfields who have discovered that the study of personality allows them to best address the issues that interest them the most. As a result, the large amount of new research is increasing in quality as well as in quantity. Now, in my fourth go-round revising this book, I am still surprised every time by how much new material needs to be included.

For example, the trait approach, too often limited in the past by an overly exclusive dependence on self-report methodology, is suddenly filled with studies that assess personality through direct behavioral observations, physiological measurements, and imaginative indicators such as music preference and the state of one's bedroom. The biological approach is moving beyond simple reductionism toward developing research programs that appreciate the complex interactions among biological systems, and between the biological systems inside the body and the larger social world outside. Psychoanalytic ideas are busily creeping into other areas of the field, especially the cognitive process approach; while such ideas sometimes get relabeled in the process of rediscovery, it is fascinating to watch formerly fringe concepts like the unconscious and attachment become routine topics for research. Humanistic psychology was almost dead at the time of the First Edition of this book, though I believed then that many of its ideas (and the philosophy behind them) were important to understand anyway. Suddenly, there has been an explosion of interest in "positive psychology" and related topics that amounts to a rebirth of the field. Cross-cultural psychology is another rapidly developing area. Research on cross-cultural issues is not only much more active, but it has also become theoretically richer and methodologically innovative, and in very recent work has begun to emphasize ways in which psychological processes may be common to people from different cultures, even when the visible outcomes of these processes are different. The study of cognitive processes has accelerated along with the rest of the field, as it gathers new insights concerning perception, thought, motivation, emotion, and the nature of the self. Finally, research on personality disorders—once clearly treated separately as a topic of abnormal psychology—is becoming increasingly integrated with mainstream personality psychology as more and more psychologists come to see these disorders as extensions of normal-range personality traits, rather than as separate and unique phenomena.

The Fifth Edition reflects these changes. In addition to continued attempts to make the writing clearer and more interesting, a large amount of new and important research is included in almost every chapter. This is particularly true of the chapters on the biology of personality (8 and 9) and cross-cultural psychology (14), two fields that continue to move so fast that it's hard to keep up. New material includes an updated summary of research on the neural correlates of personality processes using fMRI and other brain-imaging techniques, and some of the recent controversy concerning what this research really means. The Fifth Edition also includes new research on how the self-concept might vary across cultural contexts. Other prominent changes in other chapers include an expanded treatment of new developments in positive psychology, new research on the behavioral correlates of personality traits, and an expanded summary of how the important contributions of attachment theory derive from the fundamental tenets of psychoanalysis.

The most obvious change in the Fifth Edition is the look and feel of this book, which came from a major design project conducted at W. W. Norton and initiated by the editor, Sheri Snavely. The purpose of the new pictures and figures is to emphasize and clarify important points while making the overall reading experience more enjoyable. So I have worked closely with the designers to try to make sure that every picture, every figure, and even every cartoon (yes, we still have cartoons) makes a point. Pay special attention to the cartoons. One perceptive student e-mailed to tell me that her husband asked her why she was laughing while reading a previous edition. She showed him the cartoons and explained how each one was relevant. In that way, the student reported, she better learned some of the key concepts in the book! Indeed, every cartoon is there for a reason. Even the penguin in Chapter 18.

We have also expanded the support materials for the new Fifth Edition:

- The **Norton Personality Psychology in the News DVD** features nearly an hour of ScienCentral News profiles of recent research in personality psychology topics from peer-reviewed journals. Designed to relate research findings to students' lives in a concise, accessible, and engaging format, the Norton Personality Psychology in the News DVD serves as an excellent presentation tool in the lecture hall or classroom. The Norton Personality Psychology in the News DVD is available to qualified adopters only.
- The **Instructor's Manual**, which I have now authored for five editions, has been revised to coordinate with the addition of new material, research, and updated figures to the text.
- A **Test Bank**, authored by Brent Donnellan (Michigan State University) and Michael Furr (Wake Forest University), has an updated pool of available questions and has been reorganized so that questions are classified by difficulty and according to a taxonomy of educational objectives. This new reorganization of the Test Bank makes it easy for instructors to construct quizzes and exams that are meaningful and diagnostic according to their wishes.

- *The Personality Puzzle*, Fifth Edition, is accompanied by a comprehensive set of **PowerPoint lecture slides**, which integrate the art, photos, and cartoons from the text with lecture notes and examples aimed to engage students and enhance presentations. The art and photos from the book are also available separately in slide and image file format for instructors to integrate into their own lecture slide materials.

- Based on proven learning strategies, *The Personality Puzzle*, Fifth Edition, **StudySpace student Web site** contains assignments that will help students organize their study, learn essential course material, and connect knowledge across chapters and concepts. Every Study-Space contains free and open study tools such as chapter quizzes, vocabulary flash cards, and chapter reviews, as well as links to *The Personality Puzzle*, Fifth Edition, ebook.

- *The Personality Puzzle*, Fifth Edition, **ebook** provides students with a low-cost textbook option and incorporates links to review materials on the Student StudySpace. The ebook also offers many useful reading tools, such as text highlighting, search functions, and digital sticky notes to help students study more effectively.

- Dan Ozer and I are also pleased to announce that a new edition of our reader, ***Pieces of the Personality Puzzle***, Fifth Edition, will also be available for fall 2010 courses, with a number of interesting new readings included. The reader can be packaged for a substantial discount with *The Personality Puzzle* to help save students some money.

We hope that all of these support materials help instructors to teach a successful course.

Acknowledgments

It is with pleasure that I acknowledge some of the help I received with this project over the years and five editions. First of all, my wife, Patti, has been a source of emotional support, clever ideas, and critical comments throughout the process. Her insights and her skepticism about whether psychology is really a science (she was trained as a molecular biologist) continue to keep me on my toes.

Tiffany Wright (a graduate student at the University of California, Riverside), Chris Langston (a colleague), and Cathy Wick (a former editor at Norton) read the First Edition of this book and made many comments and suggestions, most of which I followed. The encouragement and advice of

Paul Rozin was particularly important, and Henry Gleitman was also generous. Traci Nagle carefully copyedited the First Edition, and a little of the prose on which she worked so hard still survives. Mary N. Babcock made an equally important contribution to the Second Edition, Anne Hellman to the Third, Sarah Mann to the Fourth, and Susan Middleton to the Fifth. Don Fusting, a former Norton editor, used the softest sell in the history of publishing to convince me to undertake this project in the first place. If not for him, this book would not exist.

When Sheri Snavely came on board as editor for the Fifth Edition, it felt like this book gained a whole new life. I am grateful for her creative ideas, good judgment, collaborative spirit, and most of all for her understanding of and enthusiasm for the distinctive kind of book *The Personality Puzzle* has strived to be. In every sense of the phrase, she "gets it." I am also appreciative of the hard work by Stephanie Romeo and Sarah England on the illustrations and design program, to Wamiq Jawaid and Josh Bisker for keeping track of a terrifying number of small details, and to Carla Talmadge for running a tight ship and keeping everything on schedule. Finally, there is no point to writing and producing a book if nobody reads it. So I am grateful to Ken Barton not only for his past advice and support, but also for helping to make the book available to readers in the United Kingdom and Europe, and to Amber Chow for her persistent travels throughout North America for the same purpose.

For this and previous editions, I was aided by the wise and knowledgeable advice of the following people:

PREVIOUS EDITIONS

Susan Basow, Lafayette College
Veronica Benet-Martínez, University of California, Riverside
Diane S. Berry, Southern Methodist University
Mia Biran, Miami University (Ohio)
Dan Boroto, Florida State University
Turhan Canli, State University of New York, Stony Brook
Brent Donnellan, Michigan State University
Peter Ebersole, California State University, Fullerton
William K. Gabrenya, Florida Institute of Technology
Jeremy Gray, Yale University
Cindy Hazan, Cornell University
Todd Heatherton, Dartmouth College
Robert Hessling, University of Wisconsin, Milwaukee
D. Brett King, University of Colorado, Boulder

Ricardo Michan, Loyola Marymount University
Dan Molden, Northwestern University
Yozan Mosig, University of Nebraska, Kearney
Denise Newman, University of Virginia
Aaron L. Pincus, Pennsylvania State University
Brian Marx, Temple University
Julie Norem, Wellesley College
Steven Richards, Texas Tech University
Rick Robbins, University of California, Davis
Joseph F. Rychlak, Loyola University of Chicago
Gerard Saucier, University of Oregon
Michele M. Tomarelli, Texas A & M University
Jeanne Tsai, Stanford University
Drew Westen, Emory University
David Williams, University of Pennsylvania
David Zald, Vanderbilt University
Marvin Zuckerman, University of Delaware

FIFTH EDITION

Sarah Angulo, Texas State University, San Marcos
Nicole B. Barenbaum, University of the South
Turhan Canli, State University of New York, Stony Brook
Colin G. DeYoung, University of Minnesota
Brent Donnellan, Michigan State University
Alisha Janowsky, University of Central Florida
Zlatan Krizan, Iowa State University
David Matsumoto, San Francisco State University
Tani McBeth, Portland Community College
Joshua Miller, University of Georgia
Douglas Mook, University of Virginia
Shigehiro Oishi, University of Virginia
Krista Phillips, York University
Janice L. Rank, Portland Community College
Steve Reise, University of California, Los Angeles
Brent Roberts, University of Illinois, Urbana-Champaign
Phillip Shaver, University of California, Davis
Kennon Sheldon, University of Missouri
Karen K. Szumlinski, University of California, Santa Barbara
Brian Tschanz, Utah State University
Simine Vazire, Washington University in St. Louis

I also have been gratified by the way I continue to receive many e-mails from students. Some of these messages arrive late at night—apparently the readers of this book and its author keep the same hours. Many have included useful questions, suggestions, and corrections that I have incorporated into this edition. More than one challenged me on key points, and if those who wrote them look closely at this edition, they will see that they had an effect. But that wasn't even the best part. I can't adequately express how encouraging it is for an author bogged down at one in the morning to have his computer suddenly beep, yielding an e-mail that says, "I really enjoyed your book and just wanted to say thanks." Thank *you*.

Finally, I want to acknowledge the very first person who read the first draft of the First Edition all the way through. He wrote comments on nearly every page. Usually, they were notations such as "What does this mean?" or "What are you talking about?" These invariably identified places where I had lapsed into incomprehensible jargon or otherwise failed to make sense. Sometimes his comments were just strong expressions of agreement or disagreement. Over the several years that I worked on the First Edition, I never once had a conversation with him that did not include the question, "How is the book coming along?" and some sort of suggestion that I really ought to be working faster. He looked forward to seeing this book in print and didn't miss it by much. My father, Elvin Funder, died in August 1995, just as I was putting the finishing touches on the First Edition. For the Second through Fifth Editions, I have had to imagine what he would say about some of my observations, but even that was helpful. I rededicate this book to him.

David C. Funder

June 2009

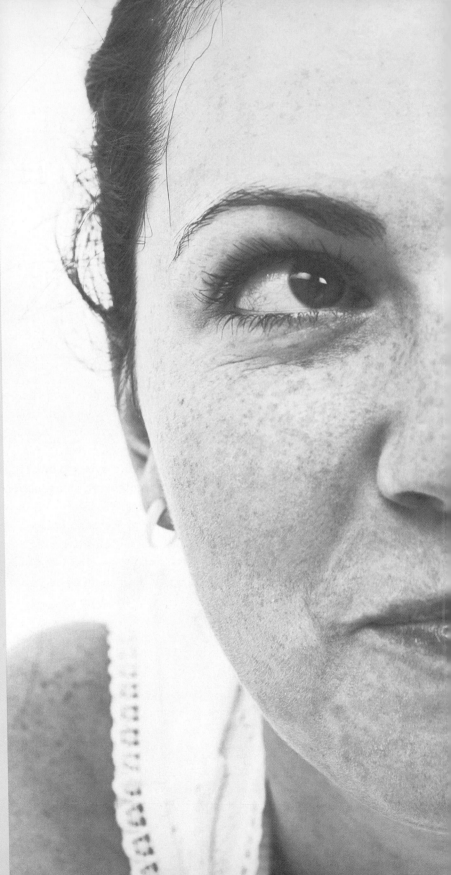

THE STUDY OF
THE PERSON

All persons are puzzles until at last we find in some word or act the key
to the man, to the woman: straightaway all their past words and actions
lie in light before us.

—RALPH WALDO EMERSON

YOU MAY ALREADY have been told that psychology is not what
you think it is. Some psychology professors delight in conveying
this surprising news to their students on the first day of the term.
Maybe you expect psychology to be about what people are thinking and feeling under the surface, these professors expound; maybe you think it is about
sexuality, and dreams, and creativity, and aggression, and consciousness,
and how people are different from one another, and interesting topics like
that. Wrong, they say. Psychology is about the precise manipulation of independent variables for the furtherance of compelling theoretical accounts of
well-specified phenomena, such as how many milliseconds it takes to find
a circle in a field of squares. If that focus makes psychology boring, well, too
bad. Science does not have to be interesting to be valuable.

Fortunately, most personality psychologists do not talk that way. This
is because the study of personality comes close to what nonpsychologists
intuitively expect psychology to be, and addresses the topics most people
want to know about (J. Block, 1993; Funder, 1998b). Therefore, personality
psychologists have no excuse for being boring. Their field of study includes
everything that makes psychology interesting.[1]

Specifically, personality psychology addresses all three parts of the **psychological triad**, the combination of how people think, feel, and behave.

---

[1] Thus, if you end up finding this book boring, it is all my fault. There is no reason it should be,
given its subject matter.

Each of these phenomena is important in its own right, but they are even more interesting in combination, especially when they conflict. For example, have you ever experienced a conflict between how you feel and what you think, such as an attraction toward someone you just *knew* was bad news? Have you ever had a conflict between what you think and what you do, such as intending to do your homework and then going to the beach instead? Have you ever found your behavior conflicting with your feelings, such as doing something that makes you feel guilty (fill in your own example here), and then continuing to do it anyway? If so (and I know the answer is yes), the next question is, why? The answer is far from obvious.

Inconsistencies between thoughts, feelings, and behaviors are common enough to make us suspect that the mind is not a simple place and that even understanding yourself—the person you know best—is not necessarily easy. Personality psychology is important not because it has solved these puzzles of internal consistency and self-knowledge, but because—alone among the sciences and even among the branches of psychology—personality psychologists regard these puzzles as worth their full attention.

When most people think of psychologists, they think first of the clinical practitioners who treat mental illness and try to help people with a wide range of other personal problems.[2] Personality psychology is not the same as clinical psychology, but the two subfields do overlap. Some of the most important personality psychologists—both historically and in the present day—had clinical training and treated patients. At many colleges and universities, the person who teaches the courses in abnormal or clinical psychology also teaches personality. When patterns of personality are extreme, unusual, and cause problems, the two subfields come together in the study of personality disorders. Most important, clinical and personality psychology share the obligation to try to understand whole persons, not just parts of persons, one individual at a time.

In this sense, personality psychology is the largest as well as the smallest subfield of psychology. There are probably fewer doctoral degrees granted in personality psychology than in social, cognitive, developmental, or biological psychology. But personality psychology is closely allied with clinical psychology, which is by far the largest subfield. Personality psychology is where the rest of psychology comes together; as you will see, personality

> Inconsistencies between thoughts, feelings, and behaviors are common enough to make us suspect the mind is not a simple place.

---

[2] This is why nonclinical research psychologists sometimes cringe a little when someone asks them what they do for a living.

psychology draws heavily from social, cognitive, developmental, clinical, and biological psychology. It contributes to each of these subfields as well, by showing how each part of psychology fits into the whole picture of what people are really like.

THE GOALS OF PERSONALITY PSYCHOLOGY

Personality refers to an individual's characteristic patterns of thought, emotion, and behavior, together with the psychological mechanisms—hidden or not—behind those patterns. This definition gives personality psychology its unique mission to explain whole persons. Of course, personality psychologists may not always succeed at this job. But that is what they are supposed to be doing—putting together the pieces of the puzzle contributed by the various other subfields of psychology, as well as by their own research, to assemble an integrated view of whole, functioning individuals in their daily environments.

Mission: Impossible

There is only one problem with this mission: It is impossible. In fact, this interesting mission is the source of personality psychology's biggest difficulty. If you try to understand everything about a person at once, you will immediately find yourself completely overwhelmed. Your mind, instead of attaining a broad understanding, may go blank.

The only way out is to choose to limit what you look at. Rather than trying to account for everything at once, you must search for more specific patterns—ways of tying together different kinds of observations. This search will require you to limit yourself to certain kinds of observations, certain kinds of patterns, and certain ways of thinking about these patterns. A systematic, self-imposed limitation of this sort is what I call a **basic approach** (another commonly used term is *paradigm*).

Some personality psychologists focus their efforts on the ways that people differ psychologically and how these differences might be conceptualized and measured. They follow the **trait approach** (the reference is to personality traits). Other psychologists try to understand the mind in terms of the body. That is, they address biological mechanisms such as anatomy,

[handwritten margin note: because one cannot understand everything about a person at once]

physiology, genetics, even evolution, and their relevance for personality. These psychologists follow the **biological approach**. Another group of psychologists is concerned primarily with the unconscious mind, and the nature and resolution of internal mental conflict. These psychologists follow the **psychoanalytic approach**. Other psychologists focus on people's conscious experience of the world, their phenomenology, and follow a **phenomenological approach**. In current research, an emphasis on awareness and experience can lead in one of two directions. The first is a program of theory and research, called *humanistic psychology*, that pursues how conscious awareness can produce such uniquely human attributes as existential anxiety, creativity, and free will, and tries to understand the meaning and basis of happiness. The other phenomenological direction emphasizes the degree to which psychology and the very experience of reality might vary across cultures, leading to an explosion in recent years of research on *cross-cultural* psychology.

Still other psychologists follow the **learning approach**: they concentrate on the ways people change their behavior as a result of rewards, punishments, and other experiences in life, a process called **learning**.[3] Classic *behaviorists* focus tightly on overt behavior and the ways it can be affected by rewards and punishments. Behaviorism was amended by a related subgroup of scientists who study *social learning*. Social learning theory attempts to draw inferences about the ways that mental processes such as observation and self-evaluation determine how behaviors are learned and performed. In the past few years, social learning theory has evolved into an influential and prolific new field of personality research focused on cognitive processes, applying insights and methods derived from the study of perception, memory, and thought. Taken together, behaviorism, social learning theory, and *cognitive personality psychology* comprise the learning and cognitive processes approaches to personality, which can also be described as the study of what personality does.

Competitors or Complements?

The different approaches to personality are often portrayed as competitors, and for good reason. The original, famous protagonist of each typically made his mark by announcing to the world that his approach finally accounted for

---

[3] This narrow use of the term *learning* by behaviorists should not be confused with its broader everyday meaning.

Figure 1.1 Freud and Skinner Sigmund Freud and B. F. Skinner each claimed that his perspective accounted for everything one might want to know about personality.

everything anybody would ever want to know about human nature, and that all other approaches were worthless. Sigmund Freud, for one, was vocal in claiming that his version of the psychoanalytic approach was the one true path, and even ostracized erstwhile followers, such as Carl Jung, who dared to differ with him on seemingly minor points. B. F. Skinner, with his very different view of human nature, was not much of an improvement in the modesty department. He announced that behaviorism explained everything relevant to psychology, and he delighted in denouncing all of the other approaches and their presumptions that people might have traits and thoughts, or even freedom and dignity.

This kind of arrogance is not limited to approaches like psychoanalysis and behaviorism that have been closely associated with famous individual founders. Biologically inclined psychologists have been known to proclaim that everything about personality reduces to a matter of genes, physiology, and brain anatomy. And trait, cognitive, and humanistic psychologists likewise sometimes have insisted their approach is the one that covers it all. In fact, major advocates of every basic approach have claimed frequently and insistently not only that their favored approach can explain everything, but also that the others are all dead wrong.

Claims like these certainly seem effective, and perhaps they are even necessary to garner attention to a point of view. But their rhetorical smoke

Each approach has its own contribution to psychology.

screen obscures an important fact. It is not obligatory, and I believe it is not helpful, to regard these approaches as mutually exclusive and forever locked in competition. They complement rather than compete with each other because each addresses a different set of questions about human psychology.

An employer trying to decide whom to hire, for instance, must compare individuals. The employer's problem is addressed by the trait approach. When a televangelist is arrested for soliciting prostitutes, questions might be raised about his motivation, especially at the unconscious level; a psychoanalytic approach seems appropriate here. A parent who is worried about aspects of a teenager's behavior and how best to make a difference probably needs a behavioral approach. A philosopher contemplating the vicissitudes of free will, or even a student considering career plans and musing on the meaning of life, might find some useful insights in the humanistic approach. And so on. Each approach to personality psychology can be useful for handling its own key concerns.

At the same time, each one typically and rather disconcertingly tends to ignore the key concerns of the other approaches (and, as I already mentioned, typically denies they are even important). For example, psychoanalysis has a lot to say about the origin of dreams, but contributes next to nothing to our understanding of behavior change. On the other hand, the principles of behaviorism can be used to teach your dog an amazing variety of tricks but will never explain why she sometimes barks and whines in her sleep.

Distinct Approaches Versus the One Big Theory

By now, the following question may have occurred to you: Why doesn't somebody come up with One Big Theory (you could call it the OBT) that explains everything now accounted for separately by trait, biological, psychoanalytic, humanistic, behavioral, and cognitive approaches? Maybe someday somebody will—and if you become a personality psychologist, it could be you!

In the meantime, you might consider a time-honored principle of engineering: A device that does one thing well tends to be relatively poor at doing anything else. A toaster that makes excellent toast is totally worthless if what you really need is to make coffee or listen to music. The converse, equally true, is that a device that does many things at the same time will probably do none of them especially well. A combination toaster, coffeemaker, and clock radio—I am sure somewhere there really is such a thing—will probably not be as good at toasting bread, making coffee, or playing music as a more modest appliance that aspires to serve only one of these functions. This principle seems also to be true within psychology, as it describes the inevitable trade-off faced by personality theorists. A theory that accounts for certain things extremely well will probably not explain everything else so well. And a theory that tries to explain almost everything—the OBT—would probably not provide the best explanation for any one thing. Maybe dreams, learning curves, free will, and individual differences in job performance could all be squeezed into one theory, but the result might not be a pretty sight.

I will return to these issues in the final chapter, but for now let me assure you that if you are confused, you are in good company. Personality psychologists have worked on this dilemma for decades and still have not come to a solution that satisfies everybody. Some really would like to develop the OBT that explains everything at least fairly well. A surprising number believe that their own currently favored approach *is* the OBT (they are wrong). Others, instead of developing a whole new theory, would like to organize all the current approaches into a single elegant framework (e.g., Mayer, 1998, 2005). Still others, like me, persist in believing that the different basic approaches address different sets of questions, and that each approach has the best answers for the questions it has chosen to address.

If you agree with—or at least understand—this final belief, then you will appreciate why this book for the most part considers each basic approach separately.[4] Personality psychology needs to look at people from all of these directions and utilize all of these approaches because different issues—for example, dreams, learning curves, and individual differences in job performance, as I just mentioned—are best viewed from different perspectives. For the present, I believe it is most useful to teach and apply these approaches one at a time and in their entirety. Perhaps someday they will become fully integrated. In the meantime, as you will see, each approach has many interesting, important, and useful things to say about the aspects of personality on which it has chosen to focus.

Advantages as Disadvantages and Vice Versa

In the introduction to his novel *Mother Night*, Kurt Vonnegut does his readers the unusual service of telling them the moral of the book they are about to read. "I don't think it's a marvelous moral," he writes, "I just happen to

---

[4]The major exception to this practice will come near the end, in Chapter 18, where I draw on various approaches when considering the personality disorders.

know what it is" (Vonnegut, 1966, p. v). My guess is that he hoped to save hundreds of English classes thousands of hours of trying to figure out what he "meant to say." (I doubt he succeeded.)[5]

As a writer I do not much resemble Vonnegut (though I wish I did), but I too think I know the moral of my book, or at least one of its major themes: In life and in psychology, advantages and disadvantages have a way of being so tightly interconnected as to be inseparable. *Great strengths are usually great weaknesses, and surprisingly often the opposite is true as well.* Sometimes I enjoy calling this observation **Funder's First Law** (there will be several other such "laws" in this book).[6] This first law applies to fields of research, theories, and individual people.

Personality psychology provides an excellent example of Funder's First Law. As I already noted, personality psychology's biggest advantage over other areas of psychology is that it has a broad mandate to account for the psychology of whole persons and real-life concerns. This mandate makes the study of personality more inclusive, interesting, important, and even more fun than it would be otherwise. But guess what? This mandate is also personality psychology's biggest problem. In the wrong hands it can lead to overinclusive or unfocused research. Even in the best hands, personality psychology can seem to fall far short of what it ought to accomplish. The challenge for a personality psychologist, then, is to maximize the advantages of the field's broad mandate and try to minimize the disadvantages, even though the two are related and perhaps inseparable.

The same is true about the various approaches within personality psychology. Each is good at addressing certain topics and extremely poor at addressing others. Actually, as we have already discussed, each basic approach usually ignores the topics it is not good at explaining. For example, behaviorism is so effective at changing behavior in part because it ignores everything else, whereas the phenomenological approach is able to offer a coherent account of free will because it ignores how reinforcements can shape behavior. The good points come with—and are even sometimes a consequence of—the bad points, and vice versa.

---

[5] For the record, Vonnegut wrote that the moral of *Mother Night* is that "we are what we pretend to be, so we must be careful about what we pretend to be" (Vonnegut, 1966, p. v). Come to think of it, this would not be a bad moral for a psychology textbook.

[6] Please don't memorize these laws. I haven't memorized them myself. They are just my attempt to distill a few of my favorite observations into fortune-cookie-sized sayings.

This connection between strengths and weaknesses can even occur within individuals. According to one analysis, the personality and ethical "flaws" of several presidents of the United States were precisely the same attributes that allowed them to attain and effectively use power (Berke, 1998). For example, a certain amount of shiftiness—generally considered a character flaw—might enable a president to respond flexibly to changing circumstances. A certain amount of stubbornness—also usually considered a flaw—might enable a president to remain steadfastly committed to important principles. On the other hand, some traits usually considered virtues, such as truthfulness and consistency, might sometimes actually be a handicap in trying to be an effective president.

The same principle may apply to other areas of life, such as basketball coaching. Bobby Knight, the longtime coach at Indiana University (and later at Texas Tech), was once described as vulgar, sarcastic, and intimidating—and also, in the same newspaper article, as "loyal, intelligent, charitable, and [a] principled perfectionist who graduates more players than most college basketball coaches" (T. Jones, 2003, p. 6E). Are these two aspects of Knight's character connected? They certainly are, in the sense that they belong to the same person; a college that hires one of these Bobby Knights gets the other one for free. A deeper sense in which they are connected is that *everybody's* personality comes as a package deal. Personality is coherent, and each part stems from and depends on the others (J. Block, 2002).

You may or may not ever become president or a Big 10 basketball coach yourself, but take a moment and think about your own strongest point. Is it

Figure 1.2 **Great Strengths Can Be Great Weaknesses** President Nixon's devious nature allowed him to surprise the world with a breakthrough in relations with China, but also led to the Watergate scandal that drove him from office.

*"Do you mind if I say something helpful
about your personality?"*

ever a problem for you? Now think about your own weakest point. What are its benefits for you? Given the necessary trade-offs, would you really like to lose all of your weaknesses and keep all of your strengths? Given the way your strengths and weaknesses are interconnected, is this even possible?

Personality psychology is perpetually faced with a similar dilemma. If its scope were narrowed, the field would be more manageable and research would become easier. But then the study of personality would lose much of what makes it distinctive, important, and interesting. Similarly, each basic approach to personality has made a more or less deliberate decision to ignore some aspects of psychology. This is a heavy cost to pay, but so far it seems to be necessary in order for each approach to make progress in its chosen area.

THE PLAN OF THIS BOOK

This book begins with a brief introduction and an overview of personality psychology that you have almost finished reading. The next two chapters concern how personality psychologists do their research, and will be useful for understanding the chapters that follow. Chapter 2 describes the different kinds of *data*, or information, that psychologists use to better understand personality, and discusses some of the advantages and disadvantages of each kind. The chapter's goal is to indelibly engrave the following idea into your psyche: *There are no perfect indicators of personality; there are only clues, and clues are always ambiguous.*[7] Chapter 3 describes some of the ways these data can be analyzed and considers several issues particular to the analysis of personality data.

The second section comprises four chapters that address how people differ from one another, the central concern of the trait assessment approach. Chapter 4 discusses the basic question of whether differences between peo-

---

[7] This is actually Funder's Second Law, which won't be officially introduced until Chapter 2.

ple significantly influence behavior and important life outcomes. (*Hint*: the answer is yes.) Chapter 5 describes several ways in which psychologists measure such differences, the topic of *personality assessment*. Chapter 6 carries that topic further by describing research on *personality judgment*—how we all assess personality in our daily lives. Chapter 7 describes specific examples of how personality traits have been used to understand behavior, and discusses how traits develop over the life span.

An exciting new direction in psychological research is emerging from rapid advances in biology. These discoveries are increasingly applied to the study of personality traits and human nature, and some of that research is surveyed in Chapters 8 and 9. Chapter 8 reviews current knowledge about how the architecture and physiology of the nervous system affect behavior and personality. Chapter 9 considers the possibility that personality is inherited to some degree, by looking at two branches of biology: *behavioral genetics*, which studies how parents might pass on personality traits to their offspring, and *evolutionary psychology*, which tries to find the origins of human nature in the evolutionary history of the species.

The next three chapters consider the psychoanalytic approach, closely identified with Freud. Chapter 10 is a basic introduction to psychoanalysis that describes the structure of the mind and psychological development. Chapter 11 describes how psychoanalytic theory addresses defense mechanisms, mistakes, and humor, and offers an evaluation of this perspective. Chapter 12 concludes the story of psychoanalysis by bringing it into the present day, with some consideration of the neo-Freudians (psychoanalysts who came after Freud), object relations theory, attachment theory, and modern research relevant to psychoanalytic ideas.

The next pair of chapters considers the topics of thought, experience, and existence. Chapter 13 describes how the phenomenological aspects of existential philosophy that emphasize individual experience developed into an approach called humanistic psychology. The theme is that an individual's particular worldview or way of understanding reality is the central aspect of her personality. Chapter 14 takes this phenomenological point one step further, by considering how individuals' personalities and worldviews—and maybe the whole notion of personality itself—may vary across cultures.

The next three chapters describe behaviorism and later approaches to personality that emphasize the cognitive and perceptual processes underlying what personality does. About 70 years ago, several influential psychologists decided to focus on what people (and animals) do rather than on what might be going on in the hidden recesses of their minds. The original psychologists who took this approach were the classic behaviorists such as John Watson and B. F. Skinner. Over the later decades of the 20th century, three different derivative theories grew out of behaviorism—theories focused on social interaction and cognitive (mental) processes. Interestingly, all three—the theories of John Dollard and Neal Miller, Julian Rotter, and Albert Bandura—were called "social learning theory." Walter Mischel added a cognitive and phenomenological flavor to social learning theory to produce a version that is currently influential. Behaviorism and the various social learning theories are described in Chapter 15. Over time, these theories became increasingly influenced by the rapidly developing field of cognitive psychology. The resulting research applies some of the concepts and methods of cognitive psychology to personality, and adds insights from the other basic approaches to consider topics including perception, memory, motivation, and emotion, summarized in Chapter 16, and the collection of thoughts and feelings called *the self*, discussed in Chapter 17.

As a way of summing up and using what we have learned, the last substantive chapter in the book considers the extremes of individual differences that are called the personality disorders. The major disorders and some of their implications are discussed in Chapter 18. The very last chapter, Chapter 19, offers an overall evaluation of the different perspectives of personality psychology, revisits some of the issues raised in this chapter, and offers a brief summary of what I hope you will remember long after reading this book.

PIGEONHOLING VERSUS APPRECIATION OF INDIVIDUAL DIFFERENCES

Personality psychology tends to emphasize how individuals are different from one another. A critic who wanted to use a pejorative term could even say that personality psychology tends to "pigeonhole" human beings. Some people are uncomfortable with this emphasis on categorization, perhaps because they find it implausible, undignified, or both.[8]

Other areas of psychology, by contrast, are more likely to treat people as if they are the same or nearly the same. Not only do the various experimental subfields of psychology, such as cognitive and social psychology, tend to

---

[8] I cannot help recalling the old saying that there are two kinds of people in the world: those who think there are two kinds of people in the world, and those who don't.

ignore differences, but also the statistical analyses central to their research literally put individual differences into their "error" terms (see Chapter 3).

But here is yet another example of a potential disadvantage working as an advantage. (Remember that this process can work in either direction, according to Funder's First Law.) Although the emphasis of personality psychology often entails categorizing and labeling people, it also leads the field to be extraordinarily sensitive—more sensitive than any other area of psychology—to the fact that people really are different from each other. We do not all like the same things, we are not all attracted to the same people (fortunately), and we do not all want to enter the same occupation or pursue the same goals in life (again, fortunately). This fact of individual differences is the starting place for all of personality psychology and gives the field a distinctive and humanistic mission of appreciating the uniqueness of each individual.[9] People are different, and it is necessary as well as natural to wonder how and why.

SUMMARY

The Goals of Personality Psychology

- Personality psychology's unique mission is to address the psychological triad of thought, feeling, and behavior, and to try to explain the psychological functioning of whole individuals. This is an impossible mission, however, so different approaches to personality must limit themselves by emphasizing different psychological topics.

- Personality psychology can be organized into five basic approaches: trait, biological, psychoanalytic, phenomenological, and learning and cognitive processes. Each addresses certain aspects of human psychology quite well and ignores others. The advantages and disadvantages of each approach are probably inseparable.

The Plan of This Book

- This book is grouped into six sections, beginning with a section on research methods and continuing with five sections that survey the basic approaches to personality. It ends with a chapter on the personality disorders and a final summing up.

---

[9] The focus on individual differences is obvious in the trait and psychoanalytic approaches to personality, which concentrate, respectively, on the quantitative measurement of individual differences and on individual psychological case studies. But less obviously, it is also true—even especially true—about behaviorism, which sees the person as the product of a unique learning history and therefore like nobody else (see Chapter 15).

Pigeonholing Versus Appreciation of Individual Differences

- Sometimes regarded as a field that seeks to pigeonhole people, personality psychology's real mission is to appreciate the ways in which each individual is unique.

THINK ABOUT IT

1. What do we know when we know a person?
2. What is the purpose of psychology? What questions should the science of psychology seek to answer?
3. Why are you taking this course? What do you hope to learn? Of what use do you expect it to be?
4. If you could choose what this course (or book) would be about, what would you ask for? Why?
5. Are psychology textbooks and courses more boring than they should be? If so, why do you think that is? Can something be done about it? Should something be done about it? (Perhaps "boring" just means that a complex topic is being rigorously studied. Do you agree?)
6. Which is more important, answers or questions?

EMEDIA

 Go to StudySpace, wwnorton.com/studyspace, to access additional review and enrichment materials.

PART I

RESEARCH METHODS

A colleague of mine once was choosing what to teach in a general psychology course. She decided to poll her students to find out what they wanted to learn, and listed all the standard topics. One scored so low it wasn't even funny. The all-time least-favorite topic in psychology is . . . research methods.

This finding helps explain why students so often think their psychology professors are strange. Almost without exception, the people who are trained to do psychological research and who teach most college courses seem obsessed with methods. In course after course, hours if not days are spent talking about statistics, data, and research design, leaving some students to wonder, not unreasonably, "What does any of this have to do with psychology?" They might even begin to suspect that they are the victims of a diabolical plot to turn psychology—a topic that should be easy and fun—into something difficult and boring.

Part of the reason for this, I think, is that research methods are often taught in a narrow and needlessly technical manner that is almost guaranteed to be discouraging. Rules, procedures, and formulas may be thrown at the student with wild abandon and scant explanation until, in a sea of confusion, the unfortunate student loses sight of the whole purpose. So, in the next two chapters, I will emphasize two points. First: the basic principles of research methods are neither obscure nor impossibly technical. Second: it is only natural that somebody who wants to learn more about psychology should find methods both interesting and useful.

To see what I mean, let's imagine an acquaintance who claims he can read minds—he has ESP. Would you be curious to find out whether he really can? Maybe not (what *does* it take to pique your interest?). But if you are, then the next question is, how would you find out? Maybe you can think of a few procedures that would test his claim. You might have him guess which playing card you are thinking of, for example. You might even do this several times and keep track of his right and wrong answers. Suddenly, by choosing which questions to ask and how to ask them, you have ventured into the realm of research design. In effect, you have designed an experiment. By writing down the number of right and wrong answers, you have gathered data. And by interpreting the numbers obtained (Do 12 right answers out of 20 qualify as ESP?), you have ventured into the world of statistics! Yet all you have done is apply some good common sense to find out something interesting.

That is what research methods are supposed to do: apply good sense to gather information in order to learn more about questions of interest. The only way to find out something new—about behavior, the mind, or anything else—is to fol-low a set of procedures that begins with observation—looking at what you want to know about—and ends with data analysis, which means trying to summarize and understand the observations you have recorded.

Chapter 2 presents a detailed account of the kinds of observations that are relevant to understanding personality. All observations are data, and these can be categorized into four basic kinds, called S, I, L, and B data (which when rear-ranged yield the cheerful but misspelled acronym BLIS).

Chapter 3 summarizes some issues about the quality of data—their reliability, validity, and generalizability. Chapter 3 also addresses *research design*, which is the plan for gathering data, and the issue of data analysis I believe to be the most important: how to interpret the effect size, or strength, of the results that your research has obtained. Finally, Chapter 3 considers ethics in research, an issue relevant to psychology and every other branch of science.

2

Data Are Clues

Four Kinds of Clues
- Ask the Person Directly: S Data
- Ask Somebody Who Knows: I Data
- Life Outcomes: L Data
- Watch What the Person Does: B Data
- Mixed Types of Data

No Infallible Indicators of Personality

CLUES TO PERSONALITY:
The Basic Sources of Data

MANY YEARS AGO, the prominent personality psychologist Henry Murray commented that in order to understand personality, first you have to look at it. This is a pretty obvious statement, but like many obvious statements, when thought about carefully it raises an interesting question. If you want to "look at" personality, what do you look at, exactly? The answer to this question is the topic of this chapter.

I maintain that to look at an individual's personality, you can do four different things. First, and perhaps most obviously, you can ask the person directly for her own opinion about what she is like. This is exactly what personality psychologists usually do. Second, you can find out what other people who know the person well say about her. Third, you can check on how the person is faring in life. And finally, you can observe what the person does and try to measure her behavior as directly and objectively as possible.

In the end, you need to look at personality in all of these ways, because personality is complicated. It is manifested by all of the characteristic ways in which the individual thinks, feels, and behaves—the psychological triad mentioned in Chapter 1. An individual might be deeply afraid of certain things, or attracted to particular kinds of people, or obsessed with accomplishing some highly personal and idiosyncratic goals. Patterns of thought, emotion, and behavior such as these typically are complex and may be revealed in many different areas of behavior and life. Therefore, when you try to learn about or measure personality, you cannot rely on just one kind of information. You need many kinds.

This brings us to **Funder's Second Law**: *There are no perfect indicators of personality; there are only clues, and clues are always ambiguous.*

[handwritten margin note: Observable personality aspects = clues]

[handwritten margin note: psychologist = detective]

[handwritten margin note: —Ignoring clues that "may provide misleading results" = silly.]

DATA ARE CLUES

The observable aspects of personality are best characterized as clues. These clues are always ambiguous because personality resides hidden inside each individual. Because you can never see personality directly, you must infer both its existence and its nature, and these inferences are forever uncertain.

Inferences about personality must be based on indications that can be observed. These might include how a person answers questions, what the person says to his psychotherapist, the behaviors the person performs in daily life, or how he responds to certain situations set up in a laboratory. The clues can be almost anything, but it is important to remember that any one of them, by itself, will always be ambiguous. The psychologist's task is to piece these clues together, much like pieces of a puzzle, to form a clear and useful portrait of the individual's personality.

In that sense, a psychologist trying to understand an individual's personality is a bit like a detective solving a mystery: clues may abound, but the trick is to interpret them correctly. For example, a detective arriving on the scene of a burglary finds fingerprints on the windowsill and footprints in the flower bed. These are clues. The detective would be foolish to ignore them. But it might turn out that the fingerprints belong to a careless police officer, and the footprints belong to an innocent gardener. These possibilities are not reasons for the detective to ignore the clues, but they are reasons to be wary about their meaning.

The situation is similar for a personality psychologist. The psychologist might look at an individual's behavior, test scores, degree of success in daily living, or responses to a laboratory procedure. These are possible clues about personality. The psychologist, like the detective, would be foolish not to gather as many as possible. Also like the detective, the psychologist should maintain a healthy skepticism about the possibility that some or all of them might be misleading.

But this skepticism should not go too far. It can sometimes be tempting to conclude that because one kind of clue might be uninformative or misleading, it should be ignored. At different times, various psychologists have argued that self-report questionnaires, demographic data, peers' descriptions of personality, projective personality tests, summaries of clinical cases, or certain laboratory assessment procedures should never be used. The reason given? The method might produce misleading results.

No competent detective would think this way. To ignore a source of data because it might be misleading would be like ignoring the footprints in the garden because they might not belong to the burglar. A much better strategy is to gather all the clues you can with the resources you have. Any of these clues might be misleading; on a bad day, they all might be. But this is no excuse to not gather them. The only alternative to gathering information that might be misleading is to gather no information. That is not progress.

Funder's Third Law, then, is this: *Something beats nothing, two times out of three.*

FOUR KINDS OF CLUES

"Are you just pissing and moaning, or can you verify what you're saying with data?"

Four general kinds of clues can be used to understand personality. Each provides vital information, but equally important, each has shortcomings as well. The advantages and shortcomings are probably inseparable (remember Funder's First Law). Before we begin, it is worth emphasizing once again that all of these clues are important and useful, though none is perfect. The imperfections are inevitable and are not a reason to ignore any of these sources of information. Instead, they are precisely the reason you need all of them.

The principle behind the clues is that to find out what a person is like, you can do four different things: (1) You simply ask the person for her own evaluation of her personality; (2) you ask her acquaintances for their evaluations; (3) you see how the person is faring in life; or (4) you watch, as directly as you can, what the person actually does. These four types of clues can be called S, I, L, and B data (see Table 2.1).[1] As you will see, each of them is potentially informative about personality, and each is potentially misleading.

---

[1] If you have read the writing of other psychologists or even the earlier editions of this book, you may notice that these labels keep changing, as do, in subtle ways, the kinds of data to which they refer. Jack Block (J. H. Block & J. Block, 1980) also propounded four types of data, calling them L, O, S, and T. Raymond Cattell (Cattell, 1950, 1965) propounded three types called L, Q, and T. Terri Moffitt (Moffitt, 1991; Caspi, 1998) proposed five types, called S, T, O, R, and I (or STORI). In most respects, Block's L, O, S, and T data match my L, I, S, and B data; Cattell's L, Q, and T data match my L (and I), S, and B data; and Moffitt's T and O match my B, and her R, S, and I match my L, S, and I, respectively. But the definitions are not exactly equivalent across systems. For a detailed typology of B data, see Furr (in press).

Table 2.1

ADVANTAGES AND DISADVANTAGES OF THE MAIN SOURCES OF DATA FOR PERSONALITY

	Advantages	Disadvantages
S data: Self-reports	Large amount of information Access to thoughts, feelings, and intentions Some S data are true by definition (e.g., self-esteem) Causal force Simple and easy	Maybe they can't tell you Maybe they won't tell you Too simple and too easy
I data: Informants' reports	Large amount of information Real-world basis Common sense Some I data are true by definition (e.g., likeability) Causal force	Limited behavioral information Lack of access to private experience Error Bias
L data: Life outcomes	Objective and verifiable Intrinsic importance Psychological relevance	Multi-determination Possible lack of psychological relevance
B data: Behavioral observations	Wide range of contexts (both real and contrived) Appearance of objectivity	Uncertain interpretation

Ask the Person Directly: S Data

If you want to know what a person is like, why not just ask? The easiest way to find out about somebody's personality is to go straight to the source for her own opinion, and personality psychologists often do just that. **S data** are self-judgments. The person simply tells the psychologist (usually on a questionnaire) the degree to which he is dominant, or friendly, or conscientious. This might be done on a 9-point scale, where the person indicates a number from 1 ("I am not at all dominant") to 9 ("I am very dominant"). Or the procedure might be even simpler: The person reads a statement, such as "I usually dominate the discussions I have with others," and then responds True or False. According to most research, the way people describe themselves by and large matches the way they are described by others (Funder, 1999; McCrae, 1982; D. Watson, 1989). But the principle behind the use of S data is that the world's best expert about your personality is very probably you.

It is important to understand that there is nothing the least bit tricky or complicated about S data. S data are straightforward and simple because the psychologist is not interpreting what the participant says or asking about one thing in order to find out about something else. The questionnaires used to gather S data have what is called **face validity**—they are intended to measure what they seem to measure, taken at face value. They ask questions that are directly and obviously related to the construct they are designed to measure.

For instance, right here and now you could make up a face-valid S-data personality questionnaire. How about a new "friendliness" scale? You might include items such as "I really like most people" and "I go to many parties" (to be answered True or False, where a True answer is assumed to reflect friendliness), and "I think people are horrible and mean" (where answering False would raise the friendliness score). There is nothing subtle or tricky about a scale like this; the more ways in which the participant describes herself as friendly (or as not unfriendly), the higher a friendliness score that person earns. In essence, all our new questionnaire really does is ask, over and over in various phrasings, "Are you a friendly person?"

Another kind of S data can be obtained by asking questions that are more open-ended. For example, one current research project asks participants to list their "personal strivings" (see Chapter 16). These are defined as "objectives you are typically trying to accomplish or attain." Some of the strivings college students have reported include "make my mother proud of me," "be honest in my speech and behavior," and "enjoy life." These responses all constitute S data because they are the participants' own descriptions of goals they are trying to accomplish, and the responses are used simply to assess the nature of people's goals (Emmons & King, 1988; Emmons & McAdams, 1991).

By far, S data are the most common basis for personality assessment. Not only are the questionnaires in magazines such as *Self* and *Cosmopolitan* ("Rate your love potential!") based on S data, but so are most of the questionnaires used by personality researchers, although the latter are usually more careful in their methods of test construction and validation. (For more on these methods, see Chapter 5.) Self-report personality questionnaires have been used with children as young as 5 years old, yielding surprisingly

> The world's best expert about your personality is very probably you.

"Next question: I believe that life is a constant striving for balance, requiring frequent tradeoffs between morality and necessity, within a cyclic pattern of joy and sadness, forging a trail of bittersweet memories until one slips, inevitably, into the jaws of death. Agree or disagree?"

Ya ar the only one who is to ya all the tine!

accurate results (Measelle, John, Ablow, Cowan, & Cowan, 2005; see also Markey, Markey, Tinsley, & Ericksen, 2002).

Do we really know ourselves better than anybody else does? Our intuitions would seem to say yes (Vazire & Mehl, 2008). But the truth of the matter is less simple. This is because as a source of information for understanding personality, S data have four advantages and four disadvantages.

ADVANTAGE: A LARGE AMOUNT OF INFORMATION

While a few close acquaintances might be with you in many situations in your life, you are present in all of them. In the 1960s, a book called the *Whole Earth Catalog* was popular. Aphorisms were sprinkled throughout the margins. My favorite read, "Wherever you go, there you are." This aphorism describes an important advantage of S data. You live your life in many different settings; even your closest acquaintances see you only within one or at most a few of them. The only person on earth in a position to know how you act at home, and at school, and at work, and with your enemies, and with your friends, and with your parents is you. This means that you have a unique perspective on the general nature of your personality and that the S data you can provide can reflect complex aspects of character that no other data source could access.

ADVANTAGE: ACCESS TO THOUGHTS, FEELINGS, AND INTENTIONS

A second informational advantage of S data is that much, though perhaps not all, of your inner mental life that would be invisible to anyone else is visible to you. You know your own fantasies, hopes, dreams, and fears; you directly experience your emotions. Other people can know about these things only if you reveal them somehow, intentionally or not. Since these aspects of inner mental life are private yet important to an understanding of personality, S data seem to provide a unique and indispensable route for finding out about them (Spain, Eaton, & Funder, 2000). You also have unique access to your own intentions. The psychological meaning of a behavior lies in what it was intended to accomplish; other people must infer this intention, whereas your knowledge is more direct.

↳ others must attempt to infer your intentions

ADVANTAGE: DEFINITIONAL TRUTH

Some kinds of S data are true by definition—they have to be correct, because they are themselves aspects of the self-view. If a person reports having a high degree of self-esteem or self-liking, for example, or conversely, reports feeling highly incapable of ever accomplishing anything, then he must be right, because these aspects of personality *are* self-views. If you think you have high self-esteem, then you do—it doesn't matter what anyone else thinks.

↳ good example

ADVANTAGE: CAUSAL FORCE

Because S data reflect what you think of yourself, they have a way of creating their own reality. What you will attempt to do depends on what you think you are capable of, and your view of the kind of person you are has important effects on the goals that you set for yourself. This idea—the role of what are sometimes called efficacy expectations—is considered more fully in Chapter 15. It is also the case that people work hard to bring others to treat them in a manner that confirms their self-conception, a phenomenon called **self-verification** (Swann & Ely, 1984). For example, if you think you are a friendly person, or intelligent, or ethical, you might put forth extra effort to make sure other people see you that way too. Part of the reason S data are important is that your view of yourself doesn't just reflect what you think about yourself—it may be among the causes of what you do.

ADVANTAGE: SIMPLE AND EASY

For cost-effectiveness, S data cannot be beat. As you will see, other kinds of data require the psychologist to recruit informants, look up information in public records, or find some way to observe the participant directly. These procedures are time-consuming and therefore expensive. But to obtain S data, all the psychologist has to do is write up a questionnaire that asks about what he wants to know, for example, "How friendly or how conscientious are you?" Then the psychologist prints copies of the questionnaire and hands them out to everybody within reach. Or, increasingly often, the psychologist may set each person in front of a computer terminal or post the questionnaire on the Internet (Gosling, Vazire, Srivastava, & John, 2004). The psychologist will obtain a great deal of interesting, important information about a lot of people quickly and at relatively little cost. As was mentioned earlier, even 5-year-old children can provide self-judgments that have a surprising degree of validity (though 12-year-olds do better; see Markey, Markey, Tinsley, & Ericksen, 2002; Quartier & Rossier, 2008).

Psychological research is low budget compared with research in the other sciences; the research of many psychologists is "funded" essentially by whatever they can cadge from the university's supply closet along with what they can spare from their own salaries. Even psychologists with government research grants usually have much less money to spend than their counterparts in biology, chemistry, and physics.[2] The importance of the inexpensive nature of S data, therefore, is crucial. Sometimes, for very real and compelling reasons, it is the only kind of data a psychologist can get.

DISADVANTAGE: MAYBE THEY WON'T TELL YOU

A person's knowledge about how she acts in all of the situations of her life and about the nature of her private experience translates into S data only if the individual is willing to reveal it. There is no way to force a person to provide an accurate account of her personality if she does not want to.

For example, two advantages of S data already mentioned are that people have unique knowledge of their intentions, and that some aspects of personality *are* self-views so the person's own judgment is true by definition. The big catch in both of these advantages is that the person might not choose to tell the researcher (or anybody else) the real intention behind her behavior. She might even be unwilling to brag about her stellar opinion of herself or, conversely, be unwilling to admit that she has profound doubts about her own abilities. More generally, it is highly possible that the person from whom the psychologist is obtaining S data is ashamed of some aspect of her personality or behavior, or might wish to claim some virtue that she does not actually possess. Perhaps she just prefers to keep some aspects of her personality and experience private. There is no way to prevent a participant from withholding information for any of these reasons (in fact, one can sympathize with these reasons), but if the person does, the accuracy of the

[handwritten note: if a person withhold information, data can be compromised]

---

[2] This discrepancy might make sense (a) if people were easier to understand than cells, chemicals, or particles, or (b) if it were less important to understand people than cells, chemicals, or particles. Both of these presumptions—if indeed anybody holds them—are highly doubtful. Write your congressperson.

S data she provides will be compromised. The psychologist can't do anything about it, and in many cases won't even know.

DISADVANTAGE: MAYBE THEY CAN'T TELL YOU

Even if an individual is—for some reason—willing to tell a psychologist everything about himself, he may not be able to do it. A person's memory of his behavior (or anything else, for that matter) is finite and imperfect; the information he happens to remember is not necessarily the most important or characteristic. Exceptional events and experiences tend to stand out in memory. As a result, a characteristically stingy person might remember the rare time he was generous to somebody; the normally courageous person might never forget the one time he was truly afraid. But an accurate personality judgment captures what is generally true about the person—not so much the exceptions.

The general truth might have a surprising amount of trouble emerging because of a common failing of self-judgment called the *fish-and-water effect*, named after the (presumed) fact that fish are not aware they are wet (Kolar, Funder, & Colvin, 1996). Similarly, people may be so used to the way they characteristically react and behave that their own actions stop seeming remarkable. A consistently kind person might fail to perceive that her kind behavior is to any degree unusual—she has been that way for so long it never occurs to her to act in any other fashion. In this small way, her own personality becomes invisible to herself. This kind of process can happen with a wide range of negative as well as positive traits: You might know people who are consistently manipulative, domineering, fearful, or rude, or courageous, friendly, or kind, who have acted this way for so long that they are no longer aware that this behavior is a distinctive aspect of their personalities.

Another variation on the fish-and-water effect can arise because of the way we become used to the customary behaviors of our own culture. A Danish mother visiting New York once parked her baby's carriage outside a restaurant while she ate, the usual practice in Copenhagen (see Chapter 14). In New York, she was arrested! It had probably never occurred to her that to trust her baby would be safe was in any way unusual or distinctive to Danish culture. The assumptions that surround us all the time may be the most difficult to see.

> The assumptions that surround us all the time may be the most difficult to see.

Information might be actively distorted in memory as well. The Freudians would point out that some particularly important memories may be actively repressed; they might be so painful to remember that the ego prevents them from emerging into consciousness (see Chapter 11). To the extent that this kind of repression takes place, self-judgments might be wrong about some of the most important aspects of personality.

Another factor is simple lack of insight. Some people—maybe all people—lack the ability to see all aspects of their own personality accurately. The self-judgment of personality, like the judgment of personality more generally, can be a complex and difficult undertaking that is unlikely to be 100 percent successful (Funder, 1999; see Chapter 17). For most if not all people, there are important aspects of their personalities that they are simply the last to know about, even though these aspects might be obvious to everyone else.

For example, research has identified a certain kind of person, called the *narcissist*, who characteristically has an exaggerated idea of his own abilities and accomplishments (John & Robins, 1994; Vazire & Funder, 2006; I will say more about narcissism in Chapters 17 and 18). As a result, anything he says about himself must be taken with a grain of salt. Do you know anybody like this?

Concealment, failure of memory, active repression, and lack of insight can cause S data to provide less accurate renditions of personality than psychologists might wish.

DISADVANTAGE: TOO SIMPLE AND TOO EASY

You have already seen that the single biggest advantage of S data, the one that makes them the most widely used form of data in personality psychology, is that they are so cheap and easy. If you remember Funder's First Law (about advantages being disadvantages), you can guess what is coming next: S data are so cheap and easy that they are probably overused (Funder, 2001). According to one analysis, 70 percent of the articles in one important personality journal were based on self-report and nothing else (Vazire, 2006).

The issue is not that anything is especially problematic about S data; like all of the other types of data, they have their advantages and disadvantages. Moreover, Funder's Third Law (about something usually beating nothing) comes into play here; a researcher definitely should gather S data if that is all her resources will allow. The problem is that S data have been used by so many investigators, to the exclusion of other kinds of data, that some investigators seem to have forgotten that the other kinds even exist. But three other kinds of data are relevant to personality psychology, and each has its own special advantages and disadvantages, which I will now consider.

[handwritten margin note: self report data is too often used & other types neglected]

Ask Somebody Who Knows: I Data

A second way to learn about an individual's personality is to gather the opinions of the people who know that person well in daily life. *I* stands for "informant"; **I data** are judgments by knowledgeable informants about general attributes of the individual's personality, such as traits. There are many ways to gather such judgments. Most of my research has focused on college students. To gather information about the personalities of these students, I ask each to provide the names and phone numbers of the two people on campus who know him the best. These people are then called and asked to come to the lab to describe the student's personality. The informants are asked questions such as "On a 9-point scale, how dominant, sociable, aggressive, or shy is your acquaintance?" The numbers yielded by judgments like these constitute I data.

The informants might be the individual's acquaintances from daily life (as in my research), or they might be coworkers or clinical psychologists who have worked with the individual for an extended period of time. The key aspect of the informants' knowledge base is that they know the person well, not that they necessarily have a great deal of formal knowledge about psychology—usually they do not. Moreover, they may not need it; usually, close acquaintanceship paired with common sense is enough to allow people to make judgments of each other's attributes with impressive accuracy (Funder, 1993). Only when the judgments are of a technical nature (e.g., the diagnosis of a personality disorder) does psychological training become relevant.

Another important element of the definition of I data is that they are **judgments**; they derive from somebody observing somebody else in whatever contexts they happen to have encountered them and then rendering a general opinion (e.g., how dominant the person is) on the basis of such observation. In that sense, I data are judgmental, subjective, and irreducibly human.[3]

I data, or their equivalent, are frequently used in daily life. The ubiquitous "letter of recommendation" that employers and schools often insist on receiving is intended to provide I data—the writer's opinion of the candidate—to the personnel manager or admissions committee.[4] Ordinary gossip

---

[3] Their use is not restricted to describing humans, though. I-data personality ratings have been successfully used to assess the personalities of chimpanzees, gorillas, monkeys, hyenas, dogs, cats, donkeys, pigs, rats, guppies, and octopuses (Gosling & John, 1999)!

[4] In many cases, the letter writer is also asked to fill out a form rating the candidate, using numerical scales, on attributes such as ability, integrity, and motivation.

example of I data: letter of recommendation, gossip.

is filled with I data because few topics of conversation are more interesting than evaluations of other people. And the first thing some people do, when invited out on a date, is to ask around: "Do you know anything about him? What's he like?" The answers are I data, and these data can be useful.

As a source of information for understanding personality, I data have five advantages and four disadvantages.

ADVANTAGE: LARGE AMOUNT OF INFORMATION

A close acquaintance who provides a description of someone else's personality is in a position, in principle, to base that description on hundreds of

TRY FOR YOURSELF 2.1

S-data and I-data Personality Ratings

Self descriptions (S data) and descriptions of a person by others (I data) can both be valuable sources of information. But the points of view can be quite different. Try rating yourself and then rating someone else you know quite well, on the scales above. Then, if you dare, have the other person do the same to you!

S Data

Instructions: Rate each of the following items according to how well it describes you. Use a scale of 1 to 9 where 1 = "highly uncharacteristic," 5 = "neither characteristic nor uncharacteristic," and 9 = "highly characteristic."

1. Is critical, skeptical, not easily impressed	1 2 3 4 5 6 7 8 9
2. Is a genuinely dependable and responsible person	1 2 3 4 5 6 7 8 9
3. Has a wide range of interests	1 2 3 4 5 6 7 8 9
4. Is a talkative individual	1 2 3 4 5 6 7 8 9
5. Behaves in a giving way to others	1 2 3 4 5 6 7 8 9
6. Is uncomfortable with uncertainty and complexities	1 2 3 4 5 6 7 8 9
7. Is protective of those close to him or her	1 2 3 4 5 6 7 8 9
8. Initiates humor	1 2 3 4 5 6 7 8 9
9. Is calm, relaxed in manner	1 2 3 4 5 6 7 8 9
10. Tends to ruminate and have persistent, preoccupying thoughts	1 2 3 4 5 6 7 8 9

I Data

Instructions: Think of a person you feel you know quite well. Rate each of the following items according to how well it describes this person. Use a scale of 1 to 9 where 1 = "highly uncharacteristic," 5 = "neither characteristic nor uncharacteristic," and 9 = "highly characteristic."

1. Is critical, skeptical, not easily impressed		1 2 3 4 5 6 7 8 9
2. Is a genuinely dependable and responsible person		1 2 3 4 5 6 7 8 9
3. Has a wide range of interests		1 2 3 4 5 6 7 8 9
4. Is a talkative individual		1 2 3 4 5 6 7 8 9
5. Behaves in a giving way to others		1 2 3 4 5 6 7 8 9
6. Is uncomfortable with uncertainty and complexities		1 2 3 4 5 6 7 8 9
7. Is protective of those close to him or her		1 2 3 4 5 6 7 8 9
8. Initiates humor		1 2 3 4 5 6 7 8 9
9. Is calm, relaxed in manner		1 2 3 4 5 6 7 8 9
10. Tends to ruminate and have persistent, preoccupying thoughts		1 2 3 4 5 6 7 8 9

Source: The items come from the California Q-set (J. Block, 1961, 2008) as revised by Bem & Funder (1978). The complete set has 100 items.

behaviors in dozens of situations. The typical informant in my research is a college roommate. This person would have observed the "target" of her judgment working, relaxing, interacting with a boyfriend or girlfriend, reacting to an A grade, receiving medical school rejection letters, and so on. Such behaviors in context not only are commonly observed by acquaintances but also are important.

The information advantage of I data goes beyond the degree of knowledge attained by any single acquaintance. Almost everybody has many acquaintances, which opens the possibility of obtaining more than one judgment of the same person. (This is not possible using S data, for obvious reasons.) In my research, I routinely try to find at least two acquaintances of each of my research participants to judge their personalities, and then I usually average them into a single, aggregate rating. (More would be even better, but usually two is all I can afford.) As we will see in Chapter 3, taking the average of several judgments yields ratings that are much more reliable than the ratings of any single judge, and this fact gives I data a powerful advantage (Hofstee, 1994).

ADVANTAGE: REAL-WORLD BASIS

The second advantage of most I data is that they are derived from the observation of behavior in the real world. Much of the other information about people that psychologists use is not; psychologists often base their conclusions on information that comes from contrived tests of one kind or another, or on the observation of behavior in carefully constructed and controlled environments. Because I data derive from behaviors informants have seen in daily social interactions, they enjoy an extra chance of being relevant to aspects of personality that affect important life outcomes.

ADVANTAGE: COMMON SENSE

Recall that I data are not simply counts or mathematical combinations of the behaviors the informant has seen; they comprise the informant's judgments about what the behaviors mean, in general, about the individual's personality. A third advantage of I data derives from this basis in human judgment. In the final analysis, I data are distillations of behavioral observations that are filtered through the informant's common sense. This fact allows I data to take account of the context and the intention of behavior to a degree that no other external source of information can equal. In other words, people are smart. I data take advantage of this fact.

An informant with ordinary common sense who transforms an observation of behavior into a judgment of personality will take two kinds of contexts into account (Funder, 1991). The first is the immediate situation. The psychological meaning of an aggressive behavior, for example, can change radically as a function of the situation that prompted it. It makes a difference whether you screamed and yelled at somebody who accidentally bumped you in a crowded elevator, or who deliberately rammed your car in a parking lot. And, if you see an acquaintance crying, you will—appropriately—draw different conclusions about his personality depending on whether the crying was caused by the death of a close friend or by the fact that it is raining and your acquaintance was really hoping to play Ultimate Frisbee today.

A second kind of context is provided by other behaviors that an informant might know about. Imagine that you see an acquaintance give a lavish gift to her worst enemy. Your interpretation of the meaning of this behavior may (and should) vary depending on whether this acquaintance is someone who, in the past, has been consistently generous, or someone you know to be sneaky and conniving. In the first case, the gift may be a sincere peace offering. In the second case, there are grounds for suspecting that some sort

[handwritten margin note:] Contexts taken into account:
- immediate situation
- other behaviors an informant might know about [eg, past behaviors such as "she does all the time"]

of manipulative scheme may be afoot (Funder, 1991). Or say your acquaintance is upset after an argument with a friend. Your interpretation of this reaction, and even your conclusion about how serious the argument was, depends on whether you know this acquaintance to be someone who is easily upset, as opposed to someone who tends to be disturbed only under extreme circumstances.

Applying information about these two kinds of contexts to the judgment of personality is a complicated matter. The science of psychology has not even come close to developing a formal set of rules, procedures, or computer programs for interpreting behavioral observations in this manner, and is unlikely to do so anytime soon. The considerations are just too complex; an overwhelming number of possible situational and contextual variations interact with the implications of too many different kinds of behavior. Yet, surprisingly, integrating diverse information into a coherent impression of personality is not so difficult for the average human judge. The intuitions provided by ordinary common sense allow people to make these judgments easily, naturally, and almost automatically.

ADVANTAGE: DEFINITIONAL TRUTH

Like S data, some kinds of I data are true almost by definition. The reason is that some aspects of your personality reside in the reactions of other people. For example, take a moment and try to rate yourself on how "charming" you are. Can you do it? How? It isn't by looking inside oneself—charm only exists in the eyes of other people, and to assess your own charm you can do little other than try to recall whether people have ever told you or reacted to you as if you were charming. If a psychologist wanted to assess this attribute of your personality, he would probably do better to ask your acquaintances than to ask you. The same is true about other traits such as likeability, sense of humor, attractiveness, obnoxiousness, and other aspects of character that reside in the reactions of others.

"Of course. Your reputation precedes you, sir."

ADVANTAGE: CAUSAL FORCE

The final consideration that makes I data important for understanding personality is quite different from the other three. Because I data are, in a sense, a reflection of the social world of the individual being described—they represent opinions of people who interact with her daily—their importance goes beyond their value as a description of the person. I data are the person's reputation, and as one of Shakespeare's characters once noted, reputation may be a person's most important possession (see also R. Hogan, 1998). In *Othello*, Cassio laments,

> Reputation, reputation, reputation! O, I have lost my reputation! I
> have lost the immortal part of myself, and what remains is bestial.
> My reputation, Iago, my reputation![5]

Why does reputation matter so much? The opinions that others have of your personality greatly affect both your opportunities and expectancies. If a person who is considering hiring you believes you to be competent and conscientious, you are much more likely to enjoy the opportunity of getting the job than you would be if that person thought you did not have those qualities. This will be true no matter how competent and conscientious you are. Similarly, someone who believes you to be honest will be more likely to lend you money than someone who believes otherwise. Your actual honesty is a separate matter. If you impress people who meet you as warm and friendly, you will develop more friendships than if you appear cold and aloof. If someone you wish to date asks around and gets a good report, your chances of romantic success can rise dramatically—the reverse will happen if your acquaintances describe you as creepy. Again, these appearances may be false and unfair, but their consequences will nonetheless be important.

Moreover, there is evidence (considered in Chapter 6) that, to some degree, people become what others expect them to be. If others expect you to be sociable, aloof, or even intelligent, you may tend to become just that! This phenomenon is sometimes called the **expectancy effect** (Rosenthal & Rubin, 1978) and sometimes called **behavioral confirmation** (M. Snyder & Swann, 1978). By either name, it provides another reason to care about what others think of you.

Now consider some disadvantages of I data as sources of information about personality.

---

[5] Iago was unimpressed. He replied, in part, "Reputation is an idle and most false imposition, oft got without merit, and lost without deserving" (*Othello*, act 2, scene 3).

DISADVANTAGE: LIMITED BEHAVIORAL INFORMATION

One disadvantage of I data is the reciprocal of the first advantage considered. Although the acquaintance who might be a source for I data has seen a person's behavior in a large number and variety of situations, he still has not been with that person all of the time. There is a good deal that even someone's closest friends do not know. Their knowledge is limited in two ways.

The first limitation is that there is a sense in which each person lives inside a series of separate compartments, and each compartment contains different people. For instance, much of your life is probably spent at work or at school, and within each of those environments are numerous individuals whom you might see quite frequently there but no place else. When you go home, you see a different group of people; at church or in a club you see still another group; and so forth. The interesting psychological fact is that to some degree, you may be a different person in each of these different environments. As William James, one of the first American psychologists, noted long ago,

> Many a youth who is demure enough before his parents and teachers swears and swaggers like a pirate among his "tough" young friends. We do not show ourselves to our children as to our club-companions, to our customers as to the laborers we employ, to our masters and employers as to our intimate friends. (James, 1890, p. 294)

One telling example of what James was getting at concerns an experience that is typical of modern college students. When a student leaves his parents' home to attend college, his social environment changes drastically. The essence of the change is not so much that college towns are unique places, but that nearly everybody in this new environment is a stranger. The student is suddenly surrounded by a large number of people of about his same age who have no preexisting knowledge of him; they do not know (yet) whether he is the class clown, a workaholic, a jock, a preppy, or an artist. (A similar situation can result from joining the military.)

This experience can be disorienting but also liberating, especially for students who have lived for a long time in a small town, with the same group of people, or perhaps in a constraining family. They are suddenly free of the expectations of others and have an opportunity to design a whole new personality for themselves. Many students do just that, trying out new identities that have long been latent within their characters, in front of a new audi-

ence of peers who do not know that they are seeing something new. The students who avail themselves of this opportunity learn at least as much from the experience as from any of their classes.

Now consider a new college student's first visit home. The person who returns for winter break may seem very different from the one who left in August. The parents and perhaps even the student's hometown friends may become frustrated and angry when they try to deal in their accustomed way with someone who no longer fits their image of her; the student may be equally frustrated and perhaps also anxious about the stability of her new identity among people with old expectations. Although this experience can be traumatic, the personality experimentation and growth that it allows are probably good. If parents, friends, and the student are all patient, they eventually can get used to the "new" person, or in some cases, once the period of experimentation is over, the "old" person might return (but they shouldn't get their hopes up). In the present context, the point to appreciate is that neither a description of the student's personality provided by parents and hometown friends nor the description drawn by college friends will tell the whole story of what that student is really like.

Another example of the complexities introduced by the compartmentalization of lives is what happens when people, whose knowledge of one another has developed in and adapted to one life environment, confront each other in a different environment where they have developed very different identities. You may be a conscientious and reliable employee much appreciated by your boss, but you will probably be disconcerted if you suddenly encounter her at a wild Friday night party where you are dancing with a lampshade on your head. (Does anyone actually do this?) At work seeing your boss is not a problem, but at that party, what do you do? In general, people are more comfortable if those who inhabit the compartments of their lives just stay put and do not cross over into compartments where they do not belong.

Occasionally, I have found myself standing with my daughters at the supermarket, contemplating the latest sale on hamburger, when I realize that one of my university students is right next to me, doing exactly the same thing. Although in general I like my students, I think this kind of encounter is mildly uncomfortable for us both. At best we exchange awkward greetings; more often we continue to gaze vaguely forward and pretend not to have seen each other.

Why? Is either of us really so ashamed to be seen in the supermarket? No, but at the university both of us have well-defined roles that we know how to perform. I know how to relate to a student; most students know how to act with a professor. At the supermarket these roles are irrelevant, so we are left without a script and suddenly neither of us knows quite what to do.

The point here is that people, to a certain degree, are different in different environments. I am not exactly the same person in the classroom as I am at the supermarket—though surely there is some resemblance—nor are students always as studious as they appear in the lecture hall. Any acquaintance who might provide I data about you is likely to know you in one or, at best, a few of your different environmental compartments. To the extent that you are a different person in these different compartments, the I data provided by any one person will have limited validity as a description of what you are like in general.

DISADVANTAGE: LACK OF ACCESS TO PRIVATE EXPERIENCE

A related limitation is that some of every person's life is private, even from a close acquaintance. Each person has an inner mental life that is shared sparingly, if at all. Each has private fantasies, fears, hopes, and dreams. These provide important information about personality, but they can be reflected in I data only to the extent that they have been revealed or shared with somebody. I data provide a view of personality from the outside; information about the inner psychology of thoughts, emotions, and perceptions must be obtained in some other manner—in most cases via S data (McCrae, 1994; Spain, Eaton, & Funder, 2000), and in some cases perhaps not at all.

DISADVANTAGE: ERROR

Because informants are only human, the judgments of personality that they offer will sometimes be mistaken. The previous section proposed that I data provided by a close acquaintance can be based on the observation of hundreds of behaviors in dozens of situational contexts. But that is just in principle. As in the case of S data, where it simply is not possible to remember everything you have ever done, no informant can remember everything he has ever seen another person do either. The capacity of human memory is remarkable, but it is neither infinite nor perfect. Therefore, an informant's judgment is based on what he happens to remember about the person being described and will necessarily overlook some information that might be relevant.

The behaviors that are most likely to stick in memory are those that are extreme, unusual, or emotionally arousing (Tversky & Kahneman, 1973). This fact could have important consequences for I data. An informant judging an acquaintance might have a tendency to forget the ordinary events he has observed but remember vividly the fistfight the acquaintance got involved in (once in 4 years), or the time she got drunk (for the first and only time), or how she accidentally knocked a bowl of guacamole dip onto the white shag carpeting (perhaps an unusually clumsy act by a normally graceful person). And, according to some psychologists, people have a tendency to take single events like these and imply a general personality trait where none may actually exist (Gilbert & Malone, 1995). It is the behaviors that a person performs consistently, day in and day out, that are most informative about personality. As a result, the tendency by informants to especially remember the unusual or dramatic may to lead to judgments that are less accurate than they could be.

DISADVANTAGE: BIAS

The term *error* refers to mistakes that are essentially random: events fail to be noticed, are misperceived, or are forgotten. The term *bias* refers to something more systematic, such as seeing someone in more positive or negative terms than they really deserve. In other words, personality judgments can be unfair as well as mistaken. Because I data consist of acquaintances' and other informants' judgments of personality, they can be affected profoundly by whatever biases these informants may have about the person whose traits they are judging. In my research, as I mentioned, I try to find the two available people who know the person best.

But this practice has potential pitfalls. Perhaps the informant I recruit, unknown to me and to the participant, does not like, or even detests, the person he is being recruited to describe. On the other hand, perhaps he is secretly in love with the participant! Perhaps the informant is in competition with the participant for some prize, job, boyfriend, or girlfriend—all quite common in college. Detesting, loving, or competing with someone can, and typically does, greatly damage the ability to judge personality accurately. For this reason, the researcher should always get at least two informants when-

at least two informant can help solve problem w bias

ever possible. This practice does not solve the problem of potential bias, but it does help a little.

Biases of a more general type are also potentially important. Perhaps the participant is a member of a minority racial group and the informant is racist. Perhaps the informant is sexist, with strong ideas about what all women are like. If you are a college student, and are from an area where few people go to college, you may find that people have an image of you largely based on your student status. If you are studying psychology, you may have experienced another kind of bias. Your relatives and acquaintances might have all sorts of ideas about your personality based on their knowledge that you are a "psych major." Is there any truth to their ideas?

Life Outcomes: L Data

Have you ever been arrested? Have you graduated from high school? Are you married? How many times have you been hospitalized? Are you employed? What is your annual income? Even, what is your zip code? The answers to questions like these constitute **L data**, which are verifiable, concrete, real-life outcomes that may hold psychological significance. The *L* stands for "life."

This type of data can be obtained from archival records such as a police blotter, a medical file, or a tax return, or by asking the participant directly. An advantage of using archival records is that they are almost always accurate and are not prone to the potential biases of self-report or the judgments of others. But the process of getting access to archival data can be tricky and sometimes raises ethical issues concerning privacy. An advantage of asking the participants for this information directly is that access is easier and raises fewer ethical issues, because if participants don't want the researcher to know, they don't have to provide the information. But participants sometimes have faulty memories (e.g., Exactly how old were you when you had the measles?), and also may distort their reports of some kinds of information (e.g., Why were you arrested? What is your income?).

L data can be thought of as the results, or "residue," of personality rather than a direct reflection of personality itself. They are manifestations of how what a person has done has affected her world, including important life outcomes, health, and physical environment. A person who is low in the trait of conscientiousness may perform less well at work and therefore be less likely to be promoted (Barrick & Mount, 1991); her L data of annual income will be a lower number. A person who has smoked for many years is likely to have poorer lung health than someone who has managed to avoid this dangerous habit. Even your zip code can be informative. In California, many auto insurance companies use zip codes to predict the probability that the policyholder will get into an accident, and they set premiums accordingly. (It is not clear whether accident-prone people move to certain zip codes, or living in certain zip codes makes you accident-prone. For their purposes, the insurance companies don't care.) For a final example, consider the condition of your bedroom. Because you live there, its current state is determined by what you have done in it, which is in turn determined by the kind of person you are. To the degree the claim I just made is true, then your personality could be assessed through another bit of L data—a survey of your bedroom!

Recent research has attempted to do just that. A study of college students sent observers into their bedrooms to rate their appearances on several different dimensions. These ratings were then compared to personality

> Conscientious people make their beds. Curious people read a lot.

Figure 2.1 What Your Personal Space Says About You   One example of L data (life-outcome data) that may reveal something about personality is the physical space an individual creates. One of these dorm rooms belongs to someone high in the trait of "conscientiousness," the other to someone low in this trait. Can you tell which is which? (Yes, you can: It's obvious.)

assessments obtained separately. It turns out that people with tidy bedrooms tended to be conscientious, and people whose rooms contained a wide variety of books and magazines tended to be open to experience (Gosling, Ko, Mannarelli, & Morris, 2002; see Figure 2.1). Conscientious people make their beds. Curious people read a lot. But a person's degree of extraversion cannot be diagnosed from looking at her bedroom—the rooms of extraverts and introverts looked about the same.

No matter how L data are gathered, as information about human personality, they have three advantages and one big disadvantage.

ADVANTAGE: OBJECTIVE AND VERIFIABLE

The first and perhaps most obvious advantage of L data is their specific and objective nature. The number of times someone has been arrested, his income, his marital status, his health status, and many other psychologically important outcomes are admirably specific and may even be expressable in exact, numeric form. This kind of precision is rare in psychology.

[handwritten margin note: — e.g. the number of x someone has been arrested]

ADVANTAGE: INTRINSIC IMPORTANCE

An even more important reason L data are significant is that often—when they concern outcomes more consequential than the condition of one's bedroom—they constitute exactly what the psychologist needs to know. To an applied psychologist working as a parole officer, a social worker, a school counselor, an insurance underwriter, or a medical researcher, L data justify her professional existence. The goal of every applied psychologist is to predict, and even have a positive effect on, the real-life outcomes such as criminal behavior, employment status, success in school, accident-proneness, or the health of her clients. Those real-life outcomes are L data.

ADVANTAGE: PSYCHOLOGICAL RELEVANCE

The third reason L data are significant is that in many cases they are strongly affected by, and uniquely informative about, psychological variables. Some people have a psychological makeup that makes them more likely than others to engage in criminal behavior. Other psychological attributes, such as a certain amount of conscientiousness, are necessary to hold a job or to graduate from school (Borman, Hanson, & Hedge, 1997). As we just learned, conscientious people also keep their rooms neat. And, an increasing amount of research is showing that an individual's personality can have an important

L data = reliable markers for psychopathology eg. unmarried 40 yr old = more likely to be mentally ill.

effect on his health (e.g., H. S. Friedman et al., 1995; Horner, 1998; Twisk, Snel, Kemper, & van Mechelen, 1998).

Clinical psychologists have long believed that a simple bit of L data—having never been married by age 40—is a fairly reliable marker of psychopathology. That is to say, people who reach the age of 40 having never married are more likely to exhibit one or more forms of mental illness than are those who have been married at least once by then. However, one must be careful with this little nugget of psychological lore. Lots of people who are unmarried at age 40 are not mentally ill. It is also important to realize that mental illness is quite rare among both married and unmarried 40-year-olds. It just seems to be less rare among the unmarried ones. Moreover, there are many reasons besides mental illness why one might never have married by age 40, such as working in a single-sex workplace, being economically unable to support a family, or simply having given other goals a higher priority than finding a spouse.

This observation is true about the other varieties of L data as well; they are often influenced by many factors that are not psychological. A person's criminal behavior is affected to an important degree by her neighborhood and degree of economic opportunity. During a recession, many people lose their jobs for reasons that have nothing to do with their degree of conscientiousness or any other psychological attribute. Whether one graduates from school may depend on finances rather than dedication. It can be very frustrating to be a careful driver who lives in the same zip code as people who are continually wrecking their cars. A messy room may be the result of messy guests, not the personality of the inhabitant. And health might be affected by behavior and mental outlook, but it is also a function of sanitation, exposure to toxins, and the availability of vaccines, among other factors.

DISADVANTAGE: MULTIDETERMINATION

These observations bring us directly to the biggest disadvantage of L data: They have many causes, so trying to establish direct connections between specific attributes of personality and life outcomes can be extraordinarily difficult. Consider the number of times a person has been arrested: Is this a function of the person's aggressiveness, impulsivity, greed, energy level, carelessness, or a combination of these and still other traits? Similarly, other important life outcomes such as income and physical health, while clearly relevant to personality, are probably not associated with just one or even a few traits.

— non personality factors that can easily affect L data

To make matters even more complicated, in some cases L data may not even be determined by personality at all. Frequently, L data are influenced by too many other factors to reveal much, by themselves, about a person's psychology. These can include social class, childhood circumstances, educational opportunities, economic circumstances, and many, many more factors. Even an arrest record doesn't mean much if, as occasionally happens, the person was arrested for a crime she didn't commit.

This disadvantage has an important implication: If your business is to predict L data from an understanding of a person's psychology, no matter how good you are at this job, your chances of success are severely limited. Even if you fully understand an individual's psychological makeup, your ability to predict his criminal behavior, employment status, school graduation, health, accidents, marriage, or anything else is constrained by the degree to which any of these outcomes is affected by the individual's personality in the first place.

This fact needs to be kept in mind more often. Psychologists who have the difficult job of trying to predict L data are often criticized severely for their limited success, and they are sometimes even more severe in their criticism of themselves. But even in the absolute best case, a psychologist can predict a particular outcome from psychological data only to the degree that the outcome is psychologically caused. L data often are psychologically caused only to a small degree. Therefore, a psychologist who attains any degree of success at predicting criminality, employment, school performance, health, or marriage has accomplished something rather remarkable.

Watch What the Person Does: B Data

When you are trying to get to know somebody, you will naturally watch her actions very closely. This makes sense, because the most visible indication of an individual's personality is what she does. The final way to try to learn about someone's personality, therefore, is to observe her as directly as possible. One might watch the person's behavior in a setting in real life or in a laboratory experiment (Furr, in press). Either way, the information recorded from direct observation constitutes **B data**; the *B*, as you probably have figured out already, stands for "behavior."

The idea of B data is that participants are found, or put, in some sort of a situation, sometimes referred to as a *testing situation*, and then their behavior is directly observed.[6] The situation might be a context in the person's real life (e.g., a student's classroom) or some more artificial setting that a psychologist has set up in an experimental laboratory. B data also can be derived from certain kinds of personality tests. What all these cases have in common, as you will see, is that the B data derive from the researcher's direct observation and recording of what the participant has done.

B data can be gathered in two kinds of contexts: natural and contrived.

NATURAL B DATA

handwritten note (left margin): direct observation 24/7 would be the ideal

In principle, it is possible to gather B data from direct observations of the participant's behavior in real life. Ordinary acquaintance with the people we know gives us access to some amount of B data about them, and we indeed do draw conclusions based on these observations. If you see someone do something exceptionally kind, or disturbingly dishonest, or astonishingly energetic, you will naturally conclude something about his kindness, integrity, or energy level. But these observations are unsystematic and also limited to the situations we share with the people we know; maybe this person is usually unkind, honest, or lazy, and we just happened to see him on an unusual day. So, ideally, as researchers we would wish for more.

First, B data should be carefully and systematically recorded, and each bit of data should refer to a directly observed behavior. The unrealistic ultimate in collecting B data would be to hire a private detective, armed with state-of-the-art surveillance devices and a complete lack of respect for privacy, to secretly follow the participant around night and day. The detective's report would specify in exact detail everything the participant said and did, and with whom, in all of the contexts of the participant's life. Ultimate, but impossible—and unethical too. So psychologists have to compromise.

handwritten note (left margin): —diary and experience sampling —not necessarily "S" data—direct indications of what one did (eg. # hours of sleep)

One compromise form of B data is provided by diary and experience-sampling methods. Research in my own lab has used both. Participants fill out daily diaries that detail what they did that day: how many people they talked to, how many times they told a joke, how much time they spent studying or sleeping, and so on. In a sense, these data are self-reports (S data), but they are not self-judgments; they are reasonably direct indications of what the participant did, described in specific terms. But they are a compromise kind of B data because the participant rather than the psychologist is the one who actually makes the behavioral observations (Spain, 1994).

---

[6] Other writers, and the First Edition of this book, have called this kind of data T (for "test") data. This label turned out to be hopelessly confusing because most personality tests are not T data.

Experience-sampling methods try to more directly get at what people are doing and feeling moment by moment (Tennen, Affleck, & Armeli, 2005). The original technique of this sort was called the "beeper" method (Csik-szentmihalyi & Larson, 1992; Spain, 1994) because participants wore radio-controlled pagers that beeped at several randomly selected times during

"You're a good listener."

the day. The participants then wrote down exactly what they were doing (and with whom) when the beeper sounded. Recent technological innovations have updated this procedure, so that participants carry around handheld computers and enter their reports directly into a database (Feldman-Barrett & Barrett, 2001). Either way, one might suspect that participants would edit what they report, producing sanitized versions of their life events. Based on the reports I have read, I think this is unlikely. At least I hope so! A colleague of mine once did a beeper study at his university just after sending his own 18-year-old twin daughters to college in another state. After reading the unvarnished reports of his own students' activities, he came very close to ordering his daughters back home.

Another kind of hybrid B data involves reports of specific behaviors offered by the participant or by one of her acquaintances. A person might record how many phone calls she made in a day or parties she went to in a week, or a close acquaintance or perhaps her spouse might provide the same information. But this kind of data is a good distance away from the B-data ideal of the researcher directly observing the participant's behavior. Now the researcher must rely on the report of the participant or of her acquaintance (a mixture of B data with S data or I data), and must therefore be mindful of the potential biases in their accounts (Schwarz, 1999).

For example, when people report on their own behaviors, they may exaggerate the number of socially desirable behaviors they performed. One study asked participants to report the number of their "agreeable" acts during a group discussion (Gosling, John, Craik, & Robins, 1998). This self-report was then compared with counts made by four observers who watched a videotape of the discussion. Participants tended to describe themselves as more agreeable than the observers did. Still, for most kinds of acts, the self-reports and the "truth" as revealed by videotape matched fairly well. This last result is encouraging because under real-life circumstances, counts of specific behaviors are very difficult to obtain, and researchers have no

Figure 2.2 Naturalistic and Laboratory B Data Observations of children at play can yield valuable data whether they are viewed in a natural school situation or a contrived laboratory setting.

choice but to settle for reports of act frequencies provided by the people who performed them.

One recently developed technique for gaining access to behavior in daily life is the electronically activated recorder (EAR) developed by psychologist Matthias Mehl and his colleagues (Mehl, Pennebaker, Crow, Dabbs, & Price, 2001). The device is a digital audio recorder that a research participant carries in a pocket or purse, and is programmed to sample the sounds around him at preset intervals such as, in one study, for 30 seconds at a time, every 12.5 minutes (Vazire & Mehl, 2008). The participant might carry this device for several days, and afterward research assistants would listen to the recordings and note down what the person was doing during each segment, using categories such as "on the phone," "talking one-on-one," "laughing," "singing," "watching TV," "attending class," and so forth. This technique still has limitations, two of which are that the record is audio only (no pictures), and that for practical reasons the recorder can sample only intermittently during the research participant's day. Still, it is probably the closest technique psychologists have yet developed to the hypothetical ideal, mentioned earlier, of having a detective follow the participant around day and night. And there is more to come. The development of techniques for what has begun to be called *ambulatory assessment*—using computer-assisted methods to assess behaviors, thoughts, and feelings during participants' normal daily activities—is progressing rapidly (Fahrenberg, Myrtek,

Pawlik, & Perrez, 2007). Indeed, a Society for Ambulatory Assessment was recently founded and has begun to hold an annual conference![7]

Another possibility is to watch what participants do in the not-quite-natural contexts to which a psychologist can gain access. Years ago, I did a study in a nursery school that was operated by a university psychology department. From the children's point of view, this place was simply their nursery school. But from a psychologist's point of view, it was a gold mine of data. Each classroom was equipped with one-way mirrors and listening devices, and one could observe any of the children unobtrusively, all day long, as they went about their nursery school business. One could gather data that reflected these direct behavioral observations, such as the number of times a child asked a teacher for help, or disagreed with another child, or played with crayons. These data reflected directly and in quantifiable terms what the child had been observed doing in a specific context, which is the hallmark of B data.

The great thing about B data gathered from real life is that they are realistic; they describe what the participants actually do in their daily activities. The disadvantages of naturalistic B data are their considerable cost—even the compromise forms just described are difficult and expensive—and the fact that some contexts in which one might wish to observe a participant may seldomly occur in the participant's daily life. For both of these reasons, B data derived from laboratory testing contexts are more common than those from natural contexts.

LABORATORY B DATA

Behavioral observations in the laboratory come in three varieties.

Experiments   The first kind is the psychological experiment. A participant is put into a room, something is made to happen in the room, and the psychologist directly observes what the participant then does.[8] The "something" that happens can be dramatic or mundane. The participant might be given a form to fill out, then suddenly smoke begins pouring under the door. The psychologist, sitting just outside holding a stopwatch, intends

---

[7] The first meeting, in 2009, was held in Greifswald, Germany.

[8] By this definition, nearly all data gathered by social and cognitive psychologists are B data, even though those psychologists are ordinarily not accustomed to classifying their data as such. They also do not usually devote much thought to the fact that their technique of data gathering is limited to just one of four possible types.

to measure how long it will take before the participant goes for help, if she ever does. (Some sit there until the smoke is too thick to see through.) If a researcher wanted to assess the participant's latency of response to smoke from naturalistic B data, he would have to wait a long time for the appropriate situation to come along. In an experiment, the psychologist can make it happen.

Experiments also provide opportunities to find out how people react to very subtle aspects of situations, and the behaviors that are measured can be surprisingly revealing. In one recent study, researchers activated, or *primed*, subconscious thoughts about old age by having participants solve puzzles that included the words *gray, wise, bingo, forgetful, lonely, retired, wrinkle,* and (I love this one) *Florida* (Hull, Slone, Meteyer, & Matthews, 2002). The participants, with these words presumably floating in their heads, were sent to walk down the hall. The B data recorded was their walking speed. The results showed that people high in the trait of "self-consciousness" walked more slowly (compared with people high in this trait who had read neutral words), whereas people low in this trait were unaffected. The theoretical explanation was that self-conscious people translated these elderly-relevant words into thoughts about themselves, and this unconsciously caused them to walk slower, as if they were elderly (more will be said about this study in Chapter 17). Admittedly, the chain of inference is complex, but these results imply it might be possible under some circumstances to assess the degree to which someone is self-conscious by measuring how quickly he walks!

> It might be possible under some circumstances to assess the degree to which someone is self-conscious by measuring how quickly he walks.

Experimental situations can also be straightforward and intended to represent real-life contexts that are difficult to observe directly. In my research, I often have participants meet partners of the opposite sex and simply engage in a conversation. I assume this is not a completely bizarre situation, although it is unusual because the participants know it is an experiment and know it is being videotaped. My purpose is to directly observe aspects of my participants' interpersonal behaviors and styles. In other videotaped situations, my participants compete with each other, cooperate in building with Tinkertoys, or engage in a group discussion. All of these settings are artificial but are designed to allow direct observation of various aspects of the participants' interpersonal behaviors that would be difficult to access otherwise. I put my participants in these situations because I want to see what they will do. My observations become B data (Funder & Colvin, 1991; Funder, Furr, & Colvin, 2000; Furr & Funder, 2004, 2007).

(Certain) Personality Tests   Certain kinds of personality tests also yield B data. Many—and probably most—personality questionnaires simply ask the participants what they are like, and the psychologist chooses to believe whatever the participants say. These kinds of personality tests yield S data. B-data personality tests are different.

For example, the most widely used personality test, the **Minnesota Multiphasic Personality Inventory (MMPI)**, is an example of B data (Dahlstrom & Welsh, 1960). The original version of this test (it was since revised) included this true-false item: "I am a special messenger of the Lord."[9] The presence of an item like this usually signals that the test is looking for B data. Why? Because the psychologist is not actually seeking bearers of heavenly messages. This item was included because people who answer it True tend to be a little unusual. It appeared on the MMPI's schizophrenia scale because schizophrenics are more likely to answer it True than are nonschizophrenics.

Another kind of B-data personality test is the **projective test**, such as the **Thematic Apperception Test (TAT)** (Murray, 1943), or the famous **Rorschach test** (Rorschach, 1921). In the TAT, the participant is shown a picture of some people doing something. In the Rorschach, the participant is shown a symmetrical print made from a blob of ink. In both cases, the participant is asked to describe what she sees. Much like in any other sort of contrived psychological experiment, the psychologist has put the participant in a situation in which she is confronted with a stimulus that she might not otherwise have confronted, and then watches the participant closely to see what she will say and do. The responses to the TAT or to the Rorschach are carefully recorded and, eventually, interpreted. (More will be said about projective tests in Chapter 5.)

In my experience, students find the distinction between S-data personality tests and B-data personality tests confusing. But the distinction is important. One way to clarify the distinction may be to look at it in the following way: If, on a personality test, a psychologist asks you a question because he wants to *know* the answer, the test constitutes S data. If, however, the psychologist asks the question because he wants to see *how* you will answer, the test constitutes B data.

In an S-data test, when the psychologist wants to know something about you, she simply asks you about it. To diagnose sociability, the psychologist asks you how friendly you are. To assess your goals, she asks you to list them.

---

[9] The item was removed from the revised MMPI because it was deemed an illegal inquiry into religious beliefs!

In a B-data test, by contrast, the psychologist gives you a stimulus—perhaps a question, perhaps a picture—to see how you will respond. Your behavior is directly observed and precisely measured—which makes it B data—but your answer is not necessarily believed. Instead, it is interpreted; your claim that you are a special messenger of the Lord (on the old MMPI) means not that you are such a messenger, but that you may be a schizophrenic. In the case of an S-data test, by contrast, the psychologist will assume that what you say about yourself is basically true.

Physiological Measures   In recent years, another kind of B data has begun to be gathered increasingly often in laboratory settings: physiological measures. These include measures of blood pressure, galvanic skin response (which varies according to moisture on the skin, that is, sweating), heart rate, and even highly complex measures of brain function such as pictures derived from CT scans or PET scans (which detect blood flow and metabolic activity in the brain). In our system, all of these are classified as B data because they are things the participant does—albeit via his autonomic nervous sytem—and are measured directly in the laboratory. (In principle, these could be measured in real life as well, but the technical obstacles are obvious.) For example, in the same priming study mentioned earlier, the experimenters also showed their participants words meant to evoke thoughts of anger, such as *ANGRY* (in capitals), and found that highly self-conscious individuals responded with changes in blood pressure and heart rate, whereas low-self-conscious individuals did not (Hull et al., 2002). Data like these will be discussed further in Chapter 8, but for now the important point is that B data can come directly from physiological measurements of the biological "behavior" of the participant, and be surprisingly informative about personality.

B data have two advantages and one big disadvantage.

ADVANTAGE: RANGE OF CONTEXTS

Some aspects of personality are regularly manifest in people's ordinary, daily lives. Your degree of sociability, for instance, is probably evident during many hours every day. But other aspects are hidden or, in a sense, latent. How do you know how you would respond to being alone in a room with smoke pouring under the door unless you are actually confronted with that situation? One important advantage of laboratory B data is that the psychologist does not have to sit around waiting for a situation to happen; if people can be enticed into an experiment, the psychologist can make it happen.

Similarly, a psychologist might believe that the way people interpret certain pictures or inkblots can provide important information about aspects of their personalities that are ordinarily hidden. In an assessment or research context, this psychologist can present these stimuli to the participants and see how they react. The variety of B data that can be gathered are limited only by the psychologist's resources, imagination, and ethics (see Chapter 3).

ADVANTAGE: APPEARANCE OF OBJECTIVITY

Probably the most important advantage of B data, and the basis of most of their appeal to scientifically minded psychologists, is this: To the extent that B data are based on direct observation, the psychologist is gathering his own information about personality and does not have to take anyone else's word for it. This is an advantage because other people may distort or exaggerate their reports, as we have already discussed. Perhaps even more importantly, the direct gathering of data makes it possible for the psychologist to devise techniques to increase their precision.

Often the measurement of behavior seems so direct that one may forget that it is an observation. For example, when a cognitive psychologist measures how long it takes, in milliseconds, for a participant to respond to a visual stimulus flashed on a tachistoscope, this measurement is simply a behavioral observation: How long did it take the participant to respond? A biological psychologist can take direct measurements of blood pressure or metabolic activity. Similarly, when a social psychologist measures a participant's "conformity" or "aggression," the measurement is essentially an observation of behavior. In my laboratory, from the videotapes taken of my participants' conversations, I can derive measurements of how long each one talked, how much each one dominated the interaction, how nervous each one seemed, and so forth (Funder et al., 2000). All of these measurements—from cognitive, social, or personality psychology—are expressed in numeric form and, when appropriate care is employed, can be gathered with high reliability (see Chapter 3 for more on reliability).

The combination of direct assessment, numeric expression, and high reliability is almost irresistible. It seems like a direct pipeline to behavioral truth. Of course, this view is naïve. B data are not quite as objective as they might appear because many subjective judgments must be made on the way to deciding which behaviors to observe and for how long and how to rate them. Even the definition of what constitutes a behavior is tricky when looked at closely. Is "arguing with someone" a single behavior? Is "raising one's left arm" also a single behavior? How about "completing a painting"?

However one chooses to answer these questions, B data have one powerful disadvantage that deserves special attention.

DISADVANTAGE: UNCERTAIN INTERPRETATION

Whether it reflects a response to an MMPI item, a description of a Rorschach inkblot, a phone call to a friend, a moment of social behavior in the laboratory, a reading of blood pressure, or a measurement of brain activity, a bit of B data is just that: a bit of data. It is usually a number, and a number cannot interpret itself. Worse, when it comes to B data, appearances are often ambiguous or even misleading, and so it is impossible to be entirely certain what they mean.

For example, consider again the situation in which someone gives you an extravagant gift. Do you immediately conclude that this person is generous, very much likes you, or both? Perhaps, but you are probably sensible enough to wonder about other possibilities. Are you being manipulated, for example? The conclusion you draw about this behavior will be based on much more than the behavior itself; it depends on the context in which the gift was given and, even more importantly, what else you know about the giver. Is this someone well known to be generous, or well known to be sneaky?

> A number cannot interpret itself.

Or consider that strange MMPI item that was mentioned earlier. How do we know what it means when someone claims that she is a special messenger of the Lord? Certainly nothing in the content of the item tells us; we need further information, such as the empirical fact that schizophrenics respond True to this item more often than nonschizophrenics. Once we know that, we might conclude, after the fact, that it really is a rather crazy thing to say. But the point is, we cannot conclude that the participant is schizophrenic without further information.

The same thing is true of any kind of behavior seen in real life or the laboratory. The person may give a gift, claim to be a messenger of the Lord, say an inkblot looks like a dragon or some favorite relative, or have a sudden intense spike in heart rate or metabolic activity in the prefrontal cortex; or the person may simply sit and wait a long time for a small reward. These are all behaviors that can be measured with great precision. But what these behaviors might *mean*, psychologically, is another question entirely.

A particular example from a study I did some years ago concerned a behavior called "delay of gratification." A large number of laboratory procedures have been developed for measuring this in children (e.g., Mischel &

Ebbesen, 1970). One procedure is to show the child two treats, ask the child which he prefers, and then say, "Okay, I am going to leave the room now, but you can bring me back at any time by ringing this bell. If you do, you can have the [less preferred treat]. But if you don't ring the bell, and wait for me to come back by myself, you can have the [more preferred treat]." The measure of the child's delay of gratification is how long, in minutes and seconds, he waits before ringing the bell. This measure is a prototypical example of contrived B data.

It is easy to see how this measure of behavior got the label "delay of gratification." That is certainly what it looks like, and even seems to be built into the experimental procedure. If the child waits, he gets something better; if the child does not wait, he gets something worse. The test is how long the child can wait. What could be more obvious?

However, the measure here is simple only if we are content to regard it purely operationally and therefore nonpsychologically. If we were to call this measurement "delay time," there would indeed be no room for controversy. But if we label this minutes-and-seconds measurement "delay of gratification," we risk making a deeper psychological claim. We are now asserting, in effect, that what the child is experiencing during that delay time is a psychological tension between desiring the better treat and not wanting to wait, a tension that is mediated according to the child's ability to delay gratification. But what if the child doesn't mind waiting? Or what if the child doesn't really like the "better" treat all that much? Then it would seem misguided to call this behavioral measure of waiting time "delay of gratification."

In the study that Daryl Bem and I did some years ago, we put a group of children through the procedure just described and also gathered personality descriptions of the children from their parents. We then analyzed our data to see how the children who waited the longest in our laboratory were described by their parents as acting at home (Bem & Funder, 1978).

The results surprised us: The most notable attribute of the longest-delaying children was not their ability to delay gratification in other contexts—this ability was a correlate, but a relatively minor one. More importantly, the longest-delaying children were likely to be described as helpful, cooperative, obedient, and not particularly interesting or intelligent. Our interpretation of these correlates was that the minutes and seconds of waiting that we measured were not so much a measure of the children's ability to delay gratification, but of their tendency to cooperate with adults. Because these children were offered something better if they waited, they thought we wanted them to wait. (After all, isn't that how life usually works?) The ones inclined to be obedient and cooperative did what they thought we wanted.

This study demonstrated that while a precise behavioral measurement may be easy to make, its meaning can be far from obvious. At the operational level, it is obvious that the minutes and seconds measured in this study did tick off the exact amount of waiting time. It is at the psychological level, when these minutes and seconds are interpreted as a measure of "delay of gratification," that matters suddenly become ambiguous.

The bottom line is that no one can know what a bit of B data means and measures, psychologically, just by looking at it or even by designing it. (This caution is true for the other kinds of data as well, but it is more frequently forgotten with regard to B data because B data can seem so objective.) To find out what a B-data behavioral measurement means, other information is necessary. The most important information is how the B data correlate with the other kinds: S, I, and L data.

> While a precise behavioral measurement may be easy to make, its meaning can be far from obvious.

Mixed Types of Data

It is easy to come up with simple and obvious examples of S, I, L, and B data. With a little thought, it is almost as easy to come up with confusing or mixed cases. For example, a self-report of your own behaviors during the day is what kind of data? As mentioned earlier, it seems to be a hybrid of B data and S data. Another hybrid between B data and S data is the kind sometimes called *behavioroid*, in which participants report what they think they *would* do under various circumstances. For example, if someone tried to rob you at gunpoint, what would you do? The answer to this kind of question can be interesting, but what people think they would do and what they actually would do are not always the same. What about a self-report of how many times you have suffered from the flu? This might be regarded a mixture of L data and S data. What about your parents' report of how healthy you were as a child? This might be a mixture of L data and I data. You can probably invent many more examples on your own.

The point of the four-way classification offered in this chapter is not to place every kind of data neatly into one and only one category. Rather, the point is to illustrate the wide range of possible types of data that are relevant to personality and to show how any source of data will have both advantages and disadvantages. S, I, L, and B data—and all their possible combinations and mixtures—each provide information missed by the other types, and each type raises its own distinctive possibilities for error.

NO INFALLIBLE INDICATORS
OF PERSONALITY

There are no infallible indicators of personality. There are only clues, and clues are always ambiguous. All four kinds of clues and data for personality psychology are valuable and important. But all four have major disadvantages that cause each to fall far short of being a perfect source of information about personality. The fact that all possible sources of data about personality are incomplete, ambiguous, and even potentially misleading means, ironically, that none of them can be spared. The investigation of personality, and of psychology in general, requires that all of these sources of data be employed. Only then can the different advantages and disadvantages of each type of data begin to compensate for each other.

When all the different types of data point to the same conclusion, a researcher can be especially confident that the conclusion is valid. For example, S data generally tend to agree with I data: people tend to see themselves as others see them (Funder, 1980). And both kinds of data appear to be about equally valid for predicting behavior in daily life assessed via the EAR technique, and they do best of all when combined (Vazire & Mehl, 2008). However, discrepancies are useful too. When a person says different things about herself than other people say—when S data conflict with I data, in other words—that finding can be informative in its own right. The hallmark of narcissism, for example, is that the individual thinks more highly of herself than other people do (Morf & Rhodewalt, 2001; Vazire & Funder, 2006). For another example, when children and their mothers have extremely different views of each other, the degree of this discrepancy is associated with poor parenting, maternal stress, and parent-child conflict (e.g., Chi & Hinshaw, 2002; Ferdinand, van der Ende, & Verhulst, 2004; see De Los Reyes & Kazdin, 2005, for a review). Gathering different kinds of data is useful when they agree, perhaps potentially even more so when they disagree.

All of which brings us to **Funder's Fourth Law**: *There are only two kinds of data.* The first kind is Terrible Data: data that are ambiguous, potentially misleading, incomplete, and imprecise. The second kind is No Data. Unfortunately, there is no third kind, anywhere in the world.

I am not trying to be cynical here. It is simply a fact, perhaps a sad fact, that no data, no matter what kind, point directly and unerringly toward Truth. But this message does not need to be discouraging. Rather, the potential shortcomings of all kinds of data are precisely what require researchers to always gather every kind they possibly can.

If data are potentially misleading, some people would prefer not to gather them at all. They prefer No Data to Terrible Data. It is tough to be a research psychologist if you have that attitude (consider a career in engineering). My own preference is derived from Funder's Third Law, already expounded: Something will beat nothing, perhaps not always, but two times out of three.

SUMMARY

Data Are Clues

- In order to study personality, first you must look at it: All science begins with observation. The observations a scientist makes are called data.

Four Kinds of Clues

- For the scientific study of personality, four types of data are available. Each type has advantages and disadvantages.

- S (self-judgment) data comprise a person's assessments of his own personality. The advantages of S data are that each individual has (in principle) a large amount of information about himself; that each individual has unique access to his own thoughts, feelings, and intentions; that some kinds of S data are true by definition (e.g., self-esteem); that S data also have a causal force all their own; and that S data are simple and easy to gather. The disadvantages are that people sometimes will not, or cannot, tell researchers about themselves, and that S data may be so easy to obtain that psychologists rely on them too much.

- I (informant) data comprise the judgments of knowledgeable acquaintances about the personality traits of the person being studied. The advantages of I data are that there is a large amount of information on which informants' judgments are potentially based; that this information comes from real life; that informants can use common sense; that some kinds of I data are true by definition (e.g., likeability); and that the judgments of people who know the person are important because they affect reputation, opportunities, and expectancies. The disadvantages of I data are that no informant knows everything about another person; that informants' judgments can be subject to random errors, such as forgetting; and that judgments can be systematically biased.

- L (life) data comprise observable life outcomes such as being arrested, getting sick, or graduating from college. L data have the advantages of being objective and verifiable, as well as being intrinsically important and potentially psychologically relevant, but they have the disadvantages of being determined by many different factors, and sometimes not even being psychologically relevant.

- B (behavioral) data comprise direct observations of a person doing something in a testing situation. This situation may involve the person's real-life environment, an artificial social setting constructed in a psychological laboratory, a personality test such as the Rorschach inkblot, or a physiological measurement of variables such as heart rate, blood pressure, and even brain activity. The advantages of B data are that they can tap into many different kinds of behaviors, including those that might not occur or be easily measured in normal life; and that they are obtained through direct observation, and so are in that sense objective. The disadvantage of B data is that for all their superficial objectivity, it is still not always clear what they mean psychologically.

No Infallible Indicators of Personality

- Because each kind of data for personality research is both potentially valuable and potentially misleading, discrepancies among data sources can be as informative as agreement between them. Therefore, researchers should gather and compare as many different types of data as possible.

THINK ABOUT IT

1. If you wanted to know all about the personality of the person sitting next to you, what would you do?
2. In your opinion, is there anything about another person that is impossible to know? Is there anything that is *unethical* to know?
3. Can you think of kinds of observations—data—that you could gather about a person that would fall outside of the BLIS scheme? Which of the four categories comes closest to describing these data?
4. An experimenter gives a subject a set of 10 impossible-to-solve mathematical problems. The experimenter times how long the subject works on the problems before giving up on the task. The minutes-and-seconds measure the experimenter has taken is, of course, B data. The experimenter calls this measure "a real, behavioral measure of persistence." What is right and wrong about this label?
5. People sometimes describe themselves differently than they are described by others (a discrepancy between S data and I data), and they sometimes describe themselves differently from how they act (a discrepancy between S data and B data). Why might this happen? When these kinds of data disagree with each other, which would you tend to believe?

6. Are some kinds of data "privileged" for some kinds of questions? For example, if a person says he is happy (S data), but his acquaintances say he is unhappy (I data), is it possible that the I data could be more valid than the S data? Would it be meaningful to say something like, "He's not as happy as he thinks he is"?

7. If an attribute like "happiness" is most appropriately (or solely) assessable with S data, are there other attributes of personality best (or solely) assessable via I data, L data, or B data?

SUGGESTED READINGS

American Psychological Association (2009). *Publication manual of the American Psychological Association*. Washington, DC: American Psychological Association.

> *This book is the bible for psychological researchers. It sets the standards that must be followed for all articles in journals published by the American Psychological Association, and most other psychological journals also follow it. The book is full of information and advice on the proper conduct, analysis, and reporting of psychological research. Every aspiring psychologist should have a copy.*

Block, J. (1993). Studying personality the long way. In D. C. Funder, R. D. Parke, C. Tomlinson-Keasey, & K. Widaman (Eds.), *Studying lives through time: Personality and development* (pp. 9–41). Washington, DC: American Psychological Association.

> *A survey of his own approach to research by one of the most respected modern personality psychologists. Jack Block describes his approach to data gathering and research design, including longitudinal research (which follows individuals over long spans of time to see how they develop).*

EMEDIA

 Go to StudySpace, wwnorton.com/studyspace, to access additional review and enrichment materials.

3

PERSONALITY PSYCHOLOGY AS SCIENCE: Research Methods

I F DATA ARE the ingredients of scientific knowledge, then research methods provide the recipe. These recipes are sometimes quite complex and can take a long time to learn. The topic of research methods ranges broadly to include specific procedures, sophisticated statistics, and even aspects of the philosophy of science, so obviously the topic involves much more than can be covered fully here. Still, certain aspects of research methodology are particularly important for personality psychology and need to be considered before we begin to study the topic in earnest. This chapter will consider the quality of data, the research designs by which data can be gathered and analyzed, the question of how one knows whether one has a good "strong" result, and, finally, the issue of research ethics.

PSYCHOLOGY'S EMPHASIS ON METHOD

It is sometimes said that the main thing psychologists know is not content but method. This statement is not usually meant as a compliment. When all is said and done, psychologists do not often seem to provide firm answers to questions about the mind and behavior. What they offer instead are methods for generating research aimed at these questions. Indeed, sometimes psychologists seem more interested in the research process itself than in the answers their research is supposed to be seeking.

Such a characterization is not entirely fair, but it does have its kernel of truth. Psychologists, like other scientists, never really expect to reach a final answer to any question. For a researcher, the real thrill is in the chase, not the capture, and the goal is to improve on the tentative answers (hypotheses) constantly being developed, rather than to settle anything once and for all.

Another kernel of truth in the caricature is that, more than any other kind of scientist, psychologists are sensitive and sometimes even self-conscious about research methodology, about the way they use statistics, and even about the basic procedures they use to draw theoretical inferences from empirical data. Issues like these don't seem to worry biologists and chemists so much. They have fewer debates about methodology, and introductory biology or chemistry textbooks usually do not contain an introspective chapter—like the one you are reading now—on research methods, whereas no psychology text seems complete without one. Why do you think this is?

Sometimes, the emphasis on methods and process is seen as a sign of weakness, even by psychologists themselves. One might even say that many psychologists suffer from "physics envy." But psychology's self-consciousness about method is one of my favorite things about it. I remember beginning to study chemistry and finding that one of my first assignments was to memorize the periodic table of elements. Where did this table come from, I immediately wanted to know, and why should I believe it? But no answers were forthcoming. They were not part of the introductory curriculum in chemistry. Certain things, at least early in the study of the subject, were just to be memorized and accepted without question. This was understandable, I suppose, but it did not seem like much fun.

When I took my first psychology course, I found the approach was different. Although I was somewhat disappointed that the professor did not immediately teach me how to read people's minds (even though I was sure he was reading mine), I was engaged by the approach to knowledge he employed. Everything was open to question, and almost no "fact" was presented without both a description of the experiment that found it, and a discussion of whether or not the experiment's evidence was persuasive. Some students did not like this approach. Why not just tell us the facts, they complained, like the professor does in chemistry class? But I loved it. It allowed me to think for myself. Early in the semester, I decided that some of the facts of psychology did not seem solidly based. Later on, I even began to imagine some ways in which I could find out more myself. I was hooked. It could happen to you. Read on.

SCIENTIFIC EDUCATION AND TECHNICAL TRAINING

Some people think that psychology is not really scientific because it has so few hard facts, and even the knowledge it has gathered seems always open to question. This view is ironic because it has things precisely backward. Real science is the seeking of new knowledge, not the cataloging of facts already known for certain. This distinction is the fundamental difference between scientific education and technical training. Technical training conveys what is already known about a subject, so that the knowledge can be applied. Scientific education, by contrast, teaches not only what is known, but also (and much more importantly) how to find out what is not yet known.

> Real science is the seeking of new knowledge, not the cataloging of facts already known for certain.

By this definition, medical education is technical rather than scientific—it focuses on teaching what is known and how to use it, and so medical doctors learn to be practitioners rather than scientists. Physicians in-training do an astonishing amount of sheer memorization, and the last step in medical education is an internship, in which the future doctor shows that she can

"Certainly. A party of four at seven-thirty in the name of Dr. Jennings.
May I ask whether that is an actual medical degree or merely a Ph.D.?"

apply what she has been taught, with actual patients. Scientists-in-training, by contrast, do much less memorization; instead they are taught to question what is already known and how to find out more. The last step in scientific education, including in psychology, is the dissertation, a research project in which the future scientist must add something new to the knowledge in her field.

The contrast between technical and scientific approaches applies in many other areas, such as the distinction between pharmacists and pharmacologists, gardeners and botanists, or computer operators and computer scientists. In each case, the issue is not which is "better"; each member of the pair is necessary, and each depends on the other. The biologist goes to a physician when sick; most of what the physician knows was discovered by biologists. But they are importantly different. Technical training teaches one to use what is already known; scientific training teaches one to explore the unknown. In science, the exploration of the unknown is called **research**. The essential aspect of research is the gathering of data.

QUALITY OF DATA

One of the best-known chefs in the world is Alice Waters, the owner of Chez Panisse in Berkeley, California. Waters is famous for her passion about ingredients. She insists on personally knowing everybody who supplies her fruits, vegetables, and meats, and frequently visits their farms and ranches. If the ingredients are good, she believes, superb cooking is possible, but if they are bad, you might as well give up. If we want to learn from her example, before we consider research design—the recipe—we should probably first put more thought into the quality of the ingredients—the data. In Chapter 2 we looked at four basic types of data for personality research: S, I, L, and B data. For each of these—and indeed, for any type of data in any field—two aspects of quality are paramount: (1) Are the data reliable? (2) Are the data valid? These two questions can be combined into a third question: (3) Are the data *generalizable*?

Reliability

In science, the term **reliability** has a technical meaning that is narrower than its everyday usage. The common meaning refers to someone or something that is dependable, that you can count on, such as a reliable person who is always on time or a reliable car that never breaks down. Reliable data are sort of like that, but more specifically they are measurements that reflect what you are trying to assess and are not affected by anything else. For example, if you found that a personality test taken several times by the same person gives different scores on different days, you might worry, with good reason, that the test is not very reliable. Probably, in this case, the test score is being overly influenced by things it shouldn't be, which might be anything from the participant's passing mood to the temperature of the room—you may never know. The cumulative effect of such extraneous influences is called **measurement error** (also called *error variance*), and the less there is of such error the more reliable the measurement is.

The influences that are considered extraneous depend on what is being measured. If you are trying to measure a person's mood—a current and presumably temporary **state**—then the fact that he won the lottery 10 minutes ago is highly relevant and not at all extraneous. But if you are trying to measure the person's general, or **trait**, level of emotional experience, then this sudden event is extraneous, the measurement will be misleading, and you might choose to wait for a more ordinary day to administer your questionnaire.

When trying to measure a stable attribute of personality—a trait rather than a state—the question of reliability reduces to this: Can you get the same result more than once? A method or an instrument that repeatedly provides the same comparative information is reliable; one that does not is unreliable. For example, a personality test that, over a long period of time, repeatedly picked out the same individuals as the friendliest in the class and others as the least friendly would be a reliable test (although not necessarily valid—that's another matter that we will get to shortly). However, a personality test that on one occasion picked out one student as the most friendly, and on another occasion identified a different student as the most friendly, would be unreliable. A test that is unreliable in this way could not possibly be a valid measure of a stable trait of friendliness. Instead, it might be a measure of a state or momentary level of friendliness, or (more likely in this case) it might not be a good measure of anything at all.

Reliability is something that can and should be assessed with any scientific measurement, whether the measurement is a personality test, a thermometer reading, a blood-cell count, or the output of a brain scan (Vul, Harris, Winkielman, & Pashler, 2009). This point is not always appreciated. For example, an acquaintance of mine, a research psychologist, once had a vasectomy. As part of the procedure, a sperm count was determined before and after the operation. He asked the physician a question that is natural for a psychologist to ask: "How reliable is a sperm count?" What he wanted to know was, does a man's sperm count vary widely according to time of day, or what he has eaten lately, or his mood? Moreover, does it matter which technician does the count, or does the same result occur regardless of who the counter is? The physician, who apparently was trained technically rather than scientifically, failed to understand the question and even seemed insulted. "Our lab is perfectly reliable," he replied. My acquaintance tried to clarify matters with a follow-up question: "What I mean is, what's the measurement error of a sperm count?" The physician really was insulted now. "We don't make errors," he huffed.

But every measurement includes a certain amount of error. No instrument or technique is perfect. In psychology at least four things can undermine reliability. First is low precision. Measurements should be taken as exactly as possible, as carefully as possible. This might seem to go without saying, but nonetheless it is all-important that great care be taken in recording data, scoring them correctly, and entering them carefully into the database. Every experienced researcher has had the nightmarish experience of discovering that a research assistant wandered away for a drink of water when she was supposed to be timing how long it took a participant to solve a problem, or that answers given on a 1–7 scale were entered into the computer as if the scale went from 7 to 1. Mishaps like this happen surprisingly often; be careful.

> "We don't make errors," he huffed.

Second, the state of the participant[1] in the study might vary for reasons that have nothing to do with the study itself. Some participants show up ill, some well; some are happy and others are sad; many college student participants are amazingly short on sleep. From a research perspective, the problem is that they might have behaved or performed differently, and therefore have given different results for the research, had they been feeling differently or more rested. There is not much researchers can do about this; variations in the state of the participants are a source of error variance or random "noise" in almost every psychological study.

A third potential pitfall for reliability is the state of the experimenter. One would hope that experimenters, at least, would come to the lab well rested and attentive, but alas, this is not always the case. Variation due to the experimenter is almost as inevitable as variation due to the participants;

---

[1] The term *subjects* became largely passé in psychological research when the *Publication Manual of the American Psychological Association* mandated that the term *participants* be used instead. However, the very latest edition of the manual, issued in 2009, announced a change in policy: Both terms are now acceptable.

experimenters try to treat all participants the same but, being human, will fail to some extent. Moreover, participants may respond differently to an experimenter depending on whether the experimenter is male or female, of a different race than the participant—or even depending on how the experimenter is dressed. It is very difficult to control all these factors. B. F. Skinner famously got around this problem by having his subjects—rats and pigeons—studied only in the environment of a mechanically controlled enclosure, the *Skinner box*. But for research with humans, we usually need them to interact with other humans, including research assistants.

A final potential pitfall can come from the environment in which the study is done. Experienced researchers have all sorts of stories that never make it into textbooks on research methods, involving fire alarms (even sprinklers) that go off in the middle of experiments, noisy arguments that suddenly break out in the room next door, laboratory thermostats gone berserk, and so forth. Events like these are relatively unusual, fortunately, and when they happen, all one can usually do is cancel the study for the day, throw the data out, and hope for better luck tomorrow. But minor variations in the environment are constant and inevitable; noise levels, temperature, the weather, and a million other factors vary constantly during a research project and provide another potential source of data unreliability.

At least four things can be done to try to enhance reliability (see Table 3.1). One, obviously, is just to be careful. Double-check all measurements, have someone proofread (more than once!) the data-entry sheets, and make sure the procedures for scoring data are clearly understood by everyone

Table 3.1

RELIABILITY OF PSYCHOLOGICAL MEASUREMENT

Factors that undermine reliability	Low precision
	State of the participant
	State of the experimenter
	Variation in the environment
Techniques to improve reliability	Care with research procedure
	Standardized research protocol
	Measure something important
	Aggregation

who works for your project. A second way to improve reliability is to use a constant, scripted procedure for all participants. The procedure written on the research protocol should be followed, no matter what happens. I once did a study in which participants watched a long videotape of a behavioral episode; in another condition, other participants watched a much shorter tape. Among the hypotheses of the study was that participants would stop paying attention to a very long episode, and the accuracy of their ratings of that episode would, instead of getting better over time, start to deteriorate. One of our research assistants, eager to go home, watched participants in the long-episode condition until they seemed bored. Then he would go in, say, "Well, you're not paying attention anyway," stop the tape, and end the experiment! By the time we discovered his procedural innovation, several participants' worth of data was ruined—an expensive mistake. But the real mistake was mine. The aspect of the procedure that prescribed "let the tape run to the end even if the participant doesn't seem to be paying attention" seemed so obvious to me that I failed to teach it adequately to at least one of my research assistants. It turns out, no aspect of experimental procedure is so obvious that it can be taken for granted.

A third way to enhance reliability in psychological research is to measure something that is important, rather than something that is trivial. For example, an attitude about an issue that matters to someone is easy to measure reliably, but if the person doesn't really care (What's your opinion on lumber tariffs?), then the answer is worth little more than the paper the questionnaire is printed on. Experimental procedures that engage participants will yield better data than those that fail to involve them; measurement of big important variables (e.g., the degree of a person's extraversion) will be more reliable than narrow trivial variables (e.g., whether the person is chatting with someone at 1:10 P.M. on a Saturday).

The fourth and most useful way to enhance the reliability of measurement in any domain is **aggregation**, or averaging. When I was in high school, a science teacher who I now believe was brilliant (I failed to be impressed at the time) provided students in the class with the best demonstration of aggregation that I have ever seen. He gave each of us a meterstick, a piece of wood cut to the length of 1 meter. We then went outside and measured the distance between our school and the elementary school down the street, about a kilometer (1,000 meters) away. We each did this by laying our meterstick down, then laying it down again against the end of where it was before, and counting how many times we had to do this before we reached the elementary school.

In each class the counts varied widely—from about 750 to over 1,200, as I recall. The next day, the teacher wrote all the different results on the blackboard. It seemed that the elementary school just would not hold still! To put this observation another way, our individual measurements were unreliable. It was hard to keep laying the meterstick down over and over again with precision, and it was also hard not to lose count of how many times we did it.

But then the teacher did an amazing thing. He took the thirty-five measurements from the 9:00 A.M. class and averaged them. He got 957. Then he averaged the thirty-five measurements from the 10:00 A.M. class. He got 959. The thirty-five measurements from the 11:00 A.M. class averaged 956. As if by magic, the error variance had almost disappeared, and we suddenly had what looked like a stable estimate of the distance to the elementary school.

What had happened? The teacher had taken advantage of the power of aggregation. Each of the mistakes we made in laying our metersticks down and losing count was essentially random. And over the long haul, random influences tended to cancel one another out. (Random influences, by definition, sum to zero—if they didn't, they wouldn't be random!) While some of us may have been laying our metersticks too close together, other classmates were surely laying them too far apart. When all the measurements were averaged, the errors canceled each other out. With thirty-five measurements per class being averaged, the result became pretty stable.

This is a basic and powerful principle of measurement. If you have doubts about the precision of your measurement, take as many measurements as you can and average them. The **Spearman-Brown formula** in **psychometrics**, the technology of psychological measurement, quantifies exactly how this works. The principle is simple: Random errors tend to cancel one another out. So the more error-filled your measurements are, the more measurements you need. The "truth" will be in there someplace, near the average. This is the best way to deal with some of the problems discussed earlier, such as the inevitable fluctuations in the states of the participants, experimenter, and environment. (For further discussion of

> Personality psychologists once got into a bitter debate, just because single behaviors are difficult to predict.

applications of the Spearman-Brown formula to personality measurement, see Chapter 5; also Burnett, 1974; Epstein, 1980; and Rosenthal, 1973a.)

The principle of aggregation is particularly important if your goal is to predict behavior. Personality psychologists once got into a bitter debate (the "consistency controversy," see Chapter 4), just because single behaviors are difficult to predict accurately from personality measurements. This caused some critics to conclude that personality itself did not exist! However, based on the principle of aggregation, it should be much easier to predict the average of a person's behaviors. Maybe a friendly person is more friendly at some times than at other times—everyone has bad days. But the average of the person's behaviors over time should be reliably more friendly than the average of an unfriendly person (Epstein, 1979).

Validity

Validity, as I indicated earlier, is different from reliability. It also is a more slippery concept. **Validity** is the degree to which a measurement actually reflects what one thinks or hopes it does. The concept of validity is slippery for a couple of reasons.

One reason is that, for a measure to be valid, it must be reliable. But a reliable measure is not necessarily valid. Should I say this again? A measure that is reliable gives the same answer time after time. If the answer is always changing, how can it be the right answer? So for a measure to be valid, it must first be reliable. But even if a measure is the same time after time, that does not necessarily mean it is correct. Maybe it reliably gives the wrong answer (like the clock in my old Toyota, which was correct only twice each day). People who study logic distinguish between what they call *necessary* and *sufficient* conditions. An example is getting a college education: It might be necessary to get a good job, but it is surely not sufficient. In that sense, reliability is a necessary but not a sufficient condition for validity.

A second and even more difficult complication to the idea of validity is that the concept seems to invoke a notion of ultimate truth. On the one hand, you have ultimate, true reality. On the other hand, you have a measurement. If the measurement matches ultimate, true reality, it is valid. Thus, an IQ measure is valid if it really measures intelligence. A sociability score is valid if it really measures sociability, the trait that helps to cause people to act friendly toward each other (Borsboom, Mellenbergh, & van Heerden, 2004). But here is the problem: How does anyone know what intelligence and sociability "really" are?

Some years ago, the psychologists Lee Cronbach and Paul Meehl (1955) proposed that attributes like intelligence or sociability are best considered to be **constructs**.[2] A construct is something that cannot be directly seen or

---

[2] Sometimes the term *hypothetical construct* is used, to underline that the existence of the attribute is not known for certain but instead is hypothesized.

touched, but which affects and helps to explain many different things that are visible. A common example is gravity. Nobody has ever seen or touched gravity, but we know it exists from its many effects, which range from causing apples to fall on people's heads to keeping the planets in their proper astronomical paths. Nobody has ever seen or touched intelligence, either, but it affects many aspects of behavior and performance, including test scores and achievement in real life (G. Park, Lubinski, & Benbow, 2007). This range of implications is what makes intelligence important. An old-time psychologist once said, "Intelligence can be defined as what IQ tests measure." He was wrong. If IQ affected only test scores and not performance in life, there would be no reason for anybody to care about it.

Personality constructs are the same as gravity or IQ in this sense. They cannot be directly seen and are known only through their effects. And their importance stems from their wide implications—they are much more than test scores. They are ideas about how behaviors hang together and are affected by a particular attribute of personality. For example, the invisible construct of "sociability" is seen through visible behaviors such as going to parties, smiling at strangers, and making numerous telephone calls. And the idea of sociability implies that these behaviors, and more, should tend to correlate with each other—somebody who does one of these behaviors probably does the others as well. This is because they all are assumed to have the same cause: the personality trait of sociability (Borsboom et al., 2004).

As you can now see, using a construct is much the same as proposing a theory (R. Hogan & Nicholson, 1988). Here, the theory is that sociability is a trait that can affect many different behaviors that all reflect an inclination to be with other people.

Of course, that's just a theory. Theories must be tested. The process of testing the theory behind a construct such as intelligence or sociability is called **construct validation** (Cronbach & Meehl, 1955). This research strategy amounts to gathering as many different measurements as you can of the construct you are interested in, such as intelligence or sociability. The measurements that start to hang together—to consistently pick out the same people as intelligent or sociable—begin to validate each other as measurements of the construct, and at the same time validate the construct as relevant to each of the measurements.

For example, you might give participants a sociability test, ask their acquaintances how sociable they are, and count the number of phone calls they make and parties they go to in a week. If these four measures correlate—if they all tend to pick out the same individuals as being highly sociable—then you might start to believe that each of them has some degree of validity as a measure of the construct of sociability. At the same time, you would become more confident that this construct makes sense, that sociability is a useful idea for predicting and explaining behavior. Even though you never reach an ultimate truth, you can start to reasonably believe you are measuring something real when you can develop a battery of measurements, all quite different, that yield more or less the same result.

Generalizability

Traditional treatments of psychometrics regarded reliability and validity as distinct from one another. When two tests that were supposed to be "the same" were compared, the degree to which they actually yielded the same result indicated their degree of reliability. For example, reliability would be gauged by the degree to which a test given at one time gives the same scores to the same people when exactly the same test is given again, a week later.

The constancy between scores on one form of a test, and scores on another form of the same test (maybe consisting of the same items, only slightly rephrased), would also be considered a gauge of reliability. But if the two tests are different, then their relationship is taken to indicate the first test's degree of validity. For example, if a friendliness test is correlated with the number of phone calls one makes in a week, then this correlation would indicate the test's validity. But most real cases are not so clear-cut. When one begins to look at it closely, the distinction between which tests should be considered "the same" and which "different" turns out to be rather fuzzy.

In recent years, therefore, psychometricians have started to regard the distinction between reliability and validity as also being rather fuzzy. They now tend to view both concepts as aspects of a single, broader concept called **generalizability** (Cronbach, Gleser, Nanda, & Rajaratnam, 1972). The question of generalizability, applied to a measurement or to the results of an experiment, asks the following: To what else does the measurement or the result generalize? That is, is the result you get with one test equivalent, or generalizable, to the result you would get using a different test? Does your result also apply to other kinds of people than the ones you assessed, or does it apply to the same people at other times, or would the same result be found at different times, in different places? All of these questions regard facets of generalizability.

GENERALIZABILITY OVER PARTICIPANTS

One important facet is generalizability over participants. For example, you might do a case study of a single individual, but then wonder about whether your findings apply to everybody or just to this one person. Most psychological research is done by university professors, and most participants in the research are college students. (There tend to be a lot of students in the vicinity of professors, and gathering data from anybody else—such as randomly selected members of the community—is much more difficult and expensive, even when it is possible.) This fact raises a basic question of generalizability: To what degree can researchers draw valid conclusions about people in general if all they study are college students? After all, college students are not representative of the broader population. They are somewhat more affluent, more liberal, and less likely to belong to ethnic minorities. They are also younger than average. These facts call into question the degree to which research results found with such students will prove to be true about the national population, let alone the world (D. O. Sears, 1986).

Gender Bias   An even more egregious example of conclusions based on a limited sample of humanity comes from the fact that until well into the 1960s, it was fairly routine for American psychological research to gather data only from male participants. Some of the classic empirical investigations of personality, such as those by Henry Murray (1938) and Gordon Allport (1937), examined only men. I once had a conversation with one of the major contributors to personality research during the 1940s and 1950s who admitted frankly that

> "It never occurred to any of us . . . to include women in the groups we studied."

he was embarrassed to have used only male participants in his research. "It is hard to recall why we did that," he said in 1986. "As best as I can remember, it simply never occurred to any of us to do anything different—to include women in the groups we studied."

   In recent years, the problem may have reversed in an ironic way. There is one particular fact about recruiting participants, rarely mentioned in methods textbooks, that nearly all psychologists have known for years: Females are more likely than males to sign up to be in experiments, and once signed up they are more likely to appear at the scheduled time. This difference is not small. From my desk in the psychology department, I used to look directly across the hallway at a sign-up sheet for my research project, which uses paid volunteer participants.[3] Because my work needs an exactly equal number of males and females, the sign-up sheet had two separate columns. At any hour of any day, there would be more than twice as many names in the "women" column as in the "men" column, sometimes up to five times as many.

---

[3] These days, of course, we sign up participants via the Internet.

This big difference raises a couple of issues. One is theoretical: Why this difference? One hypothesis could be that college-age women are generally more conscientious and cooperative than men in that age range (which I believe is true), or the difference might go deeper than that. A second issue is that this difference raises a worry about the participants that researchers recruit. It is not so much that samples are unbalanced. Researchers can keep them balanced; in my lab, I simply call all of the men who sign up and about one in three of the women. Rather, the problem is that because men are less likely to volunteer than women, the men in the studies are, by definition, unusual men. They are the kind of men who are willing to be in a psychological experiment. Most men aren't, yet researchers generalize from their willing male participants to men in general.[4]

Shows Versus No-Shows   A related limitation of generalizability is that the results of psychological research depend on the people who show up at the laboratory. Anyone who has ever done research knows that a substantial proportion of the participants who are scheduled never appear. The results of the research, in the end, depend on the attributes of the participants who do appear. This presents a problem if these two groups of people are different.

There is not much research on this issue—it is difficult to study no-shows, as you might expect—but there is a little. According to one study, the people who are most likely to appear for a psychological experiment at the scheduled time are those who adhere to standards of "conventional morality" (Tooke & Ickes, 1988). In another, more recent study, 1,442 college freshmen consented to be in a study of personality, but 283 of these never showed up (Pagan, Eaton, Turkheimer, & Oltmanns, 2006). However, the researchers had personality descriptions of everybody from their acquaintances. It turned out that the freshmen who showed up for the study were more likely to be described as having tendencies to be histrionic (emotionally expressive), compulsive, self-sacrificing, and needy. The freshmen who never appeared were more likely to be described as narcissistic (self-adoring) and low on assertiveness. It is not clear to me how to put these two studies together, but they do serve as warnings that the relatively small number of people who are included in psychology studies may not be representative of the much larger number of people who aren't.

---

[4] It was once suggested to me, quite seriously, that the imbalance would be fixed if we paid male participants three times as much as female participants. Is this is a good idea?

Cohort Effects   Another possible failure of generalizability stems from the fact that research results may be historically limited. It has been argued that much of psychology is really history, meaning it is the study of a particular group of people in a particular place and time (Gergen, 1973). The research that fills psychological journals today may be interesting as a historical artifact concerning what North American college students of the early 21st century were like, but according to this argument, it says little about what people are like in general or what they may have been like across the years and centuries.

Some evidence indicates that aspects of personality can be affected by the specific historical period in which one lives. One study of Americans who grew up during the Great Depression of the 1930s found that they took from that experience certain attitudes toward work and financial security that were distinct from the outlooks of those who grew up earlier or later (Elder, 1974). More recent research has suggested that young adults in the early 21st century—including current college students—are especially self centered, materialistic, and "narcissistic" (Twenge, Konrath, Foster, Campbell, & Bushman, 2008). Psychologists call the tendency of a group of people living at a particular time to be different in some way from those who live earlier or later a **cohort effect**.

> Recent research has suggested that young adults in the early 21st century—including current college students—are especially self-centered, materialistic, and "narcissistic."

Psychologists worry about cohort effects more often than they deal with them directly. The reason is that the necessary research is prohibitively expensive, insofar as it is even possible. The only way to find out which research results are true across time, and which are just characteristics of the cohort being studied, is to study participants from other eras. This is nearly impossible. To some degree, one can use data archives and try to go back a little ways in time. For the future, one must begin new studies and just wait. None of these tactics is terribly practical, and all of them are expensive.

Ethnic and Cultural Diversity   A generalizability issue that is receiving increased attention concerns the fact that most modern empirical research in psychology is based on a limited subset of the modern population—specifically, the predominantly white, middle-class college students referred to earlier. This is becoming a particular issue in the United States, where ethnic diversity has always been wide, and where various minority groups are becoming more assertive about being included in all aspects of society— including psychological research. The pressure to include minority participants is political as well as scientific. One place to see the results of such political pressure is in the grant application guidelines published by one branch of the U.S. government:

> Applications for grants . . . that involve human subjects are required to include minorities and both genders in study populations. . . . This policy applies to all research involving human subjects and human materials, and applies to males and females of all ages. . . . Assess carefully the feasibility of including the broadest possible representation of minority groups. (Public Health Service, 1991, p. 21)

This set of guidelines addresses the representation of American ethnic minorities in research funded by the U.S. government. As the tone of this directive hints, such representation is difficult. But notice that even if every goal it espouses were to be achieved, the American researchers subject to its edict would still be restricted to studying residents of a modern, Western, capitalist, postindustrial society. This may be an interesting society to study, but its denizens are a global minority, since 70 percent of the world's population lives outside Europe and North America (Triandis, 1994).

THE BURDEN OF PROOF

It is easy to get carried away with these kinds of worries. The concern with generalizability, the degree to which one's results apply to all people around the world at all times, is a fundamental issue for psychological research. But two points are worth bearing in mind.

First, getting the facts straight about members of our own culture in our own time seems to be difficult enough, so we should resist making facile and simplistic generalizations about members of other cultures—including jumping to conclusions about ways they might be different. To really understand the psychological differences between cultures will require a vast amount of further research more equally spread across cultures and less concentrated in Europe, North America, Australia, and New Zealand. Such research is beginning to appear, but we still have much to learn about cross-cultural differences, including how pervasive they really are (see Chapter 14).

Second, it is one thing to worry that our results or theories might not generalize, and quite another to propose just how and why a particular result or theory might not apply to another culture. Not all of the burden of proof should be on those who are trying to do research that is generalizable. Some should be shared by those who claim it is not generalizable to show when, how, and why it is not. Simply to observe that psychological data are limited, and then to conclude that all research and theory are therefore worthless is—as the old saying goes—to throw the baby out with the bathwater.

RESEARCH DESIGN

Data gathering must follow some sort of plan, the *research design*. No one research design is suitable for all topics—according to what one wants to study, different designs may be appropriate, inappropriate, or even impossible. Research designs in psychology (and all of science) come in three basic types: case, experimental, and correlational.

Case Method

The simplest, most obvious, and most widely used way to learn about something is, as Henry Murray advised, just to look at it. Even seemingly mundane events, when looked at closely, can have important implications. According to legend, Isaac Newton was sitting under a tree when he was hit on the head by an apple, and that got him thinking about laws of gravity. A scientist who keeps her eyes and ears open can find all sorts of phenomena to examine that can stimulate new ideas and insights. The **case method** involves closely studying a particular event or person of interest in order to find out as much as possible.

This method is used all the time. When an airplane crashes, the National Transportation Safety Board (NTSB) sends a team to the site and launches an intensive investigation. In January 2000 an Alaska Airlines plane went down off the California coast; almost three years later the NTSB concluded this happened because a crucial part, the jackscrew assembly in the plane's tail, had not been properly greased (Alonso-Zaldivar, 2002). This conclusion answered the specific question of why this particular crash happened, and it also had implications for the way other, similar planes should be maintained (i.e., don't forget to grease the jackscrew!). At its best, the case method yields not only explanations of particular events, but also general lessons and perhaps even scientific principles.

All sciences use the case method. When volcanoes erupt, geologists rush to the scene with every instrument they can carry. When a fish previously thought long extinct is pulled from the bottom of the sea, ichthyologists stand in line to get a closer look. Medical practice has a tradition of "case conferences" where individual patients are presented and discussed at length. Even business school classes spend long hours studying cases of companies that succeeded and failed. But the science best known for its use of the case method is psychology, and in particular personality psychology. Sigmund Freud built his famous theory of personality from his experience with particular patients who offered interesting phobias, weird dreams, and hysterical illnesses (see Chapter 10). Most of psychoanalytic theory from other theorists such as Carl Jung, Alfred Adler, and Karen Horney is likewise based on their experiences with the cases they treated. Psychologists who are not psychoanalytically inclined have also used cases; Gordon Allport, for example, argued for the importance of studying particular individuals in depth, and even wrote a whole book about one person (Allport, 1965).[5] More recently, the psychologist Dan McAdams has argued that it is important to listen to and understand "life narratives," the unique stories individuals construct about their lives (McAdams et al., 2004).

> A particularly interesting and important case study could be done on the person who shares your name, address, and social security number—that is, you.

A particularly interesting and important case study could be done on the person who shares your address, name, and social security number—that is, you. Every person is both complex and unique, and the effort to understand oneself can be a hobby that lasts a lifetime. I am not recommending that degree of self-absorption, but it is true that understanding why you do things can help you understand why others do what they do. Freud said that an important basis of his theories was his own introspection. We cannot all be theorists of Freud's caliber, but looking into ourselves from time to time to figure out why we think and behave the way we do can help us understand not just ourselves, but other people as well.

The case method has several advantages. One is that, above all other methods, it is the one that feels as if it does justice to the topic. A well-written case study can be like a short story or even a novel; Freud wrote extensively and well about many of his patients and, in general, the best thing about a

---

[5] The identity of this person was supposed to be secret. Years later, historians established it was Allport's college roommate's mother.

case study is that it describes the whole phenomenon and not just isolated variables.

A second advantage is that a well-chosen case study can be a source of ideas. New ideas have to come from somewhere, and the best source is probably life's specific events in all their complexity. A case study can illuminate why planes crash (and perhaps prevent future disasters) and reveal general facts about the inner workings of volcanoes, the body, businesses, and of course the human mind. These ideas may not have occurred to anyone unless the case was studied. Newton's apple got him thinking in a whole new direction; nobody suspected that grease on a jackscrew could be so important; and Freud generated an astounding number of ideas just from examining himself and his patients.

A third advantage of the case method is often forgotten: Sometimes the method is absolutely necessary. A plane goes down; we must at least try to understand why. A patient appears, desperately sick. The physician cannot say, "More research is needed"; rather, she must try to understand the problem at hand as thoroughly as possible and then do something. Psychologists, too, sometimes must deal with particular individuals, in all their wholeness and complexity, and base their efforts on the best understanding they can quickly achieve.

The big disadvantage of the case method is obvious. It is not controlled. Each case contains numerous, and perhaps literally thousands, of specific facts and variables. Which of these are crucial, and which are incidental? An insightful scientist might be able to perceive important patterns, but to really become confident about what one has learned from a case requires further confirmation. Once a specific case has suggested an idea, the idea needs to be checked out, and for that the more formal methods of science are required, the **experimental method** and the **correlational method**.

For example, let's say you know someone who has a big exam coming up. It is very important to him, and he studies very hard. He also becomes anxious. He takes the test and freaks out. Even though he knows the subject matter, he performs badly and gets a poor grade. Have you ever seen this happen? If you have (I know I have), then this case might cause you to think of a general hypothesis: Anxiety harms test performance. That sounds reasonable, but does this one experience prove that it is true? Not really, but it was the source of the idea. The next step is to find a way to do research to test this hypothesis. You could do this in either of two ways: with an experiment or a correlational study.

An Experimental and a Correlational Study

The experimental way to examine the relationship between anxiety and test performance would be to get a group of research participants and randomly divide them into two groups. It is important that they be assigned randomly because then you can presume that the two groups are more or less equal in ability, personality, and other factors. If they aren't, then something wasn't random. For example, if one group of subjects was recruited by one research assistant and the other group was recruited by another, the experiment is already in deep trouble, because the two assistants might—accidentally or on purpose—tend to recruit different kinds of participants. A similar problem arises if one group was recruited on one day, and the other group on a different day. It is critical to be sure that nothing beyond sheer chance affects whether a participant is assigned to one condition or the other.

Now it's time for the experimental procedure. Do something to one of the groups that you expect will make the members of that group anxious, such as telling them, "Your life depends on your performance on this test" (but see the discussion on ethics and deception later in this chapter).

Table 3.2

PARTIAL DATA FROM HYPOTHETICAL EXPERIMENT ON THE EFFECT OF ANXIETY ON TEST PERFORMANCE

Participants in the High-Anxiety Condition, No. of Correct Answers	Participants in the Low-Anxiety Condition, No. of Correct Answers
Sidney = 13	Ralph = 28
Jane = 17	Susan = 22
Kim = 20	Carlos = 24
Bob = 10	Thomas = 20
Patricia = 18	Brian = 19
Etc.	Etc.
Mean = 15	Mean = 25

Note: Participants were assigned randomly to either the low-anxiety or high-anxiety condition, and the average number of correct answers was computed within each group. When all the data were in, the mean for the high-anxiety group was 15 and the mean for the low-anxiety group was 25. These results would typically be plotted as in Figure 3.1.

Say nothing to the other group (the control group). Then give both groups something like a 30-item math test. If anxiety hurts performance, then you would expect the participants in your "life depends" group to do worse on the test than the participants in the control group, who did not hear this dire message.

To test whether you got the results you predicted, you might write them down in a table like Table 3.2 and then display them on a chart like Figure 3.1. In this example, the mean (average) score of the high-anxiety group indeed seems lower than that of the low-anxiety (control) group. You would then do a statistical test, probably one called a t-test in this case, to see if the difference between the means is larger than one would expect from chance variation alone.

The correlational way to examine the same hypothesis would be to measure the amount of anxiety that your participants already have. Give all of them a questionnaire asking them to rate, for example, how anxious they feel right then on a scale of 1 to 7. Then give them the math test. Now the hypothesis would be that if anxiety hurts performance, then those who scored higher on the anxiety measure will score worse on the math test than will those who received lower anxiety scores. The results typically are pre-

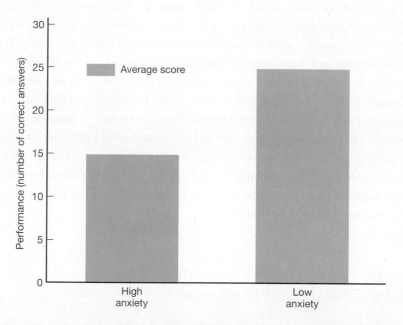

Figure 3.1 **Plot of the Results of a Hypothetical Experiment** Participants in the high-anxiety condition got an average of 15 out of 30 answers correct on a math test, and participants in the low-anxiety condition got an average of 25 correct.

Table 3.3

PARTIAL DATA FOR A HYPOTHETICAL CORRELATIONAL STUDY OF THE RELATIONSHIP BETWEEN ANXIETY AND TEST PERFORMANCE

Participant	Anxiety (x)	Performance (y)
Dave	3	12
Christine	7	3
Mike	2	18
Alex	4	24
Noreen	2	22
Jana	5	15
Etc.	. . .	. . .

Note: An anxiety score (denoted x) and a performance score (denoted y) are obtained from each participant. The results are then plotted in a manner similar to that shown in Figure 3.2.

sented in a table like Table 3.3 and then in a chart like Figure 3.2. Each of the points on the chart, which is called a **scatter plot**, represents an individual participant's pair of scores, one for anxiety (plotted on the horizontal, or x-axis) and one for performance (plotted on the vertical, or y-axis). If a line drawn through these points leans left to right in a downward direction, then the two scores are *negatively correlated*, which means that as one score gets higher, the other gets smaller. In this case, as anxiety gets higher, performance tends to get worse, which is what you predicted. A statistic called a correlation coefficient (discussed later in this chapter) reflects just how strong this trend is. The statistical significance of this correlation can be checked to see whether it is large enough, given the number of participants in the study, to conclude that it would be highly unlikely if the real correlation, in the population, were zero.

Comparing the Experimental and Correlational Methods

The experimental and correlational methods are often discussed as if they were utterly different and diametrically opposed. I hope this example makes clear that they are neither. Both methods attempt to assess the relationship

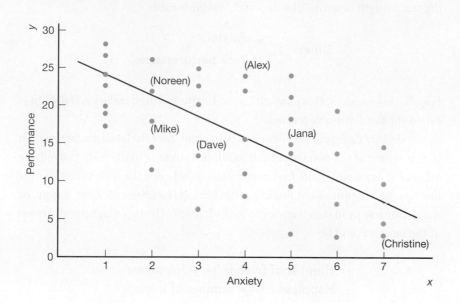

Figure 3.2 Plot of the Results of a Hypothetical Correlational Study Participants who had higher levels of anxiety tended to get lower scores on the math test. The data from the participants represented in Table 3.3 are included, along with others not represented in the table.

between two variables; in the case just discussed, they were "anxiety" and "test performance." A further, more technical similarity is that the statistics used in the two studies are interchangeable—the *t* statistic from the experiment can be converted, using simple algebra, into a correlation coefficient (traditionally denoted by the italicized letter *r*), and vice versa. (Footnote 11 later in this chapter gives the exact formula.) The only real difference between the two designs is that in the experimental method, the presumably causal variable—anxiety—is manipulated, whereas in the correlational method, the same variable is measured as it already exists, without manipulation.

This single difference is very important. It gives the experimental method a powerful advantage: the ability to ascertain what causes what. Because the level of anxiety in the experiment was manipulated by the experimenter, and not just measured as it already existed, you know what caused it. The only possible path is anxiety → performance. In the correlational study, you can't be so sure. Both variables might be the result of some other, unmeasured factor. For example, perhaps some participants in your correlational study were sick that day, which caused them to feel anxious and perform poorly. Instead of a causal pathway with two variables,

Anxiety ⟶ Poor performance

the truth might be more like the three-variable case:

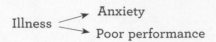

For obvious reasons, this potential complication with correlational design is called the *third-variable problem*.

A slightly different problem arises in some correlational studies, which is that either of the two correlated variables might actually have caused the other. For example, if one finds a correlation between the number of friends one has, and happiness, it might be that having friends makes one happy, or that being happy makes it easier to make friends. Or, in a diagram, the truth of the matter could be

Number of friends ⟶ happiness
Happiness ⟶ number of friends

The correlation itself cannot tell us the direction of causality—indeed, it might (as in this example) run in both directions.

Number of friends ⟵⟶ happiness

You may have heard the statement "Correlation is not causality." It's true. Correlational studies are informative, but raise the possibility that both of two correlated variables were caused by an unmeasured third variable, that either of them might have caused the other, or even that both of them cause each other. Teasing these possibilities apart is a major methodological task, and complex statistical methods such as *structural equation modeling* have been developed to try to help.

The experimental method is not completely free of complications either, however. One problem with the experimental method is that you can never be sure exactly what you have manipulated and, therefore, of where the actual causality was located. In the earlier example, it was presumed that telling participants that their lives depend on their test scores would make them anxious. The results then confirmed the hypothesis: Anxiety hurts performance. But how do you know the statement made them anxious? Maybe it made them angry or disgusted at such an obvious lie. If so, then it could have been anger or disgust that hurt their performance. You only know what you manipulated at the most trivial, operational level—you know what you said to the participants. The psychological variable that you manipulated, however—the one that actually affected behavior—can only be inferred. (This difficulty is related to the problem with interpreting B data that was discussed in Chapter 2.) You might also recognize this difficulty as the third-variable problem just discussed. Indeed, the third-variable problem affects both correlational and experimental designs, but in different ways.

A second complication with the experimental method is that it can create levels of a variable that are unlikely or even impossible in real life. Assuming the experimental manipulation worked as intended, which in this case seems like a big assumption, how often is your life literally hanging in the balance when you take a math test? Any extrapolation from the results of this experiment to the levels of anxiety that ordinarily exist during exams could be highly misleading. Moreover, maybe in real life most people are moderately anxious. But in the experiment, two groups were artificially created: One was presumably highly anxious; the other (again, presumably) was not anxious at all. In real life, both groups may be rare. Therefore, the effect of anxiety on performance may be exaggerated in this experiment, with respect to the degree of importance it has in real life; differences in anxiety level are typically less extreme. The correlational method, by contrast, assesses levels of anxiety that already exist in the participants. Thus, these levels are not artificial, and they are more likely to represent anxiety as it really exists in "average" people. Also, notice how the correlational study included seven levels of anxiety (one for each point on the anxiety scale), whereas the experimental study included only two (one for each condition). Therefore, the results of the correlational study may reflect more precisely the degree to which anxiety affects performance in real life.

This conclusion highlights an important way in which experimental and correlational studies complement each other. An experiment can determine whether one variable *can* affect another, but not how often or how much it actually *does*, in real life. For that, correlational research is required.

A third disadvantage particular to the experimental method is that, unlike correlational studies, experiments often require deception. I will discuss deception later, but for now just note that psychological experiments often require experimenters to lie to participants. Correlational studies rarely do.

The final disadvantage of the experimental method is the most important one. Sometimes experiments are simply not possible. For example, if you want to know the effects of child abuse on self-esteem in adulthood, all you can do is try to assess whether people who were abused as children tend to have low self-esteem, which would be a correlational study. The experimental equivalent is not possible. You cannot assemble a group of children and randomly abuse half of them just to see what happens to their self-esteem later in life. Moreover, in personality psychology the topic of interest is often the effect of personality traits or other stable individual differences on behavior. You cannot make half of the participants extraverted and the other half introverted; you must accept the traits that the participants bring into the laboratory.

Many discussions of correlational and experimental designs, including those in many textbooks, conclude that the experimental method is obviously superior. This is not correct. Experimental and correlational designs both have advantages and disadvantages, as we have seen, and ideally a complete research program would include both, for two reasons. First, the two designs serve different goals. Experiments can show whether a variable can have an effect on another variable; correlational studies are needed to assess how often and how much, as we have seen.

> Experimental and correlational designs both have advantages and disadvantages, and ideally a complete research program would include both.

Second, in some cases important effects are invisible if only one method is employed (Revelle & Oehlberg, 2008). In a classic example, participants in an experimental study were given caffeine or put under time stress, to assess the effect of these variables on performance on test performance. Surprisingly, there was no effect of either variable at all! The puzzle was solved when further analyses examined individual differences using the correlational method. It turned out that the effect of caffeine and time stress depends on personality. Performance gets worse for introverts, but actually gets better for extraverts (Revelle, Amaral, & Turriff, 1976).[6] This important finding would never have become visible through experimental or correlational studies alone—they had to be used together. The moral of this story is, I think, pretty obvious.

Representative Design

Do the results of a study have any implications beyond its own particular implications or participants? In other words, are the results *representative* of what happens beyond the confines of the laboratory? A great psychologist who studied perception and judgment in the 1940s and 1950s, Egon Brunswik (1956), spent a great deal of effort trying to deal with this question. As discussed earlier, researchers frequently are concerned with

---

[6] Later research showed that the situation is even more complicated, because time of day is important too (Revelle, Humphreys, Simon, & Gilliland, 1980).

whether their research participants are fairly representative of people in general, which is why they include a sample of participants, not just one. Brunswik pointed out that participants are not the only factor across which researchers must generalize. Equally pressing, though less often addressed, are concerns about generalizability across **stimuli** and **responses**.

For example, a researcher might use one particular method to induce a state of "anxiety" in participants. The expected results are obtained, but what if a different method had been used to induce anxiety? In the hypothetical example earlier in the chapter, the researcher tried to make participants anxious by saying, "Your life depends on your test performance." What if, instead, the researcher had arranged for an artificial earthquake to hit the testing room, or had parked a cageful of snakes in the corner? Would the effects of these other kinds of "anxiety" be the same? The research cannot say. Or, maybe one particular behavior (perhaps test performance) is measured to detect whether the experimental manipulation has affected how well people perform. Again, good results are obtained, but what if a different method or a different kind of test performance had been used? Does anxiety affect free-throw shooting the same way it affects performance on a math test? Unless both kinds of performance are assessed, the research cannot say. This is an important issue, because without evidence that different ways of creating anxiety have the same effect, it is hazardous to interpret the results as showing the effects of anxiety—they only really show the effects of telling people the test is vital, or of introducing a cageful of snakes, or whatever particular method was used to try to arouse anxiety.

Brunswik said that the solution to this dilemma should be the use of *representative design*—that is, research should be designed to sample across the domains to which the investigator will wish to generalize the results. A researcher who wishes to generalize to all people who might serve on juries, for example, ideally should draw participants randomly from a sample of those who are subject to jury duty. It also means that if a researcher intends to generalize her experimental manipulation to all methods of producing anxiety, the research should employ a sample of possible methods. (It is not necessary to use all methods any more than it is necessary to recruit every person on earth to be in the experiment, but the ones that are used should be representative.) Representative design further means that in order to generalize results to all types of performance, research needs to sample from those as well; it should try to affect several different kinds of performance that reflect the range of anxiety effects that you think exist in real life. So a study of the effect of anxiety on performance should ideally include several different ways to induce anxiety and several different measures of performance.

Perhaps you will be surprised to learn that up to and including the present day, Brunswik's advice is seldom followed, despite the efforts of a small group of psychologists who call themselves "Brunswikians" (see Hammond & Stewart, 2001). Researchers do tend to sample a group of participants—they usually do not study just one. (Although they don't often worry about the fact that their college students are not really representative of people in the real world, at least they use more than one participant). In the other domains of generalizability, sampling is almost nonexistent. The typical experimental study uses one kind of experimental manipulation and measures just one kind of behavior. This makes the research less generalizable—less broadly relevant—than it might otherwise be.

Brunswik's notion of representative design, though it strikes me as elementary good sense, has yet to significantly affect the practice of psychological research. One major obstacle is that the employment of representative design, or anything close to it, would make research much more expensive and time-consuming. In the long run, the solution is probably to think of research as consisting of programs of many studies, rather than as putting too much trust in the result of one single study. Over the course of many studies by many different scientists, we can hope that anxiety and its effects, for example, would be manipulated and measured many different ways. As results begin to cohere into a consistent pattern, we can become more confident that research has established findings that are fairly representative of reality.[7]

EFFECT SIZES

Psychologists, being human, like to brag about their results. Often—maybe too often—they describe the effects they have discovered as being "large," "important," or even "dramatic." Nearly always, they describe their results as "significant." These descriptions can be very confusing because there are no rules about how the first three terms can be employed. "Large," "important," and even "dramatic" are just adjectives and can be used at will. However, there are formal and rather strict rules about how the term *significant* can be employed.

---

[7] The technique of *meta-analysis* is increasingly often used to synthesize the results of large numbers of studies by many different investigators. For a review, see Rosenthal & DiMatteo, 2001.

Significance Testing

A significant result, in research parlance, is not necessarily large or important, let alone dramatic. But it is a result that is unlikely to appear if everything were due to chance. This is important to determine, because in any experimental study the difference between two conditions will almost never[8] turn out to be exactly zero, and in correlational studies an *r* of precisely zero is equally rare. So, how different do the means of the two conditions have to be, or how big does the correlation coefficient need to be, before we will conclude that these are numbers we should take seriously?

"The figures for the last quarter are in. We made significant gains in the fifteen- to twenty-six-year-old age group, but we lost our immortal souls."

The most commonly used method for answering this question is *null-hypothesis significance testing (NHST)*. NHST attempts to answer the question, "What are the chances I would have found this result if nothing were really going on?" The basic procedure is taught in every beginning statistics class. A correlation (in a correlational study) or a difference between experimental conditions (in an experimental study) that is said to be significant at the 5 percent level is different from zero to a degree that, by chance alone, would be expected about 5 percent of the time. A difference or correlation significant at the 1 percent level is different from zero to a degree expected by chance about 1 percent of the time, and so this is traditionally considered a stronger result. Various statistical formulas, some quite complex, are employed to calculate the likelihood that experimental or correlational results would be expected by chance. The more unlikely, the better.

For example, the results in Figures 3.1 and 3.2 might be evaluated by calculating the **p-level** (probability level) of the difference in means (in the experimental study) or of the correlation coefficient (in the correlational study). In each case, the *p*-level would give the probability of getting a difference of the size that was found, if the actual size of the difference were to be zero. (The possibility that the actual size of the difference between conditions or of the correlation is zero is called the *null hypothesis*.) If the result is significant, the common interpretation—which is technically incorrect,

---

[8] Actually, never.

as we shall see—is that the statistic probably did not arise by chance; its real value (sometimes called the *population value*) is probably not zero, so the null hypothesis is incorrect, and the result is big enough to take seriously.

This traditional method of statistical data analysis is deeply embedded in the psychological research literature and in current research practice. But I would not be doing my duty if I failed to warn you that insightful psychologists have been critical of this method over the years (e.g., Rozeboom, 1960), and the frequency and intensity of this criticism have increased recently (e.g., G. R. Loftus, 1996; Haig, 2005). Indeed, some psychologists have seriously suggested that significance testing like this should be banned (Hunter, 1997; F. L. Schmidt, 1996)! That may be going a bit far, but NHST does have several serious problems. This chapter is not the place for an extended discussion, but it might be worth a few words to describe some of the more obvious difficulties (see also R. J. Harris, 1997; Haig, 2005).

One problem with NHST is that it is very difficult to describe the logic precisely, and common descriptions—including those found in textbooks—are frequently wrong. It is not correct, for example, to say that the significance level gives the probability that the null hypothesis is true. Instead, the significance level gives the probability of getting the result one found, *if* the null hypothesis were true. In other words, a p-level is the probability of the data given the (null) hypothesis, not the probability of the hypothesis given the data. And the latter is what we really want to know.

An analogy might help. Suppose our datum is the fact that a person is a U.S. citizen, and our "hypothesis" is that she is a member of Congress. The probability of the data given the hypothesis is very high—all members of Congress are U.S. citizens. The probability of the hypothesis given the data, however, is very low—the vast majority of U.S. citizens are not members of Congress. So the probability of the data given the hypothesis, and of the hypothesis given the data, are entirely different things.

Believe it or not, I really did try to write the preceding paragraphs as clearly as I could. But if you found them confusing, you are in good company. One study found that 97 percent of academic psychologists, and even 80 percent of methodology instructors, misunderstood NHST in an important way (S. Krauss & Wassner, 2002). This finding is not a reflection on their intelligence, I believe. Instead, it shows that the logic of the most widely used method for interpreting research findings is so confusing that even experts often get it wrong. This cannot be a good thing.

Another problem with NHST is that even if a "significant" result were one that probably did not occur by sheer chance, that would not necessarily mean that the result was strong or important. Most measures used in psychological research have arbitrary scales where the numbers have no intrinsic meaning beyond being relatively high or low (Blanton & Jaccard, 2006). For example, a person might score 17 points out of a possible 25 on a "friendliness" scale, but does this mean he is friendly or unfriendly? There is no way to know without further research that seeks to provide specific descriptions of the behaviors associated with different points on the scale. For another example, one group of people may score 2 points higher on a measure of ability, attitude, or even racial prejudice than another group, and this difference might be statistically significant, but the implications of this difference will remain unclear without further research to find out how much a 2-point difference affects behavior. An important direction for future research will be to find ways to clarify the meanings of otherwise arbitrary psychological measurements.

> The logic of the most widely used method for interpreting research findings is so confusing that even experts often get it wrong.

Another, more obvious difficulty with NHST is that the criterion for a significant result is little more than a traditional rule of thumb. Why is a result of $p < .05$ significant, when a result of $p < .06$ is not? There is no real answer, and nobody seems to even know where the standard .05 level came from (though I strongly suspect it has something to do with the fact that we have five fingers on each hand). Another obvious difficulty is that, strangely, the chances of getting a significant result vary with how many participants are in the study. The very same strength of an effect that is nonsignificant with 30 participants might suddenly become highly significant if there are 50 participants. This is worrisome because nature hasn't changed, just the conclusion the scientist reaches about it. Yet another common difficulty is that even experienced researchers too often misinterpret a nonsignificant result to mean "no result." If, for example, the obtained p-level is .06, researchers sometimes conclude that there is no difference between the experimental and control conditions or no relationship between two correlated variables. But actually, the probability is only 6 out of 100 that, if there were no effect, a difference this big would have been found.

This observation leads to one final difficulty with traditional significance tests: The p-level addresses only the probability of one kind of error, conventionally called a **Type I error**. A Type I error involves deciding that one variable has an effect on, or a relationship with, another variable, when really it does not. The p-level is typically interpreted (incorrectly) as giving the odds of making this kind of error (e.g., a p-level of .05 is commonly taken to mean you have a 5 percent chance of being wrong if you conclude you have a real effect). But there is another kind of error: A **Type II error** involves deciding that one variable does *not* have an effect on, or relationship with, another variable, when it really *does*. Unfortunately, there is no way to estimate the probability of a Type II error without making extra assumptions (J. Cohen, 1994; Gigerenzer, Hoffrage, & Kleinbolting, 1991).

What a mess. The bottom line is this: When you take a course in psychological statistics, if you haven't done so already, you will have to learn about significance testing and how to do it. Despite its many and widely acknowledged flaws, NHST is still in wide use (S. Krauss & Wassner, 2002). But it is probably not as useful a technique as it looks to be at first, and psychological research practice seems to be moving slowly but surely away (Abelson, Cohen, & Rosenthal, 1996; Wilkinson & the Task Force on Statistical Inference, 1999).

We usually want to know two things from our data. First, is the result stable, or did it occur by chance? NHST was designed to help answer this question, but it is not really up to the job. A much better indication of the stability of results is *replication*. In other words, do the study again. Statistics are all well and good, but there is nothing quite so persuasive as finding the same result repeatedly, with different participants and in different labs. The second thing we want to know from our data is, are our results important? For that we need to turn to an altogether different kind of statistic.

Correlations

Psychologists who are better analysts of data do not just stop with significance. They move on to calculate a number that will reflect the size, as opposed to the likelihood, of their result. This number is called an **effect size**. An effect size is more meaningful than a significance level. Indeed, the *Publication Manual of the American Psychological Association* (which sets the standards that must be followed by almost all published research in psychology) explicitly says that the probability value associated with statistical significance does not reflect "the magnitude of an effect or the strength of a relationship. For the reader to fully understand the importance of your findings, it is almost always necessary to include some index of effect size or strength of relationship" (American Psychological Association, 2001, p. 25).

Many measures of effect size exist, the most commonly used (and my personal favorite) being the **correlation coefficient**. Despite its name, its use is not limited to correlational studies. The correlation coefficient can be used to describe the strength of the effect in either a correlational or an experimental study (Funder & Ozer, 1983).

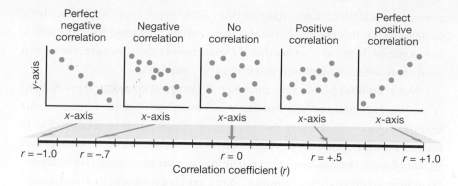

Figure 3.3 Correlation Coefficient The correlation coefficient is a number between −1.0 and 1.0 that indicates the relationship between two variables, traditionally labeled x and y.

CALCULATING CORRELATIONS

To calculate a correlation coefficient, in the usual case, you start with two variables. For example, in Table 3.3 the two variables were "anxiety" and "performance." The first step is to arrange all of the scores on the two variables into two columns, with each row containing the scores for one participant. Traditionally, these columns are labeled x and y, and also traditionally, the variable you think is the cause is put in the x column and the variable you think is the effect is put in the y column. So, in this example, x is "anxiety" and y is "performance." Then you apply a common statistical formula (found in any statistics textbook) to these numbers or, perhaps more commonly these days, you punch the numbers into a computer or maybe even a handheld calculator.[9]

The result is a correlation coefficient (the most common kind of correlation coefficient is called the *Pearson r*). This is a number that—if you did the calculations right—is somewhere between +1 and −1 (Figure 3.3). If two variables are unrelated, the correlation between them will be near zero. If the variables are positively associated—as one goes up, the other tends to go up too, like height and weight—then the correlation coefficient will be greater than zero (i.e., a positive number). If the variables are negatively associated—as one goes up, the other tends to go down, like "anxiety" and "performance"—then the correlation coefficient will be less than zero (i.e.,

---

[9] Programs to calculate the correlation coefficient are also available online. One easy-to-use calculator can be found at faculty.vassar.edu/lowry/corr_stats.html.

a negative number).[10] Essentially, if two variables are correlated (positively or negatively), this means that one of them can be predicted from the other. For example, Figure 3.2 shows that if I know how anxious you are, then I can predict (to a degree) how well you will do on a math test.

Not everybody knows this, but you can also get a correlation coefficient from experimental studies. For the experiment on test performance, for example, you could just give everybody in the high-anxiety condition a "1" for anxiety and everybody in the low-anxiety condition a "0." These 1s and 0s would go in the x column, and participants' corresponding levels of performance would go in the y column. There are also formulas to directly convert the statistics usually seen in experimental studies into correlations. For example, the t or F statistic (used in the analysis of variance) can be directly converted into an r.[11] It is good practice to do this conversion whenever possible, because then you can compare the results of correlational and experimental studies using a common metric.

INTERPRETING CORRELATIONS

To interpret a correlation coefficient, it is not enough to just use statistical significance. An obtained correlation becomes significant in a statistical sense merely by being unlikely to have arisen if the true correlation is zero, which depends as much on how many participants you managed (or could afford) to recruit as on how strong the effect really is. Instead, you need to look at the actual size of the correlation. Some textbooks provide rules of thumb. A textbook I happen to own says that a correlation (positive or negative) of .6 to .8 is "quite strong," one from .3 to .5 is "weaker but still important," and one from .3 to .2 is "rather weak." I have no idea what these phrases are supposed to mean. Do you?

Another commonly taught way to evaluate effect sizes is to square them, which tells "what percent of the variance the correlation explains." This cer-

---

[10] Also, if you draw a line through the points on a scatter plot, such as those in Figure 3.3, and the line slopes upward (left to right), then the correlation is positive. If the line slopes downward (as in Figure 3.2), then the correlation is negative. If the line is flat (horizontal), then the correlation is zero.

[11] The most commonly used statistic that reflects a difference between two experimental groups is the t (the outcome of a t-test). The standard symbol for the commonly used Pearson correlation coefficient is r. The experimental t can be converted to the correlational r using the following formula:

$$r = \sqrt{\frac{t^2}{t^2 + (n_1 + n_2 - 2)}}$$

where n_1 and n_2 are the sizes of the two samples (or experimental groups) being compared.

tainly sounds like what you need to know, and the calculation is wonderfully easy. For example, a correlation of .30, when squared, yields .09, which means that "only" 9 percent of the variance is explained by the correlation, and the remaning 91 percent is "unexplained." Similarly, a correlation of .40 means that "only" 16 percent of the variance is explained and 84 percent is unexplained. That seems like a lot of unexplaining, and so these correlations are often viewed as small.

Despite the wide popularity of this squaring method (if you have taken a statistics course you were probably taught it), I think it is a *terrible* way to evaluate effect size. The real and perhaps only result of this pseudo-sophisticated maneuver is to make the correlations typically found in psychological research seem trivial. It is the case that both in correlational research in personality and in experimental research in social psychology, the effect sizes expressed in correlations rarely exceed .40 (Funder & Ozer, 1983; see also Richard, Bond, & Stokes-Zoota, 2003, which gives the average effect size in social psychology as .21). Indeed, many important findings have effect sizes in about this range, or smaller, some of which are listed in Table 3.4. If results like these are considered to "explain" (whatever that

Table 3.4

EFFECT SIZES OF SOME IMPORTANT RESEARCH FINDINGS

Finding	Effect Size (r)
People are aggressive when they are in a bad mood.	.41
The higher a person's credibility, the more persuasive s/he will be.	.10
Scarcity increases the value of a commodity.	.12
People attribute failures to bad luck.	.10
People behave as others expect them to behave.	.33
Men are recommended for jobs over women.	.20
Members of a group influence one another.	.33
Married people report higher life satisfaction than others.	.14
People are likely to help others when they are in a good mood.	.26
People usually prefer their own group to other groups.	.35
Boys are more competitive than girls.	.03
Females smile more than males.	.23

Source: Richard et al. (2003), pp. 353–363.

means) "16 percent of the variance" (whatever that means), leaving "84 percent unexplained," then we are left with the vague but disturbing conclusion that research has not accomplished much. Yet this conclusion is not correct. It is statistically confusing and substantively misleading (Ozer, 1985). Worst of all, it is almost impossible to understand. What is really needed is a way to evaluate the size of correlations to help understand the strength and, in some cases, the usefulness of the result obtained.

THE BINOMIAL EFFECT SIZE DISPLAY

What is needed is a method, other than squaring, to demonstrate in some concrete manner how big these effect-size correlations really are. Rosenthal and Rubin (1982) provided a brilliant technique for doing just that, called the **Binomial Effect Size Display (BESD)**. Let's use Rosenthal and Rubin's favorite example to illustrate how it works.

Assume you are studying 200 participants, all of whom are sick. An experimental drug is given to 100 of them; the other 100 are given nothing. At the end of the study, 100 are alive and 100 are dead. The question is, how much difference did the drug make?

Sometimes the answer to this question can be reported in the form of a correlation coefficient that is calculated from the data on how many participants lived and died. For example, you may be told that the data show that the correlation between taking the drug and recovering from the illness is .40. If the report stops here (as it usually does), you are left with the following questions: What does this mean? Was the effect big or little? If you were to follow the common practice of squaring correlations to yield "variance explained," you might conclude that "84 percent of the variance remains unexplained" (which sounds pretty bad) and decide the drug is nearly worthless.

The BESD provides another way to think about the size of a correlation coefficient. Through some simple further calculations, you can move from a report that "the correlation is .40" to a concrete display of what that correlation means in terms of specific outcomes. For example, as shown in Table 3.5, a correlation of .40 means that 70 percent of those who got the drug are still alive, whereas only 30 percent of those who did not get the drug are still alive. If the correlation is .30, those figures would be 65 percent and 35 percent, respectively. As Rosenthal and Rubin pointed out, these effects might only explain 16 percent or even 9 percent of the variance, but in either case, if you got sick, would you want this drug?

Table 3.5

THE BINOMIAL EFFECT SIZE DISPLAY

	Alive	Dead	Total
Drug	70	30	100
No drug	30	70	100
Total	100	100	200

Life and death outcomes for participants in a hypothetical 200-person drug trial, when the correlation between drug administration and outcome $r = .40$.
Source: After Rosenthal & Rubin (1982), p. 167.

The computational method begins by assuming a correlation of zero, which gives each of the four cells in the table an entry of 50 (i.e., if there is no effect, then 50 participants receiving the drug will live and 50 will die—it does not matter whether they get the treatment or not). Then we take the actual correlation (in the example, .40), move the decimal to produce a two-digit number (.40 becomes 40), divide by 2 (in this case yielding 20), and add it to the 50 in the upper-left-hand cell (yielding 70). Then we adjust the other three cells by subtraction. Because each row and column must total 100, the four cells, reading clockwise, become 70, 30, 70, and 30.

This technique works with any kind of data. "Alive" and "dead" can be replaced with any kind of dichotomized outcomes—"better-than-average school success" and "worse-than-average school success," for example. The treatment variables could become "taught with new method" and "taught with old method." Or the variables could be "scores above average on school motivation" and "scores below average on school motivation," or any other personality variable (see Table 3.6). One can even look at predictors of success for major-league baseball teams (see Figure 3.4).

The fundamental message of the BESD is that correlational effects need to be interpreted more carefully than they usually are. It is both facile and misleading to use the frequently taught method of squaring correlations if the intention is to evaluate effect size. (Squaring, however, is useful for other, more technical purposes.) The BESD, by contrast, shows vividly both how much of an effect an experimental intervention is likely to have, and how well one can predict an outcome from an individual measurement of difference. So, when you read—later in this book or in a psychological

Table 3.6

THE BINOMIAL EFFECT SIZE DISPLAY USED TO INTERPRET SCHOOL DATA

School Motivation	School Performance		Total
	Above Average	Below Average	
Above average	50	50	100
Below average	50	50	100
Total	100	100	200

School performance outcomes for 200 students above and below average on school motivation when correlation between the two variables r = 0.

School Motivation	School Performance		Total
	Above Average	Below Average	
Above average	65	35	100
Below average	35	65	100
Total	100	100	200

School performance outcomes for 200 students above and below average on school motivation when correlation between the two variables r = .30.

research article—that one variable is related to another with a correlation of .30 or .40 or whatever, you should construct a BESD in your mind and evaluate the size of the correlation accordingly.

ETHICS

The Uses of Psychological Research

Like any other human activity, research involves ethical issues. Some issues are common to all research. One is the concern that the results may be used for harmful purposes. Just as physicists who develop atomic bombs should worry about what their inventions can do, so too should psychologists be aware of the consequences of what their research might discover.

For example, one field of psychology—behaviorism—has long aimed to develop a technology to control behavior (see Chapter 15). The technology is not available yet, but if it ever arrives, it will raise ethical questions about who decides what behaviors to create and whose behavior should be controlled. The main figure in behaviorism, B. F. Skinner, wrote extensively about these issues (e.g., Skinner, 1948, 1971). Questions about how research is used also sometimes arise in the field of personality assessment. For example, during the 1930s and 1940s some employers used personality tests to try to screen out job applicants inclined to be pro-union (Zickar, 2001). Does this seem ethical to you?

Yet another issue arises when psychologists choose to study racial differences and sex differences. Putting aside whatever purely scientific merits this work might have, it raises a fundamental question about whether its findings are likely to do more harm than good. If some racial group really is lower in intelligence, or if men really are better (or worse) at math than women, do we really want to know? The arguments in favor of exploring these issues are that science should study everything, and (on a more applied level) that knowing the basic abilities of a group might help in tailoring educational programs specifically to the needs of its members. The arguments against this research are that such findings are bound to be misused by racists and sexists and therefore can become tools of oppression themselves, and that knowledge of group characteristics is not really very useful for tailoring programs to individual needs.

When the question comes down to whether to study a given topic or not, psychologists, like other scientists, almost always come down on the side of studying it. After all, ignorance never got anybody very far. Still, there are an infinite number of interesting, unanswered questions out there that one could usefully investigate. When a psychologist devotes research time trying to prove that one race is smarter than another, or that one gender is superior to the other in some respect, it

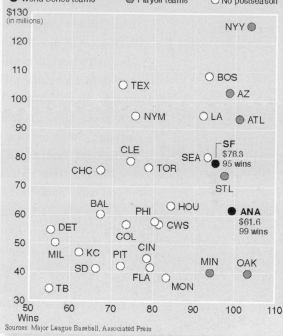

Highest performers not highest paid

Spending doesn't guarantee success in Major League Baseball. The Anaheim Angels' payroll in 2002 is half that of the Yankees, who were defeated by Anaheim in the first round of playoffs.

Team payrolls versus total wins

● World Series teams   ● Playoff teams   ○ No postseason

Sources: Major League Baseball; Associated Press

Figure 3.4 Statistics on the Sports Page An analysis of the relationship between total payrolls of major-league baseball teams and total number of games won in the 2002 season. This chart appeared in the sports section of the *Los Angeles Times*. Notice the conclusion expressed by the headline. Is it valid? The correlation between payroll and games won is .44, which, according to the Binomial Effect Size Display, means that a team that pays above-average salaries has a 72 percent chance of winning more than half its games, whereas a team that pays below-average salaries has only a 28 percent chance.

is hard not to wish that the psychologist had found some other worthwhile topic to investigate instead.

Truthfulness

Truthfulness is another ethical issue common to all research. The past few years have seen a number of scandals in physics, medicine, and psychology in which researchers either plagiarized the work of others or fabricated their own data. Lies cause difficulty in all sectors of life, but they are particularly worrisome in research because science is based on truth and trust. Scientific research is the attempt to seek truth in as unbiased a way as one can manage. Scientific lies, when they happen, undermine the very foundation of the field. Science without truthfulness is completely meaningless.

All scientists must trust each other for the process to work. If I report to you some data that I have found, you might disagree with my interpretation—that is fine, and in science this happens all the

....

Science without truthfulness is completely meaningless.

....

time. Working through disagreements about what data mean is essential scientific activity. But if you cannot be sure that I really found those data, then there is no basis for further discussion. Even scientists who vehemently disagree on fundamental issues generally take each other's truthfulness for granted (contrast this with the situation in politics). If they cannot, then science stops dead in its tracks.

Deception

The fundamental reliance of science on truth makes the use of deception in research somewhat worrisome. Quite frequently, psychologists tell their research participants something that is not true.[12] The purpose of such deception usually is to make the research "realistic." A participant might be told—falsely—that a test she is taking is a valid IQ or personality test, for example, so that the experimenter can assess the participant's reaction when she receives a poor score. Or a participant might be told that another person was described by a "trained psychologist" as "friendly" and "unsociable," to

---

[12]This is not the same as simply withholding information, as in a double-blind drug trial, in which neither the patient nor the physician knows whether the drug or placebo is being administered. Deception involves knowingly telling a lie.

see how the participant resolves this type of inconsistency. One of the most famous deception experiments was the one in which Stanley Milgram (1975) led participants to believe they were administering fatal electric shocks to an innocent, screaming victim; the "victim" was actually an actor. But most deception in psychological research is not so dramatic. The most common deceptive practice is probably the "cover story," in which participants are misinformed about the topic of the study. For example, they might be told the study is examining intellectual aptitude, when actually the purpose is to see how participants react when told they performed well or poorly.

The American Psychological Association has developed a detailed set of ethical guidelines that psychological researchers are supposed to follow. Research universities also all have institutional review boards (called IRBs) that review the ethics of all procedures conducted with human participants. The decisions made by IRBs, in turn, are increasingly guided by federal regulations. The guidelines used by the American Psychological Association and by most IRBs do allow deception, although the limits on its use are narrower than they used to be. Milgram's experiment probably would not be allowed today, although studies like the others described are still conducted frequently.

Three arguments are usually given for why deception should be allowed. The first is that participants gave their "informed consent" to be deceived. The second is that the lies usually do no harm. Indeed, some research indicates that participants report enjoying and profiting more from studies in which they were deceived than from those in which they were not (S. S.

Figure 3.5 Was This Experiment Ethical? In a famous series of experiments, the psychologist Stanley Milgram put ordinary people in a situation where they were ordered to give an innocent victim electric shocks that appeared to be dangerous or even fatal. Such a degree of emotionally significant deception would probably not be allowed by ethics committees today.

"Remember when I said I was going to be honest with you, Jeff? That was a big, fat lie."

Smith & Richardson, 1983). The third argument is that certain topics cannot be investigated without the use of a little deception. For example, if you want to know whether people will stop and help when confronted by an unconscious stranger, the only real way to know is to put such a stimulus in front of a participant and see what happens (Darley & Batson, 1967; Darley & Latané, 1968). It would not do to let people know that the passed-out victim is really the researcher's accomplice.

Are these convincing arguments? Decide for yourself. For my part, I do not see how one can give "informed consent" to be deceived; the situation seems oxymoronic (Baumrind, 1985). But more important, I think that excuses for deception that focus on the probable lack of harm to the participant miss the point. Indeed, the experience of being in most experiments is probably too mild and too infrequent to generate much in the way of consequences for participants. The real victim of a deception experiment, it seems to me, is the psychologist. The problem with lying is that once it begins, you never know when it has stopped. In a deception experiment, one person (a psychologist) has told a lie to another person (the participant). When the experimenter says, "I lied to you, but the experiment is now over," is it really over? (In at least one experiment I know of, it wasn't! See Ross, Lepper, & Hubbard, 1975.) And, on a broader scale, the psychologist has been exposed as somebody who, for a "right" end, will lie to you. What does this do to the credibility of psychology as a science (Greenberg & Folger, 1988)?

One small area in which I see this harm is in my research. Although I have not done any deception experiments in a long time (and since I made that decision, I have never really felt the lack), often my participants do not believe me! They spend the experimental hour trying to see through my cover story, even though I don't use one. Being sophisticated about psychologists and what they do, my participants find it hard to believe that I am actually studying what I have said I am studying. And I cannot blame them one bit. Until psychologists stop employing deception as a matter of routine, why should anybody believe a word they say? (For a contrary view on this matter, see Sharpe, Adair, & Roese, 1992.)

The most powerful defense of deception in psychological research is that, without it, certain topics cannot be investigated. For example, without the use of deception, important research on obedience, bystander intervention, and aggression could never have been conducted. Of course, these and other topics could still be studied in the real world. Instead of showing your participants a hypothetical stimulus person who does not exist and probably never could (as many studies do), let your participants watch and judge somebody who is real. Instead of constructing artificial situations where people are led to think they have succeeded or failed (assuming they believe you), follow them into their real lives where success and failure happen all the time. Obedience, bystander intervention, and aggression can be observed in daily life as well. This is sometimes done, but notice how research that follows this advice is restricted to correlational studies. The powerful advantage of the experimental method—its determination of the direction of causality—is lost.

The trade-offs are difficult to evaluate. In my research, as I mentioned, I no longer use deception. But other psychologists have come to other conclusions, and deceptive research is still quite common. I do know this: The issue of using of deception in psychological research is not simple. There is plenty of room for reasonable disagreement, and my own strong misgivings are fairly rare within the field. Most psychologists believe that, with proper controls, the use of deception in research is perfectly safe and ethical. They further believe that deception is necessary to allow psychological research to address certain important issues. If you are reading this book as part of a personality course, your instructor probably has a strong opinion about the permissibility of deception. Why not ask your instructor what that opinion is, and why? Then, draw your own conclusions.

TOOLS OF EXPLORATION

As one of my mentors often pointed out, data are messages from the real world that, if decoded, may tell you what is really going on. But the messages are typically confusing, contradictory, and full of static, as anyone who has spent a frustrating afternoon poring over a computer printout of her data can tell you. That is why we need to use all the ingenuity we can muster to increase the reliability and validity of our data. Nature does not give up its secrets easily. Research entails finding out something about the world that nobody ever knew before—research methods are tools of exploration, which is always difficult and, by definition, mysterious.

SUMMARY

Psychology's Emphasis on Method

- Psychology emphasizes the methods by which knowledge can be obtained, and in general is more concerned with better understanding human nature than with cataloging specific facts.

Scientific Education and Technical Training

- Real science is the seeking of new knowledge, not the cataloging of facts already known for certain. Technical training conveys what is already known about a subject, so that the knowledge can be applied. Scientific education, by contrast, teaches not only what is known but also how to find out what is not yet known.

Quality of Data

- The essence of science is that conclusions should be based on data. Data can vary widely in quality; in personality psychology the important dimensions of data quality are reliability, validity, and generalizability.

- Reliability refers to the stability or repeatability of measurements. Validity, on the other hand, refers to the degree to which a measurement actually measures what it is trying to measure. Generalizability is a broader concept that subsumes both reliability and validity, and it refers to the kinds of other measurements to which a given measurement is related.

Research Design

- The plan one uses for gathering psychological data is the research design; the three main methods are case, experimental, and correlational.

- Case studies examine particular phenomena or individuals in detail, and can be an important source of new ideas that might apply more generally. To test these ideas, correlational and experimental studies are necessary. Each of the three methods has advantages and disadvantages, but the experimental method is the only one that can be used to determine the direction of causality.

- Representative design is a technique used to maximize the generalizability of research results.

Effect Sizes

- The statistical significance of a result represents the probability that the data would have been obtained if the "null hypothesis" were true, but it is typically misinterpreted as the probability that the null hypothesis is true. Null-hypothesis significance testing (NHST) has many problems that are increasingly being acknowledged. In particular, statistical significance is not the same as the strength or importance of the result.

- The best way to evaluate research results is in terms of effect size, which describes numerically the degree to which one variable is related to another. One good measure of effect size is the correlation coefficient, which can be evaluated with the Binomial Effect Size Display (BESD).

Ethics

- Ethical issues relevant to psychology include the way research results are used, truthfulness in science, and the use of deception in research with human participants.

Tools of Exploration

- Knowledge of research methods is critical because nature does not give up its secrets easily. It is important to do everything possible to enhance the reliability and validity of data to have any hope of using them to understand how the world works.

THINK ABOUT IT

1. Is there a cohort effect between your generation and that of your parents? Do you think differently than they do? Would the conclusions of research done with college students apply to their parents? Can you think of any particular areas where they would be most likely to be different?

2. Is research done with the predominantly white college students in Western cultures also relevant to members of ethnic minorities or to people who live in other cultures? In what areas would you expect to find the most differences?

3. If you have taken a statistics course: What does a significance level tell you? What does it *not* tell you? If we were to stop using significance levels to evaluate research findings, what could we use instead?

4. Let's say we find that you score 4 points higher on a "conscientiousness" test than does another person. Alternatively, imagine that women score 4 points higher on the same test, on average, than men do. In either case, is this difference important? What else would we have to know to be able to answer this question?

5. Is deception in psychological research justified? Does it depend on the research question? Does it depend on the specific kind of deception? Does it depend on the kind of informed consent offered by the research participant? Who, if anybody, is harmed by the use of deception in research?

6. Some psychologists do research on differences between races in intelligence. Let's say members of one race really do have higher IQ scores than members of another race. Consider the issues raised above, in question 4. Then consider: Is this the kind of research psychologists should be doing, or is the issue better left alone? Once the research is done, how will the results be used?

7. Repeat question 6, but substitute *gender* for *race*.

SUGGESTED READINGS

Cronbach, L. J., & Meehl, P. E. (1955). Construct validity in psychological tests. *Psychological Bulletin*, 52, 281–302.

> *A difficult article, but the classic presentation of how personality psychologists think about the validity of their measurements. One of the most influential methodological articles ever published.*

Goodman-Delahunty, J. (Ed.) (2005). *Psychology, Public Policy, and Law*, 11, 233–336.

> *This entire issue of a journal of the American Psychological Association is devoted to an article summarizing research on race differences in cognitive ability, several rebuttals to this article, and a rejoinder by the authors of the original article. Taken together, the articles raise important issues concerning the meaning and ethics of research on racial differences, and the reasons why one would, or would not, choose to investigate this or any other topic.*

Rosenthal, R., & Rosnow, R. L. (1991). *Essentials of behavioral research: Methods and data analysis* (2nd ed.). New York: McGraw-Hill.

> *One of the best primers for a beginning researcher. This book includes many topics (such as effect size) not handled well in other methods or statistics texts. You will have to read this book to see what its authors mean by the advice "Think Yiddish, write British."*

Rozeboom, W. W. (1960). The fallacy of the null-hypothesis significance test. *Psychological Bulletin*, 57, 416–428.

> *One of the first, and still one of the clearest and most persuasive, critiques of the traditional method of hypothesis testing in psychology. After years of being ignored, the issues raised long ago by Rozeboom are finally beginning to receive more attention, but standard research practice still has not changed.*

Wilkinson, L., & The Task Force on Statistical Inference (1999). Statistical methods in psychology journals: Guidelines and explanations. *American Psychologist*, 54, 594–604.

> *In response to rising controversy about the use of significance testing in psychology, including a proposal to ban such testing altogether, the American Psychological Association put together a task force of distinguished methodologists to*

examine the issue. This article is their final report. In a subtle but strong way it argues for moving significance testing out of its traditionally central role in psychological data analysis. It includes wise commentary on a number of issues concerning how psychologists analyze their data.

EMEDIA

 Go to StudySpace, wwnorton.com/studyspace, to access additional review and enrichment materials.

PART II

HOW PEOPLE DIFFER:
The Trait Approach

P eople are different. It is obvious that no two individuals look precisely alike—not even "identical" twins—and it is almost as obvious that no two individuals behave, think, or feel exactly the same way. Everyday language contains many words to describe these differences in personality. Some years ago, the pioneering personality psychologist Gordon Allport sent his assistant, Henry Odbert, to count exactly how many of these words he could find in an unabridged English dictionary. A few weeks later, Odbert, red-eyed and weary, reported the answer: 17,953 (Allport & Odbert, 1936). The words included familiar terms such as *arrogant, shy, trustworthy,* and *conscientious,* and also more obscure entries such as *delitescent, vulnific,* and *earthbred.*[1] All of these words can describe personality traits, and the fact that the dictionary includes so many suggests that traits are an important part of how people intuitively think and talk about each other.

The trait approach to personality psychology attempts to build on this intuition by translating the natural, informal language of personality traits into a formal psychology that measures traits and uses them to predict and explain human behavior. The assessment and use of personality traits are the topics of the next four chapters. And, in a broader sense, they are the topics of the entire rest of this book, because the *personality trait* is the necessary, basic concept for measuring and understanding individual differences. As you will see, all personality psychologists focus on how people are different from each other, in one form or

---

[1] Meaning, respectively (and approximately), *secretive, wounding,* and *vulgar,*

another, whether these differences are manifested in their genes, the biology of their nervous systems, their unconscious mental processes, or their styles of thinking. All of these approaches are ways of explaining the stable patterns of cognition and behavior that make one person different from another. Therefore, they require a way to conceptualize and measure these patterns—and that is where personality traits come in.

But first, we need to address a basic question: Do personality traits even exist? If they didn't, of course, using traits to understand behavior wouldn't make much sense, and the book you are reading would already be almost over. But a debate over this very issue occupied many psychologists for years, continues to arise in one form or another in modern theory and research and, as you will learn in Chapter 4, the lessons from this debate have important implications for understanding personality.

Chapter 5 describes how psychologists construct and use personality tests. Chapter 6 describes how laypersons—nonpsychologists—assess personality in their daily lives without ever using personality tests, and considers the circumstances under which such everyday assessments are, and are not, likely to be accurate. Chapter 7 describes the way personality traits have been used to understand several important kinds of human behavior, including self-control, drug abuse, and racial prejudice. The chapter also considers the following questions: Are all 17,953 personality traits really necessary? Can this list be reduced to just a few that are really essential? The chapter concludes with a discussion of personality development, and how personality changes and remains the same from youth to old age.

The overall goal of Chapters 4 through 7 is to provide an introduction to the way personality psychologists try to measure and understand people's psychological differences, and how they apply this knowledge.

4

PERSONALITY TRAITS, SITUATIONS, AND BEHAVIOR

SOME OF THE WORDS that describe how people psychologically differ from each other were invented by psychologists. These include terms such as *neuroticism*, *ego control*, and *self-monitoring*, along with more obscure labels like *parmia*, *premsia*, and *alexithymia*.[1] More often, psychologists who follow the trait approach begin with common sense and ordinary words (e.g., Gough, 1995), and their work seeks to base the scientific measurement of individual differences on familiar concepts such as sociability, reliability, dominance, nervousness, and cheerfulness (Funder, 1991).

As a result, personality psychology and everyday human observation are in some ways not so different. Both seek to characterize people using similar kinds of terms, and it is even possible to compare one approach to the other. For example, research on accuracy in personality judgment, to be considered in Chapter 6, compares everyday judgments that people make of each other to personality assessments based on research and standardized instruments (Funder, 1995, 1999).

As we begin to consider the trait approach to personality psychology, two points are important to keep in mind. The first is that this approach is based on empirical research that mostly uses correlational designs (see Chapter 3). Trait psychologists put a great deal of effort into the careful construction of methods, such as personality tests, for accurately measur-

---

[1] To score high in these traits means, respectively (and approximately), to be "uninhibited," "sensitive," and "deficient in emotional understanding."

Handwritten margin notes (left):

Trait approach
1) Based on correlational research.
2) Focuses exclusively on individual differences.
↳ eg. are they more or less dominant vs someone else? (cannot simply see a "0" on the dominance scale)

disadvantage

---

how people differ. As we will see, some of these methods are complex and statistically sophisticated. Whether the method is beguilingly simple or fearsomely complex, however, an ultimate criterion for any measurement of a personality trait is whether it can be used to predict behavior (Wiggins, 1973). If a person scores high on a measure of "dominance," can we accurately predict that she will act in a dominant manner (relative to other people) in one or more life situations? The answer to this question will be indexed statistically by the correlation between the dominance score and some separate indication of the person's dominant behavior.

> "Every man is in certain respects (a) like all other men, (b) like some other men, (c) like no other man."

The second notable aspect of the trait approach is that it focuses exclusively on individual differences. It does not attempt to measure how dominant, sociable, or nervous anybody is in an absolute sense; there is no zero point on any dominance scale or on any measure of any other trait. The trait approach does try to measure the degree to which a person might be more or less dominant, sociable, or nervous than someone else. (Technically, therefore, trait measurements are made on ordinal rather than ratio scales.[2])

This focus on comparisons is one of the great strengths of the trait approach. It is important to understand and to be able to assess how people differ from one another. But as so often happens (remember Funder's First Law), it must also be considered a weakness: The trait approach, by its very nature, is prone to neglect those aspects of human psychology that are common to all people, as well as the ways in which each person is unique. (Other approaches, considered later in this book, do focus on those aspects of human nature.)

---

[2] A measurement is said to lie on an *ordinal scale* when its value reflects the rank ordering of each entity measured. For example, three racers would earn values of 1, 2, and 3 if they placed first, second, and third. There is no zero point on this scale (you can't place "0th"), and the numbers 1 and 3 do not imply that the third-place runner was three times slower than the first-place runner. A measurement lies on a *rational scale* if the scale has a true zero point and the measurement's value can be assessed in terms of ratios with other measurements. For example, one runner might go 3 miles an hour, a second runner 2 miles an hour, and a third (rather slow) runner might go 1 mile an hour. These measurements are rational because there is such a "pace" as zero miles an hour, and because the first runner can be said to be going 3 times faster than the third runner. Trait measurements are ordinal rather than rational because there is no such thing as "zero dominance," for example, and if one person has a dominance score of 50 and another has a score of 25, this implies the first person is more dominant than the second but not necessarily twice as dominant, whatever that might mean. (See Blanton & Jaccard, 2006, for an interesting discussion of the difficulties in expressing psychological attributes in terms of numbers.)

THE MEASUREMENT OF INDIVIDUAL DIFFERENCES

One of my favorite quotes from the personality literature comes from an old chapter by Clyde Kluckhohn and Henry Murray. In elegant (albeit sexist) phrasing, the quote reads:

> Every man is in certain respects (a) like all other men, (b) like some other men, (c) like no other man. (Kluckhohn & Murray, 1961, p. 53)

What Kluckhohn and Murray meant, first, is that certain psychological properties and processes are universal. All people have biologically based needs for food, water, and sex, for example. Their second point is that other properties of people differ but in ways that allow individuals to be grouped. People who are consistently cheerful, for instance, might be essentially alike in a way that allows them to be meaningfully distinguished from those who are gloomier (although they might still differ among themselves in other respects). And third, in still other ways, each individual is unique and cannot be meaningfully compared with anyone else. Each person's genetic makeup, past experience, and view of the world are different from those of anyone else who ever lived or ever will (Allport, 1937).

The trait approach comes in at the second, middle level of this analysis, while at the same time (necessarily) neglecting the other two. Because the trait approach is based on the ideas that all men are "like some other men" and that it is meaningful and useful to assess broad categories of individual difference, it assumes that in some real sense people *are* their traits. Theorists differ on whether traits simply describe how a person acts, are the sum

"I love the little ways you're identical to everyone else."

of everything a person has learned, are biological structures, or are some combination of all of these concepts. But for all trait theorists, these dimensions of individual differences are the building blocks of which personality is constructed.

Which raises a fundamental problem.

PEOPLE ARE INCONSISTENT

You can judge or measure the degree to which someone is shy, conscientious, or dominant, but even minimal experience will reveal that whatever you conclude the truth to be, there will be numerous exceptions. The individual may be shy with strangers but warm, open, and friendly with family members. The individual may be conscientious at work but sloppy and disorganized at home. The individual may be dominant with people of the same sex but deferential to people of the opposite sex, or vice versa. This kind of inconsistency is seen all the time.

Casual observation, therefore, is sufficient to confirm that personality traits are not the only factors that control an individual's behavior; situations are important as well. Some situations will make a person more or less shy, more or less careful, more or less friendly, and more or less dominant. This is because situations vary according to the people who are present and the implicit rules that apply (Price & Bouffard, 1974; Wagerman & Funder, 2007). You act differently at home than you do at work partly because you share your home with your family members, but you share your workplace with your coworkers (and perhaps, competitors). You act differently at a party than at a church because some pretty specific, albeit usually implicit, rules of decorum limit what is acceptable behavior in a church. Parties have implicit rules, too, but they offer more leeway (M. Snyder & Ickes, 1985).

If situations are so important, then what role does personality play? One possible answer is, not much. Perhaps individuals' behavior is so inconsistent and apt to change according to the given situation that there is no use characterizing them in terms of broad or global personality traits. If correct, this answer would imply, not only that the personality assessments that many professional psychologists do are a colossal waste of time, but also that much of the everyday thinking and talking about people is fundamentally wrong. You should consider the possibility, therefore, that traits do not exist, that people continually change who they are according to the situation, and that everybody is basically the same.

Do you find this idea outrageous? The answer you give may depend on your age and stage in life. When I teach personality psychology to college undergraduates, who are typically 18 to 22 years old, I find most students nod and calmly accept the possibility raised in the preceding paragraph. The suggestion that people have few consistent attributes to their personality and change who they are from moment to moment depending on the imme- diate situation sounds about right to them—or at least it does not immedi- ately strike them as preposterous.

Thus, I was somewhat taken aback the first time I presented this same possibility to a night-school class. The course was ostensibly the same as the one I was teaching during the daytime that semester, but the night-school students were for the most part adult, working professionals from the met- ropolitan area, rather than dorm-dwelling 18- to 22-year-olds. These older students had the opposite reaction to the idea that individual differences are not important and that how you act depends on the situation you happen to be in at the moment: "Are you crazy?"

The reason for their different point of view may be that older persons are themselves more consistent than younger ones. Research shows that the stability of the differences between people increases with age: 30-year-olds are more stable across time than are children and adolescents, and people between the ages of about 50 and 70 are the most stable of all (McCrae, 2002; Caspi, Roberts, & Shiner, 2005; see Chapter 7 for a more detailed discus- sion). Older persons who have embarked on a career track, started fami- lies, undertaken adult roles and responsibilities, and established consistent individual identities may find it hard to imagine (or remember) the fluctuating, even erratic, personalities they had when they were younger. In contrast, stu- dents who are still financially dependent on their par-

> "Are you crazy?"

ents, have not yet found spouses or started families, and perhaps have not yet even settled on their career goals find the idea that people are the same, and that how you act depends on the situation, to be quite reasonable—indeed, they wonder why anybody would make a fuss. After all, their own personali- ties are still in the design stage (Roberts, Walton, & Viechtbauer, 2006).

What I am proposing, therefore, is that people differ from each other in the degree to which they have developed a consistent personality for themselves (Baumeister & Tice, 1988; Bem & Allen, 1974; M. Snyder & Monson, 1975). This difference might be related to psychological adjust- ment as well as age: Several studies suggest that the consistency of person- ality is associated with general mental health (e.g., Asendorpf & van Aken, 1991; Schuerger, Zarrella, & Hotz, 1989). More-consistent people appear to be less neurotic, more controlled, and more pro-social (Roberts, Caspi, & Moffitt, 2001).

THE PERSON-SITUATION DEBATE

Whether or not it violates your intuition to claim that behavior is so inconsistent that, for all intents and purposes, personality traits do not exist, an argument about just this point occupied a large number of personality psychologists for more than two decades (and it continues to preoccupy some—see Cervone, 2005). These psychologists were, and are, the protagonists in the *person-situation debate*, which focuses on this very question: Which is more important for determining what people do, the person or the situation?

To a considerable degree, the debate was triggered by the publication in 1968 of a book by Walter Mischel entitled *Personality and Assessment*.[3] Mischel argued that behavior is too inconsistent from one situation to the next to allow individual differences to be characterized accurately in terms of broad personality traits. Other psychologists—including, not surprisingly, those who were heavily invested in the technology and practice of personality assessment—emphatically disagreed. Thus was the person-situation debate joined.

The rest of this chapter reviews the basis and resolution of this debate. Ordinarily, arguments among psychologists are one of the things I try to spare you in this book. I would rather teach you about psychology itself than about what psychologists do, much less what they argue about. But I hope to convince you that this particular argument is different. It is not just a tempest in a teapot, as arguments among specialists can be, nor is it even one of those issues that we can simply settle and then move on. Rather, the consistency controversy goes to the heart of how everybody thinks about people, and the way we resolve it has important implications for how we understand the bases of individual differences and important life outcomes.

There are really three issues here. The first is: Does the personality of an individual transcend the immediate situation and provide a consistent guide to her actions, or is what a person does utterly dependent on the situa-

---

[3] Ironically, given its title, the book usually is interpreted as arguing that personality does not exist and that assessment is impossible.

tion she is in at the time? Because our everyday intuitions tell us that people have consistent personalities (everybody uses personality-trait terms all day long), this question leads to a second issue: Are common, ordinary intuitions about people fundamentally flawed, or basically correct? The third issue goes even deeper: Why do psychologists continue to argue about the consistency of personality, year after year, decade after decade, when the basic empirical questions were settled long ago?

When I talk about the debate that was, to some extent, triggered by Mischel's book, I want to avoid the trap of focusing too much on Mischel and his particular arguments, and not enough on the issues that continue to make the debate they triggered both interesting and important. A small cottage industry sprang up within personality psychology during the 1970s, the main activity of which seemed to be to figure out what Mischel did and did not actually say. I was briefly a member of this enterprise myself (Funder, 1983).

But figuring out what Mischel did and did not say is a frustrating way to spend your time, both because the original book contained many qualifying phrases and escape clauses, and because Mischel seems to have changed his position on some fundamental issues during the intervening years (e.g., Mischel & Shoda, 1995). Mischel frequently has claimed that his views are less extreme than portrayed by others. He often protests, for example, that he never meant to say that personality does not exist, even though many readers (including me) interpreted the overall message of his book as being exactly that. At one psychologists' meeting attended by Mischel years ago, the chairperson looked up and down the table and then intoned, ironically, "We don't seem to have a Mischelian here with us today" (E. R. Hilgard, personal communication, October 1975).

Nevertheless, the issues in the person-situation debate are important, regardless of what Mischel or others said or now say about them, because they are aimed at the very foundations of the trait approach. In the discussion that follows, I believe that my presentation of the situationist position is faithful to its basic tenets. Stripped to its essentials, the situationist argument has three parts:

3 Arguments of situationalist approach.

1. A thorough review of the personality research literature reveals that there is an upper limit to how well one can predict what a person will do based on any measurement of that person's personality, and this upper limit is rather low.

2. Therefore, situations are more important than personality traits in determining behavior. (This is the origin of the term **situationism** [Bowers, 1973].)

3. Therefore, not only is the professional practice of personality assessment mostly a waste of time, but also, everyday intuitions about people are fundamentally flawed. The trait words used to describe people are not legitimately descriptive, because people generally tend to see others as being more consistent across situations than they really are.

Let us consider each part separately.

Predictability

THE SITUATIONIST ARGUMENT

The definitive test of the usefulness of a personality trait is whether it can be used to predict behavior. If you know somebody's level or score on a trait, you should be able to forecast what that person will do in the future. Situationists argue that this predictive capacity is severely limited. There is no trait that you can use to predict someone's behavior with enough accuracy to be useful.

Mischel's book surveys some of the research concerning the relationships between self-descriptions of personality and direct measurements of behavior, between others' descriptions of personality and direct measurements of behavior, and between one measurement of behavior and another.

Or, to use the terms introduced in Chapter 2, Mischel looked at the relationships between S data and B data, between I data and B data, and between some B data and other B data. The first two comparisons address the ability of personality-trait judgments to predict behavior—for example, can an acquaintance's judgment of your sociability predict how sociable you will be at Friday's party? The third comparison addresses the consistency of behavior across situations—for instance, if you are sociable at Friday's party, will you also be sociable at Tuesday's work meeting?

The data reported in the studies that Mischel reviewed were not, for the most part, taken from real life. Nearly all of the behav-

"Can I call you back, R.B.? I've got a situation here."

ioral measurements—the B data—were gathered in laboratory settings. Some studies measured "attitude toward authority" by asking participants for their opinions of photographs of older men, some measured "self-control" by seeing how long children could wait for candy treats provided by the experimenters, and so forth. Only rarely was behavior assessed in more or less natural situations, such as measures taken of cheating on games at a summer camp. Such naturalistic studies were (and remain) rare, primarily because they are so difficult and expensive (see the discussion of B data in Chapter 2). Either way, the critical result is how well a person's behavior in one situation can be predicted either from his behavior in another situation or from his personality trait scores.

In the research literature, predictability and consistency are indexed by the correlation coefficient. As you will recall from Chapter 3, this is a number that ranges from +1 to −1, and indexes the association or relationship between two variables, such as a personality score and a behavioral measurement. If the correlation is positive, it means that as one variable increases, so does the other; the higher someone's "sociability" score, for example, the more parties she is likely to attend. If the correlation is negative, it means that as one variable increases, the other decreases; the higher someone's "shyness" score, for example, the fewer parties he or she is likely to attend. Both positive and negative correlations imply that one variable can be predicted from a knowledge of the other. But if the correlation is near zero, it means the two variables are unrelated; perhaps, for example, scores on this particular sociability test have nothing to do with how many parties one attends.

Mischel's original argument was that correlations between personality and behavior, or between behavior in one situation and behavior in another, seldom exceed .30. Another prominent situationist, Richard Nisbett (1980), later revised this estimate upward, to .40. The implication in both cases was that such correlations are small, and that personality traits are unimportant in the shaping of behavior.

This claim concerning the unpredictability of behavior hit the field of personality psychology in the early 1970s with surprisingly devastating force, and continues to echo through the modern research literature. Some personality psychologists, and even more psychologists outside the field of personality, concluded that for all intents and purposes, personality did not exist. This conclusion was based on two premises. The first was that situationists are right, and .40 is the upper limit for the predictability of a given behavior from personality variables or behavior in other situations. The other implicit but necessary premise was that this upper limit is low.

THE RESPONSE

It took the representatives of the pro-personality side of this debate a few years to get their rebuttals in line, but when they finally did, they came up with three.

Unfair Literature Review   The first counterargument was that Mischel's review of the personality literature, which kicked off the whole controversy, was selective and unfair. After all, the relevant research literature goes back more than 60 years and contains literally thousands of studies. Mischel's review, by contrast, is quite short (only 16 pages [pp. 20–36] of his book, about the length of a typical undergraduate term paper) and concentrates on a few studies that obtained disappointing results rather than on the (perhaps more numerous) studies that obtained more impressive findings.

This is a difficult point to prove or disprove, however. On the one hand, it is obvious that Mischel's review was selective because it is so short. Moreover, he did not exactly go out of his way to find the best studies in the literature; the very first empirical study that Mischel cited (Burwen & Campbell, 1957) was less than exemplary. The study was filled with methodological and empirical flaws (e.g., a number of the participants deliberately sabotaged the research questionnaires), yet still managed to find a bit of evidence in favor of the trait it examined, which was "attitude toward authority." Many of the other studies Mischel cited were little better; moreover, even some of those managed, despite everything, to find evidence for the consistency of personality and behavior (J. Block, 1977).

On the other hand, some studies are bound to find positive results on the basis of chance alone. And although it would be easy to put together a short literature review that looks much more positive than Mischel's, it is not clear how one would prove that such a review was any more fair or less selective. It is extremely difficult to characterize the findings of entire research literatures (see Rosenthal, 1980), and the literature on behavioral consistency is no exception.

I frankly do not know how to establish whether the literature supports consistency with a few exceptions, or whether it supports inconsistency with a few exceptions. So, to move the argument along, let me just "stipulate" (as lawyers say) the Mischel-Nisbett figure: Assume that a correlation of about .40 is the upper limit for how well personality traits can predict behavior, as well as for how consistent behavior is from one situation to another.

We Can Do Better   A second counterargument to the situationist critique grants the .40 upper limit, as I just did, but claims that this limit is a result

[handwritten margin note: literature review was selective/unfair. review was extremely short.]

Figure 4.1 Personality in the Laboratory and in Real Life Much psychologi cal research is done in controlled laboratory settings. The influence of personality may be more likely to emerge in settings that are more emotionally involving.

of poor or less than optimal research methodology. The weak findings summarized by Mischel do not imply that personality is unimportant, merely that psychologists can and must do better research.

One way in which research could be improved, according to this counterargument, is for it to move out of the laboratory more often. As I mentioned earlier, nearly all of the behavioral measurements that formed the basis for the situationist critique were made in laboratory situations. Some of these situations were probably dull and uninvolving for the participants. How about behavior in real life? Personality is much more likely to become relevant, it has been argued, in situations that are real, vivid, and important to the individual in question (Allport, 1961). For example, when a person in a laboratory is asked to respond to a picture of an older individual, his personality may or may not become involved (Burwen & Campbell, 1957). But when a person is about to make his first parachute jump, personality seems likely to play a more important role (Epstein, 1980; Fenz & Epstein, 1967).

A second kind of research improvement that frequently has been advocated takes into account that some people might be more consistent than others. For example, one study asked participants how consistent they were on the trait of "sociability," and found that the behavior of those who said they were consistent was easier to predict accurately than the behavior of those who said they were inconsistent (Bem & Allen, 1974).[4] Research on

---

[4] Although this was an influential finding and an important idea, Chaplin and Goldberg (1985) provided evidence that the finding is difficult to replicate. Later, Zuckerman et al. (1988) surveyed a broad range of research literature and concluded that this effect of self-rated consistency on behavioral predictability is small but probably real.

— expressive behavior likely to be consistent across situations (eg. hand gesture wage)

— goal directed behaviors = ~~place~~ situation-based (eg. trying to impress someone).

the trait of self-monitoring suggests that some people, called "high self-monitors," quickly change their behavior according to the situation, whereas "low self-monitors" are more likely to express their personality consistently from one situation to the next (M. Snyder, 1987; see also Chapter 7). Finally, some behaviors might be more consistent than others. Elements of expressive behavior, such as how much a person gestures or how loudly a person talks, are likely to be consistent across situations, whereas more goal-directed behaviors, such as trying to impress someone, are more likely to depend on the situation (Funder & Colvin, 1991; see also Allport & Vernon, 1933).

A third possible research improvement is to focus on general behavioral trends instead of single actions at particular moments. Thus, rather than try to predict whether somebody will act friendly next Tuesday at 3:00 P.M., one might be better off trying to predict how friendly that person will behave, on average, over the next year. Do you remember the metersticks that were used to illustrate the idea of aggregation, in Chapter 3? Just as my fellow high school students and I sometimes placed our sticks too close together, and sometimes too far apart, in measuring the distance to the other school, so, too, do behaviors of a person vary around their average level from occasion to occasion. Sometimes you are a little more aggressive than usual, for example, and sometimes less; sometimes you are more shy than usual, and sometimes less, and so on. This is why your *average* level of aggressive or shy behavior is much more predictable than what you will do in any particular moment or place—on average, random variations tend to cancel out (Fishbein & Ajzen, 1974; Epstein, 1979).

The issue is more than just a matter of statistics. It concerns the whole meaning and purpose of personality-trait judgments. When you say that somebody is friendly or conscientious or shy, are you trying to predict one specific behavior at one specific time, or are you expressing a prediction of how that person will generally act over the long haul (McCrae, 2002)? In most cases, I think, the answer is the latter. When you wish to understand someone, or wish to select a roommate or an employee, it is not so critical to know what the person will do at a specific place and time, because that will always depend on the exact situation at the moment. Rather, you need to know how the person will act, in general, across the various relevant situations of life. You understand that somebody might late on rare occasions because her car won't start; you know that anybody can have a bad day and be grouchy. But when choosing an employee or a roommate, what you really need to know is: How reliable will the person be in general? Or, how friendly is the person, usually?

These three suggestions—measure behavior in real life, check for varia-tions in consistency, and seek to predict behavioral trends rather than sin-gle acts—are all good ideas for improving personality research. However, they represent potential more than reality. To follow any of these sugges-tions is difficult. Real-life behaviors are not easy to assess (see Chapter 2), individual differences in consistency may be subtle and difficult to mea-sure (Chaplin, 1991), and the prediction of behavioral trends requires, by definition, that the researcher make many direct observations of behavior, not just a few. So, although these suggestions provide good reasons that the situationist critique may underestimate the level of consistency in people's behavior, there is not yet enough research to prove that behavioral consis-tency regularly gets much higher than what is reflected by the correlations around .40 that the situationists now concede.

Besides, both of the first two responses to the situationist critique miss a more basic point, discussed next.

A Correlation of .40 Is Not Small   Remember that to be impressed (or depressed) by the situationist critique of personality traits, you must believe two things: (1) A correlation of .40 represents the true upper limit to which one can predict behavior from personality, or see consistency in behavior from one situation to another; and (2) this is a *small* upper limit. The dis-cussion so far has concentrated on responses to point 1. But if you were to conclude that a correlation of .40 was not small in the first place (point 2), then the limit would cease to be so worrisome, and the force of the situation-ist critique would largely dissipate.

Thus, it is critical to evaluate how much predictability a correlation of the size granted by the situationist critiques really represents. But to evalu-ate whether .40 is big or little, or to assess any other statistic, you need a standard of comparison.

Two kinds of standards are possible: absolute and relative. To evalu-ate this correlation against an absolute standard, you would calculate how many correct and incorrect predictions of behavior a trait measurement with this degree of validity would yield in a hypothetical context. To evaluate this correlation against a relative standard, you can compare this degree of predictability for personality traits with the accuracy of other methods used to predict behavior. Let's do both.

An absolute evaluation of a .40 correlation can be obtained from Rosenthal and Rubin's (1982) Binomial Effect Size Display (BESD), which was described in Chapter 3. I won't repeat the description here but will go straight to the bottom line: According to the BESD, a correlation of .40

means that a prediction of behavior based on a personality trait score is likely to be accurate 70 percent of the time (assuming a chance accuracy rate of 50 percent).[5] Seventy percent is far from perfect, but it is enough to be useful for many purposes. For instance, an employer choosing who to put through an expensive training program could save large amounts of money by being able to predict with 70 percent accuracy who will or will not be a successful employee at its conclusion.

Let's work through an example. Say a company has 200 employees being considered for further training, but the budget only allows for training 100 of them. Let's further assume that, overall, 50 percent of the company's employees could successfully complete the program. The company picks 100 employees at random and spends $10,000 to train each one. But, as I said, only half of them are successful. So the company has spent a total of $1 million to get 50 successfully trained employees, or $20,000 each.

Now consider what happens if the company uses a selection test that has been shown to correlate .40 with training success.[6] By selecting the top half of the scorers on this test for training, the company will get 70 successful trainees (instead of 50) out of the 100 who are trained, still at a total cost of $1 million but now at only about $14,300 per successful trainee. In other words, using a test with a .40 validity could save the company $5,700 per successful trainee, or about $400,000. That will pay for a lot of testing.

What about a relative standard? Well, what is the most appropriate basis for comparison when trying to evaluate the predictive ability of personality traits? Situationists, you will recall, believe that the situation, not the person, is all-important in the determination of behavior. To evaluate the ability of personality traits to predict behavior, therefore, it seems appropriate to draw a comparison with the ability of situational variables to predict behavior. That is the topic of the next section.

Situationism

A key tenet of the situationist position is that personality does not determine behavior—situations do. To evaluate the degree to which a behavior is

---

[5] This figure should not be confused with the "percentage of variance explained" discussed in Chapter 3, which is computed in a different way and has a more obscure interpretation.

[6] This is not an unreasonable number. Ones, Viswesvaran, & Schmidt (1993) reported that, across a large of number of tests and measures of job performance, the predictive validity of some kinds of tests averaged .41. See Chapter 7 for more on the prediction of job performance.

affected by a personality variable, the routine practice is to correlate a measure of behavior with a measure of personality. But how do you evaluate the degree to which behavior is affected by a situational variable?

This question has received surprisingly little attention over the years. When it has been addressed, the usual practice was rather strange: The power of situations was determined by subtraction. Thus, if a personality variable was found to correlate .40 with a behavioral measurement and it therefore "explained 16 percent of the variance," the other 84 percent was assumed, by default, to be due to the situation (e.g., Mischel, 1968).

Of course, this is not a legitimate practice, even though it used to be common. I have already protested the needlessly misleading obscurity of the whole "percent of variance" language (see Chapter 3). But even if you accept this terminology, it would be just as reasonable to attribute the "missing" variance to other personality variables that you did not measure as it would be to attribute it to situational variables that you also did not measure (Ahadi & Diener, 1989). Moreover, to assign variance by subtraction in this way does not allow you to say anything about which aspects of the situation might be important, in a way parallel to how trait measures tell you which aspects of personality are important.

It has long seemed remarkable to me that the situationists have been willing to claim that situations are important, yet have been seemingly unconcerned with measuring situational variables in a way that indicates precisely how or how much situations affect behavior. After all, not everybody responds to a particular situation in the same way. When situationists claim that situations are important but do not specify what is important about them or to what extent, then, as one trait psychologist pointed out,

> situations turn out to be "powerful" in the same sense as Scud missiles [the erratic weapons used by Iraq during the Persian Gulf wars] are powerful: They may have huge effects, or no effects, and such effects may occur virtually anywhere, all over the map. (Goldberg, 1992, p. 90)

Moreover, there is no need for the situationists to sell themselves so short—to be so vague about what specific aspects of situations can affect behavior. A large and impressive body of psychological research allows the effects of situations to be directly calculated. The data come from nearly every study in experimental social psychology (e.g., Aronson, 1972).

In the typical social psychological experiment, two (or more) separate groups of participants are placed, randomly and usually one at a time, into

social psych experiments

example (using monetary rewards)

one of two (or more) different situations, also called *conditions*. The social psychologist measures what the participants do. If the average behavior of the participants who are placed in one condition turns out to be significantly different (statistically speaking—see Chapter 3) from the average behavior of the participants placed in the other condition, then the experiment is deemed successful.

For example, you might be interested in the effect of incentives on attitude change. In an experiment, you could ask participants to make a statement they do not believe—for example, that a dull game was really interesting. Then, you could test to see if they come to believe these statements—that the game was not dull after all. Some of your participants could be offered a large incentive (say, $20) to make the counter-attitudinal statement, while the rest are offered a smaller incentive (say, $1). If the two groups of participants change their attitudes about the game to different degrees, then you can conclude that the difference in incentives between the two conditions was the effective cause of this difference in attitudes (although the exact process by which this happened would still be open to question). The differences between the two situations must have led the participants to respond differently, and therefore the experiment demonstrated an effect of a situational variable on behavior (Festinger & Carlsmith, 1959).

> "Situations . . . may have huge effects, or no effects, and such effects may occur virtually anywhere, all over the map."

Social psychologists pay attention to statistical significance, not the situational effects.

The literature of experimental social psychology offers a vast trove of specific examples of situational effects of this sort. For present purposes, the question is, how large are those effects, compared to the effects of personality variables? Perhaps surprisingly, social psychologists historically have paid very little attention to the size of the situational effects they study. They have concentrated on statistical significance, or the degree to which their results would not have been expected by chance. As was discussed in Chapter 3, this is a separate matter from effect size or what one might consider "actual" significance, because even a small effect can be highly significant statistically, if one has studied a large enough number of participants.

Personality psychologists, by contrast, have always focused on the magnitude of their ability to predict behavior. The key statistic in personality research, the correlation coefficient, is a measure of effect size and not of statistical significance. The "personality coefficient" of .40 is ordinarily not comparable with the effects found in social psychological studies of situational variables, therefore, because the two styles of research do not employ a common metric.

Fortunately, this difficulty can be easily remedied. As mentioned in Chapter 3, the experimental statistics used by social psychologists can be converted algebraically into correlations of the sort used by personality psychologists. Some years ago, my colleague Dan Ozer and I did just that (Funder & Ozer, 1983). From the social psychological literature, we chose three prominent examples of the power of situations to shape behavior. We then converted the results of those studies to effect-size correlations.

The first classic study that we chose concerned the "forced compliance" effect demonstrated by Festinger and Carlsmith (1959) in a study similar to the one I just described. Participants were induced to tell unwitting new participants that a dull experiment was actually interesting. The participants were offered either $20 or $1 for doing this. The counterintuitive result was that the participants paid $1 actually changed their attitudes after telling the lie, to believe that the experiment was more interesting than they had originally thought. The participants paid $20, in contrast, did not change their attitudes—they still thought the experiment had been boring.

This study was one of the early important demonstrations of the workings of cognitive dissonance. The explanation given by Festinger and Carlsmith was that participants felt dissonance as a result of saying something they did not believe, but that a payment of $20 was sufficient to reduce their uneasy feelings. One measly dollar was not enough to make them feel better, however, so the lower-paid participants had to change their own attitudes in order that their words would not be so out of line with their beliefs.

This effect is a classic of the social psychological literature and perhaps one of the most important and interesting findings in the field. Yet the statistical size of this effect had seldom been reported. Ozer and I performed the simple calculation: The effect of incentive on attitude change following counter-attitudinal advocacy turns out to correspond to a correlation of $r = -.36$. (The correlation has a negative sign because more incentive leads to less change.) This is a direct statistical measure of how strongly rewards can affect attitude change.

A second important program of research in social psychology has concerned bystander intervention. John Darley and his colleagues staged several faked but dramatic incidents in which participants came upon apparently distressed individuals lying helplessly in their path (Darley & Batson, 1967; Darley & Latané, 1968). The research was intended to find out whether the participants would stop and help.

The answer turned out to depend, among other things, on whether other people were present and whether the participant was in a hurry. The more people present, the less likely the participant was to stop and help; the correlation indexing the size of this effect was $r = .38$. Also, the greater the participant's hurry, the less likely the participant was to help; the correlation indexing the size of this effect was $r = .39$.

The third program of research we examined was Stanley Milgram's classic investigation of obedience. In a famous series of studies, Milgram's research assistants ordered participants to give apparently painful and dangerous (but fortunately bogus) electric shocks to an innocent "victim" (Milgram, 1975). If the participants objected, the assistant said, "The experiment requires that you continue."

Milgram identified two variables as relevant to whether a participant would obey this command. The first was the isolation of the victim. When the victim was in the next room and could not be heard protesting, or could be heard only weakly, obedience was more likely than when the victim was right in front of the participant. The correlation that reflects the size of the effect of victim isolation is $r = .42$. The second important variable was the proximity of the experimenter. Obedience was more likely if the research assistant giving the orders was physically present than if he gave orders over the phone or on a tape recorder. The correlation that reflects the size of the effect of experimenter proximity turned out to be $r = .36$.

Recall that the size of the personality coefficient that was supposed to reflect the maximum correlation that can be obtained between personality variables and behavior is about .40. Now, compare that to the effects of situational variables on behavior, as just surveyed: .36, .38, .39, .42, and .36.

One can draw two different conclusions from these results. This little reanalysis by Ozer and me has been summarized by others as implying that neither personality variables *nor* situational variables have much of an effect on behavior. Well, it's nice to be cited, but not so nice to be misunderstood; the weakness of situations or of these experimental effects was *not* the point we were trying to make. Rather, we reanalyzed these particular experiments precisely because, as far as we knew, nobody had ever doubted that each and every one of them demonstrated a powerful, important influence of a situational variable. These experiments are classics of social psychology—they are found in any textbook on the subject and have contributed important insights into social behavior.

We prefer a second conclusion, therefore: that these situational variables are important determinants of behavior, but that many personality variables are important as well. When put on a common scale for comparison, the size of the effects of the person and of the situation are much more

It's nice to be cited, but not so nice to be misunderstood.

similar than many had assumed. Indeed, a wide-ranging literature review concluded that the typical size of a situational effect on behavior, in a social psychological experiment, corresponds to an r = .21,[7] noticeably lower than the average of the three classic studies Dan Ozer and I reanalyzed (Richard et al., 2003).[8] In this light, calling a correlation of .40 a "personality coefficient" loses a little of its pejorative edge.

Now we are ready to consider the third part of the situationist argument.

Are Person Perceptions Erroneous?

Recall the situationist argument that the ability of personality variables to predict behavior is limited if not nonexistent; that situations are much more important; and that people's everyday perceptions of one another, which consist to a large degree of judgments of personality traits, are therefore largely erroneous. Now that we have dealt carefully with the first two parts of this argument, the third falls apart of its own weight. The effects of personality on behavior do seem sufficient to be perceived accurately. Despite the situationist critique, our intuitions probably are not that far off base.

Both everyday experience and any fair reading of the research literature make one thing abundantly clear: When it comes to personality, one size does not fit all. People really do act differently from each other. Even when they are all in the same situation, some individuals will be more sociable, nervous, talkative, or active than others. And when the situation changes, those differences will still be there (e.g., Funder & Colvin, 1991). The 17,953 trait terms in the English language did not appear out of thin air. Ideas about personality traits are an important part of Western culture (and perhaps all cultures, as we shall see in Chapter 14). Consider Eskimos and snow: It has long been noted that the Eskimo languages have many more words to describe snow than do the languages of those who live in warmer

---

[7] The standard deviation was .15, which means that about two thirds of social psychological experiments yield an effect size between .06 and .36.

[8] For another comparison in a very different domain, consider the correlation between a weather station's elevation above sea level and its average daily temperature. As everyone knows, it tends to be cooler at higher elevations; the actual correlation between these variables is −.34 (Meyer et al., 2001, p. 132).

Eskimos have more words for snow; as such, we have words to not differences in personality.

climes (Whorf, 1956; H. H. Clark & E. V. Clark, 1977).[9] This is assumed to be because snow is important to Eskimos; they build shelters from it, they travel across it, and so forth. (Skiers also have a specialized vocabulary for types of snow.) The need to discriminate between many different kinds of snow has led Eskimos to develop words to describe each kind, in order to communicate better with one another about this important topic.

The same thing seems to have happened with the language of personality. People are psychologically different, and it is important and interesting to note just how. Words arose to describe these differences—words that make us more sensitive to the differences and that make it possible to talk about them.

The proliferation of trait words is not finished yet; consider the relatively new words *jock*, *geek*, *preppy*, and *Val*.[10] Personality psychologists are not leaving the language alone either. They have introduced the terms *self-monitoring* and *parmia*, as we have seen, and others such as *private self-consciousness*, *public self-consciousness*, and *threctia* to delineate aspects of personality that they did not believe were described precisely enough by the existing language (Cattell, 1965).

PERSONALITY AND LIFE

After this survey of the ins and outs of a debate that occupied psychologists for decades, a reader could be forgiven for asking the following rude question: Who cares? Does the existence of personality even matter to anyone other than a personality psychologist who needs something to study? To be sure, since the debate was more or less resolved, personality psychologists have brought about a resurgence of research on topics such as personality

---

[9] This long-standing, famous claim stirred a controversy when the linguist Geoffrey Pullum (1991) claimed that the Eskimos do not have a particularly large number of words for snow. In response, Cecil Adams (2001), author of the Chicago newspaper column *The Straight Dope*, reported that he was able to find "a couple of dozen terms for snow, ice and related subjects" in an Eskimo dictionary and that Eskimo languages are "synthetic," meaning new words are constructed as the need arises, making it impossible to count how many snow words actually exist. Another observer counted 49 words for snow and ice in West Greenlandic, including *qaniit* (falling snow), *qinuq* (rotten snow), and *sullarniq* (snow blown in a doorway) (Derby, 1994).

[10] In a bit of regional (California) slang that is probably already passing out of use, a Val (short for "Valley Girl") is a teenage girl from the San Fernando Valley (just north of Los Angeles) who is stereotyped as being empty-headed, materialistic, and boy-crazy. More recently, I have heard the term *bro* used to describe a certain kind of young male, but I don't really understand it.

processes, personality structure, and the stability and change of personality over time (e.g., see Chapter 7). But what if—shocking thought—you just don't care about personality processes, structure, or stability? Does personality matter, even so?

You knew I was going to say yes. Personality matters on more than just theoretical grounds, and in ways that go beyond what some critics have called a "romantic" conception of human nature (Hofstee & Ten Berge, 2004). Personality affects life outcomes that matter to people, or, as two distinguished psychologists once wrote, "We assert, without providing evidence, that most people care about their own health and well being, care about their marital relationships, and care about success and satisfaction in their career" (Ozer & Benet-Martínez, 2006, p. 402).

They are right: Who needs evidence to "prove" that the most important outcomes in their lives matter to people? In their article, Ozer and Benet-Martínez proceed to summarize an impressively wide range of research documenting the effects of personality on these outcomes. They organized the traits they surveyed into five large categories (the so-called Big Five discussed in Chapter 7), and associated them with individual outcomes such as happiness and long life, interpersonal outcomes such as good relationships and peer acceptance, and what they called "institutional" outcomes including leadership and career success. Some of their major conclusions are summarized in Table 4.1.

As you can see, all five of these broad traits have impacts on several different, important life outcomes. For example, people who score high on the trait of extraversion tend to be happier than people who score low on this trait. Extraverts also enjoy better psychological health, live longer lives, are more popular, and are seen as better leaders. Agreeable people have healthier hearts than disagreeable people do, are less likely to get arrested, and go farther in their careers (I'm guessing those last two outcomes might be related). Conscientious people show an even stronger tendency to achieve career success, and conscientiousness is also associated with religious beliefs and stronger family ties. They also tend to be politically conservative, as opposed to people who score high on measures of openness, who are more likely to be liberal. Neuroticism is associated with a whole host of negative outcomes including just plain unhappiness.

The reason that personality affects so many important outcomes is that it is present throughout life. Moment by moment, people might do any of a wide variety of things for an equally wide variety of reasons. But over time, a conscientious person, for example, will act in ways that are different enough that the effects of thousands of little behaviors accumulate into life out-

Table 4.1

LIFE OUTCOMES ASSOCIATED WITH PERSONALITY TRAITS

	Individual Outcomes	Interpersonal Outcomes	Institutional Outcomes
Extraversion	Happiness Gratitude Longevity Psychological health	Peer acceptance Success in dating and relationships Attractiveness Status	Occupational satisfaction Community involvement Leadership
Agreeableness	Religious involvement Forgiveness Humor Heart health, longevity Psychological health	Peer acceptance Dating satisfaction	Social interests Job attainment Avoidance of criminal behavior
Conscientiousness	Religious beliefs Good health habits, longevity Avoidance of drug abuse	Family satisfaction Dating satisfaction	Job performance Occupational success Political conservatism Avoidance of criminal behavior
Neuroticism	Unhappiness Poor coping	Poor family relations	Occupational dissatisfaction Criminal behavior
Openness	Forgiveness, inspiration Substance abuse		Artistic interests Political liberalism

Source: Adapted from Ozer & Benet-Martínez (2006), p. 415.

comes that may be very different from those of an unconscientious person. Ozer and Benet-Martínez summarize the implications this way:

> Arguments about whether personality is consistent over time and context . . . have had one . . . unfortunate effect: they have obscured the reasons why proponents of different positions cared about personality in the first place, and first and foremost among these reasons is that personality matters. (Ozer & Benet-Martínez, 2006, p. 416)

PERSONS AND SITUATIONS

So, the evidence is overwhelming that people are psychologically different from one another, that personality traits exist, that people's impressions of each others' personalities are based on reality more than cognitive error, and that personality traits affect important life outcomes. It is important to be aware of this evidence in order to be able to counter the argument, still sometimes heard, that traits are little more than illusions. Having achieved this awareness, it is also important to put the relative role of personality traits and situations into perspective. Situational variables are relevant to how people will act *under specific circumstances*. Personality traits are better for describing how people act *in general* (Fleeson, 2001).

Relationships and Jobs

For example, consider relationships. Every person you have a relationship with—your parents, your siblings, your friends, the people you date—is different, and you act differently with each of them, to some degree. You might date three different people or have six good friends, and treat no two of these persons in quite the same way. One might say each of them presents you with a different situation, and you respond accordingly. At the same time, aspects of your behavior are more general and are likely to remain consistent across relationships. Research has shown that broad traits such as extraversion, sociability, and shyness predict how many friends you are likely to have overall and the degree to which, in general, you will find yourself in agreement or conflict with them (Asendorpf & Wipers, 1998; Reis, Capobianco, & Tsai, 2002). The most basic aspect of your relationship behavior might be simply the degree to which you tend to be happy. Three personality variables—a low level of negative emotionality, a high level of positive emotionality, and "constraint"—tend to predict the degree to which people have successful and nonabusive relationships regardless of whom the relationship is with (Robins, Caspi, & Moffitt, 2002).

Another good example can be found in the workplace. Every job is a special situation with its own requirements; some require careful attention to detail, some require mechanical skill, some require good relations with customers, and so forth. But as the industrial psychologists Walter Borman and Louis Penner have noted, certain aspects of good job performance are general across almost all jobs. One of these is a behavioral pattern they call "citizenship performance," in which the employee tries in various ways to promote the goals of the organization. This might include behaviors such as helping to teach new employees their jobs, alleviating conflicts in the workplace, being aware of problems and opportunities as they arise and trying to respond to them, and having the kind of positive attitude that makes everything go better. This pattern of behavior is predicted by traits such as conscientiousness and is a boon to organizational performance, regardless of whether the work setting is a store, a factory, or an office (Borman & Penner, 2001).

The aspects of how people relate to their relationship partners are important, as are the special requirements that arise for every type of job. Personality variables are also important since they comprise the psychological aspects of a person that she carries along throughout life, from one relationship, job, and situation to the next. This is why in the *long run*—not always in the short run—personality affects so many outcomes.

Interactionism

A sad legacy of the person-situation debate is that many psychologists became used to thinking of the person and the situation as being in opposition—that as one becomes more important, the other must become less so. A more accurate view is to see persons and situations as constantly interacting with each other to produce behavior together. This view is called **interactionism** (Funder, 2008).

Persons and situations interact in three major ways (Buss, 1979). First, the effect of a personality variable may depend on the situation, or vice versa. To use again an example from Chapter 3, a classic study showed that caffeine had no overall effect on participants' ability to solve some complex cognitive tasks (Revelle et al., 1976). But when personality was taken into account, the results were very different. It turned out that after consuming large amounts of caffeine, the performance of introverts got worse, while the performance of extraverts actually got better. This is a true person-situation interaction: Neither variable has an effect by itself; they work together.

Moreover, situations are not randomly populated: Certain types of people go to or find themselves in different types of situations. This is the second kind of person-situation interaction. A biker bar might be a situation where fights reliably break out every Saturday night, but only certain kinds of people would choose to go into this situation in the first place.

The third kind of interaction stems from the way people change situations by virtue of what they do in them: The situation in the biker bar changes abruptly once somebody has chosen to swing that first punch. The process by which people change situations, and then react to those changes, can accelerate quickly. According to one study, when two hostile people find themselves in a situation where they can punish each other with blasts of noise, they quickly ramp up their level of mutual aggressiveness as one punishes the other, the other punishes back, but even more strongly, and so on up the scale. People low on hostility were better able to avoid this vicious circle. As the authors of the study noted, "aggressive individuals created a more hostile and aggressive environment for themselves" (C. A. Anderson, Buckley, & Carnagey, 2008).

A good example of where interactions like these can lead is provided by the famous Stanford Prison experiment (C. Haney, Banks, & Zimbardo, 1973) and how it has been interpreted over the years. As you may already know, college students were recruited via a notice advertising "a psychological study of prison life." Once they arrived, they were randomly assigned to the role of guard or prisoner, taken into a simulated prison setting, and confined there for several days. The guards became surprisingly abusive to the prisoners, to the extent that the study was halted early. The psychologist who conducted this study, Philip Zimbardo, drew the lesson that

> Good people can be induced, seduced, initiated into behaving in evil (irrational, stupid, self-destructive, anti-social) ways by immersion in "total situations" that can transform human nature in ways that challenge our sense of the stability and consistency of individual personality, character, and morality. (Zimbardo, Maslach, & Haney, 2000, p. 206)

In other words, this study is a powerful demonstration of the power of the situation. It is indeed that, but subsequent research has shown that matters are more complex. For one thing, not all the guards were equally abusive, nor were all the prisoners completely subservient. A recent study added another important wrinkle: It appears that certain kinds of people are more likely to have agreed to participate in a study of "prison life" in the first place (Carnahan & McFarland, 2007). Specifically, the new study found that people who responded to an ad very much like the one Zimbardo used to recruit his participants, compared with a more neutral ad, attracted people who were relatively high on the traits of aggressiveness, authoritarianism (see Chapter 7), Machiavellianism, narcissism, and social dominance—all traits shown in prior research to be associated with aggressive abuse. People who responded to the ad were relatively low on the traits of empathy and altruism, two traits that are *negatively* associated with abusive behavior. So the "propensity to abuse" that the Stanford Prison experiment evoked might to some extent have already been there, in the participants' personalities, before the experiment even began. Moreover, it is plausible to think that an environment populated with similar kinds of people with a tendency toward abuse—the other kind of person-situation interaction—might become even more dangerous than it was to begin with.

The implications of this discussion go far beyond what one thinks of the Stanford Prison experiment. In 2003, many Americans and people around the world were shocked by revelations of abuse of Iraqi prisoners by young American soldiers at Abu Ghraib prison. The images were truly horrifying. But what explains this abusive behavior? Philip Zimbardo, the Stanford Prison experiment scientist, wrote in the *Boston Globe*

> The terrible things my guards did to their prisoners were comparable to the horrors inflicted on the Iraqi detainees. . . . Human behavior is much more under the control of situational forces than most of us recognize or want to acknowledge. (Zimbardo, 2004, p. D11)

He may be right, but the study by Carnahan and McFarland suggests there is more to the story. The guards at Abu Ghraib prison who participated in the abuse did not arrive there randomly—they volunteered (A. Cohen, 2004). One woman guard in particular, who became famous from some photographs of her abusing prisoners, spent nights in the prison even though she had been reprimanded for being there when off duty (Zernike, 2005). And

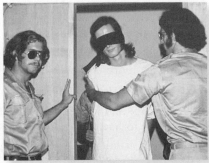

Figure 4.2 Stanford Versus Abu Ghraib The abuse of Iraqi prisoners by American guards at Abu Ghraib prison shocked the world (left), and in some ways was anticipated by the results of the Stanford Prison experiment decades earlier (right). However, the "power of the situation" may not be quite what it seems, because certain kinds of people were attracted both to the experiment and to guard duty at Abu Ghraib, and their behavior changed both situations to make violent behavior increasingly likely.

then, there are the changes that occurred in the guards' environment from the mutual presence of people who might have been prone to abuse in the first place, as they disinhibited and even encouraged each others' behavior.

Prisons are powerful situations, and Abu Ghraib was surely an overwhelming environment, one prone to lead to violence. It is highly unlikely its guards would have abused prisoners as they did in a different atmosphere or with better supervision. But personality is important too. While situations like Abu Ghraib are nearly impossible to study directly, research suggests that the personality traits of the guards helped lead to the problems there, as did the changes in the environment that those guards themselves produced. Situations and persons work *together*—for good or for ill.

Persons, Situations, and Values

When I look back on the history of the person-situation debate, I am struck by two things. First, Mischel's argument that personality did not exist impacted the world of psychology with shocking force, even though the original argument in his 1968 book was brief and not very well supported. Second, the controversy persists—less pervasively than before, but still active—into the present day. Right now you could look into the current psychological literature and find, here and there, remarks about how little personality can tell us about behavior, and how much behavior changes according to even minor alterations in situations. The implication of these remarks, still and despite everything, is that what people do is determined almost exclusively by the situations they are in.

The beginning and the lingering end of the person-situation debate suggest that deeper issues may be at stake (Funder, 2006). This is just a suspicion, so take it as you will, but I think many psychologists were eager to accept situationism because the view of human nature it implies was attractive to their philosophical and perhaps even political outlooks. A situationist view of the world, at a superficial level at least, implies that people are free to do whatever they want in every situation they encounter, rather than having their behavior determined by their consistent personality. Situationism also implies that everybody is equal to everybody else and that differing outcomes for different people are a function solely of the situations in which they find themselves. Some people get rich and others fall into poverty, some are popular and some are shunned,

> I think many psychologists were eager to accept situationism because the view of human nature it implies was attractive to their philosophical and perhaps even political outlooks.

Situationist view:
implies free will,
equality and
absolves people
from blame
↳ much more attractive
than trait approach

personality view:
1) appreciates uniqueness
2) consistant identity

and, overall, some succeed while others fail. A situationist view implies this is all due to circumstances, and further implies that under the right circumstances anybody could be rich, popular, and successful—a pleasant thought. The alternative view—that people really are different from each other—implies that, even under the best of circumstances, some people have traits that make bad outcomes relatively likely—not as attractive a prospect. A situationist view can also—and somewhat paradoxically—help to absolve people from blame. If the guards in the Stanford Prison experiment or at Abu Ghraib prison were helpless in the face of powerful situational forces, then what they did was not really their fault.

Still, the view from the personality side of the fence has its attractions too. For example, it begins with the idea that understanding human nature demands more than a "one size fits all" approach, and it appreciates the unique aspects of every individual. It also offers the possibility that an individual might be able to develop a consistent identity and personal syle that allows him to be consistently himself in a way that transcends the moment, rather than being continuously or even helplessly tossed about by situational forces. Some of the most inspirational people in history, from Nathan Hale ("I only regret that I have but one life to give for my country") to the unknown hero who stood in front of the tank during the 1989 crackdown on dissidents in Tiananmen Square in Beijing, are inspirational precisely because they found an inner determinant for their behavior that overrode what would seem to be overwhelmingly powerful incentives to act otherwise. In contrast, while we admire people who are flexible, a person can be flexible to the point of seeming manipulative, two-faced, untrustworthy—in a word, inconsistent.

So, when psychologists—or nonpsychologists—debate the importance of the person versus the situation, they may really be arguing, implicitly, about their fundamental values and even the meaning of life! And beliefs like these are deeply held indeed, which may be why the controversy refuses to go away, no matter what the data seem to demand.

Perhaps the resolution of the person-situation debate can help to reconcile this clash of fundamental values. We have seen that people maintain their personalities even as they adapt their behavior to particular situations (e.g., Funder & Colvin, 1991; Fleeson, 2004; Roberts & Pomerantz, 2004). Thus, the view of a person as flexibly adaptive to situations *and* generally consistent in personal style are not in conflict after all. If this point ever becomes fully understood and widely accepted, then psychology can offer some further lessons: Acknowledging the influence of social conditions on life outcomes does not make personal responsibility irrelevant. Individual freedom is not incompatible with being true to oneself. We do not need to

Figure 4.3 Does This Behavior Come From the Person or the Situation? As part of a crackdown on protestors in China, the government sent tanks into Tiananmen Square on June 5, 1989. A lone protestor—whose name is unknown—stood in front, stopped their advance, and became an international hero.

choose between these core values because they do not really conflict. If the resolution of the person-situation debate can help us understand this point, then personality psychology can claim an important insight into human nature.

PEOPLE ARE DIFFERENT

Late in his career, the distinguished Harvard social psychologist Roger Brown wrote:

> As a psychologist, in all the years . . . I had thought individual differences in personality were exaggerated. I compared personality psychologists to cultural anthropologists who took pleasure in, and indeed derived status from, the exoticism of their discoveries. I had once presumed to say to Henry A. Murray, Harvard's distinguished personologist: "I think people are all very much the same." Murray's response had been; "Oh you do, do you? Well, you don't know what the hell you're talking about!" And I hadn't. (Brown, 1996, p. 169)

(a)   (b)

Figure 4.4 Murray Versus Brown The personality psychologist Henry Murray (a) once got in an argument with the social psychologist Roger Brown (b) over whether everybody was basically the same. Years later, Brown concluded Murray was right: People really are different from each other.

This little exchange captures the person-situation debate in a nutshell. Historically, and even to some extent to the present day, social psychologists have tended to regard individual differences as being relatively unimportant, while personality psychologists, of course, put such differences front and center. Near the end of his career, Roger Brown decided the personality psychologists were right, and in that decision he finally came to agree with what most nonpsychologists have intuitively believed all along, as well as with the central lesson of the person-situation debate: People are psychologically different from each other, and these differences matter. This conclusion implies that it is important for psychologists to think long and hard about the best concepts to describe these differences, to develop appropriate technologies to measure them, and finally, to find ways to use them to predict and to understand what people do. These are the topics of the next three chapters.

SUMMARY

The Measurement of Individual Differences

- The trait approach to personality begins by assuming that individuals differ in their characteristic patterns of thought, feeling, and behavior. These patterns are called personality traits.

People Are Inconsistent

- Classifying people according to traits raises an important problem, however: People are inconsistent. Indeed, some psychologists have suggested that people are so inconsistent in their behavior from one situation to the next that it is not worthwhile to characterize them in terms of personality traits. The controversy over this issue is called the person-situation debate.

The Person-Situation Debate

- Situationists, or opponents of the trait approach, argue (1) that according to a review of the personality literature, the ability of traits to predict behavior is extremely limited; (2) that situations are therefore more important than personality traits for determining what people do; and (3) that not only is personality assessment (the measurement of traits) a waste of time, but also many of people's intuitions about each other are fundamentally wrong.

- The rebuttals to the first situationist argument are that a fair review of the literature reveals that the predictability of behavior from traits is better than is sometimes acknowledged; that improved research methods can increase this predictability; and that the putative upper limit for predictability (a correlation of about .40) yields better outcomes than is sometimes recognized.

- The response to the second situationist argument is that many important effects of situations on behavior are no bigger statistically than the documented size of the effects of personality traits on behavior.

- If the responses to the first two situationist arguments are valid, then the third argument—that both assessment and people's intuitions are fundamentally flawed—falls apart of its own weight.

- The large number of personality-trait terms supports the importance of traits as a useful way to predict behavior and understand personality.

Personality and Life

- A wide-ranging survey of the research literature shows that personality traits affect important life outcomes including health, longevity, and interpersonal and career success.

Persons and Situations

- Situational variables are best suited for predicting behavior in specific situations, whereas personality traits are more relevant to patterns of behavior that persist across relationship partners, work settings, and other life situations.

- The resolution of the person-situation debate requires recognizing that persons and situations do not compete for which one determines behavior more. Instead, persons and situations interact to produce behavior together.

- "Interactionism" recognizes that (1) the effect of a person variable may depend on the situation, and vice versa, (2) people with different personalities may choose, or find themselves in, different situations, and (3) situations are affected by the personalities of people who inhabit them.

- The person-situation debate may have been instigated and maintained, in part, because of deeply held philosophical beliefs. Emphasizing the effect of the situation implies personal equality and individual flexibility, along with avoidance of personal blame, whereas emphasizing the person accentuates the importance of self-determination and personal responsibility. The resolution of the debate may imply that these values are not as incompatible as people sometimes assume.

People Are Different

- The psychological differences among people matter. The business of personality psychology is to describe and measure these differences, and to use them to predict and understand what people do.

THINK ABOUT IT

1. What are the most consistent aspects of the personalities of the people you know? What are the most inconsistent aspects?
2. Do you use personality traits when describing yourself or other people? Or do you describe yourself and others in some other way? What other ways are there?
3. Have you ever misunderstood someone's personality by expecting it to be more consistent than it really is?
4. The next time you talk with your parents, explain the consistency issue to them and ask whether they think people have consistent personality traits. Then do the same with college friends who have not taken this course. Are their answers different? How?
5. What situation are you in right now? Is it determining your behavior? What situation were you in at 10:00 A.M. yesterday? Did it determine your behavior?
6. What important life outcomes—besides the ones in Table 4.2—do you think might be affected by personality?
7. During the Nuremberg trials after World War II, some participants in wartime atrocities defended themselves saying they were "only following orders." Is this the same thing as saying that the situation was so strong, their behav-

ior was not determined by their own personal characteristics? What do you think of this defense?

8. Sociologists point out that criminal behavior is much more likely from people who come from crime-prone neighborhoods, low economic levels, and unstable family backgrounds. These are all situational factors. Does this fact imply that crime comes from the situation and not from the person? If so, how can we hold a person responsible for criminal actions?

9. How are the cases described in questions 7 and 8, above, similar to and different from each other?

SUGGESTED READINGS

Kenrick, D. T., & Funder, D. C. (1988). Profiting from controversy: Lessons from the person-situation debate. *American Psychologist, 43,* 23–34.

> *A review of the person-situation debate written for a general audience of psychologists (not just for specialists in personality). Kenrick and I attempted to declare the person-situation debate finished; it almost worked.*

Mischel, W. (1968). *Personality and assessment.* New York: Wiley.

> *The book that launched a thousand rebuttals—this is the volume that touched off the person-situation debate. It is well written and, in its key sections, surprisingly brief.*

Ross, L., & Nisbett, R. E. (1991). *The person and the situation: Perspectives of social psychology.* New York: McGraw-Hill.

> *A clearly written exposition of the situationist position.*

EMEDIA

 Go to StudySpace, wwnorton.com/studyspace, to access additional review and enrichment materials.

5

PERSONALITY ASSESSMENT I: Personality Testing and Its Consequences

> If something exists, it exists in some quantity, and if it exists in some quantity, it can be measured.
>
> —EDWARD LEE THORNDIKE[1]

ARE YOU MORE OR LESS extraverted than the person sitting next to you? Are you more or less conscientious? If you accept the conclusion of Chapter 4—that personality traits like these are real and affect important life outcomes—then this Thorndike quote implies that the next task is to measure them. To decide who is the most extraverted or conscientious person in the room, or, more broadly, for personality traits to be useful for the scientific understanding of the mind, the prediction of behavior, or any other purpose, the essential task is *measurement*. The next two chapters explore personality assessment, the enterprise of trying to accurately measure characteristic aspects of personality.

THE NATURE OF PERSONALITY ASSESSMENT

Personality assessment is a professional activity of numerous research, clinical, and industrial psychologists, as well as a prosperous business that seems to fulfill a persistent need. Clinicians may measure how depressed someone is in order to plan treatment, whereas potential employers are

---

[1] As cited in Cunningham, 1992, p. 35.

eg. of personality variables:
—motives
—goals.

probably more interested in measuring the person's conscientiousness to decide whether to offer her a job. An individual's **personality** consists of characteristic patterns of behavior, thought, or emotional experience that exhibit relative consistency across time and situations (Allport, 1937). These patterns include many kinds of variables, including motives, intentions, goals, strategies, and subjective representations (the ways in which people perceive and construct their worlds; see Chapter 17). They indicate the degree to which a person desires one goal over another, or thinks the world is changeable as opposed to fixed, or is generally happy, or is optimistic as opposed to pessimistic, or is sexually attracted to members of the same or the opposite sex. All of these variables and many others are relatively stable attributes of the psychological makeup of individuals, so in that sense they are all personality traits, and any attempt to measure them necessarily entails personality assessment. As a result, assessment is relevant to a broad range of research, including nearly every topic in personality, developmental, and social psychology.

Moreover, personality assessment is not restricted to psychologists. It is practiced by you, your friends, your family—and by me, in my off-duty hours—all day long, every day. As mentioned at the beginning of Chapter 4, personality traits are a fundamental part of how we think about each other and ourselves. We choose whom to befriend and whom to avoid on the basis of our assessments—will this person be reliable or helpful or honest?—and others make the same judgments and choices about us. We even base our feelings about ourselves partly on our beliefs about our personalities: Am I competent or kind or tough? The judgments we make of one another's personalities and of ourselves are more consequential than those any psychologist will ever make.

Regardless of whether the source of a personality assessment is a psychologist, an acquaintance, or a psychological test, the most important thing to know about that assessment is the degree to which it is right or wrong. Evaluations of professional personality judgments or personality tests are said to appraise their *validity*, whereas evaluations of amateur judgments generally use the term *accuracy*.

"He looks very promising—but let's see how he does on the written test."

The basis of the evaluation is the same either way. Two basic criteria are available: agreement and prediction (Funder, 1987, 1995, 1999). The agreement criterion asks: Does this judgment agree with other judgments obtained through other techniques or from other judges (whether professional or amateur)? The prediction criterion asks: Can this judgment of personality be used to predict behavior or other life outcomes?

The topic of this chapter and the next is personality assessment—how personality is judged by professionals and by amateurs. The remainder of this chapter considers the business of personality assessment and how psychologists construct and use personality tests, as well as some of the consequences of testing. Chapter 6 considers personality assessment by ordinary people—people who are not trained or paid to be psychologists, but who nonetheless use psychology every day.

THE BUSINESS OF TESTING

The American Psychological Association (APA) holds a convention every year. It's quite an event. Thousands of psychologists take over most of the downtown hotels in a major city, such as San Francisco, Boston, or Washington, DC, for a week of meetings, symposia, and cocktail parties. One of the biggest attractions is always the exhibit hall, where dozens of high-tech, artistically designed booths fill a room that seems to go on for acres. These booths are set up, at great expense, by several kinds of companies. One group is textbook publishers; all the tools of advertising are applied to the task of convincing college professors like me to get their students to read (and buy) books such as the one you now hold in your hands. Another group is manufacturers of videos and various, sometimes strange gadgets for therapy and research. Yet another group is psychological testers. Their booths typically distribute free samples that include not only personality and ability tests, but also shopping bags, notebooks, and even beach umbrellas. These freebies prominently display the logo of their corporate sponsor: the Psychological Corporation, Consulting Psychologists Press, the Institute for Personality and Ability Testing, and so on. These goodies are paid for by what they are intended to sell: personality tests.

You don't have to go to the APA convention to get a free "personality test." On North Michigan Avenue in Chicago, on the Boston Common, at Fisherman's Wharf in San Francisco, and in Westwood in Los Angeles, I have seen people distribute brightly colored brochures that ask, in huge letters, "Are you curious about yourself? Free personality test enclosed." Inside is something that looks like a conventional personality test, with 200 questions to be answered True or False. (One item reads, "Having settled an argument out do you continue to feel disgruntled for a while?") But as it turns out, the test is really a recruitment pitch. If you take it and go for your "free evaluation"—which I do not recommend—you will be told two things. First, you are all messed up. Second, the people who gave you the test have the cure: You need to join a certain "church" that can provide the techniques (and even the strange electrical equipment) needed to cure you.

> The brochure labeled "Are you curious about yourself?" asks a pretty irresistible question.

The personality testers who distribute samples at the APA convention and those who hand out free so-called personality tests on North Michigan Avenue have a surprising amount in common. Both seek new customers, and both use all the techniques of advertising, including free samples, to acquire them. The tests they distribute look superficially alike. And both groups exploit a nearly universal desire to know more about personality. The brochure labeled "Are you curious about yourself?" asks a pretty irresistible question. The more staid tests distributed at the APA convention likewise offer an intriguing promise of finding out something about your own or somebody else's personality that might be interesting, important, or useful.

Below the surface, however, they are not the same. The tests peddled at the APA convention are, for the most part, well-validated instruments that are useful for many purposes. The ones being pushed at tourist destinations from coast to coast are frauds and potentially dangerous. But you cannot tell which is which just by looking at them. To tell a valid test from an invalid one, you need to know something about how personality tests and assessments are constructed, how they work, and how they can fail. Let's take a closer look.

PERSONALITY TESTS

The personality testing companies that are so well represented at APA meetings do a good business. They sell their products to clinical psychologists, to the personnel departments of large corporations, and to the military. You have probably taken at least one personality test, and you are likely to encounter more in the future.

One of the most widely used personality tests is the Minnesota Multiphasic Personality Inventory (MMPI),[2] introduced in Chapter 2. This test was designed for use in the clinical assessment of individuals with psychological difficulties, but it has also been widely used for many other purposes, such as employment screening. Another widely used test is the California Psychological Inventory (CPI); it is similar to the MMPI in many ways but is designed for use with nondisturbed individuals. Others include the Sixteen Personality Factor Questionnaire (16PF); the Strong Vocational Interest Blank (SVIB), used for vocational guidance in school settings; the Hogan Personality Inventory (HPI), used by employers for personnel selection; and many more.

Many personality tests, including those just listed, are *omnibus* inventories, which means they were designed to measure a wide range of personality traits. The NEO Personality Inventory, for instance, measures five broad traits along with a large number of subscales (Costa & McCrae, 1997).[3]

Others are designed to measure just one trait. Tests measure shyness, self-consciousness, self-monitoring, empathy, attributional complexity, nonverbal sensitivity, "Type A" personality (a pattern of hostility that makes the person vulnerable to heart attack), "Type C" personality (a pattern of passivity that supposedly makes the person vulnerable to cancer), and so on. No one has done an exact count, but there must be thousands of such tests, and new ones appear every day.

S-Data Versus B-Data Personality Tests

To use the terms introduced in Chapter 2, most personality tests provide S data. They ask you about what you are like, so the score you receive amounts to a summary of how you have described yourself. The "shyness" scale asks a bunch of questions about how shy you are, the "attributional complexity" scale asks questions about the level of complexity in your thinking about the causes of people's behavior, and so forth. Other personality tests yield B data. The MMPI is a good example. It presents items—such as "I prefer a shower to a bath"—not because the tester is interested in the literal

---

[2] By a tradition of mysterious origin, nearly all personality tests are referred to by their initials, in capital letters with no periods.

[3] NEO originally stood for Neuroticism, Extraversion, and Openness. Later versions of the test added Agreeableness and Conscientiousness, but it wasn't renamed OCEAN even though it could (and maybe should) have been (John, 1990).

answer, but because answers to this item are informative about some aspect of personality, in this case, empathy; preferring a shower is the empathic response, for some reason (Hogan, 1969).

Another kind of B-data personality test has been introduced relatively recently. The Implicit Association Test (IAT) measures how quickly participants respond to instructions to discriminate between terms that apply to "me" or to "others," and between terms that are relevant, or not, to the trait being measured (Greenwald, McGhee, & Schwartz, 1998). One study measured shyness in this way (Asendorpf, Banse, & Mücke, 2002). Each participant sat at a computer and responded as quickly as possible to whether terms (e.g., "self," "them") referred to "me" or "others," and then to whether other terms (e.g., "inhibited," "candid") referred to "shy" or "nonshy." Finally, participants did both tasks at the same time. The theory is that people who implicitly, but not necessarily consciously, know they are shy will have faster associations between "me" and "shy" than between "me" and "nonshy." The same study also gathered more conventional S data, self-ratings of shyness. Finally, the participants were videotaped as they chattted with an attractive stranger of the opposite sex, a task selected as one that just might induce shyness in some people.

The fascinating result is that aspects of shyness that participants consciously controlled, such as how long they spoke, could be predicted by the S-data "shyness" scores. (Shy people spoke less.) However, more spontaneous indicators of shyness, such as facial expressions and tense body posture, were predicted much better by the IAT measure. This result suggests that, although people's awareness of their own shyness is only partially conscious, their deeper, underlying knowledge can be not only measured, but also used to predict behavior. (This idea will be discussed further in Chapters 12 and 17.)

Is intelligence a personality trait? Psychologists have differing opinions about this. Either way, it can be noted that tests of intelligence, or *IQ tests*, also yield B data. Imagine trying to assess intelligence with an S-data test. Such a test would include questions such as "Are you an intelligent person?" and "Are you good at math?" Researchers have actually tried this, but simply asking people whether they are smart turns out to be a poor way to measure intelligence (Furnham, 2001). So instead, IQ tests ask people questions of varying difficulty, which have fixed and specific correct answers, such as reasoning or math problems. The more questions the test takers get right, the higher is their (tested) IQ. These right or wrong answers comprise B data.

In my opinion, the distinction between S-data tests and B-data tests is important, but this distinction is rarely drawn in the conventional literature on personality testing. More common is the distinction between projective and objective tests.

Projective Tests

PROJECTING THE MIND

Projective tests are based on a particular theory, called the *projective hypothesis*, of how to see into someone's mind (Frank, 1939). The theory is this: If somebody is asked to describe or interpret a meaningless, ambiguous stimulus—such as an inkblot—her answer cannot come from the stimulus itself, because the stimulus actually does not look like, or mean, anything. The answer must instead come from (be a "projection" of) her needs, feelings, experience, thought processes, and other hidden aspects of the mind (see also Murray, 1943). The answer may even reveal something the person does not know about herself.

This is the theory behind the famous Rorschach inkblot test (Rorschach, 1921; Exner, 1993). The Swiss psychiatrist Hermann Rorschach dropped blots of India ink onto note cards, folded the cards in half, and then unfolded them. The result was a set of complicated-looking blots.[4] Over the years, uncounted psychiatrists and clinical psychologists have shown these blots to their clients and asked what they saw.

Of course, the only literally correct answer is "an inkblot," but that is not considered a cooperative response. Instead, the examiner is interested in whether the client will report seeing a cloud, a devil, his mother, or whatever. The idea is that whatever the client sees, precisely because it is not actually shown on the card, must reveal something about the contents of his mind.

The same logic led to the development of numerous other projective tests. The Draw-A-Person test requires the client to draw (you guessed it) a person, and the drawing is interpreted according to what kind of person is drawn (e.g., a man or a woman), which body parts are exaggerated

---

[4] According to legend, Rorschach made many blots in this way but kept only the "best" ones. I wonder how he chose them.

(a)   (b)

Figure 5.1 Two Projective Tests (a) Rorschach inkblot: This picture resembles—but is not—one of the inkblots in Rorschach's famous test. The real blots traditionally are not published so that someone taking the test will see them for the first time. (b) Thematic Apperception Test: The task is to make up stories about a series of pictures like these. Themes in the stories are interpreted as indicating "implicit motives" of which the person might not himself be aware.

or omitted, and so forth (Machover, 1949). Large eyes might be taken to indicate suspiciousness or paranoia; heavy shading might mean aggressive impulses, and numerous erasures might be a sign of anxiety. The classic Thematic Apperception Test (TAT) asks clients to tell stories about a set of drawings of people and ambiguous events (Morgan & Murray, 1935; Murray, 1943). A recent version uses pictures that include "a boy in a checked shirt, . . . a woman and a man on a trapeze, two men in a workshop, and a young woman working on the [balance] beam" (Brunstein & Maier, 2005, p. 208). The themes of these stories are used to assess the client's motivational state (e.g., McClelland, 1975; Smith, 1992). If a person looks at an ambiguous drawing of two people and thinks they are fighting, for example, this might reveal a need to be aggressive; if the two people are described as in love, this might reflect a need for intimacy; if one is seen as giving orders to the other, this might reflect a need for power.

Projective tests of a sort can even be administered to people "from a distance," without them getting near a psychologist (Winter, 1991). Psycholo-

research on test validity
= scarce.

gists have tried to assess needs and other aspects of personality by analyzing the content of stories, essays, letters, and even political speeches.

The projective hypothesis behind all these tests is an interesting and seemingly reasonable idea, and interpretations of actual responses can be fascinating. A large number of practicing clinicians swear by their efficacy. However, research data on the validity of these tests—the degree to which they actually measure what they are supposed to measure—is surprisingly scarce (Lilienfeld, Wood, & Garb, 2000).

To again use the terminology introduced in Chapter 2, all projective tests provide B data. They are specific, directly observed responses to particular stimuli, whether inkblots, pictures, or instructions to draw somebody. All the disadvantages of B data therefore apply to projective tests. For one thing, they are expensive. For example, it takes around 45 minutes to administer a single Rorschach and another 1.5 to 2 hours to score it (Ball, Archer, & Imhof, 1994). Compare this to the time needed to hand out a pile of questionnaires and score them with a machine. This is a serious issue because it is not enough for projective tests to have some small (and even surprising) degree of validity. For their continued use to make any sense, they should provide extra information that justifies their much greater cost (Lilienfeld et al., 2000).

The even more fundamental difficulty with projective tests is that, perhaps even more than other kinds of B data, a psychologist cannot be sure what they mean. What does it mean when somebody thinks an inkblot looks like genitalia, or imagines that an ambiguous picture portrays a murder, or draws a person with no ears? The answer and the validity of the answer depend critically on the test interpreter (Sundberg, 1977). Two different interpreters of the same response might come to different conclusions unless a standard scoring system is used. Of the projective tests, only the TAT is consistently scored according to a well-developed system (e.g., McAdams, 1984). While scoring systems have been developed for the Rorschach (Exner, 1993; Klopfer & Davidson, 1962), not everybody uses them, and even for those systems, the training most practitioners get is not exactly ideal (Guarnaccia, Dill, Sabatino, & Southwick, 2001). Many of the remaining projective tests are interpreted according to the predilections of the individual examiner.

The survival of so many projective tests into the 21st century is something of a mystery. Even literature reviews that show projective tests to have some degree of validity tend to conclude that other, less expensive techniques work as well or even better (Garb, Florio, & Grove, 1998, 1999; Lilienfeld et al., 2000). Even more disturbing, projective tests of dubious validity, such as ones that ask clients to draw human figures, are sometimes used as evidence in court cases (Lally, 2001).[5] As the measurement expert Ann Anastasi wrote more than several decades ago, "projective techniques present a curious discrepancy between research and practice. When evaluated as psychometric instruments, the large majority make a poor showing. Yet their popularity in clinical use continues unabated" (Anastasi, 1982, p. 564). Her comment remains true today (Camara, Nathan, & Puente, 2000).

Perhaps projective tests endure because some clinical psychologists have fooled themselves into thinking they are valid. One writer has suggested that these clinicians may lack "a skill that does not come naturally to any of us: disregarding the vivid and compelling data of subjective experience in favor of the often dry and impersonal results of objective research" (Lilienfeld, 1999, p. 38). Perhaps the problem is not that the tests are worthless, but that they have been used for inappropriate purposes (Wood, Nezworski, & Garb, 2003). Perhaps, as others have suggested, the validity of these tests is beside the point. They simply serve a useful, if nonpsychometric, function of "breaking the ice" between client and therapist by giving them something to do during the first visit. Or, just possibly, these instruments have a certain, special validity in their actual application by certain skilled clinicians that cannot be duplicated by other techniques and has not been fully captured by controlled research studies.

EVALUATING THE RORSCHACH AND THE TAT

It is probably fair to say that only two projective tests have produced evidence that comes even close to establishing validity according to conventional standards, so let's take a closer look at them. One of these tests is the Rorschach, when it is scored according to one of two specific techniques—either Exner's Comprehensive System (Exner, 1993) or Klopfer's system (Klopfer & Davidson, 1962). According to one comprehensive review of research using the Rorschach, the correlation coefficient between scores garnered from one of these systems and various criteria relevant to mental

---

[5] This use of projective tests has produced something of a backlash among people who feel they have been victimized by the tests' poor validity. Test stimuli such as inkblots and TAT pictures, which in the past were closely held secrets, are now available on several websites that also offer advice on the best responses to give to them.

health averaged about .33 (Garb et al., 1998).[6] As you will recall from the BESD in Chapter 3, this means that a dichotomous (Yes or No) diagnostic decision made using the Rorschach will be correct about 66 percent of the time. Recent research also suggests that the Rorschach might be particularly valid—and somewhat better than the MMPI—for predicting certain objective outcomes such as commitment to a mental hospital or suicide (Hiller, Rosenthal, Bornstein, Berry, & Brunell-Neuleib, 1999).[7]

In one survey, 82 percent of clinical psychologists reported using the Rorschach at least occasionally (Watkins, Campbell, Nieberding, & Hallmark, 1995). It remains clinical psychology's fourth most used test,[8] and continues to be widely taught in clinical graduate programs (Childs & Eyde, 2002). But despite hundreds of studies, little evidence has been found that the Rorschach provides information that goes much beyond that provided by easier, cheaper tests such as the MMPI (Hunsley & Bailey, 1999; Parker, Hunsley, & Hanson, 1999; Garb, 2003). So, even though under ideal circumstances the Rorschach does seem to have a degree of validity, this degree of widespread use is rather astonishing. Other techniques are more valid, for most purposes, and the Rorschach is, at best, extremely expensive.

The other projective test with some degree of established validity—probably better than the Rorschach—is the TAT (McClelland, 1984). In current research, the test is often administered in a newer, shorter form called the Picture Story Exercise (PSE) (McClelland, Koestner & Weinberger, 1989). The stimuli for this test are from four to eight (versions vary) drawings or photographs that show scenes such as a ship captain talking to a passenger or two women working in a laboratory, and the scoring of clients' responses can be highly reliable (Schultheiss, 2008). The purpose is to measure *implicit motives*, meaning motivations concerning achievement, intimacy, power, and other matters that the participant might not be aware of. Studies have shown these motives to be related to complex thinking (cognitive complex-

TAT short form = PSE (Picture Story Exercise)

---

[6] The main points the authors of this review intended to make were that the validity of the MMPI is even higher (the parallel $r = .55$ in their analysis), and that, since the MMPI is much cheaper to administer, it should be used instead. At the same time, and perhaps unintentionally, they also provided the most convincing demonstration I have seen that the Rorschach has more than zero validity.

[7] The MMPI has been found better for predicting psychiatric diagnoses and self-report scores. If you want to see the argument that broke out over these findings, compare the paper by Garb, Wood, Nezworski, Grove, and Stejskal (2001) with the response by Rosenthal, Hiller, Bornstein, Berry, and Brunell-Neuleib (2001). As you can see, many people jumped into the fray.

[8] In case you are curious, the top three are (1) the Wechsler Intelligence Scale for adults, (2) the MMPI, and (3) the Wechsler Intelligence Scale for children (Camara et al., 2000).

ity), the experiences one finds most memorable, and other psychological outcomes (Woike, 1995; Woike & Aronoff, 1992).

It is possible that the TAT (and its relatives such as the PSE) and more conventional objective tests (discussed in the next section) get at slightly different aspects of personality. It is certainly the case that projective and questionnaire measures of the same attribute—such as "need for achievement"—typically do not correlate highly (Schultheiss, 2008). It is not uncommon for the same person to score high on an implicit (projective) measure and low on an explicit (questionnaire) measure, or vice versa. Researchers have proposed that this is because the motives measured by the TAT reflect what people want, whereas traits as measured by questionnaires predict how these motives will be expressed. For example, the TAT might reveal that a person has a great need for power, whereas a more conventional test might reveal how she will go about trying to obtain power (Winter, John, Stewart, Klohnen, & Duncan, 1998). Or, a questionnaire measure of need for achievement might predict what a person consciously chooses to work on, whereas a TAT measure might predict how much effort she will put into the job (Brunstein & Maier, 2005). One study found that the implicit need for achievement measured by the PSE predicted good performance on an arithmetic test, but not whether a person would volunteer to take a leadership post. On the other hand, a questionnaire measure of an explicit need for achievement predicted seeking leadership but not arithmetic performance (Biernat, 1989).

These last findings might seem a bit difficult to explain, but they fit into one view of what the implicit need for achievement is all about. Summarizing a wide range of studies, Schultheiss (2008) theorized that people high in this need are successful in work contexts where they have full control over setting goals and receive frequent feedback on how well they are doing. For example, they are in their element when running a small business where they have power over all its operations and can check the daily cash flow. But as people high in the need for achievement move into larger organizations, where less activity is under their personal control and more depends on the efforts of others, they become less successful because of their lack of managerial, or "people" skills (McClelland & Boyatzis, 1982). They also may not make particularly good presidents of the United States. David Winter (1981) showed that presidents who revealed a large need for achievement in their inaugural speeches (e.g., Presidents Wilson, Hoover, Nixon, and Carter) began with a flurry of activity, became frustrated with political obstacles, and ended up achieving little.

(a)   (b)   (c)

Figure 5.2 Analyzing Presidential Needs Based on an analysis of their inaugural addresses, psychologist David Winter rated (a) Jimmy Carter as the president of the United States who was highest in need for "achievement," (b) George H.W. Bush as highest in need for "affiliation," and (c) John F. Kennedy as highest in need for "power." (Barack Obama had not yet been elected.)

Objective Tests — *yes/no, true/false, computer-scored test.*

The tests that psychologists call "objective" can be detected at a glance. If a test consists of a list of questions to be answered Yes or No, or True or False, or on a numeric scale, and especially if the test uses a computer-scored answer sheet, then it is an **objective test**. The term comes from the idea that the questions making up the test seem more objective and less open to interpretation than the pictures and blots used in projective tests.

VALIDITY AND THE SUBJECTIVITY OF TEST ITEMS

It is not clear that the term "objective" is really justified, however (Bornstein, 1999a). Consider the first item of the famous MMPI. The item reads, "I like mechanics magazines," which is to be answered True or False (Wiggins, 1973). The item may seem objective compared with a question like, "What do you see in this inkblot?" But the appearance may be misleading. For instance, does "like" mean interest, fondness, admiration, or tolerance? Does liking such magazines require that you regularly read them? Are *Popular Mechanics* and *High Fidelity* mechanics magazines? How about *Computer World*? Are only popular magazines included in the classification, or does the item also refer to trade journals of professional mechanics or to the research literature produced by professors of mechanical engineering? This example is not an unusually problematic item; it is rather typical. And it illustrates how objectivity is harder to attain than it might seem.

commonality
scale
– 95% answered
the same way

It is difficult to escape the conclusion that the items on objective tests, while perhaps not as ambiguous as those that constitute projective tests, are still not absolutely objective. Writing truly objective items might be impossible, and even if it were possible, such items might not work. Think about this for a moment: If everybody read and interpreted an item in exactly the same way, then might everybody also tend to answer the item in the same way? If so, the item would not be very useful for the assessment of individual differences. In some cases, the ambiguity of an objective item might not be a flaw; its interpretation might have to be somewhat subjective in order for responses to imply anything about personality.

Harrison Gough, inventor of the California Psychological Inventory, included on his test a scale called *commonality*, which consists solely of items that are answered in the same way by at least 95 percent of all people. He included it to detect illiterates who are pretending they know how to read and individuals deliberately trying to sabotage the test. The average score on this scale is about 95 percent, but an illiterate answering at random will score about 50 percent (since it is a True-False scale) and therefore will be immediately identifiable, as will someone who (like one of my former students) answered the CPI by flipping a coin—heads True, tails False.

These are interesting and clever uses for a commonality scale, but its properties are mentioned here to make a different point. Gough reported that when individuals encounter a commonality item—one being, "I would fight if someone tried to take my rights away" (keyed True)—they do not say to themselves, "What a dumb, obvious item. I bet everybody answers it the same way." Instead, they say, "At last! A nonambiguous item I can really understand!" People enjoy answering the commonality items because they do not seem ambiguous (J. A. Johnson, 2006).[9] Unfortunately, commonality items are not very useful for personality measurement, because few people differ. A certain amount of ambiguity may indeed be useful (Gough, 1968; J. A. Johnson, 1981).

WHY SO MANY ITEMS?

If you look at an objective test, one of the first things you will notice is how many questions it asks. This number may be very large. Some of the shorter

---

[9] Another item from the "commonality" scale reads, "Education is more important than most people think." Paradoxically, almost everybody responds True.

personality tests have around a dozen items, but most have far more, and some of the most famous personality tests (e.g., MMPI and CPI) have hundreds. To complete a test like the MMPI can take an hour or more, and a fairly tedious hour at that.

Why so many items? The answer lies in the principle of aggregation (see Chapter 3). The answer an individual gives to any one question might not be particularly informative; it might vary according to exactly how he interprets the item or other extraneous factors. In the terminology used in Chapter 3, a single answer will tend to be unreliable. But if a group of similar questions is asked, the average of the answers ought to be much more stable, or reliable, because random fluctuations tend to cancel each other out.

For this reason, one way to make a personality test more reliable is simply to make it longer. If you add items that measure the trait in question as accurately as the existing items do—something easier said than done, frankly—then the improvement in reliability can be estimated rather precisely using the Spearman-Brown formula,[10] introduced in Chapter 3. The improvements in reliability can be remarkable. For example, if a 10-item test has a reliability of .60—which would be considered rather poor for an objective test—adding 10 more items can raise the reliability to .75, which would be considered much better. Double the number of items again, to 40, and the reliability increases to .86.

As you will recall from Chapter 3, a reliable test is one that gives close to the same answer time after time. However, you will also recall that, while reliability is necessary for validity, it is no guarantee. The validity of an objective test depends on its content. The crucial task in test construction, then, is to write and select the right questions. That is the topic of the next section.

---

[10] Here is some more specific information for the statistically inclined. The reliability of a test is measured in terms of *Cronbach's alpha* according to the following formula: If n is the number of items in the test, and p is the average correlation among all of the items, then the reliability (alpha, or α) $= np / [1 + p(n-1)]$ (Cronbach, 1951). The Spearman-Brown formula, just mentioned, predicts the increase in reliability you get when you add equivalent items to a test (W. Brown, 1910; Spearman, 1910). If $k = n_1/n_2$, the fraction by which the number of items is increased, then the reliability of the longer test is estimated by

$$\alpha_{longer\ test} = \frac{k \times \alpha_{shorter\ test}}{1 + (k-1)\,\alpha_{shorter\ test}}$$

In both formulas, alpha is the predicted correlation between a score on your test and a score on another test of equivalent content and length.

Methods of Objective Test Construction

Three basic methods are commonly used for constructing objective personality tests: the rational method, the factor analytic method, and the empirical method. Sometimes a mixture of methods is employed, but let's begin by considering the pure application of each.

THE RATIONAL METHOD

Calling one method of test construction "rational" does not mean the others are irrational. It simply means that the basis of this approach is to come up with items that seem directly, obviously, and rationally related to what the test developer wishes to measure. Sometimes this kind of test development is based on a preexisting theory of the trait or psychological construct the researcher is interested in. Thus, test developer Douglas Jackson (1971) wrote items to capture the "needs" postulated years earlier by the psychologist Henry Murray. Other times, the process of writing the items is less systematic, reflecting whatever the researcher finds relevant to ask. The data gathered are S data (see Chapter 2), or direct and undisguised self-reports.

An early example of a test constructed by the rational method is one used during World War I. The U.S. Army discovered, not surprisingly, that certain problems arose when individuals who were mentally ill were inducted as soldiers, housed in crowded barracks, and given loaded weapons. To avoid these problems, the army developed a structured interview consisting of a list of questions that a psychiatrist could ask each potential recruit. As the number of inductees increased, this long process became impractical. There were not enough psychiatrists, nor was there enough time to interview everybody.

To get around these limitations, a psychologist named R. S. Woodworth (1917) proposed that the interview questions could be printed on a sheet, and the recruits could check off their answers with a pencil. His list, which became known as the Woodworth Personality Data Sheet (or, inevitably, the WPDS), consisted of 116 questions, all of which were deemed relevant to potential psychiatric problems. The questions included "Do you wet your bed?" "Have you ever had fits of dizziness?" and "Are you troubled with

The U.S. Army discovered, not surprisingly, that certain problems arose when individuals who were mentally ill were inducted as soldiers, housed in crowded barracks, and given loaded weapons.

dreams about your work?" A recruit who responded Yes to more than a small number of these questions was referred for a more personal examination. Recruits who answered No to all the questions were inducted forthwith into the army.

Woodworth's idea of listing psychiatric symptoms on a questionnaire was not unreasonable, yet his technique raises a variety of problems that can be identified rather easily. For the WPDS to be a valid indicator of psychiatric disturbance—for any rationally constructed, S-data personality test to work—four conditions must hold (Wiggins, 1973).

First, each item must mean the same thing to the person who takes the test as it did to the psychologist who wrote it. For example, in the item from the WPDS, what is "dizziness" exactly? If you have been sitting down for a long time, suddenly stand up, and feel a little bit dizzy, does that count?

Second, the person who completes the form must be able to make an accurate self-assessment. He (only men were being recruited at the time the WPDS was administered) must have a good enough understanding of what each item is asking, as well as the ability to observe it in himself. He must not be so ignorant or psychologically disoriented that he cannot report accurately on these psychological symptoms.

Third, the person who completes the test must be willing to report his self-assessment accurately and without distortion. He must not try to deny his symptoms (e.g., in order to get into the army) or to exaggerate them (perhaps in order to stay out of the army). Modern personality tests used for selecting employees encounter this problem frequently (Rosse, Stecher, Miller, & Levin, 1998; Griffith & Peterson, 2006).

Fourth and finally, all of the items on the test must be valid indicators of what the tester is trying to measure—in this case, mental disturbance. Does dizziness really indicate mental illness? What about dreams about work?

For a rationally constructed test to measure accurately an attribute of personality, all four of these conditions must be met. In the case of the WPDS, none of them probably were.[11] In fact, most rationally constructed personality tests fail one or more of these criteria. One might conclude, therefore, that they would hardly ever be used anymore.

Wrong. Up to and including the present day, self-report questionnaires that are little different, in principle, from the WPDS remain the most com-

---

[11] On the other hand, given how inexpensive it was to administer the WPDS and how expensively problematic it could be to add a mentally ill person to an armed combat unit, the WPDS may well have been cost-effective if it caught just a few serious cases.

mon form of psychological measurement. Self-tests in popular magazines are also always constructed by the rational method—somebody just thinks up some questions that seem relevant—and they almost always fail at least two or three of the four crucial criteria.

Rationally constructed personality tests appear in psychological journals too. Such journals present a steady stream of new testing instruments, nearly all of which are developed by the simple technique of thinking up a list of questions that seem relevant. These questions might include measures of health status (How healthy are you?), self-esteem (How good do you feel about yourself?), or goals (What do you want in life?).

For example, research has addressed the differences between college students who follow optimistic or pessimistic strategies in order to motivate themselves to perform academic tasks (such as preparing for an exam). Optimists, as described by this research, motivate themselves to work hard by expecting the best outcome, whereas pessimists motivate themselves by expecting the worst to happen unless they work hard. Both strategies seem to be effective, although optimists may have more pleasant lives (Norem & Cantor, 1986). (These strategies are considered in more detail in Chapter 16.) For purposes of this chapter, the question is, how are optimists and pessimists identified? The researchers in this study used an eight-item questionnaire that included self-ratings such as "I go into academic situations expecting the worst, even though I know I will probably do OK" (see Try for Yourself 5.1).

By the definitions I have been using, this is a rationally constructed, S-data personality test. And in fact, it seems to work fairly well at identifying students who approach academic life in different ways. So clearly, tests like this can be valid, even though the four criteria for validity raised earlier should always be kept in mind.

A slightly different case is presented by the technique used in some research to measure "personal strivings." In this research, participants are asked to list the "objective[s] you are typically trying to accomplish or attain" (Emmons & King, 1988, p. 1042). This measure is rational in the sense that it directly asks about what the researchers are trying to find out. But unlike the rational method considered previously, this measure is open-ended. Instead of answering a set of printed questions by marking True or False, or by choosing a point on an 11-point scale, the participant writes her strivings on a blank piece of paper. This assessment technique, like other rational approaches, will work only to the degree a participant can and will report accurately what she is trying to accomplish. (Research indicates that

TRY FOR YOURSELF 5.1

Optimism-Pessimism Test

Instructions: Respond using an 11-point scale ranging from "not at all true of me" (1) to "very true of me" (11). Add up your scores for items 1, 4, 6, and 8, and then subtract your scores for items 2, 5, 7, and 9. The average score for all college students is about 7. According to the authors of the test, optimists have an average score of about 25, and pessimists have an average score of about –11.

1. I go into academic situations expecting the worst, even though I know I will probably do OK.
1 (2) 3 4 5 6 7 (8) 9 10 11

2. I generally go into academic situations with positive expectations about how I will do.
1 2 3 4 5 6 (7) 8 9 10 11

3. I've generally done pretty well in academic situations in the past.
1 2 3 4 5 6 7 8 9 (10) 11

4. I often think about what it will be like if I do very poorly in an academic situation.
1 2 3 4 (5) 6 7 8 9 10 11

5. I often think about what it will be like if I do very well in an academic situation.
1 2 3 4 (5) 6 7 8 9 10 11

6. I often think about what I would do if I did very poorly in an academic situation.
1 2 3 4 5 6 (7) 8 9 10 11

7. I often try to figure out how likely it is that I will do very well in an academic situation.
1 2 3 4 5 6 7 8 9 10 (11)

8. When I do well in academic situations, I often feel relieved.
1 2 3 4 5 6 7 8 9 10 (11)

9. When I do well in academic situations, I feel really happy.
1 2 3 4 5 6 7 8 9 10 (11)

Source: Norem & Cantor (1986), pp. 352–353.

most participants can and do accurately report the strivings that guide much of their lives; see Emmons & McAdams, 1991.) This technique gets around some of the problems found in other rationally constructed questionnaires that ask participants questions that may be ambiguous or of dubious relevance. Yet it poses a different problem: that of figuring out the relevance and decoding the ambiguity of what the participant has written.

THE FACTOR ANALYTIC METHOD

The factor analytic method of test construction is an example of a psychological tool based on statistics. **Factor analysis** is a statistical method for finding order amid seeming chaos. The factor analytic technique is designed to identify groups of things—such as test items—that seem to be alike. The property that makes these things alike is called a *factor* (e.g., Cattell, 1952).

Factor analysis might seem esoteric, but it is not much different from the way people intuitively group things. Consider the rides at Disneyland. Some—the Matterhorn ride, for example—are fast, scary, and enjoyed by teenagers. Others—the It's a Small World ride—are slow, include sweet songs, and are enjoyed by young children. Because certain properties seem to occur together (e.g., the slow rides are usually accompanied by sweet songs) and others rarely occur together (e.g., few rides include sweet songs and are scary), the groupings of properties constitute factors.[12] The properties of being fast, scary, and appealing to teenagers all go together, forming a factor you might call "excitement." Likewise, the properties of being slow, having sweet music, and being appealing to young children form a factor you might call "comfort." You could now go out and measure all the rides at Disneyland—or even anticipate the score of a new ride—according to both of these factors (see Figure 5.3). Then you could use these measurements for the purposes of prediction. If a new ride gets a high "excitement" score, you would predict long lines of teenagers. If it gets a high "comfort" score, you would predict long lines of small children and frazzled parents.

To use this technique to construct a personality test, researchers begin with a long list of objective items of the sort discussed earlier. The items can come from any place; the test writer's own imagination is one common source. If the test writer has a theory about what she wants to measure, that theory might suggest items to include. Another surprisingly common way to get new items is to mine them from old tests. (Items from the MMPI, in particular, have a way of reappearing on other tests.) The goal is to end up with a large number of items; thousands are not too many.

The next step is to administer these items to a large number of participants. These participants are recruited in any convenient manner, which is why they are often college students. Sometimes, for other kinds of tests, the participants are mental patients. Ideally, they should represent the kind of people with whom you hope to use this test.

(handwritten margin note: disneyworld ride example!)

---

[12] This is why I avoid the Splash Mountain ride. It confuses me.

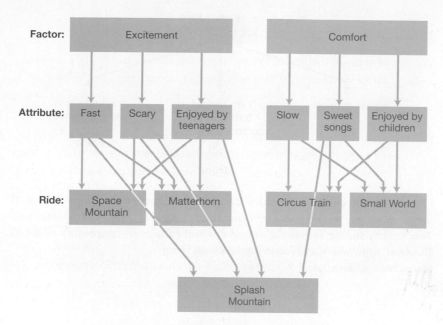

Figure 5.3 A Factor Analysis of Some Rides at Disneyland Some rides are fast, scary, enjoyed by teenagers, and fit well to the "excitement" factor. Other rides are slow, have sweet songs, are enjoyed by small children, and fit well to the "comfort" factor. A few rides have mixes of attributes of both factors, and so do not fit well to either one.

After your large group of participants has taken the initial test that consists of these (maybe) thousands of items, you and your computer can sit down together and do the factor analysis. The analysis is based on calculating correlation coefficients (see Chapter 3) between each item and every other item. Many items—probably most—will not correlate highly with anything and can be dropped. But the items that do correlate with each other will begin to group together. For example, if a person answers True to the item "I trust strangers," you might find that he is also likely to answer True to "I am careful to turn up when someone expects me" and answer False to "I could stand being a hermit." Such a pattern of likelihood, or co-occurrence, means that these three items are correlated. The next steps are to consider what the items have in common, and then name the factor.

The three correlated items just listed, according to Cattell (1965), are related to the dimension "cool versus warm," with a True-True-False pattern of responses indicating a "warm" personality (see Figure 5.4). (Cattell decided on this label simply by considering the items, as you just did.) The factor represented by these items, therefore, is "warm-cool," or, if you pre-

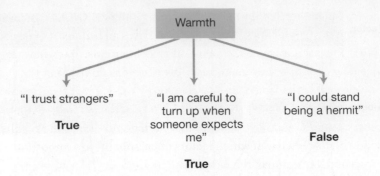

Figure 5.4 Three Questionnaire Items That Measure the Same Factor If these three items are correlated with each other—people who answer True to the first item tend to answer True to the second one and False to the third—they might all "load on," or measure, a common psychological factor.
Source: Based on Cattell (1965).

[handwritten margin notes: Limitations to FAT: 1) quality of info = quality of items put in (GIGO) 2) Computer finds statistically related items - researcher must find conceptual relation which is subjective 3) Some factors do not make sense]

fer to name it by just one pole, "warmth." These three items now can be said to form a "warmth" scale. To measure this dimension in a new participant, you would administer these three items, as well as other items in your original list that correlated highly with them, and discard the rest of the thousands of items you started with.

Factor analysis has been used not only to construct tests, but also to decide how many fundamental traits exist—how many out of the thousands in the dictionary are truly essential. Various analysts have come up with different answers. Cattell (1957) thought there were 16. Eysenck (1976) concluded there are just 3. More recently, prominent psychologists such as Lewis Goldberg (1990), Robert R. McCrae, and Paul Costa (e.g., 1987) settled on 5; this is perhaps the most widely accepted answer at present. These five traits—sometimes called the Big Five—are extraversion, neuroticism, conscientiousness, agreeableness, and openness (see Chapter 7).

At one point, some psychologists hoped that factor analysis might provide an infallible mathematical tool for objectively determining the most important dimensions of personality and the best questions with which to measure these dimensions. They were disappointed. Over the years, it has become clear that the factor analytic technique for constructing personality tests and identifying important dimensions of personality is limited in at least three important ways (J. Block, 1995).

The first limitation is that the quality of the information you get from a factor analysis will be limited by the quality of the items you put into it in the first place—or, as they say in computer science, GIGO ("garbage in, garbage out"). In theory, a factor analysis requires an initial set of items that are fairly representative of the set of all possible items. But where are you supposed to find that? Although most investigators do the best they can, it is always possible that some types of items are overrepresented in the initial pool while other important types are left out. If either of these things happens—and there is no way to ensure that both do not—then the results will provide a distorted view of which factors of personality are important.

A second limitation of the factor analytic approach is that once the computer has identified a cluster of items as being related statistically, a human psychologist must still decide how they are related *conceptually*. This process is highly subjective, so the seeming mathematical rigor and certainty of factor analysis are to some extent an illusion. The items used earlier, for example, could be named "warmth," but they could just as easily be called "sociability" or "interpersonal positivity." Any choice between these labels is a matter of taste as much as of mathematics or science. And disagreements over labels are common. For example, the same factor called "agreeableness" by some psychologists has been called "conformity," "likeability," "friendliness," and "friendly compliance" by others. Another factor has been called variously "conscientiousness," "dependability," "super-ego strength," "constraint," "self-control," and even "will to achieve." All of these labels are reasonable, and there are no firm rules for choosing which one is best (Bergeman et al., 1993).

A third limitation of the factor analytic approach is that sometimes the factors that emerge do not make sense, not even to the psychologist who did the analysis. Years ago, the psychologist Gordon Allport complained about one such failure to make sense of a factor analysis:

> Guilford and Zimmerman (1956) report an "unidentified" factor, called C_2, that represents some baffling blend of impulsiveness, absentmindedness, emotional fluctuation, nervousness, loneliness, ease of emotional expression, and feelings of guilt. When units of this sort appear [from factor analyses]—and I submit that it happens not infrequently—one wonders what to say about them. To me they resemble sausage meat that has failed to pass the pure food and health inspection. (Allport, 1958, p. 251)

Matters are not usually as bad as all this. But it is not unusual for the personality dimensions uncovered by factor analysis to include perplexing combinations of traits that are difficult to name precisely (J. Block, 1995).

It is important to remember that factor analysis is a statistical rather than a psychological tool. It can *identify* traits or items that go together. As in the example just described, however, figuring out the *meaning* of this grouping will require some difficult psychological thinking.

Factor analysis continues to have important uses. One, which will be described in Chapter 7, is to help reduce the long list of personality traits from the dictionary down to an essential few that are really useful. Another important application is for the refinement of personality tests, where it is used in conjunction with the other techniques of test construction. How many different factors are in a new personality test is useful to know because some tests turn out to measure more than one trait at the same time. A routine step in test development, therefore, is to factor-analyze the items (Briggs & Cheek, 1986).

THE EMPIRICAL METHOD

The empirical strategy of test construction is an attempt to allow reality to speak for itself. In its pure form, the empirical approach has sometimes been called "dust bowl empiricism." The term refers to the origin of the technique at Midwestern universities (notably Minnesota and Iowa) during the Depression, or "dust bowl," years of the 1930s. Intentionally or not, the term also serves as a reminder of how dry, or atheoretical, this approach is.

Like the factor analytic approach described earlier, the first step of the empirical approach is to gather lots of items. The methods for doing this can be just as eclectic—or haphazard—as described earlier.

The second step, however, is quite different. For this step, you need to have a group of participants who have already independently been divided into the groups you wish to study with your test. Occupational groups and diagnostic categories are often used for this purpose. For example, if you wish to measure the aspect of people that makes them good and happy religious ministers, then you need at least two groups of participants—happy, successful ministers and a comparison group. (Ideally the comparison group would be miserable, incompetent ministers, but typically the researcher will settle for people who are not ministers at all.) Or, you might want a test to detect different kinds of psychopathology. For this purpose, you would need groups of people who have been diagnosed as suffering from schizophrenia, depression, hysteria, and so forth. A group of normal people—if you can find them—would also be useful for comparison purposes. Whatever groups you wish to include, their members must be identified before you develop your test.

Then you are ready for the third step: administering your test to your participants.

The fourth step is to compare the answers given by the different groups of participants. If schizophrenics answer a certain group of questions differently from everybody else, those items might form a "schizophrenia" scale. Thereafter, new participants who answer questions the same way as diagnosed schizophrenics did would score high on your "schizophrenia" scale. Thus, you might suspect them of being schizophrenic too. (The MMPI, which is the prototypical example of the empirical method of test construction, was built using this strategy.) Or, if successful ministers answer some items in a distinctive way, these items might be combined into a "minister" scale. New participants who score high on this scale, because they answer the way successful ministers do, might be guided to become ministers themselves. (The SVIB was constructed this way.)

The basic assumption of the empirical approach, then, is that certain kinds of people have distinctive ways of answering certain questions on personality inventories. If you answer questions the same way as members of some occupational or diagnostic group did in the original derivation study, then you might belong to that group too. This philosophy can be used even at the individual level. The developers of the MMPI published an atlas, or casebook, of hundreds of individuals who took this test over the years (Hathaway & Meehl, 1951). For each case, the atlas gives the person's scoring pattern and describes his clinical case history. The idea is that a clinical psychologist confronted with a new patient can ask the patient to take the MMPI, and then look up those individuals in the atlas who scored similarly in the past. This might provide the clinician with new insights or ideas.

Items are selected for empirically derived personality scales solely on the basis of whether they are answered differently by different kinds of people. Then the scale is *cross-validated*, that is, used to predict behavior, diagnosis, or category membership in new samples of participants. If the cross-validation succeeds, the scale is deemed ready for use. At each step of the process of test development, the actual content of the items is purposely ignored. In fact, empirical test constructors of the old school sometimes prided themselves on never actually reading the items on the tests they developed!

This lack of concern with item content, or with face validity (discussed in Chapter 2), has four implications. The first is that empirically derived tests, unlike other kinds, can include items that seem contrary or even absurd. As I mentioned a few pages back, the item "I prefer a shower to a bath," answered True, is correlated with empathy. Similarly, the item "I like tall women" tends to be answered True by impulsive males. Why? According to the empirical approach to test construction, the reason does not matter in the slightest.

Consider some other examples. People with psychopathic personalities (those who have little regard for moral or societal rules and lack "conscience") tend to answer False to the item "I have been quite independent and free from family rule." Paranoids answer False to "I tend to be on my guard with people who are somewhat more friendly than expected." One might surmise they do this because they are paranoid about the question itself, but they also answer True to "I believe I am being plotted against." Even though the relationship between item content and meaning seems counterintuitive, faithful adherents to the empirical strategy of test construction are not supposed to even care.

....

The item "I like tall women" tends to be answered True by impulsive males. Why?

....

Here are a few other examples, all taken from the excellent discussion in Wiggins (1973): "I sometimes tease animals" is answered False by depressives. "I enjoy detective or mystery stories" is answered False by hospitalized hysterics. "My daily life is full of things to keep me interested" is answered True by dermatitis patients. "I gossip a little at times" is answered True by people with high IQs. "I do not have a great fear of snakes" is answered False by prejudiced individuals, whose prejudices apparently extend even to reptiles. Again, in each case the indicated people are more likely to answer in the indicated direction; they do not always do so.

A second implication of this lack of concern with item content is that responses to empirically derived tests are difficult to fake. With a personality test of the straightforward, S-data variety, you can describe yourself the way you want to be seen, which is indeed the score you will get. But because the items on empirically derived scales sometimes seem backward or absurd, it is difficult to know how to answer in such a way as to guarantee the score you want. This is often held up as one of the great advantages of the empirical approach.

The psychologist interpreting a person's responses to an empirically derived personality test does not care whether the person told the truth in her responses. The literal truth does not matter because the answers on such a test are not considered important for their own sake. They matter only as indicators of what group the person belongs to. Thus, empirically derived personality tests give B data instead of S data.

The third implication of the lack of concern with item content is that, even more than tests derived through other methods, empirically derived tests are only as good as the criteria by which they are developed or against which they are cross-validated. If the distinction between the different kinds of participants in the derivation or validation sample was not drawn correctly, the empirically derived test will be fatally flawed. For example, the original MMPI was derived by comparing the responses of patients who had been diagnosed by psychiatrists at the University of Minnesota mental hospitals. If those diagnoses were incorrect in any way, then diagnostic use of the MMPI will only perpetuate those errors. The theory behind the SVIB is that if the participant answers questions the way a successful minister (or member of any other occupation) does, he too will make a successful minister (or whatever vocation) (Strong, 1959). But perhaps the theory is false—perhaps new ministers who are too much like the old ministers will not be successful. Or perhaps some of the "successful" ministers in the derivation sample were not really successful. Such difficulties would undermine the SVIB as a source of vocational advice.

A more general problem is that the empirical correlates of item responses by which these tests are assembled are those found in one place, at one time, with one group of participants. If no attention is paid to item content, then there is no way to be confident that the test will work in a similar manner at another time, in another place, with different participants. The test must be continually validated and revalidated over time, for different geographic regions, and for different groups of participants (e.g., those of different ethnicity or gender mix than the original derivation sample). A particular concern is that the empirical correlates of item response might change over time. The MMPI was developed decades ago and revised only recently (it is now called the MMPI-2) (Butcher, 1999). The revision will take a long time to revalidate before psychologists can be confident it works the same way the old test did.

The fourth and final implication of the empirical approach's lack of concern with item content is that it can cause serious problems with public relations and even with the law—explaining to a layperson why certain questions are being asked can be difficult. As was mentioned during the discussion of rationally designed tests, face validity is the

"Give me a hug. I can tell a lot about a man by the way he hugs."

lack of content validity = skepticism.

External validity (what the test items can predict) is what you all that matters)

property that a test appears to measure what it is supposed to measure. A similar property is **content validity**, in which the content of the test matches the content of what it is trying to predict. For example, the WPDS has content validity for the prediction of psychopathology; the MMPI does not. Many psychologists would consider this difference to work to the advantage of the MMPI, but it also has caused problems. A lack of content validity not only can lead to skeptical reactions among the people who take the test, but also can raise legal issues that have become increasingly troublesome in recent years.

The original MMPI, for example, contained questions about religious preference and health status (including bowel habits). According to some readings of antidiscrimination law, such questions can be illegal in applied contexts. In 1993, Target stores had to pay a $2 million judgment to job applicants to whom it had (illegally, the court ruled) asked questions such as "I am very strongly attracted to members of my own sex," "I have never indulged in unusual sex practices," "I have had no difficulty starting or holding my urine," and "I feel sure there is only one true religion" (Silverstein, 1993). (These items all came from a test called the Rodgers Condensed CPI-MMPI Test, which included items from both the MMPI and the CPI.)

As Target found to its dismay, it can be difficult for users of the MMPI, CPI, or similar tests to explain to judges or congressional investigating committees that they are not actually manifesting an unconstitutional curiosity about religious beliefs or bowel habits, and that they are merely interested in the *correlates* of the answers to these items. Target may have asked these questions not because its management cared about sexual or bathroom behavior, but because the scale scores built from these items (and many others—the test they used had 704 items) showed validity in predicting job performance, in this case as a security guard. Indeed, reports from tests like these typically include only total scores and predictions of job performance, so the responses to the individual items might not have even been available to Target's personnel department. Nevertheless, in many cases it would not be difficult for an interested test user to extract applicants' responses to individual questions and then to discriminate illegally on the basis of religious or sexual orientation or health status. For this reason, developers of new tests, such as the MMPI-2, are attempting to omit items of this sort while still trying to maintain validity.

Developers and users of empirically derived tests have reversed themselves over the last 50 years or so. They began with an explicit and sometimes vehement philosophy that item content does not matter; all that mattered was the external validity, or what the test items could predict. As the social and legal climate has changed over time, however, developers of empirical tests have been forced, to some degree against their will, to acknowledge that item content does matter after all. Regardless of how their responses are used, individuals completing any kind of personality test are revealing things about themselves.

A COMBINATION OF METHODS

In modern test development, a surprisingly large number of investigators still use a pure form of the rational method: They ask their participants the questions that seem relevant and hope for the best. The factor analytic approach still has a few adherents. Pure applications of the empirical approach are rare today. The best modern test developers use a combination of all three approaches.

A good example is the way Douglas Jackson developed the Personality Research Form (known as the PRF, of course). He came up with items based on their apparent relevance to the theoretical constructs he wished to measure (the rational approach), administered them to large samples of participants and factor-analyzed their responses (the factor analytic approach), and then correlated the factor scores with independent criteria (the empirical approach) (see D. N. Jackson, 1967, 1971). Jackson's approach is probably close to ideal. The best way to select items for a personality scale is not haphazardly, but with the intent to sample a particular domain of interest (the rational approach). Factor analysis should then be used to confirm that items that seem similar to each other actually elicit similar responses from real participants (Briggs & Cheek, 1986). Finally, any personality measure is only as good as the other things with which it correlates or that it can predict (the empirical approach). To be worth its salt, any personality scale must show that it can predict what people do, how they are seen by others, and how they fare in life.

PURPOSES OF PERSONALITY TESTING

According to one wide-ranging survey, the validity of well-developed psychological tests is comparable to that of the most widely used medical tests (Meyer et al., 2001). If we can assume that a personality test has a modicum of validity, then a further question must be considered: How will this test be used? This is an important question that some psychologists engrossed

"Here's a little test I like to give prospective employees, Phil: let's see if you can grab this twenty-dollar bill before I can."

in the techniques and details of test construction may forget to ask. The answer has practical and ethical implications (Hanson, 1993).

The most obvious uses for personality tests are those to which they are put by the professional personality testers—the ones who set up the booths at APA conventions—and their customers. The customers are typically organizations such as schools, clinics, corporations, or government agencies that wish to know something about the people they encounter. Sometimes this information is desired so that, regardless of the score obtained, the person who is measured can be helped. For example, schools frequently use tests to measure vocational interests to help their students choose careers. A clinician might administer a test to get an indication of how serious a client's problem is, or to suggest a therapeutic direction.

Sometimes the testing is for the benefit of the tester, not necessarily that of the person being tested. An employer may test an individual's "integrity" to find out whether he is trustworthy enough to be hired (or even to be retained), or may test to find out about other personality traits deemed relevant to future job performance. The Central Intelligence Agency (CIA) routinely uses personality testing when selecting its agents (D. Waller, 1993).

Reasonable arguments can be made for or against any of these uses. By telling people what kind of occupational group they most resemble, vocational-interest tests provide potentially valuable information to individuals who may not know what they want to do (D. B. Schmidt, Lubinski, & Benbow, 1998). On the other hand, the use of these tests rests on the implicit theory that any given occupation should continue to be populated by individuals like those already in it. For example, if your response profile resembles those obtained from successful mechanics or jet pilots, then perhaps you should consider being a mechanic or a jet pilot. Although this approach seems reasonable, it also could keep occupational fields from evolving and prevent certain individuals (e.g., women or members of minority groups) from joining fields from which they traditionally have been excluded. For example, an ordinarily socialized American woman may have outlooks or responses that are very different from those of the typical garage mechanic or jet pilot. Does this mean that women should never become mechanics or pilots?

Similarly, many "integrity" tests administered in preemployment screenings seem to yield valuable information. In particular, they often provide good measures not so much of integrity, but of broader traits related to job performance. People who score high on integrity scales often also score high on the trait of conscientiousness and other traits, which in turn predict learning on the job and good performance in many fields (Ones, Viswesvaran, & Schmidt, 1993; see Chapter 7 for a more detailed discussion). Moreover, an advantage of integrity and other, related personality tests is that they do not discriminate against women, minorities, or other groups: All groups, on average, tend to score about the same (Sackett, Burris, & Callahan, 1989).

Still, many of these integrity tests ask questions about minor past offenses (e.g., "Have you ever taken office supplies from an employer?"), which puts nonliars into the interesting dilemma of whether they should admit past offenses, thereby earning a lower integrity score for being honest, or deny them and thereby earn a higher integrity score for having lied. Liars, by contrast, experience no such dilemma; they can deny everything and yet earn a nice, high integrity score.

A more general class of objections is aimed at the wide array of personality tests used by many large organizations, including the CIA, major automobile manufacturers, phone companies, and the military. According to one critic, almost any kind of testing can be objected to on two grounds. First, tests are unfair mechanisms through which institutions can control individuals—by rewarding those with the institutionally determined "correct" traits (such as high "conscientiousness") and punishing those with the "wrong" traits (such as low "conscientiousness"). Second, perhaps traits such as "conscientiousness" or even "intelligence" do not matter until and unless they are tested, and in that sense they are constructed by the tests themselves (Hanson, 1993). Underlying these two objections seems to be a more general sense, which I think many people share, that there is something undignified or even humiliating about submitting oneself to a test and having one's personality described by a set of scores.

All of these objections make sense. Personality tests—along with other kinds of tests such as those measuring intelligence, honesty, and even drug tests—do function as a part of society's mechanism for controlling people, by rewarding the "right" kind (e.g., those who are intelligent, honest, and don't do drugs) and punishing the "wrong" kind. It is also correct to note the interesting way in which a trait can seem to spring into existence as soon as a test is invented to measure it. Did traits like "parmia" or even "self-monitoring" (see Chapters 4 and 7) exist before there were scales to measure them? Perhaps they did, but you can see the argument here. Finally, it is true that many individuals have had the deeply humiliating experience of subjecting themselves to testing "voluntarily" (in order to get a badly needed job), only to find out that they somehow failed to measure up. It's bad enough to lack the right skills or relevant experience. But to be the wrong kind of person? That hurts.

On the other hand, these criticisms are also overstated. A relatively minor point to bear in mind is that, as we have seen in the preceding sections of this chapter, personality traits are not merely invented or constructed by the process of test development; they are also, to an important degree, discovered. That is, the correlates and nature of a trait measured by a new test cannot be presumed. They must be discovered empirically by examining what life outcomes or other attributes of personality the test can predict. For example, psychologists did not know until doing research that integrity tests are better measures of conscientiousness than of integrity, and this finding forced them to change their conception of what the tests measure. The fact that the interpretation of psychological tests depends critically on the gathering of independent data undermines the argument that personality traits are mere social constructions.

But there's a more basic and important point here: Criticisms that view personality testing as undignified or unethical, when considered, appear rather naïve. These criticisms seem to object to the idea of determining the degree to which somebody is conscientious, or intelligent, or sociable, and then using that determination as the basis of an important decision (e.g., employment). But if you accept the fact that an employer is not obligated to hire randomly anybody who walks through the door, and that the employer only uses good sense in deciding who would be the best person to hire (If you were an employer, wouldn't you do that?), then you also must accept that applicants' traits like "conscientiousness," "intelligence," and "sociability" are going to be judged. The only real question is how. What are the alternatives? One alternative seems to be for the employer to talk with the prospective employee and try to gauge his conscientiousness by how well his shoes are shined or his haircut or some other such clue. (Employers frequently do exactly that; see Highhouse, 2008.) Is this method an improvement?

You may argue that you would rather be judged by a person than by a computer scanning a form, regardless of the demonstrated invalidity of the former and validity of the latter (Ones, Viswesvaran, & Schmidt, 1993). Although that is a reasonable position, it is important to be clear about the choice being made. One cannot choose for personality never to be judged—judgments will happen even if all of the tests are burned tomorrow. The only real choice is this: *How* would you prefer to have your personality judged?

SUMMARY

The Nature of Personality Assessment

- Any characteristic pattern of behavior, thought, or emotional experience that exhibits relative consistency across time and situations is part of an individual's personality. These patterns include personality traits as well as psychological attributes such as goals, moods, and strategies.

- Personality assessment is a frequent activity of industrial and clinical psychologists and researchers. Everybody also assesses the personalities of the people they know in daily life.

The Business of Testing

- Personality testing is a big business that can have important consequences. But some personality tests are useless or even fraudulent, so it is important to understand how they are constructed and how they are used.

- An important issue for assessments, whether by psychologists or by laypeople, is the degree to which those assessments are correct. Do they correlate as expected with other assessments of related traits, and can they be used to predict behavior or important life outcomes?

Personality Tests

- Some personality tests yield S data and others yield B data, but a more common distinction is between projective tests and objective tests.

- Projective tests try to grant insight into personality by presenting participants with ambiguous stimuli and interpreting the participants' open-ended responses. To the extent they are valid—and many are not—they appear to tap into aspects of personality not captured by questionnaire measures.

- The Rorschach test appears to have some degree of validity, but may not offer enough information beyond what can be gained from quicker, easier tests to justify its added expense. The Thematic Apperception Test (TAT) appears to measure aspects of needs (e.g., the need for achievement) that are missed by questionnaire measures.

- Objective tests ask participants specific questions and assess personality on the basis of the participants' choices among predetermined options such as True or False, and Yes or No.

- Objective tests can be constructed by rational, factor analytic, or empirical methods; the state of the art is to combine all three methods.

Purposes of Personality Testing

- Some people are uncomfortable with the practice of personality assessment because they see it as an unfair invasion of privacy. However, because people inevitably judge each other's personalities, the real issue is whether personality assessment should be based on informal intuitions or formalized techniques.

THINK ABOUT IT

1. If you wanted to understand someone's personality and could ask the person only three questions, what would those questions be? What traits would the answers reveal?
2. How would you choose someone to be your roommate? Your employee? A date? Would personality traits be relevant to your choice? How would you evaluate those traits?
3. Have you ever taken a personality test? Did the results seem accurate? Were the results useful? Did they tell you anything you did not already know?
4. How many uses can you think of for knowing someone's scores on the MMPI? Are any of these uses unethical?
5. If you were being considered for a job you badly wanted, would you prefer the decision to be based on a personality test score or the employer's subjective judgment of you?

SUGGESTED READING

Wiggins, J. S. (1973). *Personality and prediction: Principles of personality assessment.* Reading, MA: Addison-Wesley.

> *The classic textbook for personality psychologists, including material of methodological as well as substantive interest. The book is now slightly out of date, but like a true classic, has maintained its interest and value with age.*

EMEDIA

 Go to StudySpace, wwnorton.com/studyspace, to access additional review and enrichment materials.

Consequences of Everyday Judgments of Personality

- Opportunities
- Expectancy Effects

The Accuracy of Personality Judgment

- Criteria for Accuracy
- Snap Judgments
- Moderators of Accuracy
- The Realistic Accuracy Model

Accuracy Matters

PERSONALITY ASSESSMENT II: Personality Judgment in Daily Life

YOU DON'T NEED A LICENSE to practice personality assessment. Everybody does it. Trying to figure out what other people are like is one of the most interesting, important, and widespread things that people do. With luck, you might go many years without being assessed by a psychologist. But there is no chance whatsoever that you can long escape being assessed by your friends, enemies, romantic partners—and yourself.

The present chapter has two parts. The first part considers how and why the assessments others make of your personality and the assessments you make of others (and yourself) are important. The second part addresses the validity—or, in the synonymous term traditionally used when considering nonprofessional judgments, the *accuracy*—of these assessments. To what degree and under what circumstances do everyday judgments of personality agree with each other? To what degree and under what circumstances can they accurately predict behavior? And finally, how is accurate personality judgment possible? How might we become more accurate in knowing other people?

CONSEQUENCES OF EVERYDAY JUDGMENTS OF PERSONALITY

The judgments other people make of your personality reflect a significant part of your social world, so their importance goes beyond their value as accurate (or inaccurate) descriptions. Your reputation among those who know you matters because, as was mentioned during the survey of I data in Chapter 2, it greatly affects both opportunities and expectancy effects.

Opportunities

Reputation affects opportunities in numerous ways. If a person who is considering hiring you believes that you are competent and conscientious, you are much more likely to get the job than if that person thinks you do not have those qualities. This will be true regardless of how competent and conscientious you really are. Similarly, if someone believes you to be honest, she will be more likely to lend you money than if she believes you to be dishonest. Your actual honesty is immaterial. If you impress people who meet you as being warm and friendly, you will develop more friendships than if you seem cold and aloof. These appearances may be false and unfair, but their consequences are important nonetheless.

Consider the case of shyness. Shy people seem to be quite common in American society; one estimate is that about one person in four considers himself to be chronically shy (Zimbardo, 1977). Shy people are often lonely and may deeply wish to have friends and normal social interactions, but they are so fearful of the process of social involvement that they become isolated. In some cases, they won't ask for help when they need it, even when a person who could easily solve their problem is nearby (DePaulo, Dull, Greenberg, & Swaim, 1989). The typical consequence is that shy people spend a lot of time by themselves, staying in their rooms and denying themselves the opportunity to develop normal social skills. When they do venture out, they are so out of practice they may not know how to act. In one study, shy and nonshy persons called individuals of the opposite sex to ask them to return a simple questionnaire. While everybody said they would return the questionnaire, the people called by the shy persons were less likely to actually do it, apparently because shy persons' speech was hesitant and halting (DePaulo et al., 1989). This kind of negative response to their attempts at social behavior only reinforces the shyness that caused them problems in the first place (Cheek, 1990).

Appearances may be false and unfair, but their consequences are important nonetheless.

A particular problem for shy people is that, typically, other people do not perceive them as shy. Instead, to most observers they seem cold and aloof. This is understandable when you consider how shy people often behave. A shy person who lives in your dormitory sees you coming across campus, and you see her. She would actually like to talk to you and perhaps even try to develop a friendship, but she is extremely fearful of rejection or of not knowing quite what to say. (This apprehension may be realistic, given her lack of social skills.) So, she may pretend not to see you or suddenly reverse course and dodge behind a building. This kind of behavior, if you detect it, is unlikely to give you a warm, fuzzy feeling deep inside. Instead, there is a good chance that you will feel insulted and even angry. You may be inclined thereafter to avoid *her*.

Thus, shy people generally are not cold and aloof, or at least they do not mean to be. But that is frequently how they are perceived. That perception, in turn, affects the lives of shy people in important negative ways and is part of a cycle that perpetuates shyness. This is just one example of how the judgments of others are an important part of the social world and can have a significant effect on personality and life.

Expectancy Effects

Judgments of others can also affect you through "self-fulfilling prophecies," more technically known as expectancy effects, which were mentioned in Chapter 2.[1] These effects operate in both the intellectual and the social domains.

INTELLECTUAL EXPECTANCY EFFECTS

The classic demonstration of expectancy effects in the intellectual domain is the series of studies by Rosenthal and Jacobson (1968). These investigators gave a battery of tests to a group of schoolchildren and then told their teachers, falsely, that the tests had identified some of the children as "bloomers" who were likely to show a sharp increase in IQ in the near future. These children were actually selected at random. But when the actual IQs of the so-called bloomers were compared to those of other children at the end of the school year, the bloomers had actually bloomed! That is, the first-grade children whose teachers expected them to show an increase in IQ actually did, by about fifteen points, and the IQs of the second-graders increased by about ten points, even though these expectations were introduced randomly.

---

[1] As mentioned in Chapter 2, some psychologists call the expectancy phenomenon "behavioral confirmation."

The exact process behind this effect has been a matter of some controversy. At least four different theoretical models of expectancy effects have been proposed (Bellamy, 1975; Braun, 1976; Darley & Fazio, 1980; Rosenthal, 1973b, 1973c). The one that has garnered the most evidence in its support seems to be a four-factor theory proposed by Robert Rosenthal, one of the original discoverers of the effect (M. J. Harris & Rosenthal, 1985).

According to Rosenthal's theory, high-expectancy students perform better because their teachers treat them differently in four ways. The first, *climate*, refers to the way that teachers project a warmer emotional attitude toward the students they expect to do well. The second, *feedback*, refers to the way teachers give feedback that is more differentiated—varying according to the correctness or incorrectness of a student's response—to their high-expectancy students. The third, *input*, refers to the way teachers attempt to teach more material and more difficult material to high-expectancy students. Finally, the fourth way high-expectancy students are treated differently, called *output*, reflects how teachers give them extra opportunities to show what they have learned. Each of these aspects of teaching leads students to perform better (M. J. Harris & Rosenthal, 1985). This is important research not only because it helps to explain expectancy effects, but also because it demonstrates some of the basic elements of good teaching: It might be better if all students could be treated in the ways that high-expectancy students are treated.

SOCIAL EXPECTANCY EFFECTS

A related kind of expectancy effect has been demonstrated in the social rather than the intellectual realm. Mark Snyder and his colleagues (M. Snyder, Tanke, & Berscheid, 1977) performed the following remarkable experiment. Two previously unacquainted college students of opposite sexes were brought to two different locations in the psychology building. The experimenter immediately took a Polaroid picture of the female participant, saying, "You are about to meet someone on the telephone, but before you do this, I need to give him a picture of you so he can visualize who he is talking to." The male participant was not photographed.

The female's real photograph, just taken, was thrown away. Instead, the experimenter gave the male participant one of two photographs of other female undergraduates who previously had been identified as either highly attractive or less attractive. "This is who you will be meeting on the phone," the male participant was told. The telephone connection was then established, and the two students chatted for several minutes as a tape recorder whirred.

Later, the researchers erased everything that the male student had said from the tape recording of this chat. (Remember, he is the one who saw the bogus photograph.) Then they played the edited tape, which contained only the female's voice, for a new group of students, and asked them to rate, among other things, how warm, humorous, and poised she seemed.

The result: If the male had seen an attractive photograph, the female was more likely to have behaved in a manner rated as warmer, more humorous, and more poised than when the male student saw an unattractive photograph. This finding means that when the male student spoke to a woman he thought to be attractive, his behavior caused her to respond in a warmer and more friendly manner than she would have if he had considered her unattractive. Snyder interpreted this effect as another form of self-fulfilling prophecy: Attractive females are expected to be warm and friendly, and those considered attractive are treated in such a manner that they indeed respond that way.[2]

In some ways, this is an even more disturbing finding than Rosenthal's results concerning IQ. This study suggests that, to some degree, our behavior with other people might be determined by how they expect us to act, perhaps based on such superficial cues as physical appearance. Snyder's results imply that to some extent we will actually become what other people perceive, or even misperceive, us to be.

EXPECTANCY EFFECTS IN REAL LIFE

Research on expectancy effects is interesting and important, and the two studies just described are classics of the genre. However, there has been a further important development in this area of research that I need to tell you about. The psychologist Lee Jussim (1991) asked an important ques-

---

[2] Two complications are worth brief mention. The first is that a slightly different process may lie behind the result. Rather than males directly inducing the females to confirm their expectancies, it may be the case that males are more friendly to attractive females because they are hoping for a date, and colder and more aloof with unattractive females with whom they do not have such hopes. The women then respond in kind. Such a process would technically not be an expectancy effect, although the result would be the same.

A related complication concerns the question of whether this effect works the other way around, when female students see pictures of attractive or unattractive males, and the effects on male participants' behavior are examined. A study by Andersen and Bem (1981) addressed this issue. The conclusions were not completely clear, but it did seem to some degree that male and female perceivers could, through what they expected of the other, affect the behavior of opposite-sex targets.

B. Smaller

"Maybe it's not a wrong answer—
maybe it's just a different answer."

tion about expectancy effects that, surprisingly, had seldom been considered: Where do expectancy effects generally come from?

The usual experiments do not address this question because the expectancy effects they study are induced experimentally; Rosenthal's teachers believed that some students would improve academically because that is what Rosenthal told them. Snyder's male participants expected some females to be warm and friendly because of stereotypes the males held about attractiveness, which Snyder elicited with a misleading photograph.

Jussim suggested that the situation in real life is usually quite different. A teacher who expects a child to do well might base that expectation on the child's actual test results rather than bogus ones, as well as on his observation of the child's performance in previous classes and what he has been told about the child by other teachers. A male undergraduate who expects a female undergraduate to be warm and charming might base this assumption on how he has seen her act with other people and what he has been told about her by mutual friends. Moreover, research has shown that, to some degree, physically attractive women really are more socially skillful and likable on the telephone (Goldman & Lewis, 1977). Therefore, these expectancy effects, although false in the lab, might be correct in real life. When this is the case, the self-fulfilling prophecies just described might have the effect of slightly magnifying or even just maintaining behavioral tendencies that the participant has had all along (e.g., Jussim & Eccles, 1992).

This observation challenges the traditional interpretation of expectancy effects. It implies that rather than restrict themselves to introducing expectancy effects in the lab, researchers also should study expectancy effects in real life to assess how powerful these effects are. Research is also needed to learn how strong these effects can be under realistic circumstances. The studies to date show that expectancy effects are consistently greater than zero, but are they ordinarily strong enough to change a low-IQ child into a high-IQ child, or a cold, aloof person into a warm and friendly one, or vice versa? It is difficult to be sure because until recently, most research has been more concerned with discovering whether expectancy effects exist than with assessing how important the effects are in relation to other factors that influence behavior.

Two recent studies suggest that expectancy effects are especially strong when more than one important person in an individual's life holds the expectancy effects for a long period of time. When over a period of several years, both parents hold the same expectancy effects for a child's alcohol use, the effects of these expectancy effects on the child's behavior appear to accumulate and increase (Madon, Guyll, Spoth, & Willard, 2004; Madon, Willard, Guyll, Trudeau, & Spoth, 2006). This appears to be especially true, unfortunately, for negative expectancy effects. When a mother and father both overestimate their child's tendency to drink, the child has a particularly strong tendency to "live down" to this expectation.

Understanding expectancy effects sheds valuable light on the more general question of how people affect each other's performance and social behavior. Rosenthal's research revealed four basic factors that probably ought to be a part of all good teaching. Snyder's research suggests that if you want to be treated in a warm and friendly manner, it might not be a bad idea to expect the best, and act warm and friendly yourself. And parents who do not want their children to become problem drinkers should not begin by assuming the worst.

THE ACCURACY OF PERSONALITY JUDGMENT

Because people constantly make personality judgments, and because these judgments are consequential, it would seem important to know when and to what degree these judgments are accurate. It might surprise you, therefore, to learn that for an extended period of time (about 30 years) psychologists went out of their way to avoid researching accuracy. Although research on the accuracy of lay judgments of personality was fairly busy from the 1930s to about 1955, after that the field fell into inactivity, from which it began to emerge only in the mid-1980s (Funder & West, 1993).

There are several reasons why research on accuracy experienced this lengthy hiatus (Funder & West, 1993; Funder, 1995). The most basic reason is that researchers were stymied by a fundamental problem: By what criteria can the personality judgments made by somebody else be judged right or wrong (Hastie & Rasinski, 1988; Kruglanski, 1989)? Some psychologists believe this question is unanswerable, that any attempt to answer it would simply pit one person's set of criteria for accuracy against another's. Who says which set of criteria is right?

This point of view is bolstered by the philosophy of **constructivism**, which is widespread throughout modern intellectual life (Stanovich, 1991). Slightly simplified, this philosophy holds that reality, as a concrete entity, does not exist. All that does exist are human ideas, or *constructions*, of reality. This view finally settles the age-old question, "If a tree falls in the forest with no one to hear, does it make a noise?" The constructivist answer is no. A more important implication is that there is no way to regard one interpretation of reality as accurate and another interpretation as inaccurate, because all interpretations are mere "social constructions" (Kruglanski, 1989).

This idea—that since there is no reality, judgmental accuracy cannot be assessed meaningfully—has become quite fashionable. Nevertheless, I reject it (Funder, 1995). I find the philosophical outlook of **critical realism** more reasonable. Critical realism holds that the absence of perfect, infallible criteria for determining the truth does not mean that all interpretations of reality are equally correct (Rorer, 1990). Indeed, even psychological researchers who argue that accuracy issues can never be settled (constructivists) still find themselves choosing which research conclusions to believe and not believe—even though their choices might sometimes be wrong. As researchers, they recognize that they must make such choices as reasonably as possible, based on whatever information is at hand or can be gathered. The only alternative is to cease drawing conclusions altogether.

Evaluating a personality judgment is no different. You must gather all the information that might help you determine whether or not the judgment is valid, and then make the best determination you can. The task remains perfectly reasonable, even necessary, though the accuracy of the outcome will always be somewhat uncertain (Cook & Campbell, 1979; Cronbach & Meehl, 1955).

Criteria for Accuracy

There is a simpler way to think of this issue. A personality judgment rendered by an acquaintance or a stranger can be thought of as a kind of personality assessment, or even a personality test. If you think of it as a test, then the considerations discussed in the previous two chapters immediately come into play, and assessing the accuracy of a personality judgment becomes exactly equivalent to assessing the validity of a personality test. And there is a well-developed and widely accepted method for assessing test validity.

The method is called **convergent validation**. It can be illustrated by the duck test: If it looks like a duck, walks like a duck, swims like a duck, and quacks like a duck, it is very probably—but still not absolutely positively— a duck. (Maybe it's a Disney audio-animatronic machine built to resemble a duck, but probably not.) Convergent validation is achieved by assembling diverse pieces of information—such as appearance, walking and swimming style, and quackiness—that "converge" on a common conclusion: It must be a duck. The more items of diverse information that converge, the more confident one is in the conclusion (J. Block, 1989, pp. 236–237).

For personality judgments, the two primary converging criteria are **interjudge agreement** and **behavioral prediction**. If I judge you to be conscientious, and so do your parents, and so do your friends, and so do you, it is likely that you *are* conscientious. Moreover, if my judgment that you are conscientious converges with the subsequent empirical fact that you arrive on time for all your class meetings for the next three semesters, and thereby demonstrate **predictive validity**, then my judgment of you is even more certainly correct (although 100 percent certainty is never attained).

In sum, psychological research can evaluate the accuracy of personality judgments by asking two questions (Funder, 1987, 1995, 1999): (1) Do the judgments agree with one another? (2) Can they predict behavior? To the degree the answers are yes, the judgments are probably accurate.

Snap Judgments

As soon as you meet a person, you very likely begin to make judgments of his personality—and that person is probably doing exactly the same thing to you. Neither of you can really help it. Personality judgments are made quickly and almost automatically, without thinking (Hassin & Trope, 2000). This fact is obviously important; you have no doubt heard the cliché that a person doesn't get a second chance to make a first

"We have testimony that you walk like a duck and you quack like a duck. Tell the court—are you a duck?"

impression. The widespread reliance on first impressions might be the reason why the more "competent-looking" candidate (judged from still photographs) won in more than 70 percent of the 2004 races for the U.S. Senate (Todorov, Mandisodza, Goren, & Hall, 2005). Are these first impressions at all accurate?

THE FACE

According to one survey, about 75 percent of college undergraduates believe that personality can be judged, to some extent, from facial appearance (Hassin & Trope, 2000). Until recently, psychologists have tended to disagree (Alley, 1988). Studies assessing whether you could tell anything about personality from, say, the size of someone's nose yielded almost uniformly negative results. More recent studies, however, have begun to focus on what are called *configural* properties of faces, or overall arrangements of features rather than single body parts (Tanaka & Farah, 1993). And when studied in this way, the validity of first impressions seems more promising.

One early study found that after undergraduates sat together in small groups for 15 minutes without talking, their ratings of each other correlated better than $r = .30$ on the traits of "extraversion," "conscientiousness," and "openness to experience" (Passini & Norman, 1966). Referring to the Binomial Effect-Size Display (BESD) described in Chapter 3, this means that rating a stranger in this situation on these three traits is about twice as likely to be right as wrong (see Table 6.1). Similar findings were obtained by other later studies (e.g., Albright, Kenny, & Malloy, 1988; D. Watson, 1989). A glance at someone's face can be enough to make surprisingly accurate judgments of the degree to which someone is dominant or submissive (Berry & Finch Wero, 1993), heterosexual or homosexual (Rule & Ambady, 2008a), or even, in the case of business executives, how much profit his[3] company makes (Rule & Ambady, 2008b).

How is this degree of accuracy possible? Apparently, there really are configural aspects of the face that allow a number of psychological aspects of people to be judged with some degree of validity. One fascinating study tried to find out what some of those aspects are (Penton-Voak, Pound, Little, & Perrett, 2006). Researchers obtained personality scores from a large

---

[3] All the business executives in this study were male.

Table 6.1

ACCURACY OF STRANGERS' JUDGMENT OF PERSONALITY

Other's Judgment	Self-Judgment		Total
	High	Low	
High	65	35	100
Low	35	65	100
Total	100	100	200

Note: These are results of a hypothetical study with 200 participants, where self-other *r* = .30 (e.g., Passini & Norman, 1966).

sample of participants, and then selected those in the top and bottom 10 percent of males and females on five different traits (15 persons in each group). Using a computer imaging program, the 15 faces in each group were averaged into a composite portrait of a generalized—not actual—person who scored high and low on each trait. Figures 6.1 and 6.2 show the results for the traits of "agreeableness," "conscientiousness," "extraversion," "emotional stablity" (the flip side of "neuroticism"), and "openness." High scorers are in the top row, and low scorers are in the bottom row. Can you tell which trait is which? The participants in the study could, some of the time. On average, they were able to tell apart the high- and low-scoring males on "agreeableness," "extraversion," and "conscientiousness," but not the other two traits. For females, participants could tell high from low scorers on "agreeableness" and "extraversion."

What do these findings mean? First, they mean that it is apparently possible for us to tell whether a person is high or low in two traits—"extraversion" and "agreeableness"—just from looking at the face. In addition, for "conscientiousness" we can do this in males but not females. Second, this level of accuracy is impressive, and even surprising: The average effect size of the successful discriminations works out to about *r* = .80. However, it is important to remember that these findings come from *averaged* faces of *extreme* scorers—a very artificial situation. What the findings probably mean in practice is that, from looking at someone's face, we are somewhat able to accurately detect the difference between someone who is extremely extraverted and someone who is extremely introverted, or extremely agreeable versus

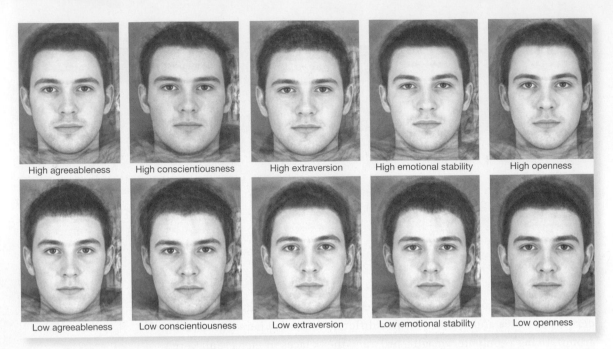

| High agreeableness | High conscientiousness | High extraversion | High emotional stability | High openness |

| Low agreeableness | Low conscientiousness | Low extraversion | Low emotional stability | Low openness |

Figure 6.1 Personality Revealed in the Face: Men These faces are composite portraits of the 10 percent of men who scored highest and lowest on five major personality traits.
Source: Penton-Voak, Pound, Little, & Perrett (2006), p. 622.

extremely disagreeable. Accurate discrimination in the middle range—where most people are found—is surely more difficult.

Still, the message from a number of recent studies is that the human face contains far more information about personality than psychologists would have guessed just a few years ago. This fact may be one reason that research has shown that job interviews done over the telephone are not as valid for judging personality as those that are conducted—you know the phrase—"face to face" (Blackman, 2002a, 2002b).

OTHER VISIBLE SIGNS OF PERSONALITY

Visible signs of personality go beyond the face. The degree to which someone dresses fashionably and has a stylish haircut can lead lay perceivers to infer that she is extraverted, and they are correct more often than not (Borkenau & Liebler, 1993). When a person speaks in a very loud voice, judges are apt to infer that he is extraverted, and that inference is usually accurate, too

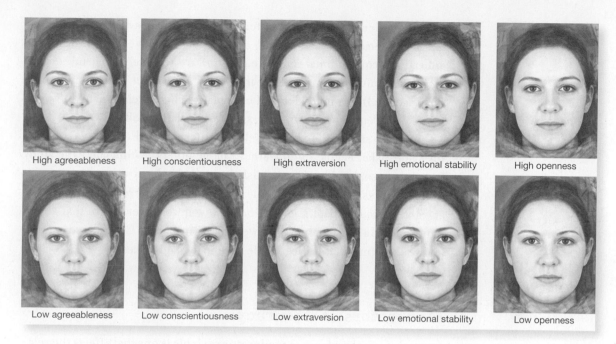

Figure 6.2 **Personality Revealed in the Face: Women** These faces are composite portraits of the 10 percent of women who scored highest and lowest on five major personality traits.

Source: Penton-Voak, Pound, Little, & Perrett (2006), p. 623.

(Funder & Sneed, 1993; Scherer, 1978). In general, judges will reach more accurate conclusions if the behaviors they observe are closely related to the traits they are judging.

Here's a novel idea for judging someone's personality. Instead of looking at the person directly, look at the person's bedroom instead. As we saw in Chapter 2, people whose bedrooms house a variety of reading material are likely to be open to experience, whereas people who carefully make their beds and are otherwise neat tend to be conscientious (Gosling, 2008b). I don't know whether most people are aware of these signs, but it does seem to be true that we are often curious to see where someone lives.

People also often assume they can judge a person by the kind of music she listens to. They may be right! When two strangers are in the process of becoming acquaintances and possibly friends, a common topic of conversation is music: which artists and styles each likes, and why. This conversation can yield information about personality (Rentfrow & Gosling, 2006). According to one recent study, people who enjoy reflective, complex music (e.g., New Age) tend to be inventive, imaginative, tolerant, and liberal. People who prefer aggressive and intense music (e.g., heavy metal) are more likely to be curious, risk-taking, and physically active. People who like upbeat and conventional music (e.g., pop) are relatively cheerful, outgoing, and helpful, but are not very interested in abstract ideas (Rentfrow & Gosling, 2003). For more detailed information on the relationship between music preference and personality, see Zweigenhaft (2008).

Another study examined the classic interpersonal cue to personality: the handshake. People often claim to judge others by this cue. One study found that people with a firm handshake tended to be extraverted and emotionally expressive, whereas people with a weak grip were more likely to be shy and anxious (Chaplin et al., 2000). If you were ever taught that a firm handshake is a sign of honesty, however, forget about it. Go to a used-car lot, and you will find all the salespeople have firm handshakes.

Moderators of Accuracy

In psychological parlance, a **moderator variable** is one that affects the relationship between two other variables. A moderator of accuracy, therefore, is a variable that changes the correlation between a judgment and its criterion. Research on accuracy has focused primarily on four potential moderators: properties (1) of the judge, (2) of the *target* (the person who is judged), (3) of the trait that is judged, and (4) of the information on which the judgment is based.

THE GOOD JUDGE

The oldest question in accuracy research is this: Who is the best judge of personality? Clinical psychologists have long postulated that some people are better at judging personality than others are, and numerous studies tackled this question during the pre-1955 wave of research on accuracy (Taft, 1955). A satisfying answer has turned out to be surprisingly difficult to reach. Early studies seemed to show that a good judge in one context or of one trait might not be a good judge in other contexts or with other traits. The only somewhat consistent finding seemed to be that highly intelligent and conscientious individuals rendered better judgments—but then again, such individuals are good at nearly any task you give them, so it was not clear that these traits were a functional part of an ability to judge people. Disappointment with this vague conclusion may be one reason why the first wave of accuracy research waned in the mid-1950s (Funder & West, 1993). But the pessimism may have been premature, because the original research was conducted using inadequate methods (Colvin & Bundick, 2001; Cronbach, 1955; Hammond, 1996).

Recent research has renewed the focus on this important topic and begun to ask some important questions. For example, who are the better judges of personality, women or men? The results on this question are mixed. One study gathered personality ratings from strangers who had sat around a table together for a few minutes but not had a chance to speak. In this setting, women were better than men on judging two traits (extraversion and positive emotionality), but not others (Ambady, Hallahan, & Rosenthal, 1995). Another study looked at ratings that were made after students actually had a chance to interact for about 5 minutes, and compared the ratings with the students' own self-judgments and with their observed behavior directly in three laboratory situations (Kolar, 1996). Men and women did not differ in their degree of accuracy in this study, but the personality correlates of accuracy were different by sex. The most accurate male judges of personality tended to be extraverted, well adjusted, and relatively unconcerned by what other people thought of them. The most accurate female judges tended to be open to new experiences, have a wide range of interests, and value their independence. These results suggest that, for men, accurate personality judgment is part of an outgoing and confident interpersonal style, whereas for women it is more a matter of openness to and interest in other people.

> If you were ever taught that a firm handshake is a sign of honesty, forget about it.

Either way, the good judge appears to be someone who is invested in developing and maintaining interpersonal relationships, a style sometimes called "communion" (Bakan, 1966). One recent study found that both women and men who tested high on "communion"—who put a particular emphasis on interpersonal relationships—were more accurate judges of personality (Vogt & Colvin, 2003), and another study found that accuracy was associated with the related traits of "social skill," "agreeableness," and "adjustment" (Letzring, 2008). Moreover, the behavior of people who score high in "attributional complexity"—an ability associated with accurate personality judgment—is described by observers as open, positive, expressive, and socially skilled (Fast, Reimer, & Funder, 2008).

Good judges of personality may be more positive in general. People whose general or "stereotypic" judgments tended to describe others in favorable terms also tended to be more accurate, because most people actually *are* generally honest, friendly, kind, and helpful, which is good to know (Letzring & Funder, 2006). People who described others—accurately—in positive terms were themselves described by people who knew them as warm, compassionate, and sympathetic. They tended to *not* be seen as arrogant, anxious, impulsive, or distrustful.

The study of the good judge lay dormant for too long. As researchers follow up on and extend these intriguing new findings, we can expect a rapid increase in our understanding of what makes some people better judges of personality than others.

THE GOOD TARGET

Another potential moderator of accuracy is the flip side of the good judge: the good target. Some people seem readable as an open book, whereas others seem more closed and enigmatic. This observation implies that some individuals are judged more easily than others. As the pioneering personality psychologist Gordon Allport asked in this context, "Who are these people?" (Allport, 1937, p. 443; Colvin, 1993b).

"Judgeable" people are those about whom others reach agreement most easily. Naturally, these tend to be the same people whose behavior is most predictable from judgments of their personalities. As follows from this definition, judgeable people are those with whom "what you see is what you get." Their behavior is organized coherently, in such a way that even different people who know them in separate settings describe essentially the same person. Furthermore, the behavior of such people is consistent, which means that we can predict what they will do in the future by taking note of what they have done in the past. We could say that these individuals are stable and well organized, or even that they are psychologically well adjusted (Colvin, 1993b).[4] Judgeable people also tend to be extraverted and agreeable (Ambady, Hallahan, & Rosenthal, 1995).

Theorists have long postulated that it is psychologically healthy to conceal very little from those around you, to exhibit what is sometimes called a "transparent self" (Jourard, 1971). To the extent that you exhibit any kind of psychological facade and that there are large discrepancies between the person "inside" and the person you display "outside," you are likely to experience excessive isolation from the people around you, which can lead to unhappiness, hostility, and depression. There is also evidence that conceal-

---

[4] It is reasonable to wonder whether this can go too far. A person who is rigid and inflexible might be judged easily but would not be well adjusted. However, research has not yet identified any real cases of such hypothetical judgeable but maladjusted individuals.

ing one's emotions can actually be harmful to physical health (D. S. Berry & Pennebaker, 1993; Pennebaker, 1992).

Recent research builds on this theory by pointing out that **judgeability** itself—the "what you see is what you get" factor—is a part of psychological adjustment precisely because it stems from behavioral coherence and consistency. This is a pattern with roots that reach into early childhood, and the association between judgeability and psychological adjustment appears to be particularly strong among males (Colvin, 1993a).

THE GOOD TRAIT

All traits are not created equal—some are much easier to judge accurately than others. For example, more easily observed traits, such as "talkativeness," "sociability," and other traits related to extraversion, are judged with much higher levels of interjudge agreement than are less visible traits, such as cognitive and ruminative styles and habits (Funder & Dobroth, 1987). For example, you are more likely to agree with your acquaintances, and they are more likely to agree with each other, about whether you are talkative than about whether you tend to worry and ruminate. This finding holds true even when the people who judge you are strangers who have observed you for only a few minutes (Funder & Colvin, 1988; see also D. Watson, 1989), or even less (Carney, Colvin, & Hall, 2007). In general, a trait like extraversion, which is reflected by overt behaviors such as high energy and friendliness, is easier to judge than a trait like "emotional stability," which is reflected by anxieties, worries, and other mental states that may not be visible on the outside (S. S. Russell & Zickar, 2005).

This conclusion might seem rather obvious. I once admitted that the main discovery of the study by Kate Dobroth and me is that more-visible traits are easier to see. We needed federal funding to learn that? (Don't worry—our grant was very small.) But it does have some interesting implications. One concerns the basis of personality judgments by acquaintances. Some psychologists, reluctant to concede that peer judgments of personality can have any accuracy, have proposed that interjudge agreement is merely the result of conversations judges have with one another or the participants. Thus, these psychologists conclude, peer judgments are not based on the participants' personalities but on their socially constructed reputations (McClelland, 1972; Kenny, 1991).

This idea seems plausible, but I doubt it is true. If peers based their personality judgments only on reputation and not on observation, then there would be no reason for observable traits to yield more consistent agreement than unobservable ones. Other people can manufacture a reputation about your ruminativeness just as well as they can about your talkativeness. But while all traits are equally susceptible to being talked about, certain traits are much harder to actually observe. Therefore, the finding that observable traits yield better interjudge agreement implies that peer judgment is based more on direct behavioral observation than on mere reputation (J. M. Clark & Paivio, 1989).

Another investigation addressed a trait the researchers called "sociosexuality," or the willingness to engage in sexual relations with minimal acquaintanceship with, or commitment to and from, one's partner (Gangestad, Simpson, DiGeronimo, & Biek, 1992). It seems reasonable to speculate that the accurate perception of this trait may have been important across the history of the human species. According to evolutionary theory, the traits and abilities that make individuals more likely to reproduce are more likely to be present in later generations. (For a more detailed discussion of this issue, see Chapter 9.) A crucial part of reproduction is figuring out who might be willing to mate with you. The hypothesis of this study, therefore, was that, for evolutionary reasons, people should be particularly good at judging this trait as opposed to other traits presumably less important for reproduction.

> Males—probably to their eternal regret—were not particularly good at judging the sociosexuality of females.

The study found that individual differences in this trait, as measured by self-report, were detected more accurately by observers than were traits less directly relevant to reproduction, such as "dominance" and "friendliness." In an interesting corollary, although this finding held true regardless of the sexes of the judge and the target, females judging the sociosexuality of males were especially accurate, and males judging the sociosexuality of other males were even more accurate!

This last finding presents a minor problem for the evolutionary explanation: What would be the reproductive advantage for a male to know the mating availability of another male? After thinking about it for a moment, you might be able to answer this question. The problem is that this is a finding evolutionary theory probably would not have predicted. (In case you are wondering, males—probably to their eternal regret—were not particularly good at judging the sociosexuality of females.)

GOOD INFORMATION

The final moderator of judgmental accuracy is the amount and kind of information on which the personality judgment is based.

Amount of Information   Despite recent findings about snap judgments summarized earlier in this chapter, it still seems to be the case that more information is usually better, especially when judging certain traits. One study found that, while traits such as "extraversion," "conscientiousness," and "intelligence" could be judged with some degree of accuracy after only 5 seconds of observations, traits such as "neuroticism" (emotional instability), "openness," and "agreeableness" took considerably more time (Carney et al., 2007). In another study that examined more-extended acquaintanceship, participants were judged both by people who had known them for at least a year and by strangers who had viewed the participants only for about 5 minutes on a videotape. Personality judgments by the close acquaintances agreed much better with the participants' self-judgments than did judgments by strangers (Funder & Colvin, 1988).

But this advantage of longer acquaintanceship did not hold under all circumstances. The videotapes that the strangers watched showed the participant conversing for 5 minutes with a peer of the opposite sex. This video was the sole basis for the strangers' personality judgments. The acquaintances, by contrast, never saw the videotape. Their judgments were based, instead, on their own knowledge of the participant obtained through observations and interactions in daily life over an extended period of time. Interestingly, when the judgments by the strangers and those by the acquaintances were used to try to predict what the participant would do in a separate videotaped interaction with a different opposite-sex peer, the two sets of judgments performed at about the same level of accuracy. That is, the advantage of acquaintances over strangers vanished when the criterion was the ability to predict behavior in a situation similar to one that the strangers had seen but that the acquaintances had not (Colvin & Funder, 1991).

Let me clarify this finding with a personal example. I regularly lecture before 150 or more undergraduates two or three times a week. As a result, a lot of people have seen me lecture but have no way of knowing what kind of person I am in other settings. My wife, on the other hand, has known me well for more than 20 years but has never seen me deliver a lecture (a not uncommon situation among college professors and their spouses). If one of my students and my wife are asked to predict how I will behave in lecture next week, whose predictions will be more accurate? According to Colvin and Funder (1991), the two predictions will be about equally valid. On the other hand, according to Funder and Colvin (1988), if you ask these two people to predict what I will do in any other context, my wife will have a clear advantage.

In our 1991 article, Randy Colvin and I called this phenomenon a *boundary* on the acquaintanceship effect, because we seemed to have found the one circumstance under which strangers could provide personality judgments with a predictive validity equal to those offered by close acquaintances. But this finding may be even more remarkable from a reversed perspective. Even though a close acquaintance—such as a spouse—has never seen you in a particular situation, that person will be able to generalize from observations of you in other situations with sufficient accuracy to predict your behavior in that situation as accurately as someone who has actually seen you in it. From casual observation in daily life, for example, the acquaintances were able to extract information about the participants' personalities that was just as useful in predicting how they would behave under the gaze of a video camera as was strangers' direct observation of behavior in a highly similar situation. The real news of this research may be this ability of acquaintances to go from their specific experiences to judgments that are generally accurate.

Another study added a further wrinkle to the effect of the quantity of information on accuracy. It turns out that if judges are given more information, this will improve the agreement between their judgments and the target individual's self-judgments, but it does not affect their agreement with each other (Blackman & Funder, 1998). Judges watched a series of videotapes of pairs of people having conversations. Some judges saw only one 5-minute tape, some saw two tapes (for a total of 10 minutes), and so on, up to those who saw six tapes for a total of 30 minutes of observation. Then they tried to describe the personality of one person they watched.

The results are illustrated in Figure 6.3. Consensus, or the agreement among judges, was almost as good at the beginning as it became by the end; it did not change significantly between the judges who watched 5 minutes versus those who watched 30 minutes of videotape. But accuracy, here indexed by the agreement between their descriptions and the targets' own self-descriptions, did improve both noticeably and significantly.

What caused this difference between consensus and accuracy? The cause seems to be that judges' first impressions of their target agree with each other because they are based on superficial stereotypes and other potentially misleading cues. Because these stereotypes are shared among judges, the judges tend to agree with each other even if they are largely wrong. After observing the target for a period of time, however, judges begin to discard these stereotypes and see the person as he really is. The result is not so much increased agreement among the judges, as it is an improvement in the accuracy of what they agree on.

A hypothetical example may clarify these findings. Consider two owners of a garage, Sue and Sally. They need a new mechanic, so they interview an applicant named, say, Luther. Luther's hair is neatly combed and he arrives

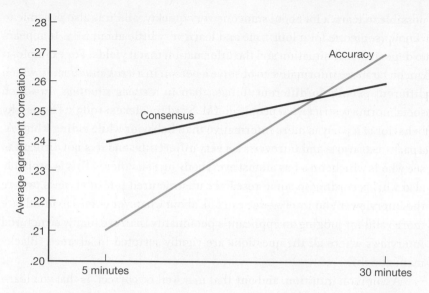

Figure 6.3 Accuracy and Consensus at 5 and 30 Minutes of Acquaintance
Blackman and Funder (1998) evaluated how consensus (interjudge agreement) and accuracy (self-other agreement) changed according to the length of time that judges watched videotapes of the target participants' behavior. The results show that while accuracy improved significantly with longer observation, consensus did not.
Source: Adapted from Blackman & Funder (1998), p. 177.

on time for his appointment, so they decide he is conscientious and give him the job. Sadly, after a few weeks they realize that he is chronically late for work and leaves his repairs only half done, and that customers are starting to complain about finding beer cans in their backseats. Sue and Sally have a meeting and agree that, contrary to their first impression, Luther is unreliable and must go.

In technical terms, consensus did not change during this sad story, even though accuracy did. Sue and Sally agreed at the beginning, and they agreed at the end. However, the content of what they agreed about changed dramatically. At the beginning they agreed about an erroneous assumption based on superficial stereotypes; at the end, with the benefit of some actual observations of his performance, they agreed about what Luther was really like. This is the kind of process, I believe, that explains why the accuracy line leans upward in Figure 6.3, even though the consensus line lies almost flat.

Quality of Information   Quantity is not the only important variable concerning information. Common experience suggests that sometimes it is possible to learn a lot about someone very quickly, and it is also possible to "know" someone for a long time and learn very little about him. It appears to depend on the situation and the information that it yields. For example, it can be far more informative to observe a person in a *weak situation*, in which different people do different things, than in a *strong situation*, in which social norms restrict what people do (M. Snyder & Ickes, 1985). This is why behavior at a party is more informative than behavior while riding a bus. At a party, extraverts and introverts act very differently, and it is not difficult to see who is which; on a bus almost everybody just sits there. This is probably also why, according to some research, unstructured job interviews, where the interviewer and interviewee can talk about whatever comes to mind, are more valid for judging an applicant's personality than are highly structured interviews where all the questions are rigidly scripted in advance (Blackman, 2002b).

A common intuition, and one that may well be correct, is that you learn something extra about a person if you see her in a stressful or emotionally arousing situation. Watching how someone acts in an emergency or how she responds to a letter of acceptance—or rejection—from medical school, or even having a romantic encounter with someone can reveal things about the person that you might not have suspected. By the same token, it is possible to sit next to a person in a class day after day for months and know next to nothing about him. The best situation for judging someone's personality is one that brings out the trait you want to judge. To evaluate a person's approach toward his work, the best thing to do is to observe him working. To evaluate a person's sociability, observations at a party would be more informative (Freeberg, 1969; Landy & Guion, 1970).

The effect of the quality of information on judgments was evaluated in an interesting study using recorded interviews. Judges of personality listened to targets being asked either about their thoughts and feelings or about their daily activities. The judges then tried to describe the targets' personalities using a set of 100 traits. The researchers found that listening to the thoughts-and-

"When you picked up your car, Mr. Ferguson, after we did the hoses, did you see Luther's shoes?"

feelings interview "produced more 'accurate' social impressions, or at least impressions that were more in accord with speakers' self-assessments prior to the interviews and with the assessments made by their close friends, than did [listening to] the behavioral . . . interviews" (Andersen, 1984, p. 294). A more recent study found that people who met in an unstructured situation, where they could talk about whatever they wanted, made more-accurate judgments of each other than did those who met under circumstances that offered less room for idle chitchat (Letzring, Wells, & Funder, 2006). The study also found that people who were instructed to deliberately try to get to know each other made judgments that were just a little more accurate than those who simply chatted.

The accurate judgment of personality, then, depends on both the quantity and the quality of the information on which it is based. More information is generally better, but it is just as important for the information to be relevant to the traits that one is trying to judge.

The Realistic Accuracy Model

To bring sense and order to the wide range of moderators of accuracy, it is helpful to back up a step and ask how accurate personality judgment is possible in the first place. At least sometimes, people manage to accurately evaluate one or more of the aspects of the personalities of the people they know. How do they do it? One explanation is in terms of the *realistic accuracy model (RAM)* (Funder, 1995).

In order to get from an attribute of an individual's personality to an accurate judgment of that trait, four things must happen (see Figure 6.4). First, the person being judged must do something *relevant*, that is, informative about the trait to be judged. Second, this information must be *available* to a judge. Third, this judge must *detect* this information. Fourth and finally, the judge must *utilize* this information correctly.

For example, consider an attempt to judge someone's degree of courage. This may not be possible unless the situation comes along that allows a courageous person to reveal this trait. But if the target of judgment encounters a burning building, rushes in, and saves the family inside, then she has done something relevant. Next, this behavior must occur in a manner and place that makes it possible for you, as the judge, to observe it. Someone might be doing something extremely courageous right now, right next door, but if you can't see it, you may never know and never have a chance to accurately assess

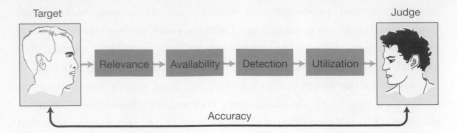

Figure 6.4 **The Realistic Accuracy Model** For an attribute of an individual's personality to be judged accurately, four things must happen. First, the individual must do something relevant to the attribute. Second, this behavioral information must be available to the judge. Third, the judge must detect this information. Fourth, the judge must utilize this information correctly.

Source: Adapted from Funder (1995), p. 659.

that person's courage. But let's say you happen by just as the target of judgment rescues the last member of the family from the flames. Now the judgment has passed the availability hurdle. That is still not enough: Perhaps you were distracted, or you are perceptually impaired (e.g., you forgot to wear your glasses), or for some other reason you failed to register the dramatic rescue. But if you did notice, then the judgment has passed the detection hurdle. Finally, you must accurately remember and correctly interpret the relevant, available information that you have detected. If you infer that this rescue means the target person rates high on the trait of courage, then you have passed the utilization stage and achieved, at last, an accurate judgment.

This model of accurate personality judgment has several implications. The first and most obvious implication is that accurate personality judgment is difficult. Notice how all four of the hurdles—relevance, availability, detection, and utilization—must be overcome before accurate judgment can be achieved. If the process fails at any step—the person in question never does something relevant, or does it out of sight of the judge, or the judge doesn't notice, or the judge makes an incorrect interpretation—accurate personality judgment will fail.

The second implication is that the moderators of accuracy discussed earlier in this chapter—good judge, good target, good trait, and good information—must be a result of something that happens at one or more of these four stages. For example, a *good judge* is someone who is good at detecting and utilizing behavioral information. A *good target* is someone who behaves in accordance with her personality (relevance) in a wide range of situations (availability). A *good trait* is one that is displayed in a wide range of contexts (availability) and is easy to see (detection). Similarly, knowing someone for a long time in a wide range of situations (*good information*) can enhance the range of behaviors a judge sees (availability) and the odds that the judge will begin to notice patterns that emerge (detection).

A third implication of this model is the most important. According to RAM, the accuracy of personality judgment can be improved in four different ways. Traditionally, efforts to improve accuracy have focused on attempts to get judges to think better, to use good logic and avoid inferential errors. These efforts are worthwhile, but they address only one stage—utilization—out of the four stages of accurate personality judgment. Improvement could be sought at the other stages as well (Funder, 2003).

For example, consider the disadvantages of being a "touchy" person. Someone who easily takes offense will find that people are more cautious or restrained when he is around: They avoid discussing certain topics and doing certain things whenever he is present. As a result, his judgment of these acquaintances will become stymied at the relevance stage—relevant behaviors that otherwise might have been performed in his presence will be suppressed—and he likely will be unable to judge these acquaintances accurately. For example, a boss who blows up at bad news will lead employees to hide evidence of their mistakes, thus interfering with the availability of relevant information. As a result, the boss will be clueless about the employees' actual performance and abilities—and maybe even about how well the company is doing.

The situation in which a judgment is made can also affect its accuracy. Meeting someone under tense or distracting circumstances is likely to interfere with the detection of otherwise relevant and available information, again causing accurate judgment to be stymied. People on job interviews or first dates may not always be the most accurate judges of the people they interact with.

Becoming a better judge of personality, then, involves much more than "thinking better." You should also try to create an interpersonal environment where other people can be themselves and where they feel free to let you know what is really going on. It may be difficult to avoid situations where tensions and other distractions cause you to miss what is right in front of you. But it might be worth bearing in mind that your judgment in such situations may not be completely reliable, and to try to remember to calm down and be attentive to the other person as well as to your own thoughts, feelings, and goals.

ACCURACY MATTERS

There is no escaping personality assessment. If you manage to evade having your personality judged by tests or by psychologists, you still will find that your personality is judged every hour of every day by your acquaintances, coworkers, friends, and yourself. Furthermore, these judgments will matter just as much as, and probably more than, any that will ever be rendered by tests or psychologists. This is why it matters whether they are accurate. We need to understand others in order to interact with them and make decisions ranging from to whom to lend $10 to whom to marry. Improving accuracy requires better thinking, but it also depends on our acting in a way that allows other people to be themselves.

SUMMARY

Consequences of Everyday Judgments of Personality

- People judge the personalities of each other and of themselves all the time, and these judgments have important consequences.

- Other people's judgments of an individual can affect that person's opportunities and can create self-fulfilling prophecies or expectancy effects. Therefore, it is important to examine when and how judgments are accurate.

The Accuracy of Personality Judgment

- Recent research has evaluated the accuracy of personality judgments in terms of consensus and predictive validity. Judgments that agree with judgments from other sources (such as other people) or that are able to predict the target person's behavior are more likely to be accurate than judgments that do not agree with each other or cannot predict behavior.

- First impressions of personality can be surprisingly accurate. Valid information about some attributes of personality can be found in the face, tone of voice, mode of dress, and even the condition of someone's bedroom. However, such judgments are more accurate for some traits than others, and tend to become more accurate with more extended acquaintanceship.

- Research has examined four variables that seem to affect the likelihood of accurate personality judgment: (1) the good judge, or the possibility that some judges are more accurate than others; (2) the good target, or the possibility that some individuals are easier to judge than others; (3) the good trait, or the possibility that some traits are easier to judge accurately than others; and (4) good information, or the possibility that more or better information about the target makes accurate judgment more likely.

- This research leads to the realistic accuracy model (RAM) of the process of accurate personality judgment, which describes accuracy as a function of the relevance, availability, detection, and utilization of behavioral cues.

- RAM implies that accurate personality judgment is difficult, helps to explain the four moderators of accuracy, and suggests some ways in which one might be able to judge others more accurately.

Accuracy Matters

- Judgments of personality rendered by ordinary people in daily life are more frequent and more important than those made by psychologists, so it matters whether they are accurate.

THINK ABOUT IT

1. How often do you make judgments of the personalities of other people? When you do, are you usually right or wrong? How can you tell?
2. What did you think about the data on first impressions summarized in this chapter? Have you found that you can judge someone from their facial appearance, tone of voice, or other easily observed clues? What are the potential pitfalls of relying too much on first impressions?
3. Think of a time when you made a personality judgment of someone that turned out to be wrong. What was the cause of your mistake?
4. When other people make judgments of your personality, are they usually right or wrong? Is there any aspect of your personality that people are apt to get wrong?
5. When are other people easiest to judge? Does it depend on when or how you met them?
6. What does it really mean to be "accurate" about judging someone's personality? If you think a person is dishonest, say, and the person thinks herself honest, can this kind of discrepancy ever be resolved? How?
7. Have you taken a course in social psychology? If so, how is the approach of social psychology to the topic of person perception similar to, and different from, the approach taken in this book?

SUGGESTED READING

Funder, D. C. (1999). *Personality judgment: A realistic approach to person perception.* San Diego: Academic Press.

> *A more detailed, somewhat more technical, and slightly dated presentation of personality judgment and the issues concerning accuracy that are covered in this chapter.*

EMEDIA

 Go to StudySpace, wwnorton.com/studyspace, to access additional review and enrichment materials.

7

USING PERSONALITY TRAITS TO UNDERSTAND BEHAVIOR

TRAITS EXIST (Chapter 4) and can be assessed by psychologists (Chapter 5) as well as by everybody else in daily life (Chapter 6). But that really is just the beginning. It is time to ask one of the most challenging questions that can be addressed to any area of research: Who cares? What is the point of measuring traits? Is it just to pigeonhole people, or is there a larger purpose? I would argue that there are actually a pair of larger purposes for measuring traits, namely (1) to predict behavior and (2) to understand behavior. While these two purposes are not exactly the same, the trait approach is built on the twin assumptions that the best way to test the accuracy of a psychological understanding of an individual's personality is to use it to (try to) predict what he will do, and that learning which traits predict a behavior can lead to insights as to why. Are these assumptions correct?

The only way to find out is to look at the research that examines how traits and behavior are connected. Does the research seem valid? And, more importantly, are the conclusions of the research useful or interesting?[1] After reading this chapter, you will be in a good position to answer these questions.

The research that seeks to connect traits with behavior has used four basic methods: the single-trait approach, the many-trait approach, the essential-trait approach, and the typological approach.

---

[1] Even when research isn't useful in any obvious way, it at least ought to be interesting.

- looks at one trait and assesses implication eg. authortananism. "what do people like that do?"

The **single-trait approach** examines the link between personality and behavior by asking, What do people like that do? where "that" refers to a (hopefully) important personality trait. Some traits have seemed so important that psychologists have devoted a major amount of effort to assessing as many of their implications as possible. For example, research programs have examined authoritarianism, conscientiousness, and self-monitoring, to name only three.

- looks @ behavior first
- "who does that" ↳ which traits correlate w given behavior

The **many-trait approach** works from the opposite direction, beginning with the (implicit) research question, Who does that? where "that" is an important behavior. Researchers attack the behavior of interest with long lists of traits intended to cover a wide range of personality. They determine which ones correlate with the specific behavior, and then seek to explain the pattern of correlations. For example, a researcher interested in the behavior of "self-control" might measure how long each member of a group of children can wait for a reward (a behavior called *delay of gratification*) and also measure up to 100 traits in each child. The researcher could then see which of these traits tended to characterize the children who delayed the longest and the shortest lengths of time. The researcher hopes that the results will reveal how and why the longest-delaying children did so, as well as illuminate the psychological mechanisms that underlie self-control.

- which traits are the most important? - eg. big 5 traits

The **essential-trait approach** addresses the difficult question, Which traits are the *most* important? The dictionary includes thousands of traits, and this embarrassment of riches has sometimes led to confusion about which ones ought to be studied and measured. Certainly not all of them. One hopes! The essential-trait approach, which has made considerable headway in recent years, tries to narrow the list to the traits that really matter. Most prominently, the *Big Five* list includes the traits of *extraversion*, *neuroticism*, *conscientiousness*, *agreeableness*, and *openness*. Are these traits the most important ones to know about a person? We will consider this question later in the chapter.

- focuses on trait patterns that characterize a whole person
- tries to sort patterns into "types"

But does it *really* make sense to array everybody in the world along the various trait scales that psychologists have developed? Even psychologists have sometimes wondered. The **typological approach** stems from a doubt and a hope. The doubt is whether it is really valid to compare people with each other quantitatively on the same trait dimensions. Perhaps they are so qualitatively different—because they are different types of people—that comparing their individual trait scores makes as little sense as the proverbial comparison between apples and oranges. The hope is that researchers can identify groups of people who resemble each other enough, and are different enough from everybody else, that it makes sense to conclude they belong to the same "type." Instead of focusing on traits directly, this approach focuses on the patterns of traits that characterize whole persons, and tries to sort these patterns into types. Which type are you? If you read to the end of this chapter, you might find out.

THE SINGLE-TRAIT APPROACH

Some of the most influential research in personality has focused on the nature, origins, and consequences of single traits of special importance. Let's begin by considering three of these. Each has been examined in hundreds of studies over several decades. Psychologists view all of them as important for different reasons. The first trait, authoritarianism, has implications for social problems: it has been theorized as a basis of racial prejudice and even fascism. The second trait, conscientiousness (and a related package of qualities sometimes called "integrity"), has turned out to be surprisingly useful for predicting who will be productive employees. The third trait, self-monitoring, is important because it addresses fundamental issues concerning the relationship between one's private inner reality and the external self presented to others.

Authoritarianism

Racial prejudice and obedience to tyrannical government have been persistent problems throughout human history. These phenomena reached particularly horrifying dimensions in Europe in the 1930s and 1940s. The rise of Adolf Hitler and Nazism in Germany produced not only a repressive, dictatorial state bent on conquering its neighbors, but also a massive wave of ethnic oppression that led to the extermination of millions of Jews and members of other disfavored minority groups, such as Roma ("gypsies") and homosexuals. For this to happen, the German people had to cooperate with, or at least accept, atrocities committed by their own government.

While this was still going on, the philosopher and psychologist Erich Fromm began to wonder how civilized people could participate in such barbarism. Fromm formulated an explanation in terms of the influence of history and society. He theorized that the demise of Catholicism and the rise of Protestantism in Germany, combined with the rise of capitalism, gave individuals unprecedented freedom to conceive of God as they wished and

Fromm = "Escape from freedom"

> To avoid frightening personal choices, some people turn their will over to an external authority, such as a government or church, and take the comforting attitude that they are "just following orders."

↓ catholicism
↑ protestants
↑ capitalism
= unprecedented freedom that scared people, caused them to turn toward external authority.

A-S scale = anti semitism.

to direct their economic activity any way they chose. But with this freedom came a frightening degree of responsibility: to conceive of God without the comforting certainty of religious dogma and to choose an occupation in which to thrive rather than starve. Many individuals, according to Fromm, fear this degree of freedom and seek to escape it—hence the title of his book, *Escape from Freedom* (1941). To avoid these frightening personal choices, some people turn their will over to an external authority, such as a government or church, and take the comforting attitude that they are "just following orders." In turn, such individuals enjoy giving orders—which they expect to be unquestioned—to those below them in the hierarchy. Fromm coined the term *authoritarian character* to describe these personalities. It was the widespread presence of such individuals in Germany, Fromm guessed, that could explain how Nazism arose there.

Fromm's analysis concentrated on societal influences that affect people in general. However, he also acknowledged that not everybody becomes an authoritarian under the circumstances he described, not even in 1930s Germany. This observation suggests that personality might be involved. A decade later, the "Berkeley group" of psychologists (Adorno, Frenkel-Brunswik, Levinson, & Sanford, 1950) attempted to understand the difference between authoritarians and nonauthoritarians (Dillehay, 1978). These psychologists had been commissioned by the American Jewish Committee to search for the psychological causes of the anti-Semitism that produced so much death and suffering during the 1930s and 1940s. Their efforts were detailed in a book called *The Authoritarian Personality*, a classic of psychological research.

The Berkeley group began by constructing a questionnaire to measure anti-Semitism. Called the *A-S scale*, it included items such as "Jews seem to prefer the most luxurious, extravagant, and sensual way of living," and "In order to maintain a nice residential neighborhood it is best to prevent Jews from living in it," and "The Jews should give up their un-Christian religion with all its strange customs (Kosher diet, special holidays, etc.) and participate actively and sincerely in the Christian religion" (Adorno et al., 1950, pp. 68–69). The people who scored highest and lowest on this scale were singled out for extensive clinical interviews and other tests.

The first thing the psychologists noticed was that individuals who endorsed anti-Semitic statements also tended to be prejudiced against other minority groups; anti-Semitism is part of a pattern that goes beyond attitudes toward Jews. So the next step was to construct a general ethnocentrism scale, called the *E scale*. It added items such as "Negroes have their rights, but it is best to keep them in their own districts and schools to prevent too much contact with whites" and "The worst danger to real Americanism during the last 50 years has come from foreign ideas and agitators" (Adorno et al., 1950, p. 142). The researchers found that scores on the E scale were correlated very highly, in the range from .63 to .75, with scores on the A–S scale.

[handwritten margin note: E scale = ethnocentricism scale]

The psychologists of the Berkeley group also believed that a more general political outlook was associated with both anti-Semitism and ethnocentrism, and in an attempt to tap it they developed the *Politico-Economic Conservatism* (PEC) scale. It was a short step from the PEC scale to the development of the *California F scale* (F meaning "fascism"), which aimed to measure the basic antidemocratic psychological orientation that these researchers believed to be the common foundation of anti-Semitism, racial prejudice, and political *pseudoconservatism*.

[handwritten margin note: PEC = politico-economic conservatism]

The authors of *The Authoritarian Personality* carefully tried to distinguish pseudoconservativism from genuine conservatism. Genuine conservatives, according to Adorno (1950), hold an internally consistent set of political beliefs, all of which support institutions and the traditional social order while seeking to protect individual rights, property, and initiative. There is no necessary connection between these beliefs and racism or psychopathology. Pseudoconservatives, by contrast, "show blatant contradictions between their acceptance of all kinds of conventional and traditional values—by no means only in the political sphere—and their simultaneous acceptance of the more destructive [attitudes] . . . such as cynicism, punitiveness, and violent anti-Semitism" (Adorno, 1950, p. 683). They also often hold radical positions that are anything but truly conservative—that the Bill of Rights should be abolished, for example, or that all taxes should be eliminated or all politicians impeached. This is the sense in which Adorno claimed authoritarians are pseudoconservative rather than genuinely conservative.

More than 50 years after the concept was introduced, research on authoritarianism and related concepts continues at a steady pace, with more than four thousand articles and counting. Instead of the classic F scale, much of this research uses an updated measure of "right-wing authoritarianism" (RWA) developed by the Canadian psychologist Bob Altemeyer (1981, 1998). Several different versions of the RWA scale have been developed over the years; if you dare, you can take one of the more recent ones (see Try for Yourself 7.1).

[handwritten note: RWA = right wing authoritarianism]

TRY FOR YOURSELF 7.1

Public Opinion Study

Instructions: This survey is part of an investigation of general public opinion concerning a variety of social issues. You will probably find that you agree with some of the statements, and disagree with others, to varying extents. Please indicate your reaction to each statement by circling a number on the scale that follows.

Very Strongly Disagree	Strongly Disagree	Moderately Disagree	Slightly Disagree	Exactly Neutral	Slightly Agree	Moderately Agree	Strongly Agree	Very Strongly Agree

1. The established authorities generally turn out to be right about things, while the radicals and protestors are usually just "loud mouths" showing off their ignorance.

    -4   -3   -2   -1   0   +1   +2   +3   +4

2. Women should have to promise to obey their husbands when they get married.

    -4   -3   -2   -1   0   +1   +2   +3   +4

3. Our country desperately needs a mighty leader who will do what has to be done to destroy the radical new ways and sinfulness that are ruining us.

    -4   -3   -2   -1   0   +1   +2   +3   +4

4. Gays and lesbians are just as healthy and moral as anybody else.

    -4   -3   -2   -1   0   +1   +2   +3   +4

5. It is always better to trust the judgment of the proper authorities in government and religion than to listen to the noisy rabble-rousers in our society who are trying to create doubt in people's minds.

    -4   -3   -2   -1   0   +1   +2   +3   +4

6. Atheists and others who have rebelled against the established religions are no doubt every bit as good and virtuous as those who attend church regularly.

    -4   -3   -2   -1   0   +1   +2   +3   +4

7. The only way our country can get through the crisis ahead is to get back to our traditional values, put some tough leaders in power, and silence the troublemakers spreading bad ideas.

    -4   -3   -2   -1   0   +1   +2   +3   +4

8. There is absolutely nothing wrong with nudist camps.

    -4   -3   -2   -1   0   +1   +2   +3   +4

Very Strongly Disagree	Strongly Disagree	Moderately Disagree	Slightly Disagree	Exactly Neutral	Slightly Agree	Moderately Agree	Strongly Agree	Very Strongly Agree

9. Our country needs free thinkers who have the courage to defy traditional ways, even if this upsets many people.

| −4 | −3 | −2 | −1 | 0 | +1 | +2 | +3 | +4 |

10. Our country will be destroyed someday if we do not smash the perversions eating away at our moral fiber and traditional beliefs.

| −4 | −3 | −2 | −1 | 0 | +1 | +2 | +3 | +4 |

11. Everyone should have their own lifestyle, religious beliefs, and sexual preferences, even if it makes them different from everyone else.

| −4 | −3 | −2 | −1 | 0 | +1 | +2 | +3 | +4 |

12. The "old-fashioned ways" and the "old-fashioned values" still show the best way to live.

| −4 | −3 | −2 | −1 | 0 | +1 | +2 | +3 | +4 |

13. You have to admire those who challenged the law and the majority's view by protesting for women's abortion rights, for animal rights, or to abolish school prayer.

| −4 | −3 | −2 | −1 | 0 | +1 | +2 | +3 | +4 |

14. What our country really needs is a strong, determined leader who will crush evil, and take us back to our true path.

| −4 | −3 | −2 | −1 | 0 | +1 | +2 | +3 | +4 |

15. Some of the best people in our country are those who are challenging our government, criticizing religion, and ignoring the "normal way things are supposed to be done."

| −4 | −3 | −2 | −1 | 0 | +1 | +2 | +3 | +4 |

16. God's laws about abortion, pornography, and marriage must be strictly followed before it is too late, and those who break them must be strongly punished.

| −4 | −3 | −2 | −1 | 0 | +1 | +2 | +3 | +4 |

17. There are many radical, immoral people in our country today, who are trying to ruin it for their own godless purposes, whom the authorities should put out of action.

| −4 | −3 | −2 | −1 | 0 | +1 | +2 | +3 | +4 |

18. A "woman's place" should be wherever she wants to be. The days when women are submissive to their husbands and social conventions belong strictly in the past.

| −4 | −3 | −2 | −1 | 0 | +1 | +2 | +3 | +4 |

TRY FOR YOURSELF 7.1

Public Opinion Study (Continued)

| Very Strongly Disagree | Strongly Disagree | Moderately Disagree | Slightly Disagree | Exactly Neutral | Slightly Agree | Moderately Agree | Strongly Agree | Very Strongly Agree |

19. Our country will be great if we honor the ways of our forefathers, do what the authorities tell us to do, and get rid of the "rotten apples" who are ruining everything.

    −4   −3   −2   −1   0   +1   +2   +3   +4

20. There is no "ONE right way" to live life; everybody has to create their own way.

    −4   −3   −2   −1   0   +1   +2   +3   +4

21. Homosexuals and feminists should be praised for being brave enough to defy "traditional family values."

    −4   −3   −2   −1   0   +1   +2   +3   +4

22. This country would work a lot better if certain groups of troublemakers would just shut up and accept their group's traditional place in society.

    −4   −3   −2   −1   0   +1   +2   +3   +4

Scoring Instructions: Do not score items 1 and 2—they are warm-ups to accustom test takers to the response scale. For Items 3, 5, 7, 10, 12, 14, 16, 17, 19, and 22:

Score −4 as 1	Score −1 as 4	Score +2 as 7
Score −3 as 2	Score 0 (or no answer) as 5	Score +3 as 8
Score −2 as 3	Score +1 as 6	Score +4 as 9

For Items 4, 6, 8, 9, 11, 13, 15, 18, 20, and 21:

Score −4 as 9	Score −1 as 6	Score +2 as 3
Score −3 as 8	Score 0 (or no answer) as 5	Score +3 as 2
Score −2 as 7	Score +1 as 4	Score +4 as 1

Interpreting Scores: Highest possible score = 180 and lowest possible score = 20. Average of Canadian college students is approximately 75. Average of adults in general, in the United States and Canada, is approximately 90. This means most people in these countries are not authoritarians. For a score to be interpreted as indicating authoritarianism in absolute terms, it would need to be 120 or higher.

Source: Adapted from Altemeyer (2007), pp. 10–13.

RWA is made up of three clusters of attitudes and behaviors:

1. **Authoritarian Submission:** the tendency to be obedient and submissive to established leaders of the government and other important institutions (e.g., the church).

2. **Authoritarian Aggression:** the tendency to act with aggressive hostility toward anybody perceived as a deviant or a member of an outgroup, or anyone who is described by authorities as someone to be despised (e.g., designated "enemies" a country might be warring against).

3. **Conventionalism:** the tendency to follow traditions and social norms that are endorsed by society and by the people in power.

Research since the time of the classic studies has shown that authoritarians tend to be uncooperative and inflexible when playing experimental games, and they are relatively likely to obey an authority figure's commands to harm another person (Elms & Milgram, 1966). They experience fewer positive emotions than nonauthoritarians (Van Hiel & Kossowska, 2006), are likely to oppose equal rights for transsexuals (Tee & Hegarty, 2006), and (if they are Americans) tend to favor the 2003 American military intervention in Iraq (Crowson, DeBacker, & Thoma, 2005). Authoritarians also watch more television (Shanahan, 1995)!

Other recent research has explored the underlying fearfulness of authoritarians. When society is in turmoil and basic values are threatened, authoritarians become particularly likely to support "strong" candidates for office (McCann, 1997). When authoritarians feel their standard of living is declining, that crime is getting worse, and that environmental quality is declining, they become six times as likely[2] to favor restrictions on welfare and eight times as likely to support laws to ban abortions (Rickert, 1998). And when they feel their nation might be in danger, they are ready to go to war.

On the other hand, there seems (perhaps surprisingly) to be little correlation between authoritarianism and political party affiliation. It appears that authoritarians prefer whatever candidate they feel projects the more powerful image, regardless of the candidate's party (McCann, 1990). Indeed, even communists can be authoritarian. A study conducted in Romania 10 years after the collapse of communist rule found that people who scored high on authoritarianism still believed in communist ideas (such as government

[2]Compared with nonthreatened authoritarians or nonauthoritarians.

ownership of factories), but also supported fascist political parties and candidates whose positions were at the opposite extreme (S. W. Krauss, 2002). The common thread seemed to be that the personalities of these people led them to crave strong leaders and even to support dictatorship. They rather missed their communist dictators, it seemed, and wouldn't have minded substituting fascist dictators.

Two points are important to remember about authoritarianism. The first is that authoritarianism is an individual-difference construct, and thus it cannot—and is not supposed to—explain why Nazism arose in Germany rather than in America, or why it arose in 1932 rather than 1882 or 1982 (Sabini, 1995). Instead, it tries to explain which individuals within any society—whether in Germany, Romania, or America—would be most likely to follow a leader like Hitler. Second, authoritarianism provides an example of how a personality trait can be helpful for understanding a complex social phenomenon. After all, as I noted, not all Germans became Nazis in the 1930s. An examination of the differences between those who did and those who did not might help us understand who is most and least susceptible; it could also help us understand why some people are dangerously swayed by the charms of leaders who seek to lead them into dictatorship (S. W. Krauss, 2002).

"Integrity" and Conscientiousness

When employers select new employees, what are they looking for? According to one survey in which over three thousand employers ranked the importance of 86 possible employee qualities, 7 out of the top 8 involved conscientiousness, integrity, trustworthiness, and similar qualities (the eighth was general mental ability) (Michigan Department of Education, 1989). When deciding whether to hire you, therefore, almost any prospective employer will try to gauge these traits. As job interview workshops repeatedly tell you, employers will pay close attention to how you are groomed, how you are dressed, and whether you show up on time. (Showing up late or in ragged jeans is not recommended.)

Sometimes employers go beyond these casual observations by administering formal personality tests. In many cases, these are called *integrity tests*, but they typically measure a wide range of qualities, including responsibility, long-term job commitment, consistency, moral reasoning, friendliness, work ethic, dependability, cheerfulness, energy level, and even-temperedness (O'Bannon, Goldinger, & Appleby, 1989). The qualities measured by these tests are partially described by the broad traits of *agreeableness* and *emotional stability*. But the trait most closely associated with integrity tests is *conscientiousness* (Ones, Viswesvaran, & Schmidt, 1993, 1995).

How well do these tests predict job performance? To some extent, the answer depends on what you mean by job performance. In many studies in industrial psychology, the criterion of interest is supervisors' ratings, often offered about a year after the person is hired. This criterion might seem subjective—and it is—but from a supervisor's point of view is probably exactly what she wishes to know when considering a job candidate: If I hire this person, a year from now will I be glad or sorry? Ones and coworkers reviewed more than 700 studies that used a total of 576,460 subjects in assessing the validity of 43 different tests for predicting supervisors' ratings of job performance. The validity was equivalent to a correlation of .41. Recall the discussion of the Binomial Effect Size Display (BESD) in Chapter 3, and the example in Chapter 4: If an employer's predictions of future job performance, made without using one of these tests, are accurate 50 percent of the time (e.g., if half of the candidates are qualified, but she makes hiring decisions by flipping a coin), her predictions if she uses the test instead will have an accuracy rate of greater than 70 percent. As we saw in Chapter 4, given the costs of training (and, when necessary, firing) employees, this difference could prove financially significant.

A more specific criterion of job performance is absenteeism. Obviously, if someone does not show up for work, he is not doing a very good job. Another, later meta-analysis by the same researchers examined twenty-eight studies with a total sample of 13,972 participants, and found the overall correlation between "integrity" test scores and absenteeism to be equivalent to a correlation of .33[3] (Ones, Viswesvaran, & Schmidt, 2003). To use the BESD yet again, this means that high scorers on this test would be in the more reliable half of employees about two thirds (or 67 percent) of the time.

The tests do less well at predicting employee theft, with a mean validity of .13 (about 58 percent accuracy as defined earlier). This may be an underestimate because theft is difficult to detect, so the criteria used in these studies may have been flawed. Still, Ones and coworkers concluded that so-called integrity tests are better viewed as broad measures of personality traits related to job performance, especially conscientiousness, than as narrow

---

[3] Actually, of course, this is a negative correlation. People with higher integrity scores have less absenteeism.

"I've been up all night drinking to prepare for this interview."

tests of honesty, and are impressively valid. Indeed, according to another review of the literature (which included 117 different studies), "conscientiousness showed consistent relations with all job performance criteria for all occupational groups" (Mount & Barrick, 1998, p. 849). This finding holds for both genders and even after controlling for age and years of education (Costa, 1996).

This finding not only gives employers a potentially useful tool, but has other implications as well. One surprising implication is that personality assessment could help alleviate the effects of bias in testing. It is well known that African Americans, as a group, score lower than white Americans on many so-called aptitude tests used by businesses to select employees. (Although a few psychologists believe this difference to be genetic, more believe it to be a by-product of discrimination in educational and social environments; see Sternberg, 1995.) The results of such tests can damage employment prospects and financial well-being, and lead to illegal and unwise discrimination. Tests of integrity, conscientiousness, and most other personality tests, however, typically do *not* show racial or ethnic differences (Sackett et al., 1989). Thus, if more employers could be persuaded to use personality tests instead of, or in addition to, ability tests, racial imbalance in hiring could be addressed without affecting productivity (Ones et al., 1993). The same lesson applies to college admissions. Conscientious students do very well in college, and the trait is a better predictor of academic success than either SAT scores or high school grade-point averages (Wagerman & Funder, 2007).

For many years, employers and organizational and educational psychologists have tried to find and measure the elusive "motivation" variable that distinguishes good workers and good students from poor ones. Perhaps it has been found. General conscientiousness might be not only a good predictor of job and school performance, but also a cause of excellence (F. L. Schmidt & Hunter, 1992). For example, highly conscientious employees seek out opportunities to learn about the company they work for, and to acquire skills and knowledge that go beyond their present job. As a

[handwritten margin note:] - integrity tests often do not show racial differences

[handwritten margin note:] - conscientiousness can be a predictor for greatness.

result, guess who gets promoted? Similarly, highly conscientious individuals tend to do well in interviews, not just because they present themselves well, but because they spend more time seeking information and preparing themselves before the interview begins (Caldwell & Burger, 1998). They do so well in advance—highly conscientious people tend not to procrastinate (D. C. Watson, 2001). And any student who has ever been assigned to a team to do a group project knows that one member—the most conscientious one—will probably wait a while for the others to do something, and then (sadly but effectively) end up doing most of the work herself.

Conscientiousness has a surprisingly wide range of implications beyond job performance. For example, economic theorists have long puzzled over the paradox that the people with the lowest risk are the ones most likely to buy insurance, when it would make more economic sense for high-risk people to do so. After all, who needs car insurance more than a reckless driver? Perhaps all is explained by conscientiousness: Highly conscientious people both avoid risks and seek to protect themselves just in case, so they are the ones who drive carefully *and* carry lots of insurance (Caplan, 2003).

Moreover, conscientious people live longer, and not just because they drive more carefully—though that surely helps (H. S.Friedman et al., 1993). A recent major analysis of 194 studies found that highly conscientious people are more likely to avoid many kinds of risky behavior as well as engage in activities that are good for their health (Bogg & Roberts, 2004). Conscientious people are less likely to smoke, overeat, or use alcohol to excess. They avoid violence, risky sex, and drug abuse. They are more likely to exercise regularly.

People with higher conscientiousness tend to accumulate more years in school even though the trait is uncorrelated with IQ (Barrick & Mount, 1991). This finding might imply that years of education can be used as a *marker variable*, or signal of conscientiousness. An employer might be wise to hire someone with more schooling, not necessarily because of what he has learned, but because a person who has completed—and survived!—many years of education is likely to be highly conscientious (Caplan, 2003, p. 399). Another implication is that if you are a college student or graduate, this just might be a sign that you will enjoy a long life—a cheerful thought.

Self-Monitoring

Mark Snyder, developer of the concept and test of self-monitoring, has long been interested in the relationships and discrepancies between the

TRY FOR YOURSELF 7.2

Personal Reaction Inventory

Instructions: The statements on this page concern your personal reactions to a number of different situations. No two statements are exactly alike, so consider each statement carefully before answering. If a statement is True or Mostly True as applied to you, circle the **T** next to the statement. If a statement is False or Usually Not True as applied to you, circle the **F** next to the statement.

T   F   1. I find it hard to imitate the behavior of other people.

T   F   2. My attitude is usually an expression of my true inner feelings, attitudes, and beliefs.

T   F   3. At parties and social gatherings, I do not attempt to do or say things that others will like.

T   F   4. I can only argue for ideas which I already believe.

T   F   5. I can make impromptu speeches even on topics about which I have almost no information.

T   F   6. I guess I put on a show to impress or entertain others.

T   F   7. When I am uncertain how to act in a social situation, I look to the behavior of others for cues.

T   F   8. I would probably make a good actor.

T   F   9. I rarely seek the advice of my friends to choose movies, books, or music.

T   F   10. I sometimes appear to others to be experiencing deeper emotions than I actually am.

T   F   11. I laugh more when I watch a comedy with others than when I am alone.

T   F   12. In a group of people I am rarely the center of attention.

T   F   13. In different situations and with different people, I often act like very different persons.

T   F   14. I am not particularly good at making other people like me.

T   F   15. Even if I am not enjoying myself, I often pretend to be having a good time.

T   F   16. I'm not always the person I appear to be.

T   F   17. I would not change my opinions (or the way I do things) in order to please someone else or win their favor.

T   F   18. I have considered being an entertainer.

T   F   19. In order to get along and be liked, I tend to be what people expect me to be rather than anything else.

T   F   20. I have never been good at games like charades or improvisational acting.

T   F   21. I have trouble changing my behavior to suit different people and different situations.

T   F   22. At a party I let others keep the jokes and stories going.

T   F   23. I feel a bit awkward in public and do not show up quite as well as I should.

T   F   24. I can look anyone in the eye and tell a lie with a straight face (if for a right end).

T   F   25. I may deceive people by being friendly when I really dislike them.

Note: Score one point for each answer that matches the key.
Key: 1-F, 2-F, 3-F, 4-F, 5-T, 6-T, 7-T, 8-T, 9-F, 10-T, 11-T, 12-F, 13-T, 14-F, 15-T, 16-T, 17-F, 18-T, 19-T, 20-F, 21-F, 22-F, 23-F, 24-T, 25-T.
Source: M. Snyder (1974), p. 531.

inner and outer selves. For example, a person might drink beer at a fraternity party because the situation calls for being a beer drinker, but the same person might be studious, serious, and intelligent in a research seminar because that is the kind of person this academic situation calls for. And yet inside, in her heart of hearts, this individual might be still another kind of person. Snyder theorized that the degree to which this is true varies across individuals. Some really do vary in their inner and outer selves and in how they perform in different settings. Snyder called these individuals "high self-monitors." Others are largely the same outside as they are inside, and do not vary much from one setting to another. Snyder called these individuals "low self-monitors" (M. Snyder, 1974, 1987).

Consider Try for Youself 7.2, which lists 25 items from a personality test that has been used widely for research purposes. Before reading beyond this paragraph, take a moment to respond True or False to these statements as they apply to you, and then calculate your score according to the key at the bottom of the box.

The list of statements you have just responded to is the original measure of self-monitoring; indeed, when it is administered, its standard title is the Personal Reaction Inventory. In samples of college students, the average score falls between 12 and 14. A score of 14 or more is interpreted as implying high self-monitoring; 12 or below implies low self-monitoring. (If your score is 13, I don't know what to tell you—in theory everybody is either "high" or "low.")

High self-monitors, according to Snyder, carefully survey every situation looking for cues as to the appropriate way to act, and then adjust their behavior accordingly. Low self-monitors, by contrast, tend to be more consistent regardless of the situation, because their behavior is guided more by their inner personality. As a result, one would expect a low self-monitor to be more judgable, in the sense discussed in Chapter 6, and a high self-monitor to be much less judgable (Colvin, 1993b).

Snyder has always been careful not to apply value judgments to high or low self-monitoring. One can say good or bad things about either. High self-monitors can be described as adaptable, flexible, popular, sensitive, and able to fit in wherever they go. They can be described just as accurately as wishy-washy, two-faced, lacking integrity, and slick. Low self-monitors, for their part, can be regarded as being self-directed, having integrity, and being consistent and honest. Or they can be described as insensitive, inflexible, and stubborn.

One nice thing about the self-monitoring scale is that you probably got the score you wanted. If the description of high self-monitors sounded better to you than the description of low self-monitors, the odds are very good that you are a high self-monitor. If you preferred the description of the low self-monitor, then probably you are one.

Research has demonstrated a number of ways in which high and low self-monitors differ. Some studies gathered descriptions of both kinds of people from those who know them well. In some of my own research (Funder & Harris, 1986), high self-monitors were more likely than low self-monitors to be described with Q-sort items such as the following:

high self monitors

- Skilled in social techniques of imaginative play, pretending, and humor (e.g., is good at the game charades)
- Talkative
- Self-dramatizing, histrionic (exaggerates emotion)
- Initiates humor
- Verbally fluent
- Expressive in face and gestures
- Having social poise and presence

Low self-monitors, by contrast, were more likely to be described as

low self monitors

- Distrustful
- Perfectionist
- Touchy and irritable
- Anxious
- Introspective
- Independent
- Feeling cheated and victimized by life

It is clear from these lists that high self-monitors are described more favorably and are more popular than low self-monitors. However, according to the construct, the difference arises because being positively regarded and popular is more important to high self-monitors. So although the description of low self-monitors might seem more negative, the low self-monitor probably doesn't care, finding other things such as independence more important.

A second kind of research borrows a leaf from the empiricists' book (recall Chapter 5) by comparing the self-monitoring scores of members of different criterion groups—groups that, according to the theory of self-monitoring, should score differently. For instance, Mark Snyder (1974) administered his scale to professional stage actors. Because their profession involves putting on the persona called for by a script, he expected them to score high on his scale—and they did. He also examined hospitalized mental patients, who typically are hospitalized because their behavior has been seen as inappropriate. Snyder expected them to get low scores on self-monitoring—and they did. (Please note: This does not mean that low self-monitors are mentally ill!)

Snyder also performed some interesting experiments. He asked his participants to read the following passage into a tape recorder: "I'm going out now, I won't be back all day. If anyone comes by, just tell them I'm not here." Each participant had to read this passage six times, each time trying to project a specific emotion—either happiness, sadness, anger, fear, disgust, or remorse—by using tone of voice, pitch, speed of talking, and so forth. (Try it yourself, right now—unless you are reading at the library.) It turns out to be easier to figure out which emotion is being projected when the reader is a high self-monitor (M. Snyder, 1974).

Studies have demonstrated relationships between self-monitoring scores and numerous other behaviors. For example, compared to low self-monitors, high self-monitors perform better in job interviews (Osborn, Feild, & Veres, 1998), place themselves in central positions in social networks (Mehra, Kilduff, & Brass, 2001), use more strategies to influence their coworkers (Caldwell & Burger, 1997), are willing to lie in order to get a date (Rowatt, Cunningham, & Druen, 1998), and even masturbate more often (Trivedi & Sabini, 1998).

Research also indicates that self-monitoring is related to the experience of emotion. In one study, men put on headphones and, while being shown a series of pictures of women, heard a tape of heartbeats that they were told (falsely) were their own. High self-monitors reported feeling most attracted to the women whose pictures they saw when they thought their hearts had sped up. Low self-monitors were less likely to be influenced by the bogus heart-rate feedback. In a second study, high self-monitors thought that

[handwritten margin note: laugh track experiment]

jokes were funnier when accompanied by a laugh track; low self-monitors were less prone to this effect (Graziano & Bryant, 1998). These findings imply that high self-monitors look to the environment for clues to how they are feeling, whereas low self-monitors are more prone to look within.

The concept of self-monitoring has raised some controversy. Critics have factor-analyzed the scale (see Chapter 5) and found that its items break into three separate factors (Briggs, Cheek, & Buss, 1980). One measures acting ability; one measures extraversion; and one measures "other directedness," a tendency to be concerned about what other people think. The appearance of the latter two factors could be viewed as a serious problem for the self-monitoring construct, because extraverts tend to use an aggressive, assertive style of getting along with others, whereas "other-directed" people try to get along by going along. These are opposite styles, and they may be mutually exclusive,[4] yet either kind of person could score high on self-monitoring. This possibility makes scores difficult to interpret. The controversy illustrates the important role that factor analysis plays in the development and interpretation of personality scales (Briggs & Cheek, 1986).

[handwritten margin note: scale factors 1) acting ability 2) extraversion 3) "other directedness" and concern for what others think. 2 and 3 can contradict]

The scale has since undergone further refinement. Mark Snyder recommended that the original 25-item scale be reduced to only 18 items (Gangestad & Snyder, 1985, 2000).[5] A series of complex analyses indicates that this abbreviated scale is a purer measure of the core idea behind self-monitoring: the degree to which behavior and emotion are controlled by the environment (high self-monitoring) or by the person (low self-monitoring).

[handwritten margin note: core idea of SM: degree to which behavior and emotion are controlled by environment (h) or person (L)]

THE MANY-TRAIT APPROACH

As we have seen, it can be highly informative to explore the implications of single traits in depth. However, a number of personality psychologists—including me—enjoy looking at many traits at once. Several lists of traits have been developed for this purpose (including Allport and Odbert's list of 17,953, which is a bit long for practical purposes; Allport & Odbert, 1936). My favorite is the list of 100 traits called the **California Q-Set** (Bem & Funder, 1978; J. Block, 1961/1978).

---

[4] When I once suggested this in class, a student came up afterward and said, "It is possible to get along *and* get ahead. I am the highest-selling saleswoman at Nordstrom's, and I am also by far the most popular!" All I could do was congratulate her.

[5] See Try for Yourself 7.2. The seven items Snyder now recommends omitting are 2, 7, 9, 10, 11, 15, and 19.

The California Q-Set

Maybe *trait* is not quite the right word for the items of the Q-set. The set consists of 100 phrases printed on separate cards. Each phrase describes an aspect of personality that might be important for characterizing a particular individual. The phrases are more complex than personality traits, which are usually expressed in single words. For example, Item 1 reads, "Is critical, skeptical, not easily impressed"; Item 2 reads, "Is a genuinely dependable and responsible person"; Item 3 reads, "Has a wide range of interests"; and so forth, for the remaining 97 items (see Table 7.1 for more examples).

   Both the way this list of items is used and its origin are rather unusual. Raters express judgments of personality by sorting the items into nine categories ranging from highly uncharacteristic of the person being described (Category 1) to highly characteristic (Category 9). Items neither character-

Table 7.1

SAMPLE ITEMS FROM THE CALIFORNIA Q-SET

1. Is critical, skeptical, not easily impressed
2. Is a genuinely dependable and responsible person
3. Has a wide range of interests
11. Is protective of those close to him or her
13. Is thin-skinned; sensitive to criticism or insult
18. Initiates humor
24. Prides self on being "objective," rational
26. Is productive; gets things done
28. Tends to arouse liking and acceptance
29. Is turned to for advice and reassurance
43. Is facially and/or gesturally expressive
51. Genuinely values intellectual and cognitive matters
54. Emphasizes being with others; gregarious
58. Enjoys sensuous experiences—including touch, taste, smell, physical contact
71. Has high aspiration level for self
75. Has a clear-cut, internally consistent personality
84. Is cheerful
98. Is verbally fluent
100. Does not vary roles; relates to everyone in the same way

Source: Adapted from J. Block (1961/1978), pp. 132–136.

(a)

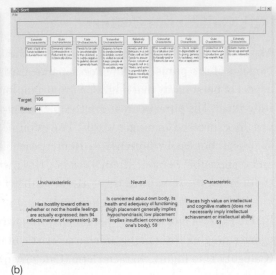

(b)

Figure 7.1 The California Q-Sort To describe an individual, the rater places the items of the Q-set into a symmetrical, forced distribution ranging from "highly uncharacteristic" (Category 1) to "highly characteristic" (Category 9). (a) This rater is in the process of laying the Q-set cards into the appropriate categories. (b) Recently, programs have become available to allow these ratings to be made on a computer screen rather than with paper cards (see, e.g., http://rap.ucr.edu/qsorter/).

[handwritten note left margin:] 5 of 100 are placed on each end (normal dist, forced)

[handwritten note left margin:] Adv Q data: — Compares all items directly vs. each other vs. relative comparison — only a few items can characterize the person

istic nor uncharacteristic are placed in or near Category 5. The distribution is forced, which means that a predetermined number of items must go into each category. The usual Q-set distribution is peaked, or "normal," meaning that most items are placed near the center and just a few (just 5 of the 100) can be placed on each end (see Figure 7.1).

The rater who does this sorting might be an acquaintance, a researcher, or a psychotherapist; in these cases the item placements constitute I data. Alternatively, a person might provide judgments of his own personality, in which case the item placements constitute S data. The most important advantage of Q-sorting[6] is that it forces the judge to compare all of the items directly against each other within one individual, rather than making a relative comparison across individuals. Furthermore, the judge is restricted to identifying only a few items as being important for characterizing a particular person. Nobody can be described as all good or all bad; there simply is not enough room to put all the good traits—or all the bad traits—into Categories 9 or 1. Finer and subtler discriminations must be made.

---

[6] A note on terms: A *Q-set* is a set of items (such as the 100 items of the California Q-Set) that a rater then sorts into categories in order to describe someone. A *Q-sort* is the resulting arrangement. And *Q-sorting* is the process of turning a Q-set into a Q-sort.

The items of the California Q-Set were not derived through factor analysis or any other formal, empirical procedure. Rather, a team of researchers and clinical practitioners developed a comprehensive set of terms sufficient to describe the people they interacted with every day (J. Block, 1961/1978). After formulating an initial list, the team met regularly to try to use the items to describe their clients and research participants. When an item proved useless or vague, they revised or eliminated it. When the set lacked an item that was necessary to describe a particular person, they wrote a new item. The resulting set of 100 items emerged after numerous such revisions and refinements. Later, other investigators further revised the Q-set so that its sometimes-technical phrasing could be understood and used by non-psychologists; this slightly reworded list is excerpted in Table 7.1 (Bem & Funder, 1978).

Delay of Gratification

One behavior that has been investigated frequently through the many-trait, Q-sort approach is delay of gratification. Delay is a classic topic for psychological research because denying oneself immediate pleasure for long-term gain seems opposed to basic human nature, yet it is also necessary for many important goals including holding a job, staying in school, and investing rather than spending money.

A particular line of research has focused on sex differences. It has long been known that males in our society are less prone to delay gratification than are females (J. H. Block, 1973; Maccoby, 1966). Why?

One study tried to answer this question using the many-trait approach (Funder, Block, & Block, 1983). One hundred and sixteen 4-year-old children (59 boys and 57 girls) were tested in two delay-of-gratification experiments. In one experiment, each child was shown a festively wrapped gift, promised after completing a puzzle. The gift was set down just within reach, and then the researchers measured how long the child was able to resist before reaching out and grabbing it. In the other experiment, the researcher told each child that he or she was forbidden to play with an attractive toy. The experimenters then left the room but secretly observed whether the child approached the toy anyway. The more the child moved toward playing with the forbidden toy, the lower the child's delay-of-gratification score. The two delay scores were then averaged and correlated with Q-sort personality descriptions obtained when the children were 3 years old (a year before the delay experiments were conducted), 4 years old (about the time the delay

Notes!
- consistant aspects of personality.

experiments were conducted), and years later, when the children were 7 and 11 years old. The results are shown in Tables 7.2 and 7.3.

These two tables can seem overwhelming at first glance, but please bear with me and take a few minutes to examine them closely. The perusal of tables of correlates like these is a crucial part of the work many personality psychologists do. The most important thing is not the exact correlations or the specific items. The trick is to look for general patterns. Which items are stable over time? What do those items mean? When Tables 7.2 and 7.3 are examined in this way, a couple of clear patterns emerge.

One pattern revealed by both tables is that the personality correlates of a behavior measured when the children were 4 years old could be detected

Table 7.2

CHILD Q-SORT CORRELATES OF DELAY OF GRATIFICATION: GIRLS

	Age at Personality Assessment			
Q-Set Item	3	4	7	11
Positive Correlates				
Appears to have high intellectual capacity	.27	.51	.27	.24
Is competent, skillful	.37	.28	.39	.19
Is planful; thinks ahead	.38	.28	.32	.16
Is attentive and able to concentrate	.19	.41	.43	.07
Develops genuine and close relationships	.18	.32	.35	.24
Is reflective; thinks before acting	.22	.30	.22	.29
Is resourceful	.37	.23	.18	.18
Uses and responds to reason	.13	.37	.28	.14
Negative Correlates				
Has transient interpersonal relationships	−.24	−.30	−.31	−.41
Is emotionally labile	−.39	−.24	−.43	−.07
Is victimized by other children	−.19	−.17	−.35	−.39
Tries to take advantage of others	−.04	−.23	−.33	−.44
Goes to pieces under stress	−.25	−.25	−.30	−.14
Seeks reassurance from others	−.02	−.39	−.12	−.29
Is easily offended	−.32	−.25	−.11	−.01
Tends to be sulky or whiny	−.30	−.26	−.02	−.09

Source: Adapted from Funder, Block, & Block (1983), p. 1203.

through personality assessments made one year earlier and as much as seven years later. This evidence, which some psychologists find surprising, indicates that many aspects of personality remain fairly consistent even throughout the rapid development and changes that occur during childhood.

Table 7.3

CHILD Q-SORT CORRELATES OF DELAY OF GRATIFICATION: BOYS

	Age at Personality Assessment			
Q-Set Item	3	4	7	11
Positive Correlates				
Is shy and reserved	.40	.36	.42	.51
Keeps thoughts and feelings to self	.41	.32	.35	.51
Is obedient and compliant	.24	.25	.53	.34
Prefers nonverbal communication	.26	.08	.47	.53
Is reflective; thinks before acting	.32	.34	.36	.30
Is inhibited and constricted	.38	.23	.25	.46
Withdraws under stress	.31	.41	.18	.42
Is indecisive and vacillating	.14	.35	.32	.45
Is physically cautious	.37	.21	.18	.39
Uses and responds to reason	.20	.22	.36	.19
Is fearful and anxious	.32	.02	.21	.35
Is planful; thinks ahead	.30	.26	.03	.22
Negative Correlates				
Is vital, energetic, lively	-.39	-.32	-.44	-.40
Tries to be the center of attention	-.37	-.23	-.39	-.46
Is physically active	-.34	-.15	-.51	-.29
Is self-assertive	-.25	-.21	-.36	-.45
Has rapid personal tempo	-.41	-.28	-.22	-.38
Characteristically stretches limits	-.28	-.16	-.43	-.31
Is emotionally expressive	-.34	-.20	-.36	-.29
Is talkative	-.23	-.10	-.35	-.47
Is curious and exploring	-.21	-.22	-.21	-.39
Is emotionally labile	-.38	-.07	-.39	-.12
Is unable to delay gratification	-.31	-.30	-.17	-.16
Is restless and fidgety	-.27	-.20	-.34	-.16

Source: Adapted from Funder, Block, & Block (1983), p. 1204.

[Handwritten margin note: M : F who wanted longest displayed ego control. —only Females also showed ego resiliency]

The second interesting facet of these tables is that the correlates of delay of gratification are both similar and different between the sexes. Girls and boys show a similar pattern in that those who are planful, reflective, reasonable, and not emotionally unstable (*labile* is the term on the tables) are likely to delay most in the experimental tests. However, girls who delay the most are also intelligent, competent, attentive, and resourceful—correlates missing among the boys. Boys who delay the most are also shy, quiet, compliant, and anxious—all correlates missing among the girls. This finding can be interpreted in terms of two broader personality attributes: **ego control** (sometimes called *self-control*, *impulse control*, or *inhibition*) and **ego resiliency** (similar to healthy psychological adjustment). In both sexes the children who delayed the longest had the highest levels of ego control, just as one would expect. But in the girls—and only in the girls—ego resiliency, or adjustment, was also related to delay. The boys who delayed the most, by contrast, varied in their level of adjustment. This difference may arise because in our society girls are taught that they must learn self-control and delay of gratification, whereas boys do not receive this lesson. The result is that the girls most able to absorb society's lessons—the well-adjusted, resilient ones—accordingly best absorb the lesson about delay and therefore manifest the behavior more. Since no such lesson is aimed at boys, their resiliency (adjustment) ends up being irrelevant, or even (especially by age 11) negatively correlated with their tendency to delay gratification (Funder, Block, & Block, 1983).

Drug Abuse

[Handwritten margin note: —individuals showed common warning signs almost a decade before hard drugs @ age 14]

Who is at risk to abuse drugs? One study looked at adolescents who were already using illegal drugs by age 14. These adolescents had been described with Q-sort items *nearly a decade earlier*, when they were small children, as being relatively restless and fidgety, emotionally unstable, disobedient, nervous, domineering, immature, aggressive, teasing, and susceptible to stress. These correlates imply that, regardless of the immediate effects of peer pressure and other external influences, the adolescents most likely to use drugs suffered from other significant problems that had been visible years earlier. This in turn implies that some of the effort to prevent drug abuse should be redirected away from campaigns such as "just say no" and other short-term interventions, and toward identifying and remedying the longer-term problems and the susceptibility to stress that underlie drug abuse (J. Block, Block, & Keyes, 1988; Shedler & Block, 1990; Walton & Roberts, 2004).

Depression

Depression is another common problem among young adults that turns out to have deep roots (J. Block, Gjerde, & Block, 1991). In one long-term study, young women who were seriously depressed at age 18 had been described as early as age 7 by such Q-sort items as "shy and reserved," "oversocialized," "self-punishing," and "overcontrolled." Young men who experienced depression at age 18 had been identified at age 7—and in some cases as early as age 3—as "unsocialized," "aggressive," and "undercontrolled." This pattern implies that women may be at risk for depression when they are overcontrolled and never venture outside of the limits society traditionally sets for them. For young men, the risk factor is undercontrol; unless they can control their emotions and behavior, they may get into trouble constantly and have difficulty finding a useful or comfortable niche in life. These findings show how society's different expectations for women and men can affect their psychological development and psychological health, and how such expectations can lead some personality traits to have opposite implications in the two sexes.

Political Orientation

An individual's political beliefs might be the last thing you would expect to be related to her childhood personality. Well, you would be wrong. The psychologists Jack and Jeanne Block assessed the personalities of a group of children in nursery school (J. Block & Block, 2006a, 2006b). Almost 20 years later, the same children, now grown up, completed a measure of their political beliefs. The measure included questions about abortion, welfare, national health insurance, rights of criminal suspects, and so forth. Each individual earned a score along a dimension from "liberal" to "conservative." This score that turned out to have a remarkable set of personality correlates. Children who grew into political conservatives were likely to have been described *almost 20 years earlier* as tending to feel guilty, as anxious in unpredictable environments, and as unable to handle stress well. Those who grew into liberals, by contrast, were more likely to have been described years earlier as resourceful, independent, self-reliant, and confident.

What do these findings mean? Drawing on some prior theoretical writings (including an article by Jost, Glaser, Kruglanski, & Sulloway, 2003, and work on the authoritarian personality described in the previous section of this chapter), the Blocks surmise that conservatism seems to be partially motivated by fear:

. . . Timorous conservatives of either gender will feel more comfortable and safer with already structured and predictable—therefore traditional—environments; they will tend to be resistant to change toward what might be self-threatening and forsaking of established modes of behavior; they will be attracted by and will tend to support decisive (if self-appointed) leaders who are presumed to have special and security-enhancing knowledge. (J. Block & Block, 2006a, p. 746)

Liberals, by contrast, are motivated more by what the Blocks call "under-control," a desire for a wide range of gratifications soon. They seek and enjoy the good life, which is perhaps why so many of them drive Volvos and sip excellent Chardonnays.[7] As a result,

Various justifications, not necessarily narrowly self-serving, will be confidently brought forward in support of alternative political principles oriented toward achieving a better life for all. Ironically, the sheer variety of changes and improvements suggested by the liberal-minded under-controller may explain the diffuseness, and subsequent ineffectiveness, of liberals in politics where a collective singlemindedness of purpose so often is required. (J. Block & Block, 2006a, p. 746)

The Blocks' subjects grew up in the San Francisco Bay area during the 1960s and 1970s, a time and place when political conservatism was an unusual and perhaps even shunned perspective, and where expressing conservative views might have been socially risky. Thus, these correlates might reflect a tendency to adhere to or oppose the dominant political perspective. If so, perhaps the same kind of study done in conservative regions such as Idaho or Utah in the early years of the 21st century might get the opposite results. But that study has not been done; indeed, longitudinal research like the Blocks'—wherein the same people are followed and measured repeatedly over extended periods of time—is still much too rare.

---

[7] This is my observation, not the Blocks'.

Recent research has seen an upsurge of interest in the study of the relationship between personality and political ideology, using methods including the Implicit Association Test (IAT, described in Chapter 5) and more conventional trait measures (Jost, Nosek, & Gosling, 2008). These studies show that, compared to conservatives, liberals are relatively likely to prefer change over stability, and progress over tradition. Liberals also are more likely to support using policies such as welfare and affirmative action to achieve social and economic equality, and have more favorable attitudes toward groups such as gays and members of ethnic minorities (Jost et al., 2008).

You might notice a common thread in the findings summarized so far. They echo, more or less faintly, the conclusion of much earlier work on the authoritarian personality, which is that there is something almost psychologically wrong about being conservative. While this might or might not be true, it is the sort of conclusion that ought to make a reader wary. Most psychologists are political liberals, and so have a built-in readiness to accept a conclusion like this. Would research done by a conservative psychologist—if you could find one—reach the same conclusion?

The psychologist Jonathan Haidt (who says he is *not* a conservative himself) has argued that, rather than focus on what is wrong with people on one side of the ideological divide, it might be more fruitful to understand how they favor different but equally defensible values (Haidt, 2008). He argues that both liberals and conservatives are likely to endorse values he calls *harm/care* (e.g., kindness, gentleness, nurturance) and *fairness/reciprocity* (justice, rights, and fair dealing). However, conservatives are also likely to strongly favor three other values that liberals regard as less important: *in-group loyalty* (taking care of members of one's own group and staying loyal), *authority/respect* (following the orders of legitimate leaders), and *purity* (living in a clean, moral way). These differences in values help to explain, for example, why conservatives get upset seeing someone burn an American flag, whereas liberals are more likely to wonder what the big deal is.

Haidt's argument provides a useful counterpoint to the usual assumption of political psychology, which sometimes comes close to treating conservatism as a pathology (Jost et al., 2003). But it is not clear how far it can go toward explaining findings such as the childhood predictors and adult personality correlates of adult conservativism summarized above, which remain data that need to be accounted for. The next few years promise to be an exciting time at the intersection of politics and personality, both because more data and theory are coming out of psychological research, and because rapidly changing events in the outside world[8] are altering the context in which we think about politics.

THE ESSENTIAL-TRAIT APPROACH

The 100 personality characteristics in the Q-sort are a lot, and a thorough survey of the literature of personality and clinical psychology would find measures of thousands of different traits. Recall Allport and Odbert's famous estimate of traits in the dictionary: 17,953. For a long time, psychologists have suspected that this is entirely too many. As I discussed in the first part of this chapter, some psychologists have been happy to work with a still-lengthy list of 100 personality characteristics. But several important efforts have been made over the years to dismantle the Tower of Babel of traits by reducing them to the ones deemed truly essential.

Reducing the Many to a Few: Theoretical and Factor Analytic Approaches

More than half a century ago, the psychologist Henry Murray (inventor of the Thematic Apperception Test described in Chapter 5) theorized that 20 traits—he called them *needs*—were essential for understanding personality (Murray, 1938). His list included needs for aggression, autonomy, exhibition, order, play, sex, and so on. Murray came up with this list theoretically—that is, by thinking about it.

Later, the psychologist Jack Block developed a theory that proposed just two essential characteristics of personality, called "ego resiliency" (or psychological adjustment) and "ego control" (or impulse control) (J. H. Block & Block, 1980; J. Block, 2002; Letzring, Block, & Funder, 2005). Note that these constructs were mentioned earlier in the chapter, in discussions of delay of gratification and of political orientation. A fundamental idea behind these constructs is the psychoanalytic—or Freudian (see Part IV)—concept that people constantly experience needs and impulses ranging from sexual drives, to the desire to eat doughnuts. Whatever the impulses are, they must be channeled or expressed somehow. *Overcontrolled* people (those high in the ego-control dimension) tend to inhibit these impulses,

_____

[8] By which I mean, the world outside the buildings that house university psychology departments.

while *undercontrolled* individuals (low in ego control) are more prone to act on them immediately. Is it better to be undercontrolled or overcontrolled? It depends on the situation—if nice things are safely available, you may as well take advantage of them, but if gratification is risky under the circumstances, self-control may be advisable. People high in Block's other personality dimension, ego resiliency, can adjust their level of control from high to low and back again as circumstances warrant. For example, an ego-resilient student might be able to study hard all week (and thus be temporarily overcontrolled), and then cut loose on the weekends (and become temporarily, but appropriately, undercontrolled). As Jack Block once remarked, "ego undercontrol gets you into trouble, but ego resiliency gets you out" (personal communication).

Another pioneer, Hans Eysenck, drew on biology to decide which aspects of personality were most important. In a time beginning in the 1940s, long before biological thinking began to widely influence personality psychology, he argued that the most important personality traits should be heritable— that is, passed on genetically from parents to children and shared among biological relatives (see Chapter 9)—and associated with particular aspects of physiology or brain functioning. Some aspects of Eysenck's system will be considered in Chapter 8, but for now we can note that most essential aspects of an individual's personality, in his conclusion, could be reduced to just three traits: *extraversion*, *neuroticism* (or "unstable emotionality"), and a trait he (rather confusingly) labeled *psychoticism*, which he saw as a blend of aggressiveness, creativity, and impulsiveness (H. J. Eysenck, 1947; S. B. G. Eysenck & Long, 1986). Extraverts like to be surrounded by people, activity, noise, and all sorts of stimulation. Introverts (the opposite of extraverts) prefer being solitary or around just a few close other people, and quieter settings where less is going on. People high in neuroticism are, in a word, worriers, and also tend to be irritable and easily upset by circumstances that would not faze more stable people. The psychoticism factor is the most puzzling one, and Eysenck admitted it was the least well established (H. J. Eysenck, 1986). People high in this trait are unorthodox and creative, and tend not to be sociable or empathic. The stereotype of the "mad artist"—who is wildly creative, self-indulgent, and inconsiderate to others—seems to be well described by this factor. However, the label might be poorly chosen, because people high in "psychoticism" are by no means necessarily psychotic.

More recently, the psychologist Auke Tellegen offered a related three-factor theory. Tellegen's Multidimensional Personality Questionnaire (MPQ; Tellegen, 1982; for a shorter version see Donnellan, Conger, & Burzette, 2005) is organized around three "superfactors" he calls *positive emotionality*,

Tellegen (on MPQ)
-positive emotionality
-negative emotionality
-constraint.
↳ better defined versions
of Eysenck

negative emotionality, and *constraint*. These three factors seem basically similar to Eysenck's.[9] However, Tellegen's terminology is a significant improvement. *Positive emotionality* is a more precise description of the first factor than *extraversion* because it describes the aspects of emotional experience that appear to be central to the trait. In a similar way, *negative emotionality* is a more precise label than *neuroticism* and also avoids implying that people high in this trait are neurotic (which in most cases they are not). Finally, even Eysenck admitted that *psychoticism* was a problematic label for the third factor; *unconstrained* is a more descriptive term that manages to avoid implying severe mental illness ("psychosis").

Eysenck and Tellegen both relied heavily on factor analysis (discussed in Chapter 5) to refine the definitions of their essential traits, and both are known for their contributions to this method. However, the most significant early proponent of using factor analysis to find the essential traits of personality was Raymond Cattell. He observed that the most important factors of personality ought to be found across different sources of data, and he developed a typology of data—including self-report, peer-report, and behavioral observations—that has become part of the foundation of the distinctions between S, I, L, and B data

....

Cattell had to borrow the basketball court at the University of Illinois to find a floor large enough to lay out all of his calculations.

....

Cattell
-16 traits, correlation
matrix
-called an "overextraction"
of factors.

presented in Chapter 2. He also pioneered the development of statistical techniques of factor analysis prior to the computer age. As discussed in Chapter 5, factor analysis involves correlating every measured variable with every other variable. The result is a *correlation matrix*. Correlation matrices can quickly get very large and, according to legend, Cattell had to borrow the basketball court at the University of Illinois to find a floor large enough to lay out all of his calculations.[10] Beginning with a large number of traits that he considered important, Cattell concluded that 16 traits were essential. These included "friendliness," "intelligence," "stability," "sensitivity," and "dominance," among others (Cattell & Eber, 1961). However, in recent years many psychologists have concluded that Cattell's work "was characterized by an *overextraction* of factors" (Wiggins & Trapnell, 1997, p. 743)—that is, 16 is probably too many for a list said to be fundamental. Moreover, while

---

[9] That is, Eysenck's factors of extraversion, neuroticism, and psychoticism have some resemblance to—though they are not exactly the same as—Tellegen's factors of positive emotionality, negative emotionality, and constraint, respectively.

[10] As you might expect, this cumbersome method appears to have led to some serious computational errors—which were not detected until years later (Digman & Takemoto-Chock, 1981).

psychologists admire Cattell's many statistical contributions, his "conceptual and methodological preferences are far from being universally shared" (Wiggins & Trapnell, 1997, p. 743), and, as one psychologist wrote, "it is difficult to avoid the conclusion that Cattell's lists of variables and factors primarily represent those traits that he himself considered the most important" (John, 1990, p. 71).

The Big Five and Beyond

DISCOVERY OF THE BIG FIVE

At present, the most widely accepted factor analytic solution to the problem of reducing the trait lexicon is also the one that has the deepest historical roots. The search for the solution began with a simple but profound idea: If something is important, then people will have invented a word for it. For example, over the course of history people have observed water falling from the sky and found it useful to be able to talk about it; the word *rain* (and its equivalents in every other language) was invented. But that's not all: Water from the sky is so important that people also developed words for different forms, including sleet, drizzle, hail, and snow. The **lexical hypothesis** (e.g., Goldberg, 1981) is that the important aspects of human life will be labeled with words, and furthermore that if something is truly important and universal, many words for it will exist in all languages.

　　This hypothesis provides a unique route for finding which personality traits are the most important. Which ones have the largest number of relevant words, and which ones are the most universal across languages? In principle, answering this question is rather straightforward, but psychologists have been working on it for more than 60 years (John & Srivastava, 1999). As Gordon Allport observed, after cataloging (with Henry Odbert's help) almost 18,000 personality-descriptive English words, finding the essential needles in that haystack could be the work of a lifetime. He was right: Allport started the project by identifying about 4,500 words (still a lot) that he thought were particularly good descriptors of personality traits. Raymond Cattell selected from that list 35 traits he thought were particularly important and focused his analyses on those. Donald Fiske (1949) chose 22 traits from Cattell's list that Fiske then used in studies that analyzed self-ratings along with ratings by peers and by psychologists. Fiske's analyses found five factors that may have been the first emergence of the list now known as the Big Five. Later, a team of two psychologists examined data

[handwritten margin notes:] ∴ which traits are most important?

18,000 personality descriptive english words.

from eight different samples, including graduate students and Air Force personnel; they, too, found the same five basic factors (Tupes & Christal, 1961). While the basis of the traits found in these early studies was questionable at first, the Big Five have been found again and again over the years, using many different lists of traits and a wide range of samples of people (e.g., Saucier & Goldberg, 1996).[11]

In recent years, work on the Big Five has become a major focus of personality research. One reason is that when personality tests—not just words in the dictionary—are factor analyzed, a common finding is that they, too, tend to fall into groups defined by the Big Five (e.g., McCrae & Costa, 1987). These include the other lists of basic traits discussed earlier—Eysenck's three, Tellegen's three, and Cattell's sixteen traits, among others, can be described in terms of one or more of the Big Five (John & Srivastava, 1999). As a result, the Big Five can be viewed as an integration rather than an opponent of these other systems (Saucier & Goldberg, 2003).

IMPLICATIONS OF THE BIG FIVE

Although some researchers have suggested that the Big Five be referred to by Roman numerals I–V (see John, 1990), the most common labels are *neuroticism*, *extraversion*, *agreeableness*, *conscientiousness*, and *openness* (or *intellect*); the labels vary somewhat from one investigator to the next. One idea behind the way these five basic factors are used is that they are *orthogonal*, which means that getting a high or low score on any one of these traits does not determine whether a person will get a high or low score on any of the others. That property makes this short list of traits useful because, together, they cover a wide swath that can summarize much of what any test can measure about personality. See Table 7.4. As part of the research summarized earlier in this chapter, Ones and coworkers integrated numerous, widely varying tests of "integrity" by relating them to measures of the Big Five traits of conscientiousness, agreeableness, and (low) neuroticism, and thereby brought order to a previously confusing field of research. We also saw, in Chapter 4, how the Big Five are useful in compiling lists of outcomes associated with personality, because they can bring a large number of otherwise divergent traits together under a few common labels (see Table 4.2).

---

[11] You can take one of the most widely used measures, the Big Five Inventory (John, Donahue, & Kentle, 1991), online, for free, at http://www.outofservice.com/bigfive/.

Table 7.4

TRAITS ASSOCIATED WITH EACH OF THE BIG FIVE

Extraversion	Agreeableness	Conscientiousness	Neuroticism	Openness/Intellect
Positive Correlates				
Talkative	Sympathetic	Organized	Tense	Wide interests
Assertive	Kind	Thorough	Anxious	Imaginative
Energetic	Appreciative	Planful	Nervous	Intelligent
Outgoing	Affectionate	Efficient	Moody	Insightful
Dominant	Softhearted	Responsible	Worrying	Curious
Enthusiastic	Warm		Touchy	Sophisticated
Negative Correlates				
Quiet	Fault-finding	Careless	Stable	Commonplace
Reserved	Cold	Disorderly	Calm	Narrow interests
Shy	Unfriendly	Frivolous	Contented	Simple
Silent	Quarrelsome	Irresponsible	Unemotional	Shallow
Withdrawn	Hard-hearted	Slipshod		Unintelligent

Note: These items were correlated with total factor scores in ratings by psychologists of 140 men and 140 women studied at the University of California, Berkeley.

Source: Adapted from John & Srivastava (1999), Table 2, p. 113.

Still, the Big Five are not quite as simple as they may seem; their commonplace labels hide a good deal of complexity. As researchers Gerard Saucier and Lewis Goldberg have written, "a broad factor [like one of the Big Five] is not so much one thing as a collection of many things that have something in common" (2003, p. 14). So, although the labels are useful, they are also necessarily oversimplified and potentially misleading (which is precisely why some psychologists have suggested using Roman numerals instead). With that in mind, let's give each of the Big Five—except for conscientiousness, considered earlier in this chapter—a brief look under the hood.

Extraversion   *Extraversion* commonly refers to being sociable and outgoing, but in the Big Five it encompasses much more than that, including traits such as "active," "outspoken," "dominant," "forceful," "adventurous," and even "spunky" (John & Srivastava, 1999). It is a trait that shows up in just about every broad-based personality inventory, including Cattell's

(handwritten margin notes:)
- risk taking unreliable
- popular
- cheerful, upbeat

Based on emotions extraverts experience; even w a held amt of social activity, extraverts still had a higher happiness correlation
- more successful attractive

16PF, Tellegen's MPQ, Douglas Jackson's Personality Research Form (PRF), Gough's CPI, and the MMPI (D. Watson & Clark, 1997). Still, psychologists have sometimes viewed extraversion in different ways. Some regard extraverts as impulsive, risk taking, and unreliable (e.g., H. J. Eysenck & Eysenck, 1975). Others view them as cheerful, upbeat, and optimistic (Costa & McCrae, 1985). Still other psychologists describe extraverts as ambitious, hardworking, and achievement oriented (Hogan, 1983; Tellegen, 1985; see D. Watson & Clark, 1997, p. 769). Extraverts are prone to make moral judgments that hold people responsible for the effects of their actions, even if the effects were unintentional (Cokely & Feltz, 2009). Both male and female extraverts achieve higher status (C. Anderson, John, Keltner, & Kring, 2001). Extraverts are consistently rated as more popular (e.g., Jensen-Campbell et al., 2002) and more physically attractive than introverts (they also exercise more); this may be why they attend more parties, where incidentally they drink more alcohol (Paunonen, 2003). But they had better be careful, because research also shows that extraverts are more likely to be on the receiving end of attempts to steal them away from their steady romantic partners (Schmitt & Buss, 2001). Some of these attempts at "mate poaching" (as the researchers call it) occur at parties, where drinking is involved.

The psychologists David Watson and LeeAnna Clark argue that the best way to conceive of extraversion is in terms of the positive emotions that extraverts tend to experience (Watson & Clark, 1997). This propensity is what causes them to be energetic, effective, engaged, sociable, and ambitious. Is this because extraverts are more sociable and their social activity makes them happy, or is it because extraversion has a direct, perhaps even biological, connection with positive emotions? One recent study suggests the latter: Even when the amount of social activity was (statistically) held constant, extraversion still correlated with happiness (Lucas, Le, & Dyrenforth, 2008).

Put all the aspects of extraversion together, and they produce several important life outcomes. According to the research summary by Daniel Ozer and Verónica Benet-Martínez (2006), extraverts are more likely than introverts to be happy, long-lived, healthy—and grateful (see Table 4.2). They have more success in dating and relationships, and are viewed as more attractive. They are more satisfied with their jobs, more involved in their communities, and more likely to attain positions of leadership.

Neuroticism   Another Big Five trait with wide implications is neuroticism. Persons who score high on this trait tend to use ineffective means for dealing with problems in their lives and have stronger negative reactions to stressful events (Bolger & Zuckerman, 1995; Ferguson, 2001). They are particularly sensitive to any kind of social threat, such as indications that other people do not accept or support them (Denissen & Penke, 2008).

It turns out that numerous questionnaires intended to assess happiness, well-being, and physical health correlate strongly (and negatively) with neuroticism (also called negative emotionality). The higher the level of neuroticism, the more likely people are to report being unhappy, anxious, and even physically sick (McCrae & Costa, 1991; D. Watson & Clark, 1984). This finding implies that many of these instruments, despite their different intentions and titles, may be to some degree measuring the same underlying tendency. Some people (those scoring high on neuroticism) complain a lot about nearly everything; others (those low in neuroticism) complain less.

Because it correlates with so many other measures of unhappiness, anxiety, and other indicators of psychological difficulty, neuroticism appears to capture a general tendency toward psychopathology. In the long run, this tendency may make someone scoring high on neuroticism at risk for developing a serious mental illness. In the short run, it can make a person vulnerable in other ways. For example, people scoring high on neuroticism are not especially likely to have people try to "poach" them away from their romantic partners. But if someone does, they are less likely to resist (Schmitt & Buss, 2001).

Not surprisingly, neuroticism is associated with several undesirable life outcomes (Ozer & Benet-Martínez, 2006). People who score high on this trait are more likely to be unhappy and to cope poorly with the stresses of life, to have problems in their family relationships, to be dissatisfied with their jobs, and even to engage in criminal behavior. This last finding requires a reminder of how to interpret correlations such as those summarized in this chapter: Most neurotics are not criminals! However, people who score high on measures of neuroticism are *more* likely to engage in criminal behavior than people who score lower. It is this kind of relative likelihood that is reflected by correlations between traits and life outcomes.

Agreeableness   This dimension of the Big Five has carried a number of labels over the years including *conformity*, *friendly compliance*, *likeability*, *warmth*, and even *love* (Graziano & Eisenberg, 1997). Hogan (1983) suggests that this trait is associated with a tendency to be cooperative, an essential behavior in the small social groups in which human beings evolved. Thus, the emergence of the term *agreeableness*—or roughly synonymous terms—

women > men

agreeable children are less vulnerable

- religious activity
- sense of humor
- well adjusted
- peer / partner acceptance

→ most controversial
→ generally, but not always, viewed as intelligent

may reflect how important it is for people to get along and work together. People are highly attentive to this trait in others, and tend to agree with each other about who in their social circle is easy to get along with—in other words, who is agreeable (Graziano & Eisenberg, 1997). Agreeable people smoke less than disagreeable people do (for some unknown reason), and women tend to score higher on this trait than men (Paunonen, 2003). Agreeableness has its limits. When agreeable people who are married or in committed relationships are approached by somebody attempting to entice them into an affair, they are likely to successfully resist (Schmitt & Buss, 2001).

Agreeableness can make children less vulnerable. One study examined children who had "internalizing problems," which meant that other children described them using phrases such as "on the playground, she/he just stands around," "she/he is afraid to do things," "she/he seems unhappy and looks sad often," and "when other kids are playing, she/he watches them but doesn't join in" (Jensen-Campbell et al., 2002, p. 236). In general, this pattern described children who tended to be victims of bullying, but *not* if they were also agreeable! Similarly, children who were physically weak or otherwise lacked social skills managed to avoid being bullied if they were high in agreeableness. Apparently, a friendly and nonconfrontational outlook can help protect you from abuse—but it won't win you social status. For that, extraversion is necessary too (Anderson et al., 2001). Research has not yet addressed whether these findings apply to college students or older adults. Do you think they would?

An individual's degree of agreeableness predicts a large number of life outcomes (Ozer & Benet-Martínez, 2006). People high in this trait are more likely to be involved in religious activities, have a good sense of humor, be psychologically well adjusted, and have a healthy heart. They enjoy more peer acceptance and dating satisfaction, have a large number of social interests, and are unlikely to engage in criminal behavior. Clearly, it is important—and usually beneficial—to be easy to get along with.

Openness to Experience (Intellect)   *Openness to experience*, sometimes called *intellect*, is the most controversial of the Big Five, as is perhaps revealed by the fact that I felt obligated to label this paragraph with two different terms. People scoring high on openness are viewed by others who know them as creative, imaginative, open-minded, and clever. They are more prone than most people to be politically liberal, to use drugs, and to play a musical instrument (Ozer & Benet-Martínez, 2006; Paunonen, 2003). But, as the prominent Big Five researchers Robert McCrae and Paul Costa have written, "the concept of Openness appears to be unusually difficult to grasp" (1997, p. 826). This difficulty arises in part because researchers think of this trait differently: Some view it as reflecting a person's approach to intellectual matters or even her basic level of intelligence. Others see it as a result of the degree to which one has been taught to value cultural matters such as literature, art, and music. Still others see it as a basic dimension of personality that underlies creativity and perceptiveness. Another reason this dimension is controversial is that, among the Big Five, it has the spottiest record of replication across different samples and different cultures (John & Srivastava, 1999). This last trait may not be as broadly applicable as the others.

Still, it is an interesting dimension. McCrae and Costa (1997) argue that people can score high on openness to experience *without* necessarily being "cultured" in their education and background, and even without being particularly intelligent! Being open-minded does not mean you are right, and it sometimes implies the reverse. College students higher in openness to experience are more likely to believe in dubious phenomena such as UFOs, astrology, and the existence of ghosts (Epstein & Meier, 1989). At the same time, persons high in this trait are described as imaginative, intelligent original, curious, artistic, inventive, and witty, and they are unlikely to be viewed as simple, shallow, or unintelligent (see Table 7.4). So McCrae and Costa (1997) may be correct that you don't have to be intelligent to be open to experience, but people high in openness are generally viewed as intelligent. People high in openness to experience are more likely to report having artistic interests and being politically liberal (Ozer & Benet-Martínez, 2006). They also report more substance abuse and a tendency to feel "inspired"—I won't comment on any possible connection between these last two findings.

UNIVERSALITY OF THE BIG FIVE

One prominent researcher believes that the Big Five may correspond to five essential, universal questions people need to ask about a stranger they are about to meet:

(1) Is X active and dominant or passive and submissive (Can I bully X or will X try to bully me)? [This question corresponds to extraversion.] (2) Is X agreeable (warm and pleasant) or disagreeable (cold and distant)? [agreeableness] (3) Can I count on X (Is X responsible and conscientious or undependable and negligent)? [conscientiousness] (4) Is X crazy (unpredictable) or sane (stable)? [neuroticism] (5) Is X smart or dumb (How easy will it be for me to teach X)?

[openness, or intellect] Are these universal questions? (Goldberg, 1981, p. 161)

Maybe they are. Several attempts have been made to see whether the Big Five can be found outside American and European cultures and in languages other than English. As was mentioned above, the appearance of the Big Five across different languages would be powerful evidence that they are fundamental attributes of personality. The results so far have been mostly encouraging. Personality questionnaires translated into various languages have yielded at least four of the five factors (all except openness) in the Philippines (Guthrie & Bennett, 1971), Japan (Bond, Nakazato, & Shiraishi, 1975), and Hong Kong (Bond, 1979). All five factors appeared when the questionnaires were translated into German (Ostendorf & Angleitner, 1994), Hebrew (Montag & Levin, 1994), Chinese (McCrae, Costa, & Yik, 1996), Korean (Piedmont & Chae, 1997), and Turkish (Somer & Goldberg, 1999).

An even more ambitious study moved beyond translating questionnaires and began with an analysis of the Chinese language to find the terms commonly used to describe personality in that culture (Yang & Bond, 1990). An analysis of personality descriptions by residents of Taiwan yielded five factors labeled *social orientation*, *competence*, *expressiveness*, *self-control*, and *optimism*. While the Chinese five factors seemed to overlap to some degree with the English five factors (e.g., expressiveness in the Chinese solution seems similar to extraversion in the English solution), there wasn't a one-to-one correspondence across the entire list. The researchers concluded that the central attributes of personality are similar to an important degree, yet are also different from one culture to another (see Chapter 14 for a discussion of cross-cultural issues). This conclusion seems rather vague, but it is probably the only reasonable one under the circumstances.[12]

There is a different sense in which the Big Five are not universal, which is that the average scores on these traits may vary by geographic region (Florida, 2008). A recent national survey in the United States found that highly agreeable people are more likely to be found in the eastern half of the country than in the western half, that people in the southwestern states are unusually conscientious, and that openness to experience is highest in areas near New York City, Los Angeles, San Francisco, and Miami (see Fig-

---

[12]This is another manifestation of Funder's Third Law, which I would interpret here as implying that you do what you can with what you have.

ure 7.2). Why do you think this might be? Around the world, sex differences vary geographically as well. While, in general, women score higher than men on neuroticism, extraversion, agreeableness, and conscientiousness, these differences tend to be larger in wealthier, more developed nations (Schmitt, Realo, Voracek, & Allik, 2008).

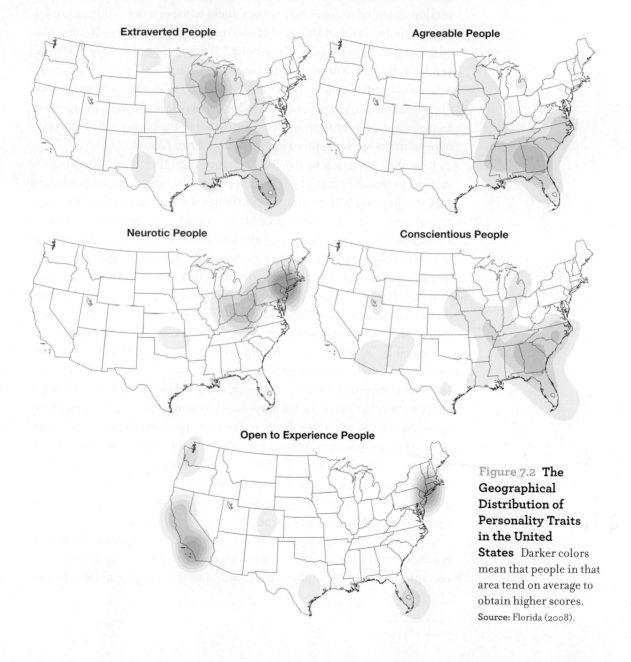

Figure 7.2 **The Geographical Distribution of Personality Traits in the United States** Darker colors mean that people in that area tend on average to obtain higher scores.

Source: Florida (2008).

BEYOND THE BIG FIVE

Although the Big Five have proved useful, they also remain controversial (J. Block, 1995). One issue is that the Big Five correlate with each other to some degree. People who score low on neuroticism tend to score high on agreeableness and conscientiousness, and people who score high on extraversion also tend to score high on openness to experience (Digman, 1997). The psychologist Colin DeYoung (2006) calls the first of these factors "stability" and the second factor "plasticity." Big Five advocate Robert McCrae and his colleagues interpret these factors as arising from raters' tendencies to see socially desirable traits as going together, rather than as meaning that the five traits can be reduced to two (McCrae et al., 2008). So an argument has arisen—and is far from settled—as to whether the biologically based core of personality can be reduced from five to just two factors.

Another objection to the Big Five goes the other direction: There is more to personality than just five traits. Even advocates have acknowledged that the list may not encompass attributes such as sensuality, frugality, humor, and cunning (Saucier & Goldberg, 1998). The psychologists Sampo Paunonen and Douglas Jackson performed factor analyses aimed at the part of personality missed by the Big Five, which produced 10 additional factors including seductiveness, manipulativeness, integrity, and religiosity (Paunonen & Jackson, 2000). Studies conducted in several languages suggest that a sixth factor called "honesty-humility" should be added (Ashton & Lee, 2005), and further analyses suggest that many traits Paunonen and Jackson identified as "missing" from the Big Five can be included under this label (K. Lee, Ogunfowora, & Ashton, 2005). For example, highly religious people tend to score high on honesty-humility, whereas manipulative people score low. On the other hand, the honesty-humility dimension correlates with the agreeableness factor of the Big Five (honest and humble people are more agreeable), so we can look forward to years of debate as to whether the Big Five has to be expanded to a Big Six.[13] Actually, the proposed label is not Big Six, but rather HEXACO, which stands for honesty-humility (H), emotionality (E), extraversion (X), agreeableness (A), conscientiousness (C), and openness (O) (K. Lee & Ashton, 2004).

A further issue concerns the degree to which broad traits at the level of the Big Five (or six) are sufficient for conceptual understanding. For example, one could summarize "authoritarianism," discussed earlier in this chapter,

---

[13] Won't that be fun.

as a combination of high neuroticism, high conscientiousness, low openness, and low agreeableness, but that summary seems to miss the essence of the construct. It fails to account for authoritarians' tendency to be deferential and agreeable with those of higher rank but mean and nasty to those of lower rank, and it says nothing about their psychodynamic motivations. Similarly, self-monitoring could be recast as a combination of high extraversion and high agreeableness, but that summary also seems insufficient to describe the psychological processes characteristic of high self-monitors.

Because the Big Five traits keep popping up no matter what measures are used or which populations are studied, some psychologists consider these traits to comprise the essential "structure" of personality. But, as Costa and McCrae noted,

> The organization of specific traits into broad factors [such as the Big Five] is traditionally called the *structure of personality*, although it refers to the structure of traits in a population, not in an individual. (Costa & McCrae, 1998, pp. 107–108)

In other words, the Big Five are types of traits, not of people. Are there types of people, and can their distinct personality structures be characterized? That is the next question we shall consider.

TYPOLOGICAL APPROACHES TO PERSONALITY

Over the years of successfully applying the three trait approaches, some psychologists have occasionally expressed misgivings about the whole enterprise. First, as just noted, the structure of personality traits across many individuals is not the same thing as the structure of personality as it resides *within* a person, and it seems a little strange to call the former the "structure of personality" (Cervone, 2005). Second, it is at least possible that important differences between people are not just quantitative but qualitative. The trait approach usually assumes that all people can be characterized on a common scale. You might score high on extraversion and I might score low, but we are compared on the same scale. But what if some differences between people are matters not of degree but of kind? If your extraversion is fundamentally different from my shyness, then to summarize this difference by comparing our extraversion scores might be a little like comparing

[handwritten margin notes:] Misgivings of trait approach 1) structure of personality does not consider the traits within a person └ only across people 2) differences are relative (not qualitative) — fundamental differences

"As an orange, how much experience have you had working with apples?"

apples to oranges by giving both of them scores in "appleness" and concluding that oranges score lower.

Of course, it is one thing to raise doubts like these and quite another to say what the essential types of people really are. To typify all individuals, one must "carve nature at its joints" (as Plato reportedly said). Just as an expert turkey carver, by knowing where to cut, can give all the guests a nice, clean piece of breast or a neatly separated drumstick, a scientist must find the exact dividing lines that distinguish one type of person from another in order for these types to be clearly identified. The further challenge is to show that these divisions are not just a matter of degree, that different types of people are qualitatively—rather than quantitatively—distinct. Repeated attempts at this carving did not achieve notable success over the years, leading one review to summarize the literature on personality types in the following manner:

> Muhammad Ali was reputed to offer this typology: People come in four types, the pomegranate (hard on the outside, hard on the inside), the walnut (hard-soft), the prune (soft-hard), and the grape (soft-soft). As typologies go, it's not bad—certainly there is no empirical reason to think it any worse than those we may be tempted to take more seriously. (Mendelsohn, Weiss, & Feimer, 1982, p. 1169)

Nonetheless, interest in typological conceptions of personality has revived in the past decade or so (Kagan, 1994; Robins, John, & Caspi, 1998). For example, Mark Snyder and his colleague Steve Gangestad proposed that self-monitoring, considered earlier in this chapter, is actually a type (Gangestad & Snyder, 1985, 2000). They suggested that people do not differ from one another in how high or low they are across the spectrum of self-monitoring; rather, people fall into one of two types: high or low self-monitors. Your score, in their interpretation, does not reflect the *degree* to which this construct describes you, but rather the *probability* that you are a high self-monitor. The higher your score, the more likely this is. Regardless whether Gangestad and Snyder's interpretation is correct, this particular typology is relatively limited. The real challenge of the typological approach is to come up with basic types of people that characterize the whole range of personality.

Avshalom Caspi (1998) reported some surprising progress in this direction. He surveyed several attempts to find the basic types of people. In each study he examined, psychologists correlated whole descriptions of people with each other. For example, J. Block (1971) used the 100 items of the Q-set described earlier in this chapter. He compared each person in his sample to every other person by correlating the 100 scores that characterized each individual. He then examined the subgroups of people who resembled each other the most and gave them labels. Block identified five personality types among male participants. *Ego resilients* were well adjusted and interpersonally effective; *vulnerable overcontrollers* were rigid, uptight, and maladjusted; *unsettled overcontrollers* were impulsive and antisocial; *belated adjusters* were maladjusted during childhood but functioning effectively in adulthood; and *anomic extraverts* were well adjusted in childhood but maladjusted as adults.

This is an interesting typology, but as Caspi noted, it was found only among males who were almost all white, intelligent, and relatively affluent. So we would want to look at other studies to see if this typology holds up across other kinds of populations. It turns out that across seven different studies with diverse participants all over the world, three types out of the five identified by Block show up again and again. The basic results of this review are summarized in Table 7.5. The terms used by specific researchers to summarize their results have varied, but underneath, the three types seem to be the same.

One of the types (denoted Type I in Table 7.5) is the *well-adjusted* person, who is adaptable, flexible, resourceful, and interpersonally successful. Then there are two maladjusted types: The *maladjusted overcontrolling* person (Type II) is too uptight for his own good, denying himself pleasure needlessly, and being difficult to deal with at an interpersonal level. The *maladjusted undercontrolling* person (Type III) has the reverse problem. She is too impulsive, prone to be involved in activities such as crime and unsafe sex, and tends to wreak general havoc on other people and herself.

These types have received wide attention by researchers and have been found repeatedly in samples of participants in North America and Europe (e.g., Asendorpf & van Aken, 1999; Asendorpf, Borkenau, Ostendorf, & van Aken, 2001). But recent work has also limited the conclusions about these and other personality types in an important way. When thinking about personality types, one should keep two questions in mind. The first is, are different types of people, as identified by the typological approach, qualitatively and not just quantitatively different from each other? That is, are they different from each other in ways that conventional trait measurements cannot capture? The possibility that this is the case—the apples-versus-oranges issue—was one basis of the sudden renewed excitement about personality types. However, the answer to this question has turned out to be no. The latest evidence indicates that knowing a person's personality type adds nothing to the ability to predict his behavior, beyond what can be done using the traits that define the typology (Costa, Herbst, McCrae, Samuels, & Ozer, 2002; McCrae, Terracciano, Costa, & Ozer, 2006).

This finding is a blow to the typological approach, but a second question still remains: Is it useful to think about people in terms of personality types? The answer to this question may be yes (Asendorpf, 2002; Costa et al., 2002). Each personality type serves as a summary of how a person stands on a large number of personality traits. The adjusted, overcontrolled, and undercontrolled patterns in the typology described earlier are rich portraits that make it easy to think about how the traits within each type tend to be found together, and how they interact. In the same way, thinking of people in terms of whether they are "military types," "rebellious student types," or "hassled suburban soccer mom types" brings to mind an array of traits in each case that would be cumbersome, though not impossible, to summarize

Table 7.5

SEVEN VIEWS OF THE THREE BASIC TYPES OF PERSONALITY

Types	J. Block (1971)	Klohnen & Block (1995)	Robins et al. (1996)	Van Lieshout et al. (1994)	York & John (1992)	Caspi & Silva (1995)	Pulkkinen (1995)
I	Ego resilients	Resilients	Resilients	Resilients	Individuated	Well-adjusted	Resilient/individuated
II	Vulnerable over-controllers	Over-controllers	Over-controllers	Over-controllers	Traditional	Inhibited	Introverts/anxious
III	Unsettled under-controllers	Under-controllers	Under-controllers	Under-controllers	Conflicted	Under-controlled	Conflicted/under-controlled

Source: Adapted from Caspi (1998).

in terms of ratings on each dimension. Advertisers and political consultants, in particular, often design their campaigns to appeal to specific types of people. For this reason, it has been suggested that types may be useful in the way they summarize "many traits in a single label" (Costa et al., 2002, p. 573) and make it easier to think about psychological dynamics. Even though types may not add much for conventional psychometric measurement and prediction, they still may have value as aids in education and in theorizing.

PERSONALITY DEVELOPMENT OVER THE LIFE SPAN

Where does personality come from? Where does it go? These questions of **personality development** concern the origins of personality, and the degree to which it is stable or changeable from childhood through old age. The short answer to the first question is that personality traits develop from a combination of genetic factors and early experience, as will be discussed in detail in Chapter 8. The short answer to the second question is that personality just keeps developing, as a function of physical and psychological maturation, and the different experiences and challenges that characterize different periods of the life span.

This second question is interesting because it concerns the degree to which people are psychologically the same throughout life. Do personalities change from childhood to adolescence, adolescence to young adulthood, and adulthood to old age? The research literature has two clear answers to this question: no and yes.

No, personality does not change much, in the sense that people show a strong tendency to maintain their individual differences throughout life. A child who is more extraverted than most children is likely, when she gets older, to be more extraverted than most other adolescents, than most other adults, and finally, when the time comes, than most fellow residents of the Golden Acres Retirement Home. Likewise, a child who is either more or less neurotic, agreeable, conscientious, or open than his peers is likely to maintain this distinction throughout life, too (Costa & McCrae, 1994). As we saw earlier in this chapter, it is even possible to predict outcomes later in life on the basis of ratings of personality in childhood. For example, 4- to 6-year-old children rated as "more inhibited" than most of their peers were slower to find a stable romantic partner and slower to find a first job 19 years later (Asendorpf, Denissen, & van Aken, 2008).

Psychologists call this *rank-order consistency*, or the stability of individual differences. According to a major summary of the literature, the correlation coefficient (see Chapter 3) reflecting consistency of individual differences in personality was .31 across childhood, .54 during the college years, and .74 between the ages of 50 and 70 (Roberts & DelVecchio, 2000). While all three figures indicate impressive stability, it does appear that individual differences in personality become more consistent as one gets older. This conclusion has been called the *cumulative continuity principle*, which asserts not only that personality traits are consistent across the life span, but that consistency increases with the passing years (Roberts, Wood, & Caspi, 2008).

The other answer—that yes, personality does change—emerges from analyses of a different kind of stability. At each age, it is possible to calculate the mean level of various personality traits to see whether people change as they get older. This is an entirely different issue than the stability of individual differences. For illustration, imagine that three young children had mean agreeableness scores of 20, 40, and 60 (on whatever test was being used), but when they were measured again later, as young adults, their scores were 40, 60, and 80, respectively. Notice that their rank-order consistency is perfect—the correlation between the two sets of scores is $r = 1.0$. But each individual's agreeableness score has increased by 20 points. So, at the same time, they are showing high rank-order consistency *and* a strong increase in their mean level of the trait.

One recent analysis based on Internet surveys of more than 130,00 respondents in North America found that people at different ages do show different levels of the Big Five personality traits (Srivastava, John, Gosling, & Potter, 2003; see Figure 7.3). Scores on agreeableness increased significantly between ages 31 and 60 among men and women. Neuroticism among women declined consistently across the ages examined, whereas men's neuroticism stayed constant (and generally lower). Openness declined in both sexes after age 30, and extraversion declined a bit for women between ages 31 and 60, whereas it increased slightly for men in the same period. The strongest and most noticeable result was for conscientiousness, which increased across all ages for both sexes. A similar study conducted in Germany and Great Britain found essentially the same results (Donnellan & Lucas, 2008). The design of these studies was *cross-sectional*, meaning that people of different ages were surveyed at the same time. Slightly different conclusions emerged from a major review of *longitudinal* studies, where the same people were repeatedly measured at different ages. That review concluded that, on average, older people tend to become more socially dominant, agreeable,

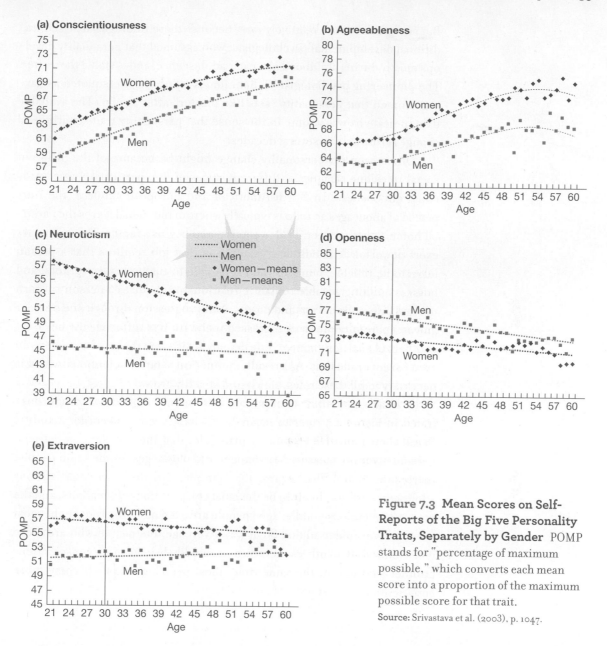

Figure 7.3 Mean Scores on Self-Reports of the Big Five Personality Traits, Separately by Gender POMP stands for "percentage of maximum possible," which converts each mean score into a proportion of the maximum possible score for that trait.

Source: Srivastava et al. (2003), p. 1047.

conscientious, and emotionally stable (less neurotic) (Roberts et al., 2006). In a word, they become more mature (Roberts et al., 2008).

Several comments can be made about these conclusions. First, the data refer to mean levels of traits, so the changes do not apply to everybody—some people actually become less agreeable or less conscientious as they get older.

But such patterns are relatively rare. Second, these findings surprised traditional developmental psychologists, who assumed that personality develops mostly during childhood and early adolescence, and is stable thereafter. The pioneering psychologist William James (1890) is often quoted as having claimed that personality "sets like plaster" after age 30. The available data indicate he was wrong, in the sense that personality traits continue to change across at least several decades.

One reason for personality change might be because of the different social roles one occupies at different stages of life, particularly as regards conscientiousness. In North American and European cultures, the time period of about ages 20 to 30 is typically when an individual leaves the parental home, starts a career, finds a spouse, and begins a family. These changes exert powerful demands. For example, a first job requires that a person learn to be reliable, punctual, and agreeable to customers, coworkers, and bosses. Building a stable romantic relationship requires a person to learn to regulate emotional ups and downs. And progression through one's career and as a parent requires an increased inclination to influence the behavior of others (social dominance). Life demands different things of you when you are a parent or the boss. As a result, inclination to be conscientious, which is necessary to fill these roles, slowly and steadily grows.

A final comment: It is important to remember that the findings illustrated in Figure 7.3 refer to mean-level change, not rank-order stability. Recall the cumulative continuity principle, that the correlations between personality traits measured at younger and older ages, in the same people, increase with age. This means, for example, that the most conscientious adolescents are also likely to be the most conscientious older adults, and the most conscientious middle-aged people are even more likely to be the most conscientious older adults. So at any given age, the people who are more conscientious than others their own age are likely to be more conscientious at other ages too. At the same time, most people gradually become more conscientious as they grow older.

FROM ASSESSMENT TO UNDERSTANDING

The usefulness of personality assessment goes beyond its ability to predict behavior, performance, and life outcomes. When we learn which personality traits are associated with certain behaviors, and how those traits change over the life course, we can learn much about why people do what they do. We have seen how personality assessment can shed light on how children delay gratification, why some people are prejudiced, use drugs, or are depressed, and how the tasks of different stages of life affect the kinds of people we become. This kind of increased understanding is the most important goal of science.

SUMMARY

- Traits are useful not just for predicting behavior, but also for increasing our understanding of the reasons for behavior. This chapter examined four basic approaches to the study of traits.

The Single-Trait Approach

- The single-trait approach zeros in on one particular trait and its consequences for behavior; this approach has been used to study "authoritarianism," "conscientiousness," and "self-monitoring," among others.

The Many-Trait Approach

- The many-trait approach looks at the relationship between a particular behavior and as many different traits as possible. One test used in this approach, the California Q-Sort, assesses different traits at once. The Q-sort has been used to explore the bases of gratification delay, drug use, depression, and political ideology.

The Essential-Trait Approach

- The essential-trait approach attempts to identify the few traits, out of the thousands of possibilities, that are truly central to understanding all of the others. The most widely accepted essential-trait list is the Big Five, which identifies "extraversion," "neuroticism," "conscientiousness," "agreeableness," and "openness" as broad traits that can organize the understanding of personality.

Typological Approaches to Personality

- The typological approach attempts to capture the ways people might differ in kind, not just in degree. Recent research has identified three basic types of personality: well adjusted, maladjusted overcontrolled, and maladjusted undercontrolled. However, while these types may be useful for thinking about how traits work in combination, they add little, if any, predictive validity to what can be achieved using trait measures.

Personality Development Over the Life Span

- Personality development concerns the questions of where personality comes from, and how it changes over the life span.

- Individual differences in personality are highly stable across the life span, becoming more stable as one gets older.

- At the same time, the mean levels of some personality traits show substantial changes for most people, with a particularly noticeable increase in "conscientiousness" across the decades.

From Assessment to Understanding

- Personality assessment is not an end in itself but should be a vehicle toward psychological understanding.

THINK ABOUT IT

1. From the examples in this chapter, which approach do you find yields the most insight—the single-trait, the many-trait, or the essential-trait approach?
2. The concept of the authoritarian personality is half a century old. Is it still useful? Can you think of current examples of authoritarians besides those in the text?
3. If you could choose, would you rather be a high or low self-monitor?
4. Do you know people who abuse drugs? From your experience, what personality traits are associated with drug use? Are these traits a cause of drug abuse, a result of drug abuse, or both?
5. Do you know a male student who is depressed? A female student? If so, would you say their depressions differ? How?
6. It has been suggested that the study of the personality antecedents for political orientation tends to paint an unfair picture of political conservatives. Do you agree? What other interpretations could be made of the data?
7. Rate yourself or a good friend on the five essential traits of personality (the Big Five). You can use a 1–5 scale or rate your target as "high" or "low" on each. Do these ratings contain useful information? What aspects of personality do they leave out?
8. If you have ever lived in a different country than you do now, or in different parts of the country, have you found that people in different places have different personalities? If so, in what ways? Why do you think this is?
9. Do you think it is possible to be creative (e.g., artistic) without being particularly intelligent?

10. Have you ever observed a change in someone else's personality? What do you think caused the changed?

11. Has your own personality ever changed? Is it changing now? Why?

SUGGESTED READINGS

Adorno, T. W., Frenkel-Brunswik, E., Levinson, D., & Sanford, N. (1950). *The authoritarian personality*. New York: Harper.

> *The classic work describing the Berkeley group's research on the psychological underpinnings of Nazism. An important part of this project was the development of the California F scale, which the book describes in detail.*

Allport, G. W. (1937). *Personality: A psychological interpretation*. New York: Holt, Rinehart, & Winston.

> *The classic and perhaps still best presentation of how trait psychologists think about personality.*

Snyder, M. (1987). *Public appearances, private realities: The psychology of self-monitoring*. New York: Freeman.

> *A summary, by the test's originator, of the research stimulated by the self-monitoring scale. The book goes beyond test-relevant issues and has much to say about basic topics in social psychology, notably self-presentation.*

EMEDIA

 Go to StudySpace, wwnorton.com/studyspace, to access additional review and enrichment materials.

PART III

THE MIND AND THE BODY: Biological Approaches to Personality

Let's face it: People are animals. From a biological point of view, human beings are members of the class Mammalia, and the human body, especially its internal anatomy including the brain and nervous system, resembles the bodies of other species in many ways. One anatomical researcher concluded that one part of the human brain resembles the brain of a reptile, a second part resembles the brain of most mammals, and a third part is uniquely human (the *triune brain* hypothesis; see MacLean, 1990). This description may be oversimplified (Buck, 1999; Fridlund, 1994), but the superficial resemblances across the brains and nervous systems of many species is striking.

The resemblances are chemical as well as anatomical. My elderly dog was once put on a thyroid medication that, it turned out, was identical to one prescribed for a relative of mine who was the same age, adjusting for dog years. The only difference was that the human version was about 10 times more expensive. (On the upside, it was covered by Medicare.) The slightly unsettling fact that most medicines prescribed by veterinarians have similar effects on people reminds us that our physiology is not unique. We humans share with our fellow mammals many of the same or similar chemicals that sustain and regulate the body and, yes, the mind. The familiar antidepressant Prozac works just fine on vervet monkeys (Raleigh, 1987; Raleigh, McGuire, Brammer, Pollack, & Yuwiler, 1991), and our family cat was once prescribed a popular antianxiety drug to help her deal with our two new dogs (though they never did become friends).

A third area of cross-species similarity is the way so much of human nature and personality seems to be biologically inherited. The family resemblance that can be observed at many holiday gatherings illustrates how traits such as hair and skin color, body size, and perhaps even abilities and behavioral styles are transmitted from one generation to the next. Animal breeders have known for a long time how to accentuate or minimize various behavioral tendencies as well as aspects of appearance through careful selection of parental matches. Not only will the offspring of two poodles surely have curly fur, but they will also probably have gentler dispositions than the offspring of two rottweilers. Evidence summarized in the following chapters suggests that personality traits of humans are to some degree inherited as well.

Finally, and perhaps most controversially, all of life—plant, animal, and human—is the product of a long process of biological evolution. Evolution is more than just a theory: It is the fundamental principle that organizes biology, systematizes the taxonomy of species, and accounts for their origin. The process of evolution has worked for millions of generations over hundreds of millions of years to produce a wide diversity of life, and it continues today (e.g., in bacteria that quickly evolve immunity to overused antibiotics). The implication of evolution for psychology is that attributes of any species—including behavioral patterns in humans—may be present because of advantages they offered for the survival and reproduction of members of past generations.

The principle of evolution sometimes evokes opposition because it seems, to some, to violate religious beliefs. As William Jennings Bryan said in 1922, the "evolutionary hypothesis . . . takes from man the breath of the almighty and substitutes the blood of a brute" (Bryan, 1922/2009). But the underlying issue goes beyond dogma. Bryan reportedly offered $100 to anyone who would sign an affidavit acknowledging having personally descended from an ape. Apparently he had no takers, which illustrates that people are reluctant to think of themselves as animals. I confess that I was disturbed when I found the same drug in my aunt's medicine chest that, at home, I stored next to the dog food. Besides the possible loss of dignity in thinking of oneself as an evolved ape (or a dog who walks upright), the topic of evolution returns us to the statement with which we began this section: Are people really just animals?

The question raises one of the oldest issues in philosophy, one with particular importance for psychology: the *mind-body problem.* To what degree is the human mind—including behavior, emotion, thought, and experiences ranging from the appreciation of beauty to moral reasoning—a direct product of physical, biological processes? This question has become more acute for psychology because, until about a decade ago, so little was known about the biological basis of personality that the issue could be safely ignored. This is no longer possible. Rapidly developing, sophisticated technology is uncovering relationships between brain processes and psychological functioning, while at the same time it is becoming apparent that personality traits are to an important degree inherited and that some aspects of human nature are rooted in our evolutionary history.

These intersections between the study of biology and the study of personality—anatomy, physiology, genetics, and evolution—are the topics of the next two chapters. More will be said near the end of Chapter 9 about the degree to which biology could subsume psychology; in the meantime, I urge you keep the mind-body question in the back of your mind as you read.

To what degree is human psychology—behavior, emotion, thought, and experience—reducible to processes of the body and the brain? It is not difficult to find people willing to argue that the answer is 100 percent (this is the *reductionist* position), and others who maintain that the answer is 0 percent (this is the *humanist* position). As we shall see, both of these answers are too simple.

THE ANATOMY AND PHYSIOLOGY OF PERSONALITY

FOR A LONG TIME, people have suspected that the brain is important for the mind and behavior. In the fourth century B.C., the Greek physician Hippocrates maintained that "from the brain and from the brain only arise our pleasures, joys, laughter and jests, as well as our sorrows, pains, secrets, and fears. Through it, in particular, we think, see, hear and distinguish the ugly from the beautiful, the bad from the good, the pleasant from the unpleasant" (Hippocrates, 1923, p. 175). However, realizing that the brain is important and figuring out how it functions are two very different matters.

To appreciate the plight of anyone who would seek to solve this problem, picture the following scenario: Imagine we could travel to ancient Greece and give Hippocrates an MP3 player loaded with a selection of early 21st-century music. As Hippocrates listened through the earbuds to some of Usher's additions to the musical canon, he would likely be amazed and perplexed. Then, being curious, he might try to figure out how this remarkable device works.

What would he do? He could try dismantling the MP3 player, though it is unlikely he would recognize anything he saw inside, and once he took it apart, it is even more unlikely he would get it back together again. But if he were too cautious to probe the device's innards, his only recourse would be to observe it, listen to it, and fiddle with its various controls. Only after the battery runs down might he dare open the device (rechargers being unavailable in ancient Greece). Unfortunately, all he would see would be the inner workings of a mechanism that no longer functioned.

Part of Hippocrates' problem here is that his tools would be limited. What if we also used our time transporter to send him a voltmeter and an X-ray machine? Now Hippocrates might have a chance to get somewhere, though he would still face many conceptual problems in trying to understand the meaning of X-ray images and voltmeter readings.

Anyone seeking to understand the physical basis of the mind faces a situation every bit as difficult as the imaginary quandry we gave to Hippocrates. Here stands a living, thinking person who possesses a functioning brain that can do amazing things, more amazing than anything an MP3 player can do by far. How would you go about figuring out how it works? You could say or do things to the person and note how he replies and what he does. This is a little like Hippocrates pushing "play" and noticing that he hears music. It is a useful start but tells you little about what is going on inside. Still, sometimes observing from the outside is all you can do. You cannot easily open up a person's brain, especially while that person is alive. And even when the brain is opened, all you see is squishy, bloody tissue, the function of which is far from obvious. Again, the problem may lie in the limitations of the available tools. For centuries, people curious about brain function were limited to studying either people with brain damage or the bodies of people who had died, using tools such as scalpels and magnifying glasses. But a dramatic revolution has begun in the past decade with the invention and availability of new tools such as EEG machines, PET scanners, fMRI magnets, and other devices that can provide information about the activities of intact, living brains.

Modern technology allows close examination of two aspects of the brain: its anatomy and its biochemistry. Anatomical researchers examine the function of different parts of the brain and try to determine the timing and physical location of various brain processes. Researchers of brain biochemistry examine the effects of two fundamental groups of chemicals, neurotransmitters and hormones, on brain processes. These two kinds of research are related; neurotransmitters and hormones have varying effects on different parts of the brain, and different parts of the brain secrete and respond to specific neurotransmitters and hormones. Brain anatomy and biochemistry have been found to be related to behavior and personality in many ways. These relationships are the topic of this chapter.

We will consider two main questions. First, what can the structure of the brain tell us about personality? Just about every part of the brain, from the brain stem (the portion between the brain and the spinal cord) to the frontal cortex (the portion just behind the forehead) has been related to personality in one way or another. The research literature is vast, complex, sometimes

[handwritten: Interactions between parts of the brain are critical to understanding]

contradictory, and changing rapidly, but a few conclusions are beginning to come through loud and clear. One is that, while particular parts of the brain may be important for certain aspects of personality, the interactions *between* different parts of the brain—which are just beginning to be understood—are probably even more critical.

The second question is, to what degree is personality a matter of chemistry? The brain is filled with blood and many chemicals including a wide range of neurotransmitters and hormones, each of which has complex relationships with behavior. This chapter will consider some of the more important ones, along with a discussion of the drugs used, increasingly often, to affect the chemistry of the brain in order to change how people feel, what they do, and (maybe) even who they are.

This last topic is a reminder that one reason for the fascination with the biology of the brain is the potential to use new knowledge to make things better—to cure mental illness, for example, or at least to lessen anxiety, alleviate depression, and improve quality of life. Not too long ago, surgery was used fairly often to change the physical structure of the brain in an attempt to treat mental illness. These days, drugs are commonly used to alter the chemistry of the brain, with the same goal. The history of psychological surgery was not a happy one, as we shall see, and drugs have drawbacks too. But one thing is clear: As our understanding of the biological bases of emotion, behavior, and personality improves, the potential to use that knowledge to help people improves as well.

[handwritten: nerve cell projections = dendrites → receive stimulations and axons → pass message on]

THE BRAIN AND PERSONALITY

The physical basis of personality is the brain and its tentacles, the nerves that reach into every corner of the body right down to the tip of the big toe. Nerve cells typically have projections called *dendrites*, which receive stimulation, and *axons*, which pass the message on. The dendrites of *afferent* nerves, which can be extremely long, extend from the central nervous system to every part of the body; messages travel up these dendrites to the brain to report what the body is feeling and doing. At the same time, *efferent* nerves, with extra-long axons, send impulses and instructions from the central nervous system back to the muscles, glands, and other organs. In between, *interneurons*, which have short axons or none at all, organize and regulate transmissions between nerve cells. The biggest bundle of interneurons is found in the large, wrinkled organ known as the brain (see Figure 8.1).

[handwritten: afferent nerves = central nervous system to other body parts]

[handwritten: XL efferent = CNS to muscles, glands, organs. Interneurons: organize and regulate between nerve cells]

—Thalamus = regulate arousal
—Hypothalamus = hormone secretion, highly connected
—Amygdala = emotion
—Hippocampus = memory processing

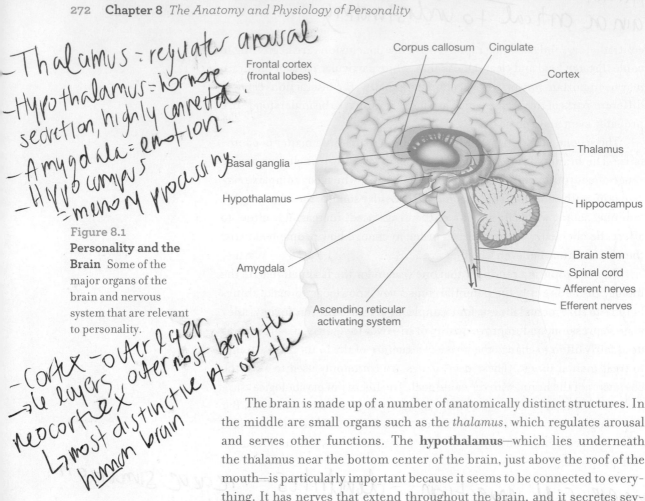

Figure 8.1
Personality and the Brain Some of the major organs of the brain and nervous system that are relevant to personality.

— Cortex — outer layer
→ 6 layers outermost being the neocortex
↳ most distinctive pt of the human brain

—Frontal cortex
↳ frontal lobes
= contain uniquely human aspects such as the ability to plan ahead or ability to be empathic

The brain is made up of a number of anatomically distinct structures. In the middle are small organs such as the *thalamus*, which regulates arousal and serves other functions. The **hypothalamus**—which lies underneath the thalamus near the bottom center of the brain, just above the roof of the mouth—is particularly important because it seems to be connected to everything. It has nerves that extend throughout the brain, and it secretes several hormones that affect the entire body. Behind and to the outer sides of the hypothalamus is wrapped the amygdala, which (as we shall see later in the chapter) has an important role in emotion, and near the amygdala is a tube-shaped structure called the **hippocampus**, which seems to be especially important in processing memories. Wrapped all around these inner organs is the outer layer of the brain called the **cortex** (or *cerebral cortex*), which itself has six layers that differ somewhat in anatomy and function. The outermost layer of the cortex, called the neocortex, is the most distinctive part of the human brain. It is more complex—and also more wrinkled—than the cortex in other animals. Another distinctive aspect of the human brain is the large size of the **frontal cortex**, which is the part that (not surprisingly) lies in front. The frontal cortex, like the rest of the brain, is divided into two lobes on the right and left sides. The two *frontal lobes* appear to be crucial for such uniquely human aspects of cognition as the ability to plan ahead and to anticipate consequences, and for aspects of emotional experience, such as empathy and moral reasoning, that may be uniquely human.

Research Methods for Studying the Brain

Knowledge about the brain comes from three principal sources: brain damage; brain stimulation; and the newest technique, brain imaging.

BRAIN DAMAGE *— oldest source*

The oldest source of knowledge about the brain is the study of people who have suffered head injuries. If enough such people are observed, it becomes possible to draw conclusions by keeping track of the specific problems caused by damage to different parts of the brain. As will be described later in the chapter, more than 100 years ago a man named Phineas Gage survived having a steel rod accidentally driven through his head, and psychologists have been talking about the effects on him ever since.

Sometimes researchers damage brains deliberately; in other words, they perform brain surgery. Parts of the brain are deliberately *lesioned* (destroyed) by being cut off from other brain structures or even removed completely. Nearly all of this kind of research has been done on animals such as rats, dogs, and (more rarely) monkeys. This is a reasonable place to begin because, as we have already mentioned, brains across mammalian species show obvious structural and functional similarities. There appear to be psychological similarities as well; for example, it is possible to assess personality traits in chimpanzees, hyenas, dogs, and tortoises (Gosling, 1998; Gosling & Vazire, 2002; J. E. King & Figueredo, 1997; Sahagun, 2005). Even squid have personality differences, it appears: Some are bold and some are shy (Sinn, Gosling, & Moltschaniwskyj, 2008), and research on "animal personality" is expanding at a rapid rate (Gosling, 2008a). So knowledge about animal brains is surely relevant to understanding the human brain. In addition, there is a smaller amount of research on the effects of surgery on human brains, mostly stemming from attempts to lessen the spread and impact of epileptic seizures. We will consider some of this work later in the chapter. *— also includes animal research*

BRAIN STIMULATION *— again, mostly done on animals*

A particularly intriguing—but difficult and rare—approach to studying the brain is to stimulate its parts directly with electrodes to see what happens. For obvious reasons, most of this research, too, is done on animals, and as a result, researchers have published detailed atlases of the brains of animals such as rats along with descriptions of how the animals respond to stimulation of each brain region. In the middle of the 20th century the

Wilder Penfield
Lsimulated brains
to have patients
report dreams, visians,
sounds, memory
flash backs.

Simulating the
substantia nigra
can produc symptoms
of depressi on

neurosurgeon Wilder Penfield performed brain surgery on patients while they were conscious and asked what they experienced when he stimulated various areas of their brains. Depending on where he placed his probe, his patients reported visions, sounds, dreams, and memory flashbacks (Penfield & Perot, 1963). More recently, surgeons unexpectedly discovered that stimulating a particular area of the brain (the central region of the left *substantia nigra*, deep in the middle of the brain) could produce symptoms of depression (Bejjani et al., 1999). A 65-year-old woman, who had electrodes inserted into her brain in an attempt to control her Parkinson's disease, was electrically stimulated in this area, and researchers described her response:

> Although still alert, the patient leaned to the right, started to cry, and [said] . . . "I'm falling down in my head, I no longer wish to live, to see anything, hear anything, feel anything. . . ." When asked why she was crying and if she felt pain, she responded, "No, I'm fed up with life, I've had enough. . . . I don't want to live any more, I'm disgusted with life. . . . Everything is useless, always feeling worthless, I'm scared in this world." (Bejjani et al., 1999, p. 1477)

Figure 8.2
Depression and Recovery From Brain Stimulation
The woman in the photographs had electrodes planted in her brain to try to control Parkinson's disease, but stimulating them triggered an acute episode of depression. (a) Her usual expression. (b) Her face 17 seconds after stimulation began. (c) Crying after 4 minutes and 16 seconds of stimulation. (d) Fully recovered and smiling, 1 minute 20 seconds after the stimulation was turned off.

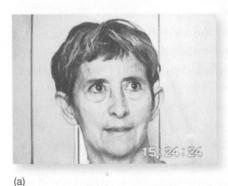
(a)

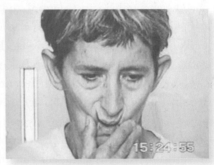
(b)

(c)

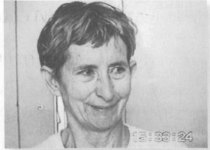
(d)

TMS—can temporarily "knock out" a certain part of the brain to see if it is essential for a psychological task = "virtual lesion"

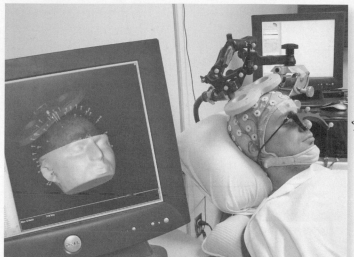

Figure 8.3 Transcranial Magnetic Stimulation Rapidly changing magnetic fields can be used to stimulate the brain for therapeutic and research purposes.

Less than 90 seconds after the stimulation was turned off, the depression went away, and within 5 minutes the patient became cheerful, laughing and joking with the researcher and even "playfully pulling his tie."

While studies like this are understandably rare—and, as in this case, may examine just a single patient—when combined with other research, they can add important knowledge about brain function. The areas of the substantia nigra relevant to this case are associated with neurotransmitters such as dopamine, norepinephrine, and serotonin, which other research has shown to be involved in depression (as will be discussed later), so this is an example of one patient adding an important piece of information to the puzzle.

A new way to stimulate the brain, called *transcranial magnetic stimulation (TMS)*, induces electrical responses in the brain using rapidly changing magnetic fields (see, e.g., Fitzgerald, Fountain, & Daskalakis, 2006). In research, TMS is used to temporarily "knock out" (turn off) areas of brain activity to see whether a particular part of the brain is essential for a psychological task. In this way, researchers can create a "virtual lesion," cutting off part of the brain without really having to cut anything. For example, if the areas of the brain essential for speech are turned off using TMS, the individual will (temporarily) be unable to talk (Highfield, 2008). While the use of this technique to study personality is just beginning, it may turn out to be useful for treating brain disorders as diverse as migraine headaches, effects of strokes, hallucinations, or depression.

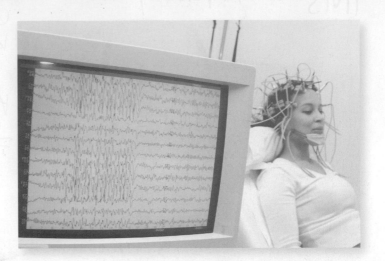

[handwritten: aka EEG]

[handwritten: oldest technique]

Figure 8.4 Electroencephalography
Electrodes placed on the outside of the
scalp pick up minute electrical signals
from the brain that are displayed as
wiggly lines on a screen or printout.

[handwritten margin notes:
Magnetoencephalography (MEG)
—similar to EEG, detects magnetic vs. electrical
— Both determine when the brain is especially active
—Easy to tell that something happened, hard to decipher exactly what it was.
—tomographs — thinly sliced images of the brain, allowing very minute structures to be examined.
CT = computed tomography. scans.]

BRAIN IMAGING

A third approach to studying the brain is to observe its function directly—
to view what the brain is doing while it is doing it. The oldest technique
is **electroencephalography (EEG)**, in which electrodes are placed on the
scalp to pick up electrical signals generated by the brain activity underneath. A newer, related technique is **magnetoencephalography (MEG)**,
which uses delicate sensors to detect magnetic (as opposed to electrical)
indications of brain activity. Both of these techniques are good for determining when the brain is especially active, but they are not very specific as
to just where in the brain the activity is concentrated, or exactly what it is
doing. I once heard the analogy that trying to understand brain activity by
looking at an EEG is a little like trying to follow a football game by standing
outside the stadium and listening to the cheering. It will be easy to tell *when*
something important happens but more difficult to know precisely *what* it
was: a touchdown, an interception, or something else.

The ability to see what is going on inside the living brain began to
change drastically as a result of rapid technological developments near the
end of the 20th century. The most important development may have been
the rapid increase in the availability and power of computers, to the point
where nearly every researcher has one with capabilities that could only be
dreamed of a few decades ago. Computers are important for a couple of reasons. One is that they allow many different images from multiple angles—
X-rays, for example—to be combined into representations of very thin slices
(*tomographs*) of the brain, allowing minute structures to be examined. These
computed tomography (*CT*) scans are now ubiquitous in medicine as well as

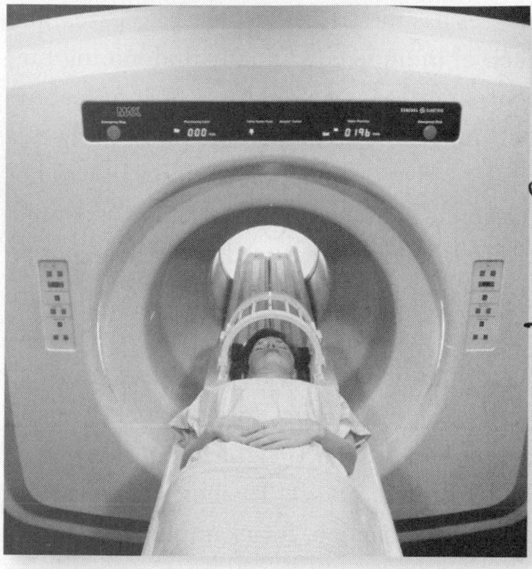

[Handwritten annotations:]

PET scans → follows bloodflow
→ see what brain is most active during certain tasks.
↓
similar to FMRI
— DTI and MRS are new methods.

Figure 8.5 An fMRI Scan A research participant entering an MRI scanner.

brain science. Another reason computers have become crucial is that the construction of images of the brain requires complex data analyses that compare many images to each other, analyses that would be impossible without massive amounts of computing power.

CT scans can be used with different data sources, including **positron emission tomography (PET)**, which was developed in the late 1980s. A PET scan creates a map of brain activity by following the location of a harmless radioactive tracer injected into the bloodstream. The assumption is that the harder the brain works, the more blood it needs, so by following blood flow, researchers can learn where the brain is most active when doing various sorts of tasks. Some PET studies use radioactive molecules that bind to, or collect at, particular brain structures, allowing studies to focus on specific regions. Another way to image the workings of the brain is **functional magnetic resonance imaging (fMRI)**, which monitors magnetic pulses generated by oxygen in the blood to map where the brain is most active at a given moment.[1] New methods continue to be developed, including *diffusion tensor imaging (DTI)* and *magnetic resonance spectroscopy (MRS)*.[2]

---

[1] Most researchers agree that blood oxygenation as shown by fMRI indicates the degree to which neurons are stimulating each other (excitatory activity), but there is debate over whether it also can indicate the degree to which neurons are inhibiting each other (inhibitory activity). Since both kinds of neural interaction are important, it is currently not clear how complete a picture of brain activity can be provided by fMRI (Canli, 2004).

[2] Despite its abbreviation, this technique is not wedded to any of the others.

BOLD (blood oxygen level dependent)
→ measured by fMRI
— calculated as a difference
  not a #
— Similar = perfusion imaging

Each of these imaging techniques has its strengths and weaknesses, and there is no one best method. Each of them is continually undergoing further development and refinement, and their use entails a host of technical difficulties. Perhaps the most important difficulty is that all parts of a living brain are always metabolically active to some degree, so a researcher must do more than simply measure what the brain does. For example, the *blood oxygen level dependent (BOLD)* signal measured by fMRI is not an absolute number; rather, it is calculated as a difference in levels of brain activity between experimental conditions, or between different individuals (Zald & Curtis, 2006). A new technique called *perfusion imaging*, which uses something called *arterial spin labeling*, appears to yield more precise measures of blood flow in the brain than do BOLD signals, but it relies on the same experimental logic (Liu & Brown, 2007). To show that a certain brain region is relevant to emotional experience, for example, it is necessary for the researcher to come up with a stimulus that evokes an emotion in the participant (e.g., a photograph of the participant's child) and a stimulus that is as similar as possible without being emotionally affecting (perhaps a picture of a stranger). Then the areas where brain activation differs between the two conditions must be mapped. These parts of the brain might be—but very possibly are not—specifically relevant to emotion.

There are a couple of reasons why the areas that differentially "light up" (as it is often said) in response to emotional stimuli might not be specifically relevant to emotion (Barrett & Wager, 2006). One reason is that the data in most studies allow an inference in only one direction: An area of the brain responds to emotional stimuli. But this does not necessarily mean that a person feels an emotion whenever this area of the brain is active. A second difficulty is that most studies necessarily look at small areas of the brain at a time. Therefore, such studies cannot show which other areas may be active, or whether the area in question becomes active only if another area is (or is not) active at the same time, a phenomenon called *neural context* (McIntosh, 1998). In other words, the function of activity in one part of the brain may depend on what is happening elsewhere in the brain (Canli, 2004, p. 1118). I will return to this point later in the chapter.

Another difficulty in brain imaging research is that, as the technology to image brain activity becomes both more powerful and more sensitive, it also becomes increasingly difficult to use. An fMRI scan requires the research participant to lie still inside a cramped cylinder filled with loud buzzing noises that might distract her from the stimulus presented by the researchers. The magnetic field generated by the scanner is so strong that, in one terrible accident, it caused a heavy oxygen tank to fly across the room

— When a brain responds to emotional stimuli, it doesn't mean a person feels emotion whenever that area is active.
— neural context; function of one pt. may depend on another pt.
— technology is highly sensitive and increasingly difficult; distracts subjects.

at almost 30 feet per second, killing a small boy (Chen, 2001). So the room in which the scanner is housed must be carefully shielded, and the building itself must be specially constructed with, for example, an extrasolid floor (the machine is almost always located in the basement). Despite special construction and expensive shielding, MEG scans, for example, are so sensitive that they can be disrupted by someone elsewhere in the building turning on a light at the wrong moment. Data from these various imaging devices must be carefully analyzed to eliminate as much interference as possible. It's not like snapping a photograph.

Indeed, the images that are published from fMRI and other scans are not photographs at all; they are color-coded data summaries, and their construction is the result of a complex set of analyses fraught with statistical difficulties (D. P. McCabe & Castel, 2008). One recent critique suggested that some of the commonly used data analytic techniques are questionable, leading to results that might be misleading at worst and exaggerated at best (Vul, Harris, Winkielman, & Pashler, 2009). As if that weren't bad enough, another recent paper has questioned the assumption that signals such as BOLD actually reflect specific areas of brain activity (Sirotin & Das, 2009). So even as the research rockets ahead, some of its basic assumptions remain in flux.

Given all these difficulties, it is remarkable how quickly findings have begun to accumulate. A review published in 2000 summarized 275 studies

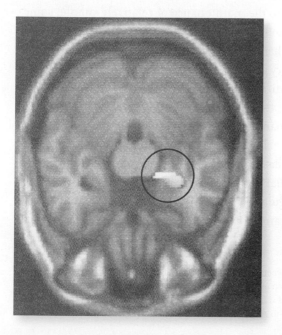

Figure 8.6 fMRI Data This picture is a graphic summary of data obtained from fMRI scans of participants who viewed happy faces. The differences in brain activation are averaged across subjects and represented as colors on an image of an average brain. The bright spot (circled) near the amygdala indicates where the brains of participants high on extraversion responded more than introverts. This result suggests that the amygdala plays an important role in the response of extraverts to pleasant stimuli.

that used fMRI and PET scans to study cognition and the brain (Cabeza & Nyberg, 2000). Strong and replicated findings identified areas associated with perception, visualization, attention, language, and several types of memory. Another, more recent review summarized more than 100 studies specifically relevant to personality (Whittle, Allen, Lubman, & Yücel, 2006). As methods improve and the psychological implications of the data become more clear, the knowledge that will be gained in the next few years is likely to change as well as far surpass what we think we know now. With all that in mind, let us turn to some current conclusions concerning the parts of the brain relevant to personality.

The Ascending Reticular Activating System

Many personality psychologists agree that one basic dimension of personality is the distinction between extraverts and introverts, as we saw in Chapter 7. A trailblazer in the attempt to relate personality to biology, British psychologist Hans Eysenck developed an interpretation of the basis for this distinction, focusing on a structure called the **ascending reticular activating system (ARAS)**. (The following discussion of his ideas is largely based on H. J. Eysenck, 1967, 1987.)

At the point where the spinal cord enters the base of the skull, it grows thicker and more complex, forming a structure called the *brain stem*. Some of the brain stem is devoted to the maintenance of relatively simple, sometimes automatic activities such as breathing and swallowing. Another part, the ARAS, has connections that lead up into the cerebral cortex and the rest of the brain. Eysenck's theory gave the ARAS a central role. The theory was based on a simple assumption. The human brain has excitatory mechanisms that arouse and stimulate brain activity and inhibitory ones that calm the brain down. Excitatory mechanisms cause an individual to be awake, energetic, and alert; inhibitory mechanisms have the reverse effect.[3] The balance between these mechanisms has important psychological implications.

Eysenck hypothesized that this balance is regulated by the ARAS, which some evidence suggests regulates the amount of information and stimulation that goes into the brain. Sometimes the information channels are

---

[3] In this context, the distinction between excitatory and inhibitory mechanisms refers to systems that serve to stimulate versus dampen overall levels of mental and behavioral activity. This is not the same as the distinction between excitatory and inhibitory functions in transmissions between neurons, which often work together to stimulate or inhibit cognition or behavior.

overarousal = introvert.
underarousal = extravert.

(Introverts are overaroused, and they don't "crave" further arousal).
↳ extraverts = "sensation seekers".

opened wide (allowing a lot of sensory stimulation to flow into the brain) and sometimes they are more closed down (limiting sensory stimulation). Eysenck's conjecture was that each individual's ARAS functions differently. Some persons' systems let in a great deal of information and stimulation nearly all the time. Other persons' systems are prone to reduce the amount of sensory stimulation.

Eysenck theorized that this difference is the basis of the difference between introverts and extraverts, although the way it works might seem counterintuitive at first: A person whose ARAS causes chronic overarousal is an introvert, whereas one whose ARAS causes chronic underarousal is an extravert. The reason is that when your ARAS opens you up to a large amount of sensory input, you end up getting more stimulation than you need—perhaps more than you can stand. As a result, you will seek to avoid exciting situations, loud noises, and social stimulation. You may turn down invitations to noisy parties, finding it stimulating enough to stay home with a good book (perhaps an unexciting book at that).

On the other hand, when your ARAS closes off much of the sensory stimulation your brain would otherwise receive, you find yourself craving more. So you seek out stimulation, perhaps going to as many loud parties as you can find. You might become a *sensation seeker*, not only in terms of parties but by taking up activities such as race-car driving or parachute jumping (Zuckerman, 1984). According to Eysenck, you seek such activities just to maintain the level of sensory input that makes you feel good—a threshold that is higher for extraverts than for introverts.

Best study = lemon juice test.
↳ introverts salivated more!

The best-known study supporting Eysenck's theory of extraversion may be the famous lemon juice test, in which researchers dropped small amounts on the tongues of introverts and extraverts (as assessed by the Eysenck Personality Inventory) and then measured the resulting amount of salivation. (Notice how, using the terms introduced in Chapter 2, the study compared S data with B data.) Would you expect introverts to salivate more or less than extraverts? Eysenck predicted that introverts, because of their wide-open ARAS, would experience the sour taste more strongly and as a result would produce more saliva in response. That is indeed the result he found (S. B. G. Eysenck & Eysenck, 1967; G. D. Wilson, 1978).

More recent studies have used other techniques such as brain-wave amplitude (measured by EEG), cardiovascular reactivity, and fMRI scans to measure arousal. For example, one study identified introverts and extraverts using the Eysenck Personality Inventory, and then gave them caffeine and made them do demanding tasks such as completing complex puzzles quickly (Bullock & Gilliland, 1993). Then the researchers measured each

Caffiene test; introverts showed faster neural transmission.

overall, introverts react more strongly and negatively to sensory stimulation. — in a neutral environment, both parties are equally aroused.

person's neurological arousal through *brain-stem auditory evoked responses*, which show how quickly and strongly the electrical activity of the brain stem, as seen on an EEG, responds to noises. The most important result was that introverts showed faster neural transmission (via their auditory evoked responses) than did extraverts; the researchers concluded that this finding was consistent with Eysenck's theory that introverts are more sensitive to stimulation.

Additional supporting data have been provided by two fMRI studies, which found that individuals who scored higher on a self-report test of "behavioral approach sensitivity" (a construct similar to "extraversion") showed *less* activity in three areas of the brain while working on a difficult memorization task (J. R. Gray & Braver, 2002; J. R. Gray et al., 2005). Another recent fMRI study showed participants pictures depicting "nudity, erotica, extreme sports, violence, bodily mutilation, insects and snakes" (Joseph, Liu, Jiang, Lynam, & Kelly, 2009).[4] In high sensation seekers, areas of the brain associated with arousal and reward responded strongly to these stimuli, whereas those low in sensation seeking showed more response in parts of their brains associated with emotional self-control.

Taken as a whole, the evidence seems to indicate that Eysenck's theory is about half right. It does not seem to be the case, as Eysenck surmised, that introverts are chronically more aroused than extraverts (Stelmack, 1990). The ARAS is not as general a system as was first believed; it does not turn neural stimulation to the entire brain on and off like a faucet (Zuckerman, 1991). One part of the brain can be stimulated, aroused, and active at the same time that another part is almost inactive. In fact, levels of arousal typically vary across different parts of the brain. On the other hand, there seems to be a good deal of evidence—including the studies just summarized—that introverts react more strongly and often more negatively to sensory stimulation than extraverts—a general idea that can be traced back to early work by Ivan Pavlov (1927). In other words, when the environment is quiet and calm, extraverts and introverts are about equally aroused. But when loud, bright, or exciting stimuli are present, introverts react more quickly and more strongly (Zuckerman, 1998). These reactions apparently lead them to withdraw—the crowds, noise, and excitement are just too much—and exhibit the pattern of behavior we identify as introverted. This same level of stimulation may be just what the sensation-seeking extravert needs to perform at her

---

[4] These pictures were drawn from something called the International Affective Picture System, which apparently is unpublished. Too bad: It has all the makings of a best seller.

best (Geen, 1984)—a need that, according to one writer, can even lead to a life of crime. "The vandal is a failed creative artist," who is bored, needs to be constantly stimulated, and "does not have the intellectual or other skills and capacities to amuse or occupy himself" (Apter, 1992, p. 198; Mealey, 1995).

Indeed, Eysenck argued in some of his later writings that a nervous system requiring extra stimulation can make a person dangerous. According to the "general arousal theory of criminality" (H. J. Eysenck & Gudjonsson, 1989, p. 118), such a person may seek out high-risk activities such as crime, drug use, gambling, and promiscuous sex. To prevent these people from becoming dangerous, according to another psychologist, perhaps they should be encouraged to enter stimulating but harmless professions such as stunt person, explorer, skydiving exhibitionist, or radio talk-show host (Mealey, 1995)! Personally, I question this advice. Are radio talk-show hosts really harmless?

> Are radio talk-show hosts really harmless?

The Amygdala — *links perceptions; thoughts to emotional meaning.*

The **amygdala** is a small structure located near the base of the brain, behind the hypothalamus. It is found in humans and in many other animals, and it appears to link perceptions and thoughts about the world with their emotional meaning (Adolphs, 2001). When the amygdala is surgically removed from rhesus monkeys, they become less aggressive and less fearful, they sometimes try to eat inedible things (even feces and urine), and they may exhibit increased and unusual sexual behavior. Research on humans and other animals indicates that the amygdala has important effects on negative emotions such as anger and fear. In shy people, the amygdala becomes highly active when they are shown pictures of people that they don't know, while nonshy participants show no such effect (Birbaumer et al., 1998), and people with anxiety disorders such as panic attacks and post-traumatic stress disorder (PTSD) tend to have an active amygdala, even at rest (Drevets, 1999). Its functioning is also related to positive emotions such as social attraction and sexual responsiveness (Klein & Kihlstrom, 1998; Barrett, 2006), as well as reactions to pleasurable stimuli such as photographs of happy scenes (Hamann, Ely, Hoffman, & Kilts, 2002), words describing positive emotions (Hamann & Mao, 2002), and pleasant tastes (Small et al., 2003). From this varied evidence, the psychologist Lisa Feldman Barrett concludes that the amygdala plays an important role in computing the degree to which a stimulus, whether a person or a thing, offers impending

— anxiety disordered people have an active amygdala even @ rest.

[Handwritten margin notes, left side top:]
computes the degree to which a stimulus is impending threat/reward
→↑HR, blood pressure.

- personality traits to amygdala
= anxiety, fearfulness, sociability, sexuality.
→attractive vs. threatening.

- People high in neuroticism respond strongly to stimuli designed to evoke "emotional conflict".

threat or reward (2006; Barrett & Wager, 2006). After assessing the situation, the amygdala may respond by making the heart beat faster, raising blood pressure, and releasing hormones such as cortisol and epinepherine (Bremner, 2005).

This hypothesis helps to explain the wide variety of personality traits that appear to be relevant to the amygdala, which include chronic anxiety, fearfulness, sociability, and sexuality (Zuckerman, 1991). What all these traits have in common relates to whether other people are generally seen as attractive (e.g., "sociability," "sexuality") or threatening ("anxiety," "fearfulness"). Other traits and stimuli are related to the amygdala too. A study using a PET scan found that the amygdala of pessimistic individuals responded more strongly to pictures of snakes than did the amygdala of optimists (Fischer, Tillfors, Furmark, & Fredrikson, 2001)! On the other hand, the amygdala of extraverted persons responded more strongly to photographs of happy faces than did the amygdala of introverts (Canli et al., 2002). More generally, the amygdala of people who score high in neuroticism responds strongly to stimuli designed to evoke "emotional conflict," such as the word "party" superimposed on a sad face (Haas, Omura, Constable, & Canli, 2007).

The importance of the amygdala and related structures was dramatically illustrated by an incident at the University of Texas on July 31, 1966. A graduate student named Charles Whitman wrote a letter that read, in part,

[Handwritten margin notes, left side bottom:]
Whitman (grad student) - murdered wife; killed mother; 14 people and wounded 32.

- "visible physical disorder" was a malignant tumor n right next to the amygdala

> I have been a victim of many unusual and irrational thoughts. These thoughts constantly recur, and it requires a tremendous mental effort to concentrate on useful and productive tasks. . . . After my death I wish that an autopsy would be performed on me to see if there is any visible physical disorder. . . . It was after much thought that I decided to kill my wife, Kathy, tonight after I pick her up from work. . . . I love her dearly, and she has been as fine a wife to me as any man could ever hope to have. I cannot rationally pinpoint any specific reason for doing this. . . . (Johnson, 1972, as cited in Buck, 1999, p. 312)

That night, Whitman did murder his wife, and then his mother. The next day he took a high-powered rifle and climbed to the top of a tower at the center of campus and began firing at random, killing 14 more people and wounding 32 before police managed to shoot him. The autopsy he wished for found the "visible physical disorder" Whitman suspected. He had a malignant tumor in the right hemisphere of his brain, in the basal ganglia next to the amygdala (see Figure 8.1).

[handwritten: amygdala + core of the brain = motivation + emotion.]

This finding implies that lower parts of the brain near and including the amygdala may be capable of producing motivations for actions like killing one's wife and mother along with innocent strangers (Buck, 1999). But these motivations, powerful as they are, might arise without the understanding, or even the emotional experiences (e.g., rage), usually associated with killing. For comprehension and emotion, other brain structures must become involved. Whitman did not know why he was motivated to do what he did. The rest of his brain did not understand the strange impulses produced by his amygdala any more than outside observers did; in that sense, the rest of his brain *was* an outside observer.

[handwritten margin note: — other parts of the brain are required to understand these thoughts/emotions.]

Just as the frontal cortex has been viewed as the seat of uniquely human cognitive functions such as thinking and planning, the amygdala and associated structures near the core of the brain have become widely accepted as contributing to motivations and emotions. The case of Charles Whitman adds an important wrinkle to this idea. In order to understand, to consciously experience or "feel" these emotions, other brain structures such as the cerebral cortex may be necessary. The fact that many animals, including reptiles, have an amygdala suggests that the basic foundation of emotional processes is ancient, evolutionarily speaking, and functions similarly across species. But the unique development of the neocortex in humans suggests that other animals might not understand or experience emotions as humans do.

The Frontal Lobes and the Neocortex

[handwritten note: important for cognitive function (speech, planning, interpreting the world).]

The **neocortex**, which forms the outer layer of the brain, is its most uniquely human part. Spread out flat, it would be about the size of a sheet of newspaper, but to fit inside the skull it is scrunched around the brain in a way that explains its wrinkled appearance. Psychologists have long accepted the idea that the frontal lobes, the two parts of the neocortex at the left-front and right-front of the brain, are particularly important for higher cognitive functions such as speech, planning, and interpreting the world.

THE FRONTAL LOBES AND EMOTION

[handwritten: left lobe = pleasant, right lobe = unpleasant]

The two lobes appear to be somewhat specialized. EEG studies suggest that the left frontal lobe is more active when a person experiences pleasant emotions, whereas unpleasant emotions are associated with activity in the right frontal lobe (Davidson, Ekman, Saron, Senulis, & Frisesen, 1990). This observation is consistent with findings that activity on the left side of

LS = approach people
RS = withdraw

2 sides responding differently = brain asymmetry.

Phineas Gaye - Iron rod through frontal lobe ok his brain. - became "a child in his intellectual capacity and manifestation) → the animal passions of a strong man.

the cortex is associated with motivations to approach people and objects, whereas activity on the right side is associated with motivation to withdraw (Hewig, Hagemann, Seifert, Naumann, & Bartussek, 2004). Also, activity in the left side of the frontal lobe is associated with the ability to inhibit responses to unpleasant stimuli, so the left frontal cortex may be able to both promote good feelings and dampen bad ones (D. C. Jackson et al., 2003). This may be why an especially active left brain seems to be associated with a propensity to feel happiness and enjoyment, whereas an active right brain seems associated with feelings of disgust and fear (Tomarken, Davidson, & Henriques, 1990; Wheeler, Davidson, & Tomarken, 1993).[5] The degree to which the two sides of the brain respond differently—called *brain asymmetry*—may itself be an important difference among people who vary in emotional sensitivity (Davidson, 1993).

> Spread out flat, the neocortex would be about the size of a sheet of newspaper, but to fit inside the skull it is scrunched around the brain in a way that explains its wrinkled appearance.

THE FRONTAL LOBES, SOCIAL UNDERSTANDING, AND SELF-CONTROL

Another clue to the particular importance of the frontal lobes for social understanding, self-control, and judgment comes from observations of patients with brain injuries and from fMRI studies.

Studies of Brain Damage   One famous case began in 1848, when a railroad construction supervisor named Phineas Gage stood in the wrong place at the wrong time, near a dynamite explosion that sent a 3½-foot iron rod through his left cheek, into the frontal lobes of his brain, and out through the top of his head. Remarkably, he survived and lived another 15 years. According to some preliminary reports, after his injury Gage was fine in all respects. He could speak and move normally, and his memories were intact. Some observers noted that he was perhaps a little less emotional than he used to be (Harlow, 1849; Bigelow, 1850).

These early reports had an unfortunately long-lasting influence. A century later, they reassured some surgeons that it was OK to remove large portions of the human brain in attempt to "cure" excessive emotionality

---

[5] The results of this research, conducted almost entirely with the EEG method, has not yet been confirmed using imaging techniques.

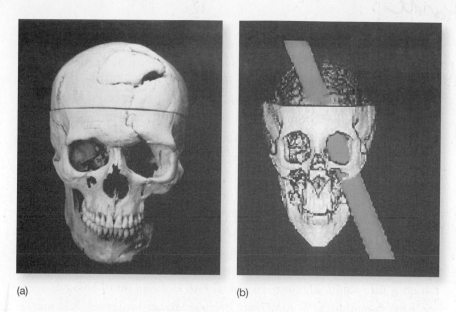

(a)   (b)

Figure 8.7 **Phineas Gage** (a) This photograph shows the incredible damage to Phineas Gage's skull. (b) The computer image reconstructs the path of the rod that caused the injury.

(Freeman & Watts, 1950). But these impressions were incorrect (Klein & Kihlstrom, 1998). In his final reports, Gage's physician, who seems to have been an astute observer, recorded that although Gage retained some reasonable degree of mental functioning, his personality was noticeably changed—and not for the better (Harlow, 1868, 1869). According to this physician, Gage's behavior became "fitful, irreverent, indulging at times in the grossest profanity (which was not previously his custom), manifesting but little deference for his fellows, impatient of restraint or advice, . . . at times pertinaciously obstinate, yet capricious and facillating [*sic*]. . . . " Overall, Gage had become "a child in his intellectual capacity and manifestations . . . [yet had] the animal passions of a strong man" (Harlow; quoted in Valenstein, 1986, p. 90).

Indeed, the long-term outcome for Gage was disastrous. His emotional life flattened out—nothing ever made him either very happy or very upset. The rest of his life fell apart. Before the accident, he was one of the most valued employees of the Rutland & Burlington Railroad. Afterward, he was unable to perform his duties and never managed to hold another job. He made one unwise decision after another, and both his professional and personal lives disintegrated.

less excitable/emotional
post-damage
- inability to understand
the emotions of others.
- inability to regulate own
emotions.

└→psychopathic.

"Elliott = cortical
tissue removed + tumor.
- unable to allocate
time properly

Gage was not the only person in history to suffer accidental brain injury, although his case became one of the more notable ones. Gunshot wounds to the head, and other kinds of injuries as well, have shown that people can live despite having remarkable amounts of tissue removed or severed. According to some accounts—similar to the first impressions of Gage—when these accidents involved the frontal lobes, the victims could still function but were less excitable and emotional than prior to the injury (e.g., Brickner, 1936). Overall, however, people with frontal-lobe damage—including damage due to brain surgeries such as lobotomies (considered later in this chapter)—appear to suffer from an inability to understand the emotions of others and to appropriately regulate their own impulses and feelings.

The well-known neuroscientist Antonio Damasio and his colleagues reported two cases of individuals who suffered damage to the frontal contex when they were very young; they enjoyed normal childhood environments but grew into adults who were inconsiderate to the point of being dangerously psychopathic (S. W. Anderson, Bechara, Damasio, Tranel, & Damasio, 1999). Perhaps they failed to experience negative emotions, such as guilt and fear, when they should. One patient neglected her baby, and the other lied frequently without any apparent motive; neither expressed any guilt or remorse for these actions.

Another of Damasio's patients, known as "Elliott," was a good husband and father and held a responsible job in business, when he began to report headaches and an inability to concentrate (Damasio, 1994). His family physician suspected a brain tumor; unfortunately, that turned out to be correct. Elliott had a large tumor right above the nasal cavities, at the midline of the brain. The surgery to remove the tumor also had to remove a good deal of cortical tissue.

After the surgery, Elliott seemed much improved and showed no obvious mental defects. Like Gage, he could move and speak normally, and his memory was unimpaired. Also like Gage, however, he had become peculiarly unemotional—he seemed not to experience strong positive or negative emotions. Over time, it became apparent that something was seriously wrong with his judgment. At a restaurant he might sit for an hour, unable to decide between different dishes as he weighed the advantages and disadvantages of each. At work, he might begin to sort through papers for a client, and then stop to read one and spend the rest of the day deeply analyzing that single paper instead of completing his main mission. He seemed unable to allocate his time and effort appropriately between important tasks and activities and those that were trivial. He lost his job and, in the end, his family as well.

Difficulties similar to the effects of Elliott's surgery have been reported as a result of accidental brain damage. Two different high-level executives suffered damage to their right frontal lobes, and afterward both seemed to recover the ability to speak, remember, and perform other cognitive tasks. They even could recognize some of their own failings, show concern about them, and express intentions to do better. But they could no longer function as executives. They seemed to lack full understanding of problems that arose—though they could speak about them almost as if they understood—and therefore, they were unable to make appropriate decisions or even act wisely in their own self-interest (Stuss & Levine, 2002).

According to Damasio's analysis, Gage's and Elliott's flattened emotional landscape and their problems with decision making, like those of the executives, stemmed from the same kind of neural damage (Damasio, 1994). The damage to tissue in the right frontal lobes impaired their ability to use their emotional reactions in decision making. According to Damasio's **somatic marker hypothesis**, emotions enable people to make decisions that maximize good outcomes and minimize bad ones, and to focus on what is really important. Feelings tie the body to the brain. Without the ability to connect emotions to thinking, Gage and Elliott lost not only an important part of life's experience but also a crucial component of the ability to make decisions. They treated important tasks and unimportant ones with equal urgency, and failed to do obvious things to create positive outcomes and avoid negative ones. The price of their disconnect between cognition and emotion was one of the worst things that can happen to a mortal: they wasted their time.

Studies Using fMRI fMRI studies add to the evidence that the prefrontal cortex is especially important for emotional regulation and social interaction. For example, while the prefrontal cortex is active during almost all high-level cognitive tasks (Cabeza & Nyberg, 2000), people who are prone to negative emotions tend to have an especially high level of activity in this area (Zald, Mattson, & Pardo, 2002). On the other hand, fMRI studies of people who are consistently cooperative have shown their brain activity in this area to be particularly high when they are interacting with other people (K. McCabe, Houser, Ryan, Smith, & Trourard, 2001), and that this activity in the frontal lobes is associated with simultaneous activity in areas of the brain known to be sensitive to reward. This pattern suggests that people cooperate because they find it rewarding (Decety, Jackson, Sommerville, Chaminade, & Meltzoff, 2004; Rilling et al., 2002). In sum, the prefrontal cortex is espe-

handwritten margin note: - people are cooperative because they find it rewarding

cially busy when a person is getting along well with others—an activity that may involve sensitivity to negative as well as positive emotions—which may be why damage to this area of the brain can lead to severe social problems.

A TMS Study   One recent study used transcranial magnetic stimulation (TMS), a new technique mentioned earlier in this chapter. People rated themselves and a best friend on a set of desirable and undesirable traits while magnetic stimulation was used to temporarily "shut off" brain activity in the medial prefrontal cortex (Kwan et al., 2007). Their tendency to describe themselves in more favorable terms—to "self-enhance"—was lessened as a result, compared with ratings given in a control condition where the equipment was noisily activated but no actual stimulation was delivered. These intriguing findings suggest that activity in the middle front part of the brain is a necessary part of the natural tendency describe ourselves more positively than we describe others.

handwritten margin note: - tendency to "self enhance" lessened when brain activity was shut off in the medial prefrontal cortex.

COGNITION AND EMOTION

A wide range of case studies as well as the rapidly accumulating literature of fMRI studies show how cognition and emotion are inextricably intertwined. The full functionality of each depends on the other.

A particularly fascinating problem that can result when cognition and emotion are detached is *Capgras syndrome*, named after one of the first doctors to identify it. An early case involved a 53-year-old woman who believed that her husband, daughter, and other important persons in her life had disappeared, replaced by doubles who were merely impersonating them (Capgras & Reboul-Lachaux, 1923, as cited in Doran, 1990). In a more recent case, a 20-year-old man received a severe blow to the head and subsequently came to believe that his parents and siblings had been shot by Chinese communist spies. The similar-looking people caring for him and worrying about him, he concluded, were imposters (Weston & Whitlock, 1971, as cited in Doran, 1990). In yet another case, a victim of severe head injury returned home from the hospital to a wife and four children who, he insisted, were an entirely different family from the one he had before the accident, although he admitted they looked very similar.

handwritten margin note: Capgras Syndrome → injury to right, frontal lobe → important in emotional response - recognize family members but felt no emotional response to them. (I cannot possibly be the people they care about so becomes the conclusion).

What all of these Capgras cases appeared to have in common was an injury to the right frontal lobe, which a large amount of evidence indicates is particularly important in emotional response (Sautter, Briscoe, & Farkas, 1991; Stuss & Levine, 2002). Apparently, when these patients recognize a loved one, they fail to feel any emotional response to this recognition. Imagine, if you can, seeing your parents, your siblings, or your boyfriend or girlfriend and feeling nothing emotional at all. What would you think? What these patients conclude, it seems, is that these cannot possibly be the people they appear to be, and that the most likely explanation (conjured up by the uninjured left frontal lobe) is that they must have been replaced by nearly identical doubles.

More broadly, cognitive understanding is important for full emotional experience, and emotional experience is crucial for real understanding. Recognizing someone who is emotionally significant to you is not just a judgment; it is also a feeling, without which the judgment may be impossible. The connection between cognition and emotion may also help explain why many people who excel at what they do are involved with their work not just intellectually but emotionally. The best physicists become excited as they talk about black holes, multidimensional space, and string theory. The best football coaches care deeply about every step taken by every player during every play. Their emotions motivate their thinking and guide their strategic decision making. This does not mean that people "think with their gut," but it is clear that the gut—emotional experience is an important part of thinking, and you cannot have full functionality of one without the other.

"I make decisions as much with my gut as I do with my brain. Let's eat."

The Anterior Cingulate

The *cingulate* is a brain structure in the cortex, just on top of the **corpus callosum** (which connects the two halves of the brain) and extending all the way from the front of the brain to the back. The back of this structure, or *posterior cingulate*,[6] appears to be important for processing information about time and space and in reacting rapidly to threatening situations, while the front,

---

[6] A number of words, commonly used in anatomy, refer to directions within the brain. For example, posterior = toward the rear, anterior = toward the front, ventral = lower, lateral = out to the side (or both sides since the brain, like the body, is mostly symmetric), and medial = toward the middle. Directions can also be combined; for example, ventromedial = lower but more toward the middle.

the **anterior cingulate**, appears to be especially important for the experience of normal emotion, in part because it projects inhibitory circuits into the amygdala (Bremner, 2005). This interaction between the cingulate, in the frontal lobes, and lower areas in the brain such as the amygdala, may be critical for controlling emotional responses and impulsive behavior (Ochsner & Gross, 2005). Charles Whitman, the University of Texas graduate student discussed earlier, appears to have suffered from a brain tumor's interference with precisely this circuit, which is what made his emotional experience both incomprehensible and eventually uncontrollable.

Recent studies have implicated the anterior cingulate in two different personality traits, but the results are complex. One fMRI study found that the anterior cingulate in extraverts responded more strongly to positive and neutral words than did this part of the brain in introverts, but that neuroticism was not related to the anterior cingulate's response to negative or neutral words (Canli et al., 2004). Another study found that the anterior cingulate in people who scored higher on measures of neuroticism was significantly more active than usual during "oddball" tasks, in which they had to detect stimuli (e.g., letters) that were different from what they expected (Eisenberger, Lieberman, & Satpute, 2005). Taken together, these studies may show that the anterior cingulate is not directly responsible for negative emotional responses but *is* important for computing mismatches between expected and actual states of the world. These mismatches sometimes trigger negative emotions (e.g., when you do not get what you hoped for). When the anterior cingulate is overactive, the result may be neuroticism. However, these results are new, the picture is not yet clear, and, as always, further research is needed.

The Lessons of Psychosurgery

At the 1935 World Congress of Neurology, the Yale psychologist J. F. Fulton told assembled delegates a story about two laboratory chimps named Becky and Lucy. They were difficult to handle because they were easily frustrated, and when they were frustrated, they became vicious. As part of a study on the function of the brain in learning, part of the two chimps' frontal lobes was surgically removed. The effects on learning were inconclusive, but researchers noticed something else: Becky and Lucy had become relaxed and mellow chimps, placid instead of vicious, downright pleasures to work with. According to legend, after Fulton presented these results, a Portuguese neurosurgeon named António Egas Moniz stood up and asked whether such

Moniz - first prefrontal leucotomy.
↳first psycho surgery — → done on people w such emotional issues.

- became prefrontal lobotomy - much more refined
- Rosemary Kennedy.

an operation might be helpful for controlling human psychotics. Fulton was so shocked by the question he couldn't even answer.

That didn't stop Egas Moniz. By 1937, two years later, he had performed—on a human!—the first *prefrontal leucotomy*, in which small areas of white matter behind each of the frontal lobes were deliberately damaged. This may have been the first instance of *psychosurgery*, surgery done with the specific purpose of altering personality, emotions, or behavior. The idea was that patients with pathological levels of agitation and emotional arousal had overactive frontal lobes, and this operation—aimed at the same area as Gage's iron bar—might make them less emotional, more rational, and calmer, like Becky and Lucy.

It is important to note that Egas Moniz operated only on people with severe emotional problems and may even have done most of them some good. Whatever subtle damage was done to their emotional lives or decision-making capabilities may have been outweighed by their relief from a miserable and uncontrollable degree of emotional overexcitement (Damasio, 1994). In any case, the operation quickly became popular around the world, especially in the United States, and in 1949 it received the ultimate scientific seal of approval when Egas Moniz was awarded the Nobel Prize.

But there was a dark side to this popularity. As its use spread, the surgical procedure became increasingly drastic. The standard technique changed from Egas Moniz's relatively modest leucotomy, in which small areas of tissue were damaged, to the more famous *prefrontal lobotomy*, in which whole sectors of the frontal lobes were scooped out. The results were similarly more drastic. Some lobotomy patients ended up much worse than either Gage or Elliott and became almost inert, mere shells of the people they were before. One was Rosemary Kennedy, the mentally retarded elder sister of John, Robert, and Edward Kennedy, who was operated on in 1941 in an attempt to control her "mood swings" (Thompson, 1995). She lived in an institution—a convent school in Wisconsin—for most of the next 60 years, until she died in 2005 at the age of 86.

Even the leading American advocates of the lobotomy noted that

> it is almost impossible to call upon a person who has undergone [an] operation on the frontal lobes for advice on any important matter. His reactions to situations are direct, hasty, and dependent upon his emotional set at the moment. (Freeman & Watts, 1950, p. 549)

Notice how this observation is consistent with the cases of Gage and Elliott. Evidence from a number of sources converges to suggest that the frontal

[handwritten margin notes:]
— Inability to force the future
— unable to anticipate future negative outcomes and worry.

lobes are centers of cognitive control, serving to anticipate the future and plan for it. These results also suggest that a particular function of the frontal lobes might be to anticipate future negative outcomes and respond emotionally to the possibility—in other words, worrying. This emotional aspect of forethought seems to be particularly important. Unless you have the appropriate reaction to future possibilities—pleasant anticipation on the one hand, or worrying on the other—you will not be able to plan appropriately or make the right decisions about what to do.

In the midst of the enthusiasm for what had become a trendy procedure, nobody paid much attention to this downside. Often psychosurgery was performed with an astonishing disregard for long-term results. Zuckerman summarized many of the early medical articles this way:

> The neurosurgeons' reports provide a remarkable contrast between accounts of the precise surgical techniques and the imprecise or totally absent methods of [subsequent behavioral] evaluation. Control groups were virtually nonexistent and, with the exception of an occasional use of the MMPI [Minnesota Multiphasic Personality Inventory; see Chapter 5], observations of change were based on the crudest kind of clinical observations, with no tests of reliabilities of ratings or single-blind controls. (Zuckerman, 1991, p. 147)

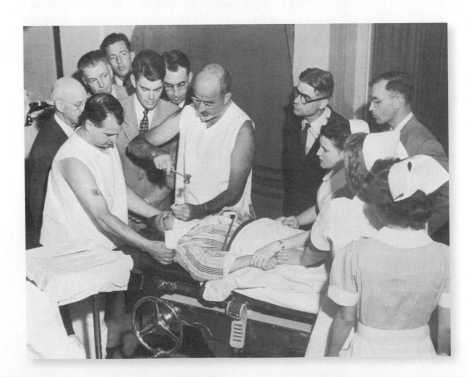

Figure 8.8

Demonstrating the Lobotomy Dr. Walter Freeman shows how to insert an instrument similar to an ice pick under the eyelid to sever nerve connections in the frontal lobe. This picture was taken in 1949 when the technique was becoming increasingly popular; such operations are rare today.

— Drug therapies are now much more popular.

Tens of thousands of lobotomies and other psychosurgeries were performed over more than four decades, but such operations are rare today. The side effects became too obvious to ignore and began to be widely publicized, not just in medical journals and newspapers but also in works such as *One Flew Over the Cuckoo's Nest*.[7] Perhaps a more important factor is that chemical therapies (drugs) were developed to make mentally ill patients manageable, if not cured. Someone like Rosemary Kennedy, who troubled her family with mood swings, would today be tranquilized rather than lobotomized. In other words, her brain would be altered with chemicals rather than with a knife. Somehow this seems less drastic and more acceptable. Is it?

The history of psychosurgery serves as a cautionary tale that illustrates not only the alarming possibility for medical practice to follow fashion rather than sound research, but also the danger of oversimplifying our still-tentative and incomplete knowledge of the brain. Entirely too many surgeons jumped to the conclusion that, because the frontal lobes have something to do with excessive worrying and neuroticism, such problems could be alleviated simply by severing or removing the frontal lobe.

This conclusion was misguided; given what we now know about brain function, it is highly unlikely that brain anatomy corresponds to psychological processes or problems in any simple, one-to-one manner (Valenstein, 1986). A more reasonable and subtle conclusion would be that the frontal lobes include among their functions the regulation of emotional responses to anticipated events. When the frontal lobes are damaged, severed, or removed, this regulatory function is disrupted. Although the result may seem to be "less worry," the evidence indicates that emotional responsiveness and future anticipation become erratic and disorganized. As a result, lobotomized people do not worry when they should, sometimes worry when they should not, and lose their ability to make decisions and to fully understand reality, as we saw with Gage, Elliott, and the Capgras patients.

Brain Systems

Most studies of brain function and personality focus on one area of the brain at a time, which is understandable because of the limits of the available technology. However, anatomists have known for a long time that

---

[7] *One Flew Over the Cuckoo's Nest*, a novel by Ken Kesey (1962/1999), was made into a play, as well as into a motion picture (starring Jack Nicholson), about life in a particularly harsh mental hospital and the disastrous effect of a lobotomy on the main character.

nearly everything in the brain is connected to everything else, which means that systems or circuits within the brain may be more important than discrete areas. Research is just beginning to address this possibility, and early results are promising. For example, one fMRI study examined *persistence*, the ability to complete a task in the face of obstacles and in the absence of immediate reward, a trait similar to "conscientiousness" in the Big Five model (see Chapter 7). This trait was associated with relatively high levels of brain activity in a complex circuit that included two areas of the frontal cortex and the ventral (lower) part of the *striatum*, which is found in the middle of the brain behind the frontal lobes (Gusnard et al., 2003). Another line of research is attempting to identify the set of structures associated with what researchers call the *C-system* (involved in effortful, reflective thinking about the self and others) and the *X-system* (involved in effortless, reflexive social thought). Early studies using fMRI have found that the C-system includes, among other areas, the lateral (side) prefrontal cortex, the hippocampus, the medial temporal lobe, and the posterior parietal cortex. The X-system includes the ventromedial prefrontal cortex, the amygdala, and the lateral temporal cortex (Lieberman, Jarcho, & Satpute, 2004).

The importance of systems rather than discrete areas in the brain helps to explain why the results of psychosurgery were so erratic (and disappointing), and why the results of the hundreds of accumulating fMRI and other imaging studies can be so difficult to integrate and assimilate. The activities of individual areas of the brain may not mean very much in the absence of knowledge about what other areas of the brain are doing at the same time. As noted earlier in the chapter, researchers call this the neural context effect (McIntosh, 1998; Canli, 2004). The effect of context is important to keep in mind; otherwise, brain science is in danger of devolving into a simplistic attempt to map traits and behaviors onto specific locations in the brain.[8] Understanding the brain is not easy. The parts of the brain work together and constantly interact with the rest of the body and with the outside world, and research to understand how these systems are coordinated is still in its early stages. In other words, the brain science of personalitiy is just starting to get interesting.

---

[8] The physiological psychologist William Uttal has gone so far as to suggest that neuroscience could be a "new phrenology," referring to the old (discredited) practice of trying to diagnose personality by feeling the bumps on a person's head (Uttal, 2002).

[Handwritten annotation at top: Galen: 4 humors: 1) Blood = cheerful, ruddy, robust. 2) Black bile = depressed, melancholy. 3) Yellow bile = angry, bitter 4) Phlegm = cold, apathetic]

BIOCHEMISTRY AND PERSONALITY

I once attended a scientific meeting where I heard the eminent psychologist Robert Zajonc cry out, "The brain is not a digital computer, it is a juicy gland!" Indeed, that is what it looks like, and to an important degree, that is exactly how it functions—through the chemicals it secretes and to which it responds.

Chemical approaches to the study of personality have a long history. The ancient Greek physician Galen (who lived between A.D. 130 and 200, practicing mostly in Rome), building on Hippocrates' earlier proposal, theorized that personality depended on the balance between four *humors*, or fluids, in the body. These humors were blood, black bile, yellow bile (also called choler), and phlegm. A person who had a lot of blood relative to the other three humors, Galen conjectured, tended to be *sanguine* (cheerful), ruddy, and robust. Excess black bile caused a person to be depressed and *melancholy*; excess yellow bile caused a person to be *choleric*, angry, and bitter; and excess phlegm made one *phlegmatic*, cold, and apathetic.

> "The brain is not a digital computer, it is a juicy gland!"

These four terms survive in the English language to this day, carrying roughly the same psychological meanings that Galen ascribed to them. Even more remarkably, this fourfold typology has undergone something of a revival among health psychologists who find it useful in connecting personality with disease (H. S. Friedman, 1991, 1992). The choleric, or chronically hostile person, for example, seems to be at extra risk for heart attack. But modern research suggests the basis of this risk is not the person's yellow bile but the stress (and hormonal reactions) caused by a life filled with tension and fights.

The Chemistry of the Mind

The physical basis of behavior is the nervous system. The nervous system is made up of billions of cells, called **neurons** (nerve cells), which connect with one another through complex pathways. The brain contains a thick bundle of neurons;[9] other neurons form the brain stem and the spinal cord, which

---

[9] Actually, neurons make up only about 10–15 percent of the cells in the brain. The rest, called *glial cells*, help to nourish and hold together the neurons, and apparently play other roles in neural transmission that are not completely understood.

connect the brain to muscles and sensory receptors all over the body. The essence of neuronal activity is communication. The activity of one neuron may affect the activity of many other neurons, transmitting sensations from the far reaches of the body into the brain; connecting these sensations with feelings, memories, and plans in the brain; and sending behavioral instructions out to the muscles, causing the body to move.

Communication between neurons is based on substances called **neurotransmitters**. As illustrated in Figure 8.9, a bioelectrical impulse causes a release of neurotransmitters at the end of the neuron. These neurotransmitters travel across the **synapse** to the next neuron in line, where they cause a chemical reaction that has either an excitatory or inhibitory effect. In an excitatory effect, the second neuron fires, which in turn causes the release of neurotransmitters at its other end, and so on down the neural network. In an inhibitory effect, the firing of the second neuron is suppressed. Although this process is often described as if neurons link to each other one-to-one, in fact the activity of one neuron might be influenced by excitatory *and* inhibitory inputs—from hundreds, or even thousands, of other neurons. As you can see, neural networks are amazingly complicated.

Hormones work slightly differently from neurotransmitters. By definition, **hormones** are biological substances that affect the body in locations different from where they were produced (Cutler, 1976). Hormones travel in the bloodstream. After release from central locations, such as the *adrenal glands* (located atop the kidneys) or the hypothalamus, they spread throughout the body. Once a hormone reaches neurons sensitive to it, it either stimulates or inhibits the activity of those neurons. The difference between neurotransmitters and hormones can be confusing because both affect the transmission of nerve impulses, and some chemicals belong to both categories. For example, norepinephrine functions within the brain as a neurotransmitter, but is also released from the adrenal glands as a hormone in response to stress. Epinephrine also works as a neurotransmitter and hormone, with diffferent associated behaviors. Both substances will be considered in detail later in the chapter.

Many neurotransmitters and hormones have been discovered, and more are still being identified: to date, researchers have counted about 60 chemicals that transmit information throughout the brain and body (Gazzaniga & Heatherton, 2003). Neurotransmitters and hormones are associated with a variety of neural subsystems and thus have many different effects on behavior. For example, norepinephrine and dopamine work almost exclusively in the **central nervous system**—the brain and spinal cord. By contrast, very little of the neurotransmitter epinephrine is found in the brain;

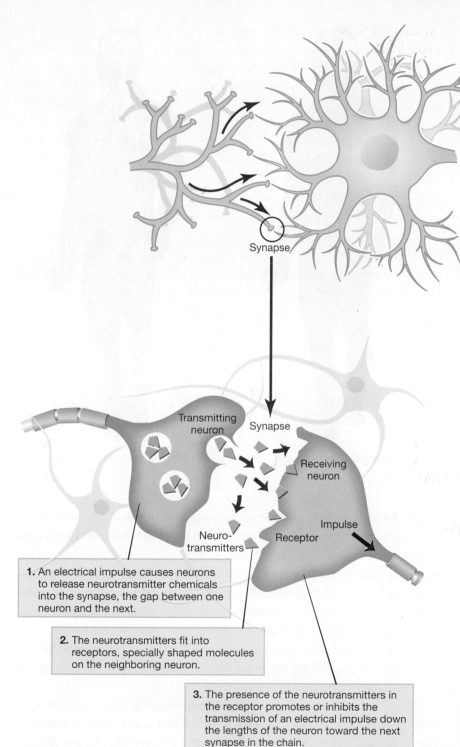

Synapse

Transmitting
neuron

Synapse

Receiving
neuron

Impulse

Neuro-
transmitters

Receptor

1. An electrical impulse causes neurons
   to release neurotransmitter chemicals
   into the synapse, the gap between one
   neuron and the next.

2. The neurotransmitters fit into
   receptors, specially shaped molecules
   on the neighboring neuron.

3. The presence of the neurotransmitters in
   the receptor promotes or inhibits the
   transmission of an electrical impulse down
   the lengths of the neuron toward the next
   synapse in the chain.

Figure 8.9

**Communication
Between Neurons**
The transmission of
impulses throughout
the nervous system is
mediated by electrical
and chemical processes
that carry impulses
across the synapses
between nerve cells.

**Figure 8.10 Two
Nervous Systems**
(a) The central nervous
system includes the
brain and spinal cord,
and (b) the peripheral
nervous system
includes the nerves
that extend throughout
the body. Different
neurotransmitters and
hormones affect the two
systems.

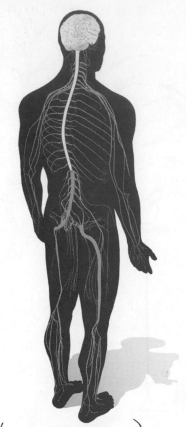

(a) Central nervous system

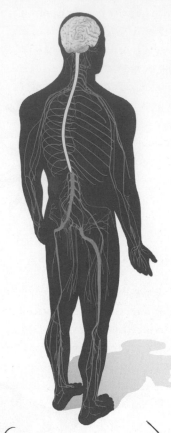

(b) Peripheral nervous system

[handwritten note:] Serotonin = wards off depression, regulates digestion

[handwritten note:] — endorphins inhibit pain. (> opiates.

mostly it is found in the **peripheral nervous system**, the neuronal networks
that extend throughout the body (see Figure 8.10). Serotonin has important
functions in the brain—it appears to help ward off depression, among other
contributions—but even more serotonin is found in the gut, where it apparently plays a role in regulating digestion. As another complication, some
neurotransmitters cause adjacent neurons to fire while, as was mentioned
earlier, others inhibit neuronal impulses. For example, the body's natural painkilling system is based on a class of hormones called **endorphins**,
which work by inhibiting the neuronal transmission of pain. Endorphins
are thus opiates produced by the body.

Many aspects of biochemistry are important in neural communication. As we have just seen, neurotransmitters play a large role in transmitting impulses. But the chemicals that make up neurotransmitters are also
important, as are the enzymes that break down neurotransmitters into their
constituent chemical parts after they have traveled across the synaptic gap

MAO (monoamine oxidase) - regulates breakdown of neurotransmitters.

between neurons. For example, the enzyme monoamine oxidase (MAO) regulates the breakdown of the neurotransmitters dopamine, norepinephrine, and serotonin. A low level of MAO in the blood, which allows higher levels of these neurotransmitters, is associated with sensation seeking, extraversion, and even criminal behavior (Zuckerman, 1998). On the other hand, a gene that promotes the action of MAO in breaking down these neurotransmitters seems to help prevent the development of delinquency among children who have been maltreated (Caspi et al., 2002; Moffitt, 2005; see Chapter 9 for more details on this research). For another example, antidepression drugs such as Paxil and Prozac increase the amount of serotonin in the body by inhibiting the chemical process that causes serotonin to break down (Kramer, 1993).

↓ MAO = ↑ sensation seeking, extraversion, criminal behavior.

Prozac inhibits process that causes serotonin to break down

Neurotransmitters

The nervous system is affected in important ways by the availability and the amounts of various neurotransmitters. This availability varies as a function of what the individual is doing and can fluctuate widely over short periods of time. But people also seem to differ in their average levels of certain transmitters, and these differences seem to be associated with particular personality traits, as we shall see in the coming pages.

DOPAMINE turns motivation → action.
↳ responds to reward, approaches attractive objects/people
— basis of sociability.

Dopamine has been described as the neurotransmitter that turns motivation into action. It plays a key role in the mechanisms that allow the brain to control body movements, and it also is involved in systems that cause one to respond to reward and to approach attractive objects and people. (Dopamine is also an important part of the chemical process that produces norepinephrine.) Research suggests that this neurotransmitter is part of the basis of sociability and general activity level, and a gene associated with response to dopamine seems to be related to the trait of novelty seeking (Ebstein et al., 1996). The exact function appears to depend on the location in the brain. In one study comparing novelty seeking and harm avoidance in people with Parkinson's disease, patients with dopamine shortages on the left side of the brain earned lower scores in novelty seeking than healthy individuals. Those who were short on dopamine on the right side of the brain had higher scores in harm avoidance (Tomer & Aharon-Peretz, 2004).

According to one theory, an inherited problem processing dopamine in the brain can produce *reward deficiency syndrome*, characterized by such diverse outcomes as alcoholism, drug abuse, smoking, compulsive over-

Reward Deficiency Syndrome = problem processing dopamine
↳ addiction.

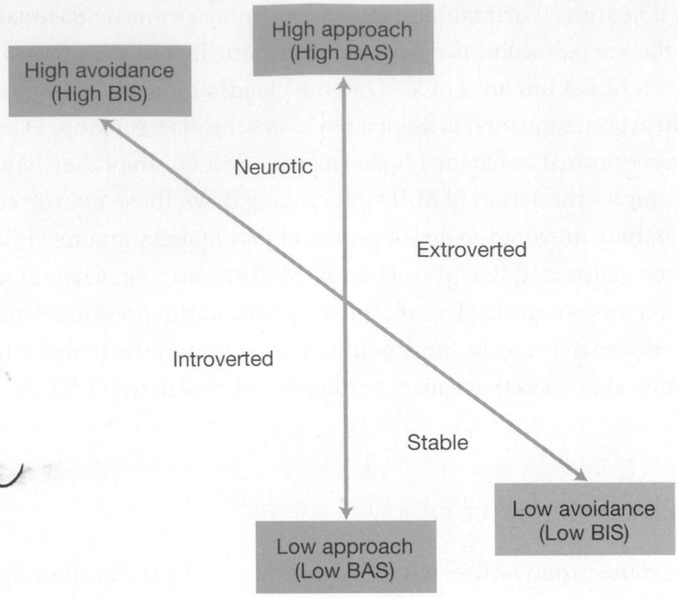

Figure 8.11 Gray's Two-Dimensional Model of Personality The dopamine-based Go system (BAS) is separate from the frontal-lobe-based Stop system (BIS). A highly active BAS makes a person sensitive to, and desirous of, reward; an active BIS makes a person fearful and avoidant of anything that might be punishing or aversive.

Handwritten notes in left margin:

—severe lack of dopamine = the basis for Parkinson's.

—Dopaminergic systems may be associated w bipolar.

eating, attention-deficit disorder, and pathological gambling (Blum, Cull, Braverman, & Comings, 1996). A severe lack of dopamine is the basis of Parkinson's disease.

In a famous case—shown, with artistic license, in the 1990 movie *Awakenings* (loosely based on the book of the same title, by neurologist Oliver Sacks, 1983)—a group of patients who developed Parkinson's disease during World War I as a result of an epidemic of encephalitis were given the new drug L-dopa 40 years later, during the 1960s. L-dopa increases the brain's production of dopamine, and for some patients who had been nearly catatonic for years, the results were dramatic. Suddenly they not only could move around much better than before, but also were able once again to experience positive emotions, motivation, sociability, and interest in and awareness of their environments.

Sadly, over time, most of these patients' conditions worsened again. They went from normal enthusiasm and energy levels into hypermanic excitement, restlessness, and grandiosity. Then, like patients with *manic-depressive disorder*, they "crashed" into deep depressions (Sacks, 1983; Zuckerman, 1991). These effects suggest that *dopaminergic* systems (systems affected by dopamine) also might be related to manic-depressive disorder (now usually referred to as *bipolar disorder*). Perhaps even more important, they suggest that dopamine might be relevant to the personality traits of extraversion, impulsivity, and perhaps others.

[handwritten: dopamine + nucleus accumbens = Go system (behavioral activation system) aka BAS — P seeks rewards]

Dopamine might affect these traits through its interactions with a part of the brain called the *nucleus accumbens*, which is located in the basal ganglia, an important junction between the cerebral cortex and the brain stem. According to neuropsychologist Jeffrey Gray, dopamine and the nucleus accumbens together form part of what is sometimes called the "Go" system (J. A. Gray, 1981). More formally called the *behavioral activation system (BAS)*, this system produces and reinforces the motivation to seek rewards. A more recent, related theory focuses directly on differences in the degree to which people develop neurons that produce and are responsive to dopamine (Depue & Collins, 1999). These individual differences might have a genetic basis, but they also might come from experience: People who have had more rewarding experiences, especially early in life, may develop more such cells, causing the dopaminergic part of their nervous systems to be well developed and active. As a result, they are motivated to seek out rewards and are capable of enjoying them strongly; they also become assertive, dominant, and outgoing—in a word, extraverts.

In some studies, BAS is measured using a questionnaire that includes items such as "When I get something I want, I feel excited and energized" and "I will often do things for no other reason than that they might be fun" (Carver & White, 1994, p. 323). People who score relatively high on BAS measures are happier when they contemplate the possibility of good things coming to them (Carver & White, 1994); they also have stronger cravings for substances such as alcohol, which (temporarily) increases dopamine levels in the brain (L. A. Clark & Watson, 1999b). On the other hand, people with low BAS scores may be at risk for depression (Harmon-Jones & Allen, 1997).

According to Gray, however, the Go system is only half the story. It is complemented by the "Stop" system, also known as the *behavioral inhibition system (BIS)*, which is comprised of the frontal lobes, which assess and respond to risk (Corr, Pickering, & Gray, 1997).[10] Items on one measure of the BIS include "If I think something unpleasant is going to happen I usually get pretty 'worked up'" and "Criticism or scolding hurts me quite a bit" (Carver & White, 1994, p. 323). Someone with a strong, active Stop system will be highly sensitive to punishment and the possibility of punishment, leading to an inhibited, anxious style of behavior and emotion.

Because the two systems are theoretically independent, any combination of BIS and BAS scores is possible (see Figure 8.11). Somebody high in approach and low in avoidance would be described as extraverted, whereas

[handwritten: "Stop" system = BIS (behavioral inhibitory system)]

---

[10] Gray's theory also includes a fight-or-flight system that he hypothesizes is the basis of emotions such as rage or panic, but he does not describe this system as thoroughly as the other systems.

someone low in approach and high in avoidance would be described as introverted (Smillie, Pickering, & Jackson, 2006). The combination of high avoidance and high approach is described as neurotic. Low approach coupled with low avoidance is sometimes labeled "stable," though the description "just doesn't care" might seem equally apt.

SEROTONIN (AND PROZAC)

Serotonin is another important neurotransmitter, one which seems to play a role in the inhibition of behavioral impulses (e.g., stopping oneself from doing something attractive yet dangerous). Serotonin is particularly relevant to the inhibition of emotional impulses. This can be useful. For example, a predator stalking its prey must inhibit the urge to leap before it is close enough to catch the prey. If you have ever watched a cat wait to pounce on a bird, you might conclude that the typical cat has a lot of serotonin in its system. The ability to inhibit emotional impulses can help humans avoid worrying too much, being too quick to anger, and being oversensitive to the minor insults of daily life.

But what happens if a person does not have enough serotonin? Problems, apparently. Dangerous criminals, arsonists, and people who commit suicide in violent ways have been found to have low serotonin levels (Virkkunen et al., 1994). According to one author, people with insufficient serotonin suffer from a syndrome called *serotonin depletion* (Metzner, 1994). The symptoms include irrational anger, hypersensitivity to rejection, chronic pessimism, obsessive worry, and fear of risk taking.

The effects of serotonin and the validity of the serotonin depletion syndrome as a clinical diagnosis are controversial topics. In 2000 the pharmaceutical company Eli Lilly sold $2.7 billion worth of Prozac, a *selective serotonin reuptake inhibitor (SSRI)*, and the entire market for related drugs (including fluoxetine, the generic version of Prozac) may be more than $20 billion per year (Druss, Marcus, Olfson, & Pincus, 2004).[11] By 1999, an estimated 22 million Americans—almost 1 person in 10—had used this drug (Shenk, 1999). The physical effect of Prozac seems fairly clear—it raises serotonin levels in the nervous system. The psychological effects, however, are more controversial, as are the implications of those effects.

---

[11] *Transporter* molecules remove up to 90 percent of the serotonin from the synapse; SSRI molecules inhibit this removal, which in turn allows more serotinin to remain available at the synapse.

In his best-selling book, *Listening to Prozac*, psychiatrist Peter Kramer (1993) claimed that Prozac can dramatically improve many people's personalities. It can stop a person from needlessly worrying and being oversensitive to minor stresses, and so provide a newly cheerful outlook on life. Some individuals who take Prozac claim that it makes them more like "themselves": They don't feel like *different* people than they were without the drug; they feel like *better* people. They get more work done and even become more attractive to members of the opposite sex. One particularly interesting study showed that normal people—that is, people with no

"Of course your daddy loves you. He's on Prozac—he loves everybody."

diagnosable personality disorders in themselves or in any of their close relatives—showed noticeable personality changes when they took paroxetine (the generic equivalent of Paxil), a drug closely related to Prozac (Knutson et al., 1998). In as little as one week, these people reported feeling less hostility and fewer negative emotions. One participant commented, "I used to think about good and bad, but now I don't; I'm in a good mood" (Knutson et al., 1998, p. 377). On the other hand, the people taking paroxetine in this study also reported side effects such as feeling sleepy and having delayed orgasms! But apparently they didn't mind.

Another researcher concluded from the evidence that SSRIs such as Prozac "are not happy pills, shifting depressed people to normalcy and normal people to bliss" (Farah, 2005, p. 36). Rather, they seem to make negative emotions less severe while leaving positive emotions unaffected. In a similar vein, the psychologist Steven Reise (2006) noted that SSRIs might be better classified as "antineurotics" than antidepressants, and that they could be helpful toward the fundamental goal of psychotherapy:

> It is not that bad turns to good, but rather bad doesn't seem so devastating (because an individual has more psychological reserve to deal with the issue). For example, in psychotherapy, low self-esteem does not magically turn into high self-esteem, but rather into an absence of devastating self-concern. Consider a man who is

in therapy because of his obsessive concern about his baldness. We do not expect such a man to ever "love baldness," but rather to not see it as such a big issue. (Reise, 2006, p. 6)

Kramer (1993) suggested that the ability of drugs to change aspects of personality may mean that, in the end, personality is primarily a matter of chemicals. He also suggested that this fact could give rise to "cosmetic psychopharmacology," the psychiatric equivalent of plastic surgery. Just as people with perfectly good noses sometimes go to a surgeon to obtain even better noses (so they think), so, too, might people with perfectly adequate personalities begin to take Prozac and other drugs to obtain even "better" personalities.

This possibility raises several issues. First, some authorities claim that the term *cosmetic psychopharmacology* is misleading because Prozac does not work on people whose personalities are adequate already (Metzner, 1994). They claim that unless the individual suffers from a disease—serotonin depletion—Prozac will have no effect. The diagnosis of this "disease" is far from clear-cut, as mentioned earlier, so this claim is difficult to evaluate; however, it seems doubtful in light of Knutson et al. (1998), the study cited earlier, which showed that the related drug Paxil had noticeable effects even on people without any serious psychological problems.

> Some individuals who take Prozac claim that it makes them more like "themselves."

A second issue is that, although chemicals clearly influence personality, the idea that personality is based so specifically on chemicals that it can be precisely adjusted is surely an exaggeration. For one thing, the effects of Prozac and related drugs on a given individual are difficult to predict and can change over time. Moreover, these effects can vary according to other factors in the patient's life, including the administration of psychotherapy. Sometimes the drugs have no effect at all, and sometimes they make things worse (Shenk, 1999). Cosmetic psychopharmacology may have side effects such as sleepiness, confusion, and sexual dysfunction. The prescription strategies of Kramer and other psychiatrists—by their own accounts—seem to be to give troubled patients some Prozac, see what happens, and then adjust the dosage of the drug accordingly, while also providing psychotherapy. Most prescriptions for Prozac are written not by psychiatrists but by primary-care practitioners, sometimes on the basis of little more than a phone call (Shenk, 1999).

Drugs that affect neurotransmitters can be remarkably beneficial for certain individuals. Still, it is difficult to avoid the conclusion that Prozac and similar products have become part of a widespread, legal drug culture in which people casually ingest a wide variety of substances with uncertain effects. They hope the drugs will make them feel better, but the ultimate consequences of such large-scale psychopharmacological intervention are presently unknown. For example, we could ask whether it is the structure of modern society that leads so many people to seek out drugs to combat depression and anxiety. If so, then maybe we ought to consider changing the structure of society rather than just medicating everybody. It is also worth pondering whether future historians will regard the present enthusiasm for psychoactive drugs such as Prozac and Paxil in much the same way we regard the previous generation's enthusiasm for psychosurgeries such as the lobotomy.

A final issue that deserves some thought concerns what chemical effects imply about the basis of personality. As the psychologist Martha Farah writes, "Are we the same person on Prozac as off? This is a good question, but so is: are we the same person after a glass of wine as before—or even during a vacation as before?" (Farah, 2005, p. 39). This notion expresses one important version of philosophy's long-standing mind-body problem: If we are what our minds do, and our minds are the product of what our brains do, then does a change to chemicals in our brains change who we are? It has often been observed that when research makes rapid progress, it typically produces more questions than answers, and in the case of brain research, some of the new questions lead into deep philosophical waters.

Hormones

As we have already seen, some neurotransmitters, such as norepinephrine, also can be considered hormones because they affect nerve cells far from their origins. The status of other chemicals as hormones, especially those produced in a central location, is clearer: Their main function is to act throughout the body, stimulating the activity of neurons in many locations in the brain and body at the same time. Different hormones affect different kinds of nerve cells, and so influence different neural systems. Hormones that are important for behavior are released by the hypothalamus, the **gonads** (testes and ovaries), and the **adrenal cortex** (part of the adrenal gland that sits atop the kidneys).

EPINEPHRINE AND NOREPINEPHRINE

Two particularly important hormones are **epinephrine** (also known as *adrenaline*) and **norepinephrine** (*noradrenaline*). Epinephrine and the neurons that respond to it are found throughout the body, while norepinephrine and its neurons work primarily within the brain, especially in the brain stem. The levels of both hormones can rise dramatically and suddenly in response to stress. When they are released into the bloodstream, the heart speeds up, digestion stops, and muscles tense, producing the well-known "adrenaline rush." At the same time, the brain becomes fully alert and concentrated on the matter at hand.[12] This sequence of events has long been called the *fight-or-flight response* (Cannon, 1932; Selye, 1956). The idea is that if the threat—such as a predator or an enemy—is one that you have a realistic chance of overcoming, you will stand and fight. If the situation seems hopeless, you will run away. Either way, the body has prepared you to react. But the response can be problematic if it is too easily triggered. People who are overly anxious and score high on measures of neuroticism may have an overactive norepinephrine system (Bremner, 2005).

The fight-or-flight response has been documented in dozens of studies over the years. However, the psychologist Shelley Taylor and her colleagues have noted that almost all of these studies—both in animals (usually rats) and in humans—have been conducted on males (S. E. Taylor et al., 2000). Why does this matter? According to Taylor et al., the response to threats may be different in men and women in important ways. They point out that during the prehistoric era when our species evolved, a man under threat had a relatively simple choice: stand and fight, or run away. For a woman—who might have been pregnant, nursing infants, or caring for children—the choice was not so simple. Either fighting or running away might put her and the children at unacceptable risk. Instead, it probably made more sense for her to respond differently, to calm everyone down and band people together to fend

---

[12] Mark Twain is said to have remarked that "the imminent prospect of hanging focuses a man's mind most wonderfully"—a classic effect of norepinephrine.

oxytoan =nurturant behavior, fear reduction.

off the threat—a response Taylor and her colleagues call *tend-and-befriend*. They point out that another hormone in the stress-response cascade is **oxytocin**, which, in females, promotes nurturant and sociable behavior along with relaxation and reduction of fear—the exact opposite of fight-or-flight. One effect of oxytocin may be to decrease anxiety and increase attachment between mothers and their children (McCarthy, 1995). This might be why primates—and, apparently, human mothers—rarely abandon their infants, even under conditions of grave danger.

This is a fascinating argument. On a methodological level, it shows the high cost of limiting research subjects to just one gender. Researchers did this not out of malicious intent, but to avoid the complications of accounting for estrous and menstrual cycles when conducting neurobiological assays. But this simplification may have come at the cost of missing a fundamental difference between the sexes. On a substantive level, moving from prehistoric environments to the modern day, Taylor's argument implies that men and women may have fundamentally different responses to threats and attacks. Men evaluate their strength relative to their opponent and assess their chances of escape. Then they either fight or run away. Women are more likely to seek out their friends and relatives and "gather their wagons in a circle," as it were. If you can't always fight or flee, at least there is some safety in numbers.

It is important to remember that this thesis, to the extent that it is correct, refers to the initial and automatic response to threat. It does not imply that further behavior is completely constrained. Men do form alliances, for example, and women sometimes stand and fight. But Taylor and her colleagues suggest that the first instinctive responses of men and women to a threatening situation may be fundamentally different (S. E. Taylor et al., 2000). A further implication—not noted by Taylor et al.—might be that the implications of neuroticism caused by an overactive norepinephrine system could be different in men and women. Neurotic men might be prone to either excessive fear or excessive aggression (or both). Neurotic women might overemphasize interpersonal attachments—including, possibly, unhealthy attachments—at the expense of doing what they need to do for themselves.

> If you can't always fight or flee, at least there is some safety in numbers.

TESTOSTERONE

Probably the best-known hormones are the gonadal, or sex hormones: **testosterone** (primarily in males) and **estrogen** (primarily in females), although both hormones are present in all humans. It has long been observed

Females-40ng testosterone

Males =300-1,000ng

Relationship between testosterone and physical aggression holds for poor, uneducated men.

that males seem generally to be more aggressive than females (e.g., Kagan, 1978; Maccoby & Jacklin, 1974), and males certainly have more testosterone in their bodies. To be exact, normal human females have about 40 ng (nanograms) of testosterone in each deciliter of their blood, whereas normal males have 300–1,000 ng per deciliter, a 10 times greater concentration.

This fact has led some psychologists to hypothesize that testosterone causes aggressive behavior, and many studies have pursued this idea. Some of these studies have found that human males with higher levels of testosterone are more likely to show aggression and other behavioral control problems than males with lower levels. In one study, male American military veterans were asked about their past behaviors. Those with higher testosterone levels reported more trouble with their parents, teachers, and classmates; a history of assaulting others; more use of hard drugs, marijuana, or alcohol; numerous sexual partners; and a "general tendency toward excessive behavior" (Dabbs & Morris, 1990, p. 209).

Findings like these, though provocative, are not always consistent from one study to the next (Zuckerman, 1991). They are also complex. For example, you should bear in mind that nearly all studies in this area—including Dabbs & Morris (1990)—measure aggression or even criminal behavior solely through self-report (S data); they do not account for people who engage in such activities but do not admit it. A more basic consideration is that while the males in many species are more aggressive than females, this is not always the case: Males are not more aggressive than females among gibbons, wolves, rabbits, hamsters, and even laboratory rats (Floody, 1983).

There is yet another important complexity. Although some extreme criminal types (e.g., rapists who also commit other kinds of bodily harm) may be likely to have high levels of testosterone (Rada, Laws, & Kellner, 1976), the reverse does not seem to be true: Men with high levels of testosterone are not necessarily aggressive. Furthermore, it has sometimes been reported that the relationship between testosterone level and physical aggression holds only (or more strongly) for poorer, relatively uneducated men (Dabbs & Morris, 1990). The presumed reason is that wealthier, more educated men have been socialized to express their aggressive impulses in less physical ways (maybe by saying something elegantly sarcastic or initiating a hostile takeover of your company).

Despite its reputation (ever heard a woman complain of a particular man suffering from "testosterone poisoning"?), the hormone is not all bad. Males with more testosterone are higher in "stable extraversion," that is, sociability, self-acceptance, and dominance. They have more restless energy, spend a lot of time thinking about concrete problems in the immediate present, and become frustrated when they can't get things done (Dabbs, Strong, & Milun, 1997). They smile less, which seems to make them appear more dominant (Dabbs, 1997); they also report having more sexual experience and more sexual partners. But again, higher testosterone levels may be a result rather than a cause of sexual activity (Zuckerman, 1991). Testosterone also has interesting interactions with personality traits. One study found that, relative to other males with similar traits, high-testosterone males who are also conscientious make better emergency medical service (EMS) providers, and high-testosterone males who are extraverted and active are better firefighters. The researchers concluded that testosterone should be thought of as an energizing factor that "appears to facilitate the behavior of individuals along directions they are already inclined to take" (Fannin & Dabbs, 2002, p. 107).

And let's not forget that women have testosterone as well. Most of their testosterone is produced by the adrenal cortex (a small amount is also produced in the ovaries), and the hormone has important behavioral effects. One study showed that female prisoners who had committed unprovoked violent crimes had higher levels of testosterone than did women who had been violent after provocation or who had committed nonviolent crimes (Dabbs, Ruback, Frady, Hopper, & Sgoritas, 1988). Lesbian women who take on the "butch" role (dressing and acting like men) have higher testosterone than either lesbians who take the "femme" role or heterosexual women (Singh, Vidaurri, Zambarano, & Dabbs, 1999). Other research showed that women who produce less testosterone (due to impaired adrenocortical functioning) seem to be less interested in sex. Moreover, the administration of testosterone injections to women can sometimes dramatically increase sexual desire (Zuckerman, 1991). These results suggest that testosterone is a chemical contributor to sexual motivation in women as well as in men.

Also similar to the findings among men, higher levels of testosterone in women are associated with higher levels of self-reported sociability and with impulsivity, lack of inhibition, and lack of conformity. In both sexes, higher testosterone is also associated with holding a blue-collar industrial job as opposed to a white-collar professional job. Among lawyers, trial lawyers who battle cases in court have higher testosterone levels than do those who work in the back room with law books (Dabbs, Alford, & Fielden, 1998).

Further evidence concerning the effects of testosterone comes from bodybuilders and athletes who take anabolic steroids to promote muscular development (H. G. Pope & Katz, 1994). *Anabolic steroids* are synthetic tes-

[handwritten: Anabolic steroids = synthetic testosterone]

tosterone; their effects include not only speedier muscle development but also a whole host of troublesome side effects. Steroid users frequently experience erratic and uncontrolled aggressiveness and sexuality. For example, male steroid users may experience erections without stimulation, but they also seem to have a lower overall sex drive and a tendency to impotence and sterility. Ben Johnson, the Canadian sprinter whose Olympic gold medal was taken away when he was found (through blood tests) to have used steroids, seemed to experience difficulty controlling aggression: He got into a lot of fights with reporters. (Then again, maybe that behavior was not drug induced.)

[handwritten: Men w too much testosterone = super extra]

What can we conclude from all this? It would be an oversimplification to conclude that testosterone causes aggression or sexuality in any direct way. Instead, it seems to play a role in the control and inhibition of aggressiveness and sexuality—including normal assertiveness and perhaps even general activity level—as well as the normal range of sexual function and responsiveness in both sexes. Recall the comment from Dabbs & Morris (1990) that in their study, males with high testosterone levels were prone to "excessive" behavior. In general, the evidence suggests that when this hormone is present in abnormally high proportions, which occurs naturally in certain individuals and artificially in steroid users, aggression and sexuality are not so much enhanced as they are messed up. Both may occur at inappropriate times and fail to occur at appropriate times. But the simple belief that testosterone makes a person either more aggressive or more sexual is probably not true.

[handwritten: - testosterone is an important part of the feedback system r: winning and boosting.]

Moreover, testosterone is not just a cause of behavior; it is also an effect. A particularly good demonstration of this was a study of World Cup soccer fans watching a playoff match (Bernhardt, Dabbs, Fielden, & Lutter, 1998). Testosterone was measured from the fans' saliva before and after the game. Afterward, the testosterone level in fans of the winning team had increased, while the testosterone level in fans of the losing team had decreased. This might help explain why riots so often break out in the winning city after an NBA championship and at colleges that win football championships, whereas the losers usually slink silently home (Gettleman, 2002). More importantly, this finding may provide insight into testosterone's regulatory function. Imagine winning a fight (Schultheiss et al., 2005). Your testosterone level goes up, and you press your advantage. But if you lose, your testosterone level goes down, and you leave the field of battle before you suffer further damage or even get killed. Testosterone is, therefore, more than a simple or unidirectional cause of behavior; it is an important part of the feedback system that affects how people respond to winning and losing.

CORTISOL *released by the adrenal system.*
↳ several metabolic processes.

In the earlier discussion of the hormones epinephrine and norepineph- *related to severe stress, anxiety and depression* rine, I described their role in the fight-or-flight response, which in women may be more of a tend-and-befriend response. Another part of this same response system is the release of a glucocorticoid hormone known as **cortisol**. Released into the bloodstream by the adrenal cortex as a response to *[↑ cortisol ↑]* physical or psychological stress, cortisol is part of the body's preparation for action as well as an important part of several normal metabolic processes. It can speed the heart rate, raise blood pressure, stimulate muscle strength, metabolize fat, and cause many other effects as well.

Individuals who suffer from severe stress, anxiety, and depression tend *infants w high cortisol* to have chronically high levels of cortisol in their blood. In this case, the *= social phobias.* rise in cortisol seems to be an effect of stress and depression rather than a cause; injecting cortisol into people does not produce these feelings (Born, Hitzler, Pietrowsky, Pairschinger, & Fehm, 1988). Infants with high levels of cortisol tend to be timid and vulnerable to developing *social phobias* (irrational fears of other people) later in life (Kagan, Reznick, & Snidman, 1988). Again, however, cortisol production may be stimulated by their fearful reactions rather than the other way around. Recent evidence suggests that excess cortisol production stimulated by too much fear and anxiety increases the risk of heart disease and may even, over time, make one's brain smaller (Knutson et al., 2001)! It seems clear that, on both a psychological and a physical level, feeling bad all the time is not good for you.

Low levels of cortisol entail risks too. Chronically low cortisol levels appear to be associated with PTSD, the collection of psychological problems that can result from experiences such as physical or sexual abuse, or harrowing experiences in war (Meewisse, Reitsma, De Vries, Gersons, & Olff, 2007). Low levels of cortisol may lead to the "sensation seeking" underreactivity syndrome noted several times already in this chapter, wherein people become impulsive and disinclined to follow the rules of society (Zuckerman, 1991, 1998). This pattern may arise because such individuals are unable, anymore, to generate the normal surge in cortisol production in response to danger, causing them to fail to respond normally to danger signals associated with high-risk activities like bungee jumping and shoplifting.

Low cortisol = PTSD, sensation seeking

BIOLOGY: CAUSE AND EFFECT

A final note: When looking deeply into the relationships between brain activity, neural chemicals, and behavior, it is tempting to believe that we are finally getting to the real causes of things. There is also something down-right seductive about the colorful brain images that appear to show the living brain at work (D. P. McCabe & Castel, 2008). Since all behavior must have its origin somewhere in the nervous system, some people infer that once the brain is understood, behavior will be demystified as well. But the situation is not so simple. The relationship between the brain and its environment works in both directions.

As we saw several times in this chapter, biological processes are the effects of behaviors or experiences as often as they are the causes (Roberts & Jackson, 2008). For example, a stressful environment will raise one's cortisol level, as will feeling depressed or anxious, and the result (not the cause) may be a smaller brain! Winning a game raises one's testosterone level; likewise, behavior and the social environment affect levels of other hormones and neurotransmitters, as well as the development and functioning of the brain. Measurable brain activity can be changed by drugs; it can also be changed by psychotherapy (Isom & Heller, 1999). So we will not fully understand the nervous system until we understand depression, anxiety, psychotherapy, stressful environments, and even why some people win fights while others lose. The workings of the brain help to explain social behavior, but a greater understanding of social behavior will also help us to better understand the brain.

Remember Hippocrates' MP3 player? Let's imagine, clever fellow that he is, that he actually manages to make progress in understanding how it works. "Ah," he realizes, "the power comes out of the battery and rotates this disk; the sensor picks up the information, and then it is amplified through this transistor and comes out through the speaker." If he figured all of this out, it would be a stunning accomplishment, comparable to modern attempts to understand the workings of the brain. Then, being wise as well as clever, Hippocrates might ask, "And who is this Usher person? What does this song mean? Who decided to record music like this, and why do people choose to listen to it?" The important questions haven't ended; they are just beginning.

SUMMARY

- Studies of the biology of personality raise the philosophical issue called the mind-body problem, which concerns the degree to which all aspects of human nature can be understood as processes of our physical brains and bodies, making humans no different from any other animal.

The Brain and Personality

- Both brain anatomy and neurophysiology are relevant to personality. Knowledge about the brain comes from studies of the effects of brain injury and brain surgery, from measurements of brain activity using relatively old techniques such as electroencephalography (EEG) and newer techniques such as magnetoencephalography (MEG), from studies of direct brain stimulation (including a new technique called transcranial magnetic stimulation, or TMS), and from newly developed imaging tools such as positron emission tomography (PET) scans and functional magnetic resonance imaging (fMRI).

- Computerized data analysis can combine data gathered from instruments such as PET and fMRI scanners to provide data summaries, represented as pictures, that identify the brain areas that are most active during various mental tasks and emotional reactions. Researchers have also used these techniques to compare brain activity in people with different personality attributes. The data analyses this research requires are complex and sometimes controversial.

- The ascending reticular activating system (ARAS), part of the brain stem, was hypothesized by Hans Eysenck to be the basis of extraversion and introversion. According to his theory, people whose ARAS cuts them off from stimulation may seek out exciting people, environments, and activities, perhaps to the point of danger.

- The amygdala plays a special role in generating emotional response. Based on its computation of whether the environment seems to offer impending threat or reward, it can respond by making the heart beat faster and raising the blood pressure, among other effects. Traits associated with functioning of the amygdala include chronic anxiety, fearfulness, sociability, and sexuality.

- The frontal lobes are the basis of uniquely human abilities such as language and foresight; they also are important for understanding the self and other people, and for regulating emotion. In fMRI studies, strong activity in this area occurs in people who are prone to negative emotions, but also in people who are consistently cooperative. Cases such as Phineas Gage, Elliott, and victims of Capgras syndrome show how basic emotional responses and cognitive functioning must work together for meaningful experiences and adaptive decision making.

- Psychosurgeries on the frontal lobes, such as lobotomies, may have helped some desperately ill people in the past, but overall seemed to damage patients' ability to reason and to function, especially in their emotional lives and relations with others.

- Recent fMRI research suggests that personality may be affected more by systems or circuits of different areas of the brain acting in concert than by the relevance of single areas to particular traits.

Biochemistry and Personality

- The chemical bases of behavior include neurotransmitters and hormones, both of which play a role in communication between and stimulation of the cells of the nervous system.

- The neurotransmitters epinephrine and norepinephrine are an important part of the fight-or-flight response to threatening situations. Some psychologists have recently proposed that tend-and-befriend better characterizes women's instinctive response to a threat.

- Dopamine is important for responding to rewards and may be the basis of "extraversion." Dopamine is an important basis of the behavioral activation system (BAS), hypothesized by Jeffrey Gray. Gray also describes a behavioral inhibition system (BIS), based mostly in the frontal lobes.

- Serotonin aids in regulating emotions. Some widely prescribed antidepressant drugs are designed to increase its prevalence in the brain. When its level is raised via selective serotonin reuptake inhibitors (SSRIs) such as Prozac, the result is often a general lessening of neurotic overreactions to negative events. However, attempts to improve personality-relevant brain functioning through cosmetic psychopharmacology may have side effects.

- The male sex hormone testosterone plays a role in sexuality, aggression, and dominance, especially in people who have not been socialized against physical aggression. Testosterone level is an effect as well as a cause of certain social behaviors; for example, it rises after the experience of victory over an opponent.

- Cortisol is an important part of the fight-or-flight (or tend-and-befriend) response. Excess production may lead to chronic anxiety and even brain damage, whereas a shortage can lead to dangerously impulsive behavior.

Biology: Cause and Effect

- It is important to remember that biological processes affect behavior, but both behavior and the social environment also affect biological processes. Understanding each is helpful for understanding the others.

THINK ABOUT IT

1. Are people just animals? In what ways—if any—are they not?

2. What do you think of Hans Eysenck's account of extraversion and introversion? Think of the people you know. Is somebody who stays at home with a book rather than going to a wild party just avoiding overstimulation? Is the chronic partygoer otherwise understimulated?

3. What if Charles Whitman had survived that awful day in Texas? Would it have been fair to prosecute him for murder?

4. Psychosurgery has mostly given way to drug therapy. Is this an improvement? Does it make a difference whether a person's mood, behavior, or personality is changed with drugs, or with surgery?

5. If you could take a pill to improve some aspect of your personality, would you do it? Would you still be the same person after taking the pill?

6. Imagine that you are involved in intense negotiations with somebody. Your adversary takes a pill to become more confident and aggressive, and thereby achieves a better outcome than you do. Did your adversary have an unfair advantage? Will you take one of those pills yourself next time?

7. In your experience, do women respond to stress and danger differently from men?

SUGGESTED READINGS

Damasio, A. R. (1994). *Descartes' error: Emotion, reason, and the human brain.* New York: Putnam.

> *A lively and highly readable summary of one neurologist's view of the relationship between the brain and behavior. It includes several compelling case studies (including that of Elliot, summarized in this chapter) and the author's somatic marker hypothesis, in which he argues that emotions are an indispensable component of rational thought.*

Valenstein, E. S. (1986). *Great and desperate cures: The rise and decline of psychosurgery and other radical treatments for mental illness.* New York: Basic.

> *A vivid history of psychosurgery, electroshock therapy, and other drastic, biologically based "psychotherapeutic" interventions that have been tried over the years. Along the way, much is taught about both biology and the sociology of psychology and medicine.*

EMEDIA

 Go to StudySpace, wwnorton.com/studyspace, to access additional review and enrichment materials.

9

THE INHERITANCE OF PERSONALITY:
Behavioral Genetics and Evolutionary Theory

THE NEXT MEMBER of New York's Rockefeller family will be born rich. Why? The reason, of course, is *inheritance*. The child's parents are already rich, so he or she will join a wealthy family and have all of the advantages (and perhaps disadvantages) that accompany large amounts of money. But why are this child's parents rich? Why are all the Rockefellers wealthy? The explanation goes back more than 100 years to the career of John D. Rockefeller, a fabulously successful and utterly ruthless businessman. Using tactics such as secret buyouts, intimidation, and market manipulation, between 1870 and 1882 he built Standard Oil of Ohio into the Standard Oil Trust, which for years held a near monopoly. After many battles with competitors and the legal system, he retired in 1911 with a fortune almost beyond imagining. His family name has been a synonym for wealth ever since.

Now consider a question that might seem unrelated. Where did your personality come from? Why are you so friendly, competitive, or stubborn? Maybe you have chosen to be this way, but we need to consider the strong possibility that answer also concerns inheritance. Are your parents especially friendly, competitive, or stubborn? If the answer is yes, as it might well be, then a further question arises: Where did this trait come from in the first place? The answer might lie in the careers of some of your ancestors who lived a very long time ago.

Two different biologically based approaches consider the ways personality might be inherited; that is, how characteristic patterns of behavior might be encoded on genes and passed from parents to children across generations. The first of these approaches, *behavioral genetics*, attempts to explain how individual differences in behavior—personality traits—are passed from parent to child and shared by biological relatives. The second approach, *evolutionary psychology*, attempts to explain how patterns of behavior that characterize all humans originated in the survival value these characteristics provided over the history of the species. These two approaches are connected: The evolutionary approach assumes that inherited personality attributes promoting survival became more prevalent across generations, and the personality attributes we inherited from our ancestors—ancient and recent—are the result. Put another way, behavioral genetics concerns how personality can be inherited much like a bank account or a great estate; evolutionary psychology asks where all this money came from in the first place.

This chapter will consider the inheritance of personality from both perspectives. First, we will survey some of the research on behavioral genetics that examine how personality traits are shared among biological relatives, including recent studies that are uncovering the molecular basis of the inheritance of personality. The chapter will also examine how the effects of inheritance interact with experience—two people with the same genes might have very different attributes, depending on the environments in which they are raised, and, as recent research is beginning to show, environments can actually change genetic expression. Second, we will summarize some recent theorizing on how human nature and personality may be a result of the evolutionary history of the human species going back hundreds of thousands of years. We will also consider some of the controversies over this evolutionary approach, and the light that evolutionary theory can shed on our understanding of human nature. The chapter ends by reconsidering the question that began this section of the book: Are people just animals? Or, to put the question another way, is an explanation of the biology of behavior sufficient for explaining human psychology?[1]

> Are people just animals?

BEHAVIORAL GENETICS

People tend to look somewhat like their biological parents, and at family reunions it can be interesting to notice how all of these aunts, uncles, and cousins share a family resemblance. While the existence of similarity may

---

[1] I will give you a hint about the answer: it's no.

be obvious, its exact basis can be surprisingly difficult to pin down. Whatever its manfestation (the shape of the eyes? a curl of the hair? a characteristic facial expression?), the cause of the resemblance among biological relatives is the genes that they share.

Physical appearance is one thing, but now consider some other questions: Is there family resemblance in personality? Did you inherit your traits from your parents? Are you psychologically similar to your brother or sister because you are biologically related? Questions like these motivate the study of behavioral genetics. This field of research examines the way inherited biological material—the genes—can influence broad patterns of behavior. A pattern of behavior relevant to more than one situation is, by definition, a **personality trait** (Plomin, Chipuer, & Loehlin, 1990). Thus, "behavioral" genetics might more accurately be called "trait" genetics, but in this chapter I will stick with the traditional term.

Controversy

The field of behavioral genetics has been controversial from the beginning, in part because of its historic association with a couple of notorious ideas. One is *eugenics*, the belief that humanity could (and should) be improved through selective breeding. This idea has led to activities ranging from campaigns to keep "inferior" immigrants out of some countries, to attempts to set up sperm banks stocked with deposits from winners of the Nobel Prize. A second controversial idea to emerge from eugenics is cloning, the belief that it might be technologically possible to produce a complete duplicate—psychological as well as physical—of a human being. Both of these ideas have dodgy histories (e.g., Adolf Hitler promoted eugenics), and seem to lead to nightmarish future scenarios.

Modern behavioral geneticists are generally quick to dissociate themselves from these ideas. They view themselves as basic scientists pursuing knowledge for its own sake, and they invoke the standard (and true) argument that ignorance never got anyone very far (see the discussion of research ethics in Chapter 3). But a more reassuring observation may be that neither eugenics nor cloning turns out to be very feasible. Because personality is the result of a complex interaction between an individual's genes and the environment, as we shall see, the chances of being able to breed people to specification or to duplicate any individual are, thankfully, slim.[2] The real contribution of behavioral genetics is the way it expands our understanding of the sources of personality to include bases in both genes and the environment.

Calculating Heritabilities

One research method in behavioral genetics is to compare similarities in personality between individuals who are and are not genetically related, or who are related to each other to different degrees. The basic question concerns the degree to which variation in the *phenotype*, the observable traits of a person, can be attributed to variation in the *genotype*, or underlying genetic structure. The classic technique for answering this question is to look at twins. As you probably know, there are two kinds of human twins: identical (also called monozygotic, or MZ) twins, and fraternal (dizygotic, or DZ) twins. Monozygotic ("one-egg") twins come from the splitting of a single fertilized egg and therefore are genetically identical. Dizygotic ("two-egg") twins come from two eggs fertilized by two different sperm, and so, although born at the same time, they are no more genetically related than any other two siblings.

Humans are highly similar to each other genetically. More than 99 percent of all human genes are identical from one individual to another. (Indeed, 98 percent of these same genes are also found in chimpanzees! See Balter, 2002.) Behavioral genetics concentrates on the less than 1 percent of the human genome that varies. MZ twins are identical in all of these varying genes; DZ twins share about half of them, on average. Thus, for example, the statement that a mother shares 50 percent of her genetic material with her child really means that she shares 50 percent of the material that varies across individuals. This rather technical point highlights an important fact: Like trait psychology (see Chapters 4 to 7), with which it is closely aligned, behavioral genetics focuses exclusively on aspects of personality that differ from one individual to another. The inheritance of species-specific traits that all humans share is addressed by evolutionary biology, which is discussed in the second half of this chapter (Tooby & Cosmides, 1990).

---

[2] However, as a colleague of mine once noted, meeting your clone would still be "pretty danged weird."

Research on behavioral genetics has made great efforts to find twins of both types (MZ and DZ), and also to seek out the rare twins separated at birth and reared apart from each other. Researchers try hard to find such twins and measure their personalities, usually with self-report instruments such as those discussed in Chapters 5 and 6. The Eysenck Personality Questionnaire (EPQ) and the California Psychological Inventory (CPI) are particular favorites. Researchers have also directly observed twins in laboratory contexts to assess the degree to which they behave similarly (Borkenau, Riemann, Angleitner, & Spinath, 2001). The next step is to compute the correlation coefficient (see Chapter 3) across the pairs of twins.[3] The basic assumption of behavioral genetics is that if a trait or a behavior is influenced by genes, then the trait and behavioral scores of identical (MZ) twins ought to be more highly correlated than scores of fraternal (DZ) twins are. Furthermore, closer relatives (e.g., siblings) ought to be more similar on a gene-influenced, inherited trait than are more distant relatives (e.g., cousins).

A statistic called the *heritability coefficient* is computed to reflect this influence (see the hypothetical example in Table 9.1). In the case of twins, one simple formula is

$$\text{Heritability quotient} = (r_{MZ} - r_{DZ}) \times 2$$

(that is, twice the difference between the correlation among MZ twins compared with the correlation among DZ twins). Across many, many traits, the average correlation across MZ twins is about .60, and across DZ twins it is about .40, when age and gender are controlled (Borkenau et al., 2001, p. 661). The difference between these figures is .20; multiply that by 2, and you arrive at a heritability coefficient of .40. This means that, according to twin studies, the average heritability of many traits is about .40, which is interpreted to mean that the proportion of phenotypic (behavioral) variance that can be explained by genetic variance is 40 percent (see also Plomin et al., 1990).[4]

Twin studies are simple and elegant, and the calculations are easy because MZ twins share exactly twice as many variable genes as do DZ twins, but these studies are not the only way to estimate heritabilities. Other kinds

---

[3] For technical reasons, a related statistic called the intraclass correlation coefficient is used.

[4] When both self- and peer reports are combined to yield more reliable measures, heritability estimates for the Big Five can increase to a range of .65–.79 (Riemann, Angleitner, & Strelau, 1997).

Table 9.1

CALCULATING HERITABILITIES

	Identical (MZ) Twins		Fraternal (DZ) Twins	
	Score of First Twin	Score of Second Twin	Score of First Twin	Score of Second Twin
Pair 1	54	53	52	49
Pair 2	41	40	41	53
Pair 3	49	51	49	52
...	x_4	y_4	x_4	y_4
...	x_5	y_5	x_5	y_5
	$r = .60$		$r = .40$	

Note: Heritability quotient = $(r_{MZ} - r_{DZ}) \times 2$

Calculation: $.60 - .40 = .20$

$.20 \times 2 = .40$

Conclusion: Heritability = 40%.

of relatives also vary in the degree to which they share genes. For example, children share, on average, 50 percent of their variable genes with their biological parents, whereas adopted children (presumably) share no more of their personality-relevant genes with their adoptive parents than they would with any other person chosen at random. Full siblings also share, on average, 50 percent of the genes that vary, whereas half-siblings (who have one parent in common) share only 25 percent. Calculating similarities in personality across these different kinds of relatives provides an alternative way to estimate heritability. Interestingly, for most traits the estimates of heritability garnered from nontwin studies are about 20 percent, or half the average heritability estimated from twin studies (Plomin et al., 1990).

Why this difference? One likely explanation is that the effects of genes are interactive and multiplicative rather than additive. That is, the twin-studies calculation assumes that because DZ twins share half the variable genes that MZ twins do, they are half as similar in genetic expression. But if genes act not just by independently adding their effects together, but also by interacting with one another, then DZ twins' similarity in genetic expression will be less than 50 percent. Though they share 50 percent of the genes, they share only 25 percent of the two-way interactions among those genes. As a result, in terms of genetic expression, identical twins will be four times as similar to each other than are fraternal twins, instead of only twice as similar. If this line of reasoning is correct, then the 20 percent figure for the heritability of many traits is probably a better estimate than the 40 percent figure often quoted.

There is at least one other good reason to conclude that genes interact with each other. The Human Genome Project concluded in 2003 that the human genome includes about 25,000 genes. For comparison, fruit flies have between 13,000 and 14,000 genes; the roundworm *Caenorhabditis elegans* has only 959 cells in its body but over 19,000 genes. The vast differences between humans and these other species, not to mention the vast diversity among humans, cannot be accounted for by adding up genetic effects (Gould, 2001). Genes interact with each other and with the environment in complex, often unpredictable ways.

"We think it has something to do with your genome."

What Heritabilities Tell You

Admittedly, these heritability calculations are rather technical, and a more basic question should be asked: Regardless of how you compute it, what does a heritability number tell you? Three things.

3 things inferred from heritability calc.

( ) GENES MATTER

First, heritabilities tell you that genes matter. For years, psychologists presumed that all of personality was determined environmentally—that is, by early experiences and parental practices. Heritability estimates challenge that presumption whenever they turn out to be greater than zero—and they nearly always do. Indeed, it has been seriously suggested that the first law of behavioral genetics should be: "everything is heritable" (Turkheimer, 1998, p. 785; Turkheimer & Gottesman, 1991). Not all of personality comes from experience; some of it comes from genes. This important realization is relatively new to psychology. It still is not accepted by everyone, and its far-reaching implications are still sinking in.

not yet widely accepted

Severe mental retardation =not heritable — moderate is. 2)

Other psych problems are often just extreme ends of the "normal" range of characteristics.

INSIGHT INTO ETIOLOGY

Heritabilities sometimes can tell you whether specific behavioral or mental disorders are part of the normal range or are pathologically distinctive. One of the more interesting findings to emerge from the behavioral genetics literature is that severe mental retardation (defined as an IQ below 50, where 100 is the average) apparently is not heritable—a rare violation of the "first law" just mentioned. The average IQ of the sibling of a severely retarded child is a perfectly normal 103. However, moderate mental retardation (IQs ranging from 50 to 69) does seem to be heritable; the average IQ of the sibling of a moderately retarded child is 85. Moderate retardation runs in families, but severe retardation surprisingly does not! This finding implies that severe mental retardation comes from something other than inheriting a very low IQ. The real cause is probably related to the environment. For example, perhaps the mother had an infection during pregnancy, or the child suffered some kind of birth trauma or head injury—these are both potential nongenetic causes of severe retardation (Plomin et al., 1990).

Other psychological problems appear to be examples of extreme ends of the normal range. One recent analysis examined the relationship between the genetics of personality disorders and the genetics of normal personality (Markon, Krueger, Bouchard, & Gottesman, 2002). Well-adjusted people vary in the degree to which they characteristically experience negative emotions, but when taken to an extreme, such experiences can turn into depression. A normal tendency to become absorbed in interesting activities and thoughts can, at the extreme, be related to psychosis. And normal variation in impulsiveness and a tendency to be uninhibited may, at the extremes, have the same genetic roots as criminal behavior and family abuse (see Chapter 18).

INSIGHT INTO EFFECTS OF THE ENVIRONMENT

3)

A third contribution of heritability studies is to provide a window into how the early environment does—or does not—operate in shaping personality development. According to some researchers, the major finding of behavioral genetics so far is this: Growing up together in the same home does not tend to make children similar to each other. The personality traits of adoptive siblings raised in the same family resemble each other with a correlation of only .05, which means that a mere 5 percent of the variation in their personalities—typically measured in terms of the Big Five traits considered in Chapter 7—is due to their common family environment. More impor-

more important:
— birth order, friendships, other outside interests
and activities.

tant, it seems, is the portion of their early environments that siblings do not share. This includes the effects of birth order (e.g., the degree to which firstborns are treated differently from those born later), friendships outside the home, and other outside interests and activities (Loehlin, Willerman, & Horn, 1985, 1989; Rowe, 1994).

Of course, these are just speculations. Research on behavioral genetics does not tell which aspects of a child's early environment are important (Turkheimer & Waldron, 2000). It does suggest that whatever the key aspects may be, they are not shared across members of a family. But there is more to this story.

Does the Family Matter?

If the shared family environment truly has little or no effect on personality development, the implications are stunning. For example, this conclusion implies that aspects of the family environment—such as neighborhood, home atmosphere, income, nutrition, parents' styles of child rearing, and even the presence or absence of one or both parents—are not important in determining the kind of adult each child grows up to be. Psychologist Judith Rich Harris followed these implications to their logical extreme. She has written professional articles and a best-selling book arguing that parents—and the rest of the family environment—don't matter at all (J. R. Harris, 1995, 1998). As she wrote in one attention-grabbing article, "Do parents have any important long-term effects on the development of their child's personality? This article examines the evidence and concludes that the answer is no" (J. R. Harris, 1995, p. 458). This seems like a radical statement (it is!), but it represents just a small step from the conclusion of the behavioral geneticists that the shared family environment—such as the fact that all siblings in an intact family are raised by the same parents—has no identifiable effect on later personality.

You can imagine the stir this statement caused when it hit both the professional literature and the popular media. At one stroke, it denies all of the fundamental assumptions that have guided the study of development for the past 50 years or more. Even more disconcerting, Harris's claim also seems to imply that people might as well not bother trying to be better parents; it could even be taken to imply that there is no reason to remove children from abusive households.

A number of questions could be raised about this conclusion, however. First, many decades of research in developmental psychology have documented the effects of child rearing, family environment, and even social class on personality (Baumrind, 1993; Bergeman et al., 1993; Funder et al., 1993; Hetherington, 1983). On the other hand, it must be admitted that research on how parental styles affect children has been *confounded*, to use a methodological term, by the fact that parents and their children are genetically related. So some of the effects that psychologists have attributed to the way parents raise their children may instead be due to the genes that parents share with their children. Still, it is difficult to believe that having an alcoholic parent, or living in substandard housing, or having parents who encourage all their children to do well has no importance for how a child turns out.

> It is difficult to believe that having an alcoholic parent, or living in substandard housing, or having parents who encourage all their children to do well has no importance for how a child turns out.

Moreover, experiments have shown that when mothers and fathers are taught how to be better parents, their children both behave better and control their emotions more effectively (Eisenberg, Spinrad, & Cumberland, 1998; Kazdin, 1994). This might be because good parents adjust their own behavior to the needs of each child, rather than treating all their children the same. This aspect of parental skill would not show up in analyses as a shared effect—because it would be different for each child—but it would be an important way in which the family environment matters.

A relatively technical complication is that because adoptive parents are often screened, chosen, and even arranged by social service agencies, the family environments they foster may be more similar to each other than are the environments encountered in families at large. Furthermore, all of the families in typical heritability studies come from the same culture. To the extent that the families in these studies resemble each other, estimates of the effects of family environment on personality tend to be underestimates (Mandler, 1997). (The technical reason for this tendency is that the range has been restricted on the "family environment" variable, lowering its chance of demonstrating an effect on any other variable.) Indeed, according to one recent reanalysis, when heritability calculations are corrected for the similarities among families, it appears that up to 50 percent of the variance in individual differences such as IQ are accounted for by the shared family environment (Stoolmiller, 1999).

The most important response to Harris's hypothesis has been to assert that the evidence from past research is not quite as strong as summaries by her and others might make it appear. Several developmental outcomes, including juvenile delinquency, love styles, and aggression, have been found—using standard methods of behavioral genetics—to be affected by

[handwritten annotation: – several developmental outcomes have been shown to be influenced by the shared family environment]

the shared family environment (Rowe, Rodgers, & Meseck-Bushey, 1992; N. G. Waller & Shaver, 1994). The results may depend on the methods used (Borkenau, Riemann, Angleitner, & Spinath, 2002). For example, when twins and other siblings rate their own personalities, they may focus on the traits that make them different from each other, rather than on broader similarities that would be obvious to outside observers. This may be why the shared family environment has been shown to be important in the development of aggression only when aggression is measured through direct observation (B data, discussed in Chapter 2) rather than through questionnaires (S data) (Miles & Carey, 1997). And the effects of the shared family environment go beyond aggression. One large, recent study obtained ratings of twins' personality traits based on the direct observations of 15 different behaviors, including introducing oneself to a stranger, building a paper tower, and singing a song. The result was that "extraversion was the only trait that seemed not to be influenced by shared environment" (Borkenau et al., 2001, p. 655). Every other trait measured in the study *was* affected by the shared environment.

As Borkenau et al. pointed out, their result has two important implications. The first is that the widely advertised conclusion that family environment is unimportant for personality development was reached too quickly, on the basis of limited data. For many years, behavioral genetics research was based almost exclusively on self-report personality questionnaires, and these S data show little similarity across siblings raised together. But when personality is assessed by directly observing behavior, the shared family environment shows important effects. The second conclusion returns us to the message of Chapter 2: Personality research can employ many kinds of data, and they all should be used. Conclusions based on only one kind are at risk; conclusions based on consistent results across several kinds of data are much more likely to hold up in the long run.

[handwritten annotation: – Implications 1) Conclusion that family environment is unimportant may reached too quickly due to limited data. 2) All type of data should be cited]

The line between provocative scientific hypothesizing and irresponsible overstatement is both thin and blurry. Some behavioral geneticists have danced right up to this line with their enthusiastic claim that the shared family environment has little or no effect on personality development. Judith Harris jumped over it with her claim that parents don't matter. The overwhelming scientific evidence is that they do (Eisenberg et al., 1998; Collins, Maccoby, Steinberg, Hetherington, & Bornstein, 2000).

Still, the discussion is worth having. Behavioral genetics research should get credit for raising this provocative issue, and much research remains to be done to ascertain how genetic factors interact with environmental factors, including the family environment, in personality development. And criticisms of the overstatements made by some behavioral geneticists cannot deny one basic fact: Personality is partially determined by genes, to an extent that psychologists just a couple of decades ago would not have believed possible.

Nature and Nurture

Ever since scientists realized the effects that heredity might have on behavior, they have longed for a simple calculation that would resolve the nature-nurture debate by indicating what percentage of any given trait was due to nature (heredity) and what percentage was due to nurture (upbringing and environment). To some, the heritability coefficient seemed like the answer, since it yields a figure between 0 and 100 percent that reflects the percentage of the variation in a trait due to variation in genes.

But consider, as an example, the number of arms you have. Was this number determined by your genes or by your childhood environment? Let's use some (hypothetical but realistic) twin data to calculate the heritability of this trait. Look again at Table 9.1. For the score of the first identical twin of Pair 1, plug in the number of arms he has, which you can presume to be 2. Do the same for the score of the second twin of Pair 1, which presumably is also 2. Repeat this process for both twins in all the identical pairs. Then do the same thing for the scores of the fraternal twins. When you are finished, all the numbers in the table will be 2. The next step is to calculate the correlation for the identical twins, and the correlation for the fraternal twins. Actually, you cannot do that in either case because the formula to calculate the correlation (not shown in Table 9.1) will require a division by 0, the result of which is undefined in mathematics. This fact makes the formula at the bottom of the table a bit awkward to use, but we can presume that the difference between two undefined numbers is 0, which multiplied by 2 is still 0, and so the heritability of having two arms is 0. Does that mean that the number of arms you have is determined entirely by the environment? Well . . .

What went wrong in this calculation? The problem is that, for the trait "arm quantity," there is practically no variation across individuals; nearly everyone has two. Because heritability is the proportion of variation due to genetic influences, if there is no variation, then the heritability will approach zero. Generally speaking, the less a trait varies across individuals, the lower its heritability is likely to be. This means that if a given trait has a high heritability, two situations are possible: The trait might vary greatly across individuals, or it might be a trait that is determined largely by genes. Likewise, if a given trait has a low heritability, that trait might vary less across individuals, or it may be a trait that depends less on one's genes.

If you are still following this discussion, you might now appreciate that your calculation of the heritability of number of arms did not go wrong at all. If you look around at people, occasionally you will see someone with one arm. Why? Almost always, it will be because of an accident—an environmental event. The *difference* between people with one arm and those with two arms—the variation in that trait—therefore is produced environmentally and not genetically. This is why the heritability coefficient for the number of arms people have is near zero.

How Genes Affect Personality

Here is a fact that may astonish you: To a statistically significant degree, television watching is heritable (Plomin, Corley, DeFries, & Fulker, 1990). Does this mean an active gene in your DNA causes you to watch television? Presumably not. Rather, there must be some related propensity—perhaps sensation seeking, or lethargy, or even a craving for blue light—that has a genetic component. And this component, interacting somehow with biological development and early experience, causes some people to watch a lot of television. Research has not yet examined any of these interactions, however, and offers not even a hint as to what the inherited propensity might actually be.

> Here is a fact that may astonish you: Television watching is heritable.

Here is another example. It turns out that divorce is heritable: If one or more of your close relatives have been divorced, you are more likely to get divorced than if none of your relatives has been divorced—even if you have never met these relatives (McGue & Lykken, 1992). What does this finding imply about the causes of divorce? Maybe not much (see Turkheimer, 1998). The finding does imply that one or more genetically influenced traits are relevant to divorce. But which traits are involved, or how they influence divorce, behavioral genetics analyses cannot say. It could be that impulsiveness is heritable and that impulsive people have affairs, which cause them to divorce. Or perhaps homosexuality is heritable, or alcoholism, or depression—any or all of which might make a person more likely to divorce. As the psychologist Eric Turkheimer pointed out, "everything is heritable" (1998, p. 785), so every personality trait that might affect divorce is probably heritable; as a result, divorce may turn out to be indirectly heritable as well. But this conclusion does not explain how genes influence divorce, and it certainly does not imply a "divorce gene."

MOLECULAR GENETICS

The field of behavioral genetics has changed dramatically in the past few years by moving into molecular biology. New research has begun to unravel the mystery of how specific genes influence life outcomes (though they have not explained TV watching or divorce yet), by diving into the actual DNA. Most studies use the **association method**, which tries to determine whether differences in a trait correlate with differences in a particular gene across individuals.

One pioneering effort explored the genetic basis of homosexuality in males (Hamer & Copeland, 1994; Hamer, 1997). First, the researchers found a group of homosexuals who were related to various degrees. Then, using microbiological techniques, they identified a gene on the X chromosome that most (but not all) of the homosexuals shared but that was not found in heterosexual members of the same family. They concluded that this genetic similarity was one basis of homosexuality.

Other, more complex studies have examined the relationship between traits associated with behavioral and emotional control and a gene called *DRD4*, which affects the development of dopamine receptors. As we saw in Chapter 8, dopamine is part of the brain system that responds to reward, and some psychologists have theorized that a shortage of dopamine, or an inability to respond to it, may lead people to crave extra stimulation to the point of engaging in risky behavior. The dopaminergic systems of the brain (the parts of the brain influenced by dopamine) also play a broad role in the control and regulation of behavior and even bodily movement. People with dopamine shortages caused by Parkinson's disease develop tremors and may eventually lose muscular control altogether. An early study found that different forms of the *DRD4* gene are associated with variations in sensation seeking, and so concluded that this gene might be a basis of sensation seeking via its effect on dopaminergic systems (Benjamin et al., 1996; see also Blum et al., 1996). A separate study confirmed that variations in the *DRD4* gene were correlated with participants' scores on a test of novelty seeking (Ebstein et al., 1996). The *DRD4* gene is also associated with the risk for attention deficit hyperactivity disorder (ADHD), which makes sense given the association between dopamine and brain regulation of cognition and behavior, as well as the related personality trait of impulsivity (Munafó, Yalcin, Willis-Owen, & Flint, 2008).

serotonin.

Rapid progress is also being made in understanding the genetics associated with serotonin (another neurotransmitter described in Chapter 8). Recall that a shortage of serotonin has been blamed for a wide variety of emotional disorders ranging from depression to anxiety and social phobia, and that drugs (such as SSRIs) that increase the level of serotonin in the brain effectively treat these disorders, at least sometimes. A certain "short" variant of a gene associated with the serotonin transporter protein 5-HTT appears to be particularly important in the development of neuroticism, a broad personality trait relevant to anxiety and overreaction to stress, as well as depression. Different forms of the same gene are called **alleles**. The 5-HTT gene has a short allele and a long allele, based on the shape of the chromosomal structure. Several studies have now shown that people with the short allele score higher on measures of neuroticism than people with the long allele (Canli & Lesch, 2007). Even more interesting, the amygdala in people with the short allele also shows stronger responses, as viewed through fMRI images, PET scans, and other imaging techniques (see Chapter 8), to fearful and unpleasant stimuli such as pictures of frightened-looking faces, accident victims, mutilated bodies, and polluted scenery (Hariri et al., 2002; Heinz et al., 2005; Munafó, Brown, & Hariri, 2008). This gene also appears to regulate the degree to which the amygdala and the prefrontal cortex work together, which may offer an important clue to the brain structure of depression (Heinz et al., 2005). Finally, possession of the short allele corre-

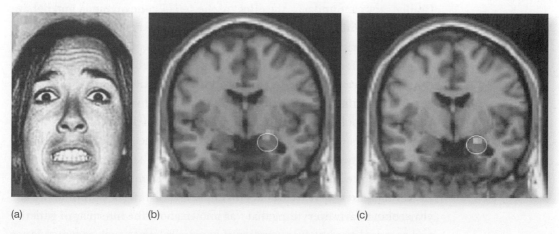

(a) (b) (c)

Figure 9.1 Genetics and Amydala Response In one experiment, the amygdala of people shown (a) frightened-looking faces (and other fear stimuli) responded more strongly if they had (b) a short allele of the 5-HTT gene than if they had (c) a long allele.

lates with how much the amygdala of people who suffer from social phobias respond when giving a public speech (Furmark et al., 2004).

A fascinating—and perhaps disconcerting—finding is that the prevalence of the short allele of the *5-HTT* gene may vary across cultural groups. In particular, the allele appears to be present in more than 75 percent of Japanese people, more than double its frequency in Caucasians (e.g., Kumakiri et al., 1999). What does this finding mean? Some writers have speculated that the allele may be one reason why Asian cultures emphasize cooperation and avoiding conflict over the kind of individualistic striving said to be characteristic of Western cultures (Chiao & Ambady, 2007). Because of the emotional sensitivity associated with this allele, Asians might tend to find interpersonal conflict more aversive than do Westerners, and so make extra efforts to smooth it over. But we are skating on thin ice here. Attempts to account for behavioral differences between cultural groups on genetic grounds has a long, nasty, and sometimes tragic history. Nonetheless, science has a tendency to lead where it leads—which is sometimes to the good and sometimes not.

It is also important to remember that, as complex as the findings linking genes to behavior have become, they are still not the whole story. One limitation, as the authors of these studies frequently acknowledge, is that they do not apply to everybody. For example, not all homosexuals share the same pattern of DNA, and at least a quarter of the Japanese population does *not* have the short allele of *DRD4*. Moreover, the effects of *DRD4* on personality and behavior are fairly small and can't always be replicated (Plomin & Crabbe, 2000). Similarly, the effect of the *5-HTT* gene on mood and behavior, while found in several studies, is not the same for everybody. In addition, the inheritance of personality goes beyond the effects of single genes. At least 10 different genes, or as many as 500, may be involved in complex traits such as sensation seeking or proneness to anxiety (Ridley, 1999). The chance of finding a single gene that has a simple, direct, and easily understood effect on homosexuality, impulsiveness, anxiety, or any other aspect of personality, therefore, seems slim. The real connection between genetics and personality will turn out to be much more complex than that.

Yet despite all the complexity, the rate of accumulation of knowledge in just the past few years has been simply astonishing. Up until about the year 2000, nearly everything that was known about the interplay of genetics and personality came from studies of genetic relatives such as twins. Since then, serious efforts to explore molecular genetics have yielded tantalizing hints concerning the biological bases of anxiety, impulsiveness, depression, homosexuality, and even criminal behavior. Recent innovations are allowing researchers to move beyond focusing on single genes, to scanning the entire human genome for clues about the determination of personality (e.g., Gillespie et al., 2008). The next few years should see further rapid advances, as well as a better understanding of how one's genes interact with experience. We consider this issue next.

Gene-Environment Interactions

It was only natural for the study of behavioral genetics, including molecular genetics of personality, to begin with the study of main effects, of how particular genes are associated with particular behavioral or personality outcomes. But in the final analysis, genes cannot cause anybody to do anything, any more than you can live in the blueprint of your house. The genotype only provides the design, and so indirectly affects the behavioral phenotype by influencing biological structure and physiology as they develop within an environment. The next challenge, therefore, after figuring out which specific aspects of the nervous system are affected by genes, is to understand how those aspects interact with environmental experience to affect behavior.[5]

The basic principle is that genes can influence the development of behavior only in people who live in some kind of environment. Without an environment, there would be no behavior, regardless of what genes and brain structures were present. The reverse is also true: Without a person (built by genes) to affect, no behavior can occur, no matter what the environment. The point has been made many times but always seems to need reemphasis: In the determination of personality, genes and the environment *interact*. Neither can do anything without the other.

The environment can even affect heritability itself. For example, in an environment where every child receives adequate nutrition, variance in height will be genetically controlled. Tall parents will tend to have tall children, and short parents will tend to have short children; the heritability coefficient for height will be a large number. But in an environment where food is scarce and some children do not have good nutrition, variance in height will fall more under the control of the environment. Well-fed children will grow to be tall while poorly fed children will be shorter, and the

---

[5] Genes can interact with the environment only via the physical bodies (the phenotypes) of the individuals carrying the genes. So, the term *gene-environment interaction* should more precisely be labeled "phenotype-environment interaction" (Turkheimer & Waldron, 2000), but for present purposes I will stick with the traditional term.

height of the parents will not matter so much; the heritability coefficient for height will be a small number.

Consider a more psychological trait such as IQ. From the logic just used, we could expect that, in an environment where intellectual stimulation and educational opportunities vary a lot from one child to the next, IQ might be under the control of the environment. The children who are stimulated and educated will grow up to be more intelligent than those who are not so lucky, and heritability of IQ will be low. But if we could achieve a society where all children received sufficient stimulation and education, then the remaining differences in IQ would be due to their genes. As the intellectual environment improves for everybody, we should expect the heritability of IQ to go up! And that is exactly what has been shown to happen. One major recent study found that, for children from improverished families, most of the variance in IQ was accounted for by their shared environments, whereas in affluent families most of the variance in IQ was due to genes (Turkheimer, Haley, Waldron, D'Onofrio, & Gottesman, 2003).

Genes and the environment interact in several other ways (Scarr & McCartney, 1983; Roberts & Jackson, 2008). For example, a boy who, as a result of his genes, is shorter than his peers may be teased in school; this teasing could have long-term effects on his personality. These effects are due in part to his genes, but they came about only through an interaction between the genetic expression and the social environment. Without both, there would have been no such effect.

Another way genes and environments interact is in how people choose their environments. A person who inherits a tendency toward sensation seeking, for example, may take dangerous drugs. This practice might harm his health or involve him in the drug culture, either of which could have long-lasting effects on his experience and his personality development. Let's say that from hanging around with criminals, he develops a criminal personality. This result is only indirectly due to the inherited trait of sensation seeking; it comes about through the interaction of the inherited trait with the environment he seeks out because of that trait.

The most important way in which genes and environments interact is that the same environment can affect individuals in different ways. A stressful environment may lead a genetically predisposed individual to develop mental illness but leave individuals without that predisposition psychologically unscathed. More generally, the same circumstances might be experienced as stressful, enjoyable, or boring, depending on the genetic predispositions of the individuals involved; these variations in experience can lead to very different behaviors and, over time, to the development of different personality traits.

Studies of the molecular genetics of personality are just beginning to account for the complexities of gene-environment interactions. Two of the leaders in this field are the psychologists Avshalom Caspi and Terrie Moffitt. Along with their colleagues, they have worked closely with a major study based in New Zealand that has followed a group of children for decades. One groundbreaking study of this group examined why stressful experiences lead to depression later in life for some people but not others (Caspi et al., 2003). The study assessed the degree to which participants experienced stresses such as unemployment, financial setbacks, housing problems, health challenges, and relationship problems between the ages of 21 and 26, and then whether they experienced depression at the end of this period. Building on the results summarized in the preceding section of this chapter, Caspi, Moffitt, and their coworkers found that people who had the short allele for the serotonin-related gene *5-HTT* were relatively likely to experience depression following stress, whereas those without this allele were not. But—and this is important—there was no difference in outcome between those with the long allele and those with the short allele if they had not suffered any stress. This is a perfect example of a genotype-environment interaction: The genotype is important, but only for people who have experienced a certain kind of environment.

Another study, similar in design, examined why some maltreated children become delinquents or adult criminals, while others do not (Caspi et al., 2002). In this case, the targeted gene is part of the X chromosone, and has been shown to affect the enzyme MAOA (monamine oxidase A), which influences functioning of a range of neurotransmitters including norepinephrine, serotonin, and dopamine (see Chapter 8). An earlier study showed that when this gene is "knocked out" (neutralized) in mice, the mice become highly aggressive, but when the gene is "turned back on," they return to normal (Cases et al., 1995). The gene might have an aggression-regulating affect in humans as well. In Caspi's study, children whose genes caused a high level of expression of this enzyme were protected to some degree from the psychological effects of maltreatment. In contrast, among maltreated boys who had the allele leading to low MAOA activity, 85 percent exhibited "some form of antisocial behavior" (Caspi et al., 2002, p. 853). The findings were replicated by a study conducted in Virginia, which found that 15 percent of boys with adverse backgrounds and the high *MAOA* gene developed antisocial behaviors, whereas 35 percent of the boys who had adverse backgrounds and the low-activity form of this gene had this outcome. In other words, the low *MAOA* gene more than doubled the risk of developing antisocial behaviors, but only if the child had suffered maltreatment. Children who enjoyed good parenting and family backgrounds were at low risk regardless of their genes.

Even at a biological level, the effect of a gene on behavior may depend on more than the gene itself. Recent work on **epigenetics** has begun to document how experience, especially early in life, can determine how or even whether a gene is expressed during development (Weaver, 2007). So far, the evidence comes largely from studies of rats, which differ in the expression of a gene related to their stress response as a function of how much licking and other grooming they received from their mothers when they were young (Weaver et al., 2004). But there is little reason to think that the basic mechanisms of epigenetics will prove to be much different in humans. The bottom line is that the term *interaction* does not really capture the complexity of relationships between effects of genes and the environment. Genes can *change* environments and, as we are beginning to discover, environments can change genes. For this reason, one scientist recently wrote that, when it comes to the nature-versus-nurture controversy, we should probably just "call the whole thing off" (Weaver, 2007, p. 22).

Behavioral genetics sometimes is portrayed as a pessimistic view of human nature, because it seems to imply that people cannot change what they were born to be. The more we learn about how genetic influence on behavior really works, the clearer it becomes that this view is mistaken. As we have seen, while two different genes seem to put a person at risk for depression or antisocial behavior, the risk goes away—regardless of genes—with good parenting and a supportive family environment.[6] For another example, in Chapter 8, I quoted a psychologist who suggests that persons with a biologically determined tendency toward sensation seeking might be deterred from crime by participating in less damaging occupations that satisfy the need for excitement (such as race-car driving or hosting a radio talk show). Frankly, I'm not sure whether this was a serious suggestion. But it makes a point: If we understand an individual's biological predispositions, we might be able to help her to find an environment where her personality and abilities lead to good outcomes rather than bad ones.

---

[6] As we also saw, in rat pups who receive a lot of love from their mothers, there is a change in the expression of a gene related to how they respond to stress later in life.

The Future of Behavioral Genetics

The most significant news from the study of behavioral genetics over the past few years is that genes are important in the determination of personality. This lesson constitutes a dramatic change, within the past couple decades, from the conventional view that psychologists held for many years. The future of behavioral genetics, however, does not lie in further documenting this fact (Turkheimer, 1998). Rather, the remaining jobs for behavioral geneticists are, first, to explain how genes create brain structures and aspects of physiology that are important to personality, and second, to explain how a person's genetically determined tendencies interact with the environment to determine behavior. You have read in the preceding pages about rapid advances in this direction, toward identifying genes associated with behavior patterns, the effects of certain genes on brain structures and behavior, and various ways in which genetically determined tendencies and environmental circumstances interact. Behavioral genetics has proved, beyond a shadow of a doubt, that personality is inherited to an important degree. Its next exciting order of business is to explain exactly how.

EVOLUTIONARY PERSONALITY PSYCHOLOGY

Evolutionary theory is the foundation of modern biology. Modern extensions of the theorizing that began with Charles Darwin's *Origin of the Species* (1859/1967) are used to compare one species of animal or plant to another, to explain the functional significance of various aspects of anatomy and behavior, and to understand how animals function within their environments. In recent years, an increasing number of attempts have been made to apply the same kind of theorizing and reasoning to human behavior and even social structure. One landmark book, E. O. Wilson's *Sociobiology: The New Synthesis* (1975), applied evolutionary theory to psychology and sociology. Other earlier efforts, such as Konrad Lorenz's *On Aggression* (1966), also explained human behavior using analogies to animals and their evolution.

In general, the evolutionary approach to personality assumes that human behavioral patterns developed because they were helpful or necessary for survival in the evolutionary history of the species. The more a behavioral tendency helps an individual to survive and reproduce, according to evolutionary theory, the more likely the tendency will be to appear in

Survival ; reproduction = most important in evolutionary theory.

subsequent generations. The evolutionary approach to explaining personality, therefore, is to identify a common behavior pattern and then ask how that pattern could have been *adaptive* (beneficial to survival and reproduction) as the human species developed (Tooby & Cosmides, 1990).

A wide range of human behavior has been examined through this evolutionary lens. For example, Lorenz (1966) discussed the possibly necessary—and sometimes harmful—role of the instinct toward aggression throughout human history. The biologist Richard Dawkins (1976) examined the evolutionary roots of the opposite behavior, altruism, and described how a tendency to aid and protect other people, especially close relatives, might help ensure the survival of one's own genes into succeeding generations (an outcome called *inclusive fitness*). It pays to be nice to your relatives, according to this analysis, because if the people who share your genes survive, then some of your genes may make it into the next generation through these relatives' children, even if you produce no offspring.

Evolutionary theory has even been used to explain why self-esteem is so important. According to the psychologist Mark Leary's "sociometer theory," our feelings of self-esteem evolved to monitor the degree to which we are accepted by others. Humans are a very social species, and few things are worse—or more dangerous—than being shunned by one's fellows. On the reality television program *Survivor*, the dreaded words "The tribe has spoken" may touch a deep, instinctual fear.[7] When we detect signs of not being adequately valued and accepted, our self-esteem goes down, motivating us to do things that will cause others to think better of us so that we can think better of ourselves. The people who did not develop this motive failed to reproduce (Leary, 1999). We, on the other hand—all of us—are the descendants of people who cared deeply what other people thought about them. And so do we.

Even depression may have evolved as a useful adaptation. According to one recent analysis, people suffer different kinds of depression as a result of different causes (M. C. Keller & Nesse, 2006). Depression that follows a social loss—such as a breakup with a boyfriend or girlfriend, or a bereavement—is characterized by pain, crying, and seeking social support. Depression that follows failure—such as flunking an exam or being fired from a job—is more often characterized by fatigue, pessimism, shame, and guilt. The psychologists Matthew Keller and Randolph Nesse speculate that, in the

---

[7] In the unlikely event you have not seen this program, the host intones the phrase just after a member of the tribe is voted off the island. He then symbolically extinguishes the ex-member's torch.

Figure 9.2 "The Tribe Has Spoken" These words may touch a deep, evolutionarily based fear of being shunned by one's social group.

history of the species, these reactions may have promoted survival. Pain signals that something has gone wrong and must be fixed. Just as it is important to be able to feel the pain of a broken leg so you won't try to walk on it, so too it may be important to feel emotional pain when something has gone wrong in your social life, because that signals that your chances for reproducing or even surviving may be at risk. This is a process similar to Leary's sociometer theory. But Keller and Nesse go further to suggest that crying may often be a useful way of seeking social support, and that fatigue and pessimism can prevent one from wasting energy and resources on fruitless endeavors. One fascinating implication is that

> in the same way that blocking fever may prolong infections, blocking normal depressive symptoms with antidepressant medication could increase the risk of chronic negative life situations or poorer outcomes in such situations, even as the sufferers feel better. Similarly, individuals who lack a capacity for depressive symptoms should be more likely to lose valuable attachments, more likely to persist at unachievable pursuits, less able to learn from mistakes, and less able to recruit friends during adverse situations. (M. C. Keller & Nesse, 2006, p. 328)

Have you ever told anyone to "go ahead, have a good, long cry"? It might have been good advice. Sometimes we need to feel the pain.

Sex Differences in Mating Behavior

A behavioral pattern that has received particular attention from evolutionary psychologists is the variation in sexual behavior between men and women. Particular differences stand out in the behaviors of **mate selection**—what one looks for in the opposite sex—and **mating strategies**—how one handles heterosexual relationships.

MATE SELECTION

First consider mate selection. When seeking someone of the opposite sex with whom to form a relationship, is an average heterosexual more likely to be interested in his or her (1) physical attractiveness or (2) financial security? Across a wide variety of cultures, including those in early-21st-century North America, men are more likely than women to place a higher value on physical attractiveness (D. M. Buss, 1989). In these same cultures, by contrast, women are more likely to value economic security in their potential mates. Indeed, there is some evidence that men and women consider attractiveness and resources, respectively, as necessary attributes of potential mates, not just nice benefits (N. P. Li, Bailey, Kenrick, & Linsenmeier, 2002).

In addition, heterosexual men are likely to desire (and typically do find) mates several years younger than themselves (the average age difference is about three years, and increases as men get older), whereas women prefer mates who are older than themselves. This difference can be documented through marriage statistics and even personal ads. When age is mentioned, men advertising for women usually specify an age younger than their own, whereas women do the reverse. The other effect mentioned earlier also can be found in the personals: Men are more likely to describe themselves as financially secure than as physically attractive, whereas women are more likely to describe their physical charms than their financial ones (Kenrick & Keefe, 1992). Presumably, individuals of each sex know what the other is looking for and so try to maximize their own appeal.

The evolutionary explanation of these and other differences is that men and women seek essentially the same thing: the greatest likelihood of having healthy offspring who will survive to reproduce. But each sex contributes to and pursues this goal differently, and thus the optimal mate for each sex is different. Women bear and nurse children, so their youth and physical health are essential. Attractiveness, according to the evolutionary explanation, is simply a display, or cue, that informs a man that a woman is indeed young, healthy, and fit to bear his children (D. M. Buss & Barnes, 1986; D. Symons, 1979).

In contrast, a man's biological contribution to reproduction is relatively minimal. Viable sperm can be produced by males of a wide range of ages, physical conditions, and appearances. For women, what is essential in a mate is his capacity to provide resources conducive to her children thriving until their own

*"Whenever Mother's Day rolls around,
I regret having eaten my young."*

reproductive years. Thus, since a woman seeks a mate to optimize her children's circumstances, she will seek someone with resources (and perhaps attitudes) that will support a family, whereas a man seeks a mate who will provide his children with the optimal degree of physical health.

We can see already that these explanations gloss over some complications. For example, a woman who lacks a certain percentage of body fat will stop menstruating and therefore will be unable to conceive children, yet many women considered by men to be highly physically attractive are thin, nearly to the point of anorexia.[8] In previous eras, much heavier women were considered ideal. Moreover, whether we consider someone attractive can be determined by whether we like them, as well as vice versa. One recent study found that when people are told someone is honest, they come to like them more, and as a result rate them as more physically attractive (Paunonen, 2006). So-called physical attractiveness is more than just physical.

Likewise, male physical attractiveness is more important to many women than the standard evolutionary explanation seems to allow. In other species, male displays of large manes or huge fans of plumage appear to be a

---

[8] However, women generally overestimate the degree of thinness that men find most attractive. Conversely, men overestimate the degree of muscularity that women find most attractive (Frederick & Haselton, 2007). Perhaps because of this, pictures of men in men's magazines are more muscular than pictures of men in women's magazines (Frederick, Fessler, & Haselton, 2005).

"Stupid—yet irresistible."

sign of health that attracts females. It is not clear why the situation would be so different in humans. However, it must be admitted that physical attractiveness does not seem to be as important to women as to men. The general trends in what men and women favor in each other are difficult to deny, despite occasional exceptions and complications.

MATING STRATEGIES

Once they have completed their mutual selection process and mated, men and women still differ in their subsequent behaviors (although the differences may not be as large as sometimes described; see Hyde, 2005). According to the evolutionary account, men tend to want more sexual partners, and are neither particularly faithful nor picky about the women with whom they will mate. This approach to life appears to be particularly likely in men characterized by traits sometimes called "the Dark Triad": narcissism, psychopathy, and Machiavellianism (Jonason, Li, Webster, & Schmitt, 2009).[9] More generally, men appear to be prone to certain kinds of wishful thinking in which they are quick to conclude that women are sexually interested in them, even when they are not (Haselton, 2002). Women, in contrast, are more selective about their mating partners and, having mated, seem to have a greater desire for monogamy and a stable relationship.

These differences also can be explained in terms of reproductive success. A male may succeed in having the greatest number of children who reproduce to subsequent generations—which evolutionarily speaking is the only outcome that matters—by having as many children by as many women as possible. In a reproductive sense, it may be a waste of his time to stay with one woman and one set of children; if he leaves them, they will probably survive somehow and he can spend his limited reproductive time trying to impregnate somebody else. A woman, however, is more likely to have viable offspring if she can convince the man to stay to support and protect her and the family they create. In that case, her children will survive, thrive, and eventually propagate her genes.

---

[9] The colloquial term for men like this is "jerks."

Another, related behavioral difference is found in the ways in which men and women experience sexual jealousy. In one study, men and women were asked to respond to the following vignette (D. M. Buss, Larsen, Westen, & Semmelroth, 1992):

> Please think of a serious committed relationship that you have had in the past, that you currently have, or that you would like to have. Imagine that the person with whom you've become seriously involved became interested in someone else. What would distress or upset you more: (Circle only one) *40% M, 82% F*
> (a) Imagining your partner forming a deep emotional attachment to that person, or
> (b) Imagining your partner enjoying passionate sexual intercourse with that person? (p. 252) *60% M, 18% F*

In this study, 60 percent of the males chose option b, whereas 82 percent of the females chose option a. In a follow-up study, the final question was changed slightly (D. M. Buss et al., 1992):

> What would upset you more: *45% M, 12% F*
> (a) Imagining your partner trying different sexual positions with that other person, or
> (b) Imagining your partner falling in love with that other person? (p. 252) *55% M, 88% F*

This time, 45 percent of the males chose option a, whereas only 12 percent of the females chose option a. In other words, option b was chosen by 55 percent of the males and by 88 percent of the females. Notice that this question does not produce a complete reversal between the sexes; most members of each sex find their partner falling in love with someone else more threatening than their partner having intercourse with him or her. But the difference is much stronger among women than men.

Why is this? Evolutionarily speaking, a man's greatest worry—especially for a man who has decided to stay with one woman and support her family—is that he might not be the biological father of the children he supports. This fact makes sexual infidelity by his mate his greatest danger and her greatest crime, from a biological point of view. For a woman, however, the greatest danger is that her mate will develop an emotional bond with some other woman and so withdraw support—or, almost as bad, that her mate will share their family's resources with some other woman and her children. This makes emotional infidelity a greater threat than mere sexual infidelity, from the woman's biological point of view.

Related evolutionary logic can even explain some seeming paradoxes or exceptions to these general tendencies. For example, why are some women attracted to men who are obviously unstable? Consider the situation described by the typical country-and-western song. Some women prefer men who may be highly physically attractive (and/or own motorcycles) even when such men have no intention of forming a serious relationship and are just "roaming around." I have no idea how common this situation is, but from an evolutionary standpoint it should never happen, right?

Wrong. The theory is rescued here by what has been called the "sexy son hypothesis" (Gangestad, 1989). This hypothesis proposes that a few women consistently—and many women occasionally—follow an atypical reproductive strategy (Gangestad & Simpson, 1990). Instead of maximizing the reproductive viability of their offspring by mating with a stable (but perhaps unexciting) male, they instead take their chances with an unstable but attractive one. The theory is that if they produce a boy, even if the father then leaves, the son will be just like his dad. When he grows up, this "sexy son" will spread numerous children (who of course will also be the woman's grandchildren) across the landscape, in the same ruthless and irresponsible manner as his father.

Some evidence does support this hypothesis, if not prove it. Women report more interest in having sex with someone other than their primary partner when the "other man" is significantly more attractive than their regular partner and they are themselves near ovulation (Pillsworth & Haselton, 2006). Moreover, women's short-term sexual partners tend to be more muscular than men with whom they have longer-term relationships (though it turns out to be important that they not be *too* muscular; Frederick & Haselton, 2007). But male attractiveness is more than a just a matter of muscles: Women in their fertile period also find creative men especially attractive (Haselton & Miller, 2006). It might be in order to attract these attractive, muscular, creative men that women tend to dress more provocatively when they are in the middle of their cycle (Durante, Li, & Haselton, 2008).

Individual Differences

Evolutionary psychology has, so far, been much more concerned with the origins of general human nature than with individual differences. Indeed, it almost implies that individual differences should be unimportant, because it would seem that maladaptive behavioral variations should have been selected out of the gene pool long ago (Tooby & Cosmides, 1990). However, it is also true that the mechanism of evolution requires individual differences to be maintained. Species change only through the selective propagation of the genes of the most successful individuals in earlier generations. So not only is it fair to expect a "theory of everything" like evolutionary psychology to explain individual differences, but such an explanation is essential for the theory to work.

One probable reason for the persistence of individual differences is basic to evolutionary theory: For a species to remain viable, it must include diversity (Nettle, 2006). A trait that is adaptive in one situation may be fatal in another. For example, the Big Five personality trait of neuroticism can cause needless anxiety in safe situations, but it might promote lifesaving worry in dangerous ones. Similarly, agreeableness can make you popular, but also vulnerable to people intent on cheating you. The end result is that, over hundreds of generations, people continue to be born who are near the extremes of both ends of every trait dimension.

Evolutionary psychology tries to account for individual differences in three additional ways (D. M. Buss & Greiling, 1999). First, behavioral patterns evolve as reactions to particular environmental experiences. Only under certain conditions does the evolved tendency come "on line," sort of like the way the skin of a Caucasian has a biological tendency to darken if it is exposed to the sun. For example, a child who grows up without a father present during the first five years of childhood may respond with an evolved tendency to act as if family life is never stable, which might in turn lead to early sexual maturity and frequent changes of sexual partners (Belsky, Steinberg, & Draper, 1991). Second, people in general may have evolved several possible behavioral strategies, and individuals just use the one that makes the most sense given their other characteristics. We may all have innate abilities to be both aggressive and agreeable, for example. But the aggressive style works only for those of us who are big and strong; otherwise, the agreeable style might be a wiser course. This may be why big, muscular boys are more likely to become juvenile delinquents (Glueck & Glueck, 1956). Third, some biologically influenced behaviors may be frequency dependent, meaning that they adjust according to how common they are in the population at large. For example, one theory of *psychopathy*—a behavioral style of deception, deceit, and exploitation—is that it is biologically determined in a small number of people (Mealey, 1995). If more than a small number of individuals tried to live this way, nobody would ever believe anybody, and a psychopathic style would become evolutionarily impossible to maintain.

These are interesting suggestions, but notice how they all boil down to an argument that human nature has evolved to be flexible. I think that is a very reasonable conclusion, but at the same time it tends to undermine the idea that evolution is the root of specific behavioral tendencies—such as self-esteem, depression, mate selection, and jealousy—which has been the whole point of the approach. This is just one reason why it is controversial. Psychologists have pointed out several difficulties with an evolutionary approach to human personality, to which we now turn.

Objections and Responses

Many objections have been raised to the evolutionary approach to human behavior. Its account of sexual behavior and sex differences, in particular, seems almost designed to set some people off, and it certainly does. At least five objections to the evolutionary approach to personality can be identified.

METHODOLOGY

The first objection concerns scientific methodology. It is indeed interesting to speculate "backward" in the way that evolutionary theorists do, by wondering about what in the past might have produced a behavioral pattern we see today. But how can such speculations be put to empirical test? What sort of experiment could we do, for example, to see whether men really seek multiple sexual partners in order to maximize their genetic propagation? Or consider the proposal that men have an instinct toward rape because it furthers their reproduction (Thornhill & Palmer, 2000), or that stepparents are prone to child abuse because of the lack of shared genes (Daly & Wilson, 1988). These are provocative suggestions, to say the least, but they also entail certain problems.

For example, there is something odd about postulating an instinctual basis for behaviors like rape or child abuse when most men are not rapists and most stepparents are not abusive. (The primatologist Frans de Waal, 2002, calls this the "dilemma of the rarely exercised option," p. 189). Furthermore, it is probably not wise to assume that every genetically influenced trait or behavior pattern has an adaptive advantage. Because of the human genome, people walk upright, and because we evolved from four-legged creatures, this design change makes us prone to backache. Apparently, walking upright had enough advantages to counteract the disadvantages, but that does not mean that lower-back pain is an evolved mechanism. In the same way, behavioral patterns such as depression, unfaithfulness, child abuse, and rape—even if they are genetically influenced—may not have emerged because they are are adaptive. Rather, they may be unfortunate side effects of other, more important adaptations. As de Waal noted, "the natural world is rampant with flawed designs" (2002, p. 188).

Evolutionary theorists usually acknowledge that criticisms such as these are fair, to a point, but those in the evolutionary camp do have a good response: For any theoretical proposal in science—not just those in evolutionary psychology—alternative explanations are always possible. Moreover, whole, complex theories are seldom judged on the basis of one crucial, decisive study. Instead, bits and pieces of these theories are tested in numerous studies as methods become available. Accordingly, complex evolutionary theories of behavior are difficult to prove or disprove in their entirety, and some alternative explanations may never be ruled out, but empirical research can address specific predictions from these theories. For example, the evolutionary theory of sex differences yields a further prediction that males should be older than their sexual partners across all cultures, because it assumes this difference is a biological, not a cultural, product (Kenrick & Keefe, 1992). In the cultures examined by researchers so far (including India, the United States, and many others), the hypothesis seems to have been supported. Even though this finding does not prove that the reproductive motives described by evolutionary theory cause the age differences, nor does it rule out all possible alternative explanations, in fairness it must be considered encouraging empirical support.

REPRODUCTIVE INSTINCT

A second objection is that evolutionary psychology's assumption that everybody wants as many children as possible seems a bit strange in an age when many people choose to limit their own reproduction. For example, how can it make sense to say that a woman who dresses provocatively is seeking an attractive mate who will provide good genes for her children, if at the same time she is on the pill? Evolutionary psychologists have a good response to this objection, too. For evolutionary theorizing about behavior to be correct, it is not necessary for people to consciously try to do what the theory says their behavioral tendencies are ultimately designed to do (Wakefield, 1989). All that is required is for people in the past who followed a certain behavioral pattern to have produced more members of the present generation than did people who did not follow the pattern (Dawkins, 1976).

Thus, although you might or might not want children, it cannot be denied that you would not be here unless somebody (your ancestors) had children. (Neither sterility nor abstinence runs in anyone's family.) The same tendencies (e.g., sexual urges) that caused them to produce offspring are also present in you. Thus, your sexual urges are based on a reproductive instinct, whether or not you are consciously aware of it or wish to reproduce. It is also the case that your sexual urges do increase your chances of reproducing, whether you want them to or not (since birth control methods sometimes fail). According to evolutionary theory, people have a tendency toward certain behaviors because of the effect of similar behaviors on past generations' reproductive outcomes—not necessarily because of any current intention to propagate.

CONSERVATISM

A third criticism of the evolutionary approach to behavior is that it embodies a certain conservative bias (Alper, Beckwith, & Miller, 1978; Kircher, 1985). Because it assumes that humans' current behavioral tendencies evolved as a result of the species' past environments, and that these tendencies are biologically rooted, the evolutionary approach seems to imply that the current behavioral order was not only inevitable but also is probably unchangeable. This conservative implication bothers some people who think that male promiscuity, child abuse, and rape are reprehensible (which they are, of course), and others who think that human tendencies toward aggression, for example, must and can be changed.

Evolutionary theorists respond that political objections like these are irrelevant from a scientific standpoint (see the discussion of research ethics in Chapter 3). They also observe that with this criticism, opponents of evolutionary theories commit the "naturalistic fallacy" of believing that anything natural must be good. But evolutionary theorists do not draw this inference (Pinker, 1997). As the philosopher Daniel Dennett, who writes frequently about evolutionary theory, has stated, "Evolutionary psychologists are absolutely not concerned with the moral justification or condemnation of particular features of the human psyche. They're just concerned with their existence" (cited in Flint, 1995). If a political bias does underlie evolutionary psychology, then it must be more subtle. The basic assumption of evolutionary analysis—that our personalities have been selected over the millennia to favor behaviors that promote our individual survival—may itself come from the larger culture. As one critic has observed, "In totalitarian regimes, dissidence is treated as a mental illness. In apartheid regimes, interracial contact is treated as unnatural. In free-market regimes, self-interest is treated as hardwired" (Menand, 2002, p. 96).

HUMAN FLEXIBILITY

[handwritten: evolutionary psych = module approach]

A fourth and more powerful objection is that evolutionary accounts seem to describe a lot of complex behavior as genetically programmed into the brain, whereas a general lesson of psychology is that humans are extraordinarily flexible creatures with a minimum of instinctive behavior patterns, compared with other species. Indeed, we saw in Chapter 8 that the neocortex (the outer part of the cortex, which is unique to humans) has the function of planning and thinking beyond simple responses and fixed patterns of behavior. Yet evolutionary accounts such as that of sex differences seem to suggest built-in behavioral patterns that cannot be overcome by conscious, rational thought.

The issue here is not whether the theory of evolution is correct; the scientific community settled that question to its satisfaction long ago. Rather, the question is whether, in the domain of behavior, people evolved general capacities for planning and responding to the environment, or specific behavioral patterns (called *modules*) (Öhman & Mineka, 2001). When evolutionary psychology tries to explain behaviors such as mate preference, sex differences in jealousy, and even child abuse and rape, it seems to favor a modular approach (C. R. Harris, 2000). But when it addresses the question of individual differences, it acknowledges that the evolution of the cerebral cortex has given the human brain the ability to respond flexibly to changing circumstances and even to overcome innate urges. These two kinds of explanation are difficult but perhaps not impossible to reconcile, and debate in the next few years is likely to focus on this issue. What is the human evolutionary heritage? Is it a collection of specific responses triggered almost automatically by particular circumstances? Or is it the ability to plan, foresee, choose, and even override instinctive tendencies?

BIOLOGICAL DETERMINISM OR SOCIAL STRUCTURE?

A final criticism of the evolutionary approach to personality is closely related to the idea that people may have evolved to be flexible. Many behavioral phenomena might be the result not of evolutionary history but of humans flexibly responding to circumstances, especially social structure. For example, the sex differences discussed earlier may be caused not by biological hard wiring, but by the current structure of society.

The psychologists Alice Eagly and Wendy Wood (Eagly & Wood, 1999; W. Wood & Eagly, 2002) have provided an alternative to the evolutionary

Eagly/Wood
on men and
women.

account of the differences in the criteria used by men and women in choosing mates. They hypothesize that because of men's greater size and strength, and women's role in childbearing and lactation, societies have developed worldwide in which men and women are assigned different jobs and social roles. Men tend to be warriors, rulers, and controllers of economic resources. Women are more likely to be restricted to staying near the home, gaining power and affluence largely as a function of the men with whom they affiliate. This difference is enough, Eagly and Wood argue, to explain why women value the wealth of a man more than his looks, and why the wealth of a woman matters less to a man. The difference comes not from a specific innate module, but from a reasonable and flexible response to the biological facts (see also Eagly, Eastwick, & Johannesen-Schmidt, 2009).

The argument is important for both theoretical and practical reasons. On a theoretical level it goes to the heart of the question of how much of human nature is evolutionarily determined and biologically inherited. Their argument is important on a practical level because the world is changing. In an industrial culture where physical strength is less important than it was and alternative child-care arrangements are possible, the traditional division of labor between men and women no longer seems inevitable. But it continues anyway, because societies are slow to change. What happens next?

Still may
be a slow
process.

According to the evolutionary view, the differences between men and women in mate selection and other behaviors are built in through biological evolution. This view implies that it might be almost impossible to change these differences; at best, any change will occur at the speed of evolution, thus likely requiring thousands of years. According to the contrary societally based view, as the necessity for a sexual division of labor melts away, societies will change, and sex differences will change (and perhaps lessen) as a result. The process may still be slow—it might take hundreds of years—but will be much quicker than the processes of biological evolution.

power difference
between cultures
shows this

It may be happening already. According to one analysis by Eagly and Wood (W. Wood & Eagly, 2002), in present-day cultures where women have power relatively equal to men, the sex differences in preference for a wealthy spouse are much smaller than in the cultures where the power difference is intact. This finding implies—but it does not prove—that if societies begin to provide equal power to women, some of the sex differences discussed earlier in this chapter may begin to erode.

The current debate about the implications of evolutionary theory for personality psychology, particularly its implications for sex differences, is lively and stimulating. It is important to note, for now, that neither side has proved its point conclusively. Even critics such as Eagly and Wood acknowledge that their explanations of the origin of sex differences are about as well supported as the explanations offered by evolutionary psychologists. We can expect further arguments, evidence, and perhaps even improved understanding over the next few years.

The Contribution of Evolutionary Theory

Researchers will continue to argue about the details of evolutionary theory as applied to human behavior for a long time to come. But one fact is already beyond argument: Since the introduction of evolutionary thinking into psychology, the field will never be the same (Pinker, 1997). Not every aspect of thought or behavior exists because it specifically evolved. But researchers have to consider the possibility. Whenever an investigator is trying to explain a brain structure, thought pattern, or behavior, he can no longer avoid asking, Is this explanation plausible from an evolutionary perspective? How might this (brain structure, thought process, or behavior) have promoted survival and reproduction in the past? Does the answer to this question help explain why people today—the descendants of past survivors and reproducers—have it?

Figure 9.3 Who Holds Power? Female political leaders have taken control in several nations, and the future seems likely to hold more women leaders rather than fewer. As the power differential between the sexes becomes smaller, mating strategies of both men and women may change.

WILL BIOLOGY REPLACE PSYCHOLOGY?

This chapter and the previous one reviewed the implications for personality of four different areas of biology: anatomy, physiology, genetics, and evolution. Each of these areas has a lot to say about personality. Indeed, the contributions from each of these fields can be taken to imply that personality is biologically based. This implication was anticipated by Gordon Allport's classic definition of personality, which predated by many years nearly all of the research just surveyed. Allport wrote that personality is "the dynamic organization within the individual of those *psychophysical systems* that determine his [or her] characteristic behavior or thought" (originally offered in Allport, 1937; also in Allport, 1961, p. 18; my emphasis).

The rapid progress of biological approaches to psychology in recent years led some observers to speculate that, as an independent field of study, psychology is doomed. Because personality is a psychophysical system, once everything is known about brain structure and physiology, there will be nothing left for psychologists to investigate! This point of view is called *biological reductionism*—in the final analysis, it reduces everything about the mind to biology.[10]

Obviously I have a vested interest in this issue; nevertheless, I will state that I do not think biology is going to replace psychology. It certainly will not do so soon. As we have seen, too many huge gaps remain in our knowledge of the nervous system to replace the other approaches to human personality—yet.

But what about the distant future? I don't think biology will replace psychology even then, and the reason is fundamental. Biological approaches to psychology, by themselves, often tell us much more about biology than about psychology. This biology is extremely interesting, but it does not provide a description of how people act in their daily social environments, or of the consistencies that can be found in their behaviors (topics we considered in Part II). A purely biological approach will never describe what psychological conflict feels like, or how such conflict might be revealed through accidental behavior, or what it means to face one's existential anxiety (topics to be considered in Parts IV and V). A purely biological approach does not address how an individual's environment can determine behavior, or explain how an individual interprets that environment or plans a strategy for success (topics considered in Part VI). It cannot even say much about what is on your mind at this moment.

> Biological approaches to psychology, by themselves, often tell us much more about biology than about psychology.

For example, the evolutionary process, as it has affected males, gives them a biological tendency to be unfaithful to their mates (according to one theory). But what happens inside the male's head at the moment he is unfaithful? What does he perceive, think, feel, and (above all) want? Evolutionary psychology not only fails to answer this question; it fails to ask it. Similarly, the other biological approaches describe how brain structures, neurochemicals, or genes affect behavior without addressing the psycho-

---

[10] A few years ago, the Department of Psychology at Dartmouth College changed its name to the Department of Psychological and Brain Sciences—a harbinger of the future?

logical processes that connect the brain, neurochemicals, or genes, on the one hand, and behavior on the other.

One theme of this book is that the different approaches to personality are not different answers to the same question; rather, they pose different questions. Thus, there is little danger of any one of them completely taking over. The biological approach to personality is becoming more important all the time, and evolutionary theory can organize a huge range of psychological knowledge (Pinker, 1997). But behavioral genetics and evolutionary theory will never supersede the other approaches by showing how behavior is "really" caused by biological mechanisms (de Waal, 2002; Turkheimer, 1998). The greatest promise of the biological approach lies elsewhere, in explaining how biology interacts with social processes to determine what people do.

PUTTING IT ALL TOGETHER: SEXUAL ORIENTATION

Consider sexual orientation, for example. What causes a person to become heterosexual, homosexual, or bisexual? A novel theory by the psychologist Daryl Bem shows how anatomical, neurochemical, evolutionary, and genetic perspectives can be combined with social psychology and even sociology to explain the processes that determine this psychological outcome (Bem, 1996).

At the outset, Bem observes that the right question is not What is the cause of homosexuality? but rather, What directs sexual orientation in general? Bem shares this point of view with Freud, who said that homosexuality and heterosexuality were equally difficult to understand, and who also speculated that the same basic processes might underlie both (S. Freud, 1905/1962). So Bem's theory tries to account for the development of all varieties of sexual orientation. The theory is outlined in Figure 9.4.

First, biological influences such as genes and prenatal hormones produce children with particular childhood personalities (which Bem calls "temperaments"); some children are aggressive and active, while others are more quietly sociable. These temperaments interact with the structure of childhood society, which strongly segregates boy and girl playgroups beginning at about age 5. A boy who enjoys rough-and-tumble play will fit in well with groups of other boys. A boy who, for reasons of his temperament, does not enjoy these activities, may seek out the company of girls. So the

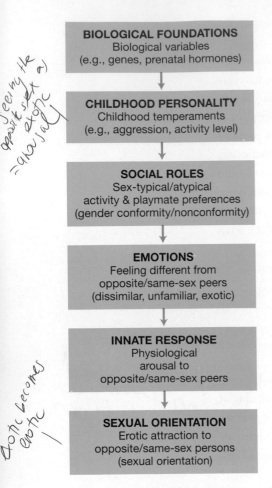

Figure 9.4 Bem's "Exotic Becomes Erotic" Theory of Sexual Orientation This flowchart shows the sequence of events over the course of development that produce the sexual orientation of most men and women in a culture that accentuates sex differences and segregates the sexes during much of childhood.
Source: Bem (1996), p. 321.

first boy will grow up around other boys; the second boy will grow up around girls. As a result, the first boy will come to see girls—with whom he has had little experience in childhood—as relatively unfamiliar and "exotic" (to use Bem's term), while the second boy will come to see other boys—with whom he may have had little experience—as exotic.

At this point, psychological mechanisms common to all members of the human species come into play. People are physically aroused by novel stimuli; when they see something unusual or strange, their heartbeat increases and their blood pressure rises. But people interpret their arousal based on the environmental context and who and what is present. For example, one classic study showed that men who were psychologically aroused by standing on a high, swaying bridge apparently came to believe they were sexually attracted to the woman standing on the bridge with them (Dutton & Aron, 1974)!

These processes lead the boy who grew up around other boys to be aroused, later in life, by the novelty of the presence of girls and, as he enters puberty, to label this arousal as sexual attraction. But the boy who grew up around girls is aroused by the novelty of the presence of boys, and through a parallel path, labels this arousal as sexual attraction. Now you can see why Bem calls this theory "exotic becomes erotic." People who belong to the group seen as exotic (whether male or female) become erotically stimulating, too. For most people, the exotic sex is the opposite one; for a substantial minority, the reverse is the case.

Notice that Bem's theory has several components, some of which are biological and others of which are social and even sociological. All four of the biological approaches we considered in this chapter and in the preceding chapter are included at least briefly. Bem assumes that hormones and the anatomical structure of the brain produce basic patterns of behavior concerning energy level, activity preferences, and so on. At another level of analysis, he assumes that these basic patterns of behavior are heritable. He also assumes that there are some "built-in" psychological mechanisms that everybody shares as the result of evolution—specifically, the mechanisms that cause arousal in response to novel stimuli and that cause arousal to be interpreted according to the situation. The truly novel aspect of Bem's theory is the way he puts all of these components together and integrates them with the experiences of a child growing up in the usual cultural context. His theory also makes the point that complex behavioral patterns such as homosexuality may be, to some extent, biologically determined, but only indirectly, through basic heritable traits that make the behavior pattern more likely to develop in a particular social context (Bem, 2001).

The evidence for Bem's theory is reasonably good. A study of Australian twins indicates that the tendency to enjoy activities conforming to traditional sex roles is biologically heritable (Bailey, Dunne, & Martin, 2000), and influenced by the level of testosterone one was exposed to in the womb (Auyeung et al., 2009). This tendency, in turn, is predictive of hetero- and homosexuality. For example, Bem reports that 63 percent of homosexual men report not having enjoyed typical "boy" activities in childhood, while only 10 percent of heterosexual men make the same report. The trend for women is almost as strong. Among lesbian women, 63 percent report not having enjoyed typical "girl" activities in childhood, while this is true of only 15 percent of heterosexual women. Parallel trends are found among many other variables that, according to Bem's theory, ought to be precursors of sexual orientation—although we can already see, from Bem's own data, that there are many exceptions.

The gender nonconformity associated with homosexuality appears to extend into adulthood. One recent study asked people about their occupational preferences, and found that the same choices that differed between men and women also tended to differ between heterosexual and homosexual individuals. For example, women were more likely than men to report wanting to be an interior decorator, a beauty consultant, or a florist, and homosexual men showed the same pattern in comparison to heterosexual men. At the other end of the scale, men were more likely than women to report wanting to be a mechanical engineer, a building contractor, or a jet pilot, and homosexual women showed the same pattern compared to heterosexual women (Lippa, 2002, 2006).

These findings are consistent with the theory, but they do not prove it. A complete test of Bem's model would require a longitudinal study that follows samples of boys and girls with varying temperaments, activity preferences, and playmate groups from childhood to adulthood, and tracks the development of their sexual orientations. Such a study would be difficult and is not likely any time soon. Moreover, complete proof of a theory this complex is probably not possible.

But for present purposes, proof of Bem's theory of sexual orientation is not really the issue. Its most important aspect may be the way it illustrates what a biologically informed theory of personality should look like. Notice how many different kinds of elements interact: the child begins with genes and hormones, which produce personality styles, which interact with the structure of society and the formation of childhood groups, which lead to certain feelings about members of the same and opposite sexes, which become eroticized through a universal emotional mechanism, which produces the sexual orientation of the adult. Wow!

Biological approaches to personality have come a long way. Their further progress will come from showing how biological influences interact with behavioral styles, social interaction, and the structure of society to produce the people we become. This could and should be done with many important personality outcomes, not just sexual orientation. Bem has shown us a way to do it.[11]

INHERITANCE IS THE BEGINNING, NOT THE END

At the end of Chapter 8, I returned to the problem of Hippocrates' MP3 player by noting that once he figured out how it worked, he still would not have begun to answer questions concerning why people like music, how the economics of the music industry works, or why some artists achieve fame and others do not—all of which are important if he wants to fully understand the sounds that come out of that box.

Let's conclude this discussion of the inheritance of personality by returning to the Rockefellers and the way they routinely inherit large amounts of money. In the short run, this is easily explained because each new Rockefeller has wealthy parents. In the longer run, the wealth of the extended clan can be traced to one spectacularly successful ancestor. But let's look at little Baby Rockefeller and ask a few more questions. What will she do with all this inherited wealth? Will she spend it on luxury, give it to charity, use it for a career in politics, or fritter it away on drugs and die broke? Previous Rockefellers have done all of these things. The inheritance is just the beginning; what she does with it depends on the society in which she lives, the way she is raised by her parents, and, yes, by her biological genes. The personality you inherited from your parents and your distant

---

[11] For a recent attempt to accomplish the same thing in explaining antisocial behavior, see Raine (2008).

ancestors may work the same way. It determines where you start, but where you go from there depends on many things, and may ultimately be up to you.

SUMMARY

- Behavioral genetics concerns the degree to which personality is inherited from parents and shared among genetic relatives.

- Evolutionary psychology concerns the ways in which human personality (and other behavioral propensities) may have been inherited from our distant ancestors, and how these propensities have been shaped over the generations by their consequences for survival and reproduction.

Behavioral Genetics

- Behavioral genetics has always been controversial because of its historical association with eugenics (selective breeding) and the concept of cloning, but modern behavioral geneticists (mostly) disavow any interest in these goals.

- The most commonly used heritability coefficient is calculated as the correlation across pairs of monozygotic twins for that trait, minus the correlation across dizygotic twins, times 2: heritability quotient = $(r_{MZ} - r_{DZ}) \times 2$.

- Heritability statistics computed from the study of monozygotic and dizygotic twins estimate that about 40 percent of the phenotypic variance in many personality traits can be accounted for by genotypic variance. Other studies suggest that the real figure may be lower because genes interact rather than simply expressing the sum total of their effects.

- Heritability studies confirm that genes are important for personality, can be informative about whether psychological disorders are distinct pathologies or extremes on the normal range of variation, and, perhaps most importantly, can provide insights into the effects of the environment on behavior and personality.

- Findings that unrelated adopted children who grow up together do not develop similar personalities led to questioning whether the family environment affects development. More thorough analyses and new data, however, suggest that the shared family environment affects many important traits, especially when they are measured via behavioral observation rather than self-report.

- Recent research is beginning to map out the complex route by which genes determine biological structures that can affect personality. For example, the

DRD4 gene is associated with dopaminergic systems that play a role in the trait of extraversion, and the *5-HTT* gene is associated with the neurotransmitter serotonin, and with the trait of impulsivity and related patterns of behavior. The amygdala in people with the short-form allele of this gene responds more strongly to unpleasant stimuli; these people are at risk for anxiety disorders.

- While research has begun to document the relationships among genes, brain function, and personality, the situation is even more complex than these relationships: Not only do genes also interact with each other, but their effects on development are also critically influenced by the environment. For example, people with the short allele for the *5-HTT* gene (which affects serotonin) appear to be at risk of depression and antisocial behavior, but only if they experience severe stress or maltreatment in childhood.

Evolutionary Personality Psychology

- Evolutionary psychology attempts to explain behavioral patterns—such as aggression, altruism, depression, mating choices, and sex differences—by analyzing how they may have promoted survival and reproduction in past generations.

- Some of these explanations are controversial. A key issue concerns the degree to which evolutionary processes have produced specific modular patterns of human behavior, as opposed to general abilities to understand and flexibly respond to changing environmental factors, including culture. Either way, research on evolutionary biology and behavioral genetics implies that biology and genetic inheritance are involved in determining personality.

- Evolutionary psychology explains individual differences as the results of interactions with the environment. In that sense, human nature may have evolved to be flexibly adaptive to specific circumstances.

Will Biology Replace Psychology?

- Some observers speculate that increases in knowledge will someday allow all psychological processes to be explained in terms of biology, a position called biological reductionism.

- However, biology will never replace psychology because biology does not and cannot, by itself, address many core psychological issues. These issues include the ways people act in their daily social environments, the basis of behavioral consistency, the experience of psychological conflict, the ways people interpret their environments and plan strategies for success, and many others.

Putting It All Together: Sexual Orientation

- The promise that biological approaches bring to personality study is their potential to illuminate the interactions between biological, psychological, social, and sociological influences on behavior. This is exemplified by Bem's theory of the development of sexual orientation.

Inheritance Is the Beginning, Not the End

- The biological aspects of personality that you inherited from your parents may determine your psychological starting point, but not your life outcomes.

THINK ABOUT IT

1. What is human nature? To understand human nature, what topics must you address?
2. Do you think your personality was shaped more by how you were raised, or by your genes?
3. When scientists learn that a particular brain structure or chemical is associated with a personality trait, how is that knowledge valuable? Does it help us to understand the trait better? Does it have practical implications?
4. If you have siblings, was the family environment in which you grew up the same as, or different from, theirs? If different, do these variations account for how you and your siblings turned out?
5. Is there anything useful about depression? Would a person who was unable to experience depression have problems as a result? Can a person learn anything, or benefit in any way, from being depressed?
6. Do you agree or disagree with evolutionary psychology's conclusions about sex differences? Do you think these differences exist in the way the theory suggests? Could they be explained as well or better by culture?
7. Do you think psychology will eventually be replaced by biology?
8. Are people just another species of animal? In what ways are people similar to, and different from, "other" animals?

SUGGESTED READINGS

Krueger, R. F., & Johnson, W. (2008). Behavioral genetics and personality: A new look at the integration of nature and nurture. In O. P. John, R. W. Robins, & L. A. Pervin (Eds.), *Handbook of personality: Theory and research* (3rd ed.), pp. 287–310. New York: Guilford.

> *A relatively brief but up-to-date and thorough review of the current state of knowledge in behavioral genetics, including the latest thinking about gene-environment interactions.*

Pinker, S. (1997). *How the mind works*. New York: Norton.

   A far-ranging, stimulating, and engagingly written survey of cognitive and social psychology from an evolutionary perspective. Pinker provides many creative and startling insights into the way evolutionary history may have shaped the ways we think.

Wilson, E. O. (1975). *Sociobiology: The new synthesis*. Cambridge, MA: Harvard University Press.

   The book that sparked the revival of interest in using evolutionary theory to explain human behavior.

EMEDIA

 Go to StudySpace, wwnorton.com/studyspace, to access additional review and enrichment materials.

PART IV

THE HIDDEN WORLD OF THE MIND:
The Psychoanalytic Approach

Eliot Spitzer was an aggressive and effective crime fighter. As a district attorney, attorney general, and then as governor of New York, he attacked securities fraud, Internet scams, predatory lending, and environmental pollution. A special focus was prostitution, which he called "modern day slavery" (Bernstein, 2008). He agreed with feminist groups that it was misguided to punish only the women while ignoring their customers, and he passed a law that increased the penalty for hiring a prostitute.

On February 13, 2008, Governor Spitzer met "Kirsten,"[1] who worked for an organization called Emperor's Club VIP, in room 871 at the Mayflower Hotel in Washington, DC. She had traveled there with the understanding that he "would be paying for everything—train tickets, cab fare from the hotel and back, minibar or room service, travel time and hotel" (Westfeldt, 2008). Afterwards he paid her $4,300 in cash, which included $1,000 as a deposit toward future services. Sadly for the governor, his attempts to conceal the source of the cash made his bank suspicious, which led to an investigation, and all was revealed in the *New York Times* on March 10, 2008. A week later he resigned. Governor Spitzer's career was over.

[1] Obviously, not her real name.

How could something like this happen? How could a dedicated and official opponent of crime and prostitution turn out to be a customer of exactly the same business he so vigorously opposed? This is not an isolated case. In 2003, William Bennett, would-be morals teacher and author of *The Book of Virtues*,[2] was forced to acknowledge a long-standing gambling habit, which had lost him millions of dollars. In 2006, a pastor of the Southern Baptist Church who had spoken out against gay marriage and urged homosexuals to reject their "sinful, destructive lifestyle" was arrested for propositioning a plainclothes police officer in an area of Oklahoma City known for "male prostitutes flagging down cars" (Green, 2006). Every few days, it seems, the news reveals yet another self-righteous politician or crusading preacher who turns out to be a regular practitioner of the same vices he (it does usually seem to be a he, but there are exceptions) made a career of denouncing. Such strange and paradoxical cases almost beg for a psychologist to explain them.

It might surprise you, therefore, to learn that most approaches to personality psychology have almost nothing to say. More than 50 years ago, the psychologist Henry Murray complained that much of psychology

> is over-concerned with recurrences, with consistency, with what is clearly manifested (the surface of personality), with what is conscious, ordered, and rational. . . . It stops short at the point precisely where a psychology is needed, the point at which it begins to be difficult to understand what is going on. (Murray, 1938, p. 715)

For most of personality psychology, his complaint is equally valid today. However, one approach has sought from the very beginning to explain thoughts and behaviors that are strange and difficult to understand. The approach is psychoanalysis, originally based on the writings of Sigmund Freud.

Psychoanalysis is more than just "Freudian" psychology, however. Freud changed his mind about important matters several times during his career, and many psychologists have continued to translate, interpret, and extend his ideas for nearly a century. Psychoanalysis concerns the underground part of the

[2] Also *The Children's Book of Virtues*, for the benefit of morally questing small fry.

mind, the part that is ordinarily hidden and, in some cases, seemingly contradictory, irrational, or absurd.

The next three chapters present a survey of classical, revised, and modern psychoanalysis. Chapter 10 provides a general introduction to Freud and to psychoanalytic thought and its view of the structure and development of the mind. Chapter 11 describes some of the workings of the unconscious mind, including defense mechanisms, parapraxes (slips), and humor. Finally, Chapter 12 brings psychoanalysis into the present day by surveying some of the prominent neo-Freudian theorists, including Adler, Jung, and Horney, along with some recent, relevant empirical research and modern psychoanalytic theorizing. Much of this new theorizing focuses on personal relationships, including object relations and attachment theory. Freud is not dead, we shall find—he lives on in a surprising number of ways.

10

BASICS OF PSYCHOANALYSIS

WHAT GOES ON in the dark, hidden, unconscious recesses of the human mind? The aim of the psychoanalytic approach, initiated by Sigmund Freud and developed by later neo-Freudian theorists, is to answer that question. Psychoanalytic theory is complex and comes in many versions, but in this chapter I keep things relatively simple. But please note I say *relatively* simple; there is no way to talk seriously about psychoanalysis without delving into some complex issues.

The present chapter progresses from a summary of key ideas and a bit of the history of Freud's life, through an account of how children develop psychologically into adults, to a description of the psychoanalytic model of how the mind is structured and how it thinks, both consciously and unconsciously. The chapter concludes by considering some of the implications of Freudian ideas for psychotherapy and modern life.

THE KEY IDEAS OF PSYCHOANALYSIS

One of the elegant aspects of the psychoanalytic approach is that all of its complexity is built on a relatively small number of key ideas. The four ideas that make up the foundation of psychoanalysis are psychic determinism, internal structure, psychic conflict, and mental energy.

Psychic Determinism

The first and most fundamental assumption of the psychoanalytic approach is **psychic determinism** (Brenner, 1974). Determinism, a basic tenet of sci-

everything has an identifiable cause — no accidents, miracles, free will, etc.

ence, is the idea that everything that happens has a cause that—in principle, maybe not always in practice—can be identified. The psychic determinism at the root of the psychoanalytic approach is the assumption that everything that happens in a person's mind, and therefore everything that a person thinks and does, also has a specific cause. This idea leaves no room for miracles, free will, or even random accidents. If it did, the entire approach would stall at the starting line. The key faith (and that is really what it is—faith) of a psychoanalyst is that psychology can explain even a prostitute-patronizing anticrime governor, a moralizing compulsive gambler, or a male antihomosexuality crusader who propositions men hanging around outside hotels. All that is needed is diligence, insight, and of course the proper psychoanalytic framework.

The nondeterministic alternative would be to say something like, "He just decided to get a prostitute [or go gambling] of his own free will, despite what he said," or, "He's just inconsistent." Those statements might be true, but they really do not explain anything, and you would never hear either one from a psychoanalyst. Only slightly better, from a psychoanalytic point of view, would be an observation such as, "This governor is a typical politician doing what is popular in order to get elected, but whatever he wants on the side," or, "The author of *The Book of Virtues* is simply a hypocrite." These explanations also might be true, but they still beg the questions of how a governor of a major state could be unable to resist behaving in a way that not only contradicted his publicly espoused values, but endangered (and ultimately ended) his career, and how moral crusading can come out of the same brain as a multimillion-dollar vice. There must be a reason, and psychoanalysts would argue that the reason lies somewhere in the structure and dynamics of personality. The trick is to find it.

Part of psychoanalytics is to determine why people do things.

From a psychoanalytic perspective, all seeming contradictions of mind and behavior can be resolved, and nothing is ever accidental. There is a reason why you preached one way and acted another; there is also a reason you forgot that name, dropped that dish, or said a word you did not intend to say. The purpose of psychoanalysis is to dig deep to find those reasons, which usually lie in the hidden part of the mind. The assumption of psychic determinism, therefore, leads directly to the conclusion that many important mental processes are unconscious.[1] Modern research tends to support this

---

[1] Freud believed that the idea of psychic determinism led so directly and necessarily to the theory of unconscious mental processes that to assume one was to assume the other. This is why, following Freud, I do not treat unconscious mental processes as a fifth and separate foundation of psychoanalysis.

conclusion—it appears that only some of what the mind does—perhaps only a small part—is available to conscious awareness (Kihlstrom, 1990; Bornstein, 1999b; Shaver & Mikulincer, 2005).

2) Internal Structure *of the mind* {id → irrational/emotional; ego → rational; superego → moral}

A second key assumption of psychoanalysis is that the mind has an internal structure made of parts that can function independently and which, in some cases, conflict with each other. We saw in Chapter 8 that this assumption is consistent with what is now known about brain function, but it is important to remember the distinction between the mind and the brain: The brain is a physical organ, whereas the mind is the psychological result of what the brain and the rest of the body do. Psychoanalytic theory sees the mind as divided into three parts, which will probably sound familiar to you. They are usually given the Latinized labels **id**, **ego**, and **superego**. These terms pertain to the irrational and emotional part of the mind, the rational part of the mind, and the moral part of the mind, respectively.[2]

The independence of these three mental structures can raise interesting problems. The id of the governor of New York compelled him to seek out prostitutes even while his superego condemned the activity. *The Book of Virtues* excoriates a long list of vices that strangely (or perhaps not so strangely) omits gambling. The author's superego enforced many prohibitions, it appears, but his id gained at least one exemption. The Oklahoma church official sought out male prostitutes at the same time he publicly denounced homosexuality. In all of these cases, the ego—the rational part of the mind—doesn't seem to have been doing its job, which is to manage the crossfire between these competing forces.

Modern research in biological and cognitive psychology has not found that the mind is actually divided neatly into three parts. However, both kinds of research support the idea that the mind includes separate and independent structures that can process different thoughts and motivations at the same time (Gazzaniga, Ivry, & Mangun, 1998; Rumelhart, McClelland, & The PDP Research Group, 1986; Shaver & Mikulincer, 2005). So while the three parts of the mind might not exist exactly as Freud envisioned them, it

---

[2] The psychoanalyst Bruno Bettelheim (1982) argued persuasively that these widely used terms mistranslate Freud's original German writing, but it is probably too late to correct that mistake here. Bettelheim's preferred translations for id, ego, and superego are the It, the I, and the Over-I.

is highly plausible to consider the mind as containing many voices, not just one, which might not all be saying the same thing.

3) Psychic Conflict and Compromise

Compromise-formation
↳ego's job.

The third assumption of the psychoanalytic approach stems directly from the second. Because the mind is divided into distinct and independent parts, it can conflict with itself, as we saw in the cases of the governor, the book author, and the church official. But psychic conflict is not always so dramatic. Let's assume, for example, that at this moment your id wants ice cream, but your superego thinks you don't deserve it because you haven't studied all week. It might fall to your ego to formulate a compromise: You get to have ice cream *after* you have finished this chapter.

The idea of **compromise formation** is a key tenet of modern psychoanalytic thought. The ego's main job, psychoanalysts now believe, is to find a middle course between the competing demands of motivation, morality, and practicality, and also among the many things a person wants at the same time. (Ego psychology will be considered again in Chapter 12.) The result of the compromise among these competing forces is what the individual consciously thinks and actually does (Westen, 1998). If the governor's and the church official's egos had been more effective, they might have been able to find some kind of compromise between their sexual motivations and their morality that would have kept them out of trouble. The ego of *The Book of Virtues* author failed him by leaving him in the awkward position of campaigning sternly against all modern vices except one. Without reasonable internal compromises, these individuals were left to flail between strong and contradictory impulses—first one way, and then the other—with disastrous results.

libido = psychic
energy.
=used to power the
mind
↳ remove neurotic
conflicts ↑ psychic
energy.

4) Mental Energy

The final key assumption of the psychoanalytic approach is that the psychological apparatus of the mind needs energy to make it go. The kind of energy required is sometimes called mental, or *psychic energy*, also known as **libido**, and only a fixed and finite amount is available at any given moment. Therefore, energy powering one part of the mind is not available for any other part; energy spent doing one thing, such as pushing uncomfortable thoughts out of memory, is unavailable for other purposes, such as having new and creative ideas. The principle of the conservation of energy applies to the mind as it does to the physical world.

This principle seems reasonable, and Freud based it on the Newtonian physics of his day, but some of its implications have not stood the test of time very well. For example, the original formulation assumed that if a psychological impulse was not expressed, it would build up over time, like steam pressure building in a boiler. If someone made you angry, then unless you expressed your anger, the associated psychic energy would build up until something snapped. This is an interesting idea that seems in accord with some real-life experience, such as the meek and mild person who allows himself to be pushed around by a bully until he bursts forth in murder. However, research suggests that it is usually wrong. Expressing anger typically makes a person more angry, not less, a direct contradiction of the original Freudian idea (Bushman, 2002).

There is another reason not to take the energy metaphor too literally. My first teaching job was at a college of engineering and science.[3] My class of engineers was dozing politely through my lecture on Freud when I mentioned psychic energy. They immediately perked up, and one student, grabbing his notebook, asked eagerly, "Psychic energy—in what units is that measured?" Unfortunately, I replied, psychic energy is not something that Freud ever measured in units of any kind. It was just a metaphor that applied in some respects but not in others—and none too precisely. At that answer, the students sighed, slouched back into their chairs, and no doubt privately redoubled their determination to become engineers rather than psychologists.

Modern psychoanalytic theory has moved away from Freud's original conception of psychic energy. In current thinking, the assumption is that it is the mind's capacity for processing information, rather than its energy, that is limited (Westen, 1998). This reformulation retains the implication that capacity used up by one purpose is not available for anything else. One goal of psychoanalysis, from the patient's perspective, is to free up more psychic energy—or computing capacity—for the challenges of daily living, by removing neurotic conflicts one by one.

CONTROVERSY

From the beginning until the present day, the psychoanalytic approach has stirred more controversy than any other approach to personality psychology.

---

[3] I recommend such a bracing experience to all of my psychologist colleagues.

Some people have even viewed it as dangerous. Objections to psychoanalysis have changed with the times. The Victorians looked at Freud's emphasis on sex and sexual energy, and complained that his theory was "dirty." We more enlightened folk of the 21st century look at Freud's emphasis on what cannot be seen and cannot be conclusively proved, and complain that his theory is "unscientific." The bases of the criticisms change, but in every age, it seems, a lot of people just don't like psychoanalysis. And many don't like Freud either. It is interesting to see how often criticisms of psychoanalysis are mixed with complaints about Freud's ethics, manners, and even personal life (e.g., Crews, 1996; see Westen, 1998, pp. 344–345; more will be said about attacks on Freud in Chapter 12).

Freud anticipated these kinds of attacks and sometimes even seemed to revel in them. His response was not exactly self-effacing. He pointed out that Copernicus became unpopular for teaching that the earth is not the center of the universe, and that Darwin was derided for his claim that humans are just another species of animal. His own insights that human nature is largely hidden, and that the motivations that drive many human behaviors are base and irrational, were not ideas he expected would win him any popularity contests. And he was right: psychoanalysis bothers people.

Let's bring this down to a personal level by considering two cautionary tales. They both exemplify the discomfort that psychoanalytic insights can cause, and the dangers of offering such insights unsolicited.

The first takes us way back to the time when I decided to major in psychology. I broke the news to my family in the traditional fashion. Returning home from college for Thanksgiving break, I waited for the inevitable question: "Have you decided on a major yet?" "Psychology," I replied. As many others making this choice have discovered, my family was not exactly thrilled. After a stunned silence, my sister spoke first. "OK," she said, "but so help me, if you ever psych me out, I will never speak to you again!"

Her comment is highly pertinent. Learning about personality psychology, especially the psychoanalytic approach, can produce irresistible urges to analyze the behavior and thoughts of those around us. It's all part of the fun. The advice you should take from my sister's warning, however, is to keep the fun private. People are typically not grateful to be analyzed. Sharing your insights into why your friends "really" did something can start real trouble. This is true even if your insights are accurate—Freud thought this was true *especially* when your insights are accurate.

My second tale is an example concerning psychoanalysis. When I get to the part of my courses when I teach about Freud, I try to do so as an advocate. I make the best, most convincing case for psychoanalytic theory that I can.

Who knows what effect this sales job has on my students, but one person I never fail to convince is myself. Thus, for a few weeks each academic year, I turn into a raving Freudian. I become temporarily unable to avoid analyzing every slip, mistake, and accident I see.

I did this once, years ago, on a date. In the course of a casual conversation, my dinner companion related something she had forgotten to do that day. Being deep in the Freudian phase of my syllabus, I immediately offered a complex (and rather clever, I thought) interpretation of the unconscious anxieties and conflicts that probably caused her memory lapse. My insight was not well received. My date vehemently replied that my interpretation was ridiculous, and that in the future I could keep my absurd Freudianisms to myself. Gesturing for emphasis, she knocked a glass of ice water into my lap. Picking up the ice cubes, but still in a Freudian frame of mind, all I could do was acknowledge the vivid, symbolic nature of the warning I had received.[4]

> Sharing your insights into why your friends "really" did something can start real trouble. This is true even if your insights are accurate—Freud thought this was true *especially* when your insights are accurate.

The moral of these two stories is the same: keep your clever analyses of other people to yourself! If you are wrong, it will make them mad. If you are right, it will make them even more mad. As they say at stunt demonstrations: "We are trained professionals. Do not try this at home."

FREUD HIMSELF

In this book, I have tried to avoid the trap of writing about psychologists instead of about psychology, because I believe that psychology is much more than "what psychologists do." An exception must be made for Freud. No other psychological approach is at once so influential and so closely identified with one individual. Freud is one of the most interesting and important people to have lived in the past couple of centuries. So let's take a moment and consider Freud and how he developed his ideas.

Sigmund Freud (1856–1939) was a medical doctor who practiced in Vienna, Austria, from the 1890s until the 1930s. Because he was Jewish, he had to flee his native country after Hitler came to power in the 1930s; he spent the last few years of his life in London. Freud died in a pessimistic frame of mind, convinced that the impending world war, following so closely on the heels of the catastrophic and tragic First World War, proved

---

[4] We later married anyway.

Figure 10.1 **Sigmund Freud at Work**

that we humans had an aggressive, destructive urge that, in the end, would destroy us.

One of Freud's less profound yet most enduring cultural legacies is the stereotype of what a psychotherapist should look like. He had a beard and small eyeglasses. He favored three-piece suits with a watch chain hanging from the vest. When he spoke English, it was with a Viennese accent. He had a couch in his office—along with some impressive African art that some patients reportedly found distracting.

Freud began his career as a research neurologist. He went to France for a time to study the newly developing field of hypnosis with Jean-Martin Charcot. He gradually moved into the practice of psychiatry, in part so he could make a living and get married. Then, as now, medical practice paid much better than theoretical research. Early in his clinical practice, Freud made a simple but fundamental discovery: When his patients talked about their psychological problems, sometimes that, by itself, was enough to help or even cure them. At first, Freud used hypnosis to get his patients to talk about difficult topics. Later, he turned to the use of *free association*, instructing the patient to say whatever came to mind, for the same purpose. One of Freud's grateful patients dubbed the results of such therapy the "talking cure." The talking cure was Freud's greatest contribution to psychotherapy. By now, it is ubiquitous. A fundamental assumption of nearly every school of psychotherapy—including many whose followers claim they have nothing in common with Freud—is that "talking about it helps."

Figure 10.2 **The Outside of Freud's Home at Berggasse 19, Vienna** His office and the apartment where he lived with his family were on the second floor. This picture was taken in 1938, shortly after the German army occupied Austria and shortly before Freud fled to London. If you look closely, you can see that someone has affixed a swastika above his door.

Freud thought he knew why talking helps. In part, it is because making one's thoughts and fears explicit by saying them out loud brings them into the open, where one's conscious, rational mind can deal with them. Your crazy thoughts won't make you so crazy once you have thought them through rationally. The other reason is that the psychotherapist can provide emotional support during the patient's difficult task of trying to figure out what is going on. Every psychotherapist keeps a box of tissues handy. In a letter to Carl Jung, Freud wrote that "psychoanalysis is in essence a cure through love" (cited in Bettelheim, 1982, epigraph). Many non-Freudian schools of psychotherapy have adopted these two ideas as well.

Freud attracted numerous disciples whom he encouraged to help him spread the ideas of psychoanalysis. Many of them had strong minds of their own, which led to some famous and bitter quarrels. Carl Jung and Alfred Adler were the most famous of Freud's followers who eventually split from their mentor (see Chapter 12).

Figure 10.3 **Freud's Famous Consulting Couch**

Freud's ideas came from the patients he treated and even more importantly from his observations of the workings of his own mind. This is something the psychoanalytic approach has in common with the humanistic approach, which is considered later in this book (see Chapter 13). Both psychoanalysts and humanists begin the psychological endeavor with the attempt to know themselves. An important part of traditional psychoanalytic training is being psychoanalyzed oneself. Other psychologists do not attempt to do this; in fact, they seem to avoid it. Trait psychologists and behaviorists, for example, generally focus their work safely outside of their own personalities, just as biological psychologists seldom cut themselves open.

Freud's ideas were influenced by the time and place in which he lived and by the patients he saw. Most were well-to-do women, a surprising number of whom reported having been sexually abused by their fathers when they were young. Freud at first believed them and saw this early abuse as a common source of early-life trauma. Later he changed his mind, and decided that these memories of early abuse were fantasies that, for psychological reasons, had come to seem real.[5]

Now that you have met Freud, let us turn to the basics of the theory he developed. It begins with the question of motivation, which asks, What do people want?

PSYCHOANALYSIS, LIFE, AND DEATH

Behind the many, sometimes contradictory things that people want, Freud believed, two motives are fundamental. The first motive impels toward life, the other toward death. Both motives are always present and competing. In the end, death always wins.

The life drive is sometimes called **libido**, also referred to as the *sexual drive*, which is what libido means in ordinary conversation.[6] In psychoanalytic writings by Freud and by those who came later, libido receives a great deal of attention. But I think it is also widely misunderstood, perhaps in part

---

[5] The critic Jeffrey Masson (1984) argued that this latter conclusion was a fundamental mistake, because it led psychoanalysts to look inside the mind instead of outside at the world for the origin of psychological problems.

[6] Freudian theory uses the term *libido* in several different, overlapping ways. Libido is the sexual drive. For Freud, this is the same as the life drive, though other psychoanalytic theorists, as we shall see, view the sexual drive as being part, but not all, of the life drive. Either way, the energy generated by this drive is source of the psychic energy (Freud's term for mental energy) that drives the whole psychological apparatus.

because so many people are easily distracted by any reference to sex. In the final analysis, sex is simply life. Sex is necessary for the creation of children, biological interventions aside, and its enjoyment can be an important part of being alive. In this sense libido is the sexual drive—Freud meant that it had to do with the creation, protection, and enjoyment of life and with creativity, productivity, and growth. This fundamental force exists within every person, Freud believed, and he called this force libido.[7]

Relatively late in his career, Freud posited a second fundamental motive, a drive toward death. He called it **Thanatos** (Greek for "death"). Although he probably did not mean to claim the existence of a "death wish," he held a fundamental belief in the duality of nature, or the idea that everything contains its own opposite. Freud observed that not only do people engage in a good deal of destructive activity that does not seem rational—wars are a good example—but also that, in the end, everybody dies. He introduced the death drive to account for these facts.

This drive, too, is sometimes misunderstood. Freud probably was not as morbid as his idea of a drive toward death makes him sound. I suspect he had in mind something like the concept of *entropy*, the basic force in the universe toward randomness and disorder. Ordered systems tend toward disorder over time, and this trend is inevitable; local, short-term increases in order only result in widespread, long-term increases in disorder.[8] Freud viewed the human mind and life itself in similar terms. We try desperately throughout our lives to make our thoughts and our worlds orderly, and to maintain creativity and growth. Although entropy dooms these efforts to failure in the end, in the meantime we may have a pretty good ride. So Freud's ultimate view of life was far from morbid; it might be better described as tragic.

The opposition of libido and Thanatos derives from another basic idea that arises repeatedly in psychoanalytic thinking: the **doctrine of opposites**. This doctrine states that everything implies, even requires, its opposite: life requires death, happiness requires sadness, and so forth. One cannot exist without the other.

An implication of this doctrine is that extremes on any scale may be more similar to each other than either extreme is to the middle. For exam-

---

[7] Here, as elsewhere, I am reinterpreting Freud in light of later developments in psychoanalytic thought and modern evidence. I think this rendition is true to the spirit of what Freud thought about libido. However, I also have to admit that Freud frequently talked about libido in a literally sexual sense, and that later psychoanalytic thinkers such as Jung thought Freud overemphasized sexuality at the expense of a broader interpretation of libido as the life drive.

[8] This is why, according to physics, the universe is doomed.

ple, consider pornographers and the leaders of antipornography censorship campaigns. The doctrine of opposites would claim that they have more in common with each other than either does with people in the middle, for whom pornography is not much of an issue. There may be something to this idea. Pornographers and censorship crusaders share not only extremism, but also a certain fascination with pornographic material—they agree that it is very important—and a tendency to spend a lot of time looking at it. Those in the middle, by contrast, may have a distaste for pornography, but are not so excited by its existence to make its prohibition a burning issue, or to immerse themselves in it all day long. Or consider an antiprostitution crusader and a regular patron of prostitutes. They could not be more different, right? Remember the sad case of Eliot Spitzer. Or consider what happens when one person stops loving another. Does her new attitude more often move to the middle of the continuum—to "mild liking"—or to the other extreme?

The juxtaposition of the life drive with the death drive is also consistent with the doctrine of opposites. But the death drive came to Freud as a sort of afterthought; he never fully worked it into the fabric of his theory, and most modern analysts do not really believe in it.[9] When I talk about psychic energy in the remainder of this book, therefore, the reference is to life energy, or libido.

PSYCHOLOGICAL DEVELOPMENT: "FOLLOW THE MONEY"

In the film *All the President's Men* (Pakula, 1976), the reporter Bob Woodward asks his secret source, Deep Throat, how to get to the bottom of the Watergate scandal embroiling the Nixon White House.[10] Deep Throat replies, "Follow the money." He means that Woodward should find out who controlled a large sum of secret cash at the Committee to Re-Elect the President, a fund-raising organization for Nixon, and find out how it was spent. This tip allows him and fellow reporter Carl Bernstein to crack the case.

When trying to understand the workings and the development of the human mind, Freud gives us similar advice. His version is, "Follow the energy." Like money, psychic energy is always both absolutely necessary and

---

[9] Personally, I find the idea useful.

[10] Decades later, in 2005, Deep Throat was revealed to have been FBI official Mark Felt.

Each stage has 3 aspects: 1) physical focus—where energy is concentrated/gratification obtained 2) Psychological theme related to PF and demands placed on child 3) Adult character type: fixated in one stage

absolutely limited, so the story of where it goes tends to be the story of what is really happening.

This principle comes into play in Freud's account of how the mind of an infant gradually develops into the mind of an adult. Psychological development is the story of how life energy, libido, becomes invested and then redirected over an individual's early years. A new baby fairly bubbles with life energy, but the energy lacks focus or direction. As the baby develops into a child and then an adult, the energy begins to focus, first on one outlet and then another. As the focus shifts, the style and type of gratification that the child seeks continually change. But no matter where it is focused, it is still libido, the same old psychic energy.

The focal points for psychic energy define the stages of psychological development. You have probably heard of them: oral, anal, phallic, and genital. Each stage has three aspects: (1) a *physical focus*, where energy is concentrated and gratification is obtained; (2) a *psychological theme*, related both to the physical focus and to the demands on the child from the outside world during development; and (3) an *adult character type* associated with being fixated (to some degree stalled) in that particular stage, rather than fully developing toward the next one. If an individual fails to resolve the psychological issues that arise at a particular stage, that person will always have some psychological scar tissue related to that stage, and those issues will be troublesome throughout life.

Oral Stage

A newborn baby is essentially helpless. It flails its arms and legs around. It cannot see clearly and cannot reach out and grab something it wants. It cannot crawl or even turn over. Its lack of motor control and physical coordination is almost total.

Almost. There is one thing a newborn baby can do as well at birth as any grown person will ever be able to do: suck. This is no small matter. The action is quite complex; the baby must develop suction with the mouth muscles and bring food into the stomach without cutting off the air supply. In a full-term baby, the necessary neuronal networks and muscles are in working order at birth. One of the many problems premature babies can have is that this complex mechanism may not yet function.

So now ask yourself, how does a new baby have any fun? It can't require the arms or legs, which don't really work yet. The primary source of pleasure for a newborn, and the one place on his body where the newborn can mean-

Birth–18 months.

PF: mouth, lips, tongue

PT: dependency – all
id

APT: "oral character"
– super independent
vs super passive

ingfully interact with the environment, is right there in the mouth. It stands to reason, therefore, that the mouth will be the first place psychic energy is focused. The **oral stage** of psychological development lasts from birth to about 18 months.

Let's consider the three aspects, described earlier, for this stage of development. The physical focus of the oral stage, as just discussed, is on the mouth, lips, and tongue. Freud sometimes said that for an infant these body parts are sexual organs—another remark that seems almost deliberately designed to be misunderstood. Freud meant that during this stage the mouth is where the life force and primary feelings of pleasure are concentrated. Eating is an important source of pleasure, but so are sucking on things and exploring the world with one's mouth.

When a baby begins to get control over her hands and arms, and sees some small, interesting object, what is the first thing she does? The baby puts the object in her mouth—often to the distress of the parents. Many parents assume the baby is trying to eat the ball, or the pencil, or the dead cockroach. But that is not the baby's real intention. The baby's hands are simply not developed enough to be of much use for exploration. When you pick up something interesting, you fondle it, turn it around, feel its texture and its heft. None of this works for a baby because too many fine motor skills are required; putting the object in the mouth can be more informative and interesting, because the mouth is more developed than the hands.

The psychological theme of the oral stage is *dependency*. A baby is utterly, even pathetically, dependent on others for everything he needs to live. The baby is passive in the sense that there is very little he can do for himself, though he may be far from passive in demands about what others should do. The baby's main psychological experience at this stage, therefore, is lying back and having others either provide everything he needs, or not. Either way, there is not much the baby can do about it, besides make plenty of noise. Another way to make the same point is to observe that, at the oral stage, the baby is all id. That is, the baby wants—full time—to be fed, to be held, to have a dry diaper, to be warm and comfortable, and to be entertained. Wanting stuff is the id's specialty. Actually doing something about those desires is the job of psychological structures that develop only later, along with the necessary physical competencies.

If a baby's needs at this stage of life are fulfilled to a reasonable degree, then attention and psychic energy will move along in due course to the next stage. Two things might go wrong, however. One is that the needs might not be fulfilled. The caretakers might be so uncaring, incompetent, or irresponsible that the baby is not fed when hungry, covered when cold, or comforted when upset. If this happens, the baby may develop a basic mistrust of other people and never be able to deal adequately with dependency relationships. The idea of depending on other people—or of being betrayed or abandoned by them—will forever make him upset, although he might not realize why.

A second thing that might happen is that a baby's needs are fulfilled so instantly and automatically that it never occurs to her that the world could respond differently. The increasing demands—and poor service—the world later provides, therefore, come as quite a shock. Such a person may wish to be back at the oral stage, where all that was necessary was to want something and it immediately appeared. Again, any issue that comes up in the baby's later life involving dependency, passivity, and activity might cause anxiety, though again she may be unaware as to just why.

Here we see the doctrine of opposites again. It will resurface many, many times: Any extreme childhood experience or its exact opposite, according to Freud, will yield equivalently pathological results. The ideal, Freud believed, lies in the middle. As a child-rearing strategy, Freud would recommend that a parent make reasonable efforts to fulfill a child's wants and needs at the oral stage but not go overboard by making sure every wish is instantly gratified, nor neglect the child so much that the child starts to doubt whether basic needs will be met.

I find it surprising that Freud gets so little credit for having been such a consistent and profound moderate. He disliked extremes of any kind— in behavior, in child-rearing styles, in personality types, in attitudes—in part because he saw both ends of most scales as equivalently pathological. Freud's ideal was always the golden mean; his adherence to this ideal is one of the most consistent and praiseworthy aspects of his approach.[11]

The adult personality type that Freud thought resulted from extreme childhood experience at this stage is the *oral character*. If you are getting used to how Freud thought about things, you will not be surprised to learn that the oral character comes in two extreme types. Both share an obsession, discomfort, and fundamental irrationality about any issue related to dependency and passivity. At one extreme are the supposedly independent souls who refuse help from everyone, who are determined to go it alone no matter what the cost. To these people, no accomplishment means anything unless it is achieved without assistance. At the other extreme are the passive individuals who wait around, seemingly forever, for their ships to come in. They

---

[11] We can see a modern version of this idea in the conclusion of most clinical psychologists that personality disorders are extreme positions on the normal range of personality trait variation (e.g., L. A. Clark, Livesley, & Morey 1997; see Chapter 18).

do nothing to better their situations, yet are continually bewildered—and sometimes angry—about their failure to get what they want. To them, wanting something should be enough to make it appear. That is how it works for babies, after all; they feel hunger or some other need, they cry, and somebody takes care of them. It is almost as if, as adults, oral characters expect the same strategy to work.

At their root, both oral types are equivalent, Freud believed. One interesting sign of their equivalence is the tendency of oral characters to flip from one oral type to the other. When they change, they go not to the middle but to the other end of the scale, which is psychologically closer to their original position. Someone who is aggressively independent, for example, may suddenly become completely passive and dependent when things do not go right. Someone who is completely passive may one day conclude that things are not going as they should and may move, not to the middle, but to the other extreme, disdaining help and trying to be independent to a degree that is not sensible.

I have a relative who, while in his thirties, was once described as the world's oldest 16-year-old, which is actually an insult to many 16-year-olds. He is an intelligent, likeable person, but he seems utterly unable to connect what he wants with what he must do. A few years ago he announced at a family gathering that he had finally formulated a career goal. We waited to hear what it was with some anticipation. He explained that he had thought about it carefully, worked out all of the figures, and decided that he wanted a job that paid $100,000 a year—after taxes. That would be enough to give him everything he wanted. "And what would the job be?" we asked. He seemed surprised by the question; he had not worked that part through, he said.

This is a classic attitude of an oral character. I think he believed, perhaps at some unconscious level, that all he had to do to get something was to make it clear that he wanted it. The idea that more planning and work might be required was somehow foreign. In general, oral characters spend much more time thinking about what they want than about how to get it.

Some students show a related attitude. At the end of the semester, they plead for a higher grade on the grounds that they need it. Often, they make an eloquent case for why they really need it. That should be enough, they seem to feel. The idea that attending class and doing the assignments is the way to earn a higher grade, rather than simply demanding it after the course is over, seems not to have occurred to them. Honestly, maybe it never did.

The reverse kind of oral character, the person who is chronically and pathologically independent, seems to be more rare. Yet I have seen the same relative whom I just described disdain even the most minor help in preparing a cookout or fixing a car. Perhaps you know people who insist, "I can do it myself," in the midst of utter failure.

Again, the ideal is the middle. A person who has resolved the oral stage accepts help gracefully but is not utterly dependent on it, and understands that people are ultimately responsible for their own outcomes.

Anal Stage — *development of the ego.*

The glory of life at the oral stage is that you do not have to do anything. Because you cannnot take care of yourself, you are not expected to. You do and express whatever you feel like, and whatever you can, whenever you want. Well and truly, this is too good to last.

Many breast-feeding mothers have had the experience of their baby, sucking away, suddenly trying out his new teeth with a good, strong bite. You can imagine how mom reacts: She yells, "Yow!" or something stronger, and instantly pulls the baby off. And you know how the baby reacts: with outrage, anger, frustration, and maybe even fear, if mom yelled loudly enough. The reaction comes to the baby as a rude shock: What do you mean—I can't bite when I feel like it? Moreover, the baby quickly discovers that until he can muster enough self-control to stop biting, the good stuff will fail to be forthcoming. This experience marks a dark day. It is an ominous forewarning of what is to come.

> Until the baby can muster enough self-control to stop biting, the good stuff will fail to be forthcoming. This experience marks a dark day.

As the child grows a little older, the demands of the world escalate rapidly. The child is expected to do a few things for herself—to start to control her emotions, for example. As the child begins to understand language, she is expected to follow orders. She learns the word *no*—a new and alarming concept. And—something that famously got Freud's attention—the child must learn to control her bowels and processes of elimination. Toilet training begins.

From all of this, the child begins to develop a new psychological structure: the ego. The ego's job is to mediate between what the child wants and what is actually possible. It is the rudimentary ego that must figure out that breast feeding will continue only as long as biting ceases. It is through painful lessons like this that the ego typically begins to develop a wide range of capabilities to rationally control the rest of the mind.

The physical focus of the **anal stage** is on the anus and associated organs of elimination. Learning the sensations of "having to go" and deal-

PF: anus and associated organs of elimination.

—begins a phase of escalated expectations child is expected to act independently.

PT: self control and obedience.

Problem: parents over a under controlling urges.
APT: anal character. control issues.

ing with them appropriately are important tasks of this stage. Freud and others pointed out that a good deal of everyday language seems to reveal an emotional resonance with the processes and products of elimination. This includes not only many standard insults and expletives with which I suspect you are familiar, but also descriptions of some people, anal characters as it turns out, as "uptight," and the common advice to "let it all out," which suggests relaxing one's self-control and acting "naturally."

But I am going to bend Freud a bit here (in the direction of Eriksonian theory, which we shall discuss in Chapter 12). I think the classic theory places a misleading degree of emphasis on literal defecation and its supposed physical pleasures. Toilet training is an important part of life during the anal stage and seems to be the source of some powerful symbolic language. But it is just one example among many increasing demands for obedience and self-control that begin around the age of 18 months. As the child develops the capacity for bowel control, the parents, tired of diapers, are eager to have the child use this new skill.[12] But this escalation of expectation applies to many other circumstances as well, from "Get your own drink of water" to "Don't touch that!" All of these experiences, happening at once and for the very first time, are part of a dramatic turning point in life tied to a powerful set of psychological themes.

The primary psychological theme of the anal stage is *self-control* and its corollary, *obedience*. At the age of about 18 months, a child begins to move around effectively and do other things independently: The child also begins to develop the ability to control urges, not only the urge to defecate but other urges as well, such as the urge to cry, or grab a forbidden object, or hit a baby sister. Authority figures—usually the parents—begin to insist that the child use these new self-control capacities.

There is a lot to learn at the anal stage, and things do not always go smoothly. Typically, a child will try to figure out just how much power the authority figures around him really have to make him do their bidding, as opposed to how much he gets to decide. The child does this by testing the parents, experimenting to find the boundaries of what he can get away with. What happens if the child pulls the cat's tail after being told not to? If the parents say, "No more cookies," what happens if the child sneaks one anyway?

In the folklore of parenthood, this testing stage is known as the "terrible twos." The child indeed can begin to seem like a little monster. But really, this behavior is perfectly rational. How will the child figure out how

---

[12] Besides the mess, diapers are shockingly expensive.

the world works without experimenting? The behavior can be exasperating, but it is normal and probably even necessary.

Two things might go wrong at the anal stage. As always in psychoanalytic thinking, the two kinds of mistakes are polar opposites, and the ideal is in the middle. Unreasonable expectations can be traumatic. If parents insistently make demands that the child is not capable of meeting—for example, that the child always obey, never cry, or hold her bowels longer than physical capability allows—the result can be psychological trauma with long-lasting consequences. And the opposite—never demanding that the child control her urges, neglecting toilet training altogether—can be equally problematic.

As at every stage, the child's developmental task is to figure out what is going on in the world and how to deal with it. At the anal stage, the child must figure out how, and how much, to control himself and how, and how much, to be controlled by those in authority. This is a thorny issue, even for an adult. A child will never work it through sufficiently if the environment is too harsh or too lenient.

Relatively recent research that followed a sample of children from childhood into late adolescence basically confirmed this Freudian view. The parents of these children were classified as authoritarian (extremely rigid and obedience oriented), or permissive (weak and lacking control), or authoritative (compromising between firm control and their children's freedom). As Freud would have anticipated, it was the authoritative parents—the ones in the middle—whose children fared the best later in life (Baumrind, 1971, 1991).[13]

Psychological mishaps at the anal stage produce the adult anal character. The *anal character* has a personality organized around control issues. As always, the outcome might go either of two ways. One way is to become obsessive, compulsive, stingy, orderly, rigid, and subservient to authority. This kind of person tries to control every aspect of her life and often seems equally happy to submit to an authority figure. She cannot tolerate disorganization or ambiguity. Long ago, one of my professors of abnormal psychology said he had a one-item test for detecting an anal character: Go to that person's room, and you will see on the desk a row of pencils or other items in a perfectly straight line. Reach over casually, turn one of the pencils at a $90°$ angle, and start timing. If within 2 minutes the person has moved the pencil back, he is an anal character. This test is too facile, of course, but you get the idea.

---

[13] This finding may be limited to the Western culture with which Freud was most familiar. Recent evidence suggests that authoritative versus authoritarian parenting may have very different implications and consequences in an Asian cultural context (Chao, 2001).

The other type of anal character is exactly the opposite. This person may have little or no self-control, be unable to do anything on time or because it is necessary, be chaotic and disorganized, and have a compulsive need to defy authority. Freud saw both types of anal characters as psychologically equivalent and further believed that such individuals would more likely flip from one anal extreme to the other than attain the ideal position in the middle.

There is a lame joke dating from the 1970s that expresses the equivalence of the two anal types:

Q: Why did the short-hair cross the road?
A: Because somebody told him to.
Q: Why did the long-hair cross the road?
A: Because somebody told him not to.[14]

Freud's point is similar. If you are rigidly, obsessively organized and obedient, you have a problem. If you are completely disorganized and disobedient because you cannot help it, you also have a problem—in fact, you have the same problem. Self-control and relations with authority should be means to an end, not ends in themselves. The ideal is to determine how and to what degree to organize your life and how you relate to authority, in order to achieve your goals.

Phallic Stage

The next stage of development begins with a realization: boys and girls are different. According to psychoanalytic theory, this fact begins to sink in at around the age of 3½ to 4 years, and dominates psychological development until about age 7.

The specific realization that occurs at the **phallic stage** for both sexes, according to Freud, is that boys have a penis and girls do not—hence the name of the stage.[15] The basic task of the phallic stage is coming to terms with sex differences and all that they imply. According to Freud, boys, hav-

---

[14] This joke relies on a stereotypical image from the late 1960s: men with short hair were viewed as conservative and subservient to authority, whereas men with long hair were assumed to be radical and disobedient. Today, hairstyles have few political implications, thank goodness.

[15] Maybe this is not as specific or universal as Freud thought. I once asked one of my daughters, then not quite 4 years old, what the difference was between boys and girls. "Boys do not have crotches," she instantly replied.

ing noticed that girls do not have penises, wonder what happened and if the same thing could happen to them. Girls just wonder what happened.

Hard-core adherents of orthodox psychoanalysis launch into a pretty complicated story at this point. The story is based on the Greek myth of Oedipus, the man who unknowingly killed his father and married his mother. According to the psychoanalytic version of the *Oedipal crisis*, young boys fall physically as well as emotionally in love with their mothers, and because of this they understandably fear their fathers' jealousy. The specific fear is that their fathers might castrate them in retaliation. For girls this crisis is less intense, but they still suffer grief over the castration they believe has

"*Why do you think you cross the road?*"

already occurred. To resolve this anxiety or grief, each child identifies with the same-sex parent, taking on many of his or her values and ideals, which lessens the child's feelings of rivalry and jealousy that might otherwise reach a critical level.

The full story of the Oedipal crisis is rich and fascinating, and the summary just presented (which you may have noticed was exactly four sentences long) fails to do it justice. Nevertheless, I will not say much more about it here, in part because the story is so well told elsewhere. The best rendition in English may be the one provided by Bettelheim (1982). A more important reason for not getting too deeply into the traditional story of the phallic stage is that it has not held up well in the light of empirical research (R. R. Sears, 1947). So, I will discuss this point in development in simpler and more modern terms.[16]

It seems obvious that the realization that the sexes differ must be an important milestone in psychological development. It also seems natural that with this realization comes the awareness that one parent is male and the other female. I do not think it is far-fetched to think that children

---

[16] Here is yet another place where I am straying from what Freud literally said, and substituting a contemporary rendition that strikes me as both more sensible in light of modern knowledge, and also consistent with the spirit of what Freud meant.

PT: gender identity
and sexuality.
— relating to samesex parent
— trying to become
more like the people
or fears
= development of the
superego.

APT: phallic character
— over or underdeveloped
superego.
↳ may be the basis of
homosexuality.
— so deeply in love w
one's mother that all
other women become
intolerable rivals.

wonder about the attraction between their parents, and that they fantasize to some degree about what a relationship with their opposite-sex parent would be like. And, although this may push the envelope a bit, I even think it's plausible that children feel guilty, at some level, about having such fantasies. The fantasies probably seem rather outlandish even to children, and they probably suspect their same-sex parent would not exactly be thrilled if he or she knew what they were thinking.

The psychological theme of the phallic stage is *gender identity and sexuality*—the need to figure out what it means to be a boy or girl. For most children, the best, or most obvious, examples are their mothers and fathers. One way to be a girl is to act like mom, and to be a boy, act like dad. This can mean taking on many of the parent's attitudes, values, and ways of relating to the opposite sex. Freud called this process **identification**.[17]

Related psychological themes of the phallic stage include love, sexuality, fear, and jealousy. The adult consequences of the phallic stage include the development of morality, which Freud saw as a by-product of the process of identification; the values of your same-sex parent provide the beginnings of your own moral outlook. Another adult consequence is the development of sexuality—what kind of person you find attractive, how you handle sexual competition, and the overall role of sexuality in your life. The most important result of the phallic stage is an image of oneself as masculine or feminine, whatever that may entail.

Additional identifications are possible and even likely. A child might take on the values and behaviors of an admired teacher, relative, religious leader, or rock star. In most cases, people identify with those whom they love and admire, but in some circumstances, individuals identify with people they loathe and fear. During World War II, inmates in Nazi death camps reportedly sometimes identified with their guards, making Nazi armbands and uniforms from scraps and giving each other the "Heil Hitler" salute. According to the psychoanalyst Bruno Bettelheim, who was an inmate at Dachau and Buchenwald himself, this seemingly strange behavior was an adaptation to deal with their profound and realistic fear of the guards; to become more like the guards was to fear them less (Bettelheim, 1943). I

---

[17] The personal lives of many students intersect with the content of a personality course at this point. I have been asked many times, "What happens at this stage if a child is raised by a single parent?" Such questions are not merely hypothetical. I wish I had a good answer. The best I can manage is that these children look elsewhere for salient models of masculinity or femininity, perhaps to relatives, friends, teachers, or (shudder) the mass media.

suspect milder forms of this behavior—trying to become more like the people one most fears—are rather common and are probably one basis for the development of the superego. People sometimes identify with a teacher they hate, a coach they fear, an older student who hazes them, or a drill sergeant or an entire branch of the military who gives them little but abuse. In the process, these characters become less fearful while the person becomes a little more like them.

Wherever they come from—and again, the usual source is the parents—the sum of one's identifications makes up the third major psychic structure after the id and ego: the superego. The superego is the part of the mind that passes moral judgment on the other parts, judgments based on a complex mixture of all the different moral lessons learned directly and by example, from everybody one has ever identified with. When successfully developed, the superego provides a conscience and a basis for reasonable morality. But as always, the development of the superego is a process that can go too far or not far enough.

An overdeveloped or underdeveloped superego yields the adult type of the *phallic character*. A person who has developed a completely rigid moral code, one that brooks no shades of gray and no exceptions, may be a phallic type. So is someone who lacks a moral code altogether. An extremely promiscuous person might be a phallic type. So, too, might someone who becomes completely asexual.

Male homosexuality might have its roots here, although in my opinion, psychoanalysis does not offer a very convincing account of just how. The story basically involves a boy who falls so deeply in love with his mother that all other women become intolerable rivals. To avoid disloyalty to mom, he turns to members of his own gender for sexual gratification. For a more plausible account, see Bem's theory summarized in Chapter 9.

A pattern of extremely "loose" sexual behavior might be one manifestation of a phallic character; so might an overly rigid and puritanical one. As always, Freud was suspicious of the extremes; the healthy place to be is in the middle.

Genital Stage

After the phallic stage, a child gets a chance to take a developmental breath and concentrate on the important learning tasks of childhood, such as learning to read, the names of plants and birds, arithmetic, and all of the

latency - period between phallic and genital.

PF = genitals
└ not only the physical organ, but reproduction.

Developmental task: add something constructive to life and society.

PT: maturity.

APT: genital character → balanced

Mental Health (Freud)
"the ability to love and work."

other important stuff taught in elementary school. This *latency* phase is a sort of psychological respite to allow the child to learn much of what he will need in adult life. The rest period ends with a bang, at puberty.

The **genital stage** of development is fundamentally different from the others in that Freud saw it not as something individuals necessarily pass through, but something they must attain. Adulthood is not inevitable; it is an achievement. Sometime after physical puberty, if all goes well, a person develops a mature attitude about sexuality and other aspects of adulthood. Freud is not explicit about when this happens; in some people, it apparently never happens.

The physical focus of the genital stage is the genitals, but notice how this label differs from that of the phallic stage. Genital describes not just a physical organ; the word also refers to the process of reproduction, or giving life. The genitals, at this stage, become not just organs of physical pleasure, but the source of new life and the basis of a new psychological theme.

The focus of the genital stage is the creation and enhancement of life. True maturity, Freud believed, entailed the ability to bring new life into the world and nurture its growth. This new life includes children, but it also can include other kinds of creativity, such as intellectual, artistic, or scientific contributions. The developmental task of the genital stage is to add something constructive to life and to society, and to take on the associated adult responsibilities. In that sense, the psychological theme of the genital stage is *maturity*. And, as I mentioned, not everybody attains it. The *genital character* is psychologically well adjusted and—here comes the familiar word—balanced.

Early in the 20th century, Freud made his only trip to the United States where he was dismayed to find himself trailed by newspaper reporters who found some of his sexual theories titillating, especially after they had finished distorting them. Freud's lifelong aversion to America and anything American seems to have been boosted by this experience. But the trip was not a total loss. At one point, a reporter asked him, "Dr. Freud, what is your definition of mental health?" Freud replied with the best answer that anybody has ever come up with. The essence of **mental health**, he said, is the ability "to love and to work."

The most important word in this definition is "and." Freud thought it was important to love, to have a mate and family to care for and nurture. He also thought it was important to work, to do something useful and constructive for society. The good life, Freud thought, would always contain both. To do just one was to be an incomplete person. The truly mature person who has attained the genital stage has learned to balance both kinds of generativity, love and work.

Many women face well-known difficulties in balancing families and careers. In our society, one often conflicts with the other, and to "have it all" seems a nearly insurmountable challenge. Freud would have approved of the way women make this struggle, I think. After all, the balance of those two things is what life is all about.[18]

Consider traditional men, by contrast. The word *workaholic* was coined to describe what many men became in the 20th century, and some still are today. These men experience little conflict between work and home because they simply give up on, or delegate, the home part. Are they better off? Freud would think not. To leave out one of the two aspects of life that a person must balance is not psychological health—it's arrested development. The balance many women have been trying to achieve, therefore, implies that they are more psychologically developed than men who have given up the struggle.

Times are changing. On the one hand, as society continues to evolve, more women are beginning to fit the workaholic mold, neglecting family in pursuit of career in the manner that once characterized men. On the other hand, a small but steadily increasing number of men are putting family ahead of their career, even becoming "househusbands" to workaholic wives. Both sexes strive to reconcile the inevitable conflict between what Freud called love and work. The perfect balance seems to elude everybody, but that is the nature of perfection. It is something we seek but never attain.

Moving Through Stages

As we have seen, an important consequence of developing through these stages is building the basic psychological structures. At the beginning of the oral stage, the newborn baby is all id—a seething bundle of wants and needs. As the baby moves into the anal stage, experiences of frustration and delay lead part of the mind to differentiate and separate from the id, taking some of its energy with it to form the ego. The ego has the duty to control and channel, to some degree, the urges of the id. At the phallic stage, the child identifies with important persons, principally her parents, and the sum of these identifications forms the third structure, the superego. The super-ego is the conscience; it morally judges the person's actions and urges, and sometimes tries to stop them.

---

[18] Actually, perhaps Freud would not have approved. In his personal life he seems to have been a typical Victorian sexist. But I think the spirit of Freudian thought implies that everybody should seek to balance love and work.

Freud once used a different analogy: A mind progressing through the stages of psychological development is a little like an army conquering a hostile territory. Periodically it encounters opposition and difficulty, and at that point a battle ensues. To secure the ground after the battle, some troops are left behind as the army advances. If the battle was particularly bitter, and if the local resistance remains strong, a larger part of the army must stay behind—leaving fewer troops to advance. Moreover, if the main army encounters severe problems later, it is likely to retreat to a stronghold at the site of a former battle.

In this analogy, the individual's store of libido is the army. It encounters "battles" at each of the developmental stages. If the battle of the oral, anal, or phallic stage is not completely won, libidinal energy must be left behind at that point. The result will be **fixation**. The adult will continue to struggle with issues from that stage, and will tend to retreat there under stress. Such retreat is called **regression**. An oral character under stress becomes passive and dependent and may even revert to thumb sucking. An anal character under stress becomes even more rigid or more disorganized than usual. A phallic character under stress may become promiscuous or completely asexual. Victory, in this analogy, means making it through all of these stages to the final (genital) stage, with as much of one's army intact as possible. The more libido available to enjoy the final stage of maturity, the better adjusted the adult will be.

THINKING AND CONSCIOUSNESS

Underneath the progression through these psychosexual stages, the mind is also undergoing a subtle, profound, but incomplete shift between two kinds of thinking: primary process thinking and secondary process thinking. **Secondary process thinking** is what we ordinarily mean by the word *think*. The conscious part of the ego thinks this way; it is rational, practical, and prudent, and it can delay or redirect gratification. It is secondary in two senses. First, it develops only as the ego begins to develop; a newborn has no capacity for secondary process thinking. Second, Freud believed it played a less important role relative to primary process thinking, which he consid-

Secondary process thinking: occurs after infancy. rational, practical, prudent.

ered more interesting, important, and powerful—throughout life, not just in infancy.

→ does not contain the idea of "no"

Primary process thinking is the way the unconscious mind operates, and how the infant's as well as the adult's id is said to operate. It is a strange sort of thinking. The fundamental aspect of primary process thinking is that it does not contain the word, or even the idea of, *no*. It is thinking without negatives, qualifications, sense of time, or any of the practicalities, necessities, and dangers of life. It has one goal: the immediate gratification of every desire.

ties disparate feelings closer together.

Primary process thinking operates by an odd shorthand that can tie the disparate feelings closely together. Your feelings about your family can affect how you feel about your house, for example. Primary process thinking can use displacement to replace one idea or image with another: Your anger toward your father, for example, might be replaced by anger at all authority figures, or your anger toward an authority might be transformed into anger at your father. (Displacement will be considered in more detail in Chapter 11.) **Condensation** can compress several ideas into one; an image of a house or of a woman might consolidate a complex set of memories, thoughts, and emotions. And through **symbolization**, one thing might stand in for another.

condensation — compresses several idea into one

At one point in his career, Freud thought there might be a universal symbolic code of the unconscious mind, in which certain symbols meant the same thing to everybody the world over. He thought people could use these symbols to interpret the meanings of dreams, and some of these are included in the little paperback books on dream analysis you can get at the supermarket. They include translations like:

House = human body
Smooth-fronted house = male body
House with ledges and balconies = female body
King and queen = parents
Little animals = children
Children = genitals
Playing with children = (You fill in this one.)
Going on a journey = dying
Clothes = nakedness
Going up stairs = having sex
Bath = birth

Intriguing as lists like this can be, Freud later dropped the idea of universal symbols. He decided that meanings vary for every individual, and therefore a general dictionary of the unconscious was not useful. The idea of unconscious universal symbols was picked up with a vengeance, however, by Carl Jung (see Chapter 12).

Primary process thinking is a very interesting concept, but one might reasonably ask, If primary process thinking is a property of the unconscious mind, then where is it ever "seen"? Freud thought that primary process thinking could emerge into consciousness under several limited circumstances. He believed that the conscious thought of very young children operates according to primary process, but because they develop secondary process thinking by the time they can talk, this hypothesis is difficult to verify (actually, it is impossible). He also thought primary process thinking could become conscious during fever delirium, and during dreams. This is consistent with the experience that in dreams or delirium, one may have no sense of time, one person can change into another, images may symbolize other things, and so on. Freud also thought that psychotics sometimes consciously experience primary process thinking; if you listen to the speech of a patient with schizophrenia, you will see where Freud got this idea.

But primary process thinking rarely emerges directly into consciousness. More important, Freud believed, are the ordinary and indirect ways that primary process thinking influences conscious thought and overt behavior. The results of primary process thinking often leak out, as slips of the tongue, accidents, lapses of memory, and the like (see Chapter 11).

Freud posited three levels of consciousness in what is sometimes called his *topographic model*[19] (see Figure 10.4). The smallest, topmost, and according to Freud, least important layer is the **conscious mind**, the part of your mental functioning you can observe when you simply turn your attention inward. A second layer, the **preconscious**, consists of ideas you are not thinking about at the moment, but that you could bring into consciousness easily. For example, how is the weather outside right now? What did you have for breakfast? Where is your car parked? Presumably, none of these things was in your conscious mind until I asked, but you probably had little trouble bringing them into your conscious awareness.

The third, the biggest, and according to Freud, the most important layer of the mind is the unconscious. The **unconscious** includes all of the id and superego, and most of the ego. The unconscious is buried deep; the only way to bring it to the surface is by digging. One method of psychologi-

---

[19]*Topography* refers to elevation; a topographic map is one that shows the elevations of the hills and valleys over an expanse of territory.

Figure 10.4 Freud's Diagram Showing the Relationship Between Consciousness and Id, Ego, and Superego
The conscious mind is denoted by *pcpt.-cs* (which stands for "perception–conscious"). Freud wrote about this diagram, "It is certainly hard to say today how far the drawing is correct. In one respect it is undoubtedly not. The space occupied by the unconscious id ought to have been incomparably greater than that of the ego or the preconscious. I must ask you to correct it in your thoughts."

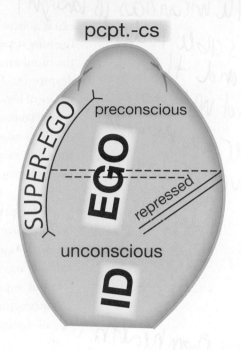

cal digging that Freud used early in his career was hypnosis. Other clues come from slips of the tongue, accidents, and lapses of memory. All have their causes in mental processes that occur outside of consciousness. Finally, Freud developed the technique of free association, in which a person is encouraged to say whatever comes to mind in relation to some concern or issue. Freud thought the mental wanderings of free association were not random—he never thought anything was random. Therefore, the way a person jumps from one thought to another offers important clues about his or her unconscious.

I know of one psychoanalyst who, following these precepts, explains to his patients that they should tell him whatever comes to mind, because their thoughts, feelings, and motives are all connected in complex networks of associations. We often lack conscious access to these networks, but they can be uncovered. One goal of psychoanalysis is to map these networks in order to see the context in which a symptom is embedded and to get a better idea of how the patient's mind works (Drew Westen, personal communication, April 28, 1994).

PSYCHOANALYIS AS A THERAPY AND AS A ROUTE TOWARD UNDERSTANDING

The purpose of psychoanalytic therapy is to use these various clues to reveal the contents of the unconscious. Freud believed that the problems that make most people anxious and unhappy have their roots in unconscious conflicts. The way to resolve these conflicts is to bring them into the open through dream analysis, analysis of slips and lapses, and free association. Once an unconscious conflict is brought into consciousness, the rational part of the

[Handwritten margin note: Once the unconscious is brought to consciousness, the ego is able to deal with it and the conflict will no longer = a problem. - power of logic.]

ego is able to deal with it, and the conflict will no longer pose a problem. In the long run of therapy, Freud believed that insight into the hidden parts of the mind would allow the patient full, rational self-control. In other words, despite his focus on irrational mental processes, Freud believed in the power of logic.

Of course, the process is a bit more complicated than that. Unconscious conflicts must be dealt with not just logically but emotionally, which takes time and can be painful. It can even be dangerous. As the psychoanalytic psychologist Robert Bornstein pointed out,

> some patients with a history of severe sexual or physical abuse do not have the psychological resources available to cope adequately with explicit memories of these experiences. For these patients, therapeutic work should focus primarily on bolstering defenses and coping mechanisms. Only when these resources have been strengthened can insight be used productively within and outside of therapy. (Bornstein, 1999b, p. 169)

[Handwritten margin note: Flight from health = "I don't want to talk about it".]

As people bring their conflicts to the surface, they often begin to feel more anxious in the short run; the prospect of losing one's neuroses can be surprisingly disconcerting. Many people avoid dealing with their unconscious anxieties for this reason; psychoanalysts call the phenomenon of running away from the solution to one's psychological problems the "flight from health." It is very common; it may be what is going on when you hear someone say, "I don't want to talk about it."

[Handwritten margin note: Therapeutic alliance = bond between therapist and patient. Loccurs through transference. patient → therapist therapist → patient = countertransference.]

To comfort, guide, and support the patient through this difficult healing process, Freud believed, there must be an emotional bond between therapist and patient. The development of this bond is called the *therapeutic alliance*. This alliance gets its power through **transference**, the tendency to bring ways of thinking, feeling, and behaving that developed toward one important person into a later relationship with a different person. One might relate to a teacher in the same way one learned years earlier to relate to one's father, for example (see Chapter 12's discussions of object relations and attachment theory). Transference is particularly important in psychotherapy, because the emotional relationship the patient develops with the therapist is built on the model of that patient's past relationships with other important people. The therapist has reactions to the patient as well, both positive and negative. The emotional response of the therapist to the patient is called *countertransference*.

The development of transference and countertransference in therapy is important, but it can also cause problems. Freud was perhaps the first psychotherapist to note that sexual attraction sometimes arises between patients and psychotherapists. He was adamant that it was the duty of the therapist to resist this attraction. The patient must become emotionally invested for the therapy to work, Freud believed, and perhaps the therapist must as well, but the therapist must, at all costs, avoid acting on those emotions. This warning applies to negative reactions as well. Therapists working with difficult patients, such as those characterized by narcissistic personality disorder (see Chapter 18), describe feeling resentful, regretful, frightened, and manipulated (Betan, Heim, Conklin, & Westen, 2005). They feel they are "walking on eggshells" around their patient (p. 893), and even dread checking their phone messages! Obviously, to even hope to be helpful to a patient like this, therapists must struggle to control their own emotions.

Psychoanalysis often is criticized for its allegedly low or even zero demonstrable cure rate, and for the fact that treatment can last for many years and perhaps never end. But recent research gave it a major and, to some observers, surprising boost. A thorough summary of 23 studies involving 1,053 patients concluded that long-term psychoanalytic therapy was more effective than shorter forms of treatment, especially for what were called "complex mental disorders." Indeed, patients who participated in long-term psychoanalysis fared better than 96 percent of the patients treated by other means (Leichsenring & Rabung, 2008).

This impressive finding does not mean that psychoanalysis always works, or that it is appropriate for everybody. As one psychiatrist recently wrote:

> Thanks to decades of clinical study, analysts are able to assess which patients are able to do better with medication or . . . [other forms of] therapy and which are likely to benefit more from analysis. Within the group for whom analysis is suitable, patients often make gains unachievable with other treatments. (J. D. Miller, 2009, p. 6)

Despite this recent attempt at resolution, the argument over the efficacy of psychoanalytic psychotherapy continues. Late in his own career, Freud began to see the issue as beside the point:

> After forty-one years of medical activities, my self-knowledge tells me that I have not been a physician in the proper sense. . . . [My real interests are] the events of the history of man, the mutual influ-

ences between man's nature, the development of culture, and those residues of prehistoric events of which religion is the foremost representation . . . studies which originate with psychoanalysis but go way beyond it. (Cited by Bettelheim, 1982, p. 48; bracketed phrasing is mine)

In the end, Freud was surprisingly uninterested in psychoanalysis as a medical or therapeutic technique, an attitude that some modern psychotherapists share (Bader, 1994). Instead, he saw its real importance as a tool for understanding human nature and culture.

SUMMARY

- Unlike many approaches to personality, the psychoanalytic approach concentrates on the cases where the cause of behavior is mysterious and hidden.

The Key Ideas of Psychoanalysis

- Psychoanalytic theory is based on a small number of key ideas, including psychic determinism, the mind's three-part internal structure (id, ego, and superego), psychic conflict, and mental energy.

Controversy

- Psychoanalysis has been controversial throughout its history, although the nature of the controversy has changed with the times. Freud was one of the geniuses of the 20th century.

Freud Himself

- Freud was a practicing psychotherapist, and developed his ideas from the cases he saw as well as from introspection and his broad knowledge of literature, art, and culture. One of his grateful patients dubbed his technique "the talking cure."

Psychoanalysis, Life, and Death

- Freud's psychoanalytic theory posits two fundamental motives: a life force (libido), and a drive toward death and destruction (Thanatos).

Psychological Development: "Follow the Money"

- Libido produces psychic energy, and the story of psychological development is the story of how this energy is focused in different areas over the course of four stages of life.

- Each developmental stage has a physical focus, a psychological theme, and an adult character type that results if that stage of development does not go well. The main theme for the oral stage is dependency; for the anal stage it is obedience and self-control; for the phallic stage it is gender identity and sexuality; and for the genital stage it is maturity, in which one ideally learns to balance "love and work."

- The different structures of the mind form during progression through these developmental stages. The newborn baby is "all id." The ego develops during the anal stage, as a result of experiences with frustration and delay, and the superego develops during the phallic stage, as a result of identifications with significant people, especially the parents.

- Fixation occurs when an individual gets, to some degree, psychologically "stuck" in a stage of development; regression is movement backward from a more advanced psychological stage to an earlier one.

Thinking and Consciousness

- Primary process thinking, assumed by Freud to be present in babies and in the unconscious part of the adult mind, is unconscious thought characterized by displacement, symbolism, and an irrational drive toward immediate gratification.

- Secondary process thinking, which develops as the child moves toward adulthood, is ordinary, rational, conscious thought.

- The three layers of consciousness are the conscious mind, the preconscious, and the unconscious. Freud thought the conscious mind was by far the smallest of the three.

Psychoanalysis as a Therapy and as a Route Toward Understanding

- Psychoanalytic therapy is performed through techniques such as dream analysis and free association in the context of a therapeutic alliance between patient and therapist. The goal is to bring the unconscious thoughts that are the source of an individual's problems into the open, so the conscious, rational mind can deal with them.

- Although psychoanalysis has become notorious for its long length and allegedly low cure rate, recent research has provided surprising support for its efficacy. Freud himself might not have cared much; he once wrote that he was interested in psychoanalysis more as a tool for understanding human nature than as a medical technique.

THINK ABOUT IT

1. Do you hear Freudian ideas used in the ways people talk about each other? Can you think of any examples beyond those presented in this chapter?

2. Has anything happened recently in the news or in your life that seems best explained from a psychoanalytic perspective?

3. Have you heard about Freud or psychoanalytic ideas in any other courses you have taken? Which ones?

4. When your instructors in other psychology courses have mentioned Freud, have they expressed a favorable or hostile attitude? On what grounds? How about your instructors in other fields, such as English?

5. What does it say about a theorist that people still argue heatedly about his ideas almost a century after his career?

6. Do you think toilet training is a big deal for children? Does the way it is handled have important consequences for psychological development?

7. Research in political science shows that most young adults belong to the same political party as their parents. How would Freud explain this? Do you think this explanation is correct, and can you think of other possible reasons?

8. Can you think of any oral, anal, phallic, or genital characters among the people you know? Without naming names, what are they like? How do you think they got this way?

9. Do you think dreams reveal anything about the mind of the dreamer? Have you ever learned something about yourself by analyzing a dream?

10. If you had a psychological problem, would you go to a psychoanalyst? Why, or why not?

SUGGESTED READINGS

Bettelheim, B. (1988). *A good enough parent*. New York: Vintage.
> *A fascinating look at childrearing from a psychoanalytic point of view, by one of the more important psychoanalysts of the latter part of the 20th century. It is never blindly orthodox and is filled with nuggets of wisdom that would interest any parent.*

Gay, P. (1988). *Freud: A life for our time*. New York: Norton.
> *A masterful, thorough, well-written biography of Freud that recounts not just his life, but the development of psychoanalytic thought. The author is clearly sympathetic to Freud and psychoanalysis, but brings a modern perspective.*

Gay, P. (1989). *The Freud reader*. New York: Norton.
> *An excellent collection of Freud's original writings, including some unusual selections translated specially for this volume.*

EMEDIA

Go to StudySpace, wwnorton.com/studyspace, to access additional review and enrichment materials.

11

THE WORKINGS OF THE UNCONSCIOUS MIND:
Defenses and Slips

Ego uses "defense mechanisms" to avoid anxiety.

DO YOU *REALLY* **WANT** to know what is going on around you, and would you like to understand the unvarnished truth about yourself? Maybe not. Some facts, thoughts, or feelings might make you feel uncomfortable or intolerably anxious if you were consciously aware of them, perhaps to the point that you could no longer function. You also may have some urges, as Freud believed, that would get you in big trouble if they were expressed. An important responsibility of the ego, therefore, is to keep these disturbing parts of mental life safely locked inside the unconscious sectors of the mind. The techniques the ego uses to keep certain thoughts and impulses hidden in order to avoid anxiety are called the **defense mechanisms**.

Defense mechanisms are not always effective. Thoughts, words, and even actions occasionally leak out. You might think something that seems strange even to you, say something you didn't mean to say, or do something against your better judgment. These "Freudian slips," also called parapraxes, can be embarrassing and even hurtful, and they also provide important clues about the activities of the unconscious part of the mind.

Freud believed that the ego sometimes permits the expression of otherwise prohibited thoughts and feelings on purpose, a sort of "venting" that allows the ordinarily forbidden to be enjoyed. The mechanism by which this is accomplished is wit or humor. A humorous action, statement, or joke allows an impulse or feeling ordinarily seen as inappropriate to be enjoyable and acceptable.

"Freudian slips" = parapraxes (provide important clues about the unconscious mind.

These three main topics comprise this chapter on the unconscious mind: anxiety and the defense mechanisms, slips, and humor. The chapter concludes with an evaluation of Freud's contribution to psychology.

ANXIETY

Anxiety is an unpleasant state. Its intensity can range from a vague and uneasy sense that not all is right with the world, to desperate and debilitating terror—the classic anxiety attack. Anxiety can be generated by stresses from the outside world, and also by conflicts within the mind itself—the kind of anxiety Freud found most interesting.

Anxiety From Psychic Conflict

There are things we each want, things that are possible, and things that are morally right. Wouldn't it be wonderful if these three were always the same? Of course, life is not so simple. To want something we can never have and to be tempted to do something we know is wrong are common human experiences. Right now, for example, the odds are high you are supposed to be reading this book. If you are a college student, then reading this book is the right thing to do: College students are expected to do their homework, and why are you or your hard-working parents investing so much money and time in your education if you don't even bother to do your reading? (Thus speaks your superego.) Moreover, it is the prudent thing to do. Flunking is bad; A's are pleasant to receive. The latter outcome becomes more likely the more diligently you do your reading. (Thus speaks your ego.) And yet, and yet . . . there is a party right down the hall. Music is playing, people are laughing, and this chapter seems to be going on *forever*. (Thus speaks your id.) All of these statements are correct, so what will you do? The answer is far from certain. The tension between these three aspects of reality—what is right, what is possible, and what you want—is a fact of life. If you stay and read, part of you will pine for the party. And, sadly, even if you throw the book down and go to the party, part of you will wish you were back in your room getting your work done.

We saw in the previous chapter that, according to psychoanalytic theory, the mind is divided into three parts with separate, specialized functions. The id generates wants; the superego provides moral judgment; and the ego tries to figure out the rational thing to do, with the id and superego

[handwritten: Psychic conflict occurs between the ego, superego and id.]

both metaphorically shouting in its ear. Because desires, morals, and possibilities so often conflict, the id, ego, and superego—likewise, and perhaps typically—also conflict. **Psychic conflict** happens when a mind battles itself. The result is *anxiety*.

[handwritten: ego = practical consequences]

Suppose you see a small boy standing with his mother and holding a delicious-looking piece of candy. You may not be aware of the feeling, but your id may immediately want that candy and create in you an impulse to reach out and grab it. If this happens, both the ego and the superego will quickly swing into action. The ego will realize that grabbing candy from a child in full view of his mother is likely to lead to serious difficulties, such as being yelled at or possibly even arrested. The superego will be horrified that the id would even think of doing such a despicable thing. Both object, but for different reasons: The ego cares about practical consequences, and the superego cares about right and wrong.

[handwritten: superego = moral consequences.]

In this example, both the ego and the superego will probably use their energy to push the id's impulse back down, not only below the threshold of action, but also below the threshold of awareness. You will never even know you were tempted. But consider what might happen if the problematic impulse and its prohibition were particularly strong. Imagine a married person, deeply committed to her family, who experiences strong lustful impulses toward an attractive, available individual of the opposite sex. This impulse creates problems because, although the temptation is real, the ego will probably calculate that acting on the impulse risks terrible damage to her family and to other areas of her life. On top of that, the superego may weigh in with the observation that acting on this impulse would violate every value she holds dear. As a result of these strong oppositions, the impulse might be pushed almost out of awareness, although it may remain present on some level; she might be conscious only of a vague feeling of uneasiness, anxiety, or guilt. Later on, she might forget having met this attractive individual or might develop a seemingly inexplicable dislike for this person. (Remembering might cause renewed anxiety; developing any sort of friendship might strengthen the forbidden impulse.) She may never know where the anxiety came from, why a seemingly routine encounter was forgotten so quickly, or what caused the dislike for someone who never did her any intentional harm.

[handwritten: → married people being tempted to commit adultery.]

Freud believed one particular conflict to be quite common. He believed that most people at times feel sexual attraction toward members of their own sex, and that these latent homosexual feelings are pushed out of action and awareness, both by the ego on practical grounds, and by the superego on moral grounds. (Most people in Freud's era were raised—as some still are today—with the idea that homosexuality is immoral.) This constant but pro-hibited impulse is a persistent source of anxiety in many individuals, Freud believed, although they may never become consciously aware of the source of their discomfort.

Modern psychoanalysts called *ego psychologists* believe that compro-mise formation is the most important function of the ego (Brenner, 1982; Westen, 1998). When parts of the mind want different things, the ego must seek some way for all of them to get a little of what they want. For example, imagine a person whose superego condemns pornography while his id loves the stuff. His ego might formulate a compromise in which he becomes an antipornography crusader. He then can satisfy his superego by loudly and frequently condemning the evils of pornography, while at the same time collecting and viewing large amounts of pornography, all in reluctant ser-vice to the battle against it. This kind of compromise can fail, however, as we saw in Chapter 10.

The modern psychoanalyst Drew Westen (1998) described the case of a man who was conflicted about whether to remain in his unhappy mar-riage. He stayed married for many years, mostly because he would have felt guilty had he left his wife. When he finally did end his marriage, he declined opportunities to date two attractive women who were interested in him and instead continued to live alone in a seedy apartment. According to Westen, it emerged in therapy that his ego had reached the following compromise between his id, which wanted freedom, and his guilty superego: He allowed himself to leave his wife only if he also did penance by never enjoying himself afterward, especially with other women. Of course, this compromise was reached unconsciously—he had no conscious idea that this is what he was doing. And while the compromise alleviated his conflicting feelings to some extent, it also left him dissatisfied and vaguely anxious.

> When a patient arrives with the complaint, "I feel bad and I don't know why," a psychoanalyst settles into the problem with relish.

Vague anxiety of unknown origin is a quintessential Freudian symptom. When a patient arrives with the complaint, "I feel bad and don't know why," a psychoanalyst settles into the problem with relish. As we saw in Chapter 10, the whole purpose of psychoanalytic therapy is to uncover—and eventu-ally relieve—hidden sources of anxiety.

Realistic Anxiety

Freud focused on psychic anxiety to the extent that he probably underem-phasized the anxiety generated by the outside world. First is the unpleasant

Terror mgmt theory: may thought processes and motivations are based on an effort to avoid thinking about death

fact that all of us are mortal and so will die at some point. According to the *terror management theory* of Tom Pyszczynski, Jeff Greenberg, and Sheldon Solomon (1997), many of our thought processes and motivations are based on an effort to deal with and avoid thinking about this literally terrifying fact (Greenberg, Koole, & Pyszczynski, 2004). Other aspects of life produce anxiety as well. Relationships (Does she really love me?), performance in school (Will I pass the course?), and career aspirations (Will I be able to get a job, or keep the one I have?) are issues that can make us realistically anxious. A particular source of anxiety, according to some writers, is any threat to self-esteem (Cramer, 1998). We sometimes receive information that—looked at objectively—suggests that we are not as smart, good looking, invulnerable, moral, or lovable as we would like to believe.

anxiety = any threat to self esteem.

This anxiety is unpleasant, which raises an interesting question. Is it good to experience it, or should we avoid these bad feelings any way we can? Psychologists continue to debate this question. According to one perspective, we should avoid anxiety even if we distort reality to do so. To be realistic about one's position and chances in life can lead to depression; people who are optimistic—even unrealistically so—are happier and experience better mental health (S. E. Taylor & Brown, 1988). From another perspective, this idea is dead wrong (Colvin & Block, 1994). The costs of unrealistic perception can be high. As mentioned in Chapter 9, anxiety is often a sign that something is not right. If we avoid feeling anxious, we might avoid dealing with the underlying problem. For example, some students deal with the anxiety of impending final exams by not thinking about them. In the short run, they are happier than students who worry about studying until the exam begins or final grades are announced. Then they are less happy. A little anxiety early can save a lot of anxiety later (Norem & Chang, 2002).

— should we experience or avoid these feelings?

The real trick, apparently, is to keep anxiety within bounds (Block, 2002). Too much anxiety and a person can become completely nonfunctional. Too little anxiety and a person might fail to sensibly handle problems. Sometimes we need to face reality directly; at other times, it seems, a little distortion becomes necessary (Paulhus, 1998). Ideally, defense mechanisms help achieve this balance.

L keep anxiety within bounds. through defense mechanisms.

DEFENSE MECHANISMS

The ego owns a variety of tools for keeping anxiety levels within a tolerable range, regardless of whether the anxiety comes from internal psychic conflict or from stressors in the external world. Sigmund Freud talked about

These tools are not used consciously.

defensive processes, but he never systematically organized them. It was left to his daughter, Anna, to create an inventory of the tools of psychological defense (A. Freud, 1936).

These tools are not used consciously—that would defeat their whole point. They are deployed by the unconscious part of the ego as soon as it detects a potential source of anxiety. The ego's defense strategies are varied and ingenious. The discussion that follows considers eight of them: denial, repression, reaction formation, projection, rationalization, intellectualization, displacement, and sublimation.

EGO DEFENSE STRATEGIES.

Denial

- failing to acknowledge one's source of anxiety.
- works well in the SR.
- perceptual defense!
- used to lessen the initial shock of an event until one can muster the psychological resources to do something about it.

The simplest defense mechanism is **denial**: A person simply refuses to acknowledge the source of anxiety, or even fails to perceive it in the first place. This tactic is common and effective in the short run, but if used for very long can lead to a serious lack of contact with reality (Suls & Fletcher, 1985).

At one time, my office was across the hall from the wall where grades for introductory psychology exams were posted.[1] So I occasionally observed the moment when someone discovered having failed an exam. How could I tell? By the audible defense mechanism of denial: these students would jump back from the grade roster and shout (at themselves more than at anybody else), "No!"

For most of these students, denial is a temporary tactic. By refusing to believe what they have seen, they give themselves a psychological breather to collect themselves before making a second run at the problem. As time passes, they probably will acknowledge that, yes, they failed the exam. They may even come back to the grade roster in a calmer frame of mind to double-check. At that point they will either deal realistically with the problem—study harder next time, for example—or invoke one or more of the more long-term defense mechanisms to deal with the anxiety produced by academic failure. In the long run, people are likely to take credit for their successes but blame their failures on external circumstances or other people (Zuckerman, 1979). According to several studies, when students perform poorly on a test, they tend to conclude that the test is invalid, but when they do well, they think the test is just fine (Schlenker, Weigold, & Hallam, 1990). These

---

[1] Now, of course, they are posted on the Internet.

skewed interpretations serve to protect self-esteem, but they also may prevent learning from mistakes.[2]

Denial can also defend against anxiety that comes from within. Suppose you unintentionally blurt out something embarrassing or even horrifying. Your next statement might be, "I didn't say that!" Or suppose you are ashamed of something you did. You might try to deny, even to yourself, that you did it.

Persistent denial may be a sign of serious psychopathology (as we shall see in Chapter 18). It is a quintessential symptom of alcoholism, for example. (Have you ever tried to tell an alcoholic that she has a drinking problem?) Used effectively, however, the primary purpose of denial is to keep an individual from being overwhelmed by the initial shock—at something that has happened or something one has done—as psychological resources are mustered to do something more permanent about it. Elisabeth Kübler-Ross (1969) noted that when someone is diagnosed with a fatal illness, the first impulse is to deny that this could be true. Only later is the person able to muster other ways of coping with such extreme news.

"I'm doing a lot better now that I'm back in denial."

2) Repression

more complex, further reaching and longer lasting then denial.

The defense mechanism of **repression** is more complex, further reaching, and longer lasting than denial. Denial generally refers to pushing a thought out of awareness or failing to perceive things that currently exist, such as anxiety-producing facts or feelings. Repression, in contrast, refers to banishing the past from your present awareness, and so repression tends to involve less outright negation of reality than does denial. When repressing something, you do not really deny it exists; you just manage not to think about it. In some cases, this results from conscious effort; some research

— banishes past events from present awareness
└ managing not to think about it.

[2] For some experimental studies of *perceptual defense*—failing to see something that might cause anxiety—see Chapter 16.

"Frankly, I've repressed my sexuality so long I've actually forgotten what my orientation is."

indicates that trying not to think about something now may prevent you from accessing that information in memory later (Levy & Anderson, 2002; M. C. Anderson & Levy, 2002).

Like denial, repression keeps out of consciousness and out of action a problematic impulse of the id; an unpleasant thought, feeling, or memory; or a potential stressor in the external world.

Freud believed that many forbidden impulses are quite common. For example, if you are a college student in your early twenties, you may resent your continued financial dependence on your parents. Your ego finds this feeling problematic, however, because its direct expression (calling your parents and announcing that you hate them) might endanger your financial support. Moreover, your superego also finds the resentment problematic because it seems shamefully ungrateful after all that your parents have sacrificed. If the resentment were to become conscious—even worse, if it were to be overtly expressed—then disapproval of the resentment by both the ego and super-ego would cause anxiety. The defense mechanism of repression may kick in to prevent this from happening.

In this case, the most direct action of repression will be to bar from consciousness any negative thoughts about your parents, which should also prevent overtly negative behavior. But repression takes no chances; it may also bar from consciousness anything that might *remind* you of how you resent your parents. In fact, the stronger the resentment, the wider and deeper the repressive wall becomes. You might find yourself forgetting to call them as you have promised, because calling them would remind you they exist, which would raise the possibility of becoming aware that you resent them. Or you might forget their phone number! And it could go further: You might forget your roommate's parents' names, because remembering her parents would remind you of your parents, which in turn would remind you of your resentment. Or you might forget to watch a favorite television show because it is also your father's favorite show. . . . You get the idea. Such elaborate secondary protection from anxiety-arousing stimuli can cause a wide range of slips and memory lapses, and the connection between the repressed actions, thoughts, and feelings, and the initial repressed source of anxiety can be so indirect as to require a good deal of psychoanalytic digging to find the cause. For instance, figuring out the real reason you forgot to relay your roommate's mother's phone message might take a long time and a lot of work.

Thus, repression is much more complicated than denial. For that reason, it is also more difficult to demonstrate with empirical research (Baumeister, Dale, & Sommer, 1998). The same complex process can work with memories as well. Suppose you did something a month ago that would cause you anxiety to remember, perhaps because it was dangerous (an ego judgment), immoral (a superego judgment), or both. It bears repeating that repression might cause you not only to forget what you did, but also to forget other things that might remind you of what you did. If you hate to think about that time you almost got into a stupid accident with your car, for example, you might find that you have forgotten where you parked it.

If the feeling, memory, or impulse is successfully repressed—locked away in the unconscious—then you are defended against the anxiety it would otherwise cause. But such defense does not come for free. The ego has a limited store of psychic energy that it takes from the id.[3] Every forbidden feeling, memory, or impulse has a certain amount of id energy forcing it toward consciousness and behavioral expression. In repression, the ego must oppose that force with an equal amount of its own energy. If the ego runs low on energy or tries to defend against too many impulses at once, it can start to lose the struggle, and these forbidden impulses will work their way toward consciousness. As they begin to surface, you will feel anxiety, typically without knowing why.

You can imagine the danger of this situation. If ego energy fails for some reason—for example, illness, stress, or trauma—a whole array of forbidden impulses might suddenly come to consciousness and even action. Or they might burst forth simply because they are too numerous and too strong, as a dam can suddenly break after years of water pressure slowly increasing behind it. The result can be violent lashing out, emotional outbursts, and a wide variety of irrational behaviors.

For example, a meek and mild-mannered man might have absorbed insults and humiliations for many years. Each insult and humiliation may have been repressed so that he does not feel the associated anxiety, until one day it has gone on too long. The defenses fail, the dam breaks, and he goes on

---

[3] As mentioned in Chapter 10, modern psychoanalytic theory, drawing from research in cognitive psychology, holds that the mind's capacity for information processing, rather than the energy itself, is limited (Westen, 1998). The consequences are the same, however: Capacity used for one purpose is not available for other purposes.

a murderous rampage. "He was always so quiet," comment the (surviving) neighbors in the newspaper the next day (see Megargee, 1966).

The danger of repression can also be more subtle. Because the ego's energy store is limited, the more energy it devotes to repression, the less it has available for other purposes. A severe shortage of free psychic energy can lead to depression, Freud believed. The modern interpretation of the same phenomenon would be that a mind preoccupied with keeping certain thoughts and memories out of awareness has less processing capacity left to deal with anything else. Either way, clinical depression is much more than just being sad. Its hallmark is a debilitating lack of motivation and energy. One purpose of psychoanalysis is to discover the areas of repression and remove their causes to free up psychic energy for constructive and creative purposes.

Repression, like denial, is a sort of brute-force defense mechanism; it builds a psychological dam between the individual and the potential sources of anxiety. But any dam can hold back only so much for so long; repression cannot be used very often. Fortunately, the ego has several other tactics in its playbook.

Reaction Formation

Reaction formation is an even more complex defense than repression. It keeps forbidden thoughts, feelings, and impulses out of awareness and action by instigating their *opposites*. The ego is particularly likely to use this tactic if the forbidden impulse is very dangerous or very strong and an extra measure of defense seems necessary. Doing or thinking the opposite of the forbidden impulse builds a safety margin, ensuring that the impulse never reaches consciousness or action. This process can protect self-esteem (Baumeister et al., 1998). If individuals are concerned that they might have some unacceptable trait, they might seek to display the opposite trait. If someone implies that you are hostile, for example, you might respond with exaggerated efforts to act agreeable and peace loving.

Unconscious homosexual impulses again provide a particularly good example. These impulses are very common, according to Freud, but are considered problematic by both the ego and the superego, and they ordinarily are constrained by repression. When the homosexual impulse is particularly strong, or the superego has developed powerful prohibitions against it—as might a superego that developed in a rigidly puritanical environment—then reaction formation may become necessary to ensure the impulse is never felt or expressed.

The most obvious manifestation of reaction formation in the case of repressed homosexual feelings would be "gay bashing." The person might loudly denounce homosexuals, write "death to queers" on bathroom walls, tell "fag" jokes frequently and loudly, or even physically attack gays.

The indication that these behaviors might stem from reaction formation is their disproportion and gratuitousness. Reaction formation is not revealed by saying something like, "Some aspects of one common gay lifestyle can lead to serious problems in an age of AIDS." Such a statement might well express a sincere and reasonable attitude. But the need to insult, belittle, and perhaps even physically assault people does not. No reasonable attitude leads to such behaviors. Thus, we are led to suspect a deeper psychological source.

Consider another example. I lived for several years in a small, peaceful, almost bucolic college town in the Midwest. The local television news one night showed a preacher crusading in front of the town's (apparently) one-and-only pornographic bookstore, which was in such an obscure location—even in this small town—that, until I saw it on television, I didn't know it existed. The preacher was screaming the dangers of smut. His face was red, his voice was hoarse, the veins stood out on his neck: The store was Sin and it was a Danger!

Again, notice that I am not talking about somebody calmly saying, "The images of women and of sexuality in most pornography are not the sorts of things to which we would wish to expose our children." Such a statement, although you might agree or disagree, is certainly reasonable. It is the preacher's almost absurdly exaggerated response that can make one suspicious of his psychological motives. How big a danger is this store, really? What harm is it actually doing if many townspeople do not even know it exists? The vehemence of this crusader's reaction suggests his emotion does not come from any danger the store poses, but rather his own temptation to rush in and buy the place out. He prevents himself from doing this, of course, in part by standing out front with a megaphone and a picket sign. Such is the purpose and mechanism of reaction formation.

The giveaway is always a lack of proportion between the provocation and the response. Homosexuality, pornography, and many other potentially threatening topics are legitimate areas for discussion. But when so much emotion is involved, psychological defense may come into play. It can be informative, but also brave to the point of foolhardiness (thus, I do not recommend it), to ask such a crusader this question: "With so many problems in the world, why do you care about this one so much?" The response is unlikely to be reasonable; it will be angry, anxious, and defensive.

An almost universal example of reaction formation, Freud believed, occurs in nearly every family. When a new baby comes home from the hospital, the natural reaction of the older sibling is hate—this is called *sibling rivalry*, and it may be biologically based. But the older sibling soon discovers that their parents are protective of the baby, and any attempts to harm the baby are met with parental disapproval and punishment, which is quite threatening. The sibling learns to repress hate for little brother or sister and, if sufficiently threatened (or if the impulse to harm is sufficiently strong), may engage in elaborate demonstrations of affection. "I love my little brother!" she might say, giving him a big kiss. In this way, she prevents herself from strangling him. The parents may approve of this affection, but they also may realize that it rings a little false. In general, behavior driven by reaction formation somehow does not look quite right.

> "I love my little brother!" the big sister might say, giving him a big kiss. In this way, she prevents herself from strangling him.

Reaction formation is a tricky phenomenon to study, but several laboratory experiments have demonstrated something that looks much like it. In one study, female participants completed a questionnaire designed to measure their degree of "sex guilt." Then they were shown graphic erotic images and asked how they felt. Women who scored higher in sex guilt reported lower levels of arousal in response to the erotic images than women who scored lower in sex guilt. However, according to physiological measures, the former were actually *more* sexually aroused. This discrepancy between self-report (S data) and physiology (B data) suggested to the investigators that the women who experienced the greatest physical arousal were so threatened by it that, through the mechanism of reaction formation, they reported (and probably consciously experienced) the least psychological arousal (Morokoff, 1985).

Apparently—and this is consistent with Freud's speculations summarized earlier—the same thing can happen with men who experience latent homosexual impulses. In one study, a group of men was given a questionnaire to measure their *homophobia* (fear of homosexuals and of being homosexual themselves). Then they were shown videotapes of homosexual activity. The men who scored highest on homophobia reported the lowest level of sexual arousal from watching the tapes, but they also showed the highest level of physiological arousal (H. E. Adams, Wright, & Lohr, 1996). Again, the conscious experience that the homophobic men reported was the opposite of the forbidden responses of their bodies. It supports Freud's opinion that homophobia is a reaction formation against homosexual impulses, since homophobics are more aroused than nonhomophobics by homosexual stimuli and also more prone to deny it.

Hamlet's mother said, "The lady doth protest too much, methinks." She was talking about reaction formation.

Projection ~ attributing to someone else a thought or behavior feared by oneself

Like reaction formation, **projection** is a defense mechanism that protects against unwanted impulses by causing a behavior that, at first glance, appears to be opposite. It is the tactic of attributing to somebody else a thought or an impulse that is feared in oneself. To yourself as much as to anybody else, you announce, "It's not me who feels (or acts) that way, it's him."

Homosexuality again provides a prototypical example. Freud believed that some people deal with threatening, latent homosexual impulses by projecting homosexual intent onto everybody else. "Gay bashers" like those described earlier are quick to claim to have spotted "another one" and may even tell you that they can identify any homosexual at a glance. They are wrong, of course, but it is revealing that they believe this.

Other kinds of self-doubt can also lead to projection. People who doubt their intelligence may deal with anxiety about their own inadequacy by claiming to be surrounded by morons. It seems to make them feel better, and for the short term, pointing out how other people are stupid makes them appear smarter (Amabile & Glazebrook, 1982).

Current research on projection suggests that the classic psychoanalytic view was close to correct, but not quite. In one recent study, participants took a personality test and then were told (falsely) that their scores indicated certain good traits as well as certain bad ones (Newman, Duff, & Baumeister, 1997). Then they were instructed to try not to think about one of the bad traits they supposedly had. Next they watched a person on videotape and rated that person on all the same traits on which they had received feedback. Participants rated that person worse than themselves on the one bad trait they were trying not to think about, but not on any of the others. This study suggests that projection—seeing one's own bad traits in another—results from trying to suppress a bad thought about oneself. It is not clear that this kind of projection lessens the tendency to see the trait in oneself—as Freud believed—but it does seem to be a by-product of trying to deny unpleasant truths.

Not all your negative opinions of others are due to projection, of course. But, you should ask yourself, Do I often characterize other people in a par-

[handwritten margin notes:]
⌐ rating others on one "bad" trait
⌐ participants rated that person lower, only on that trait.

ticular way? Am I frequently detecting "jerks," "morons," "lazy freeloaders," or the like? If so, it is fair to suspect the workings of projection. The negative attribute you tend to see in other people may be something that you actually, albeit unconsciously, fear characterizes you.

5) Rationalization

Rationalization may be the most widely used defense mechanism of all. **Rationalization** defends against the anxiety aroused by having done something that would otherwise cause you shame, by concocting a seemingly rational case for why you had to do it. A hit song a couple of decades ago proclaimed, "You've got to be cruel to be kind." That's a rationalization.

Rationalization is everywhere, and some people use it consistently (von Hippel, Lakin, & Shakarchi, 2005). Parents who harshly punish their children claim it is for the children's own good. Wealthy people give themselves tax breaks while raising the burden on the poor, then claim this will make things better for everybody. People cheat and lie, then claim it was harmless or even necessary.

The remarkable facts about rationalizations such as these are (1) that they are *obviously* rationalizations, and (2) that the people who use them seem completely sincere. If the reasoning were not so clearly flawed, you might be tempted to think these people actually believe what they say. The hallmark of rationalization is the ability—even eagerness—of otherwise intelligent people to believe the implausible when it is in their own interest. Deep inside, these people are ashamed. Rationalization protects them from the anxiety they would feel if they realized their shame.

One kind of rationalization is *trivialization*, which amounts to convincing yourself that your shortcomings or regrettable actions don't matter. Trivialization can apply to a wide range of actions. Some people steal from their employers and convince themselve it isn't important because what they stole won't be missed. Other people may hurt an acquaintance's feelings and then reassure themselves with the thought that "she'll get over it." In extreme cases, individuals with antisocial personality disorder (see Chapter 18) sometimes trivialize the emotional and even physical harm they cause other people because they regard those they harm as inferior or even as not really being human.

The process of trivialization can be even more complex. According to research in social psychology, people feel a negative emotion called **cognitive dissonance** when experimenters induce them to express opinions that are really not their own. A common result is that people then change their beliefs to match what they were made to say (e.g., Festinger & Carlsmith, 1959). A more recent study in this vein (Simon, Greenberg, & Brehm, 1995) had people write essays that contradicted their beliefs, but the experimenters allowed participants the opportunity to dismiss their counterattitudinal essay writing as a trivial exercise that meant nothing. This trivialization prevented the attitude change that would otherwise have occurred, because it apparently defended participants from the anxiety of cognitive dissonance.

Intellectualization

Yet another way to deal with a threatening emotion is to turn the feeling into a thought. This is the defense mechanism of intellectualization. **Intellectualization** can turn a heated, anxiety-provoking issue into something cool, abstract, and analytical. Using this mechanism may involve developing a technical vocabulary that allows discussion of horrifying things without using everyday, emotionally arousing language.

You see a lot of intellectualization in modern warfare. Whenever a war starts, television screens fill with retired colonels expounding on military strategy. They can talk for quite a while without using the words *kill* or *die*, though these are defining attributes of war. They use words such as *suffer* and *bleed* even more rarely. Instead, their analyses deploy maps and charts to tell an interesting story that has much of the same appeal as a good game of chess. To truly enjoy the show—and maybe even just to plot strategy—the observer must forget what is really going on.

The medical profession does much the same thing. Surgeons talk about "this gallbladder" rather than "this person," and use a vocabulary so technical as to be virtually inaccessible. Physicians are reluctant to talk about pain (they prefer "discomfort") and death (you really just "expire").

I don't mean to belittle the military or medical professions here. When the pretense and technical blather are stripped away, they both deal on a daily basis with situations that are truly horrifying. It is unlikely they could function at all without the defense of intellectualization. If the surgeon thought too directly about the life of the child on the operating table, it is doubtful she could get through the operation successfully. A general who dwells too much on the deaths his work will cause might be unable to formulate a winning strategy. Unadorned reality can be too painful to deal with effectively. Intellectualization (along with the other defense mechanisms) builds a useful barrier between you and reality, allowing you to get on with what you need

ey. military or surgeons.

to do. A recent summary of relevant research supports the idea that creating this kind of a "mental gap or barrier between some threatening cognition and other thoughts and feelings" is an effective tactic for reducing anxiety (Baumeister et al., 1998, p. 1099).

All defense mechanisms have costs, however, and intellectualization is no exception. A general who forgets that his decisions kill people might be an effective strategist, but he also might needlessly sacrifice life or even find war so interesting that he unnecessarily prolongs it. A physician who enjoys the technical aspects of surgery and forgets she is cutting real people might neglect her patients' emotional needs that are important for healing.

> To the extent that psychological theories begin to shield one from reality, psychology itself can be a defense mechanism.

Intellectualization is a particular occupational hazard of psychologists. I suspect that part of the field's appeal lies in the way it explains potent issues of emotion and experience using an abstract theoretical framework. This can be useful; Freud himself seems to have built his theory as a gigantic exercise in intellectualization. But to the extent that psychological theories begin to shield one from reality, psychology itself can be a defense mechanism.

Displacement

7)

- replaces one object of emotion w/another.
↳ relocates from an unsafe target to a safe one.
↳ ey chewing on a pen instead of sucking one's thumb.

A less intellectual defense mechanism is based on a property of the id's primary process thinking. Specifically, the id seems to have a capacity for **displacement**, which, as mentioned in Chapter 10, involves replacing one object of emotion with another. A feeling about your family might be displaced onto your house, for example, or a feeling about a parent might be displaced onto a boss, or vice versa. The defense mechanism of displacement relocates the object of an emotional response or desire from an unsafe target to a safe one. A simple example might be the urge, based on a fixation in the oral stage, that an adult might have to suck his thumb.[4] Of course, this is not acceptable behavior at a business meeting, so displacement might lead the executive to chew thoughtfully, and with impeccable dignity, on a pen or pipe instead.

The direction of displacement depends on two things. Generally, an id impulse will be displaced onto the available target that most resembles the desired object but that is also socially acceptable. Satisfying substitutes for

---

[4] Freud would observe that this impulse is itself a displacement of the desire to breast-feed.

[handwritten: Aggression is frequently displaced]

thumb sucking might include either a toe or a pipe stem. However, only the pipe is acceptable in public (it also requires less flexibility), so that is where the impulse relocates.[5]

Aggression frequently is displaced in this manner. You might become angry at your boss but fear losing your job if you confront him. So you go home and kick your dog, especially if your dog looks like your boss. Many student dormitory rooms contain professor dartboards. It is safe and legal to throw darts at a piece of cork decorated with a disliked professor's picture, and throwing darts may partially gratify an aggressive impulse. But it is not the same as throwing pointed darts at the actual professor; that is why the behavior is considered displacement.

Like all defense mechanisms, displacement has its benefits and its dangers. It is useful in redirecting forbidden and even harmful impulses onto safe targets. It can be a problem if it becomes a substitute for necessary direct action. Displacement also can be a problem if it directs aggression onto innocent targets. It is not the dog's fault that your boss is a jerk, and cruelty at home is no solution to difficulties at work.

[handwritten margin note: Problem: can substitute necessary direct action, or can direct aggression onto innocent targets]

In addition, displacement is generally ineffective. Experimental research since the time of Freud suggests that a person who expresses displaced aggression may become more inclined to be aggressive, not less (Berkowitz, 1962; Bushman, 2002). This suggests that, rather than being one of the ego's defense mechanisms, displacement might be a more primitive function of the id's primary process thinking. People who kick the wall when they are angry at someone may do so not for any functional reason, but because they cannot help it. Bad moods and aggressive impulses tend to generalize away from their original targets, but there is little, if any, evidence that this reduces anxiety (Baumeister et al., 1998).

[handwritten: ↳ displacement can be straight up ineffective]

Sublimation

To be sublime is to be elevated and noble. **Sublimation** is the defense mechanism by which base and forbidden impulses are transformed into constructive behaviors. Sublimation is a type of displacement that relocates the object of an impulse such that the result is high cultural attainment. For example, Freud believed the great works of art produced by people such as Leonardo da Vinci and Michelangelo were strongly influenced by psycho-

[handwritten: forbidden impulses = constructive behaviors]

[5] According to legend, Freud was once asked to explain the meaning of the cigars he enjoyed. He replied, "Sometimes a cigar is just a cigar."

ey. hostile people
become lawyers.

-Freud saw
sublimation as
a positive process.

primitive urges
=constructive outcomes.

logical traumas they experienced in early childhood. Freud also believed that Leonardo's prolific scientific investigations were a sublimation of his frustrated sexual passions.[6]

Occupational choice is a more mundane place to find sublimation. It can be psychologically useful to channel one's otherwise unacceptable impulses into lifelong constructive work. If you unconsciously want to cut people, poke them with needles, or see them with their clothes off, you might find yourself drawn to a career in medicine, particularly surgery. If your deep urges are to express hostility and argue, then perhaps you should become a lawyer. If you want to spend your life trying to gain power over others, then a career in politics might seem attractive. If you have anally based urges to smear feces and, via displacement, paint, then you might become an artist. And, if you want to pry into other people's minds and ask a lot of questions that are none of your business, perhaps you should consider a career in clinical psychology.

This can start to sound silly, but it may contain a kernel of truth. Every person has a unique pattern of fixations left over from childhood, which in turn results in a unique pattern of desires and interests. People who are both wise and lucky may seek careers that allow the constructive expression of these desires and interests. As discussed in Chapter 8, work you are passionate about is the kind you will do best.

It is important to realize that Freud saw sublimation as a *positive* process. It is a part of normal functioning and a useful way to translate primitive urges into constructive outcomes. Unlike the other defense mechanisms, sublimation does not have a downside. It allows psychic energy to be channeled into useful pursuits including the development of society, culture, civilization, and achievements of all sorts. We need to sublimate more often. To do this, we probably need to know ourselves better.

PARAPRAXES AND HUMOR

Defense mechanisms prevent us from acting on, or even thinking about, forbidden impulses. But sometimes feelings and thoughts that the ego and

---

[6] Freud's interpretation was presented in a short book entitled *Leonardo da Vinci and a Memory of His Childhood* and is discussed in detail by Gay (1988, pp. 268–277). A recent literature review concluded that no experimental evidence supported the idea of sublimation, but it also acknowledged that nobody has yet figured out a way to test it experimentally (Baumeister et al., 1998). For now, we are left with anecdotes like Freud's story of da Vinci, which you may or may not find convincing.

superego try to suppress make it into the open anyway. This leakage might be uncontrolled and haphazard, or it might be carefully channeled.

Parapraxes

A **parapraxis** (plural: parapraxes) is another name for what is commonly called a "Freudian slip": a leakage from the unconscious mind manifesting as a mistake, accident, omission, or memory lapse. Remember that Freud was a determinist—he thought everything had a cause. This belief comes into play when considering the causes of accidents and other slips. Freud was never willing to believe that they happened at random.

FORGETTING *often a result of repression*

According to Freud, forgetting something is a manifestation of an unconscious conflict revealing itself in your behavior. The slip, or parapraxis, is the failure to recall something you needed to remember, which can result in embarrassment or much worse. These consequences make the lapse a parapraxis; in the service of suppressing something in your unconscious mind, your slip messes up something in your life.

Usually, forgetting is a result of repression. To avoid thinking about something painful or anxiety producing, you fail to remember it. You make a date and then have second thoughts, so you forget you made it. Although you might have saved yourself some immediate anxiety, when you run into your erstwhile date the next week in the cafeteria, you will have a serious social problem. Many college students manage to forget the times that exams are held and term papers are due. Failing to remember may make the students less anxious in the short run but can produce serious problems in the long run. Occasionally a student will make an appointment with me to discuss a difficulty he or she is having in class. I know the odds are no better than 50 percent that the student will show up at the appointed time. The explanation is always the same: "I forgot."

These examples are fairly obvious. But Freud insisted that *all* lapses reveal unconscious conflicts. Now the going gets a little tougher: What about when you forget something for no reason? No such thing, according to Freud. The psychoanalytic faith declares that, with sufficient psychotherapy using free association, a therapist can eventually (and perhaps at great expense) figure out the cause of any memory lapse. The system of causal roots may be quite complex: You may have forgotten to do something because it reminds

eg, forgetting the name of an acquaintance because it is the same as an enemy's.

you of something else, which through primary process thinking has come to symbolize yet a third thing, which makes you anxious.

In one case, a psychoanalyst reported that a patient forgot the name of an acquaintance who had the same name as a personal enemy. Moreover, the acquaintance was physically handicapped, which reminded the patient of the harm he wished to do the enemy of the same name. To defend against the superego-induced guilt this wish produced, he forgot the name of his perfectly innocent acquaintance (Brenner, 1974).

SLIPS

- eg, calling your current BF your old BF's name

Slips are unintended actions caused by the leakage of suppressed thoughts or impulses. Many of them happen in speech and can be as simple as a failure to suppress what one privately wishes to say. In one of the first courses on psychoanalysis I took in college, the professor was mentioning the students who visited during his office hours. "When infants come to see me . . . ," he said, then he stopped, stammered, and his face turned bright red. His students did not fail to understand this revelation of what he really thought of them.

A more common slip is to say one name when you mean another. Saying the name of a former boyfriend or girlfriend at important and delicate moments with one's current boyfriend or girlfriend is a common and extremely embarrassing slip. Explanations are often demanded: "Why did you say her name?" "I just made a mistake—it didn't mean anything!" The current significant other is no more likely to accept this reply than would Sigmund Freud himself.

- leaving something @ someone's house.

Slips can occur in action as well as in speech. Accidentally breaking something can be a leakage of hostility against the person who owns the object, who gave you the object, or whom the object (for some reason) symbolizes. A more pleasant example is the standard interpretation of somebody accidentally leaving something at your house after a visit: It means the object's owner hopes to come back.

As already noted, the person who commits these slips of speech or action may deny that the slip meant anything. Not only does psychoanalysis not accept such a denial, but the louder and more vehement it is, the more a Freudian will suspect a powerful and important impulse.

- fatigue, inattention, excitement may ↑ probability of slips, but are not the cause of them.

But what about accidents that happen just because a person is tired, not paying attention, in a hurry, or excited? These, too, are not accidents, according to Freud. Fatigue, inattention, or excitement might make slips more likely, but they do not cause them. Freud compared the role of such factors to the way darkness helps a robber. A dark street might make a burglary more likely, but dark streets do not cause burglaries; a burglar is still required. Similarly, fatigue, inattention, and other factors might make it easier for a suppressed impulse to leak into behavior, but they are not the cause of the impulse.

Does this mean that there really are no accidents? Freud believed so. Any failure to do something you ordinarily can do—such as drive a car safely—must be due to the leakage of a suppressed impulse, according to Freud. Some examples that fit this description have been quite prominent. In the Winter Olympics a few years ago, a skier on the way to an important downhill race broke her leg when she crashed into a member of the ski patrol. This was an accident, of course, but it is also reasonable to ask how often an Olympic-level skier crashes into somebody else. How often does any skier crash into a member of the ski patrol? And, of all mornings of this skier's life, why did the accident happen on this morning? One is led to wonder if this skier did not want to show up for her race, and why.

An even more dramatic incident at the 1988 Olympics involved speed skater Dan Jansen, whose sister died of leukemia just five hours before he was scheduled to compete in the 500-meter event. Jansen was favored for the gold medal, and his sister had insisted he go to the Olympics even though the family knew she didn't have long to live. Ten seconds into the race, Jansen fell down. Four days later, in his second event, the 1,000-meter race, he fell again. A psychoanalytic perspective makes one wonder whether Jansen might have been ambivalent about coming home bedecked in gold medals at such a time. Had he fully wanted to succeed, it seems unlikely that he would have fallen down in the two most important athletic events of his life.[7]

> While there may not be many—or any—Freudians in the typical university psychology department, the physical education department may have a lot of them.

While there may not be many—or any—Freudians in the typical university psychology department, the physical education department may have a lot of them. They may not think of themselves in such terms, but coaches are often practicing Freudians. They worry about instilling in their athletes the right mental attitude, a will to win. When a basketball player at the free-throw line in a big game misses a shot she can make 20 times in a row in practice, any good coach knows the solution is not more free-throw prac-

---

[7] The sports world breathed a sigh of relief when, in the 1994 Olympics, Jansen took the gold medal in the 1,000-meter race and set a world record.

Athletic coaches are often Freudian practicers.

tice; something about the athlete's attitude needs work. If the player had fully wanted to make the basket, the ball would have gone in. Ask any coach which team will win any given game, and the coach will reply, "The team that wants it more." Freud would say, "Exactly right."

The next time you fail to perform to your ability in sports, in academics, at work, or wherever, take a moment to ask yourself: Did I really, whole-heartedly, want to succeed? If not, why not?

Humor

Humor = the expression of a motivational impulse.

Parapraxes are failures of defense and can be harmful. In wit, however, a forbidden impulse is expressed in a controlled manner. Freud saw wit as a form of sublimation: An impulse that otherwise would be anxiety provoking or harmful is vented in a way that makes it safely enjoyable. According to one modern theory, successful jokes unexpectedly juxtapose two things usually seen as distinct, allowing them to be seen in a surprising, new, and enjoyable way (Martin, 2006). This theory is fine as far as it goes, but notice how it does not explain why so much humor concerns ordinarily forbidden topics such as sex, violence, and bodily elimination. That's where Freud comes in. Humor is not merely the juxtaposition of two thoughts; it is the expression of a motivational impulse.

GOOD JOKES

— Real situation is carefully concealed to the last minute to avoid conflict from the ego/superego.

Humor allows otherwise problematic thoughts and id impulses to be enjoyed by using the tactic of surprise. In a successful joke, the impulse is disguised until the last possible moment. Then—bang!—the impulse is expressed and enjoyed before your ego or superego has a chance to inhibit it. A few seconds later, you might feel a bit sheepish or guilty about what made you laugh, but the deed is done. The impulse was expressed and enjoyed.

In one of *The Pink Panther* movies, Peter Sellers sees a dog standing next to a desk and asks the clerk, "Does your dog bite?" The clerk answers, "No, never." Sellers reaches down to pet the dog and is savagely bitten. "I thought you said your dog doesn't bite!" he cries, jumping up and down. "That," replies the clerk, "is not my dog."

Someone who laughs at this scene is enjoying the spectacle of a person fooled into being harmed by an unexpectedly vicious animal. What's funny about that? Everything, apparently. The reason this scene works is that the real situation is concealed carefully until the last possible moment. The

viewer enjoys the joke with a burst of
laughter before the superego's censors
point out how reprehensible the situation really is.

A comedian named Emo Phillips
tells the following story: "When I was
a child, my parents always said to me,
'Emo, whatever you do, don't open the
cellar door. Never open the cellar door.'
But I was curious, and after a few years I
finally snuck over and opened the cellar
door. What I saw was amazing—things
I had never seen before. Trees. Birds.
The sky."

*"You see? Once more, Wile E. Coyote is restored swiftly
and miraculously to health. His potential trauma has been
trivialized, and we are yet again amused."*

This is a child-abuse joke! What
could be funny about locking a child in
the basement for the first years of his life? Some evil impulse to enjoy such
a situation seems to exist, however, and it leaks out and causes surprised
laughter before the realization that this situation is actually tragic. Moreover, this joke is more effective than the Peter Sellers scene, for two reasons.
First, child abuse is more reprehensible than dog bites, so the release of the
impulse causes a stronger emotional response. Second—and this really is
the key—Phillips's disguise around the impulse is deeper than Sellers's. It
is less apparent at the beginning where Phillips's joke is going; when I tell
it in class, there are always several students who don't get it until someone
explains.

A joke allows a forbidden impulse to be released in a way that avoids
anxiety. For this reason, most (maybe all) jokes, when examined closely, are
"sick" jokes, based on sexual or hostile impulses. Many involve people being
duped; others indirectly express obscenity in a disguised, sudden fashion.

BAD JOKES

[handwritten annotation: Jokes aren't funny to someone who does not have the "forbidden impulse"]

Not all jokes work. A joke will not be funny to a listener who does not have
the forbidden impulse in the first place. Some people enjoy hostile jokes
more than others do, for example. Presumably, this is partly because some
people have stronger hostile impulses. The same probably goes for sexual
jokes. A particularly noticeable individual difference appears in the enjoyment of racist and sexist jokes. Enjoying them depends on underlying hostility toward the targeted minority group or gender. Someone who does not

have such underlying hostility may find such jokes mystifying and probably offensive rather than funny. For example, men and women with nonsexist attitudes do not tend to find cartoons belittling women very funny (Moore, Griffiths, & Payne, 1987).

A person's underlying attitudes may be revealed through sense of humor in other ways. I know someone who is uptight and generally rule bound—a real "anal" character. His favorite form of humor? Toilet jokes. Children not far beyond the anal stage also greatly enjoy bathroom humor. But as the libido moves into later stages, most adults find that the appeal of potty humor fades a bit.

Political humor is another problematic area. You are more likely to laugh at jokes about politicians you oppose than those you support. A political humorist, therefore, must choose whether to be a blatant partisan, and thereby limit the audience, or to joke about politicians of all persuasions, which is a difficult art because you risk offending somebody no matter what you say.

A joke can also fail by being too direct. If a joke fails to disguise the impulse and so fails to surprise the listener, expressing the impulse will cause discomfort rather than enjoyment. This is why the more times you hear a joke, the less funny it becomes. When the element of surprise is taken away, the impulse can no longer be enjoyed. Some jokes are not even surprising on first hearing. If you can see the punch line coming, it won't be very funny.

Some "jokes" do not even try to disguise the impulses they express. Such jokes rely simply on saying obscene words or graphically describing sexual acts. Some people find them funny; most do not. Other jokes amount to the undisguised expression of hostility. Jokes like these make most people squirm instead of laugh, a response that defeats the whole purpose of humor.

An example of this, to my mind, is presented by the long-running television program *America's Funniest Home Videos*. Most of the videos on this program portray people, including children, as they fall down, break things, and make huge messes. Some people—myself included—feel uncomfortable rather than entertained by this program. The events portrayed come a little too close to the line that separates a humorous incident from an event that is humiliating, disturbing, or painful.

After these examples, I should reiterate that from the psychoanalytic perspective, humor is good. It allows the harmless and even beneficial venting of forbidden impulses that otherwise would have to be repressed or defended against. But humor is also a delicate business.[8] The expressed impulse must be shared, and it must be suitably disguised. To succeed in both of these criteria is a fine and difficult art.

PSYCHOANALYTIC THEORY: A CRITIQUE

Throughout the past two chapters, I have tried to sell you Freud. Psychoanalytic theory has much to offer in understanding important aspects of daily life. The theory is dramatic and insightful, it is comprehensive, and it even has a certain elegant beauty.

Having said that, I still must warn you against taking Freud too seriously. When a student asks me, "What happens to sexual development if a boy is raised by his mother in a single-parent family?" (see Chapter 10), I want to reply, "Hey! Don't take this stuff so seriously! Freud has a neat theory, and it's fun to play around with, but don't start using it to evaluate your life." Psychoanalytic theory is far from being received truth. So, having praised Freud, let me now bury him for a bit. Psychoanalytic theory has at least five important shortcomings.

Excessive Complexity

First of all, Freud's theory is highly complex, to put it mildly. A basic principle of science, sometimes called *Occam's razor*, is that less is more: All things being equal, the simplest explanation is the best. Suppose you want to explain why boys take on many of the values and attitudes of their fathers. One possibility is that they look for guides in the world around them and choose the most obvious and prominent. Freud's theory, however, says that boys sexually desire their mothers, but they worry that their fathers will be jealous and castrate them in punishment, so they identify with their fathers in order to vicariously enjoy the mother and lessen the threat from the father. This is intriguing, and maybe it is even correct, but is it the simplest possible explanation? No way. Even modern theorists sympathetic to psychoanalysis have moved away from this story (Westen, 1998).

---

[8] According to legend, the great actor Sir Donald Wolfit, on his deathbed, was asked if he was having any difficulties. He replied, "Dying is easy. *Comedy* is hard."

theory based on
Introspections and
insights.
↳ may be biased
i take it or leave
it —

2) Case Study Method

A second tenet of science is that data must be public. The bases of one's conclusions must be laid out so that other scientists can evaluate the evidence together. Classic psychoanalytic theory never did this, and the neo-Freudians and object relations theorists (considered in Chapter 12) have generally followed suit. Their theorizing is based on analysts' (including Freud's) introspections and on insights drawn from single therapeutic cases, which are (by law) confidential. Freud himself complained that proof of his theory lay in the details of case studies that he could never reveal because of the need to protect his patients' privacy. The fact that this *case study method* is uncheckable means that it may be biased. This bias may arise out of what psychoanalysts and their patients (such as Freud's turn-of-the-century, Viennese patients suffering from hysteria) are like. Or perhaps the theorist's reasoning distorts what happens to the patients. Because the data are private, no one can ever be sure. Psychoanalytic theory's traditionally dismissive attitude toward requests for empirical proof could be summarized by the slogan "Take it or leave it." Only recently have researchers renewed efforts to test some of its key ideas.

3) Vague Definitions

eg. no measurement of
psychic energy.

Another conventional scientific standard is the *operational definition*. A scientific concept should be defined in terms of the operations or procedures by which it can be identified and measured. Psychoanalytic theory rarely does this. Take the idea of psychic energy. I mentioned that a bright student once asked me what units it was measured in. There are no units, of course, and it is not entirely clear what Freud meant by the term: Was he being literal, or did he intend "energy" as just a metaphor? Exactly how much psychic energy—what percentage, say—needs to be left behind at the oral stage to develop an oral character? As repressions accumulate, at what point will one run out of energy for daily living? And what is the difference, exactly, between denial and repression? Psychoanalytic theory does not even come close to providing specific answers to these questions.

4) Untestability

There is no set of
observations that a
psychoanalytic theory
cannot explain after
the fact ↳ can't be "proven wrong"

Freud's theory is also untestable. A scientific theory should be *disconfirmable*; that is, it should imply a set of observations or results that, if found, would prove it to be false. This is the difference between religion and science. There is no conceivable set of observations or results that would prove that God does not exist. God might always just be hiding. Therefore, the existence of God is not a scientific issue. In the same way, there is no set of observations that psychoanalytic theory cannot explain—after the fact. Because there is no experiment that would prove the theory wrong, it is unscientific. Some people have argued that perhaps it should be considered a religion![9]

Still, no single experiment is sufficient to prove or disprove any complex theory. The theory of evolution (see Chapter 9) is not testable in this sense, for example. So the real question is not whether psychoanalysis is testable in a strict sense, but whether the theory leads to hypotheses that can be tested individually. In the case of psychoanalysis, the best answer is sometimes yes and sometimes no.

Sexism *Females = altered males.*

Psychoanalytic theory is sexist; even modern writers who are highly sympathetic to Freud admit it (e.g., Gay, 1988). In psychoanalytic writing, it is abundantly clear that Freud considers males the norm and bases his theories on their psychology. He then considers females, when he considers them at all, as aberrations or deviations from the male model. For example, his Oedipal story about why children identify with their same-sex parent is much more coherent for males than for females, who seem to have been added almost as an afterthought.

Freud viewed females essentially as altered males, rather than as whole persons in their own right. In Freud's opinion, women spend much of their lives grieving about not sharing male anatomy. The side effects of being female, in psychoanalytic theory, include having less self-esteem, less creativity, and less moral fiber. Much of a female's life, according to Freud, is based on her struggle to come to terms with the tragedy that she is not male. If that's not sexism, then I don't know what is.

---

[9] Early in his career, Freud frequently expressed his desire that psychoanalytic theory be considered scientific. As he grew older, this criterion became less important to him (Bettelheim, 1982). However, he would have been horrified at the idea of psychoanalysis as a religion.

WHY STUDY FREUD?

So, with all these acknowledged problems, why study Freud? I believe there are several reasons. One is that Freud and the tradition he initiated acknowledge, and indeed focus on, ideas that are underemphasized elsewhere. Freud was right that people have conflicting motives and that sorting them out can be a source of confusion and anxiety. He was right that sex and aggression are powerful forces in psychological life. And he was right that childhood experiences shape adult personality and behavior in important ways, and that a child's relationships with his or her parents in particular form a template that is a basis of relationships throughout life. As I hope you have noticed while reading this and the previous chapter, psychoanalytic theory is full of insights, big and small, that the rest of psychology has tended to neglect, if not completely overlook.

Moreover, psychoanalysis continues to profoundly influence psychology and modern conceptions of the mind, even though few modern research psychologists—including those who teach personality psychology—consider themselves Freudians. Freud's influence shows up in many ways.

Most obviously, Freud continues to influence the practice of psychotherapy. One survey indicated that about 75 percent of practicing psychotherapists rely to some degree on psychoanalytic ideas (K. S. Pope, Tabachnick, & Keith-Spiegel, 1987). For example, even many psychotherapists who consider themselves non-Freudians practice the "talking cure" (the idea that talking about a problem helps), free association (encouraging the client to say whatever comes to mind), and transference (building an emotional relationship with the client to promote healing). According to legend, Freud also originated the practice of billing clients for their missed appointments!

Second, many of Freud's ideas have entered popular culture and provide a routine—and helpful—part of how people think and talk about each other, in ways they might not always recognize as Freudian. For instance, suppose you give somebody an expensive present. The next time you visit him, the present is nowhere in sight. "Whatever happened to . . . ?" you ask. "Oh," your friend replies nonchalantly, "It broke, so I threw it away." How does his response make you feel? If it makes you feel bad (and of course it does), one reason might be that you have made a Freudian interpretation of your friend's behavior (e.g., he has unconscious hostility toward you) without quite realizing that you have done so.

Sometimes, everyday thought is even more explicitly Freudian. Have you ever heard somebody hypothesize that, "She only goes out with that older guy because he's a father figure," or, "He's all messed up because of the way his parents treated him when he was little," or, "He never dates because his entire soul goes into programming his computer," or, "She's got too much invested in him [psychologically] to walk out now"? These are all Freudian interpretations.

So, it is probably the case that you knew a good deal of psychoanalytic theory before you read Chapter 10 and this chapter, and you may even use it every day. As a result, Freud's ideas do not always seem as original as they should. There is an old joke about the person who went to scc one of Shakespeare's plays for the first time but walked out halfway through. "It was too full of clichés," he complained. Of course, much of Shakespeare is full of clichés because so many of his lines (e.g., "To be or not to be") have made it into everyday speech. Some of Freud's most original ideas might sound mundane after all these years for the same reason.

A third consideration is that Freudian thought has undergone a revival within research psychology (see Chapter 12), and in 2006 Freud even appeared on

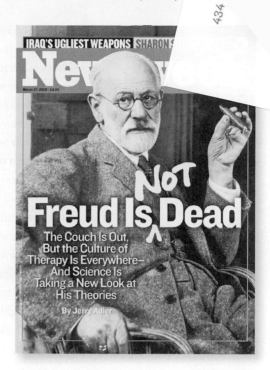

Figure 11.1 Freud Continues to Influence Popular Culture This issue of *Newsweek* was published in 2006.

the cover of *Newsweek* (see Figure 11.1). Psychologists are researching and publishing articles on defense mechanisms (see Cramer & Davidson, 1998), transference (Andersen & Berk, 1998), unconscious thought (Kihlstrom, 1990; Bornstein, 1999b), and other classically Freudian topics (Westen, 1998; Westen, Gabbard, & Ortigo, 2008). Some of these researchers vehemently deny that they are Freudians themselves, even when researching topics that seem psychoanalytic.[10] If Freud were still alive, he would surely observe that such denials only prove his continued and profound influence.

The fourth and perhaps most important way in which Freud continues to be influential is that his theory remains the only complete theory of personality ever proposed. Freud knew what he wanted to explain: aggression, sexuality, development, energy, conflict, neurosis, dreams, humor, accidents—and the list goes on. His theory offers an account for *all* these aspects. Regardless of whether he is right about every one of them, or even none of them, the theory does map out all the important questions for personality

---

[10] Do they protest too much?

psychology. In science, the most important thing is not answering questions but figuring out the right questions to ask. In this regard, Freud's theory of personality is a triumph that may stand for all time.

Among other topics, Freud theorized extensively about how experiences early in life affect personality in adulthood; we saw in Chapter 9 how this issue continues to generate research and controversy. Freud also posed questions concerning such matters as the meaning of dreams and the sources of sexual attraction, which psychologists still have not gotten around to investigating seriously. The psychoanalytic psychologist Drew Westen (1990) pointed out that "one can read a thousand pages of social-cognitive theory [arguably the dominant paradigm in social psychology today] and never know that people have genitals—or even, for that matter, that they have bodies—let alone fantasies" (p. 54). Freud's function in the Victorian age (as it is today) was to raise questions that others were too uncomfortable to think about.

For all these reasons, no education in psychology—especially personality psychology—would be complete without some grounding in psychoanalysis.

SUMMARY

Anxiety

- Anxiety can originate in the real world or in inner psychic conflict, such as that produced by an impulse of the id that the ego and superego try to combat.

Defense Mechanisms

- The ego uses several defense mechanisms to protect against the conscious experience of excessive anxiety and associated emotions such as shame and guilt. These defense mechanisms include denial, repression, reaction formation, projection, rationalization, intellectualization, displacement, and sublimation.

- Use of these defenses can reduce anxiety in the short run, but in the long run can produce problems in understanding and dealing with reality.

Parapraxes and Humor

- Forbidden impulses of the id can be expressed in thought and behavior in two ways. Parapraxes involve accidentally venting forbidden impulses in accidents of speech or action commonly called Freudian slips. In wit or humor, a forbidden impulse is deeply disguised to permit its enjoyment without anxiety.

- A joke is not funny when the listener doesn't share the forbidden impulse the joke disguises, or the disguise is insufficient.

Psychoanalytic Theory: A Critique

- Psychoanalytic theory has been criticized for its excessive complexity, its reliance on the case study method rather than on experimentation, the poor definitions of some of its concepts, its untestability, and its sexism.

Why Study Freud?

- Nonetheless, psychoanalysis is important because of its contributions to psychotherapy (in the form of "talk therapy" for example), its effect on popular culture, the increasing amount of research it has generated in recent years, and because it is a complete theory of personality that raises questions other areas of psychology do not address.

THINK ABOUT IT

1. Can you be anxious about something without knowing what it is? Or does that strike you as a nonsensical idea?
2. What examples of the various defense mechanisms—in your own behavior or that of others—can you come up with?
3. If you are or have been on an athletic team, did your coach ever give you a pep talk? What did your coach say? Was any aspect of the speech Freudian? Was it helpful?
4. What's the funniest joke you have heard lately? Can you explain, from a psychoanalytic perspective, what makes it funny? Have you heard a joke lately that you did *not* find funny? Can you explain what went wrong?
5. Do you think Freudian psychoanalysis should be considered scientific? Does the answer to this question matter?
6. Should Freudian psychoanalysis still be taught in college psychology classes?

SUGGESTED READINGS

Horney, K. (1942). *Self-analysis*. New York: Norton.
Horney, K. (1950). *Neurosis and human growth*. New York: Norton.

> *Two books by an important psychoanalytic theorist that make fascinating reading for their insights into human nature, especially the unrealistic ways people think about themselves and their goals. These are self-help books, but intellectually they are much richer than typical offerings in this category.*

EMEDIA

 Go to StudySpace, wwnorton.com/studyspace, to access additional review and enrichment materials.

12

PSYCHOANALYSIS AFTER FREUD:
Neo-Freudians, Object Relations, and Current Research

SIGMUND FREUD DIED in 1939. His theory of the human mind lives on, however, as does his style of theorizing and his approach to psychodynamics. Academic research psychology—the kind done at universities by psychology professors—does not currently emphasize Freudian theory and psychoanalysis, but more than a few modern psychologists keep Freud's legacy alive in one way or another. Some reinterpret his theory or extend it into new domains, others test his ideas with empirical research, while still others keep Freud alive just by continuing to argue about him.

Indeed, more than 70 years after his death, a surprising number of psychiatrists, psychologists, professors of English, and even Sanskrit scholars devote their careers to the seemingly never-ending project of debunking Freud. The goal of many of them is to prove that he was wrong about absolutely everything from the very beginning (e.g., Crews, 1996). A few years ago a book by the flamboyant psychoanalyst (and Sanskrit scholar) Jeffrey Masson (1984) stirred the popular media by dredging up material about some of Freud's more questionable friends and using it to attack Freud's whole theory.[1] Similar works appear on a regular basis.[2] As one reporter

---

[1] Masson also received extensive publicity when he sued *The New Yorker* magazine, which he claimed libeled him in a personality profile. He lost the case.

[2] See, for example, Sulloway (1979) or Crews (1996, 1998). The latter is a book of attacks on Freud that, in the words of the ad on its jacket, "decisively [forge] the case against the man and his creation . . . [and] reveal the fumbles and deceptions that led to the 'discovery' of psychoanalysis." On the other side of the debate, Robinson (1993) summarizes the arguments of some of Freud's main critics and offers a defense.

wrote, "To innocently type [Freud's] name into a search engine is to unleash a torrent of denunciation. . . . Merely being wrong—as even his partisans admit he probably was about a lot of things—seems inadequate to explain the calumny he has engendered" (J. Adler, 2006, p. 44).

Indeed, the most remarkable aspect of many of these efforts is their vehemence and personal tone. They don't merely and reasonably suggest that the modern evidence concerning some of Freud's ideas is weak. They go much further, arguing that Freud was a liar, a cheat, and a fraud; that he was mean to his family; and that he never had an original idea in his life. They stop just short of arguing that his books should be pulled from the library shelves and burned in the public square. Recall the discussion in Chapter 11 of reaction formation and its hallmarks. Are attacks like these a proportionate response, or might there be a deeper explanation? As psychiatrist Glenn Gabbard commented, "The unconscious is terribly threatening. It suggests we are moved by forces we cannot see or control, and this is a severe wound to our narcissism" (cited in J. Adler, 2006, p. 44). The psychoanalytically inclined psychologist Drew Westen adds that "any theory that is entirely comfortable to discuss is probably missing something very important about what it means to be human" (Westen et al., 2008, p. 86).

> More than 70 years after his death, a surprising number of psychiatrists, psychologists, professors of English, and even Sanskrit scholars devote their careers to the seemingly never-ending project of debunking Freud.

A more constructive development has been the continuing development of psychoanalytic thought by clinical practitioners and theorists who—amid varying degrees of acknowledgment of, or expressed opposition to, the "Big Guy"—have introduced a number of refinements. Some are minor adjustments made in the course of summarizing Freud's work in order to make sense of it in a modern context. I have done some adjusting of my own in the previous two chapters of this book. Other amendments are more drastic. Carl Jung set up his own version of psychoanalysis, including some mystical ideas far removed from the way Freud thought. But Jung's spiritual angle—influential as it has been—is unusual within psychoanalysis.

The theme of most post-Freudian psychoanalysts is to move away from his emphasis on built-in sexual and aggressive instincts toward a focus on the interpersonal aspects of life. A special concern is the way that early attachments, especially with parents, affect perceptions of, and relations with, other people. The important insight they take from Freud is that our relationships with other people are mediated through our mental images of them—which sometimes do not much resemble the way they actually are. These partially accurate mental images of people are called *objects*, and the modern school of psychoanalysis that deals with the origin and implications of these images is called *object relations theory*. A close relative of object relations theory is *attachment theory*, which focuses specifically on how attachments to significant other people, called *attachment figures*, and our images of such attachments can be a buffer in times of stress (e.g., Bowlby, 1988; Shaver & Mikulincer, 2005).

This chapter aims to bring Freud into the present day by summarizing some of the ways his theory has been reinterpreted and altered since his death. We will focus on a few prominent *neo-Freudian theorists* and work in object relations and attachment theory. Then we will summarize examples of modern empirical research testing psychoanalytic ideas, and conclude by placing psychoanalytic theory into perspective, by considering some of its shortcomings and accomplishments.

INTERPRETING FREUD

Modern writers who work to make sense of Freud may shade their summaries in various ways that try to maintain the spirit, if not the letter, of Freudian law. I did this in Chapter 10 when I described how a child unsure about gender roles might look to a role model, such as the same-sex parent, for guidance. The dynamic process is different from the one Freud originally envisioned, but the result is still that boys usually identify with their fathers and girls with their mothers.

Only a fuzzy boundary separates interpreting versus revising a theory. Freud wrote hundreds of articles and dozens of books over more than six decades, and he changed his mind about important issues more than once. So it is no small or insignificant activity to interpret what he said or meant to say, or to determine the overall meaning of his work, or to decide how best to summarize it. A particular challenge is to interpret Freud's theory in a way that sounds reasonable today, because that will require some changes. The original theory is, after all, nearly a century old.

Many psychologists and historians have taken on this task, with widely varying results. Peter Gay's (1988) monumental biography of Freud includes a thorough and insightful survey of the development of Freud's theory and a firm defense of it. Charles Brenner's (1974) useful outline of psychoanalytic concepts merges Freud's ideas with Brenner's own insights and updates. The preceding two chapters of this book likewise constitute more of a sympathetic interpretation than a literal retelling of Freud. I merged what Freud said with what I think he meant to say or should have said, and even mixed in some ideas contributed by later thinkers in the Freudian tradition.

For example, as mentioned, I altered the traditional story of the Oedipal crisis because I don't think the original makes much sense in light of more recent research about socialization. Thus, my version changes (some would say distorts) Freud's original theory. I also reinterpreted libido by describing it as the "life drive," rather than limiting it to something exclusively sexual. Again, this changes—in fact directly contradicts—some of Freud's writings, but I prefer to interpret them in terms of what makes sense to me today. I also changed Freud's description of the stages of personality development to emphasize, as did the great neo-Freudian theorist Erik Erikson (1963), that each stage is associated not just with physical development and bodily sensations but also with changing tasks in relating to the social world.

The more you become tempted to "fix" Freud by mixing in other thinkers and ideas, and inserting your own ideas about Freudian theory, the more you become an active developer of psychoanalytic theory yourself. It was Anna Freud, not her father, who wrote the definitive survey of the defense mechanisms, some of which were described in Chapter 11. It is probably safe to say Sigmund Freud would approve (he apparently approved of everything his favorite daughter did), since she did not deviate from the spirit of his theories. Many other thinkers have continued to write about psychoanalysis, attempting to stay true to Freud's theory while extending it.

LATTER-DAY ISSUES AND THEORISTS

The theorists who, in later years, continued to develop **neo-Freudian psychology** are an impressive crew. They include Anna Freud, Bruno Bettelheim, Erik Erikson, Carl Jung, Alfred Adler, Karen Horney, Harry Stack Sullivan, Melanie Klein, D. W. Winnicott, Henry Murray, and John Bowlby. You probably have heard of several of them; Erikson, Jung, and Adler number among the major intellectual figures of the 20th century. But it is also an important fact that every individual just named is deceased. Although some neo-Freudians are still around, their golden age has passed.

Most neo-Freudians used the same research methods as Freud himself. They saw patients, looked into themselves, read widely in history and literature, and drew conclusions. These practices are common to some of Freud's most vehement critics, such as Jung (an early dissenter) and Jeffrey Masson (a recent dissenter), as well as to those more sympathetic to him, such as Bruno Bettelheim and Anna Freud.

This method allows psychoanalysts of every stripe to cover a lot of theoretical ground. It also invokes a style of argument that more conventionally scientific psychologists find frustrating. When Jung argued with Freud, for example, he would basically say that his cases and introspection showed conclusion A, and Freud would reply no, his own cases and introspection led clearly to conclusion B, to which Jung would reply that anybody can see it's really A . . . and so forth. Anyone looking for an experiment to settle the matter would search in vain; even if somebody were clever enough to come up with one, neither Freud nor Jung—nor any of the classic neo-Freudians—would allow a mere experiment to settle such profound matters.

Common Themes of Neo-Freudian Thought

Most neo-Freudians differ from Freud in three major respects. First, they view sex as less important than Freud did. Most of them place less emphasis on the libido as the sexual wellspring of thought and behavior; instead, they reinterpret libido as a general motivation toward life and creativity. You have already seen such a reinterpretation in the preceding chapters. I view this change of emphasis as a permissible modern reinterpretation; other theorists view this issue as an example of how Freud was simply wrong.

Freud's emphasis on sexuality—even in children—was always one of the most unsettling and controversial aspects of his theory. Thus, it is not surprising that later theorists have been tempted to clean up psychoanalysis in this respect. Freud believed that those who deemphasized the psychological role of sex did so because of their own anxieties. Their defenses made them unable to directly face the importance of sex and caused them to seek the important bases of behavior elsewhere. This kind of argument is not easily settled: If I say you disagree with me because of your sexual hangups, how can you reply except, perhaps, by saying the same about me?

In a second deviation, some neo-Freudians put less emphasis on unconscious mental processes and more emphasis on conscious thought. Modern ego psychologists focus on the processes driving the perception and conscious comprehension of reality (e.g., Hartmann, 1964; Loevinger, 1976; Rapaport, 1960; G. S. Klein, 1970). **Ego psychology** looks less like classic psychoanalysis and more like current mainstream psychology (especially the cognitive process approaches considered in Chapter 16), because instead of focusing on sexuality, psychic conflict, and the unconscious, ego psychologists focus on perception, memory, learning, and rational, conscious thinking. According to Jane Loevinger's influential version, the ego's function is to make sense of everything a person experiences (Loevinger, 1987). Moreover, Loevinger's story of development is essentially the story of the development of the ego itself. Early in life, the ego struggles to understand how the individual is separate from the world and from the mother; later, the ego grapples with such issues as how to relate to society, achieve personal autonomy, and appreciate the autonomy of others. According to Loevinger's test of "ego development," most people never get much further than learning society's basic rules and appreciating that some of those rules have exceptions (Holt, 1980). Very few become truly independent people who appreciate and support the independence of others.

A third common neo-Freudian deviation puts less emphasis on instinctual drives and mental life as the source of psychological difficulties, and focuses instead on interpersonal relationships. By modern psychological standards, Freud was surprisingly uninterested in the daily lives of his patients. Whereas a modern therapist would want to know the details of a patient's interactions with his spouse, Freud would be more interested in his childhood relationship with his mother. Adler and Erikson both emphasized the way psychological problems arise from day-to-day difficulties relating with other people and with society, and object relations theorists believe that people replay certain key relationship patterns throughout their lives.

Inferiority and Compensation: Adler

Alfred Adler (1870–1937) was the first major disciple of Freud to end up at odds with the master. Like many others at the time and since, Adler thought that Freud focused too much on sex as the ultimate motivator and organizer of thought and behavior. Of equal or greater importance, Adler thought, was what he called *social interest*, or the desire to relate positively and productively with other people (A. Adler, 1939).

Adler said that individuals are motivated to attain equality with or superiority over other people, and that they try to accomplish this to compensate for whatever they felt in childhood was their weakest aspect. This idea, called **organ inferiority**, leads one to expect that someone who felt physically weak as a child will strive for physical strength as an adult, that one who feels stupid will grow into an adult obsessed with being smarter than everyone else, and so on. It matters little whether the child actually *was* physically weak or relatively unintelligent, only how the child *felt*.

A particular kind of compensation for the past is seen in the desire of an adult to act and become powerful, because of feeling inadequate or inferior. Adler called this kind of overcompensating behavior the **masculine protest**. He applied this term to both men and women, but believed the issue to be particularly acute for men. Young boys pick up from society the idea that males are supposed to be the powerful and dominant gen-

"Fill 'er up with testosterone."

der—and yet, who is the most powerful person in *their* lives? Mom, obviously. Adler believed this early experience caused some young men to develop a powerful yearning to prove their dominance, power, and masculinity. One way to do this in modern culture is to buy a pickup truck that can be entered only via a ladder, loudly rev the engine, race up and down the highway, and terrify passersby. However, this kind of behavior always rings a little false. I think most people intuitively understand that someone secure in his masculinity does not need to prove it through his choice of vehicle, manner of driving, or any other superficial means. The masculine protest, therefore, is a compensation, an expression of inferiority complex.

> One way to prove dominance, power, and masculinity is to buy a pickup truck that can be entered only via a ladder, loudly rev the engine, race up and down the highway, and terrify passersby. However, this kind of behavior always rings a little false.

Adler's point is that everyone felt inferior as a child, probably in many respects, and the quest to overcome these feelings can influence adult behavior. This quest can help explain behaviors that otherwise do not seem to make sense—such as driving an implausibly large truck to the supermarket—but also much more. Needs for power, love, and achievement all have roots in early experience. An individual's compensations for perceived childhood inferiorities coalesce into a particular mode of behavior, which Adler called that individual's "style of life." Two familiar terms with roots in Adlerian thought are *inferiority complex* and *lifestyle*.

The Collective Unconscious, Persona, and Personality: Jung

The next major rebel from psychoanalysis was Carl Jung (1875–1961). (See Jung, 1971a, for a collection of his writings.) His feud with Freud was more dramatic and bitter than Adler's because of Freud's high hopes for Jung, one of his earliest disciples. Indeed, Jung and Freud had close contact for many years; they wrote each other numerous letters and even traveled to America together. Freud declared Jung his "crown prince," and anointed him the first president of the International Psychoanalytic Association.

But over the years, Jung's theories departed more and more from Freud's, to the point that the two men couldn't get along any more. Perhaps Jung's deviation that most irritated Freud was his increasing interest in mystical and spiritual matters. Freud, a devout atheist, found Jung's ideas concerning an inner rhythm of the universe ("synchronicity"), transcendental experiences, and a collective unconscious rather hard to take. These ideas became extremely important to Jung, however, and they are an important reason why he remains famous.

Jung's best-known idea is the **collective unconscious**. Jung believed that as a result of the history of the human species, all people share inborn "racial" (by which he meant species-specific) memories and ideas, most of which reside in the unconscious. Some of these are basic images, called **archetypes**, which Jung believed go to the core of how people think about the world, both consciously and unconsciously. They include "the earth mother," "the hero," "the devil," and "the supreme being." Versions of these archetypes, sometimes disguised with symbols, show up repeatedly in dreams, thoughts, world mythologies, and even modern literature. (Indeed, a school of literary criticism active to this day seeks Jungian archetypes in novels, plays, and cinema.) This seems like an odd idea, but there may be something to it. Snakes show up frequently in cultures' foundational stories, such as the Bible, almost always in a sinister role—and research suggests that the human fear of snakes may be innate (Öhman & Mineka, 2003).

Another lasting idea of Jung's is the **persona**, his term for the social mask one wears in public dealings. He pointed out that to some degree everyone's persona is false, because everyone keeps some aspects of their real selves private, or at least fails to advertise all aspects of the self equally. This idea survives in modern social psychology and sociology (e.g., Goffman, 1959); it also influenced object relations theory, considered later in this chapter. The danger, according to Jung, is that an individual might come to identify more with the persona than with the real self. She may become obsessed with presenting a certain image instead of who she really is and what she really feels, and thus become shallow with no deeper purpose than social success. Such people become creatures of society instead of individuals true to themselves.

Another influential Jungian concept is the anima and animus. The **anima** is the idea, or prototype, of the female, as held in the mind of a male. The **animus** is the idealized image of the male as held in the mind of a female. These two images cause everyone to have some aspects of the opposite sex in their psychological makeup: a male's anima is the root of his "feminine side"; a female's animus is the basis of her "masculine side." These concepts also shape responses to the opposite sex: A man understands (or misunderstands) women through the psychological lens of his anima; a woman likewise understands or misunderstands men according to her animus. This can lead to real problems if the idealized woman or man in one's mind matches poorly with the real women or men in one's life. This is a common problem, Jung believed, and daily experience seems to support him on this.

Another key Jungian idea is his distinction between people who are psychologically turned inward (introverts) and those who are oriented toward the external world and other people (extraverts). As we saw earlier in the chapters of Part II, the dimension of extraversion-introversion is one of the Big Five personality traits and has been found in a wide range of psychometric research programs.

Yet another useful Jungian idea is his classification of four basic ways of thinking: rational thinking, feeling, sensing, and intuiting. As Jung wrote,

> Sensation establishes what is actually present, [rational] thinking enables us to recognize its meaning, feeling tells us its value, and intuition points to possibilities as to whence it came and whither it is going in a given situation. (Jung, 1931/1971b, p. 540)

Jung believed that everybody uses all four kinds of thinking, but that people vary in which kind predominates. An engineer might emphasize rational thinking while an artist emphasizes feeling, a detective emphasizes sensation, and a religious person emphasizes intuition. A modern personality test, the *Myers-Briggs Type Indicator* (*MBTI*; Myers, 1962), is sometimes used to determine which kind of thinking an individual uses most. Guidance counselors and personnel departments frequently use this test.

Jung believed that, ideally, one would achieve a balance among all four types of thinking, although he acknowledged that such an achievement is rare. The distinction between Jung and Freud could be summed up in Jungian terms by saying that Freud emphasized rational thinking, whereas Jung had a more intuitive style.

Feminine Psychology and Basic Anxiety: Horney

Karen Horney (1885–1952) did not begin publishing about psychoanalysis until late in Freud's career, and, unlike Adler and Jung, she never feuded with the master. She is one of the three most influential women in the history of psychoanalysis (the other two being Freud's brilliant and devoted daughter Anna and the object relations theorist Melanie Klein). Some of her books are among the best introductions to psychoanalytic thought (see Horney, 1937, 1950). She also wrote about self-analysis, which she thought could help people through psychological difficulties when professional psychoanalysis was impractical or unavailable (Horney, 1942).

Horney deviated from Freud over an aspect of his theory that many people—especially women—have found objectionable. She disagreed with Freud's portrayal of women as obsessed by "penis envy" and the desire to be male. As mentioned in Chapter 11, in some of his writing, Freud seems to view women as damaged creatures—men without penises—instead of as whole persons in their own right. Like many others, Horney found this view implausible and objectionable. If some women wish to be men, she theorized, it is probably because they see men as being more free than women to pursue their own interests and ambitions. Although women might lack confidence and overemphasize their love relationships with men as a source of fulfillment, this is due to the structure of society rather than the structure of bodies.[3]

Horney's other contributions fit better into the conventional Freudian mode. She emphasized that adult behavior is often based on efforts to overcome the basic anxiety acquired in childhood: the fear of being alone and

---

[3] As a counter to this observation, Westen recently noted that children tend to think in concrete terms and so might be especially prone to symbolize the relative social advantages of men and women in this literal and physical way. Before Westen became a psychologist, a coworker who knew nothing of Freudian theory

> . . . told him that her 6-year-old daughter had cried the night before in the bathtub because her younger brother, with whom she was bathing, had "one of those things" and she did not. The author [Westen] has always wondered about the impact of the mother's tongue-in-cheek reply: "Don't worry, you'll get one someday." (Westen et al., 2008, p. 65)

helpless in a hostile world. Attempts to avoid such anxiety can cause what Horney called *neurotic needs*, needs that people feel but that are neither realistic nor truly desirable. These include the needs to find a life partner who will solve all of one's problems (love-related and otherwise), to be loved by everybody, to dominate everybody, and to be independent of everybody. Not only are these needs unrealistic; they are mutually contradictory. But the mind often unconsciously tries to pursue all of them anyway, which can lead to self-defeating behavior and relationship problems.

Psychosocial Development: Erikson

Erik Erikson (1902–1994) always claimed to be a faithful, orthodox Freudian, but his innovations in psychoanalytic theory make him Freud's most important revisionist (see Erikson, 1963, 1968). For example, he pointed out persuasively that not all conflicts take place in the unconscious mind—many conflicts are conscious. A person might have to choose between two (or more) activities, careers, or even lovers. These conflicts can be painful and consequential, as well as completely conscious.

Erikson believed that certain basic conflicts arise at various stages of life. This insight led Erikson to develop his own version of Freud's theory of psychological development, in which Erikson emphasized not the physical focus of libido, but the conflicts experienced at each stage and their possible outcomes. For that reason, his theory of development is referred to as a *psychosocial*, as opposed to Freud's *psychosexual*, approach (see Table 12.1). (Erikson's psychosocial approach heavily influenced the psychoanalytic view of development presented in Chapter 10.) Erikson's theory covers not just childhood, but development throughout life.

The first stage, according to Erikson, is *basic trust versus mistrust*. This corresponds to Freud's oral stage of very early childhood, when the utterly dependent child learns whether needs and wants will be met, ignored, or overindulged. Given the appropriate ratio of satisfaction and temporary frustration, the child develops *hope* (which in Erikson's terminology refers to a positive but not arrogant attitude toward life) and confidence—but not overconfidence—that basic needs will be met.

The next stage, corresponding to Freud's anal stage, is that of *autonomy versus shame and doubt*. As the child begins to control bowels and other bodily functions, learns language, and begins to receive orders from adult authorities, an inevitable conflict arises: Who's in charge here? On the one hand,

Table 12.1

COMPARISON OF FREUD'S AND ERIKSON'S SEQUENCE OF PERSONALITY DEVELOPMENT

Approximate Age	Freudian Stage	Eriksonian Issue
0–2 years	Oral	Trust vs. mistrust
3–4 years	Anal	Autonomy vs. shame and doubt
4–7 years	Phallic	Initiative vs. guilt
8–12 years	Latency	Industry vs. inferiority
13+ years	Genital (evolves over adulthood)	Indentity vs. identity confusion
		Intimacy vs. isolation
		Generativity vs. stagnation
		Integrity vs. despair

adults pressure the child to obey, but on the other hand, that child wants control of his own life. Ideally these wills can strike a balance, but either may win out, leading in some cases to the anal character described in Chapter 10.

Erikson's third stage, corresponding to Freud's phallic stage, is that of *initiative versus guilt*. The child begins to anticipate and fantasize about life as an adult. These fantasies inevitably include sexual ones, as well as various tactics and plans to get ahead in life. Such fantasies are good for a child, Erikson believed, but if adults do not respond to them well, these thoughts can lead the child to feel guilty and to back off from taking initiative in her development toward adulthood. Ideally, the child will develop a sense of right and wrong that is derived from adult teachings but is also true to the child's developing sense of self. This development leads to a principled adult morality, in which moral rules are applied with flexibility and wisdom, rather than a merely conformist pseudomorality in which rigid rules are followed blindly and without exception. You may have noticed that this stage reinterprets Freud's phallic stage without the full Oedipal crisis (see Chapter 10).

The fourth stage is *industry versus inferiority*, during which one should develop the skills and attitudes to succeed in the world of work or otherwise contribute to society. At this time the child must begin to control his exuberant imagination and unfocused energy and get on with tasks of developing competence, workmanship, and a way of organizing life tasks. This stage corresponds roughly to Freud's latency period.

At Erikson's fifth stage, development deviates more widely from the path laid out by Freud. The Freudian account basically stops with the genital stage, which is reached at some unspecified time after puberty, if at all. In Erikson's view, however, development continues throughout life. The next crisis involves *identity versus identity confusion*, as the adolescent strives to figure out who he is and what is and is not important. At this stage, individuals choose values and goals that are consistent, personally meaningful, and useful. Close on the heels of the identity conflict comes the conflict of *intimacy versus isolation*. The task here, for young adulthood, is to find an intimate life partner to share important experiences and further development, rather than becoming isolated and lonely.

As one enters middle age, Erikson said, the next conflict is *generativity versus stagnation*. As a person's position in life becomes firmly set, does she settle into passive comfort, or begin to turn her concerns to the next generation? The challenge here is to avoid the temptation to simply cash in one's savings and go fishing, and instead to raise and nurture children and generally to do what one can to ensure the progress of the next generation. I am reminded here of the modern phenomenon of prosperous American retirees who vote overwhelmingly against taxes to support schools. At a younger age, there are "yuppies" (young urban professionals) who either don't have children, who might slow down their career, or who have children but hire people to raise them because they "don't have time" themselves. Which choice do you think these people have made between generativity and stagnation?

The final crisis in life occurs late in old age, as one begins to face the prospect of death. The choice here is between *integrity versus despair*. Does the person regret earlier mistakes and feel that, basically, he blew it? Or from experience, has the person developed wisdom? The test is: After 70, 80, or 90 years of life, does the person have anything of interest and value to say to the next generation? Or not?

As we have seen, a person progresses from one crisis to another in Erikson's scheme not according to physical or genital maturation, but according to the developmental tasks that different phases of life require because of the structure of society. This idea is consistent with the recent analysis of changes in the Big Five personality traits over the life span, which was reviewed in Chapter 7 (Roberts et al., 2006). This insight about the societal basis of psychological development was the first of two major contributions of Erikson's theory of development. Its second major contribution was Erikson's pioneering venture into what is now called *life-span development*. This idea proposes that development is not limited to little children; it is an ongoing task and opportunity throughout life, from childhood through old age. Modern developmental psychology is heavily influenced by this idea.

Object Relations Theory: Klein and Winnicott

The most important part of life, the source of its pleasure and pain, is probably relationships. In psychoanalytic terms, emotionally important people are called *objects*, and the analysis of interpersonal relationships is called **object relations theory** (J. R. Greenberg & Mitchell, 1983; see also M. Klein, 1964; Winnicott, 1958, 1965). The key insight of the object relations approach is that we can only relate to other people via the images of them we hold in our minds, and these images do not always match reality. Not surprisingly, mismatch causes problems.

Object relations theory is the most active area of psychoanalytic thinking at present and has generated a huge literature. A search for "object relations" on the PsychInfo database yields more than 6,000 articles. The core ideas go back (naturally) to Freud, who thought the superego was built from childhood identifications with important people, and who also thought that people repeat important psychological patterns in new relationships through the mechanism of transference. Anna Freud pushed this idea further by examining children's relationships with their parents. Other important object relations theorists include Melanie Klein and D. W. Winnicott. The work of many other theorists, including the neo-Freudians summarized earlier, is also relevant to object relations, to the extent that these theorists address problems of interpersonal relations (J. R. Greenberg & Mitchell, 1983).

Object relations theory comes in many forms, therefore, but almost every version includes four principal themes. The first is the observation that every relationship has elements of satisfaction and frustration, or pleasure and pain. Melanie Klein theorized that the first important object (literally) in the infant's life is the mother's breast. The infant quickly discovers that this object is a source of great delight, providing nutrition, warmth, and comfort. So the baby adores the breast. At the same time, the breast can be frustrating—it is not always available and not always full. So the baby hates the breast. The baby's demands are not reasonable—remember the description of the id's primary process thinking in Chapter 10. The baby wants everything *now*, and when the breast cannot or does not provide, the baby is angry.

This dichotomy leads to the second theme of object relations: the mix of love and hate. Just like the original object, the breast, important people are sources of both pleasure and frustration. They may give us love, support, and even sexual satisfaction. So we love them. At the same time, they may express annoyance with us, criticize us, and frustrate us. So we hate them. This sad situation is inevitable, in the view of object relations theory. You cannot satisfy someone without also frustrating her sometimes. So love will never be completely unmixed with frustration and resentment.

The third major theme of object relations is the distinction between the parts of the love object and the whole person. To the baby, the mother *is* the breast, at least at first. This is what interests and attracts the baby, not the mother as a person. It is a complex and difficult process, perhaps never completed, for the baby to come to appreciate the mother for more than just what she provides. In the same way, other people in our lives have parts and wholes. One might enjoy a partner's sense of humor, intellect, body, or money. To what degree is this the same as loving the partner himself? From an object relations perspective, it is not the same at all. Using a person's attributes for one's own enjoyment is very different from loving the whole person. Here object relations theory intersects with common sense. To love a person's physique or wallet is not the same thing as loving the person, and to move beyond appreciating superficial aspects of people to loving them as whole persons is a difficult and perhaps rarely accomplished feat.

The fourth major theme of object relations is that, to some degree, the psyche of the baby (and the adult) is aware of and disturbed by these contradictory feelings. The baby worships the mother's breast, but according to Klein, the baby also feels anger (because there is never enough), envy (because the baby desires the breast's power for herself), fear (because the baby dreads losing the breast), and guilt (if the baby harms the breast, she could lose it). It may not be particularly plausible to attribute all of these complex reactions to a baby, but the overall theme does strike a chord. Let's say you are fortunate enough to form a relationship with a truly attractive and desirable person. That's great. The downside may be a set of Kleinian reactions that are more or less unconscious. The very delight in the person's company may make you frustrated and even angry that he or she is not always available. You may envy the power this person has over you, precisely because of his or her attractiveness. You may fear losing him or her, and the fear is greater the more desirable he or she seems. And finally, you may feel secret guilt over all of these negative reactions, because if you expressed them, the relationship might be over. No wonder relationships can get so messed up.

Melanie Klein developed her theories based in large part on her work with children; she was one of the earliest psychoanalysts (along with Anna Freud) to attempt psychoanalytic treatment with the very young. Freud himself dealt almost exclusively with adults' childhood memories. One of

"I wish I'd started therapy at your age."

Klein's innovations in child therapy, still widely used, was to communicate with, and diagnose children through, play (M. Klein, 1955/1986). She usually provided a range of toys, and then observed which ones the child played with, and how; she believed play allowed the symbolic expression of emotions such as hate, anger, love, and fear. From watching children "play pretend" about their parents, for example, she observed that children divide, or *split*, their important love objects into two parts, one good and one bad. The good part of the object pleases them; the bad part frustrates them. Children wish to destroy the bad part because they fear being destroyed *by* it (Klein called this the *paranoid position*), and they wish to worship and protect the good part because they fear losing it (Klein called this the *depressive position*).

Naturally, the phenomenon of splitting applies to other love objects as well. The problem, of course, is that people are not neatly divided into good and bad parts; they are indivisible wholes. So both desires—to destroy and to worship—are contradictory and irrational. This situation can lead to some common neurotic defenses. For example, to defend against the (more or less hidden) desire to destroy (the bad part of) a parent, one may idealize him or her. Have you ever heard someone describe her father in terms that were literally too good to be true? Klein believed, in true Freudian fashion, that such idealization is a symptom of underlying hostility being defended against at all costs. She might not be able to accept that her father has flaws, because to do so would expose her anger at those flaws and threaten a loss of his love or the memory of that love. In addition, to the extent that she has identified with her father, he has become a part of her, so to criticize him is to criticize herself. She therefore constructs an image of him as having been perfect. People do this with descriptions of their parents, their boyfriends and girlfriends, and even their children. The distortions may be obvious to everyone but the person constructing these images.

The pediatrician D. W. Winnicott started his career in child psychology heavily influenced by Klein, but he soon developed his own important additions to object relations theory. One of his ideas that has come into everyday use was his description of what he called the *niffle* (Winnicott, 1996). The term came from a young patient named Tom, who at age 5 had to be hospitalized away from his family and took comfort from sleeping with his "niffle," a small piece of cloth to which he developed an emotional attachment. Tragically, the niffle got lost during his journey home. This loss so upset Tom that he became hostile, stubborn, and annoying to the point that his parents brought him to Winnicott for therapy. From this experience, Winnicott formed the idea of the *transitional object*, which may be a special blanket, stuffed animal, or niffle, that the child uses to bridge the gap between private fantasy and reality. The child endows the object with special, almost magical emotional meaning, so it can comfort the child when adult company (or, as Klein would surely say, the breast) is not available. Over time, the object loses its special meaning as the child becomes better able to handle the world without this kind of support.

Objects like these are transitional in two senses. First, they help the child make the change from the time when adults are constantly caring for him, to the time when he must face the world alone. Second, they exist in an interesting transitional state between fantasy and reality. The objects are always real in that there actually *is* a teddy bear, or a blanket, or whatever the niffle is. (For one of my daughters, the niffle was a toy dinosaur.) But the child gives it a special magic which, importantly, nobody in the family questions. Houses have been turned upside down more than once looking for lost niffles, and for good reason. Objects like this are important, and their use is not limited to children. Adults have sentimental attachments to many things that represent important people in their lives. The most obvious examples are the family pictures many people perch on their desks or living room mantels, and carry in their wallets. The purpose of these pictures and other sentimental keepsakes is to compensate in some small way for the fact that we cannot have our loved ones with us all the time, or forever.[4]

> The purpose of pictures and other sentimental keepsakes is to compensate in some small way for the fact that we cannot have our loved ones with us all the time, or forever.

Another idea Winnicott added to object relations theory was the notion of the *false self*, which children—and later, adults—learn to put on to please other people. Notice the similarity of this idea to Jung's notion of the persona. Winnicott believed that, to some degree, putting on a false self is nor-

---

[4] When people are asked what they would grab first if their house were on fire, family pictures are always high on the list.

mal and even necessary; ordinary social etiquette and politeness generally require refraining from saying exactly what you think in order to smooth interpersonal relationships. He worried more about some particularly charming children who, he feared, learned to put on a false act in a desperate attempt to cheer up their depressed mothers, at a high cost to the children's own integrity. Winnicott observed that the false self serves, in a sense, to protect the true self by keeping it invisible: No one can exploit, harm, or even touch the true self if it is hidden behind a big enough false front. The ultimate maneuver of the false self is suicide: If there seems to be no hope that the true self can ever emerge, succeed, and be accepted, then the false self prevents its exposure permanently.

The purpose of psychotherapy, from the perspective of object relations, is to help minimize discrepancies between the true and false selves and, in the classic Freudian tradition, to help the rational resources of the mind work through irrational defenses. The goal is for the client to see the important people in her life as they are, not as the client wishes them to be. Likewise, the client may need help to see these people as whole individuals with a mixture of virtues, vices, and traits in between, rather than splitting them into images of Jekyll-and-Hyde twins who are all good on one side, and all bad on the other. Overcoming these illusions is not easy. On some level, everybody would prefer their important people to be perfect and devoted, and everyone may be on some level outraged that even the most beloved people in our lives fall short of perfection and fail to satisfy us sometimes. Object relations theory retains this idea from Freud: Rationality can win over all. If we think clearly and brush away enough of the neurotic cobwebs, we can do what makes sense and relate to others as real people.

Where Have All the Neo-Freudian Theorists Gone?

As I mentioned earlier, they all seem to be dead. The chapters in personality textbooks that survey Freud and the neo-Freudians are sometimes sardonically called the "tour of the graveyard." Certainly no one of the stature of Jung, Adler, Horney, or Erikson, or even Klein or Winnicott, is actively developing psychoanalytic theory today. Although these thinkers contributed important ideas, their general approach based on informal observation, clinical experience, and personal insight is the wave of the past. The wave of the near future is conducting experimental and correlational research to scientifically confirm, disprove, or alter psychoanalytic theory using the kinds of scientific evidence that psychology generally employs.

CURRENT PSYCHOANALYTIC RESEARCH

Almost all conventional psychological research—that is, experimental and correlational studies with publicly reported data—is conducted by academic psychologists at universities or research institutes. The relations between those doing research and their colleagues who practice clinical psychoanalysis has ranged from uneasy to downright hostile. This situation has actually worsened over the years. In the 1950s, Freudian ideas predominated throughout psychology, but psychoanalysis gradually faded from view due to several trends including the rise of behaviorism (see Chapter 15), the increased separation of academic psychology from clinical practice, and the appeal of one-shot laboratory studies over difficult, complex theoretical efforts (Shaver & Mikulincer, 2005). As a result, most university psychology departments training researchers today have no Freudian faculty, so there is a remarkable amount of ignorance about psychoanalysis on the part of many research psychologists. Where would they learn about it? As psychologists Philip Shaver and Mario Mikulincer (2005) have observed, "many students specializing in personality psychology hardly know who Freud was, and most have never read his work" (p. 23). Even when academic psychologists encounter psychoanalytic research that meets their empirical standards, they often seem unwilling to believe the evidence showing aspects of psychoanalytic thought to have value.

For their part, many psychoanalysts are equally guilty (Bachrach, Galatzer-Levy, Skolnikoff, & Waldron, 1991; Westen, 1998). They often show little interest in conventional scientific research, preferring to exchange anecdotal evidence: "I had a patient once who. . . ." Freud himself thought that psychodynamic processes could be seen only through clinical case study; most modern psychoanalysts likewise seem to regard experimental and correlational research as irrelevant. For example, one modern psychoanalyst wrote the following about experimental research:

> I have been singularly uninterested in, if not contemptuous of, anything that the "number crunchers" had to say. . . . The phrase "meaningful statistical data" was, to me, an oxymoron of hilarious proportions. (Tansey, 1992, p. 539)

The result of this mutual myopia between psychoanalytic psychologists and nonpsychoanalytic psychologists is that each group mostly ignores the other, and when they do interact, they typically attack or lecture without listening to the other side.

This sorry situation may be changing, however. A few brave psychologists are pursuing research relevant to psychoanalysis, and many more are doing so without realizing the relationship between their work and neo-Freudian ideas. Westen (1998), one of the most important of these modern researchers, has pointed out that while few psychologists research Freud or psychoanalysis directly, many of them pursue work that can be considered relevant to these topics. Westen observes that any research is at least "a little" psychoanalytic, whether knowingly or not, to the extent that it includes any of the following:

1. An examination of independent mental processes that occur simultaneously in the same mind and can conflict with one another
2. Unconscious mental processes
3. Compromises among mental processes negotiated outside of consciousness
4. Self-defensive thought and self-deception
5. The influence of the past on current functioning, especially childhood patterns that endure into adulthood
6. Sexual or aggressive wishes as they influence thought, feeling, and behavior

While very little experimental or correlational research includes all of these concerns, a great deal is relevant to one or more of them. Westen contends that if a given piece of research addresses any one of these issues, it is at least a little bit psychoanalytic. The more of these issues the research includes, the more psychoanalytic that research becomes—whether the researchers know it or not. Westen's observation is extremely important because it implies that conventional experimental and correlational research may not be as irrelevant to psychoanalysis as psychologists on both sides of the fence have long assumed.

Testing Psychoanalytic Hypotheses

Using Westen's definition, it seems that a large amount of research in the psychological literature addresses psychoanalytic hypotheses. Most of this research did not explicitly set out to test psychoanalysis, and sometimes the articles do not even mention it. But a large amount of research documents and supports ideas that began with Freud and with variants on psychoanalysis. I summarized some of this evidence already during the survey in the preceding two chapters (see especially the discussion of defense mechanisms in Chapter 11), but it might be useful to look at a few more instances.

For example, a large amount of research shows that the unconscious part of the mind can perceive things without the conscious mind's awareness (Erdelyi, 1974; Bornstein, 1999b; see also Chapter 16). It appears that the unconscious mind can keep a perception from emerging into consciousness in order to prevent anxiety—the classic defense mechanism of denial (see Chapter 11). In one study, a participant watched as a "dirty" word (you know what I mean), which presumably might upset the values of the superego, was flashed on a screen. The participant reported being unable to recognize it. Then another word, the same length as the first but innocuous rather than obscene, was flashed. The participant recognized it immediately. This finding implies that some part of the mind realized that the first word was obscene *before* it was consciously perceived, and kept this realization out of conscious awareness. Furthermore, people who avoid reporting such anxiety-producing perceptions are not just trying to look good, but also appear to be actively pushing their negative experience out of conscious awareness (Erdelyi, 1974, 1985; Weinberger & Davidson, 1994).

Many modern cognitive psychologists have concluded that most of what the mind does is unconscious (usually they avoid acknowledging Freud, however). One currently dominant model of cognitive processing, called *parallel distributed processing (PDP)*, posits that the mind does many different things at once and only a small fraction of its activity is conscious. The conscious thought and actual behavior that emerges represent a compromise among the outputs of all these simultaneous processes (Rumelhart et al., 1986).

Behavior results from a similar process of compromise. As the cognitive psychologist Stephen Pinker (1997) concluded, "Behavior is the result of an internal struggle among many mental modules" (p. 42). This finding recalls Freud's idea that consciousness is just the tip of the mental iceberg, with most of its causes hidden from view (Sohlberg & Birgegard, 2003; see Chapter 16 for more research on unconscious mental life).

Modern research also supports other psychoanalytic ideas. For example, new techniques can assess the degree to which people's speech reveals their use of psychoanalytic defense mechanisms (Feldman-Barrett, Williams, & Fong, 2002). The traits of the anal personality—stinginess, orderliness, rigidity, and so on—correlate with each other just as Freud theorized, and the traits of the oral character also seem to intercorrelate as Freud predicted, though perhaps to a weaker degree (Westen, 1990). The process Freud called *catharsis*, which involves freely expressing one's psychological disturbances, has proven helpful for psychological and even physical health (Erdelyi, 1994; Hughes, Uhlmann, & Pennebaker, 1994).[5]

Not all Freudian ideas have fared so well, however. As I mentioned earlier, research has failed to support Freud's story of the Oedipal crisis at the phallic stage (Kihlstrom, 1994; R. R. Sears, 1947). Apparently, this part of Freud's theory was wrong; this is why, in Chapter 10, I offered a different account of what happens at the point when children begin to realize that boys and girls are different. Some psychologists claim that the psychoanalytic ideas best supported by research, such as the unconscious, would have been thought of even if Freud had never lived, and that most of his unique ideas, such as the Oedipal crisis, have been proven wrong. These psychologists conclude that Freud contributed nothing to modern human psychology (Kihlstrom, 1994).

This view seems unduly harsh to me. The edifice of Freudian theory has influenced modern thinking and psychology in many, many ways. Indeed, it is difficult to imagine what modern psychology would look like without Freud. Moreover, the completeness and persuasiveness of the original Freudian accounts of human nature, along with some of the neo-Freudian revisions and a bit of modern interpretation, convince me that Freudian theory offers a great deal of insight into the complex nature of ourselves and others.

Attachment Theory

As we saw in Chapter 10, a basic Freudian concept is transference, which refers to applying old patterns of behavior and emotion to relationships with somebody new. In recent years, this basic idea has blossomed into the

---

[5] Other aspects of the idea of catharsis, specifically the prediction that expressing aggression impulses will "vent"—and therefore lessen—aggressive drive, have not been supported by empirical research (Bushman, 2002).

study of **attachment theory**, which focuses on patterns of relationships with others that are consistently repeated with different partners throughout life. The consistency of attachment styles has been demonstrated in several laboratory studies (Andersen & Baum, 1994; Andersen & Berk, 1998). In addition, a wide-ranging program of research led by psychologists Philip Shaver and Mario Mikulincer is using basic concepts of attachment to integrate modern research psychology with basic concepts in psychoanalysis.

The shift from Freud's idea of transference to the much broader concept of attachment began with the English psychoanalyst John Bowlby (see Bowlby, 1969/1982; Waters, Kondo-Ikemura, Posada, & Richters, 1991; Mikulincer & Shaver, 2003; Shaver & Mikulincer, 2005). Bowlby was heavily influenced by Freud's theory but frustrated by the speculative way some of his psychoanalytic colleagues wrote about the nature of love. He was even more frustrated by what he saw as their failure to understand how a person's early experiences with love—those in infancy, usually with the mother—could shape one's future outlook on emotional attachments. In that sense, Bowlby was an object relations theorist, like those discussed earlier in this chapter, but his work and the other research it influenced have moved far beyond the concerns of those original theorists, as well as being much more firmly grounded in empirical research.

According to Bowlby, attachment is the basis of love. His description resembles some of the theorizing by evolutionary biologists described in Chapter 9. Bowlby hypothesized that, in the risky environment in which the human species developed over thousands of years, humans (indeed, all primates) evolved a strong fear of being alone, especially in unusual, dark, or dangerous places, and especially when tired, injured, or sick. This fear motivates us to desire protection from someone, preferably someone with an interest in our survival and well-being. In other words, we want someone who loves us. This desire is especially strong in infancy and early childhood, but it never truly goes away; it forms the basis of many of our most important interpersonal relationships (Bowlby, 1969/1982).

This desire for protection leads us to develop what Bowlby called *attachments*. The child forms the first attachment with the primary caregiver, usually the mother. The term *primary* implies that a child generally has other caregivers as well, and all of those relationships are important. If everything goes well, the child's attachments provide both a safe haven from danger and a secure base from which to explore in happier times. This description resembles Freud's account of successful development at the oral stage.

Unfortunately, everything does not always go well. As a result of the child's interactions with the primary and other caregivers, and the degree to which his basic needs are met, he develops expectations about attachment relationships and what they should provide. These expectations are represented in the mind as vivid images of how others can be expected to react (*working models of others*), as well as how he expects himself to feel and behave (the child's *working model of the self*).

Bowlby pointed out that a child draws two lessons from her early experiences with adult caregivers. First, the child develops a belief about whether the people to whom she becomes attached—her *attachment figures*—will generally be reliable. Second, and perhaps more important, she develops a belief about whether she is the kind of person to whom attachment figures are likely to respond in a helpful way. In other words, if a child does not receive the necessary amount of love and care, the child might conclude that he or she is not lovable or worth caring about. This inference is not logical, of course: just because a negligent caregiver fails to love and nurture the child does not mean the child is not lovable.

The American psychologist Mary Ainsworth tried to make the consequences of these expectations and conclusions concrete and visible. She invented an experimental procedure called the *strange situation*, in which a child is briefly separated from, and then reunited with, his mother. Ainsworth believed that his reactions, both to the separation and to the reunion, could be quite informative—in particular, one could determine the type of attachment relationship the child had developed (Ainsworth, Blehar, Waters, & Wall, 1978). From her research, Ainsworth classified children into three types, depending on the kinds of expectations they had about their primary caregivers and how they reacted to the strange situation.

Anxious-ambivalent children come from home situations where their caregivers' behaviors are "inconsistent, hit-or-miss, or chaotic" (Sroufe, Carlson, & Shulman, 1993, p. 320). In the strange situation, these children are vigilant about the mother's presence and grow very upset when she disappears for even a few minutes. In school, they are often victimized by other children and unsuccessfully attempt to cling to teachers and peers in a way that only drives these people away—and leads to further hurt feelings, anger, and insecurity.

Avoidant children come from homes where they have been rebuffed repeatedly in their attempts to enjoy contact or reassurance. According to one study, their mothers tend to dislike hugs and other bodily contact (Main, 1990). In the strange situation, they do not appear distressed, but measuring their heart rate reveals definite signs of tension and anxiety (Sroufe & Waters, 1977). When the mother returns from the brief separation, they simply ignore her. In their school situations, these children are often hostile and defiant, alienating teachers and peers. As they grow older, they develop an angry self-reliance and a cold, distant attitude toward other people.

The luckiest ones, *secure* children, manage to develop a confident faith in themselves and their caregivers. When the mother returns after the separation, they greet her happily, with open arms. They are easily soothed when upset, and they actively explore their environment, returning frequently to the primary caregiver for comfort and encouragement. They are sure of the caregiver's support and do not worry about it. This positive attitude carries over into their other relationships.

One remarkable aspect of these attachment styles is their self-fulfilling nature (Shaver & Clark, 1994). The anxious, clingy child annoys people and drives them away; the avoidant child makes people angry; the secure child is likeable and attracts both caregivers and friends. Thus, a child's developing attachment style affects his outcomes throughout life.

Further research is beginning to examine what happens to children with different attachment styles as they grow into adults and try to develop various elements of a mature life including satisfying romantic relationships. There are at least 21 different methods to assess someone's *adult attachment style*, the grown-up version of the childhood pattern just described. One of the simplest goes like this:

Which of these descriptions best describes your feelings?

1. I am somewhat uncomfortable being close to others; I find it difficult to trust them completely, difficult to allow myself to depend on them. I am nervous when anyone gets too close, and often, love partners want me to be more intimate than I feel comfortable being.

2. I find that others are reluctant to get as close as I would like. I often worry that my partner doesn't really love me or won't want to stay with me. I want to get very close to my partner, and this sometimes scares people away.

3. I find it relatively easy to get close to others and am comfortable depending on them. I don't often worry about being abandoned or about someone getting too close to me. (Hazan & Shaver, 1987, p. 515)

According to this measure, if you checked Item 1, you are avoidant; if you checked Item 2, you are anxious-ambivalent; and if you checked Item 3, you are secure. When this survey was published in a Denver newspaper,

55 percent of the respondents described themselves as secure, 25 percent as avoidant, and 20 percent as anxious—the same percentages found in American infants put by Ainsworth into the strange situation (Campos, Barrett, Lamb, Goldsmith, & Stenberg, 1983).

Studies that examined attachment styles in more detail found that avoidant individuals are relatively uninterested in romantic relationships; they are also more likely than secure individuals to have their relationships break up and to grieve less after a relationship ends, even though they admit to being lonely (Shaver & Clark, 1994). They like to work alone, and they sometimes use their work as an excuse to detach from emotional relationships. They describe their parents as having been rejecting and cold, or else describe them in vaguely positive ways (e.g., "nice") without being able to provide specific examples. (For example, when asked, "What did your mother do that was *particularly* nice?" they are typically stuck.) Avoidant individuals under stress withdraw from their romantic partners, and instead tend to cope by ignoring stress or denying it exists. For example, avoidant individuals who were victims of sexual abuse in childhood tend to be unable to remember it 14 years later (Edelstein et al., 2005). They do not often share personal information, and they tend to dislike people who do.

> The anxious, clingy child annoys people and drives them away; the avoidant child makes people angry; the secure child is likeable and attracts both caregivers and friends.

Anxious-ambivalent adults, in contrast, are obsessed with their romantic partners—they think about them all the time and have trouble allowing them to have their own lives. They suffer from extreme jealousy, report a high rate of relationship failures (not surprisingly), and sometimes exhibit the cycle of breaking up and getting back together with the same partner. Anxious-ambivalent adults tend to have low and unstable self-esteem, and they like to work with other people but typically feel unappreciated by coworkers. They are highly emotional under stress and have to work hard to control their emotions. They describe their parents as having been intrusive, unfair, and inconsistent.

You will be relieved to learn that secure adults tend to enjoy long, stable romantic relationships characterized by deep trust and friendship. They have high self-esteem as well as high regard for others. Under stress they seek out others, particularly their romantic partners, for emotional support. They also offer loyal support when their romantic partners are under stress. They describe their parents in positive but realistic terms, which they are able to back up with specific examples. In sum, they are people who are easy to be with (Shaver & Clark, 1994).

Secure individuals can deal directly with reality because their attachment experience has been positive and reliable. They have always had a safe refuge from danger and a secure base from which to explore the world. This idealized description does not mean that secure people never cry, become angry, or worry about abandonment. But they do not need to distort reality to deal with their sadness, anger, or insecurity.

According to attachment theory, these patterns are learned in early childhood and reinforced in an increasingly self-fulfilling manner across young adulthood. This pattern of transference can persist across a person's life span, affecting her approach to work as well as relationships (Hazan & Shaver, 1990). If an individual learns an avoidant or anxious-ambivalent style, change is difficult but perhaps not impossible. Psychotherapists who use attachment theory try to teach these people the origins of their relationship styles, the way these styles lead to self-defeating outcomes, and more constructive ways to relate to others (Shaver & Clark, 1994).

Recent years have seen a explosion of research on attachment, which is moving from a specific area of psychoanalytic research to a program that offers the potential to integrate large areas of social and personality psychology with psychoanalytic thought and the study of mental health (Dozier, Stovall, & Albus, 1999; Shaver & Mikulincer, 2005). Some of the research progress is technical. For example, researchers are moving beyond the three-category classification of attachment just described to a two-dimensional model on which people vary according to their degree of *anxiety* about relationships, and their degree of *avoidance* of relationships. Only a person low on both dimensions would be considered securely attached. A person high in attachment anxiety characteristically worries that his emotionally significant other people will not be available at times of need, and deals with it by maintaining extreme vigilance, watching for signs of rejection almost to the point of paranoia. A person high in attachment avoidance has learned to distrust other people and so strives to maintain independence and emotional distance, and tries to convince himself that close emotional relationships are unimportant.[6] According to one recent experiment, someone high in both avoidance *and* anxiety will tend to avoid paying attention to any signs of emotion from another person, such as angry *or* happy facial expressions (Dewitte & De Houwer, 2008).

Other research uses increasingly ingenious methods to demonstrate how attachment styles are invoked unconsciously. In one study, participants

---

[6] Paul Simon wrote a song called "I Am a Rock," with the refrain "I am a rock, I am an island." If you know the song, this would be a good time to hum it to yourself.

were shown on a computer screen either a neutral word (*hat*) or a threatening word (*failure*) subliminally, meaning too fast for them to read these words consciously (Mikulincer, Gillath, & Shaver, 2002, Study I).[7] Then they were asked to indicate on the keyboard, as quickly as possible, whether each string in a series of letter strings consisted of words or nonwords—and they were told that proper names counted as words. Some of the words presented to them were names of people to whom the participants were emotionally attached (according to a questionnaire they completed earlier), while other names were of people with whom they were acquainted but to whom they were not emotionally attached. The results showed that people recognized the names of attachment figures more quickly in the threat condition than in the neutral condition; this was not true for other acquaintances. The conclusion of the study was that when people feel threatened, even by the subliminal presentation of a word with unpleasant connotations, they respond by thinking of the people to whom they are emotionally attached. In other words, we go to our attachment figures when we feel under threat, and if they are not physically present, we go to them in our minds.

> We go to our attachment figures when we feel under threat, and if they are not physically present, we go to them in our minds.

Attachment theory, originated by a psychoanalyst who considered himself a neo-Freudian (Bowlby), has diverged a long way from its psychoanalytic roots. Indeed, some would argue it is no longer Freudian (Kihlstrom, 1994), although attachment theorists themselves tend to disagree (Shaver & Mikulincer, 2005). Attachment theory provides an an example of how far a group of creative psychologists can develop a basic Freudian idea. In this case, the Freudian idea is that, via transference, early relationships with parents form a template for future emotionally important relationships throughout life. Notice, too, how attachment theory provides yet another example of Freud's doctrine of opposites. There are two ways for an emotional attachment style to go wrong—too clingy or too dismissive. The ideal is in the middle, as always.

PSYCHOANALYSIS IN PERSPECTIVE

It is not easy to come to an overall evaluation of psychoanalytic thought. Freud's theory, developed and amended over several decades, is compli-

---

[7] This study was conducted in Israel, and the words were in Hebrew.

cated enough. Add in Jung, Adler, the neo-Freudians, over 6,000 studies of object relations, and the burgeoning field of attachment theory, and there is clearly no simple answer to the question of whether the psychoanalytic perspective is valid. *Which* psychoanalytic perspective? I suggest you consider carefully what you have learned in this and the previous two chapters and do some extra reading of your own, so you can come to your own conclusions about which psychoanalytic ideas make sense.

A few years ago, analyst and psychologist Drew Westen (1998) made a valuable contribution toward coming to terms with psychoanalysis. Earlier in this chapter, we considered his idea that several common research topics are a "little bit" psychoanalytic, even if the studies don't acknowledge any debt to Freud. After reviewing a large amount of this research, Westen concluded that at least five neo-Freudian propositions have been firmly established:

1. Much of mental life, including thoughts, feelings, and motives, is unconscious, which is why people sometimes behave in ways they do not understand.
2. The mind does many things at once and so can be in conflict with itself. For example, it is not unusual to want two contradictory things at the same time, and the competing desires are not necessarily conscious.
3. The events of childhood shape the personality of the adult, especially concerning styles of social relationships (e.g., attachment).
4. Relationships formed with significant other people—such as one's parents—establish patterns that repeat throughout life with new people.
5. Psychological development involves moving from an unregulated, immature, and self-centered state to a more regulated, mature state in which relationships become increasingly important.

Not everybody in psychology believes these five conclusions, or even considers all of them relevant to psychoanalysis. As Freud foresaw, psychoanalysis seems doomed to be controversial, which means some researchers and theorists will always consider it not just wrong, but dead wrong.

As you reach your own conclusions, I would suggest you keep this point in mind: The criterion for evaluating the psychoanalytic approach (as well as each of the other approaches) is not whether it is right or wrong—it has been said that all theories are wrong in the end—or even whether it is scientific. Instead, evaluate it by asking, Does the approach raise questions you did not previously consider, and offer insight into things you did not understand as well before? On those questions, I suspect, psychoanalytic theory will earn better than a passing grade.

SUMMARY

- Freud died more than half a century ago, but his theory lives on and continues to stimulate controversy and argument.

Interpreting Freud

- Many modern writers have altered Freud's ideas in various degrees through their summaries and interpretations.

Latter-Day Issues and Theorists

- In addition, neo-Freudian theorists proposed their own versions of psycho-analysis. Most of these revised theories include less emphasis on sex and more emphasis on ego functioning and interpersonal relations.

- Alfred Adler wrote about adult strivings to overcome early childhood feelings of inferiority.

- Carl Jung proposed ideas concerning the collective unconscious; the outer, social version of the self called the persona; the concepts of animus and anima, the distinction between extraversion and introversion, and four basic types of thinking.

- Karen Horney developed a neo-Freudian theory of feminine psychology and also described the nature of basic anxiety and associated neurotic needs.

- Erik Erikson developed a detailed description of the stages of psychosocial development during which children and adults must come to terms with their changing life circumstances. Unlike Freud, Erikson extended his account of development through adulthood and old age.

- The object relations theorists, notably Melanie Klein and D. W. Winnicott, described the complex relationships people have with important emotional objects; they also observed that these relationships mix pleasure and pain, and love and hate. It is difficult to relate to other people as whole and complex human beings, and people often feel guilty about their mixed emotions and need to defend against them.

Current Psychoanalytic Research

- Modern psychologists interested in psychoanalysis are bringing rigorous research methodology to bear on some of the hundreds of hypotheses that could be derived from psychoanalytic theory. Evidence has supported some of these hypotheses, such as the existence of unconscious mental processes and phenomena like repression and transference.

- A particularly fruitful area of research is attachment theory, which examines the connection between childhood patterns of attachment and adult patterns of romantic love and other relationships.

- The three basic attachment styles—anxious-ambivalent, avoidant, and secure— have important implications for interpersonal life, emotional experience, and mental health.

- Experimental research shows that when people feel threatened, they will go to their attachment figures, and if these figures are not physically available, they will go to them in their minds.

Psychoanalysis in Perspective

- In the end, psychoanalysis might best be evaluated not in terms of the answers it has offered, but in terms of the questions it continues to raise.

THINK ABOUT IT

1. Why does Freudian theory make some people so angry? Is this reaction justified? For example, Freudian theory is undeniably sexist. Is this a legitimate cause for anger?
2. Does psychoanalysis overestimate the importance of sex? How far-reaching are the effects of sex on human life?
3. Why might one buy a vehicle such as a Humvee? Is it possible that buyers might not know all of their reasons for wanting such a vehicle? Have you seen advertisements that seem to target hidden motives for buying things?
4. Have you noticed that the same character types tend to show up in books, movies, and television programs? What are some examples? Could Jung's idea of a collective unconscious have anything to do with this?
5. Are people the age of your parents (or professors) still growing and changing? In what ways? Do you see psychological differences, for example, between people the age of your parents and people the age of your grandparents?
6. Must love always be mixed somewhat with frustration and resentment (as object relations theorists claim)?

7. Do you know anybody who brought a transitional object with them to college? What purpose does it serve? Would the person be upset if the object was lost? Why?
8. Is it possible to prove psychoanalytic ideas right or wrong using experiments?
9. Can you think of (anonymous) examples of people who fit any of the three attachment styles?

SUGGESTED READINGS

Bettelheim, B. (1988). *A good enough parent*. New York: Vintage.

A fascinating look at child rearing from a psychoanalytic point of view, by one of the more important psychoanalysts of the latter 21st century. It is never blindly orthodox and is filled with nuggets of wisdom that would interest any parent.

Block, J. (2002). *Personality as an affect-processing system: Toward an integrative theory*. Mahwah, NJ: Erlbaum.

A brilliant summary of a model of personality that integrates fundamental tenets of psychoanalytic thought with the state of the art in modern personality research.

Shaver, P. R., & Mikulincer, M. (2005). Attachment theory and research: Resurrection of the psychodynamic approach to personality. *Journal of Research in Personality, 39,* 22–45.

A fairly brief but remarkably thorough summary of the argument that attachment theory can integrate psychoanalysis with a wide range of modern research in cognitive, social, developmental, and personality psychology. The article includes clear summaries of important recent experiments that are beginning to make psychoanalytic ideas increasingly susceptible to empirical investigation.

Westen, D. (1998). The scientific legacy of Sigmund Freud: Toward a psychodynamically informed psychological science. *Psychological Bulletin, 124,* 333–371.

A thorough and highly readable summary of the modern research evidence that supports many of Freud's key ideas.

EMEDIA

Ⓢ **Go to StudySpace, wwnorton.com/studyspace,** to access additional review and enrichment materials.

PART V

EXPERIENCE AND AWARENESS:
Humanistic and Cross-Cultural Psychology

Individuals have different points of view. Fans of opposing teams who watch the same game may come away with drastically different impressions of who fouled whom and which side the referees favored (Hastorf & Cantril, 1954). Or, more consequential, where one person sees a woman exercising a free choice about whether her circumstances are right to start a family, another person observing exactly the same behavior may see the murder of an unborn child.

Humanistic psychology, the subject of Chapter 13, is based on the premise that to understand a person you must understand her unique view of reality. It focuses on phenomenology, which comprises everything a person hears, feels, and thinks, and which is at the center of her humanity and may even be the basis of free will. The other basic approaches to personality tend to regard people, at least implicitly, almost like things that can be dispassionately examined under the psychological microscope. Humanistic psychology emphasizes that the object of the psychologist's scrutiny is a fellow human who can scrutinize right back and form her own opinions. Even more centrally, humanistic psychology emphasizes how people feel, think, experience, and choose, and the ways that these activities make the study of the human mind unique.

Because humanistic psychologists emphasize the part of psychology that is uniquely human, they pay particular attention to a question that other psychologists generally ignore: the meaning of life. One view is that people are essentially selfish and life itself is intrinsically meaningless. A more cheerful view is that people are basically good and they attain meaning in life by rising above selfish concerns, serving others, and making the world a better place.

Humanistic psychology has evolved in an interesting way toward an increased emphasis on the latter, optimistic view—to the extent that many of its modern proponents travel under the banner of "positive psychology." A prime concern of positive psychology is one particular aspect of phenomenology: happiness. Among the insights from this area of psychology is that two people in the same objective circumstances may vary greatly in how happy they are, which goes back to the fundamental phenomological principle that reality is what you make it.

Phenomenological considerations also raise this interesting question: If everybody's view of the world is different, which one is right? Or, in the midst of shifting perceptions, where is reality? The question turns out to be unanswerable, but it is critical nonetheless. Asking this question acknowledges that none of us has an exclusive ownership of truth, and that other points of view—even those that seem drastically different, foreign, or strange—may have an equal claim to validity.

This latter insight is the basis of the cross-cultural study of personality, the topic of Chapter 14. Not only do different individuals have different views of reality, but different cultures do too. A behavior seen as polite by a Japanese may seem frustratingly inefficient to a North American, and the same action considered ordinary by a North American may seem deeply immoral to an Indian. In recent years, psychologists have paid increasing attention to the degree to which theories of personality forged in Western cultures do or do not apply to people around the world. Cross-cultural psychologists also address a further key question raised by the phenomenological approach to personality: If different cultures have different worldviews, what happens to values? Who is to judge what is right and what is wrong?

The following two chapters, therefore, address the same phenomenological premise—that the way you experience the world is the most important psychological fact about you. Chapter 13 examines this premise at the individual level, and Chapter 14 examines the same idea at the cultural level. Both approaches pose the challenge of trying to see the world the same way as someone else— whether a close friend or a member of a different culture. From a humanistic, phenomenological perspective, this is the only way to understand a person.

13

EXPERIENCE, EXISTENCE, AND THE MEANING OF LIFE:
Humanistic and Positive Psychology

The story is told of how Watergate burglar G. Gordon Liddy liked to impress people by holding his hand steadily above a lit candle as his flesh burned. "How can you do that? Doesn't it hurt?" he was asked. "Of course it hurts. The trick," he replied, "is not to care."[1]

PSYCHOLOGY IS A FUNNY KIND of science, because the object of its scrutiny is also the one doing the scrutinizing. Psychologists typically do the best they can to ignore this little complication. Instead, they try to think about people and the human mind as interesting phenomena that can be examined from a distance in the same dispassionate, objective, and precise way that one might examine a rock, a mollusk, or a molecule. Psychologists are eager to have the prestige of "real" scientists, and psychology is even sometimes accused of suffering from "physics envy." Not all psychologists envy physicists, but many do believe that the best way to understand the human mind is by copying the physical and biological sciences and their principles of public data, objective analysis, repeatability, and so on.

---

[1] I heard this existential fable from Lily Tomlin, who told it during a performance of *The Search for Signs of Intelligent Life in the Universe*, a play by Jane Wagner. Ms. Tomlin seems reliable on other matters, so perhaps this story is true.

The contradiction built in to this approach was caricatured by the humanistic psychologist George Kelly:

> I, being a psychologist, and therefore a scientist, am performing this experiment in order to improve the prediction and control of certain human phenomena; but my subject, being merely a human organism, is obviously propelled by inexorable drives welling up within him, or else he is in gluttonous pursuit of sustenance and shelter. (Kelly, 1955, p. 5)

The goal of **humanistic psychology** is to overcome this paradox by acknowledging and addressing the ways in which the field of psychology is unique. The classic humanistic psychologists vehemently disagreed with the idea that the study of the mind is just another science, or that it could or should resemble physics or chemistry. As an object of study, they argued, the mind is not just different from things such as molecules or atoms, it is fundamentally different.

It is fundamentally different because the human mind is aware. It knows it is being studied and has opinions about itself that affect the way it is studied. This fact has two implications. First, psychology needs to address this unique phenomenon of awareness rather than brushing it under the rug. Second, and even more important, self-awareness brings to the fore many uniquely human phenomena that do not arise when the object of study is a rock, a molecule, or even another animal. These phenomena include willpower, reflective thinking, imagination, introspection, self-criticism, aspirations, creativity, happiness, and above all, free will. Self-awareness makes these possible, and, interestingly, the rest of psychology tends to ignore these topics (Maddi & Costa, 1972; Seligman & Csikszentmihalyi, 2000). That is where the humanistic psychologists come in. Their job, as they see it, is to seek to understand awareness, free will, happiness, and the many related aspects of the mind that are uniquely human and that give life meaning. But what is self-awareness? What is free will? What is happiness? And, most difficult of all, what is the meaning of life? These weighty questions of humanistic psychology are the topics of this chapter.

"The meaning of life is cats."

[handwritten margin notes: "believe that the mind is fundamentally different (because aware) it is"]

[handwritten margin notes: "self awareness makes that / quality possible"]

PHENOMENOLOGY: AWARENESS IS EVERYTHING

The central insight of humanistic psychology is that one's conscious experience of the world, also called a person's **phenomenology**, is psychologically more important than the world itself. And that summary may be an understatement. Proponents of phenomenological approaches to psychology sometimes assume that immediate, conscious experience is all that matters. Everything that has happened to you in the past, everything that is true about you now, and anything that might happen in the future can influence you only by affecting your thoughts and feelings at this moment. Indeed, from a phenomenological viewpoint, the only place and time in which you exist is in your consciousness, here, right now. The past, the future, other people, and other places are no more than ideas and, in a sense, illusions. The sense is this: A broader reality might exist, but only the part of it that you perceive—or invent—will ever matter to you. Your hand might be on fire, but the trick, as G. Gordon Liddy observed, is not to care. More importantly, the realization that only your present experience matters is the basis of free will. The past is gone and the future is not here yet. You are here now and can *choose* what to think, feel, and do.

This may all sound rather New Age, but phenomenological analysis is not a new idea. The Talmud says, "We do not see things as they are. We see them as we are." Epictetus, a Greek Stoic philosopher who lived two thousand years ago, said, "It is not things in themselves that trouble us, but our opinions of things." Likewise, Marcus Aurelius, the Roman emperor and general who seems to have been one of G. Gordon Liddy's role models, wrote, "If you are distressed by anything external, the pain is not due to the thing itself, but to your estimate of it; and this you have the power to revoke at any moment." More recently, but still more than half a century ago, Carl Rogers (1951, p. 484) wrote, "I do not react to some absolute reality, but to my perception of this reality. It is this perception which for me is reality" (see McAdams, 1990).

choosing positive or negative

Your particular experience of the world is called your **construal**. Your construals, which are different from everybody else's, form the basis of how you live your life, including the goals you pursue and the obstacles and opportunities you perceive. A chance to travel opens exciting possibilities and raises significant risks. The development of a new relationship can be the first step toward an emotionally happy life or a possible path toward rejection and despair. The positive and negative views each have an element of truth, so the choice between them is yours. It is by choosing your construal of the world—deciding how to interpret your experience—that you can achieve free will (Boss, 1963). And it is by leaving this choice to other people or to society that you lose your autonomy. (I will say more about this later.)

These observations imply that psychology has a special duty to study how people perceive, understand, and experience reality. In 19th-century Leipzig, Germany, Wilhelm Wundt founded one of the first psychological laboratories. The primary method he followed was **introspection**, in which his research assistants tried to observe their own perceptions and thought processes (Wundt, 1894). But the roots of psychology's interest in phenomenology go back even further, to the existential philosophers.

EXISTENTIALISM

Existentialism is a broad philosophical movement that began in Europe in the mid-1800s. Søren Kierkegaard, the Danish theologian, was one of its early proponents, as were Friedrich Nietzsche, Martin Heidegger, and more recently Ludwig Binswanger, Medard Boss, and Jean-Paul Sartre.

Existentialism arose as a reaction against European rationalism, science, and the industrial revolution. The existentialists thought that by the late 19th century, rationality had gone too far in its attempt to account for everything. In particular, they thought science, technology, and rational philosophy had lost touch with human experience. This point of view began to catch on among European philosophers after World War II, which seemed to have disproved much of what they previously had thought was true about human nature and the meaning of life. The purpose of existential philosophy was to regain contact with the experience of being alive and aware.

Existential analysis begins with the concrete and specific experience of a human being *existing* at a particular moment in time and space. An excel-

lent example is you, right now. (I mean, then, back when you read the words "right now," although that is already past, so maybe we should concentrate on right *now*, instead. Oops, too late.) The point is, your experience of existence happens one infinitesimally small moment at a time, which is then gone and followed by another.

The key existential questions are: What is the nature of existence? How does it feel? And what does it mean?

The Three Parts of Experience

According to the existential psychologist Ludwig Binswanger, if you look deeply into your own mind, you will find that the conscious experience of being alive has three components (Binswanger, 1958).

The first component is biological experience, or **Umwelt**, which consists of the sensations you feel by virtue of being a biological organism. Umwelt includes pleasure, pain, heat, cold, and all the bodily sensations. Poke your finger with a pin: The experience is Umwelt.

The second component is social experience, or **Mitwelt**, which consists of what you think and feel as a social being. Your emotions and thoughts about other people and the emotions and thoughts directed at you make up Mitwelt. Think about someone you love, fear, or admire. The experience is Mitwelt.

The third component is inner, psychological experience, or **Eigenwelt**. In a sense, this is the experience of experience itself. It consists of how you feel and think when you try to understand yourself, your own mind, and your own existence. Eigenwelt includes the experience of introspection (and we can presume that Binswanger himself felt it strongly when trying to figure out the components of experience). Try to watch your own mind having the experience of a pinprick, or the experience of love, or even the experience of reading this paragraph. When you observe your own mind and feelings in this way, the (often confusing) experience is Eigenwelt.

"Thrown-ness" and Angst

An important basis of your experience is your **thrown-ness**—Heidegger used the German word *Geworfenheit*. This term refers to the time, place, and circumstances into which you happened to be born (Heidegger, 1927/1962). Your experience clearly depends on whether you were "thrown" into a medieval slave society, or a 17th-century Native American society, or an early-21st-century industrialized society.

From an existential perspective, this last way of being thrown—yours—is particularly difficult. Existence in modern society is difficult because the world seems to have no overarching meaning or purpose. Religion plays a relatively small role compared with its role in the past. Its modern substitutes—science, art, and philosophy—have failed to provide an alternative worldview that can tell you the two things you most need to know:

1. Why am I here?
2. What should I be doing?

Indeed, according to existential philosophy, there are no answers to these two concerns beyond those you invent for yourself.

Failure to answer these questions leads to anxiety about the meaning of life and whether you are spending yours the right way. After all, life is short, and you get only one—waste it, and you waste everything. The unpleasant feelings caused by contemplating these concerns is called *existential anxiety*, or **Angst**. According to Sartre (1965), this Angst can be analyzed into three separate sensations: anguish, forlornness, and despair.

Every conscious human feels *anguish* because choices, though inevitable, are never perfect. A choice to do good in one way often leads to bad outcomes in other ways. For example, deciding to aid one person may leave others to suffer. Such trade-offs are inescapable, according to Sartre, so the resulting anguish is inescapable, too.

Furthermore, nothing and no one—no god, no unquestionable set of rules or values—can guide your choices or let you off the hook for what you have decided. Your choices are yours alone. (Sartre also says that even if there is a God who tells you what to do, you still must decide whether to do what God says—so you are still alone in your choice.) Furthermore, there is no escape from this existential solitude: There you remain, *forlorn*, alone with your existential choices.

Finally, any aware person realizes that many outcomes are beyond control, including some of the most important elements of life. For example, you cannot hope to change your fate and the fates of your loved ones. If you acknowledge this momentous and regrettable fact, you also will feel *despair* at your inability to change crucial aspects of the world. This inability, according to Sartre, only redoubles your responsibility to affect those aspects of the world that you can influence.

[Handwritten margin notes: "3 analyzations of angst 1) anguish 2) forlornness 3) despair" and "even if a god tells you what to do, you must still choose whether to do what they say."]

Bad Faith

What should you do about Angst and all of these other unpleasant-sounding experiences? According to existentialists such as Sartre, you must face them directly. It is a moral imperative, they believe, to face your own mortality and the apparent meaninglessness of life, and to seek purpose for your existence nonetheless. This is your existential responsibility, which requires existential courage, or what Sartre called *optimistic toughness* (1965, p. 49).

Of course, there is a way out, at least temporarily, that requires neither courage nor toughness: avoid the problem altogether. Quit worrying about what life means, get a good job, buy a big car, and advance your social status. Do not try to think for yourself. Instead, do as you are told by society, convention, your peer group, political propaganda, religious dogma, and advertising. Lead the unexamined life. Existentialists call this head-in-the-sand approach *living in bad faith*. Although the strategy of ignoring existential issues is very common, the existentialists point out that it has three problems.

The first problem, they say, is that to ignore these troubling facts of existence is to live a cowardly lie; it is immoral and amounts to selling your soul for comfort. You are given just one short life, and you are giving it up if you refuse to examine the substance and meaning of your experience. You might as well not be alive. Existentially speaking, you might as well be a rock.

In his novel *Cat's Cradle*, Kurt Vonnegut (1963) proposed that a human being is really no more than a pile of lucky mud. (After all, the human body is chemically not much different from the dirt it walks on, except that it is about 70 percent water). The only difference, says Vonnegut, is that this mass of mud is up and walking around. More important, it has awareness, so it can look around and experience the world. The other mud, that stuff underfoot, does not get to do that. It just lies there, ignorant of all the interesting things happening above.

And that is Vonnegut's good news. The bad news is that this luck cannot last. Sooner or later (at death), the chemicals that make up the body begin to break down and turn back into earth. The Bible says people come from the earth and return to it; that is Vonnegut's point as well.

Therefore, it is imperative not to waste this brief period of lucky awareness. As long as you are alive-and-aware mud, and not just regular mud, you must experience as much of the world as possible, as vividly as possible. In particular, you need to be aware of your luck and know it won't last—this is your only chance. The tragedy, from an existential perspective, is that many people never do this. They lead unexamined lives, never realizing how lucky they are to be alive and aware, and they eventually lose their awareness forever without realizing how special it was.

2) A second, more pragmatic problem with living in bad faith is that, even if you manage to ignore troubling existential issues by surrounding yourself with material comforts, you still will not be happy. Indeed, research shows that most people value a meaningful life more than being wealthy (L. A. King & Napa, 1998), and that experiences affect people's happiness more than possessions do (Van Boven, 2005).

The person who chooses the material path, therefore, might occasionally suffer from a tantalizing, frustrating glimpse of the more satisfying life that could have been if she made different choices. These dark moments of the soul may pass quickly, but until one owns up to existential responsibility and thinks seriously about what is really important, such moments will continue to sneak up when least expected.

3) The third problem with the ostrich approach to existential issues is that it is impossible, because choosing not to worry about the meaning of life and surrendering your choices to external authorities is still a choice. As Sartre (1965) put it, "What is not possible is not to choose. . . . If I do not choose, I am still choosing" (p. 54). Thus, there is no exit from the existential dilemma, even if you can fool yourself into thinking that there is.

Can't escape existential drama

Authentic Existence

The existentialists' preferred alternative to bad faith is to courageously come to terms with existence. Face the facts: You are mortal, your life is short, and you are master of your own destiny (within those limits). This approach, called *authentic existence* (Binswanger, 1963) entails being honest, insightful, and morally correct.

Authentic existence will not relieve you from loneliness and unhappiness; a courageous examination of conscious experience reveals the awful truth that every person is alone and doomed. Life has no meaning beyond what you give it, which means that any apparent meaning it might seem to have is an illusion. The essence of the human experience is this discovery: The human being is the only animal that understands it must die.

This is pretty stern stuff. Psychologists have noted that the terror inspired by the prospect of death can cause people to distort reality in many different ways in order to feel better (Pyszczynski et al., 1997), and may be the basis of culture itself as "humans must balance a propensity for life with an awareness of the inevitability of death" (Matsumoto, 2006, pp. 35–36). In other words, existentialism is not for wimps (McAdams, 1990). It takes moral courage to cast aside defense mechanisms and the veneer of culture, and peer into the void of mortality and meaninglessness. When the existentialist philosopher Friedrich Nietzsche did this, he decided the most honorable response was to rise above it all and become a *superman*. Nietzsche's superman did not wear a cape and tights, however. Instead, his ideal person sought to triumph over the apparent meaninglessness of life by developing the existential strength to face what must be faced. This is easier said than done. Neitzsche never managed to become a superman himself; instead, he went insane and died in an asylum.

"*What is this endless series of meaningless experiences trying to teach me?*"

Metzsche = superman theory,

Jean-Paul Sartre tried to be both more realistic and a little more optimistic. He sometimes expressed annoyance with people who considered existentialism gloomy, although one wonders what else he could expect, given his claim that the basic elements of existence are anguish, forlornness, and despair. Sartre lightened this load a little with his claim that only through existential analysis can people regain awareness of their freedom. He wrote that existential theory "is the only one which gives man dignity, the only one which does not reduce him to an object" (Sartre, 1965, p. 51). He believed that the existential challenge is to do all you can to better the human condition, even in the face of life's uncertainties.

—Frankel

A similar lesson was offered by the existential philosopher Viktor Frankl (1959/1992), who advised that you can become stronger in the face of difficult circumstances if, instead of asking, "What do I want from life?" you can move to asking, "What does life want from me?" Frankl's advice has some empirical support. One study found that people who endorsed statements such as "I strive to make this world a better place" and "I accept my limitations" felt more hope and less depression over the following two months (Mascaro & Rosen, 2005). They also were more likely to report that they had "found a really significant meaning for leading my life." This finding offers a place where philosophy, psychology, and the teachings of many religious traditions come together: Sometimes the best thing you can do for yourself is to do something for somebody else.

Sometimes the best thing you can do for yourself is to do something for somebody else.

The Eastern Alternative

The core view of the European existentialists summarized so far in this chapter seems rather gloomy, given the way it harps on individual isolation, mortality, and the difficulty of finding meaning in life. Whatever you think of this philosophy, it is worth noticing that it is fundamentally European, Western, and focused on the individual. We will consider cultural differences between Eastern and Western points of view in Chapter 14, but for now just notice how existentialism begins with the experience of the single individual at a single moment in time. All else, it claims, is illusion. The fundamental reality is your own experience at this moment—the past, the future, and the experiences of other people are forever closed off.

From the perspective of the Eastern religions that influence most of the people on earth (such as in China, India, and Japan) and that are often associated with collectivist cultures, this analysis is fundamentally wrong. Consider Zen Buddhism (see Rahula, 1974; Mosig, 1989, 1999). The key idea of Buddhism is **anatta**, or "nonself," the idea that the independent, singular self you sense inside your mind is merely an illusion. The French philosopher René Descartes believed that the existence of his own singular self was the one thing he could be sure of; Buddhism teaches that he was overconfident. What feels like your "self" is merely a temporary composite of many things—including your physiology, environment, social setting, and society—all of which are constantly changing. There is no unchanging soul at the center of all this, just a momentary coming together of all these influences that, in the next moment, is gone, only to be replaced by another. Gertrude Stein once said of Oakland, California, "There's no there there." That's what the Buddha says about the self.

Furthermore, Buddhism teaches that this illusion of having a separate and independent self is harmful. It leads to feelings of isolation—such as tormented the existentialists—and an excessive concern with "me" and that which is "mine." The true nature of reality is that everything and everyone are interconnected now and not only in this moment but also across time. It is not true, according to Buddhism, that all you have is your own experience, now. Rather, there is nothing special about your experience or about the moment labeled "the present." All consciousness and all of time have equal claim to existence and are equally important, and time flows not from past to present to future, but from present to present to present (Yozan Mosig, personal communication, November 6, 2000). In a similar fashion, a single person is just one of many. Your existence is no more or less real or important than anyone else's. The more important fact is that all people are interconnected.

This viewpoint might seem to diminish the importance of the self, but in a way it enhances it. The Buddhist view implies that instead of being forever alone and powerless, you are an integral and interconnected part of the universe and it is part of you, just as the present moment is made of equal parts past and future. Moreover, you are immortal in the sense that you are part of something larger than yourself that will last forever.

If you can begin to grasp these ideas, your selfish thoughts and fears about the future will fall away. You will understand the idea of **anicca**, that nothing lasts forever and it is best to accept this fact instead of fighting it. The current moment is not particularly important; all moments in the past and future have equal status. The well-being of others is just as important as your own, because the boundaries between you and them are illusory. These are difficult ideas to grasp, especially for persons raised in Western cultures, and true understanding can be the work of a lifetime. If you do achieve it, you are said to be *enlightened*. Enlightenment is manifested by caring for others the same as for yourself, which leads to universal compassion; according to Buddhism, this is the essence of wisdom and leads to a serene, selfless state called **nirvana**. This sure beats anguish, forlornness, and despair.

OPTIMISTIC HUMANISM: ROGERS AND MASLOW

America has a reputation—partially deserved—of being a cultural melting pot. So, perhaps it was only natural that two American psychologists would mix European existential philosophy, the less isolated Eastern view of the self, and a stereotypically American can-do attitude to yield an optimistic philosophy of life. Beginning in the early 1950s, Carl Rogers and Abraham Maslow developed related approaches to humanistic psychology. They began with the standard existential assumptions that phenomenology is central and that people have free will, and then added another crucial idea—that people are basically good: They seek to relate closely with one another, and they have an innate need to improve themselves and the world. It is important to bear in mind that this optimistic view is an added *assumption*; Rogers, Maslow, and other humanists believe it but can offer no proof. What kind of evidence would be relevant? All theories begin with assumptions though, and this one is not particularly extreme. So let us take a closer look at humanistic psychology and see where it leads.

[handwritten: phenomenology + free will + assumption that people are basically good]

Self-Actualization: Rogers

Carl Rogers changed the tone and much of the message of the classic existential and phenomenological analysis when he proposed that "the organism [by which he means any person] has one basic tendency and striving—to actualize, maintain, and enhance the experiencing organism [itself]" (Rogers, 1951, p. 487). According to Rogers's theory, a person can be understood only from the perspective of her *phenomenal field*, which is the entire panorama of conscious experience. This is where everything comes together—unconscious conflicts, environmental influences, memories, hopes, and so on. These mental experiences combine in different ways at every moment of a person's life, and these combinations give rise to the person's ongoing conscious experience. So far, this resembles the standard phenomenological fare we considered earlier.

Rogers added a new aspect, however, when he posited that people have a basic need to *actualize*, that is, to maintain and enhance life. (This need has much in common with Freud's notion of libido as it was interpreted in Chapter 10.) The goal of existence is to satisfy this need. This assumption led Rogers to differ sharply with traditional existentialists who believed that existence has no intrinsic goal.

the intrinsic goal of existence

The Hierarchy of Needs: Maslow

Abraham Maslow wrote at about the same time as Rogers and was almost equally influential (e.g., Maslow, 1987). His theory of humanistic psychology begins with the same basic assumption: A person's ultimate need or motive is to self-actualize. However, Maslow claimed that this motive becomes active only if the person's more basic needs are met first. According to Maslow, human motivation is characterized by a *hierarchy of needs* (see Figure 13.1). First, a person requires food, water, safety, and the other essentials of survival. When those are in hand, the person then seeks sex, meaningful relationships, prestige, and money. Only when those desires are satisfied does the person turn to the quest for self-actualization. In other words, someone starving to death is not particularly concerned with the higher aspects of existence. In this belief, Maslow is also at odds with traditional existentialists, who would believe that even an individual who is starving has free choice in what to concern himself with.

Maslow's theory has practical applications in areas such as career choice and employee motivation. Consider your own ambitions: What kind of

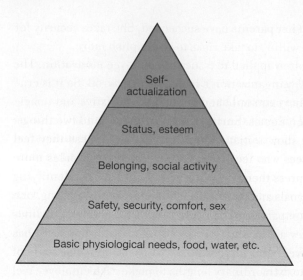

Figure 13.1 Maslow's Hierarchy of Needs As an individual's needs lower in the pyramid are fulfilled, the higher needs become more important.

career are you seeking? My parents grew up during the Great Depression of the 1930s and remained acutely aware of the dangers of being unemployed, homeless, and even starving—not that any of this ever happened to them, but they had lived through an era during which these outcomes were a real possibility for an unusually large number of Americans. As a result, like others of their generation, they put a premium on finding a career path that was, above everything else, safe. Making a lot of money was not the issue; rather, choosing a field where "you can always get a job," as they repeatedly said, was the way to ensure survival and stability. My father dreamed of being an architect. For most of his career, he worked as an accountant.

You can imagine their reaction when they found out I declared a psychology major! But the reason I felt free to do this was precisely because of their success: The issues of homelessness and survival they faced never seemed real to me. I took that level of security for granted, which, in Maslow's terms, freed me to move up the hierarchy of needs and choose a field based on its possibilities for self-expression.

At the university where I teach, a large number of students are children of first- or second-generation immigrants; many are from Asia or Mexico. Their situation is not very different from mine at their age. Their parents took risks to come to America in search of opportunity and financial security. And, like my parents, many of my students' parents do not quite understand why their children would choose a major as seemingly impractical as psychology. But again, when a child of immigrant parents chooses a career because of its opportunities for self-expression rather than financial security, this is evidence that her parents have succeeded. She takes security for granted and is therefore willing to take risks to accomplish more.

Maslow's theory is often applied to issues of employee motivation. The most expensive part of any organization's budget is its payroll. So it is crucial that employees go that extra mile and apply their initiative and imagination to the organization's goals. Smart managers understand two things: (a) Employees will not show initiative and imagination unless they feel secure, and (b) employees who feel secure want something besides more money—they want to express themselves through their work by identifying with the organization's goals and contributing to them. At this writing, one of the most successful companies in the United States is Southwest Airlines (and it is one of very few airlines not on the brink of bankruptcy). It has never laid off an employee. And while it does not pay as much as some of its competitors, it goes to extraordinary lengths to make each employee feel like a valuable part of the organization, with everything from regular company parties to open meetings with management where employees at any level can make suggestions to the boss. Most companies are less insightful and follow the conventional model: (a) When in doubt, lay off more people, and (b) if the remaining employees feel overworked and underappreciated, pay them more.

The hierarchy of needs can also be used to explain how people in different cultures may have different bases of happiness. According to one study of 39 nations (including more than 54,000 survey participants), financial status was associated with life satisfaction more often in poorer nations, whereas in richer nations one's home life was more important (Oishi, Diener, Lucas, & Suh, 1999). To be exact, according to a meta-analysis that summarized many different studies, in poorer countries the average correlation (see Chapter 3) between well-being and economic status was $r = .28$, and in richer countries the average was only $r = .10$ (Howell & Howell, 2008). These findings demonstrate one of Maslow's key points: Money is most important when you have very little. After a certain point, it begins to become irrelevant to happiness (though we often seek it anyway); our emotional needs and, in particular, our relationships with others grow to matter much more.

The Fully Functioning Person

Maslow and Rogers believed that the best way to live is to become more clearly aware of reality and of yourself. If you can perceive the world accurately and without neurotic distortion, and if you take responsibility for your choices, then you become what Rogers called a *fully functioning person*, who lives what the existentialists would call an authentic existence—except that the fully functioning person is happy. A fully func-tioning person faces the world without fear, self-doubt, or neurotic defenses. Doing this becomes possible only if you have experienced *unconditional positive regard* from the important people in your life, especially during childhood. Maslow disagreed slightly; he believed that anybody from any background could become a fully functioning person. However, if you feel that other people value you only if you are smart, successful, attractive, or good, then according to Rogers, you will develop *conditions of worth*.

> A fully functioning person faces the world without fear, self-doubt, or neurotic defenses.

— limit are freedom

Conditions of worth limit your freedom to act and think. If you believe you are valuable only if certain things about you are true, then you may dis-tort your perception of reality to believe them, even if they are not true. If you think you are valuable only if your behavior conforms to certain rules and expectations, you may lose your ability to choose what to do. Both of these limitations violate the existential imperatives to see the world as it is, choose freely, and take complete responsibility for all of your actions.

A person who has experienced unconditional positive regard from par-ents and other important people in life does not develop such conditions of worth. This leads to a life that is free from existential anxiety, because that person is confident of her value. She does not need to follow rules, because her sense of innate goodness leads her to make the right choices. A fully functioning person lives a life rich in emotion and self-discovery, and such a person is reflective, spontaneous, flexible, adaptable, confident, trusting, creative, self-reliant, ethical, open-minded—you get the idea. She is also "more understanding of others and more accepting of others as separate individuals" (Rogers, 1951, p. 520).

Psychotherapy

The goal of Rogerian psychotherapy, and humanistic psychotherapy in gen-eral, is to help the client become a fully functioning person. To achieve this goal, the therapist develops a genuine and caring relationship with the client and provides unconditional positive regard (Levine, 2006). This technique is sometimes caricatured: The patient says something like, "I would really like to kill you with a knife," and the therapist—reluctant to impose condi-tions of worth—replies, "You feel you want to kill me with a knife. Uh huh."

Rogerian psychotherapy

Problems w Rogerian

This portrayal is probably unfair—Rogers once stated he would stop a murderer—but it captures the basic idea that, in his view, the therapist's job is (1) to help the client perceive his own thoughts and feelings without the therapist seeking to change them in any way, and (2) to make the client feel appreciated no matter what he thinks, says, or does. This process allows insight and the removal of conditions of worth, the theory goes, and helps the client become a fully functioning person.

Rogerian psychotherapy requires enormous amounts of time and, from the therapist, the patience (and perhaps the courage) of a saint. What is the result of this kind of therapy? Although research on the effects of psychotherapy is extraordinarily difficult to conduct, Rogers and his followers tried to document some of them.

In a typical study, each individual in a group of people about to begin psychotherapy and in a group of people uninterested in therapy was asked to describe first himself or herself and then the ideal person they would like to be. (Often these descriptions were rendered using the Q-sort technique described in Chapter 7.) The results showed that these two descriptions diverged more among those who felt they needed therapy. When the therapy group repeated this procedure after completing a program of Rogerian treatment, their real and ideal selves aligned more closely—although still not as closely as those of the people who did not seek therapy (Butler & Haigh, 1954).

Results like these—and they have been reported frequently over the years—show that Rogerian psychotherapy makes people feel they are becoming more like their ideal selves. But critics have noted two problems. First, the results seem to be about equally due to changes in clients' ideal views as to changes in their self-views. That is, the clients not only change what they think they themselves are like, but also change how they wish to be (Rudikoff, 1954). Second, describing oneself as highly similar to one's idea of a perfect person is not always a good measure of psychological adjustment. One study found that people afflicted with paranoid schizophrenia considered themselves close to ideal, and concluded that to employ a high correlation between the self and ideal-self conceptions "as a sole criterion of adjustment" would lead to the inappropriate categorization of many people, particularly those afflicted with paranoid schizophrenia, as well adjusted (I. Friedman, 1955, p. 614). There is more to mental health than believing you are the way you would most like to be (Wylie, 1974).

Despite this ambiguity about the outcome, Rogerian psychotherapy has contributed the influential idea that any psychotherapist's first job is to listen to the client. Although not all therapists would respond "uh huh" to statements like those mentioned earlier, the Rogerian example has influenced many therapists to be more patient in listening and more hesitant to impose their own values on their clients.

PERSONAL CONSTRUCTS: KELLY

Another important phenomenological psychologist, George Kelly, also thought that a person's individual experience of the world was the most important part of her psychology. As we have seen, individual construals of the world can be general (for example, Bob sees the world as an evil place) or specific (Maria sees parties as boring, or even, Maria saw last Saturday's party as boring). Kelly's unique contribution was to emphasize how one's *cognitive* (thinking) system assembles one's various construals of the world into individually held theories called *personal constructs*. These constructs, in turn, then help determine how new experiences are construed. Accordingly, Kelly's theory of personality is called *personal construct theory* (Kelly, 1955).

Sources of Constructs

Kelly viewed constructs as *bipolar dimensions* (scales ranging between one concept and its opposite, such as "good-bad") along which people or objects can be arranged. These constructs can include paired opposites of all sorts: for example, the idea of good versus bad (as just mentioned), large versus small, weak versus strong, or conservative versus liberal. If weak versus strong is one of your constructs, you might tend to see everything and everybody in terms of individual strength. Each person's cognitive system is made of a unique set of constructs.

An individual's personal construct system can be assessed in many ways, but Kelly favored a method called the Role Construct Repertory Test, or the Rep test for short. The Rep test asks you to identify three people who are or have been important in your life. Then it asks you to describe how any two of them seem similar to each other and different from the third. Then you follow the same process with three important ideas, three traits you admire, and so on. In each case, the question is the same: How are two of these similar to each other and different from the third?

Kelly believed that the ways you discriminate among these objects, people, and ideas reveal the constructs through which you view the world. For example, if you frequently state that two of the objects are strong whereas the third is weak (or vice versa), then strong versus weak is probably one of your personal constructs. Therefore, this dimension is an important part of how you frame reality because you use it to relate different aspects of the world.

Research by those publishing after Kelly has shown that particular constructs are more readily brought to mind in certain individuals. These have been called *chronically accessible constructs* (Bargh, Lombardi, & Higgins, 1988). For example, the idea of devastating failure might be chronically accessible to one person, so that, in everything he undertakes or even considers undertaking, the idea that it will all turn into a catastrophe is never far from his mind. For another person, the idea of interpersonal power might be chronically accessible, so that every relationship she observes or enters brings up the question, "Who is in charge here?" which frames her view of these relationships.

Where do these constructs come from? Kelly believed that they come from—but are not determined by—past experience. What does that mean? Kelly relied heavily on the metaphor that every person is, in a sense, a scientist: someone who obtains data and devises a theory to explain the data. But data never determine the scientist's theory; any pattern of data could fit at least two, and perhaps an infinite number, of alternative theories. (This observation comes from elementary philosophy of science.) Therefore, the scientist always *chooses* which theory to use. To be sure, science has developed rules, such as the *principle of parsimony* (also known as "Occam's razor"): the idea that all other things being equal, the simplest theory is the best. But these canons do not ensure the right choice—sometimes a more complex theory is accurate. To choose a theory, the scientist makes a judgment call.

Kelly believed that the sum of your experiences and perceptions provides the data you use to develop an interpretation, or theory, of what the world is like. This theory is your personal construct system, which becomes the framework for your perceptions and thoughts about the world. This system is determined not by your past experience, therefore, but your—freely chosen—interpretation of past experience. No matter what has happened to you, you *could* have chosen to draw different conclusions from it. In fact, you still can.

For example, suppose you had a miserable childhood; perhaps you were even abused. You could draw from this history a personal construct system that tells you the world is unalterably evil and abusive. That conclusion would fit the data of your life experience. Just as well, you could conclude that no matter what life throws at you, you will survive. That conclusion—since you did survive—also fits the data. Therefore, your conclusion and your worldview are up to you. To pick another example, suppose you are about to go on a job interview. This situation could be viewed in several different ways, all of which are, to some degree, accurate: an opportunity to show off your talents, a normal conversation, an exhausting ordeal, or a terrifying risk of utter humiliation and career destruction. Which construal will you pick? Your performance at the interview may depend on it.

A corollary of personal construct theory, which Kelly called the **sociality corollary**, holds that understanding another person means understanding her personal construct system; you must be able to look at the world through that person's eyes. Actions that appear incomprehensible or even evil can make sense, Kelly believed, if you can see them from the point of view of the person who chose them. In addition, he believed that the primary duty of a psychotherapist was leading the client to self-understanding, and he designed the Rep test as a tool to help psychotherapists do that.

Constructs and Reality

The basic lesson of Kelly's theory is that, depending on one's personal constructs, any pattern of experience can lead to numerous construals—perhaps infinitely many. That means you choose the construals you use; they are not forced on you, since others are equally possible. Kelly called this view *constructive alternativism*, which means that your personal reality does not simply exist apart from you; you construct it in your mind. Furthermore, you can always choose to reconstruct reality differently.

This lesson has far-reaching implications. Kelly's theory draws on a part of the philosophy of science that scientists themselves sometimes forget. *Scientific paradigms* are frameworks for construing the meaning of data. The basic approaches to personality considered in this book—trait, psychoanalytic, phenomenological, and so on—are paradigms in that sense. Each is sensible, I believe, and each is consistent with the data it regards as important, but each also represents a choice by the researcher to focus on some aspects of human psychology and ignore others. This fact implies two things about scientific paradigms: (1) The choice among them is not a matter of which is right and which are wrong, but rather which paradigm addresses the topic that interests the researcher; and (2) personality psychology needs all of them because each one leaves out something important.[2]

The same two lessons apply to many other systems of constructs, or paradigms. Almost everybody—scientist and layperson alike—has developed systems of belief that affect how they understand politics, morality, economics, and many other matters. These belief systems are useful and necessary, but a narrow-minded devotion to just one paradigm can make a person forget (or worse, deny) that other ways of constructing reality—other belief systems—are equally plausible.

My favorite example concerns the economic concept of opportunity costs, which in my opinion (based on my personal belief system) is one of the most harmful ideas ever invented. The concept deals with the question of what something costs. The layperson's answer is that the cost of something is the amount of resources required to get it. A different answer is taught in business schools: The cost of something is the difference between what it brings you and what you could have gained by spending your resources on something else. The difference between these two amounts is not your ordinary cost, but your *opportunity cost*.

These two definitions of cost derive from different construals of the goal of economic life. The first construes the goal as doing what you want as long as you can pay for it. This is sometimes called a "satisficing goal." The second maintains that you must maximize your gain, and that unless you make as much money as possible, you have failed. This is an "optimizing goal." Both goals are reasonable, and neither is intrinsically right or wrong. Yet business schools often teach that the second goal is sophisticated and correct, whereas the first is hopelessly naïve.

The consequences of such construals can be real and concrete. A few years ago, the *Boston Globe* published an article about a mom-and-pop grocery store located on the ground floor of a building in Boston's Beacon Hill, which has developed into a fashionable neighborhood. The grocer, who had been running the store there for decades, was being evicted. The longtime owner of the building discovered that he could command higher rent from a clothing boutique. When neighbors protested, the owner replied, apparently with a straight face, "I couldn't afford to keep that grocery store there any longer with property values so high."

---

[2] This does not mean that each paradigm can or should be applied simultaneously, which generally would lead to incoherence. Rather, the psychologist needs to apply the appropriate paradigm for the question at hand while keeping the rest in reserve, lest the question of interest change.

He may have believed what he said, but from another point of view this man's statement was absurd: As long as he could afford to keep the building, he could afford to keep the store. He never claimed the grocer paid him less than the owner needed in order to pay for the building or to live well himself. Rather, he focused on the fact that by evicting the grocer he could make more money, and thought of the difference between what he *was* making and what he *could* make as a "cost" that he could not "afford."

This viewpoint is the reverse of a silly commercial that ran on television a few years ago. The theme of the commercial was, "What will you do with all the money you save (by buying our car)?" In one ad, a happy woman declared that with the money she saved, she was "going to Hawaii!" I have news for this person: Nobody ever went to Hawaii with the money "saved" by buying a car. The news for the Boston landlord is that nobody ever went broke from opportunity costs. You can *choose* to think about situations this way, but you are kidding yourself if you think you are getting rich by spending money, or becoming poor by not collecting as much money as possible.

The Boston landlord and the car buyer in the commercial each absorbed a particular construct about money—and thought of that construct as real. But from the perspective of another construct system, the landlord's behavior was immoral, and the car buyer's was simply ridiculous. The choice of how to think about issues like these can have far-reaching psychological consequences. One study contrasted *maximizers*—people who believe one should also seek to get as much as one possibly can—with *satisficers* who believe that some outcomes, short of the maximum, are "good enough." Compared with maximizers, satisficers enjoy more happiness, optimism, and life satisfaction, while maximizers are prone to perfectionism, depression, and regret (B. Schwartz et al., 2002).

The moral of this story is that you should probably question the construals of reality taught in business school, in science classes, or anywhere else, including in this book. Other construals are always possible, and you have the ability, the right, and perhaps the duty to choose your own. How you choose to see the world will affect everything in your life.

Early in his career, Kelly learned something else fascinating about construals. He started out as a psychoanalyst practicing in Kansas, when he began to doubt some of the exotic Freudian interpretations he was offering to his plainspoken patients. As a little experiment, he began offering deliberately random or odd interpretations to see how his patients would react. To his astonishment, he reported that even these purposely bizarre interpretations seemed to be helpful! He concluded that the important aspect of psychotherapy was not the content of the intervention, but the therapist's role in getting the patient to construe reality in a different way (Kelly, 1969). Once the patient can do this, he can choose which construals work best and make the most sense, and is then on the way to recovery.

FLOW: CSIKSZENTMIHALYI

The heart of the phenomenological approach is the conscious experience of being alive, moment to moment. The research of Mihalyi Csikszentmihalyi[3] renews the focus on this fundamental concern (Csikszentmihalyi & Csikszentmihalyi, 1988). As a phenomenologist, Csikszentmihalyi believes that your moment-to-moment experience is what really matters in life; his concern is how to make the most of it. His work focuses on *optimal experience*—understanding it and achieving it.

Csikszentmihalyi investigated the experiences of artists, athletes, writers, and so forth, as they did what they enjoyed most. He concluded that the best way a person can spend time is in *autotelic* activities, those that are enjoyable for their own sake. The subjective experience of an autotelic activity—the enjoyment itself—is what Csikszentmihalyi calls **flow**.

Flow is not the same thing as joy, happiness, or other, more familiar terms for subjective well-being. Rather, the experience of flow is characterized by tremendous concentration, total lack of distractibility, and thoughts concerning only the activity at hand. One's mood is elevated slightly (although not to the point of anything like ecstasy), and time seems to pass very quickly. This is what is experienced—when all goes well—by a writer writing, a painter painting, a gardener gardening, or a baseball player waiting for the next pitch. Flow has been reported by surgeons, dancers, and chess players in the midst of intense matches. Computers induce flow in many people. Perhaps you have seen an individual playing video games far into the night, seemingly oblivious to any distraction or to the passage of time itself. That person is likely experiencing flow. I often experience flow when lecturing to a class and sometimes while writing. To me, a 50-minute class feels as if it ends about a minute and a half after it begins. (I know it does not feel this way to my students.) Losing track of time is one sign of experiencing flow.

According to Csikszentmihalyi, flow arises in your activity when the challenges it presents are well matched with your skills. If an activity is too

---

[3] Pronounced "chick-*sent*-me-high," with the emphasis on the second syllable.

difficult or too confusing, you will experience anxiety, worry, and frustration. If the activity is too easy, you will experience boredom and (again) anxiety. But when skills and challenges are balanced, you experience flow. Achieving flow also entails staying away from television. Csikszentmihalyi found that watching television disrupts and prevents flow for long periods of time. Some people find that spending time on the Internet can induce flow, but it depends on what you do there.

> Achieving flow entails staying away from television.

Certain immersive games may put a person in flow, as was mentioned above, but the typical experience in online shopping does not. Online shopping is not challenging enough for flow, which implies that if web marketers were clever enough to turn the shopping experience into an immersive game, they could increase their sales immensely (Hoffman & Novak, 2009).

Csikszentmihalyi thinks that the secret for enhancing your quality of life is to spend as much time in flow as possible. Achieving flow entails becoming good at something you find worthwhile and enjoyable. This seems like a decent prescription for happiness, come to think of it, whether you are a phenomenologist or not.

On the other hand, flow does not work for everybody. According to one study, only people high in *locus of control*, who believe they can control their own life outcomes, benefit from activities meant to promote flow (J. Keller & Blomann, 2008). Even in the best of circumstances, flow seems to describe a rather solitary kind of happiness. In that respect Csikszentmihalyi is a true existentialist, perhaps not dwelling on forlornness like Sartre, but still regarding experience as something that happens alone. (Csikszentmihalyi does describe flow as it can occur during sex, but even here he emphasizes the experience of one individual.) The drawback with flow is that somebody experiencing it can be difficult to interact with; she may not hear you, may seem distracted, and in general may be poor company. Interrupt somebody engrossed in a novel or a video game, and you will see what I mean.

HARDINESS: MADDI

Stress has become a bad word. Many people, including psychologists, talk about the fact that the modern world is full of stress, assess the harm that stress inflicts on health and psychological well-being, and seek ways to avoid stress. According to the modern humanistic psychologist Salvatore Maddi (e.g., 2003), this is all wrong. Without stress, he argues, life would be boring and meaningless. Even worse, he says, is that so many people seek to avoid stress by developing a conformist lifestyle driven by the expectations of other people and of society (Maddi, 1985): Get an easy, well-paid (albeit boring) job, hang out with people just like you, and be sure to talk only to people you already agree with.

Despite the seeming safety and comfort of this lifestyle, Maddi believes it is likely to lead to a kind of existential psychological pathology that resembles Sartre's description of bad faith presented earlier in this chapter. In the words of another humanistic psychologist, R. D. Laing (1959), a conformist lifestyle leads to the development of a false self in which "an individual's acts are no longer self-expressions" (p. 94). According to Maddi, the most severe kind of existential pathology is *vegetativeness*, in which the person feels that nothing has meaning and so becomes listless and aimless. Slightly less severe, and more common, is *nihilism*, in which experience is dominated by anger, disgust, and cynicism. Do you know anyone who constantly seeks out the negative, and reacts with disdain and sarcasm to anybody with optimistic expectations or a positive thought? Your chronically negative acquaintance may suffer from existential nihilism. (Whatever you do, don't tell him this.)

Another potential side effect of the conformist lifestyle is an adventurousness in which only extreme thrills manage to garner one's full attention and distract from deep feelings of meaninglessness. This kind of "adventurousness"—perhaps too positive a word—can lead to promiscuous sex, drug use, and other dangerous activities. Whatever form these activities take, their purpose is the same: to conceal the emptiness at the center of life.

Maddi's prescription for curing this bad faith is to develop what he calls *hardiness*, a lifestyle that embraces rather than avoids potential sources of stress. Properly approached, stressful and challenging experiences can bring learning, growth, and wisdom, and dealing with them successfully is an important part of what gives life meaning (L. A. King, 2001). Maddi's research team has developed self-report scales to measure hardiness, and has shown that hardy people are generally healthier and better adjusted psychologically, even under stressful circumstances (Maddi et al., 2002). Maddi even helped set up a Hardiness Institute (in Newport Beach, CA), to teach people how to handle stress. But his most important contribution is bringing Sartre's notions of bad faith and authentic existence into the 21st century by reminding us that the purpose of life is not to avoid everything potentially stressful or disturbing, but rather to develop the capacity to tackle challenges with gusto and to learn from these experiences.

[handwritten: ext'rinsic goals]
[handwritten: hedonia = max pleasure]
[handwritten: intrinsic goals]
[handwritten: eudaimonia goals = minimize pain]

SELF-DETERMINATION THEORY: DECI AND RYAN

Philosophers going back at least as far as Aristotle have observed that happiness can be sought via two basic routes. One route is to maximize pleasure and minimize pain, which seems like a pretty simple and obvious way to be happy. The second route is more complex, and entails seeking a deeper meaning to life by pursuing important goals, building relationships, and being aware of taking responsibility for one's choices in life. The first route is called **hedonia** and the second is called **eudaimonia**, and the distinction between them is an important basis of Richard Ryan's and Edward Deci's *self-determination theory (SDT)* (see Ryan & Deci, 2000; Ryan, Huta, & Deci, 2008).

Hedonia is dangerous, according to SDT theorists. The more one seeks simply to maximize pleasure and minimize pain to the exclusion of other goals, the more one risks living a life "bereft of depth, meaning and community" based on "selfishness, materialism, objectified sexuality and ecological destructiveness" (Ryan et al., 2008, p. 141). Eudaimonia, by contrast, entails finding and seeking goals that are valuable in their own right (*intrinsic goals*) rather than being means to an end (*extrinsic goals*).

The most commonly sought extrinsic goal is money. In contrast, there are three central intrinsic goals, according to SDT. *Autonomy* means finding your own way in life and making your own decisions. *Competence* involves finding something you are good at, and becoming better. *Relatedness* means establishing meaningful and satisfying ties to other people. These needs are present in you whether you know it or not, according to SDT, and you cannot ever be a fully functioning person (to borrow a term from Rogers) unless you attain them.

[handwritten: 3 central intrinsic goal 1) autonomy 2) competence 3) relatedness]

Deci, Ryan, and their collaborators have amassed considerable evidence that people who follow intrinsic goals are better off than people who organize their lives around extrinsic goals. For example, one early study found that people who valued financial success over their relationships, personal growth, and community had lower well-being overall (Kasser & Ryan, 1993). A more elaborate study examined seven life goals, three of which—wealth, fame, and attractiveness—were deemed extrinsic and four—personal growth, intimacy, community, and physical health—were identified as intrinsic. People who emphasized the intrinsic goals over the extrinsic goals were higher in vitality and positive emotionality, and lower in depression, negative emotions, anxiety, and signs of physical illness (Kasser & Ryan, 1996). Such people also contributed more to the well-being of other indviduals and of their community (Ryan et al. 2008).

SDT claims that the goals of autonomy, competence, and relatedness are basic to everybody in the world regardless of circumstances or cultural background. But it is reasonable to question whether they are really as universal as the theory says. They certainly all sound good, but how do we know their attractiveness comes from some inner, essentially human source and not simply from our cultural teachings? The only possible answer at this point is, we don't. But that's what research is for. It is a good thing when a theory makes a strong claim that might be wrong, because that means the theory is not obviously or trivially true. It also makes the theory testable. Over the years to come, we can expect some interesting research around the question of whether these three goals actually apply to everybody.

POSITIVE PSYCHOLOGY

Abraham Maslow is often quoted as having said that health means more than simply the absence of disease (Simonton & Baumeister, 2005). This idea, along with humanistic psychology's traditional emphasis on growth, development, and the achievement of one's potential (Levine, 2006), has enjoyed a resurgence in recent years with the advent of the *positive psychology movement* (Gable & Haidt, 2005) of which self-determination theory, just reviewed, can be considered a part. The aim of this growing field of theorizing and research is to correct what its proponents see as a long-standing overemphasis within psychology on psychopathology and malfunction. Instead, positive psychology focuses on phenomena such as "positive subjective experience, positive individual traits, and positive institutions" in order to "improve quality of life and prevent the pathologies that arise when life is barren and meaningless" (Seligman & Csikszentmihalyi, 2000, p. 5). Sound familiar? It should: it's the theme of just about every humanistic theory reviewed in this chapter so far.

The reemergence of this theme signals a remarkable turning point in the history of psychology. For a period of several decades—from about the 1970s until just after the turn of the 21st century—humanistic psychology seemed to be dying, though a few lonely voices continued to argue for its importance (e.g., Rychlak, 1988). Their pleas have finally been answered, though perhaps not in the way they would have expected.

Positive psychology is the rebirth of humanistic psychology. As we have seen in this chapter, the humanists consistently maintained that traditional psychology, because it treats people almost as inanimate objects of study, tends to ignore uniquely human capacities for creativity, love, wisdom, and free will. Perhaps most crucial, traditional psychology ignores the question of the meaning of life. Positive psychologists place this question front and center (Baumeister & Vohs, 2002), arguing that a satisfying and meaningful life involves happiness and that true happiness comes from overcoming important challenges (Ryff & Singer, 2003). This idea is not unlike Sartre's conception of optimistic toughness, Maddi's notion of hardiness, and Deci and Ryan's idea of eudaimonic happiness.

> Positive psychology is the rebirth of humanistic psychology.

However, research in positive psychology does more than just revive old-fashioned humanism or put a positive spin on existential philosophy. Positive psychologists also investigate the traits, processes, and social institutions that promote a happy and meaningful life. For example, a good deal of research examines the factors that contribute to and detract from happiness, or *subjective well-being* (E. Diener, Lucas, & Oishi, 2002). As was mentioned earlier, this research shows that beyond a certain base level, money is not important for happiness; building relationships and overcoming challenges becomes more important, a vindication of Maslow's theory. In addition, some people characteristically think in ways that promote happiness, such as avoiding unproductive rumination about negative events and appreciating the good things in life (Lyubomirsky, 2001; Lyubomirsky, Sheldon, et al., 2005). Happiness is a centrally important component of well-being, and researchers in positive psychology are playing an increasingly important role in improving our understanding of it. Their research on happiness will be reviewed in more detail in Chapter 16.

Positive psychology seems inherently optimistic (notice its name), which raises an interesting question: Should we try to always expect the best? A specific line of research investigates the benefits of explaining and anticipating events from an optimistic viewpoint (C. Peterson & Steen, 2002). Perhaps not surprisingly, optimistic individuals are less fearful, more willing to take risks, and are usually relatively happy. On the other hand, optimism may lead one to take foolish risks or fail to anticipate problems before they arise. For that reason, the psychologist Julie Norem has made the interesting argument that the study of pessimism should also be considered a part of positive psychology (Norem & Chang, 2002).

The most distinctive feature of positive psychology is its focus on human

positive psych = focus on human strength vs. faults

strengths instead of faults. Recall from Chapters 10 and 11 how Sigmund Freud and the psychoanalytic viewpoint emphasized psychological conflict and the neuroses it produces. More generally, it would probably be fair to say that psychology focuses more on preventing or curing bad outcomes, such as mental illness, than on promoting good outcomes, such as optimal achievement and health. Positive psychology aims to fix that by identifying and promoting character strengths. Indeed, a very thick book, recently published by the American Psychological Association, catalogs and analyzes a long list of "virtues" (C. Peterson & Seligman, 2004).

This topic raises a sticky question, though: What are virtues? After all, one person's virtue might be another person's vice, and deciding how people *should* behave seems to involve making value judgments that go beyond science. One way researchers studying virtue have approached this problem is by trying to discern which attributes have been viewed as virtues in all cultures, at all times. A particularly ambitious recent project surveyed the virtues encouraged in key writings of Confucianism, Taoism, Buddhism, Hinduism, ancient Greek philosophy, Christianity, Judaism, and Islam[4] (Dahlsgaard, Peterson, & Seligman, 2005). From this survey the authors identified six *core virtues*: courage, justice, humanity (compassion), temperance, wisdom, and transcendance (see Table 13.1). Of these, the most clearly universal appeared to be justice and humanity, because these values were explicitly mentioned as important in all eight of the cultural traditions examined (see Table 13.2). Temperance, wisdom, and transcendence were *implied* to be good in the writings of those cultures that did not explicitly identify them as virtues. The only virtue that showed a notable lack of consensus was courage, which was not viewed as particularly important by Confucianism, Taoism, or Buddhism.

What makes these attributes virtues? The authors of this study speculate that their universality suggests they are evolutionarily based (see Chapter 9), because "each allows a crucial survival problem to be solved" (Dahlsgaard et al., 2005, p. 212). Specifically, each virtue counteracts a tendency that could threaten the survival of individuals and cultures. Justice prevents anarchy and chaos; humanity prevents cruelty; wisdom prevents stupidity. And, as the authors note, "We would not need to posit the virtue of courage if people were not (sometimes) swayed from doing the right thing by fear or the virtue of temperance if people were not sometimes reckless" (Dahlsgaard et al., 2005, p. 212). This point is important, because it answers the question why, if these virtues are crucial for survival, not everybody has them. If

---

[4] Apparently, Scientology was not included.

Table 13.1

Virtue	Description
Courage	Emotional strengths that involve the exercise of will to accomplish goals in the face of opposition; examples include bravery, perserverance, and honesty.
Justice	Strengths that underlie healthy community life; examples include fairness, leadership, and teamwork.
Humanity	Strengths that involve protecting and taking care of others; examples include love and kindness.
Temperance	Strengths that protect against excess; examples include forgiveness, humility, prudence, and self-control.
Wisdom	Strengths that entail the acquisition and use of knowledge; examples include creativity, curiosity, judgment, and perspective.
Transcendence	Strengths that give meaning to life by connecting to the larger universe; examples include gratitude, hope, and spirituality.

CORE VIRTUES IDENTIFIED BY POSITIVE PSYCHOLOGY

[handwritten note]: Lack of notable consensus.

Source: Adapted from Dahlsgaard, Peterson, & Seligman (2005), Table 1, p. 205.

everybody had these virtues, there would be no need to teach them, or even to label them. The key virtues identify six ways in which people try to make themselves better. Some people succeed at this kind of self-development better than others, and perhaps nobody ever quite manages to achieve all six virtues perfectly.

Despite the recent flurry of empirical and theoretical activity, the rebirth of humanism is not complete. Positive psychology has not yet had much to say about existential anxiety, for example, nor does it address the difficult dilemmas that arise from free will. It usually addresses experience in the form of "subjective well-being," which is basically the degree to which one "feels good"—a limited phenomenological analysis compared with the earlier work of existentialists and humanists—and is just beginning to focus on the difference between hedonic and eudaimonic sources of well-being.

But let's be fair. Positive psychology, by that name, is still new—its most important articles and books have all appeared since the year 2000. As Sartre mordantly observed, the dilemmas of free will and mortality cannot be wished away, even if we try to ignore them, so positive psychology likely will address these issues before long. In the meantime, it offers a powerful cor-

Table 13.2

AGREEMENT ABOUT VIRTUES ACROSS CULTURAL TRADITIONS

Tradition	Courage	Justice	Humanity	Temperance	Wisdom	Transcendence
Confucianism		E	E	T	E	T
Taoism		E	E	E	E	T
Buddhism		E	E	E	T	E
Hinduism	E	E	E	E	E	E
Athenian philosophy	E	E	E	E	E	T
Christianity	E	E	E	E	E	E
Judaism	E	E	E	E	E	E
Islam	E	E	E	E	E	E

Note: Traditions that *explicitly* endorse a virtue are identified with E; those that *implicitly* endorse the virtue are identified with T.
Source: Adapted from Dahlsgaard, Peterson, & Seligman (2005), Table 2, p. 211.

rective to psychology's emphasis on the negative side of mental life. By seeking to identify and promote human strengths, positive psychology offers psychology an important direction that is not exactly new—but does renew it.

THE IMPLICATIONS OF PHENOMENOLOGY

At the root of the existential and humanistic approach to psychology is phenomenology, the moment-to-moment experience of every aware person. This emphasis on phenomenology allows humanistic analysis to make two unique contributions. It reminds us of the mystery of experience, and it teaches that the only way to truly understand another person is to comprehend that person's unique view of reality.

The Mystery of Experience

The essential fact that phenomenologists going back to Wundt have always grasped, which all other basic paradigms neglect, is that conscious experience is both an obvious fact and a basic mystery. It cannot be explained by science or even described very well in words. Though we cannot quite describe what it is to be aware and alive, every one of us knows what it is.

Science and psychology usually choose not to address how something so familiar can be so difficult to understand; they just ignore it, which is fine, to a point. The point is reached when science and psychology seem to assume that conscious awareness is not important or even proceed as if it does not exist. Nearly as bad, psychology sometimes treats conscious experience as simply an interesting form of information processing, no different from the kind done by a computer (Rychlak, 1988). Some theories proposed by cognitive psychologists claim that consciousness is a higher-order cognitive process that organizes thoughts and allows flexible decision making. These theories hold that beyond these functions, consciousness is just a feeling (Dennett, 1994; Dennett & Weiner, 1991; Ornstein, 1977).

Of course, to say consciousness is "just a feeling" begs the main question: What does it mean to be able to consciously experience feeling? In fact, conscious awareness is not in the least similar to the kind of information processing computers perform, even if it fulfills some of the same functions. Awareness is a human experience, and science can neither credibly deny its existence nor explain just what it is or where it comes from. It is only natural, therefore, that phenomenological analysis sometimes expands into speculations that are not only philosophical, but also religious and spiritual.

Understanding Others

A corollary of the phenomenological view at the heart of humanistic psychology is that to understand another person, you must understand that person's construals (Kelly, 1955). You can only comprehend someone's mind to the extent that you can imagine life from her perspective. The adage "Do not judge me until you have walked a mile in my shoes" expresses the general idea.

This principle discourages judgmental attitudes about other people. It implies that if you could see the world through their eyes, you would realize that their actions and attitudes are the natural consequences of their understanding of reality. Furthermore, there is no way to prove your view of reality right and the views of others wrong. Thus, it is a mistake to assume that others interpret the world the same way you do, or that there is only one correct perspective. Others' opinions, no matter how strange, must be considered as valid as your own.[5]

---

[5] Extremists such as Thomas Szasz (1960, 1974) have sometimes argued that this is even true about the people usually considered mentally ill; they merely have an alternative and equally valid construal of reality. But this is an extreme position.

One direct consequence of this phenomenological principle is a far-reaching cultural and even moral relativism. You cannot judge the actions and beliefs of other people through your own moral code. For, when all is said and done, there is no objective reality—or, if there is, there is no way for anyone to know it. Furthermore, it is generally misguided to judge the values and practices of other cultures from the perspective of your own. Although there may be widespread agreement about a handful of core virtues, separate cultures still see the world very differently, and to understand other cultures, just as to understand other individuals, we must seek to understand the world from an alternative point of view. The attempt to apply personality psychology across different cultures is the topic of the next chapter.

SUMMARY

- Humanistic psychology concentrates on the ways that studying humans differs from studying objects or animals, including such issues as experience, awareness, and free will.

Phenomenology: Awareness Is Everything

- The phenomenological perspective implies that the present moment of experience is all that matters, which means that individuals have free will and that the only way to understand another person is to understand that person's construal, or experience of the world.

Existentialism

- The philosophical school called existentialism breaks experience into three types: experience of the external world, social experience, and introspective experience-of-experiencing. Existentialism also claims that existence has no meaning beyond what each person gives it.

- Existential philosophers such as Sartre concluded that a failure to face life's lack of inherent meaning constitutes living in bad faith.

Optimistic Humanism: Rogers and Maslow

- Modern humanist psychologists added to this existential analysis the assumption that people are basically good and inherently motivated to self-actualize.

- Rogers and Maslow asserted that a person who faces experience directly can become a fully functioning person. Rogers believed this outcome could only occur for individuals who had received unconditional positive regard from the important people in their lives. Maslow believed that higher needs such as self-actualization could come to the fore only after more basic needs related to survival and security became satisfied.

Personal Constructs: Kelly

- Kelly's personal construct theory says that each person's experience of the world is organized by a unique set of personal constructs. These personal constructs, which stem from, and help determine, one's construals of experience, resemble scientific paradigms.

Flow: Csikszentmihalyi

- Csikszentmihalyi's theory of flow says that the best state of experience is one in which challenges and capabilities are balanced, attention is focused, and time passes quickly.

Hardiness: Maddi

- Maddi's theory of hardiness argues that people should embrace life's challenges rather than seek to avoid all stress.

Self-Determination Theory: Deci and Ryan

- Deci and Ryan's self-determination theory asserts that happiness can be pursued through hedonic means (seeking pleasure and comfort) or eudaimonic means (seeking to fulfill one's potential).

- A solely hedonic route is ultimately self-defeating because people have universal, fundamental needs for autonomy, competence, and relatedness, which are best fulfilled by pursuing intrinsic goals (meaningful in themselves), rather than extrinsic goals (merely means to an end).

Positive Psychology

- Positive psychology represents a rebirth of humanistic psychology, focusing on the traits and psychological processes that promote well-being and give life meaning.

- An important contribution of positive psychology is its attempt to catalog universal human virtues, which research suggests include justice, humanity, temperance, wisdom, and transcendence. A sixth core virtue, courage, appears to be somewhat less universal.

The Implications of Phenomenology

- The two main contributions of humanistic psychology's phenomenological approach are the attempt to address the mystery of human experience and its emphasis on nonjudgmental understanding of individuals and cultures.

THINK ABOUT IT

1. Do people have free will? Or are they driven by their past experiences, unconscious motivations, and personality traits? If free will exists, what does this mean, and how is it possible?

2. What does it feel like to be alive and aware? Can consciousness be described in words? How could you tell whether a computer had this feeling? Can psychology further our understanding of this experience? How?

3. How can a person decide between right and wrong? Is there some authority to help sort it out? How do you know whether to heed this authority?

4. Sartre believed that God does not exist, but said that, even if God *did* exist, it wouldn't matter. What did Sartre mean?

5. How do you think Rogers and Maslow could start with existentialist ideas and develop such optimistic-sounding psychologies?

6. If a psychotherapist is treating a murderer or a child molester, do you think the therapist should give the client unconditional positive regard? Why, or why not?

7. Does everybody need autonomy, competence, and relatedness (from self-determination theory)? Is it possible to have a good life without them? Is one of them more crucial, or more expendable, than the other two?

8. Would you spend your whole life in a state of flow if you could?

9. Why are you in college? Are your goals hedonic or eudaimonic? Why do you think most students are in college?

10. Can pessimism be useful? Can stress be good for you?

11. Is it important for psychology to emphasize human strengths as well as weaknesses? What good would that do?

12. The strongest cross-cultural agreement about virtues seems to concern justice and humanity. Does this mean these are the most important virtues? Courage seems to inspire slightly less agreement. Does this mean it is less important? How can we decide which virtues are the most important?

13. When trying to identify core virtues or to explain the meaning of life, where does psychology leave off and religion—or other cultural teachings—begin?

14. We each know we are aware and consciously experiencing the world, yet psychology finds this fact difficult to study. Why? What kinds of investigations might lead to a helpful or convincing explanation of human consciousness?

SUGGESTED READINGS

Keyes, C. L. M, & Haidt, J. (Eds.). (2003). *Flourishing: Positive psychology and the life well-lived*. Washington, DC: American Psychological Association.

Peterson, C., & Seligman, M. E. P. (Eds.) (2004). *Character strengths and virtues: A handbook and classification*. Washington, DC: American Psychological Association.

> Two collections of writings organized by major figures in the modern positive psychology movement.

Maslow, A. H. (1987). *Motivation and personality* (3rd ed.). New York: Harper.

> One of the most accessible—and briefest—thorough presentations of American humanistic psychology by one of its two most important figures (the other being Carl Rogers). Maslow's writing is passionate and persuasive.

Sartre, J. P. (1965). The humanism of existentialism. In W. Baskin (Ed.), *Essays in existentialism* (pp. 31–62). Secaucus, NJ: Citadel.

> A surprisingly readable and interesting exposition of existentialism from one of its important philosophers.

EMEDIA

 Go to StudySpace, wwnorton.com/studyspace, to access additional review and enrichment materials.

14

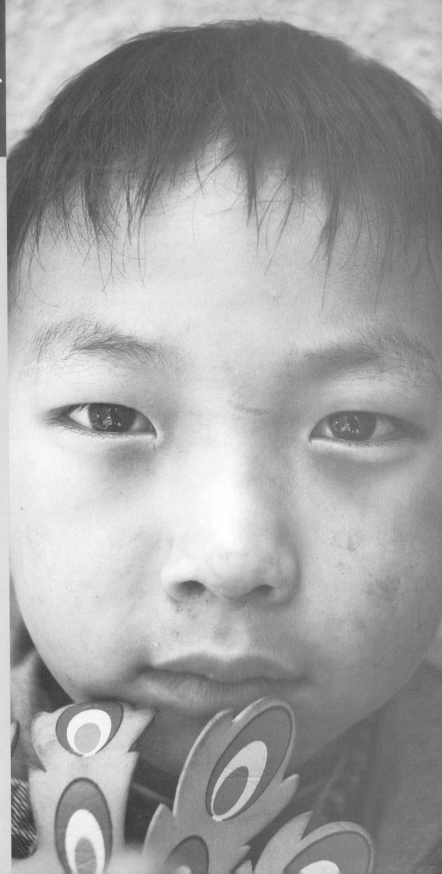

CULTURAL VARIATION IN EXPERIENCE, BEHAVIOR, AND PERSONALITY

WHAT THE WORLD ACTUALLY contains may matter less than how an individual sees or construes it, so the only way to understand a person is to get inside of his distinct view of reality. In Chapter 13, we saw the phenomenologists make a pretty good case along these lines. Construals of reality vary not just between individuals but also across cultures, and in recent years psychologists have begun to pay increasing attention to this variation. Behavior that seems the epitome of politeness in one culture may be viewed as rude by another. Ideas can take on drastically different meanings according to the cultural context. And, perhaps most important, cultures seem to differ in some of their basic values.

Few areas of psychology are more challenging than cross-cultural research, because the job often entails grappling with concepts that are both unfamiliar and difficult. For example, the psychiatrist Takeo Doi reports that the term *amae* is central for understanding personality structure in Japanese culture. *Amae* literally means something like "sweet," but in a family context the word implies indulgence and dependence, of the sort that may exist between a parent and child. This pattern of benevolent dependence is expected to continue into adult relationships, so that people treat each other thoughtfully and considerately, while appreciating how they depend on each other (Doi, 1973; Tseng, 2003). But it is difficult even to translate *amae* into English, much less to fully comprehend its implications. Does this concept have meaning outside the Japanese context? Or is the concept so embedded in the Japanese way of seeing things that it cannot be exported? Questions like these may be impossible to answer, but the business of **cross-cultural psychology**[1] is to attempt to address them anyway. The present chapter will survey some of the recent research that is beginning to work through the implications of cultural diversity for personality psychology.

CULTURE AND PSYCHOLOGY

Personality psychology focuses on psychological differences between individuals. Culture comes into play for two reasons. First, individuals may differ from each other to some extent because they belong to different cultural groups. According to one study, for example, people in China are on average more emotionally reserved, introverted, fond of tranquility, and considerate than Americans (Cheung & Song, 1989). Second, members of some groups may differ from *each other* in distinctive ways. Doi described a Japanese mother who complained that her son was not as *amae* as he should be, a complaint you would probably not hear from an American parent. An important challenge for personality psychology is to understand ways that particular personality differences vary from one culture to another, or differentiate between individuals within different cultures.

Cross-Cultural Universals Versus Specificity

To what extent are people from different cultures psychologically similar or different? Are their differences variations on a theme, or are they entirely different symphonies? To put the question one more way, does human nature have a common core? Or are people from separate cultures so fundamentally different that they cannot be meaningfully compared? Anthropologists have grappled with these issues for many years, and psychologists are relative newcomers to the fray. While both fields include plenty of proponents for both the "universal human nature" and "cultural specificity" positions, this is one of those eternal issues, like the nature-versus-nurture question (Chapter 9) or the consistency debate (Chapter 4), that seems bound never to be entirely settled.

---

[1] A note on terms: Cross-cultural psychology generally refers to research that compares different cultures. A variant sometimes called *cultural psychology* seeks to understand individual cultures in their own terms but eschews comparisons.

In what follows, we will see plenty of evidence that culture influences how people vary both across and within cultures, and evidence for a common core to human nature as well. Furthermore, while cross-cultural psychology has traditionally emphasized how people in separate cultures are different, in the past few years an increasing amount of research is emphasizing how people around the world are psychologically similar, and turning more attention to how people differ *within* cultures. An important challenge for the future will be to figure out how universal psychological processes, such as personality and emotion, play out in diverse cultural contexts (e.g., Tsai, Knutson, & Fung, 2006). We will return to these issues near the end of the chapter.

What Is Culture?

The term *culture* refers to psychological attributes of groups: according to one writer, these include "customs, habits, beliefs and values that shape emotions, behavior and life patterns" (Tseng, 2003, p. 1). Culture also may include language, modes of thinking, and perhaps even fundamental views of reality. The concept of the cultural group is difficult to pin down precisely. Any group of people who are identifiably psychologically different from another group can be a candidate. Traditionally, cultural groups are ethnic and linguistic, but important cultural differences can be found within national and linguistic borders as well as across them. Studies have compared North Americans with Asians, Japanese with Chinese, Spanish speakers with English speakers, and even residents of Manhattan with residents of Queens (Kusserow, 1999).

Differences between cultural groups are almost entirely learned, not innate. A child picks up the culture into which she is born (a process called **enculturation**), and a person who moves from one country to another may gradually pick up the culture of her new home (a process called **acculturation**). Genetics are unlikely to be the primary basis of cross-cultural differences because, according to DNA analyses, individuals within a given ethnic or racial group are only slightly more similar to each other than they are to individuals from different groups (American Anthropological Association, 1999). Another reason why genetics is unlikely to be the primary basis of cultural differences is that cultural groups are not just ethnic or linguistic, but can also be defined on the basis of history, geography, religion, philosophy, or even politics.

Psychologists are members of cultures, too. Every psychologist speaks a language and lives in a geographic area that inevitably influences his outlook. It is even possible that being a psychologist makes one a member of a certain "culture."

THE IMPORTANCE OF CROSS-CULTURAL DIFFERENCES

Until relatively recently, psychologists more or less ignored cross-cultural issues, and many still do. Most of this neglect is fairly benign. Rather than worry about cross-cultural variation at every step, especially in the absence of much relevant data, most psychologists just try to describe and explain the phenomenon at hand in the context of their own culture. Freud did not worry too much about cross-cultural concerns; he found Viennese women plenty complicated enough. Likewise, the European and North American psychologists measuring individual differences and exploring perception, cognition, and the laws of behavioral change have proceeded primarily within the Western cultural context. Research even within these limits has proven sufficiently interesting and difficult that most researchers have not attempted cross-cultural applications.

This attitude of benign neglect is rapidly becoming less tenable as research expands and accelerates. Even the Surgeon General of the United States has officially announced that "culture counts" for understanding mental health disorders, interventions, and risk factors (Public Health Service, 2001). Psychologists are interested in cross-cultural differences for three good reasons. Understanding cultural differences is important for increasing international understanding, for assessing the degree to which psychology applies to people around the world, and for appreciating the possible varieties of human experience.

> Even the Surgeon General of the United States has officially announced that "culture counts" for understanding mental health disorders, interventions, and risk factors.

Cross-Cultural Understanding

Different cultural attitudes, values, and behavioral styles frequently cause misunderstandings. The consequences can range from trivial to serious.

Near the trivial end of the spectrum, the cross-cultural psychologist Harry Triandis described a misunderstanding with an Indian hotel clerk caused by a contrast between the American practice of marking an X next to the part of a form that *does* apply, and the Indian practice of marking an X at the part that does *not* apply. He received a postcard from the hotel with an X next to "We have no rooms available," and thought he did not have a hotel reservation, when he did (Triandis, 1994). This episode was surely inconvenient, but no major tragedy.[2]

More consequential differences include the preference of business people in Thailand to try to preserve the dignity of everybody involved in a negotiation, or the tradition in Japan of getting to know a potential business partner well on a personal level before beginning to draw up a contract. The Japanese practice allows for controversial issues that might arise during a meeting to be settled beforehand, in private (L. Miller, 1999). When these styles encounter the relatively brash, direct, and even insensitive American way of doing business, the result is more conflict and probably less profit than would have been possible with a little more mutual understanding.

In 1994, an American teenager living with his parents in Singapore learned a lesson about cross-cultural differences the hard way. He was convicted of spray painting some parked cars, which in the United States probably would have been considered an act of petty vandalism (albeit an extremely annoying one). In Singapore such misbehavior is taken more seriously. He was sentenced to pay restitution, spend several months in jail, and—most surprising from an American perspective—to be hit several times with a bamboo cane, which can split open the skin and cause permanent scarring. The sentence caused an international uproar.

Behaviors that are ordinary in other cultures can also stir up a storm if they are practiced in the United States. In 1997, a Danish mother visiting New York went into a restaurant for dinner and left her fourteen-month-old daughter sleeping in a stroller parked outside. Alarmed New Yorkers saw the "abandoned" baby and called the police, who arrested the mother and placed the child in temporary foster care. Yet apparently in Denmark this is a common practice (see Figure 14.1). As one Danish writer commented,

> In Denmark, people have an almost religious conviction that fresh air, preferably cold air, is good for children. All Danish babies nap outside, even in freezing weather—tucked warmly under their plump goose-down comforters. . . . In Denmark, [this mother's] behavior would have been considered perfectly normal. (Dyssegaard, 1997/2004, p. 370)

---

[2]Another, only slightly less trivial example: On a visit to Poland I once encountered two restroom doors, one labeled with a circle and the other with a triangle. Which was which? I guessed wrong.

Figure 14.1 Nothing to Get Excited About A few days after a Danish mother visiting New York was arrested for leaving her baby parked on the sidewalk, this photograph was taken outside of the Café Sommersko in Copenhagen.

Cross-cultural misunderstandings occur within as well as across international borders. In some inner cities of North America, a subculture of violence and fear has led to the extreme valuation of receiving proper "respect." Anything that threatens such respect can literally threaten one's life, so tokens such as stylish clothing, a fear-producing appearance, and even an advertised willingness to kill become highly valued (E. Anderson, 1994). Nonverbal expressions take on added meanings, too. For example, to gaze for more than a second or so at a person from this subculture expresses disrespect and invites a violent response. Similarly, research has suggested that the American South has its own "culture of honor" that is different from the rest of the United States; it includes such behaviors as elaborate displays of mutual respect (such as calling people "sir" and "ma'am") and the obligation to respond forcefully to any insult (D. Cohen, Nisbett, Bowdle, & Schwartz, 1996).

The Generalizability of Theory and Research

Sigmund Freud's theories were largely based on his own introspections and his experience treating upper-middle-class women who lived in turn-of-the-20th-century Vienna. It is not particularly original to observe that his view of humanity may have been skewed by the limits of this database.[3]

---

[3] An early tradition in cross-cultural psychology involved trying to interpret different cultures in psychoanalytic terms. For example, Gorer (1943) claimed that Japanese people are anal-compulsive because they subject their children to early and severe toilet training. Theorizing by modern cultural psychologists is very different and seldom Freudian.

The problem is not unique to Freud, of course. As I discussed in Chapter 3, a basic worry about the generalizability of research findings concerns the degree to which the results of modern empirical research, based disproportionately on college students in North America, applies to humanity at large. This issue may be particularly acute for personality psychology, because a great deal of evidence indicates that culture affects the ways personality is expressed and emotion is experienced. The only way to incorporate this fact in psychological research is to include not only people besides college students, but also people from around the world.

The situation seems to have improved a bit in recent years. The principal psychological journals increasingly report research from psychologists in many different countries including Australia, New Zealand, many countries in Europe—Germany is particularly active in personality psychology—and a growing number of Asian countries including Japan, China, Korea, India, and Singapore. As psychology becomes more international, it will become more generalizable, and a better science.

Varieties of Human Experience

A third and more deeply theoretical issue also drives interest in cross-cultural psychology. A moment's reflection is sufficient to realize that the way you see and construe the world is, to a considerable degree, a product of your experience and cultural background. An intriguing possibility to consider is how the world might look if you were from some other cultural background. Things that are now invisible might become clear, and things you see and take for granted might become invisible. You might even, in a real sense, become a different person.

For example, a visitor from a South American rain-forest community might look at a tree and immediately see the uses for its bark and sap. That same visitor might look at an automobile or a computer and have no idea how it could be used. A native of Western culture, however, might immediately see the transportation and informational possibilities in the car and the computer, but detect little potential on beholding a teak. A ride around the block might be sufficient to acquaint the visitor from the rain forest with the possibilities of cars; imparting an understanding of computers might be a bit more difficult. And if we visited their community in the rain forest, there might be artifacts or objects they would find difficult to explain. In a similar way, an American might look at a house and never realize which way its door points. To a Chinese raised in the tradition of *feng shui*, this would be one of the first things noticed and would lead to some immediate conclusions concerning the dangers and possibilities that might exist within the house.[4]

Cross-cultural observations like these raise a profound phenomenological question: Does the human experience of life vary fundamentally across cultures? Do people raised and living in different cultural environments see the same colors, feel the same emotions, desire the same goals, or organize their thoughts in comparable ways? The cultural anthropologist and psychologist Richard Shweder called these aspects of psychology *experience-near constructs*, and proposed that they are the most fitting subject matter for cultural psychology (Shweder & Sullivan, 1993). In a somewhat more accessible phrase, Triandis (1994) claimed, "Culture imposes a set of lenses for seeing the world" (p. 13). If that description is valid—and it probably is—then the natural next question is, How different are these cultural lenses, and do they lead to views of the world that are fundamentally different or comparable?

In its ultimate form, this question is probably unanswerable. As we saw in Chapter 13, we can never know the experience of another individual in our own culture for certain, much less enter fully into the experience of a member of a different culture. But it seems to be useful to try. Recent evidence indicates that the experience of having lived abroad can make you a more creative person, especially if you made an effort to truly adapt to—rather than merely visit—the unfamiliar culture (Maddux & Galinsky, 2009). What does it mean to be more creative? The study used measures of insight, association between ideas, and generation of new ideas. One task asked participants to draw pictures of aliens from another galaxy (see Figure 14.2). People who had lived abroad drew more creative aliens!

THE CHARACTERISTICS OF CULTURES

As psychologists turn their attention to culture, the first question that arises is a difficult one: How can one culture be compared with another? Comparison has been attempted in many ways relevant to personality, including the degree and way they shape their members' behavior, experience of emotion, thoughts, and sense of connection with the larger world.

---

[4] If the American happens to live in California, the difference in perception might not be so wide. For several years, the Sunday real estate section of the *Los Angeles Times* included a "Feng Shui" column with advice on how to align one's home with the unseen forces of the universe.

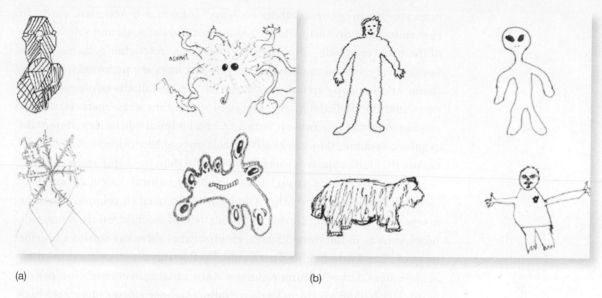

(a)   (b)

Figure 14.2 Living Abroad Enhances Creativity In one study, people who had lived abroad and adapted to the new culture were more creative than those who had stayed at home or never experienced more than a brief visit abroad. One measure of creativity asked participants to draw an alien they might see if they visited another galaxy. The drawings in panel (a) were judged more creative than those in panel (b).

The basic assumption underlying cultural comparison is that any idea or concept has aspects that are the same across cultures and aspects particular to a specific culture (J. W. Berry, 1969). The universal components of an idea are called **etics**, and the particular aspects are called **emics**.[5] For example, all cultures have some conception of duty, in the sense that a person should be responsible for doing what she is supposed to do. But beyond this basic etic, different cultures impose their own ideas of a person's actual duty. A dutiful person in New Delhi will probably behave differently from an equally dutiful person in New York (McCrae & Costa, 1995). At the same time, a renegade in New Delhi and one in New York will both break rules, but they will break different rules.

An early approach to cross-cultural psychology, still followed by some, was to attempt to characterize general differences between whole cultures. One pioneering effort more than half a century ago concluded that some cul-

---

[5] The words derive from linguistic terms that refer to *phonetics* (the universal sounds of language) and *phonemics* (the sounds of a specific language) (Tseng, 2003).

tures are "tough" whereas others are "easy" (Arsenian & Arsenian, 1948). In easy cultures, individuals can pursue many different goals and at least some of them are relatively simple to attain, whereas in tougher cultures, only a few goals are viewed as valuable and very few ways are provided to achieve them. Another early system suggested that the overall stressfulness of cultures could be indexed by the degree to which they were characterized by suicide, homicide, "drunken brawling," and a tendency to view important events as influenced by witchcraft (Naroll, 1959). According to this classification, the Ifalik culture is much less stressful than the Tupinamba culture.[6]

David McClelland (1961) believed that a central aspect of any culture was the degree to which it emphasizes the need to achieve, which he assessed by examining stories traditionally told to children. In some cultures, such as in the United States, children are told many stories along the lines of "The Little Engine That Could," reflecting a high cultural need for achievement. Other cultures tell more stories that reflect needs for love or, to use McClelland's term, *affiliation*. Cultures whose stories manifest a high need for achievement, according to McClelland, show more rapid industrial growth than those whose stories focus less on achievement, and data including measures such as amount of electrical production have tended to bear him out: more achievement stories, more electricity. Of course, the correlational nature of these data make the direction of causality unclear. Does telling achievement-oriented stories to children make them more likely to grow up to build prosperous, industrialized, electricity-using cultures? Or do prosperous cultures create an environment in which children's authors just naturally think up stories about achievement?

More recently, Triandis (1994, 1997) proposed that cultures vary along three basic dimensions: complexity, tightness-looseness, and collectivism-individualism. One can compare cultures by assessing their positions on these cultural trait scales.

Complexity

Are some cultures more complicated than others? Triandis (1997) wrote of the difference in *complexity* between "modern, industrial, affluent cultures

---

[6] To answer your next question, the Ifalik live on islands in Micronesia, in the Pacific Ocean, and the Tupinamba are from the east coast of Brazil.

[and] the simpler cultures, such as the hunters and gatherers, or the residents of a monastery" (p. 444). This difference seems plausible, but let's be careful. How do we know that modern industrial societies are more complex than hunter-gatherer cultures? Such seemingly simple cultures have their own complex patterns of interpersonal relationships and political struggles, although they may not be visible to an outsider. Things might become pretty complex, for example, when it comes time to choose a new chief. It is reasonable to wonder, too, whether monastery life looks as simple from the inside as it does from the outside. While some cultures might be more complex than others, it is not easy to be sure which those are.

Tightness and Looseness

The *tightness-looseness* dimension contrasts cultures that tolerate very little deviation from proper behavior (tight cultures) with those that allow fairly large deviations from cultural norms (loose cultures). Triandis hypothesizes that ethnically homogeneous and densely populated societies tend to be culturally tighter than societies that are more diverse or where people are more spread out. This is because in order to strictly enforce norms, people must be similar enough to agree on those norms, and because strict norms of behavior are more necessary when people must live close together. For example, cultures that developed in places such as Hong Kong would tend to be tighter than cultures in places such as Australia.

The United States, historically a diverse and geographically spread out society, is a classic example of a loose culture. But the degree of looseness varies. Having lived in both places, I can testify that east-central Illinois is a much tighter culture than Berkeley, California, even though both are in the United States. Berkeley is more densely populated than downstate Illinois, but it is also more diverse. This observation suggests that diversity may override density in determining tightness and looseness.

Boston, where I have also lived, is an even more interesting case. Tightness and looseness can vary by block. Homogeneous, ethnic Italian and Irish neighborhoods (the North End and South Boston, respectively), where cultural mores are quite tight, abut more diverse neighborhoods (e.g., Back Bay), where standards are much looser. Again, diversity seems key. All of these neighborhoods are about equally crowded. But whereas South Boston and the North End are populated mostly by people born and raised there and are each dominated by a particular ethnic group, nearly everybody I met in Back Bay seemed to be from another state—usually California!

So, is population density less important than diversity in determining whether a culture is tight or loose? Not so fast. Consider Singapore, a fairly tight culture, if you recall the incident of the spray-painting teenager. It is ethnically diverse to an amazing degree—much more so than Boston or even California. It is densely populated, however, and its tight organization appears to be an important part of what makes the country function well on a daily basis.

An interesting way to index the tightness of a culture is to examine left- and right-handedness. Worldwide, about 10 percent of the population is left-handed (Hardyck & Petrinovich, 1977). But this figure might be an underestimate of people's true propensity, because almost all cultures (including American and European) prefer that people be right-handed, and use various techniques to coerce use of the right hand. The degree of pressure to be right-handed appears to vary. One cross-cultural survey found that about 10 to 12 percent of Eskimos and Australian Aborigines were left-handed, indicating a minor coercion toward right-handedness in those two relatively loose cultures. In Western European samples, the rate was about 6 percent, and in Hong Kong, the rate was near 1 percent, suggesting that those cultures are much tighter. Interestingly, the percentage of "lefties" among women enrolled at the University of Hong Kong was zero, suggesting that they are subjected to particularly strong cultural pressures (Dawson, 1974).

Collectivism and Individualism

One of the most profound ways cultures may differ from each other is the way they view the relationship between the individual and society. Cultures can be arrayed along the collectivism-individualism dimension, which compares the Western view of the individual that is probably familiar to most readers of this book, with a viewpoint consistent with the Buddhist philosophy summarized in Chapter 13.

According to psychologists who study this dimension, in collectivist cultures such as Japan, the needs of the group (the "collective") are more important than the rights of individuals (Markus & Kitayama, 1991). Indeed, the boundary between the individual self and the others in one's group is relatively fuzzy. For example, the Japanese word for "self," *jibun*, refers to "one's portion of the shared life space." Japanese also exhibit a general desire to sink inconspicuously into the group; a Japanese proverb says, "The nail that stands out gets pounded down" (Markus & Kitayama, 1991, pp. 224, 228).[7]

In individualist cultures, such as the United States, the single person is more important. People are viewed as separate from each other, and independence and individual prominence are important virtues. Individual rights take precedence over group interests, and one has a right—indeed, an obligation—to make moral choices that are independent, not determined by cultural tradition. The willingness to stand up for one's individual rights is all-important, and an American proverb teaches, "The squeaky wheel gets the grease" (Markus & Kitayama, 1991, p. 224). As we saw in Chapter 13, an individualist view also leads to phenomena such as existential anxiety, the concern over whether one is living life in the right way. Because the philosophy of individualism isolates people from each other, members of individualist cultures may be particularly vulnerable to problems such as loneliness and depression (Tseng, 2003).

> Because the philosophy of individualism isolates people from each other, members of individualistic cultures may be particularly vulnerable to problems such as loneliness and depression.

Japan, China, and India are the most frequently discussed examples of collectivist cultures, and the United States seems like the most obvious—or glaring—example of an individualist culture. A survey of employees of IBM (which has employees all over the world) found that natives of Taiwan, Peru, Pakistan, Columbia, and Venezuela were more collectivist and less individualist in outlook than natives of Australia, Britain, Canada, the Netherlands, and the United States (Hofstede, 1984). Within the United States, Hispanics, Asians, and African Americans are more collectivist than Anglos (Triandis, 1994). Also within the United States, women seem to be more collectivist than men (Lykes, 1985).

Researchers have developed long lists of behavioral and attitudinal differences between individualist and collectivist cultures. The most far-reaching suggestion is that personality itself might have a different meaning—or no meaning at all—in collectivist, especially Asian, societies (Markus & Kitayama, 1998). One indication is the number of trait words in Eastern and Western languages. English has about 2,800 trait words that are

---

[7] New Zealand, which is also more collectivist than the United States, has a similar common saying—that tall poppies are cut first.

used in everyday speech (Norman, 1967),[8] whereas Chinese has about 557 (Yang & Lee, 1971). This is a noticeably smaller number, and has led some psychologists to suspect that personality in the Western sense is less meaningful in Eastern contexts (e.g., Shweder & Bourne, 1982, 1984). However, 557 traits words is still quite a few, and every language studied so far has at least some. Moreover, recent studies have confirmed that personality traits can predict behavior, and behavior is consistent across situations in collectivist as well as individualist cultures (Church, Henderson-Harami, et al., 2008; Church, Katigbak, et al., 2008). So it is almost certainly going too far to say that personality traits have no meaning in collectivist cultures—and wrong to the point of being troubling to claim that collectivist people have "no personalities."

One does not have go to such an extreme to notice many differences between individualist and collectivist cultures that are real, interesting, and important. For example, more autobiographies are written in individualist countries, and more histories of the group are written in collectivist countries (Triandis, 1997). In collectivist countries, satisfaction with life is based on the harmony of one's relationships with others; in individualist countries self-esteem is more important (Kwan, Bond, & Singelis, 1997). People from collectivist cultures carefully observe social hierarchies. In India, a person who is even one day older is supposed to receive more respect from a younger friend (Triandis, 1997). People in individualist cultures are less attentive to differences in status. In the United States, many students call their professors by their first names; this does not happen in China, Japan, or India.[9]

Collectivist cultures are more sociable. For example, Mexicans spend more time in social interaction than Americans (Ramírez-Esparza, Mehl, Álvarez-Bermúdez, & Pennebaker, 2008). Skiing in groups and social bathing are more common in collectivist cultures; members of individualist cultures prefer to do these activities alone (Brandt, 1974). In general, members of individualist cultures spend less time with more people; members of collectivist cultures spend more time with fewer people (L. Wheeler, Reise, & Bond, 1989). The cocktail party, where one is supposed to circulate and meet

---

[8] Most of the traits on Allport and Odbert's famous, much longer list (see the introductory text for Part II) are rarely used in ordinary conversation. When is the last time you heard someone described as *vulnific*?

[9] Calling professors by their first names also would not have happened in the United States 50 years ago. Does this means that U.S. society has become more individualist? Perhaps so; one recent book argues that young Americans are becoming increasingly self-centered (Twenge, 2006).

as many people as possible, is a Western invention. While Easterners may be relatively standoffish and shy at such gatherings, they also tend to have a few close relationships, not casually entered into, that are more intimate than usual Western friendships.

Members of individualist and collectivist cultures may experience emotion differently. People in individualist countries report experiencing more self-focused emotions (such as anger), compared with people in collectivist countries, who are more likely to report experiencing other-focused emotions (such as sympathy) (Markus & Kitayama, 1991). Furthermore, Japanese students reported more pleasant emotional lives when they felt they were fitting well into their group; for American students individual concerns were just as important (Mesquita & Karasawa, 2002). Arranged marriages are relatively common in collectivist cultures, whereas members of individualist cultures are expected to marry for self-directed love. The downside of this romantic, individualist approach is that, when a married couple falls out of love, they may get divorced and cause their family to disintegrate. In collectivist cultures this is less likely (Tseng, 2003). In general, emotional experience in collectivist cultures appears to be more grounded in assessments of social worth, to reflect the nature of social reality rather than private, inner experience, and, perhaps most importantly, to depend on relationships rather than the individual alone (Mesquita, 2001).

People in individualist and collectivist cultures also may have different fundamental motivations. According to one theory, a primary danger in collectivist society is "losing face," or respect by one's social group. While respect by others can be lost quickly, it can be increased or regained only slowly, so it makes sense to become risk-averse and attentive to the possibility of loss. In individualist cultures, the focus is more on individual achievement that stands apart from the group, so doing better for oneself is more important than the risk of losing face. In an attempt to test part of this theory, one recent study found that North Americans (Canadians) were more sensitive to information that indicated the presence or absence of possibilities for pleasure or reward, whereas Asians (in this case, Japanese) were more sensitive to information relevant to risk or loss (Hamamura, Meijer, Heine, Kamaya, & Hori, 2009). For example, when asked to memorize a long list of life events, North Americans were more likely to remember "gorgeous weather for hiking" (representing the presence of a positive outcome), and Japanese were more likely to remember "doing better than expected on a test" (the absence of a negative outcome). Similarly, North Americans were more likely to remember "a favorite class was cancelled" (absence of a positive outcome), and Japanese were more likely to remember "stuck in a traffic jam" (presence of a negative outcome) (Hamamura et al., 2009, p. 457).

This difference in motivation can have advantages. Because of their need to stand out, members of individualist cultures may *self-enhance*, that is, describe themselves as better than they really are, whereas members of collectivist cultures, free of this need, may describe themselves more accurately. One study examined the *holier-than-thou phenomenon*, in which people describe themselves as being more likely than they really are to perform acts such as donating money or avoiding being rude (Balcetis, Dunning, & Miller, 2008). Members of individualistic cultures (English and German participants) were more likely to describe themselves as better ("holier") than they really were, than were members of collectivist cultures (Spanish and Chinese-American participants). Interestingly, this bias applied only to perceptions of self: Collectivists and individualists were both fairly accurate in predicting the future virtuous behavior of their acquaintances.

Even advertising differs across cultures. An ad in a collectivist culture like Korea might say, "Our ginseng drink is produced according to the methods of 500-year tradition," or, "Seven out of ten people are using our product." An American ad is more likely to say, "Choose your own view," "The Internet isn't for everybody. But then again, you're not everybody," or, simply, "Individualize!" (Kim & Markus, 1999, p. 793).

Beyond Collectivism and Individualism

The collectivism-individualism dimension has become a staple of cross-cultural psychology. But as research has accumulated, the picture of this difference between cultures has become more complicated. For one complication, Harry Triandis has suggested that individualistic or collectivist societies can both be further categorized as either vertical or horizontal (Triandis & Gelfand, 1998; see Table 14.1). *Vertical societies* assume that individual people are importantly different from each other, whereas *horizontal societies* tend to view all persons as essentially equal. Thus, a collectivist-vertical society might enforce strong authority on its members (e.g., China), whereas a collectivist-horizontal society might have weaker authority but a strong ethic that enforces equality and sharing (e.g., Israel). An individualist-vertical society would have strong authority but also the freedom (and the obligation) to support oneself in a market economy (e.g., France), whereas an individualist-horizontal society would value individual freedom but also assume that meeting everyone's needs is a shared obligation (e.g., Norway).

Table 14.1

VERTICAL AND HORIZONTAL TYPES OF COLLECTIVISM AND INDIVIDUALISM

Dimension	Collectivism	Individualism
Vertical	Self different from others	Self different from others
	Communal sharing	Market economy
	Authority ranking	Authority ranking
	Low freedom	High freedom
	Low equality	Low equality
	e.g., China	*e.g., France*
Horizontal	Self same as others	Self same as others
	Communal sharing	Market economy
	Low freedom	High freedom
	High equality	High equality
	e.g., Israel	*e.g., Norway*

Source: The examples of countries in this tables were chosen by Triandis and Gelfand. Table adapted from Triandis & Gelfand (1998), Table 1, p. 119.

Cultures also differ from each other in other ways that do not map well onto the collectivism-individualism dimension. One study compared *self-compassion*, defined as "holding painful emotions in mindful awareness while feelings of care and kindness are extended to the self" (Neff, Pisit sungkagarn, & Hsieh, 2008, p. 267), in the United States, Thailand, and Taiwan. While self-compassion might seem like a quintessentially collectivist idea, the study found that, while the highest levels were in Thailand, the lowest levels were in Taiwan—both ostensibly collectivist societies—and individualist United States fell in the middle. The authors speculated that the basis of the difference might stem from the predominance of Buddhist philosophy in Thailand compared with Confuciansim in Taiwan.

Even when the dimension is relevant, some researchers have expressed concerns that the differences between cultures considered individualist and collectivist might be exaggerated. In cultures viewed as extreme on this dimension, such as Japan and the United States, plenty of people have individual points of view that stand outside their own cultural norms. In other words, Japan and China have a large number of individualists who are striving for personal accomplishment, and the United States includes many collectivists who are closely bound and attentive to the needs of others

(Oyserman, Coon, & Kemmelmeir, 2002; Oishi, 2004). In general, as will be discussed later in this chapter, it is easy to exaggerate differences between cultures, and the differences between those labeled collectivist or individualist may not be as clear-cut or uniform for all their members as discussions of this distinction sometimes imply.

CULTURAL ASSESSMENT AND PERSONALITY ASSESSMENT

Assessing the personality of a culture can be a little bit like assessing a person. Indeed, the three dimensions Triandis uses to describe cultures can also be used to describe individuals. The cultural complexity dimension is analogous to the personality trait of *cognitive complexity*; cultural tightness resembles the traits of conscientiousness and *intolerance for ambiguity*; the collectivist-individualist distinction is analogous to a dimension of personal values that focuses on whether one believes that the individual is more important than the group (*ideocentrism*), or vice versa (*allocentrism*). It seems that complexity, tightness, and collectivity are traits of individuals as well as cultures. As we shall see in the next section, psychologists have also used more familiar personality-trait concepts to understand cross-cultural differences.

As we saw in Chapters 4 through 7, personality traits are a central concept in psychology. Apparently, all languages have terms for traits such as *talkative*, *timid*, and *diligent*, but they differ in how many terms they include in the lexicon. So it is not surprising that cross-cultural psychologists have tried to address the degree to which certain traits apply to different cultures. Researchers have done this in two ways. The first is to try to characterize cultural differences by assessing the degree to which average levels of specific traits vary between cultures. The second is to dive a bit more deeply into the cultures being compared by assessing the degree to which the traits that characterize people in one culture can meaningfully characterize people in another.

Comparing the Same Traits Across Cultures

As an example of the first approach, psychologists have translated the MMPI (see Chapter 5) into Chinese and found that, compared with Americans,

Chinese people on average score higher on emotional reserve, introversion, considerateness, social caution, and self-restraint (Cheung & Song, 1989). At present, the most common way to compare the personalities of different cultures is using the Big Five (see Chapter 7). A study using translations of the NEO Personality Inventory (see Chapter 5) assessed extraversion in a large number of "Old World" nations, producing the map shown in Figure 14.3. Another study using the same inventory compared ethnic Chinese living in Canada with those in Hong Kong. Those who lived in Canada described themselves (S data) as being more open, cheerful, and agreeable, and these differences with people in Hong Kong increased the longer they lived in Canada—which suggests they arose because of the cultural environment (McCrae, Yik, Trapnell, Bond, & Paulhus, 1998). Personality varies within nations as well. As was mentioned in Chapter 7, one survey of more than 500,000 Americans found that (with some exceptions) extraversion, conscientiousness, and agreeableness tend to be highest in the Midwest and

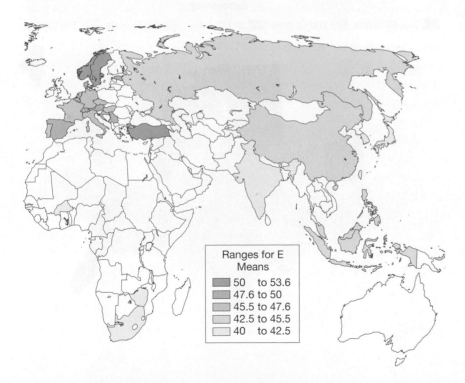

Figure 14.3 Extraversion Scores in Old World Nations The darker the color, the higher the average extraversion (E) score. No data were available for countries without shading.

Source: McCrae (2004), Figure 2, p. 11.

Southeast, neuroticism highest in the Northeast, and openness to experience highest along the two coasts (Rentfrow, Gosling, & Potter, 2008; see Figure 14.4 for a map of extraversion; see Figure 7.2 for all of the Big Five).

Cultural differences in personality are not just interesting; they can be important. People in different countries have different levels of self-esteem. According to one study, residents of Canada have higher self-esteem than those in any other country in the world, followed by Israel, Estonia, and Serbia. Residents of Japan have the lowest self-esteem, and those in Hong Kong and Bangladesh are not much higher. This fact may be significant, because one recent study found that the lower a country's average level of self-esteem, the higher the suicide rate (Chatard, Selimbegović, & Konan, 2009). In this sense, cultural differences in personality can be a matter of life and death.

> Cultural differences in personality can be a matter of life and death.

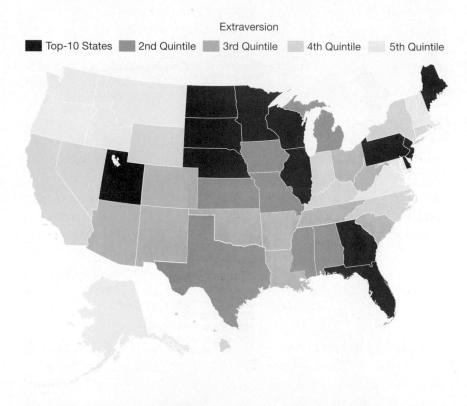

Figure 14.4 Extraversion Across the United States According to a survey of more than 500,000 people, Americans who live in the Midwest and Southeast are the most extraverted with some exceptions, as you can see.
Source: Rentfrow, Gosling, & Potter (2008), p. 352.

What about gender differences? Psychologists addressed this question by administering the NEO Personality Inventory, or translations of it, in 26 cultures to 23,031 individuals (Costa, Terracciano, & McCrae, 2001). They found that, in almost all cultures, women scored higher than men in neuroticism, agreeableness, warmth, and openness to feelings; men scored higher than women in assertiveness and openness to ideas. Surprisingly, these differences were actually larger in so-called developed societies such as Belgium, France, and the United States than in less-developed areas such as Zimbabwe and Malaysia.

Different Traits for Different Cultures?

The findings summarized above are interesting, but their meaning is not always clear, because they depend on a not-so-hidden assumption—that the same traits can be used to describe people in different cultures. This assumption is probably all right if one wishes to compare Michigan with New York,[10] but becomes more tenuous when comparing, say, China and the United States. Psychologists have put major effort into investigating the degree to which the same traits are relevant and have the same meaning across cultures. The results are mixed.

An impressive and influential program of research has shown that the Big Five traits of personality can be found in observers' personality ratings in more than 50 cultures (McCrae, Terracciano, & 78 members of the Personality Profiles of Cultures Project, 2005). But other studies have found many variations from one culture to the next. For example, one study concluded that measures of the Big Five could be effectively translated into Spanish, but that such translations also missed particular aspects of Spanish personality, such as humor, good nature, and unconventionality (Benet-Martínez & John, 1998, 2000). Building on findings like these, some researchers have argued that only three of the Big Five—conscientiousness, extraversion, and agreeableness—should be considered truly universal (De Raad & Peabody, 2005).

Translating personality-trait terms from one language to another is a hazardous enterprise because translations are always at least a little bit inexact. Some quantitatively sophisticated psychologists are attempting to improve the degree to which personality tests are comparable from one culture and language to the next, by using a technique called *item response*

---

[10] Is it?

theory (IRT). IRT analyses go deep into the analysis of personality inventories by looking not just at mean scores, but at patterns in how participants respond to specific items. One such study found that, in a scale used to measure satisfaction with life, four of the five items yielded completely different patterns of response between Chinese and American participants (Oishi, 2006). Another study found that, while Germans appeared to score higher than Minnesotans in aggression and absorption, and Minnesotans higher in well-being, control, and traditionalism, these findings might be due simply to differences in patterns of item response (W. Johnson, Spinath, Krueger, Angleitner, & Riemann, 2008). The ultimate implications of these recent findings are not clear, but they do serve as a caution that, when comparing mean trait scores between cultures, there may be more (or less) than meets the eye.

To move beyond such problems in translation, an increasing number of psychologists around the world are developing trait scales *endogenously* (from the inside), to see if personality-trait constructs that emerge in one culture also emerge in another. This approach is much more difficult because the nature of the research requires the work of psychologists who are native to each culture, and many areas of the world do not have the traditions or means to train and support homegrown psychologists. Nonetheless, rapid progress is being made.

One recent study examined personality traits in China. It began by listing the trait words found in a Chinese dictionary and then asking large numbers of Chinese participants to rate one another using those traits. The researchers found that these traits could be summarized by seven factors that they labeled "extraversion," "conscientiousness," "unselfishness," "harmfulness,"[11] "gentle temper," "intellect," and "dependency/fragility" (Zhou, Saucier, Gao, & Liu, 2009). As you can see, only three or four of these seem similar to any of the Big Five: extraversion, conscientiousness, intellect (which resembles openness), and perhaps harmfulness (as the opposite of agreeableness). A parallel study, conducted in Spain, also found seven factors in Castilian Spanish (Benet-Martínez & Waller, 1997). The Spanish personality factors were labeled "positive valence," "negative valence," "conscientiousness," "openness," "agreeableness," "pleasantness" (referring to emotional experience), and "engagement" (or "passion"). Chinese and Spanish may both have seven basic personality traits, but, to read these lists, they are not the same seven.

---

[11] They also used the label "noxious violativeness," which sounds dreadful.

Taking a different tack, a group of Chinese psychologists aimed to develop an indigenous Chinese Personality Assessment Inventory (yes, it is called the CPAI). The result was a scale that the researchers concluded measured the factors of neuroticism, conscientiousness, agreeableness, and extraversion in a manner that resembled these traits as represented in widely used instruments in English (Cheung et al., 1996). But they also found, instead of the "openness to experience" factor often found in Western samples, a factor they interpreted as reflecting an individual's degree of interpersonal relatedness. They also developed factor scores unique to the Chinese context that measured such traits as "harmony," "face" (similar to "dignity"), "thrift versus extravagance," and a trait they called *ren qing* ("interpersonal favor").

Thinking

One of the most intriguing and challenging questions facing cross-cultural psychology concerns the degree to which people from different cultures think differently. On one level, it seems safe to infer that because behavioral traits differ across cultures, as we have just seen, the thinking associated with behavior must be different too. On another level, it is difficult to specify the ways in which thought processes in one culture may differ from those in another, so research attempting to do this is opening an exciting new frontier in psychology that has important and controversial implications.

For example, one line of research suggests that East Asians think more *holistically* than Americans, explaining events in context rather than in isolation, and seeking to integrate divergent points of view rather than set one against another (Nisbett, Peng, Choi, & Norenzayan, 2001). In particular, this difference appears to characterize how they think about the self. According to one study, Japanese and Chinese people are more willing than Americans to describe themselves in contradictory terms (e.g., as friendly but shy), and also use more holistic phrases such as "I am someone insignificant in the universe" or "I am a living form" (Spencer-Rogers, Boucher, Mori, Wang, & Peng, 2009, p. 32).

These stylistic differences may be related to the collectivism-individualism distinction discussed earlier, in which collectivists feel more a part of their social environment than individualists do. This difference may reach down to the perceptual level. In one study, Japanese participants either watched animated underwater scenes or looked at photographs of wildlife; in both cases, they remembered more information about the wider context than did American participants, and were better able to recognize specific objects when they saw them in their original settings (Masuda & Nisbett, 2001). These results suggest that an American observer may look at a scene and see a specific object or person, whereas the Japanese observer is more likely to see and remember the larger context.

A controversial area of cross-cultural research on thinking concerns the degree to which Asians, compared with Americans, characteristically formulate and express independent and original points of view. Various psychologists and educators have observed that Asian students seem drawn to fields that require rote study and memorization rather than independent thinking, and that they are less willing than European Americans to speak up in class discussion (e.g., Mahbubani, 2002). One Vietnamese-American writer lamented that this occurs because

> "self-expression is largely discouraged across Asia. . . . Asia is by and large a continent where the ego is suppressed. The self exists in the context of families and clans . . . [while] America still values the maverick, the inventor, the loudmouth class clown, the individual with a vision" (Lam, 2003, p. M6).

Other observers have offered a different interpretation. One recent study showed that for Asian Americans, thinking is disrupted by trying to talk at the same time, whereas this effect was not found in Americans of European descent (Kim, 2002). Thus, a quiet Asian-American student may be silent because she is thinking! The Confucian philosophy of learning prescribes that the first thing a student should do is learn the basic facts of a field, then analyze, and finally innovate. Early in her learning career, a student is not supposed to formulate independent opinions; that should come only later, after she has sufficient knowledge (Tweed & Lehman, 2002). Another writer has observed that

> Asians are respectful not because they are afraid of their teachers or because they have no questions, but because they are brought up with the idea that humility ensures better learning. They are taught to listen attentively and to question only after they have understood others. (J. Li, 2003, pp. 146–147)

Values

The most difficult issues in cross-cultural psychology concern values. People feel deeply about matters of right and wrong, and may be not merely surprised but also upset and angry when they find that other people do not share their views. Sometimes, wars start. Thus, a particular challenge is to try to understand how even seemingly obvious and basic values can vary across cultures, and to formulate an appropriate response to these differences.

THE SEARCH FOR UNIVERSAL VALUES

Cross-cultural research on values has followed two tracks. One track seeks values that are universal to all cultures. This is similar in intent to the research summarized in the previous chapter (Chapter 13) that tried to identify traits that all cultures see as virtues. Finding universal values would have two implications. First, we might infer that a value held in all cultures is in some sense a "real" value that goes beyond cultural judgment, a value which we can be confident should be valued. (Do you agree with this inference?) Second, if we could find a set of common values, we might be able to use these to settle disputes between cultures by developing compromises based on the areas of universal agreement.

An influential study by the cross-cultural psychologists Shalom Schwartz and Lilach Sagiv (1995) identified 10 values as candidates. The 10 possibly universal values are power, achievement, hedonism, stimulation, self-direction, understanding, benevolence, tradition, conformity, and security. Another way to look at these values is to see them as goals that everybody, everywhere, wants to achieve. Schwartz and Sagiv theorize that these values can be organized in terms of two dimensions. One is the *openness to change–conservatism* dimension, and the other they called the *self-transcendence–self-enhancement* dimension. For example, stimulation is high on openness to change and low on conservatism, whereas conformity, tradition, and security are the reverse. Likewise, achievement is high on self-enhancement and low on self-transcendance, while benevolence is the reverse (see Figure 14.5). Ratings of these values followed this two-part structure, more or less, in countries including Israel, Japan, and Australia. The hope of this ongoing research is to develop not just a universal list of values, but an understanding of how these values relate to each other and apply to decisions, behaviors, and cultural priorities.

CULTURAL DIFFERENCES IN VALUES

While Schwartz and Sagiv's research seeks to identify a universal structure of values, they acknowledge that cultural differences are still important. The second track in cross-cultural research on values strives to illuminate these differences. A long-standing interest of many researchers has been

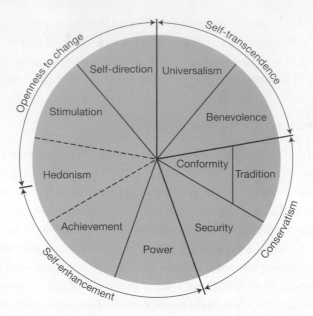

Figure 14.5 **Theoretical Structure of Values Suggested to Be Universal** The 10 terms in this figure all refer to values that, it has been theorized, people in all cultures are motivated to live by. They are arranged here in terms of their relevance to two dimensions: openness to change versus conservatism, and self-transcendence versus self-enhancement.

Source: Schwartz & Sagiv (1995), Figure 1, p. 96.

the differences between collectivist and individualist cultures in their styles of moral reasoning (J. G. Miller, Bersoff, & Harwood, 1990). While the individualist cultural ethos emphasizes liberty, freedom of choice, rights, and individual needs, some theorists claim, the collectivist cultural ethos emphasizes obligations, reciprocity, and duties to the group (Iyengar & Lepper, 1999; J. G. Miller & Bersoff, 1992). The collectivist style of moral reasoning imposes a group norm; the individualist style emphasizes independent and individual choice.

We can see this distinction even within North American culture. For example, although individualism is often viewed as a Western cultural attribute, the Roman Catholic Church—a Western institution if ever there was one—is profoundly collectivist in outlook. Individualism is really a Protestant, northwestern European idea, whereas collectivism is more Catholic and southeastern European (Sabini, 1995). Martin Luther broke with the Catholic Church over the right of individuals to interpret the Scriptures. The Catholic view was—and still is—that any interpretation must come from the Church itself.

We can hear echoes of this ancient argument, as well as of the distinction between individualism and collectivism, in the modern debate over abortion. The individualist point of view, endorsed by many (though not all) Protestant and Jewish denominations, is that abortion is a matter of individual moral responsibility and choice. One might deplore abortion and regard it as a tragic occurrence but still endorse the idea that it is the pregnant woman who is most centrally involved, and in the end it all comes down to her individual, free decision. Those who endorse the right to safe, legal abortions do not like to be called "pro-abortion"; they prefer the term "pro-choice."

The very different, collectivist point of view, strongly espoused by the Catholic Church and some of the more conservative Protestant denominations, is that abortion is morally wrong, period. The unborn fetus is already a person—a member in good standing of the collective, if you will. To abort that fetus is to kill a member of the collective, something no individual member—not even the fetus's mother—has a right to do. Indeed, it is the duty of the collective, institutionalized in the church or the state, to prohibit any such act. The matter does not come down to personal choice at all. It comes down to a collectively determined issue of right and wrong.

No wonder this debate shows no signs of subsiding, and no wonder, too, that grounds for reasonable compromise seem nonexistent. In the abortion debate, we see a head-on collision between two fundamentally different ways of addressing moral issues. Elements of both views coexist, uneasily, in North American culture, but one of them cannot be mapped onto the other. From either a collectivist or individualist perspective on the abortion debate, the other point of view is simply and deeply wrong.

THE ORIGINS OF CULTURAL DIFFERENCES

We have now surveyed ample evidence that the average personalities of people in different cultures are often different, that people differ in *how* they differ in different cultures (i.e., the same traits may not apply in all cultures), and that cultures can hold profoundly divergent basic values. So this may be a good time to step back and ask two questions that, while not often addressed, have been lurking in the background all along: *Why* are cultures so different? And what determines the specific, distinctive psychology that a particular culture develops?

Avoiding the Issue

One approach to cultural psychology, influential until fairly recently, regarded these questions as essentially unanswerable. The philosophy of **deconstructionism** holds that reality has no meaning apart from what humans invent, or "construct." This philosophy is an important part of the modern study of literature, and has also permeated some areas of anthropology (e.g., Shweder & Sullivan, 1990). Translated into cultural psychology, deconstructionism implies that any answer to why a culture is the way it is would itself have to be based on the assumptions of another culture (J. G. Miller, 1999). This is another way of saying that no meaningful answer is possible. If you recall Funder's Third Law—about something beating nothing two times out of three—you will not be surprised to learn that I do not have much patience with the deconstructionist approach to cultural comparison. Differences between cultures are real, and to ask why they exist is to ask a good question.

The Ecological Approach

The most reasonable explanation would seem to be that different cultures developed, over a long period of time, in different circumstances and with the need to deal with different problems. Triandis (1994) proposed a straightforward model that can be diagrammed as

Ecology $\longrightarrow$ culture $\longrightarrow$ socialization $\longrightarrow$ personality $\longrightarrow$ behavior

In this model, behavior comes from personality, which comes from implicit and explicit teaching during childhood (socialization is another name for enculturation in this context), which is a product of the culture. The first term in Triandis's model is *ecology*, by which he means the physical layout and resources of the land where the culture originated, together with the distinctive tasks and challenges this culture has faced.

For example, the collectivist nature of Chinese culture might be traceable to the need, thousands of years ago, to develop complex agricultural projects and water systems that required the coordination of many people. To succeed at these tasks, a culture had to develop in which people were willing to surrender some degree of self-interest in order to serve the common good. In the same historical period, people who lived in hunting or gathering societies, where individual effort is more important, did not develop the

"I don't know how it started, either. All I know is that it's part of our corporate culture."

same collectivist outlook or complex social system. While it takes thousands of people to build a water system, a hunting party that becomes too large will not catch anything. This difference, we could speculate (and honestly, that's all we are doing), may be one reason why China developed a collectivist culture while Germany developed an individualist one.

On an even broader scale, the biologist Jared Diamond has argued that European culture became a dominant colonial power around the world because of an accident of geography. Ancient Europe had native plants that were easily turned into reliable, food-giving crops and had native animals that were readily domesticated to provide food and work. Another, ironic, "advantage" is that at the same time Europeans began to travel around the world, at home they often lived close together in filthy cities. Those who survived developed wide immunity to diseases that were fatal to other peoples, such as Native Americans, who lived in cleaner environments (Diamond, 1999). The arrival of Europeans into such settings often meant the arrival of a devastating epidemic.

Disease can affect cultural development in other ways. One recent study examined the degree to which cultures differed in their average levels of extraversion, openness, and sociosexuality (which, as explained in Chapter 6, is the willingness to engage in sexual relationships in the absence of a long-term relationship) (Schaller & Murray, 2008). The average level of these traits tends to be lower, it turns out, in countries that historically have suffered from high levels of infectious disease. (Many of these countries lie near the equator,[12] where the warm climate apparently facilitates disease transmission.) Why? The authors of the study speculate that extraverted behavior, open behavior, and—perhaps most of all—"sociosexual" behavior, all increase interpersonal contact and the risk of catching a disease from someone. As a result, people who are more introverted and less open and sociosexual have better chances for survival, making their type more common as members of the culture over time.

Even small differences in ecology can lead to large cultural differences that help to shape personality. Truk and Tahiti, small islands in the South Pacific with cultures dependent on fishing, have evolved different patterns of gender roles and aggressive behavior (Gilmore, 1990). In Truk, catching fish requires venturing out to sea, which is quite hazardous. The result is a culture in which the men who must do this learn to be brave, violent, and physical, and also dominating of women. In Tahiti, fish can be caught easily in the home lagoon, which is not dangerous at all. The men in this culture tend to be gentle, to ignore insults, to be very slow to fight, and also to be respectful of women. Apparently, all this is a result of where the fish are!

It is also possible to explain the development of subcultures as a function of particular conditions experienced by groups within larger cultures. As I mentioned earlier, extreme poverty and decades of racial discrimination have led some ethnic subcultures within the United States to develop styles of self-presentation (young males seeking to appear tough and threatening) and self-definition (through identification with gangs and other sources of social support and physical protection) that strongly contrast with the mainstream culture (E. Anderson, 1994). The culture of honor in the American South may have its roots in the agrarian past of that region, where land and possessions had to be personally protected, or else lost (D. Cohen et al., 1996). Other aspects of minority subcultures in the United States and Canada stem from distinct ethnic heritages rooted in Asia, Africa, Latin America, and Europe, which have been more or less imported to the North American continent.

---

[12] Of course, the equator runs through several continents. Countries historically high in infectious disease include Nigeria, Zambia, Greece, Italy, India, China, Indonesia, Venezuela, and Brazil. Some of the lowest historic rates were in South Africa, Sweden, Norway, and Germany (Gangestad & Buss, 1993).

Cultural Differences From Personality Differences

Almost all psychologists who study cultural differences assume that they are learned, not innate. And, as was mentioned earlier, members of ethnic cultures are almost as different from each other as they are from members of other cultures—but not quite as different. In Chapter 9, we saw some evidence of different rates of a gene associated with emotional control in Japanese as compared with Caucasian samples. A separate study suggests that differences between Japan and the United States on outcomes such as depression, anxiety, optimism, and self-esteem may arise because of the personality differences between these cultures (Matsumoto, Nakagawa, & Estrada, 2009). Findings like these are leading a few psychologists, such as Robert R. McCrae and David Matsumoto, to suggest that culture → personality may not tell the whole story (McCrae, 2004; Matsumoto et al., 2009). Perhaps, to some degree, we should also consider the possibility that personality → culture.

Even proponents of this idea are quick to acknowledge its hazards. McCrae (2004, p. 8) points out that any discussion of genetic differences between cultural groups should be sure to emphasize the following:

1. The differences are small, at most.
2. Traits are likely to be even weaker predictors of behavior at the cultural level than they are at the individual level.
3. People within cultures are widely different from each other.
4. The data available so far can be explained in several different ways.

Perhaps an even more important consideration, as mentioned before, is that cultures themselves are not sharply defined categories, and many people belong to two or even more. With the basis of cultural membership so complex, it is hard to imagine how genetic differences could be a major contributor to cultural differences.

Moreover, the distinction between culture determining personality, and personality determining culture, is not clear-cut. Take, for example, the hypothesis that societies that must develop large-scale projects requiring many participants—such as ancient China—tend to develop collectivist cultures. The same pressures that push the culture in a collectivist direction may also push individuals in the same direction: Collectivists thrive, have more children, and their genes (e.g., a gene that causes one to avoid interpersonal conflict) become more widely represented in the gene pool over generations. This gradual change in genetics might, in turn, help to entrench the cultural differences even more deeply. A child born into such a culture—or someone who migrates to it—might or might not have the relevant gene, but will absorb the relevant cultural teachings. So, does culture produce personality or is it the other way around? This question might, in the end, be a lot like the classic query concerning chickens and eggs. It's not only hard to say which one came first, it's not very meaningful.

> Does culture produce personality or is it the other way around?

CHALLENGES AND NEW DIRECTIONS FOR CROSS-CULTURAL RESEARCH

Cross-cultural psychology raises several issues that make research especially challenging, and which are likely to receive increasing attention in the future. How do we avoid having our view of other cultures colored by our own cultural background? Does focusing exclusively on cultural differences lead us to exaggerate them? How can different cultures' values be reconciled? What is the right way to think about areas of the world—or even individuals—with more than one culture? Now that we have almost finished our survey of recent research, it is time to consider these questions.

Ethnocentrism

Any observation of another culture almost certainly will be colored by the observer's cultural background, no matter how hard he tries to avoid it. A truly objective point of view, free from any cultural bias, is difficult to attain, and some anthropologists argue that is it impossible. As Triandis (1994) pointed out, researchers are most in danger of committing *ethnocentrism* (judging another culture from the point of view of your own) when the "real" nature of the situation seems most obvious.

For example, Triandis considered two interviews, reported by Shweder, Mahapatra, & Miller (1990), concerning "a widow in your community [who] eats fish two or three times a week." First, a Hindu Indian was interviewed:

Q. Is the widow's behavior wrong?

A. Yes. Widows should not eat fish, meat, onions or garlic, or any "hot" foods. . . .

A. How serious is the violation?

A. A very serious violation. . . .

A. Is it a sin?

A. Yes. It's a "great" sin.

Q. What if no one knew this had been done? It was done in private or secretly. Would it be wrong then?

A. What difference does it make if it is done while alone? It is wrong. A widow should spend her time seeking salvation—seeking to be reunited with the soul of her husband. Hot foods will distract her. They will stimulate her sexual appetite. . . . She will want sex and behave like a whore.

Then an interview of an American is reported:

Q. Is the widow's behavior wrong?

A. No. She can eat fish if she wants to.

Q. How serious is the violation?

A. It is not a violation.

Q. Is it a sin?

A. No.

Q. What if no one knew this had been done? It was done in private or secretly. Would it be wrong then?

A. It is not wrong, in private or public. (Shweder et al., 1990, pp. 168–170, as quoted in Triandis, 1994.)

Triandis pointed out that the responses of the Indian informant may seem absurd and somewhat amusing, whereas those of the American informant seem obvious and even boring. It takes an intellectual struggle to consider the possibility that the Indian's responses are just as reasonable as the American's, and differ only by starting with unfamiliar cultural assumptions. The principal assumption underlying the Indian's conversation is that the relationship between a husband and wife exists for all eternity, whereas the American assumes a widow is a free and independent individual. (The Indian interview also contains assumptions about the aphrodisiac properties of fish and certain other foods.) The American point of view will be more familiar to most readers of this book, but the Indian one is not necessarily false.

The point of this example is not that we should begin worrying about widows who eat garlic, but that it is difficult, and perhaps impossible, to cast off the cultural lenses through which we see the world. The whole point of cross-cultural psychology is to attempt this anyway.

The Exaggeration of Cultural Differences

Cross-cultural research sometimes exaggerates differences by acting as if all members of a given culture are alike (Gjerde, 2004). Researchers often imply that everybody in India, Japan, or China acts or thinks in the same way; some even claim that Indians, Japanese, and Chinese all have the same, "Eastern" view of the world. Given the size and diversity of these populations, such blanket characterizations are unlikely to be correct (Matsumoto, 2004; Oishi, 2004). As one writer observed:

> For instance, we say, the Japanese culture is serene (although many Japanese are not; just look at my sisters!), or the American culture is fast-paced (although many Americans are laid-back; just look at the students in my personality course!). (Oishi, 2004, p. 69)

Cultural differences tend to be exaggerated for at least three reasons. One is that cross-cultural psychology has long been in the business of finding differences. After all, if cultures were predominantly similar, then perhaps cross-cultural psychology would not have much to do. At the same time, even cross-cultural psychologists harbor stereotypes, which may increase their tendency to exaggerate the differences they perceive (Oishi, 2004; Oyserman et al., 2002).

A second reason is statistical, and it concerns some of the issues raised in Chapter 3. Many studies of cultural differences use significance tests rather than examining effect sizes. If the cultural groups studied are large, as they often are, then statistically significant results—differences that would be unlikely if only chance were operating—are easy to find. Once found, they will be published and may be described as important. Yet the actual size of the differences may be very small. A related problem is that many analyses of cultures look for differences at the aggregate or general level, which examines an average across a large cultural context. For example, studies (including some cited earlier in this chapter) have showed that advertising is often different from one culture to the next (e.g., Han & Shavitt, 1994). But advertising targets the largest possible number of people at once and reflects general cultural views rather than individual perspectives. At the level of the individual, differences between cultures may be smaller (Oyserman et al., 2002; Oishi, 2004).

A third reason is the psychological phenomenon that social psychologists call the **outgroup homogeneity bias** (e.g., Linville & Jones, 1980; Lorenzi-Cioldi, 1993; B. Park & Rothbart, 1982). One's own group naturally seems to contain individuals who differ widely from each other. But members of groups to which one does not belong seem to be "all the same." For example, students at one college often have stereotypes about what students at another, nearby college are like. But they are well aware that the students at their own college are very different from one another. Many of us can easily describe stamp collectors, Californians, and members of the National Rifle Association—unless we happen to belong to one of those groups, in which case we may feel they are too diverse to characterize in any simple way. Even cross-cultural psychologists and anthropologists—who, of all people, should know better—sometimes fall into this bias trap. They may describe members of another culture (but never their own culture!) as if everybody in it were essentially the same. But just as Western culture contains both individualists and collectivists, the same is true about China, India, or anyplace else. Somebody who says, "Nobody in India has a sense of the self as being separate," is making the same mistake as somebody who assumes that everybody in the world senses the self as being separate.

Interestingly, to emphasize the variations between individuals within a culture is an individualist view. To emphasize variations between whole cultures is a collectivist view. Which view is yours?

Cultures and Values

Unless one is careful, cross-cultural psychology can sometimes lead to *cultural relativism*. As we saw in Chapter 13, cultural relativism is the phenomenologically based idea that all cultural views of reality are equally valid, and that it is presumptuous and ethnocentric to judge any of them as good or bad.

This is a point of view that seems fine until we begin to consider some examples. In some areas of Africa and Asia, female genitals are mutilated as part of a cultural tradition intended to preserve purity and thereby improve girls' chances for marriage. Typically, elderly village women use a razor blade or piece of glass, under unhygienic conditions and without anesthesia, to remove the clitoris or the clitoris and labia minora of a young girl. Each year, this procedure is performed on about 2 million girls between the ages of 4 and 15. Opposition expressed by the World Health Organization and some international human rights groups has sometimes been denounced as ethnocentric (Associated Press, 1994). But does our different cultural perspective truly mean that we have no grounds for condemning this tradition?

Steven Spielberg's movie *Schindler's List* describes the career of Oskar Schindler, who, by the standards of the dominant culture of his day (the Nazi culture), was a misfit and an outlaw. One of the fascinating things about this movie is its suggestion that Schindler might not have been completely well adjusted psychologically. He is shown as disorganized, deceitful, impulsive, and not very good at calculating risks. Yet it is precisely these traits that allowed him to engage in behavior—a complex and dangerous scheme to save thousands of Jewish lives over several years—that today is regarded as heroic. Being a misfit in one's culture is not always a bad thing.

> Being a misfit in one's culture is not always a bad thing.

The dangers of cultural relativism have been compellingly described by psychologists Jack and Jeanne Block:

> If the absolute definition [of psychological adjustment and of right and wrong] risks the danger of a parochial arrogance, the relative definition may be advocating the value of valuelessness. . . . To the extent that relativism implies one culture is as good as another . . . relativism provides a rationale for tolerance that is also a rationale for perpetuation of what is, rather than what might be. (J. Block, Block, Siegelman, & von der Lippe, 1971, p. 328)

This issue is what makes the search for universal values, discussed earlier in this chapter, so important. Every culture is likely to have its own values, but perhaps we can all agree about a few.

Subcultures and Multiculturalism

At the beginning of this chapter we saw how the term *culture* was surprisingly difficult to pin down. Some cultural groupings are both obvious and oversimplified, such as the difference between East and West (which neatly divides the globe in two), or (almost the same thing) collectivism and individualism. Another way to group people is on the basis of language or in terms of geography, such as political boundaries or one's continent of residence. All of these groupings have proved useful as bases of psychological comparison, but it is important to bear in mind that they are also imprecise and to some extent arbitrary. Members of the same cultural group by one definition may belong to different groups by another definition. Furthermore, cultural groups often contain distinct and important subgroups. For example, much of the research summarized in this chapter treats North Americans as a single cultural group that can then be compared with Asians, including Koreans, Japanese, Chinese, Indians, and others. But it may have occurred to Canadian readers that there are subtle but real cultural differences within North America, and to Asian readers that not all Asian groups are alike, either.

Important subcultures exist even within the political borders of the United States. I already mentioned the work on the culture of honor that describes how residents of the southern United States differ from those in the North, and patterns of the Big Five traits across different states. Research has also documented other ethnically based differences within the population sometimes described simply as "European American." One fascinating study compared American-born, second-generation-or-later descendants of immigrants from Scandinavia, with similarly distant descendants of Irish immigrants. When videotaped recounting times in their lives when they felt happiness or love, Irish Americans smiled significantly more than did Scandinavian Americans, consistent with the customs of their different ancestral cultures (Tsai & Chentsova-Dutton, 2003). This finding suggests that there may be more ethnic diversity within European-American culture than previously suspected and opens the door to future research.

Another complication to cultural grouping, especially in nations of immigrants such as the United States and Canada, is that some *multicultural* individuals may belong to more than one culture. For example, California includes many young people raised in Spanish-speaking households among extended and powerful Mexican-American family groups, who also attend English-speaking schools, watch U.S. television, and participate in other thoroughly "Americanized" aspects of U.S. culture. The same is true of many Asian Americans and first-generation children of immigrants from many different lands, not to mention the many children whose two parents come from different ethnic or cultural groups. When confronted by the typical university form that demands, "State your ethnicity," what are they supposed to put down?

According to recent research, perhaps some of them should check "all of the above" (or at least check more than one option). One study showed that bicultural Chinese Americans can switch quickly between Chinese and American ways of looking at the world, sometimes without being aware of doing so. All it takes is looking at pictures of a Chinese dragon or the Statue of Liberty. That's enough, according to one remarkable study, to invoke Chinese or American styles of perception. As was described earlier, the Chinese style is more holistic and the American style more focused on specific details (Benet-Martínez, Leu, Lee, & Morris, 2002).

Another study suggested that bilingual individuals may, in some sense, have "two personalities" (Ramírez-Esparza, Gosling, Benet-Martínez, Potter, & Pennebaker, 2006). The study had two stages. First, a test of the Big Five personality traits was administered to Americans who spoke only English and to Mexicans who spoke only Spanish. Then the same test was given, in both languages, to individuals in both countries who spoke both languages. The results showed that Americans who spoke only English, and bilinguals taking the test in English, scored higher in extraversion, agreeableness, and conscientiousness. Mexicans who spoke only Spanish and bilinguals taking the test in Spanish scored higher in neuroticism; results for openness were mixed. These results suggest that bilinguals to some degree had two personalities, higher in extraversion, agreeableness, and conscientiousness when they think about themselves in English, but higher in neuroticism when they think about themselves in Spanish. Further work is needed to see if these differences in self-report also appear when behavior is measured directly—for example, are bilinguals more agreeable when they interact with others in English than in Spanish?—but these preliminary results are intriguing.

By some estimates, about half the world's population is bilingual (Grosjean, 1982), so many individuals may have two personalities, in some sense. But such biculturalism does not always come easy. Some people integrate multiple cultural identities to gain the maximum benefit from each, while others experience conflict and even stress (Haritatos & Benet-Martínez, 2002). The concept of *bicultural identity integration (BII)* has been introduced to measure and explain this difference (Benet-Martínez et al., 2002). Individuals who score high on BII are said to see themselves as members of a combined or emergent joint culture that integrates aspects of both source cultures. For example, they might see themselves as "Mexican-American" in a way that is neither Mexican nor American but comfortably combines aspects of both cultures' traditions and languages. Individuals who score low on BII, by contrast, experience conflict between their two cultures and feel stress from being unsure which one they really belong to. Research has further refined this picture, suggesting that BII has two aspects: the degree to which bicultural individuals see their two cultures as distant from each other (as opposed to overlapping), and the degree to which they see their two cultures as being in conflict as opposed to in harmony (Benet-Martínez & Haritatos, 2005).

The study of multicultural individuals is important on both theoretical and practical grounds. On a theoretical level, the concept of two personalities within one individual is truly fascinating. An old Czech proverb says, "Learn a new language and get a new soul" (quoted in Ramírez-Esparza et al., 2006, p. 2), and psychology is just beginning to explore the ways this proverb may be correct. On a practical level, many areas of the world including the United States, Canada, and many countries in Europe are experiencing increased waves of immigration, and a major challenge in the coming years will be accommodating these multicultural citizens into the larger society in a way that minimizes stress and conflict within as well as between people. Personality psychology may be a useful tool for figuring out how to do this.

THE UNIVERSAL HUMAN CONDITION

According to the existential philosopher Sartre, discussed in Chapter 13, one fact applies across all individuals and all cultures. That fact comprises the "*a priori* limits which outline man's fundamental situation in the universe." In the same passage, Sartre wrote,

> Historical situations vary; a man may be born a slave in a pagan society or a feudal lord or a proletarian. What does not vary is the necessity for him to exist in the world, to be at work there, to be there in the midst of other people, and to be a mortal there. . . . In this sense we may say that there is a universality of man. (Sartre, 1965, pp. 52–53)

Despite cross-cultural psychology's traditional emphasis on differences between cultures, the pendulum is beginning to swing the other way, with an increasing number of psychologists emphasizing the degree to which people all over the world are psychologically similar (e.g., Matsumoto, 2004; McCrae, 2004; Oishi, 2004).

For one thing, differences between cultural rules for appropriate behavior might mask similar motivations. For example, it is easy to observe that the Chinese generally appear less extraverted than Americans. They talk less often and less loudly, among other differences. However, Chinese culture tends to restrain feelings and considers their public display inappropriate. Thus, it is possible that an extraverted American might laugh twice as much, and appear to have stronger feelings than, as an equivalently extraverted Chinese when the two feel the same way (McCrae et al., 1996). In a similar fashion, the same sensations that Americans report as emotional experiences are interpreted by members of many other cultures in a more physical manner. An American might report "feeling depressed," and a Chinese might report "feelings of discomfort in the heart" (Zheng, Xu, & Shen, 1986). Other recent research suggests that culture may influence more how a person *wants* to feel rather than how she *does* feel. For example, Asians may hope to feel positive low-arousal emotions such as calm, whereas European Americans prefer positive high-arousal emotions such as enthusiasm. Yet, when asked about their actual experience, they report feeling about the same (Tsai et al., 2006). And everybody, it seems, wants to please their parents. In one recent study, European-American and Asian-American college students both reported more life satisfaction to the degree that they felt they had fulfilled their parents' expectations—even though the contents (and intensity) of those expectations were quite different (Oishi & Sullivan, 2005).

Even seemingly obvious cross-cultural differences in behavior may be less pervasive than they appear. The psychologist Laura Miller has commented that

> in presenting the public or outside self to strangers or outgroup members, Japanese will tend to display deferential, hierarchical, and self-effacing conduct. The private personality, in which an individual may display confidence, assertiveness, and directness, will be reserved for interactions with co-workers, friends, and family. Most Americans meet only the public selves of Japan, and interpret these as the "true" personality. (L. Miller, 1999, p. 225)

In a similar vein, I once heard the psychologist Brian Little relate an unpublished result from a cross-cultural research project. He was interested in the goals or "personal projects" people pursue (see Chapter 16), and the degree to which they might vary cross-culturally. Little teaches at a university in Canada, and it was easy for him to ask his students to describe their current personal projects. At considerable expense and difficulty, he managed to have a group of Chinese students in China surveyed on a similar question. The researchers took great pains to translate the question into Chinese, then back-translate it into English to make sure it accurately crossed the cultural divide,[13] and they expended the same efforts translating

---

[13] In *back translation*, the researcher takes a phrase in one language, gets it translated into a second language, and then translated by a different translator back into the first (original) language. Finally, a native speaker of the original language judges whether the original and back-translated statements mean the same thing—as they should, if the two translations were correct.

the students' answers. Almost uniformly, the results disappointed anyone expecting large differences. The goals—get good grades, shop for tonight's dinner, find a new girlfriend—seemed more universal than culturally specific. Then, to his great excitement, Little read one particular Chinese student's response: One of her current projects, she reported, was to "work on my guilt."

Little reported his initial reaction as: Wow, what a profoundly different, non-Western type of goal. What interesting insight a goal like *working on one's guilt* provides into the fundamentally contrasting, collectivist Chinese worldview. And, not least of all, what a publication this will make! Then, good scientist that he is, Little did some checking. The statement turned out to be a misprint. The Chinese student enjoyed making homemade blankets, so she was trying to find time to work on her *quilt*.

Sometimes, cross-cultural differences in personality have a way of disappearing just when you think you have found them.

SUMMARY

- If, as the phenomenologists claim, a person's construal of the world is all-important, a logical next question concerns the variations in such construals of reality across cultures.

Culture and Psychology

- Individuals from different cultures may be psychologically different from one another, and members of particular cultural groups may differ from each other in distinctive ways.

- The process by which a child picks up the culture into which she is born is called enculturation; the process by which someone who moves into a culture picks up its mores is called acculturation.

The Importance of Cross-Cultural Differences

- It is important to examine psychological differences between cultures because misunderstandings can lead to conflict and even war, because theory and data developed in one culture might not be applicable in another, and because understanding how other peoples view reality can expand our understanding of the world.

The Characteristics of Cultures

- The comparative approach of most modern cultural psychologists contrasts *etics*, elements common to all cultures, with *emics*, elements that make cultures different.

- Cultures have been compared on emic dimensions including complexity, tightness-looseness, and collectivism-individualism.

- People in collectivist cultures are said to regard society and relations with others as more important, relative to individual experience and gain, compared with people in individualistic cultures. The usual assumption that Asian cultures are more collectivist than European or American cultures is probably too broad, given all the exceptions (e.g., Mexican culture is more collectivist than North American culture).

- A large amount of research has contrasted collectivist and individualist cultures on behavior, values, and views of the self.

Cultural Assessment and Personality Assessment

- Trait analyses have assessed the average differences between members of separate cultural groups across various personality traits, and also have evaluated the degree to which the traits that characterize people in one culture can accurately characterize people in another.

- Analyses of thinking styles have addressed hypotheses such as the idea that members of collectivist cultures think more holistically and are less prone to self-expression than members of individualist cultures.

- A few values may be universal. One analysis suggests 10 potentially global values that can be organized in terms of two dimensions: openness to change versus conservatism, and transcendence versus self-enhancement.

- Despite the evidence for a few universal values, cultural differences are still important. Collectivist cultures place group values (such as harmony) ahead of individual values (such as freedom); individualist cultures do the reverse.

The Origins of Cultural Differences

- Deconstructionists avoid the question of where cultural differences originate, but the ecological comparative approach holds that cultural differences originate in the diverse ecologies to which groups around the world must adapt. Such ecological differences may also produce small but consequential genetic differences.

Challenges and New Directions for Cross-Cultural Research

- Ethnocentrism is a constant hazard in doing cross-cultural research because one's cultural context inevitably affects one's point of view. The other extreme—cultural relativism—is also a hazard. Though difficult, it is important to find ways to make basic moral judgments while avoiding ethnocentrism.

- Cultural differences may be exaggerated in some cases, because cultural psychologists are in the business of explaining differences, because researchers can be prone to stereotyping, and because analyses of statistical significance may describe small differences as important.

- In particular, the outgroup homogeneity bias may lead to exaggerated views of the degree to which people in another culture are "all the same." Individuals differ within as well as between cultures.

- Cultures often contain subcultures; many individuals are multicultural, and in that sense may even have more than one personality. Their challenge is to successfully integrate the different cultures within themselves rather than feel conflicted by them.

The Universal Human Condition

- Although cross-cultural psychology has traditionally emphasized differences between cultures, some recent work is emphasizing psychological processes that all persons have in common. Moreover, beneath cultural differences is the existential, universal human condition noted by Sartre: Everybody everywhere must exist, work, relate to other people, and ultimately die.

THINK ABOUT IT

1. Have you ever lived in a different culture or known someone from a culture other than where you live now? Do people in that other culture view things differently? How fundamental are these differences?

2. If you wanted to understand another culture, such as one that resides on a small island in the South Pacific, what would you have to do? How could you be sure your interpretation of that culture was correct?

3. What are the pros and cons of living in an individualist culture? a collectivist culture? Which do you think you would prefer? Is your preference a result of cultural conditioning?

4. Which do you think is more important: the differences between cultures or the differences among individuals within cultures?

5. Do you know several members of a culture different from your own? To what degree and in what ways are they alike? How are they different from each other?

6. If a trait is considered to be a virtue in all cultures, does this mean we can be

certain the trait is truly virtuous? What other criteria could we use to decide whether a trait is good or bad?

7. Consider the example presented in the text of the practice of female genital mutilation. Can we judge this practice as wrong? On what grounds, if any, can we judge the practices of another culture as moral or immoral?

8. Can a person be a member of two (or more) cultures at once? To approach this issue another way: Given the definition of culture in this chapter, is it possible to be a member of just one culture? How many cultures do you belong to?

SUGGESTED READINGS

Lee, Y.-T., McCauley, C. R., & Draguns, J. G. (Eds.) (1999). *Personality and person perception across cultures*. Mahwah, NJ: Erlbaum.

> *An excellent collection of articles on cross-cultural psychology written by psychologists from around the world.*

Triandis, H. C. (1994). *Culture and social behavior*. New York: McGraw-Hill.

> *A readable introduction to comparative cross-cultural psychology, now a little out of date.*

Tseng, W.-S. (2003). *Clinician's guide to cultural psychiatry*. San Diego: Academic Press.

> *A very thorough and well-written survey of cross-cultural psychiatry that includes specific case studies. Although it focuses on mental disorders as they vary across cultures, the book includes many insights on the psychology of specific cultures and the difficulties of cross-cultural comparison.*

EMEDIA

 Go to StudySpace, wwnorton.com/studyspace, to access additional review and enrichment materials.

PART VI

WHAT PERSONALITY DOES:
Learning, Thinking, Feeling, and Knowing

In the very first psychology class I ever took, the professor decided one day to teach us about the power of reward. He produced a basket of slips of paper. Printed on each were the words, "Good for one extra point on the next exam." Did we want them? Indeed we did. He began a class discussion about what we would be willing to do for an extra point or two, and how our desire for higher grades could be used to manipulate our behavior. From time to time, he would suddenly bestow one of the precious little slips on a student. But it wasn't at all clear why. He might call out "Wrong!" in response to a comment, then give the student a slip of paper. He might say "Right!" and give nothing. Slowly, we began to catch on. First one student, then another, gradually realized that he handed out an extra point to anyone who said the word *reinforcement*. Suddenly a critical mass of awareness was achieved, and we were all screaming, "Reinforcement! Reinforcement! Reinforcement!" Game over.

This little demonstration conveyed three lessons. First, behaviors that are rewarded—reinforced, in behaviorist terminology—become more likely to occur. I think we were beginning to say "reinforcement" increasingly often even before we quite realized what the deal was. Second, this fact offers a powerful tool for influencing what people do. His little slips of paper were enough to make a room full of legal adults scream the same word over and over—a pretty weird behavior actually. The third lesson was more subtle. There was a moment, an obvious moment, when everyone in the class suddenly realized what was going on (when we began to yell "reinforcement!" in unison). This observation shows that awareness is important. People don't just respond to what is rewarded; they respond to what they *expect* will be rewarded—sometimes a very different matter.

The fact that people base their behavior on their expectations has several important implications. First, it means that behavior can change suddenly—as soon as someone "gets it," or thinks she gets it, her behavior may change immediately and drastically. Second, it means that people might sometimes change their behavior for the wrong reason. We respond to what we think will be rewarded, and expectations and reality sometimes differ. Third, it implies that our behavior might change not just because we have been rewarded, but because we have seen other people rewarded. As soon as my classmates realized that other students were getting those precious slips just for saying "reinforcement," they immediately began to do it themselves. Fourth, it means that to understand human behavior, it is not enough to map out the ways people are rewarded and punished. We must also try to understand how people think.

In one 50-minute class demonstration, my first psychology professor recreated the 50-year evolution of behaviorism, social learning theory, and cognitive conceptualizations of personality. This evolution began early in the 20th century with proud and confident behaviorist decrees that the basic facts of behavior were simple, and that anybody could be made to do anything or be anyone through reward and punishment. Then the picture became more complex, as psychologists began to demonstrate that people also learn from watching rewards and punishments administered to other people, and that expectations for reward and punishment do not always match reality. These realizations led to the development of social learning theory. Finally, by late in the century, social learning theory had evolved into theories by psychologists such as Albert Bandura, Walter Mischel, and others that focused on mental, or *cognitive*, phenomena such as perceptions, thoughts, goals, plans, and the self.

The theme underlying all of this research is that you have learned to be the person you are, and that the psychological processes that build your personality include your simple responses to reward and punishment as well as perceiving, thinking, and feeling. Through the rewards and punishments that have come your way, and the distinctive manner in which you have interpreted the experiences of your life, the world has taught you, and you have taught yourself, how to be yourself. The topic of the next three chapters is how this works.

Chapter 15 reviews some of the history of behaviorism and how it increasingly came to emphasize cognitive processes as it evolved into several versions of social learning theory, while still remaining true to its theoretical roots. Chapter 16 describes the personality processes of perception, thought, motivation, and emotion, and includes a discussion of the causes and consequences of happiness. Chapter 17 focuses on the "self," which consists of the different kinds of knowledge that you have—or think you have—about who you are.

15

LEARNING TO BE A PERSON:
Behaviorism and Social Learning Theories

Give me a dozen healthy infants, well-formed, and my own specified world to bring them up in and I'll guarantee to take any one at random and train him to become any type of specialist I might select—doctor, lawyer, artist, merchant, chief and yes, even beggarman and thief, regardless of his talents, penchants, tendencies, vocations, and race of his ancestors.

—J. B. WATSON[1]

CONSIDER TWO SIMPLE IDEAS. First, two stimuli—events, things, or people—repeatedly experienced together will eventually elicit the same response. For example, if someone puffs air into your eye at the same time he rings a bell, before too long the sound of the bell will be enough to make you blink. Second, behaviors followed by pleasant outcomes tend to be repeated, and behaviors followed by unpleasant outcomes tend to be dropped. For example, if your hard work is rewarded, you may work even harder; if your hard work goes unappreciated, you may figure, why bother?

Both of these ideas can be reduced to a single, even simpler idea: Behavior changes as a result of experience. Whether you blink at the sound of a bell, or work hard, or do any number of other things depends on what has happened to you in the past. This process—the change of behavior as a function of experience—is called **learning**, and the learning-based approaches

---

[1] J. B. Watson (1930), p. 65.

to personality attempt to explain all of the phenomena considered so far in this book in terms of this process.

Learning-based approaches to personality come in two varieties: behaviorism and the social learning theories. By carefully applying one simple idea, learning, to more and more complex situations, psychologists in these two related traditions have built theories of the basis of personality and behavior, and an effective technology for behavioral change. They also have built an approach to psychology that holds high the scientific values of objectivity, publicly observable data, and tight theoretical reasoning.

If your hard work is rewarded, you may work even harder; if your hard work goes unappreciated, you may figure, why bother?

This last-named accomplishment—an approach to psychology that seems truly scientific—has been a major attraction for many psychologists. Such researchers believe that psychology is not, and should not be, art or literature. It is science. And only psychology's unique objectivity, its basis in concrete facts rather than personal points of view, makes it scientific. The worldview of these scientifically inclined individuals—and certainly their approach to psychology—is exactly opposite the worldview of that of the humanists described in Chapter 13. Indeed, behaviorism was invented, in part, out of frustration with the focus on unobservable events inside the mind advocated by introspectionists such as Wilhelm Wundt.

The desire to bypass introspection and obtain more objective data led the behaviorists to concentrate on aspects of psychology that can be observed directly. The resulting approach focuses on the causes of behavior that lie outside the mind and are not particular to the individual. Behavioral psychologists study how a person's behavior is a direct result of her environment, particularly the rewards and punishments that environment contains. The implication is that anybody else in the same situation would do exactly the same thing. As you may recall, the protagonists of the person-situation controversy reviewed in Chapter 4 debated which were more important determinants of behavior—persons or situations. Behaviorists would definitely vote for the situation.

Despite its early success, some researchers eventually grew dissatisfied with behaviorism's rigidity and with the number of psychological phenomena it ignores. Influential figures such as John Dollard, Julian Rotter, and Albert Bandura, whose ideas are considered later in this chapter, expanded behaviorism into the broader social learning theories. Over time, these theories grew even broader and were relabeled "cognitive social learning theory" by theorists such as Walter Mischel. But while learning theory evolved

[handwritten margin note: Behaviorists believe the situation is a greater determinant of behavior (vs. the person).]

and expanded, it still held true to some basic tenets of behaviorism, as we shall see.

BEHAVIORISM

Psychology—the study of the psyche, after all—is often regarded as an attempt to "get inside the head." The personality researchers considered so far in this book—the psychoanalysts, humanists, and even most trait theorists and biological psychologists—put great efforts into understanding the unseen recesses of the mind. However, early behaviorists such as John Watson and B. F. Skinner believed that the best vantage point for understanding a person is from the outside, because that is where they assumed that all the causes of behavior were to be found. They were wary of any kind of theorizing that might imply that anything important lay inside the mind, where you couldn't see it. This theme continues to influence the writings of modern descendants such as Walter Mischel, who wrote recently, "If I have learned any lesson from my life as a scientist in psychology, it is that whatever way one chooses to define 'personality' it surely is not a de-contextualized 'entity within the mind'" (2009, p. 289). *Introspection is unreliable and? Well?!*

The behaviorists never developed an official slogan, but I will happily make one up for them: "We can only know what we can see, and we can see everything we need to know." Consider the two parts of this slogan separately. First, the behaviorist believes that all knowledge worth having comes from direct, public observation. Private introspection, of the sort practiced by Wundt (see Chapter 13), is invalid because nobody can verify it. Attempting to tap other people's thoughts, via psychoanalysis for example, is similarly suspect. The whole idea of theorizing about something we can't see—any entity within the mind—is a dubious business at best. The only valid way to know about somebody is to watch what he does—the person's behavior. That is why the approach is called **behaviorism**.

This idea implies that your personality is simply the sum of everything you do. Nothing else. Personality does not include traits, unconscious conflicts, psychodynamic processes, conscious experiences, or anything else that cannot be directly observed. If such unobservable structures and processes even exist, which traditional behaviorists tend to doubt, they are not important. A behaviorist approach to personality, then, is generally based on B data, which were described in Chapter 2.

*Based on
B data*

Close on the heels of the importance of observing behavior comes a further belief that the causes of behavior can be observed as directly as behavior itself. This is because the causes are not hidden in the mind; they can be found in the individual's environment. In this context, *environment* refers not to the trees and rivers of nature, but to the rewards and punishments in the physical and social world. The goal of behaviorism is a **functional analysis** that maps out exactly how behavior is a function of one's environmental situation.

The Philosophical Roots of Behaviorism

Behaviorism can be regarded as the American, 20th-century, scientific manifestation of some very old philosophical ideas. Three ideas in particular are fundamental: empiricism, associationism, and hedonism.

EMPIRICISM

*at birth or mind
is a "tabula rasa"
(used by
behaviorists?)*

The idea that all knowledge comes from experience is called **empiricism**. Experience, in this analysis, is not something that produces or exists separately from reality, as the phenomenologists described in Chapter 13 would argue. Experience is the direct product of reality itself. The contents of our minds are created by the contents of the world and how it has impinged on us, producing everything we have seen, heard, and felt. In this way, the structure of reality determines personality, the structure of the mind and, by extension, our behavior.

The opposing view, *rationalism*, holds that exactly the reverse is true: The structure of the mind determines our experience of reality. We saw this belief held by the phenomenologists discussed in Chapter 13, as well as the deconstructionists and some of the cultural psychologists considered in Chapter 14. Empiricism and therefore behaviorism are emphatically neither phenomenological nor deconstructionist.

Taken to its logical conclusion, empiricism implies that, at birth, the mind is essentially empty. The 19th-century philosopher John Locke called the mind of a newborn baby a tabula rasa (Latin for "blank slate"), ready to be written on by experience. The 20th-century psychologist and founder of behaviorism, John Watson, held the same belief, as the epigraph at the beginning of this chapter illustrates. Only as a person encounters reality does she begin to accumulate experiences and thereby build a characteristic way of reacting to the world, that is, a personality.

ASSOCIATIONISM

A second key philosophical idea explains how learning happens. **Associationism** is the claim that any two things, including ideas, become mentally associated as one if they are repeatedly experienced close together in time. Often, but not always, this closeness occurs as the result of a cause-and-effect relationship. Lightning flashes, then thunder booms, so thunder and lightning become associated in the minds of all who experience this combination. Other combinations are more psychological: A smile of a certain kind is followed by a kiss. Still other combinations are arbitrary or even artificial. A bell rings, and then you are fed (try to imagine yourself as a dog for this example). In each of these cases, the two things mentally become one. The thought of one conjures up the other, and a person's reaction to one tends to become his reaction to the other.

HEDONISM AND UTILITARIANISM

Taken together, empiricism and associationism form the core of the behaviorist explanation of personality's source and its components: Personality comes from experience and consists of the resulting associations between simple ideas. A third philosophical concept, hedonism, provides the remaining piece of the puzzle, namely motivation. Hedonism provides an answer for why people do anything at all.

In the context of behaviorism, **hedonism** claims that people (and organisms in general) learn for two reasons: to seek pleasure and avoid pain. These fundamental motivations explain why rewards and punishments shape behavior. They also form the basis of a value system that guides the technology of behavioral change, which is behaviorism's proudest achievement.

Hedonism is not a new idea. Epicurus, a Greek philosopher who lived from 341 to 270 B.C., claimed that the purpose of life is to be free of pain and to pursue what he called "gentle pleasure," or aesthetic enjoyment and peace of mind. Much later but still long ago (in 1781), the philosopher Jeremy Bentham wrote:

> Nature has placed mankind under the governance of two sovereign masters, *pain* and *pleasure*. It is for them alone to point out what we ought to do, as well as to determine what we shall do. (Bentham, 1781/1988, p. 1)

This hedonist philosophy leads to a surprisingly powerful principle for morality and ethics: Whatever produces the most pleasure for the most people in the long run is good. Whatever does the reverse is bad. Many actions commonly regarded as unethical or immoral fall under the umbrella of this statement. Theft, for example, benefits the thief and harms the victim, two outcomes that could be said to cancel each other out, but it also harms the social order that allows commerce and other good things to happen. So theft is, on balance, harmful. In a very different example, marital infidelity might produce short-term pleasure, but it damages a more important marital relationship (causing long-term harm to the individual) and may damage an entire family (harming the many for the advantage of the few). Lying, cheating, and complicated actions such as polluting the environment for short-term profit, or concentrating power and money in the hands of a few at the expense of the many, can be judged immoral by the same pragmatic standard. In general, the Epicurean ideal leads to a social philosophy called *utilitarianism*, which claims that the best society is one that creates the most happiness for the largest number of people.

This idea might sound uncontroversial, and the examples just listed seem pretty compelling. But it is not without problems. One complication is that utilitarianism puts the goal of the most happiness for the most people above all other goals, including truth, freedom, and dignity. The behaviorist and latter-day utilitarian B. F. Skinner wrote the book *Walden Two* about a fictional utopia (Skinner, 1948). In his Walden, everybody was happy but nobody was free, and considerations such as dignity and truth were treated as irrelevant.

Would you give up your freedom to be happy? A utilitarian would (believing freedom to be an illusion, anyway). An existentialist, by contrast, surely would not. As you will recall from Chapter 13, the ultimate purpose of life for an existentialist is to understand and face truth; "happiness" in the absence of truth, freedom, and meaning would be worthless. The modern-day positive psychologists surveyed in Chapter 13 would agree. To reuse two terms introduced in that chapter, positive psychologists generally emphasize eudaimonic well-being, which comes from seeking a truthful and meaningful life, over the simple pursuit of hedonic well-being through the experience of pleasure.

Three Kinds of Learning

The doctrine of empiricism, as we have seen, asserts that all knowledge comes from experience. The behaviorist idea of learning is similar, except that it focuses on behavior rather than on knowledge. Behaviorism traditionally identifies three types of learning: habituation, classical (or respondent) conditioning, and operant conditioning.

HABITUATION

Sneak up behind someone and ring a bell. The person will probably jump, perhaps high in the air. Then ring it again. The second jump will not be as high. Then ring it again. The third jump (assuming the person has not snatched the bell away from you by now) will be still lower. Eventually, the bell will produce almost no response at all.

This kind of learning is called **habituation**. It is the simplest way behavior changes as a result of experience. A crayfish, which has only a few neurons, can do it. Habituation even happens in single neurons and single-celled animals such as amoebas. If you repeatedly electrically stimulate a neuron or poke a crayfish, the response diminishes with each repetition until it almost disappears.

Despite its simplicity, habituation can be a powerful mechanism of behavioral change. When my wife and I moved to Boston some years ago, we had been in our new Back Bay apartment just a few minutes when we heard an earsplitting whooping and clanging sound outside. I ran to the window and saw a new Mercedes parked across the street, its alarm in full uproar. Nobody was anywhere near. Eventually, the alarm stopped. A few minutes later, it went off again. Again I went to the window, but a little more slowly. Then again, a few minutes after that. And again. After a few weeks, only the looks on our guests' faces made me aware that yet another car alarm was disturbing the neighborhood.

Experimental research on habituation has shown that a response nearly as strong as the original can be maintained, but only if the stimulus changes or increases with every repetition. Everyone has heard—too often, I'm sure—those car alarms that start with a whooping sound, then beep, then whistle, and then cycle back to whooping. The purpose of this variation in sound is not to annoy people (although it does this very effectively) but to prevent habituation.

The consequences of habituation can be not just disturbing but dangerous. Images projected in the international popular culture seem to be increasingly violent. Video games feature exploding bodies and sprays of blood. Movies display levels of mayhem and gore that at one time would have been considered unthinkable. What effect does being exposed to such images, again and again, have on people? According to recent research, it might make them "comfortably numb," and not in a good way (Bushman & Anderson, 2009, p. 273). In one study, subjects played a violent video game and then, afterward, overheard a loud fight in the hallway outside that seemed to include somebody being injured. In a second study, subjects watched a violent movie (e.g., *The Ruins*) and then, on their way out of the theater, encountered a woman with an injured ankle struggling to retrieve her crutches. In both cases, the subjects were less likely to help than were people who played a less violent game or saw a nonviolent movie (e.g., *Nim's Island*). The effect of seeing images of suffering and violence, the researchers speculate, is to become habituated to the pain of others, with the result that one becomes less likely to help them when they are in need. Indeed, according to another study, repeated exposure to violent video games can make an individual's very personality more aggressive (Bartholow, Sestir, & Davis, 2005).

Even the impact of important life events can lessen over time (Brickman, Coates, & Janoff-Bulman, 1978). For example, people who win millions of dollars in a lottery have a pretty exciting day, but over the long run end up not much happier than they were before. They become habituated to their millionaire status—it becomes the "new normal." The reverse effect sometimes happens with people who become paraplegic in accidents. They may habituate even to this momentous change and regain more happiness than they might have thought possible. This is why, according to recent research on *affective forecasting*, people tend to overestimate the emotional impact of future events, both good and bad. Winning that big promotion won't make you as happy as you expect, over time, but flunking that test won't make you as miserable as you anticipate either (T. D. Wilson & Gilbert, 2005). It seems you can get used to almost anything.

CLASSICAL CONDITIONING

You moved away 10 years ago and have not been back since, but one day you find yourself near the old neighborhood, so you drop by. As you walk down the street you used to travel every day, long-forgotten images and feelings flood your mind. It can be a strange sensation, a little like traveling back in time. You might feel emotions you cannot label but know you have not felt in years; you might surprise yourself with the strength of your reaction to a familiar mailbox or your old front door; you might even, in some inexpressible way, feel 10 years younger! What is going on here? You are experiencing the results of **classical conditioning**.

How Classical Conditioning Works   Classical conditioning is usually described in a very different context from the previous example, often involving animals—traditionally dogs. The nearly legendary story of classical conditioning involves the Russian scientist Ivan Pavlov, who was originally interested in studying the physiology of digestion. (He won a Nobel Prize for his work on that subject in 1904.) His subjects were dogs, which he hooked up to an apparatus that measured their salivation as they were fed.

He discovered some unexpected complications in this research. He wanted to study how dogs salivated while eating, but inconveniently they often started salivating *before* they were fed. They might salivate at the sight of the assistant who brought their food, or at the sound of the streetcar that passed outside at their usual feeding time. This finding forced his investigations out of the realm of pure physiology and into psychology. Against the advice of some of his colleagues in physiology, Pavlov decided that the psychological issues were more interesting, and turned his attention to the circumstances under which psychological stimuli could elicit salivation and other physical responses.

One of his first findings forced an important change in our understanding of associationism. It turns out that a bell begins to elicit salivation most quickly and reliably when it is rung not simultaneously with feeding, but slightly before. (If rung too early, the bell also loses its effectiveness.) Associationism held that two things become combined in the mind by being experienced together. Pavlov's finding showed that conditioning is more than a simple pairing of stimuli; it involves teaching the animal that one stimulus (the bell) is a warning or signal of the other (the food). The difference is subtle but fundamental, because it means that the principle of associationism is slightly wrong. Events become associated not merely because they occurred together, but because the *meaning* of one event has changed the meaning of another. The bell used to be just a sound. Now it means "food is coming."

Classical conditioning can work in a negative direction as well. If you encounter a particular food under unpleasant circumstances—for example, when you are sick, or if the food itself is dirty or smelly—you may avoid it forever after (Rozin & Zellner, 1985). Or, if you become convinced that smoking cigarettes or eating meat is immoral, you may come to find cigarettes or meat physically disgusting (Rozin, 1999; Rozin, Markwith, & Stoess, 1997). This progression is even more likely if you start calling meat "flesh" and cigarettes "cancer sticks."

Classical Conditioning and Physiology   Classical conditioning affects emotional responses and low-level behavioral responses such as salivating, as we have seen. Some research also has suggested that the workings of many organs of the body not usually considered to be under psychological control can be classically conditioned. Some "behaviors" that researchers report having classically conditioned include insulin release by the pancreas; glycogen uptake by the liver; speed of the heartbeat; and flow of secretions in the stomach, gallbladder, and endocrine glands (Bykov, 1957; Bower & Hilgard, 1981).

These findings raise some interesting possibilities concerning physical health (Dworkin, 1993; M. G. King & Husband, 1991). For example, persons undergoing cancer treatment by chemotherapy, which often creates nausea, may feel nauseated just by entering the room where the chemicals are administered. Unintentional classical conditioning also can change effects of drugs. Injecting heroin into the bloodstream triggers biological *opponent processes* that serve to lessen its effects, which is why addicts require larger doses over time. Through classical conditioning, these opponent processes might be triggered simply by the sight of the needle, or even by entering the room in which the addict usually shoots up. What happens, then, if a heroin addict shoots up in a location where he has not used drugs in the past—such as his parents' house, for example? Because this location is not classically conditioned, the opponent processes may fail to kick in before the injection, and a dose the addict could have otherwise tolerated may become fatal (Siegel, 1984; Siegel & Ellsworth, 1986). Finally, we may eventually be able to teach people, through classical conditioning, how to control their own immune systems (Ader & Cohen, 1993).

> Some "behaviors" that researchers report having classically conditioned include insulin release by the pancreas; glycogen uptake by the liver; speed of the heartbeat; and flow of secretions in the stomach, gallbladder, and endocrine glands.

Learned Helplessness   So far we have considered what happens when a person learns that one stimulus is associated with another. What about the cases where one stimulus is not associated with another—where both seem to happen randomly? This might seem like a nonsensical question, but in fact, this circumstance teaches an important lesson: The world is unpredictable. If you experience occasional, painful shocks, for example, without any stimulus to provide advance warning, you learn this: You are never safe (Gleitman, 1995).

Such a sense of unpredictability not only is unpleasant, but also can have important consequences. If one group of rats is given periodic electric shocks in which each shock is preceded by a warning light, and another group of rats is given the same shocks at the same times but without any warning, the unwarned group becomes more likely to develop stomach ulcers (Seligman, 1968; Weiss, 1970, 1977). This finding illustrates the difference between fear and anxiety. One feels fear when one knows what the danger is, and has a reason to think that danger is impending. One feels anxiety when the source of danger is unclear, or when one has no idea when the danger might actually arrive. A chronically anxious person may have experienced no more than the usual ration of "hard knocks" but never been able to learn when to expect them.

This feeling of anxiety due to unpredictability can also lead to a behavioral pattern called **learned helplessness** (Maier & Seligman, 1976; C. Peterson, Maier, & Seligman, 1993). Experiments with animals such as rats and dogs, and later with humans, suggest that receiving random rewards and punishments can lead to the belief that nothing one does really matters. In turn, this belief can lead to depression (W. R. Miller & Seligman, 1975). One long-recognized symptom of depression is the "why bother?" syndrome, where everything—including, in extreme cases, even getting out of bed—simply seems like too much trouble. The learned helplessness hypothesis is that this syndrome results from a history of unpredictable reward and punishment, leading the person to act as if nothing she does matters.

S-R Conception of Personality Principles of classical conditioning yield a distinctive personality theory. Early American behaviorists such as John Watson derived their understanding of personality directly from Pavlov's ideas. They assumed that the essential activity of life was to learn a vast array of responses to specific environmental stimuli, and that an individual's personality consists of a repertoire of learned *stimulus-response (S-R)* associations. Because everyone has a different learning history, each person's patterns will be idiosyncratic, so the S-R pattern for a given person need not have any particular structure or coherence. It will depend simply on what he happens to learn. For example, if one has learned to be dominant at home but meek at work, a business meeting might trigger a subservient response and a home situation might trigger dominance. This conception of personality is not without its influence today, as we shall see near the end of the chapter, but it is an old version of behaviorism. Skinner greatly enriched and expanded this basic behaviorism by formulating the idea of operant conditioning.

OPERANT CONDITIONING

A good cook likes to experiment. She rarely uses the same ingredients, cooking times, or methods twice. Nonetheless, every good cook also has a fairly consistent style that evolves from this process of experimentation. Things that work are repeated. Things that do not work are dropped. As a result of experience, the cook's creations constantly change and improve as she develops a distinctive style.

The Law of Effect: Thorndike   This kind of learning from experience is not limited to cooks, or even to humans. A classic early example involved cats. Early in the 20th century, even before Pavlov began his work with dogs, the American psychologist Edward Thorndike was putting hungry cats in a device he called the "puzzle box" (Figure 15.1). The cats could escape only by doing some specific, simple act, such as pulling on a wire or pressing a bar. Doing so would cause the box suddenly to spring open, and the cat would jump out to find a bit of food nearby. Then Thorndike would put the cat back in the box, to try again (Thorndike, 1911).

Thorndike found that gradually, the cats began to escape more and more quickly. What originally took 3 minutes occurred, after 25 trials or so, in less than 15 seconds.

Techniques of Operant Conditioning: Skinner   Skinner (e.g., 1938) pointed out that in the case of Pavlov's dogs, their salivating did not affect

cats escaping from a box

Figure 15.1 Thorndike's Puzzle Box Pioneering psychologist Edward Thorndike would put cats in this box and observe how long it took them to get out. A food treat was nearby. The cats learned quickly.

their situation. It was a response that, after training, happened to be followed by meat. Even if a dog did not salivate, the meat would still arrive. But when Thorndike's cats pushed the lever that opened their cage, something did happen. A closed door sprang open, allowing them to escape.

Skinner called the first kind of learning **respondent conditioning**, meaning that the conditioned response is essentially passive with no impact of its own. The second kind of learning, which he found much more interesting, he called **operant conditioning**: The animal learns to *operate* on its world in such a way as to change it to that animal's advantage.

"Oh, not bad. The light comes on, I press the bar, they write me a check. How about you?"

To work out the laws of operant conditioning, Skinner invented a device that became known as the *Skinner box*. In principle, this invention is much like Thorndike's puzzle box, but it is simpler and usually used with animals such as rats and pigeons. The Skinner box contains only a bar and a chute for delivering food pellets. Put a pigeon in there, and it begins to bump around. It does a little dance, preens its feathers, and eventually pushes the bar. A food pellet immediately rolls down the chute. The pigeon eats it and then—pigeons not being terribly bright—goes back to its pigeon activities. It dances around some more, preens some more, and eventually hits the bar again. Another food pellet. The pigeon dimly begins to catch on. The pigeon hits the bar at a steadily increasing rate, sometimes (depending on the frequency of reinforcement) to the point where it does little else.

According to the behaviorists, this pigeon and the cook with which I began this section are not all that different. Both learn from experience through operant conditioning. If an animal or a person performs a behavior, and the behavior is followed by a good result—a **reinforcement**—the behavior becomes more likely. If the behavior is followed by a punishment, it becomes less likely. (More will be said about punishment later in this chapter.)

Despite Skinner's emphasis on how reinforcement derives from the organism's effect on its environment, the results of operant conditioning are not necessarily logical. It will work on any behavior, regardless of

Figure 15.2 A Skinner Box The psychologist B. F. Skinner performed famous experiments on learning by placing pigeons inside this box.

the real connection between the behavior and the consequences that follow. As a little joke, I once rubbed a $10 bill on a colleague's grant proposal "for luck." It was funded. For months after, everyone in my department came by to have me rub money on their grants before they sent them in.

Skinner worked hard to develop practical techniques for changing behavior that can produce impressive results with both animals and humans. Consider *shaping*. A sculptor shapes a piece of clay into a statue by gradually shaving here and there until a square block comes to resemble a person or an animal. The process happens in small steps, but the result can be amazing. Behavior can be shaped in a similar manner. Begin by rewarding a pigeon for hitting a bar; this behavior becomes more frequent. Then raise the criterion for reward: Now the pigeon must step forward and back and then hit the bar. (Because a pigeon is constantly emitting different behaviors, it will do this eventually.) This behavior, too, gradually becomes more frequent. Then raise the reward criterion again. Before too long, the pigeon may be doing a complete tango, and ready to appear on *Dancing With the Stars*.[2]

According to legend—advertised as true when told to me but probably apocryphal—Skinner's students at Harvard University decided to try out his principles on their esteemed instructor. They wanted him to stop lecturing from the podium and instead speak from a spot near the door, with one foot out in the hallway. One day, as Skinner began the class, they looked bored and shuffled their feet. The first time he happened to step away from the podium, they all perked up. When he stepped back, they returned to an apathetic slouch. After Skinner had learned to lecture from a step away, the students raised the criterion. Now they did not look alert until he was two steps away from the podium. By the end of the semester, B. F. Skinner was indeed delivering his lectures from the doorway, with one foot in the hall, running occasionally to the podium to glance at his notes, then back to the doorway to continue.

---

[2] Not really.

And now, the punch line. A departmental colleague happened by the class one day. Later, he asked Skinner why he lectured from the doorway, instead of from the podium. Skinner replied, "Don't you know, the light is much better in the doorway."

Another example, which I know is true because I was there, concerns my old college roommate, Rick. A psychology major long before I was (and now a successful firefighter in Idaho—who says you can't have a valuable career with a B.A. in psychology?), Rick was given the assignment of shaping behavior in a real-life context. He chose the dorm lounge where, every night at 6:00 P.M., most of the residents gathered to watch *Star Trek*.[3] Rick was an electronics buff as well as a psychology major. He attached a wire to the innards of the television, ran the wire under the carpet to the back of the room, and there connected the wire to a button. When he pressed the button, the television picture became scrambled and unwatchable.

Now he was ready to strike. That evening, as the crowd gathered, he silently selected his victim; that person, he decided, was going to stand by the television with one hand on top, the other hand raised straight up in the air, and one foot lifted off the floor. It was easy enough. As the program began to get interesting, Rick pushed the button and scrambled the picture. Various people leapt up to fix things, but the picture cleared only when his victim stood. It scrambled again when she sat down. After she was standing, he raised the criterion. Now she had to stand closer, and then even closer to the television to clear the picture. Well before 7:00 P.M., Rick's victim was standing by the television with one hand on top, the other one up in the air, and one foot off the floor.

After *Star Trek* ended, Rick approached his victim and asked innocently why she had been standing like that. "Oh, don't you know," she replied, "the body acts like a natural antenna."

The Causes of Behavior   A number of morals can be derived from these stories including, perhaps, the moral that neither psychologists nor their students are to be trusted (see the discussion of ethics in Chapter 3). A deeper moral is that people may do things for very simple reasons of which they may be unaware. They even make up elaborate rationales for their actions that have little or nothing to do with the real causes (Nisbett & Wilson, 1977).

But let's not get too carried away. The human mind has many processes that occasionally produce errors but usually lead to correct outcomes

---

[3] Even then, it was in reruns.

"We reward top executives at the agency with a unique incentive program. Money."

(Funder, 1987). One can fool somebody—like Skinner or the dorm resident—into doing something without knowing why. But under most circumstances, it is a good bet that we know why we do certain things. In part, this is because rewards are not usually so hidden. The paycheck that causes many people to go to work is an effective and obvious reinforcement.

Punishment

He that spareth the rod hateth his own son.

—PROVERBS 13:24

There is one behaviorist approach that millions of people use every day to try to control behavior: punishment. Despite its popularity, it has some dangers. Or, to be more precise, punishment works well when it is done right. The only problem is, it is almost never done right.

A **punishment** is an aversive consequence that follows an act in order to stop it and prevent its repetition. Punishment frequently is used by three kinds of people: parents, teachers, and bosses. This may be because people in all three roles have the same goals:

1. Start some behaviors
2. Maintain some behaviors
3. Prevent some behaviors

The usual tactic for achieving goals 1 and 2 is reward. Teachers use gold stars and grades, parents use allowances and treats, and bosses use raises and bonuses. All of these people—if they are good at what they do—use praise. (Praise is an excellent behavior modification tool because it is effective and it is free.) But what about goal 3? Many people believe the only way to stop or prevent somebody from doing something is punishment.

Wrong. You can use reward for this purpose, too. All you have to do is find a response that is incompatible with the one you are trying to get rid of, and reward that incompatible response instead. Reward a child for reading instead of punishing him for watching television. Or, if you want to stop and prevent drug abuse, provide rewarding activities that are not drug related.

Offer would-be drug users recreation, entertainment, education, and useful work instead. Make these other activities as rewarding as possible, and drug use will become less attractive.

Consider the famous antidrug campaign, JUST SAY NO. Saying no to drugs is a pretty limited life unless it also includes saying yes to something else. Yet (if I may editorialize) our society seems more interested in punishing drug use than providing rewarding alternatives. The reason is not a matter of saving money—it costs taxpayers 1.5 times as much to house a prisoner for a year as it does to house and educate a student at the University of California for the same amount of time. Budget savings that result from closing schools, parks, basketball courts, and community-service programs are more than eaten up in constructing jails. I suspect the real reason has to do with a generally punitive attitude, coupled with a profound lack of imagination—and a lack of psychological education. Although I can't change the punitive attitudes or the lack of imagination, I do what I can about psychological education (writing this book, for example).

Reward is also underused in the workplace. A friend of mine from graduate school now is a psychological consultant for businesses. One of his first clients was a lumber mill. The mill operated along classic old-style management principles. The supervisor sat in a glass booth high in the rafters, from which he could see the entire production line. He scanned with binoculars until he saw something go wrong. Then he came down, yelled at the worker who was responsible, sometimes demoting or even firing the worker on the spot. Not surprisingly, the workers dreaded the supervisor's approach. Moreover, they did what they could to conceal their activities. Morale was low; absenteeism and turnover were high. Occasionally there was even sabotage.

My friend's first action was to gather the supervisors together for some instruction. (He charged a high fee, so the company would order them to follow his advice.) He told them, effective immediately, they were forbidden to punish workers. Instead, they were to sit in their little glass booths until they saw a worker doing something perfectly. Then they were to come down and praise the worker. Occasionally, if the work was truly exemplary, they were to award a bonus or a paid day off on the spot.

The supervisors were perplexed by and resistant to this seemingly crazy plan. But they followed corporate orders, and you can guess the results. At first the workers were terrified; they thought they knew what the supervisor's approach meant. But gradually they came to look forward to his visits. Then they went one step further: They started to try to show the supervisor what they were doing, in case it might be good enough to merit a reward or just some praise. They started to like the supervisor, and they started to like their jobs. Absenteeism and turnover declined. Productivity skyrocketed. My friend earned his fee.

HOW TO PUNISH

One way to see how punishment works, or fails to work, is to examine the rules for applying it correctly. The classic behaviorist analysis says that five principles are most important (Azrin & Holz, 1966):

1. **Availability of Alternatives:** An alternative response to the behavior that is being punished must be available. This alternative response must not be punished and should be rewarded. If you want to threaten kids with punishment for Halloween pranks, be certain some alternative activity is available that will not be punished, or will even be rewarding, such as a Halloween party.

2. **Behavioral and Situational Specificity:** Be clear about exactly what behavior you are punishing and the circumstances under which it will and will not be punished. This rule is the basis of the common parenting advice never to punish a child for being a "bad boy" or "bad girl." (It is also consistent with the religiously based guidance to "hate the sin but love the sinner.") Instead, punish "staying out after curfew" or "cursing at Grandma." A child who is unsure why he is punished may, just to be safe, becomes generally inhibited and fearful, not quite sure what is right and what is wrong.

3. **Timing and Consistency:** To be effective, a punishment needs to be applied immediately after the behavior you wish to prevent, every time that behavior occurs. Otherwise, the person (or animal) being punished may not understand which behavior is forbidden. And again, if a person (or animal) is punished but does not understand why, the result will be general inhibition instead of specific behavioral change.

   Have you ever made this mistake? You come home from a hard day at work and discover your dog has dug out the kitchen trash and spread it across the living room. The dog bounds to greet you, and you swat it. This is, one supposes, punishment for scattering trash, but consider the situation from the dog's point of view. The trash scattering occurred hours ago. What the dog did just before being punished was greet you. What behavioral change will result? This kind of error is common and shows the danger of applying punish-

[handwritten margin note: punishment must be applied immediately and consistently.]

ment when you are angry. The punishment might vent your emotions but is likely to be counterproductive.

4. **Conditioning Secondary Punishing Stimuli:** One can lessen the actual use of punishment by conditioning secondary stimuli to it. I once had a cat who liked to scratch the furniture. I went out and bought a plastic squirt bottle and filled it with water, and then kept it nearby. Whenever the cat started to claw the sofa, I made a hissing noise and then immediately squirted the cat. Soon I did not need the squirt bottle; my "hissss" was sufficient to make the cat immediately stop what she was doing. With people, verbal warnings can serve the same purpose. Many a parent has discovered this technique: "If you don't stop, when I get to 3, you'll be sorry. One, two, . . ."

5. **Avoiding Mixed Messages:** This is a particular warning to parents. Sometimes, after punishing a child, the parent feels so guilty that she picks the child up for a cuddle. This is a mistake. The child might start to misbehave just to get the cuddle that follows the punishment. Punish if you must punish but do not mix your message. A variant on this problem occurs when the child learns to play one parent off against the other. For example, after the father punishes the child, the child goes to the mother for sympathy, or vice versa. This can produce the same counterproductive result.

"What do I think is an appropriate punishment? I think an appropriate punishment would be to make me live with my guilt."

THE DANGERS OF PUNISHMENT

Punishment will backfire unless all of the guidelines just listed are followed. (Usually, they are not.) A punisher has to be extremely careful, for several reasons.

1. **Punishment Arouses Emotion:** The first and perhaps most important danger of punishment is that it creates emotion. In the punisher, it can arouse excitement, satisfaction, and even further aggressive impulses; the punisher may get carried away. Some years ago, the Los Angeles police pulled over an errant driver named Rod-

ney King. They yanked him out of the car and made him lie on the ground. Then they began to beat him, an act that was videotaped by a nearby resident who happened to have a camera handy. The videotape, which was then broadcast many times, provides a vivid illustration of how punishment can get out of hand. The emotions that beating King aroused in the officers seemed to cause them to lose all semblance of self-control.

Emotions are aroused in the "punishee," too. By definition, a punishment is aversive, which means that the punishee feels pain, discomfort, or humiliation, or some combination of these. Punishment also usually arouses fear of and hate for the punisher, a desire to escape, and possibly self-contempt. These powerful emotions are not conducive to clear thinking. As a result, the punishee is unlikely to "learn a lesson," which supposedly is the whole point. How well do you learn a lesson when you are fearful, in pain, confused, and humiliated? Often punishers think they are teaching what behavior not to repeat. But the punishee is too unhappy and confused to think much beyond "let me out of here!"

2. **It Is Difficult to Be Consistent:** Imagine that, in one day at work, you lose a big account, get yelled at by your boss, spill ketchup on your pants, and find a new dent in your car. When you arrive home, your child has thrown a baseball through your living-room window. What do you do?

   Now imagine another day, when you land a big account, get promoted by your boss, and take delivery on a beautiful new car that cost $5,000 less than you expected. You arrive home to find a baseball thrown through the window. Now, what do you do?

   Very few people would react to the child's behavior the same way under both circumstances. (Those who would are saints.) Yet the child's behavior was the same. Punishment tends to vary with the punisher's mood, which is one reason why it is rarely applied consistently.

3. **It Is Difficult to Gauge the Severity of Punishment:** Many cases of child abuse have occurred when what a parent thought was a mild but painful slap caused a broken bone or worse. Parents are bigger than children; this is not always easy to take into account, especially when the parent is angry. Words can hurt, too. A rebuke from a parent, teacher, or boss can cause severe humiliation. It may cause more psychological distress than the punisher imagines and can provoke desires for escape or revenge that make the situation worse.

4. **Punishment Teaches Misuse of Power:** Specifically, it teaches that big, powerful people get to hurt smaller, less-powerful people. As a result, the punishee may think, I can't wait to be big and powerful so I can punish too! Thus, parents who were abused as children may become child abusers themselves. How children are punished may have long-lasting effects on their personalities (Hemenway, Solnick, & Carter, 1994; Widom, 1989).

5. **Punishment Motivates Concealment:** The prospective punishee has good reasons to conceal behavior that might be punished. Have you ever been in an office where the boss rules through punishment? Nobody talks to anybody, least of all the boss, if they can avoid it, and the boss soon becomes detached from what is really going on in the office. Rewards have the reverse effect. When workers anticipate rewards for good work instead of punishment for bad work, they are naturally motivated to bring to the boss's attention everything they are doing, in case it merits reward. They have no reason to conceal anything, and the boss will be in close contact with the operation she is running. (This was the case in the lumber mill described earlier.)

This works in the home as well. A child who expects punishment from his parents soon cuts off as much communication as possible. A child who expects the reverse naturally does the reverse.

THE BOTTOM LINE

Punishment, used correctly, can be an effective technique for behavioral control. But to use it correctly is nearly impossible. Correct punishment requires that the punisher understand and consistently apply all of the rules just listed. It also requires that the punisher's own emotions and personal needs not affect his or her actions, which is even more difficult. So the bottom line is this: Punishment works great if you apply it correctly—but to apply it correctly, it helps to be a genius and a saint.

SOCIAL LEARNING THEORY

Behaviorism boasts high standards of scientific rigor and many practical applications, such as the tips concerning punishment that we have just reviewed. However, even in its early days, some psychologists suspected it

Köhler
=chimpanzees

did not tell the whole story. One of these was the German psychologist Wolfgang Köhler, who studied chimpazees. He would set up puzzles for them, such as hanging a banana out of reach, and then watch his chimps figure out what to do. Some of their solutions were so clever—such as stacking boxes or using a stick to pole-vault up to the banana (see Figure 15.3)—that Köhler concluded the chimps had done more than learn from reward. They actually came to understand their situation—to develop *insight*. His evidence was that once the chimps realized out what behavior would get them a banana, they used the tactic immediately, not gradually (Köhler, 1925; Gleitman, 1995). This sudden change in behavior resembles that of my classmates, years ago, when they realized they could get points just for saying "reinforcement."

Years later, the idea of insight applied to behaviorism opened the door for the introduction of social learning theory and for some of the cognitively oriented research that followed. Social learning theory arose to correct several shortcomings of orthodox behaviorism.

Figure 15.3 **Köhler's Smart Chimps** Chimps studied by the German psychologist Wolfgang Köhler figured out many ways to reach a hanging banana, including stacking boxes and using a stick to pole-vault.

The most obvious shortcoming is that behaviorism ignores motivation, thought, and cognition. Behaviorists have sometimes tried to make a virtue of this omission. The writings of Skinner and his followers typically deny that thinking is important and sometimes have tried to deny it exists. Behaviorists certainly never conduct research on it. Social learning theorists, by contrast, claim that the ways people think, plan, perceive, and believe are important parts of learning, and that research must address these processes.

Second, classic behaviorism, to a surprisingly large extent, is based on research using animals. Thorndike favored cats, Pavlov used dogs, and much of Skinner's own work was done with rats and pigeons. Behaviorists study animals so often because they hope to formulate laws of learning that are relevant to all species. This is a laudable goal, but in fact, not all species are the same. Notice how Köhler, who studied chimps, came to conclusions about the role of insight that were different from those of his colleagues who studied rats, pigeons, and even dogs and cats. Humans are an even more special case. In general, according to the social learning theorists, behaviorists have concentrated too much on elements of learning that are important for animals, such as reinforcement, and not enough on aspects that are more important for humans, such as solving a problem by thinking about it.

A third shortcoming of classic behaviorism is that it ignores the social dimension of learning. The typical rat or pigeon in the Skinner box is in there alone. It cannot interact with, learn from, or influence any other animal. In real life, however, learning tends to be social. We learn by watching others—something a pigeon isolated in a box is in no position to do even if it was capable. The social learning theorists, as their label implies, are highly sensitive to this issue.

A fourth shortcoming of classic behaviorism is that it treats the organism as essentially passive. How does a rat or pigeon get into a Skinner box in the first place? Easy—it is put there. Once there, the *contingencies* of the box—its rules for what will and will not be rewarded—are ironclad and may even be automated. The pigeon did not seek out the box, but there it is, and unless it pushes the bar, there will be no food pellets. For humans, the situation is different. To an important (if not unlimited) degree, we not only choose our environments, but also change these environments as a result of what we do in them.

Imagine if rats were allowed to choose among several Skinner boxes, and then could change the reinforcement contingencies inside. For humans, real life is rather like that. A party might bring out certain behaviors you do not do otherwise, but you can choose whether to go to the party. Moreover, once you are there, the party changes as a result of your presence. These facts complicate any analysis of how the environment affects behavior. Unlike classical behaviorists, modern social learning theorists welcome and study these complications.

Three major theories of personality have expanded behaviorism in response to one or more of these shortcomings. It seems somewhat ironic—and confusing—that although the three theories are different from each other in important ways, all were named *social learning theory* by their inventors. The three theories were developed by John Dollard and Neal Miller, by Julian Rotter, and by Albert Bandura.

Dollard and Miller's Social Learning Theory

John Dollard and Neal Miller were psychologists at Yale during the 1940s and 1950s. The key idea of their social learning theory is the concept of the **habit hierarchy**. The behavior you are most likely to perform at a given moment resides at the top of your habit hierarchy, while your least likely behavior is at the bottom. For example, at this moment the behavior at the top of your habit hierarchy seems to be reading. After all, that is what you are doing. Lower on your habit hierarchy—probably a lot lower—is dancing. It is extremely unlikely, although not impossible, that in a moment you will jump up and dance around the room. Somewhat higher in your habit hierarchy might be snacking—at any moment you really might put this book down and go get something to eat (especially now that I've mentioned it). Dollard and Miller theorized that the effect of rewards, punishments, and learning is to rearrange the habit hierarchy. If you were rewarded for dancing, this behavior might become more likely; if you were punished for reading, then reading might become less likely.

Notice how Dollard and Miller have already deviated from classic behaviorism in a major way. Skinner claimed that learning changes behavior. Dollard and Miller claimed that learning changes the arrangement of an *unobservable* psychological entity, the habit hierarchy. This habit hierarchy is, in effect, the personality. An individual's history of learning produces a distinctive arrangement of behaviors she is more and less likely to perform. Understanding that arrangement, according to Dollard and Miller, is the best way to understand the person.

MOTIVATION AND DRIVES

What do you want, and why do you want it? These are questions of motivation. According to Dollard and Miller, the answer is found in *needs*, which produce psychological drives. A **drive** is a state of psychological tension that feels good when the tension is reduced. Pleasure comes from satisfying the need that produced the drive.

Two kinds of drive are important. **Primary drives** include those for food, water, physical comfort, avoidance of physical pain, sexual gratification, and so on. **Secondary drives** include positive drives for love, prestige, money, and power, as well as negative drives such as the avoidance of fear and of humiliation. In the process of development, according to Dollard and Miller, secondary drives come later. In their own words:

> The helpless, naked, human infant is born with primary drives such as hunger, thirst, and reactions to pain and cold. He does not have, however, many of the motivations that distinguish the adult as a member of a particular tribe, nationality, social class, occupation, or profession. Many extremely important drives, such as the desire for money, the ambition to become an artist or a scholar, and particular fears and guilts are learned during socialization. (Dollard & Miller, 1950, p. 62)

no reinforcement without reducing a drive

According to Dollard and Miller, there can be no reinforcement (and hence no behavioral change) without reducing a drive, whether primary or secondary. According to their *drive-reduction theory*, for a reward to have the power to encourage the target behavior, the reward must satisfy a need (see Figure 15.4).

This principle is not as straightforward as it may sound, because it raises an important question: Is the goal of all behavior (and hence all life) really just to satisfy every desire and achieve a state of "zero need"? So far, the analysis implies that, in the ideal state of existence, all needs have been satisfied. At that point, people have no motivations and can just sit in an inert, satisfied lump. This implication is questionable, both because that

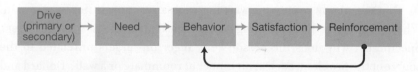

Figure 15.4 Drive Reduction Theory Drives may be primary (physiologically based) or secondary (learned). Drives create needs, which produce behaviors to satisfy them. This satisfaction produces reinforcement, which makes the behavior increasingly likely in the future.

state does not seem very desirable, and because people often go out of their way to raise their level of need.

For example, if you are going out this evening for a dinner at a four-star restaurant that will cost you $120, you are unlikely to eat a bag of potato chips at 6:00 P.M., even if you are hungry. Why not? Because it would "spoil your appetite," as your mother always said. The meal will be less fun and hardly seem worth the expense if you are not hungry. But why would that matter if the goal is simply to attain a state of zero hunger?

Sexual arousal and gratification comprise another obvious example. People go out of their way to seek sexual arousal, not just gratification. The greater the arousal and sexual need, it seems, the more gratifying the satisfaction of that need will be. Secondary drives also may work this way. Many people not only try to finish the work they have been assigned, for example, but actively look for new work. They constantly create new needs—starting new projects even as they complete earlier ones. This seeking for new challenges might be one basis of eudaimonic well-being, discussed in Chapter 13.

Observations such as these require a modification of drive-reduction theory. Perhaps true reinforcement is not a state of zero need, but the movement from a state of higher need to a state of lower need. The distance between the initial and final states matters most, according to this proposition. This principle explains why people might foster new needs in themselves as well as purposely increasing the levels of existing needs before seeking satisfaction.

FRUSTRATION AND AGGRESSION

If your roommate has had a frustrating experience—failing an exam, say, or being turned down for a date—watch out. He or she is likely to be angry. It hardly matters at what. It could be at you if you are not careful. If your socks are on the sofa, you will get yelled at. If you present no such opportunity to be targeted, then your roommate might just pound the wall instead, or steam loudly about the person who supposedly caused the problem.

Not everybody reacts this way, but such a reaction is not uncommon. When it happens, the interesting psychological question is, why the anger? Specifically, why does the person vent anger on targets unrelated to the source of the problem, such as an innocent roommate or a wall? Dollard and Miller's classic answer is the **frustration-aggression hypothesis**: The natural, biological reaction of any person (or animal, for that matter) to being blocked from a goal, is to be frustrated, with the resulting urge to lash out and injure. The more important the blocked goal, the greater the frustration, and the greater the aggressive impulse.

The preferred target of the aggression will be the source of the frustration. But Dollard and Miller borrowed Freud's idea of displacement (see Chapter 11) to describe how the aggressive impulse can be redirected elsewhere. If your boss unfairly denies you a raise, this might lead to frustration and anger, but you are unlikely to vent it at the boss if you want to keep your job. So you might come home and kick the wall or criticize your spouse out of anger displaced from its original target.

PSYCHOLOGICAL CONFLICT

Fun things can also be frightening, and experiences we look forward to can also include an element of dread. Take bungee jumping, for example. A while back, a student of mine signed up for a Sunday bungee jump. It cost him money, and he signed up of his own free will, so he must have expected it would be fun. As the day approached, however, he became noticeably more nervous (the funeral plans being made by his fellow students may not have helped). In the end, it seemed a close call whether he would go or not. In this case, he did (and survived, I should add).

This kind of conflict between desire and fear, and the way it can change over time, was addressed by Dollard and Miller's theory of **approach-avoidance conflict**. (This theory can get technical, mind you.) Consider its five key assumptions:

1. An increase in drive strength will increase the tendency to approach or avoid a goal.
2. Whenever there are two competing responses, the stronger one (i.e., the one with greater drive strength behind it) will win out.
3. The tendency to approach a positive goal increases the closer one gets to the goal.
4. The tendency to avoid a negative goal also increases the closer one gets to that goal.
5. Most important, tendency 4 is stronger than tendency 3. That is, as a negative goal becomes nearer, the tendency to avoid it becomes stronger more rapidly than does the tendency to approach a positive goal. To put this even more technically (I warned you it would get technical), the avoidance gradient is steeper than the approach gradient (see Figure 15.5).

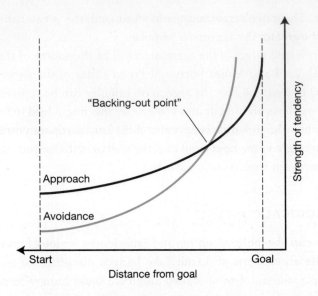

Figure 15.5 **Approach-Avoidance Conflict** Tendencies to approach or avoid a goal that is both attractive and dreaded (e.g., a bungee jump) may change over time. According to Dollard and Miller, both tendencies increase as the goal gets closer, but the avoidance gradient is steeper than the approach gradient. In this illustration, the person will try to back out of the act at the point where the two gradients cross. The bungee jump might be canceled at the last minute.

This set of principles yields some interesting predictions, particularly involving goals that have conflicting positive and negative elements. Such a goal might be a bungee jump, an airplane trip you are simultaneously looking forward to (for the vacation) and fearing (because you are afraid of flying), or a talk you have volunteered to give (because you need the practice), but that you also dread (because you have a fear of public speaking). Dollard and Miller's five-part theory predicts that in each case you will be relatively willing to commit to these behaviors if they are far off in time. But as the moment of truth approaches, you may regret having agreed to it. Even though the bungee jump, plane trip, or talk seemed like a good idea last week, with time the negative aspects are becoming more prominent than the positive aspects. In the end, you may not be able to go through with it.

This can be a useful principle. If you are responsible for arranging a series of speakers, for example, you are wise to schedule your speakers and get ironclad commitments as early as possible. Somebody will commit to something six months in advance that she might flatly refuse if you ask the week before. Dollard and Miller may have discovered the real reason dentists schedule appointments so far in advance, and why airlines make ticket refunds so difficult.

Rotter's Social Learning Theory

Julian Rotter's version of social learning theory primarily concerns decision making and the role of expectancies (Rotter, 1954, 1982).

EXPECTANCY VALUE THEORY

A woman about to graduate from college scans the list of companies interviewing on campus. She is allowed to interview for one job, and she narrows her choice down to two. One pays $35,000 a year, and the other pays $20,000. Which interview will she sign up for? Classic behaviorism predicts that she will choose the $35,000 job. But, according to Rotter's social learning theory, there is another factor to consider: What if she does not think she would get the $35,000 job, but thinks the chances are excellent that she would get the $20,000 job?

Rotter claimed that the woman's choice can be worked out mathematically. Suppose she thinks her chances of getting the $35,000 job are 50/50, whereas she thinks she is certain to get the $20,000 job. The *expected value* of the $35,000 job then becomes .50 × $35,000, or $17,500. The expected value of the other job is 1 × $20,000, or $20,000. Because the second job has a higher expected value, Rotter's theory predicts this is the interview she would choose.

This hypothetical example illustrates the core of Rotter's approach, which is **expectancy value theory**. This theory assumes that behavioral decisions are determined not just by the presence or size of reinforcements, but also by beliefs about the likely results of behavior. Even if a reinforcement is very attractive, according to this theory, you are not likely to pursue it if your chances of success seem slim. Conversely, even something not particularly desirable might motivate behavior if the chances of getting it are good enough.

EXPECTANCY AND LOCUS OF CONTROL

An **expectancy** for a behavior is an individual's belief, or subjective probability, about how likely it seems that the behavior will attain its goal. If you ask that person out, what is the probability the person will say yes? If you

Rotter: beliefs shape behavior.

apply for that job (and forgo others), will you get it? If you go to class, will that affect your score on the final exam, and if so, what are the chances? The expectancy is your belief about whether an action will pay off.

Because an expectancy is a belief, it can be right or wrong. Rotter's theory says that it does not matter whether a behavior is actually likely to bring success or not; if you think it will, you will try. The same goes for behavior that actually would bring success, if you were to make the effort; if you think it won't work, you won't even try.

Herein lies the key difference between Rotter's theory and classic behaviorism: The classic view focuses on *actual* rewards and punishments, while Rotter's social learning variant focuses on *beliefs about* reward and punishment. These beliefs shape behavior, Rotter claimed, even when they are inaccurate. Notice that, at this point in Rotter's social learning theory, a little wisp of phenomenology—that a person's impressions of reality are more important than reality itself—has drifted in (recall Chapter 13).

Rotter claimed that people actually have two kinds of expectancies: specific and general. A *specific expectancy* is the belief that a certain behavior, at a certain time and place, will lead to a specific outcome. For example, if just after lunch on Tuesday you ask Mary for a date on Friday night, will she say yes? The expected answer may depend on all of the following factors: when you ask the question, whom you ask, and when the date is scheduled. Another example: If you attend class this Monday, what are the chances you will pick up something helpful for the exam? From reading the syllabus, you might have reason to think that Monday's material is going to be essential, but that you can safely skip on Wednesday.

At the other extreme, people have *generalized expectancies*. These are general beliefs about whether anything you do is likely to make a difference. Some people, according to Rotter, believe that they have very little control over what happens to them; they have low generalized expectancies. Others believe that the reinforcements they enjoy (and the punishments they avoid) are directly a function of what they do; these people have high generalized expectancies. Not surprisingly, the latter tend to be energetic and highly motivated, while the former are more likely to be lethargic and depressed. Generalized expectancy is a broad personality variable, and in fact can be considered a trait exactly like those discussed in Chapters 4 through 7.

Rotter sometimes referred to generalized expectancy as *locus of control*. People with internal locus of control are those with high generalized expectancies and thus tend to think that what they do affects what happens to them. Those with external locus of control have low generalized expectancies and tend to think that what they do will not make much difference.

Later investigators have emphasized how locus of control (and generalized expectancy) can vary across the domains of one's life. For example, some people have internal academic locus of control (they believe they have control over their academic outcomes), but external locus of control otherwise. Other psychologists have studied health locus of control, which involves the difference between people who believe that their daily actions importantly affect their health, as opposed to those who think they have very little control over whether they get sick or stay well (e.g., Rosolack & Hampson, 1991; Lau, 1988). Even dating locus of control can vary. Maybe not everybody is willing to go out with you, but hopefully you realize that somebody somewhere is eager to do so.

Bandura's Social Learning Theory

The third and probably most influential social learning theory comes from the Stanford psychologist Albert Bandura. Bandura's version of social learning builds directly on Rotter's (Bandura, 1971, 1977). Many of the same ideas appear in both theories, but there are also important differences. Rotter's concepts of generalized expectancies and locus of control lead to theories about, and measurement of, individual differences. Bandura's theory gives less emphasis to stable differences between people—in fact, it generally ignores them. Where Bandura has gone beyond Rotter is in his emphasis on the social nature of learning and the ways people interact with the situations in their lives.

EFFICACY EXPECTATIONS

What Rotter called expectancies, Bandura reinterpreted as **efficacy expectations**. Both terms not only refer to the belief that one can accomplish something successfully, but also carry the phenomenological implication that one's interpretation of reality matters more than reality itself. The two concepts are not exactly the same, however. Rotter's notion of expectancy is the perceived conditional probability that *if* you do something, you will attain your goal. Bandura's efficacy is the perceived probability that you can do something in the first place.

Recall the example of the woman deciding which job to seek. Rotter's analysis assumes that she can apply for any job; the issue is whether she thinks she will get the job if she applies. Her perception of the probable result of her behavior determines what she will do.

[handwritten margin note: Bandura – can you even do "it" in the first place]

A more typical case for Bandura's analysis is someone with a snake phobia. He wishes not to fear snakes yet does not believe he could ever get near one. If this belief changes, he will be able to approach snakes and conquer his phobia. The issue for Bandura is not what happens after he handles a snake, but whether he can get close to a snake in the first place.

Bandura takes a step further away than Rotter does from the classic behaviorism with which both theories began. Rotter's expectancy is a belief about reinforcement, which was classically seen as the key agent of behavioral change. Bandura's efficacy expectation, or **self-efficacy**, is a belief about the self, about what the person is capable of doing. For example, you might have the efficacy expectation that you will someday be able to finish reading this book. As I am writing these words, I am trying to maintain the efficacy expectation that I can finish writing this book. In either case, our beliefs about our own capabilities are likely to affect whether we persist. Since you are holding this book in your hands, we can presume that my efficacy expectations held up. How are yours doing?

Efficacy expectations can interact with, or be determined by, other kinds of self-judgments (see Chapter 17). For example, if you think you are extremely attractive, you are more likely to attempt to date someone who interests you than you would be if you saw yourself as unattractive. In other words, your **self-concept** affects your efficacy expectation in this domain. Of course, both of these—your self-concept and your efficacy expectation—can be independent of how attractive you really are. A person's actual physical attractiveness might matter less than people sometimes believe; individuals who merely think they are attractive often do surprisingly well, it seems.

Bandura emphasized that efficacy expectations should be the key target for therapeutic interventions. If you achieve a better match between what you think you can accomplish and what you really can accomplish, Bandura believed, your life will be more rational and productive. Moreover, efficacies can create capacities. A snake phobic who is persuaded, by whatever means, that he can handle a snake subsequently will be able to handle a snake. The target of therapy, therefore, should not be the behavior of handling a snake, but the client's beliefs about his ability to handle a snake.

Research suggests that increases in self-efficacy can increase both motivation and performance. One study compared leg strength and endurance in men and women as a function of self-efficacy (Weinberg, Gould, & Jackson, 1979). Efficacy was manipulated experimentally. In one experimental condition, participants who lifted weights with their legs were told they were competing against someone with a knee injury, a belief that presumably increased their own self-efficacy. In the other condition, participants were told they were competing against a member of the varsity track team, a belief that presumably decreased their self-efficacy. Participants in the high-efficacy condition outperformed those in the low-efficacy condition, even though their actual strength (before the study) was about the same. This effect was quite impressive. In general, men have stronger legs than women. But in this study, the women in the high-efficacy condition demonstrated slightly more leg endurance than the men in the low-efficacy condition.

Increasing efficacy expectations seems to be a useful approach, therefore. A psychotherapist in Bandura's mold will use all sorts of tactics to accomplish this goal, including verbal persuasion ("You can do it!") and *modeling*, which means allowing the client to watch somebody else (the model) accomplish the desired behavior. Therapy for snake phobics may involve watching somebody else cheerfully handle a snake. The most powerful technique is to actually have the client perform the behavior. The goal of therapy, therefore, is to build up to the point where the client can handle a snake. This is the most effective way to convince the client that such a thing is possible.

Bandura's prescription for self-change follows the same pattern. If you are reluctant to do something, force yourself to do it. It will be less difficult next time. A small example: Suppose you know you should exercise more but do not think you are really the type. Take control of your life and go exercise anyway. This experience, if you can keep it up, will change your view of yourself, allowing exercise to become a natural part of your day rather than something strange that you must force yourself to do. In its brilliant way, Madison Avenue created a commercial for an athletic shoe that boiled this principle down to three words: "JUST DO IT."

> If you are reluctant to do something, force yourself to do it. It will be less difficult next time.

OBSERVATIONAL LEARNING

One of the most influential aspects of Bandura's theory has been its emphasis on **observational learning**, that is, learning a behavior vicariously, by seeing someone else do it. It is very different from what happens inside a Skinner box. At one time, psychologists believed that only humans could learn from observation, but recent research has indicated otherwise. Learning by songbirds is a frequently cited example. Some bird species seem to learn their songs simply by listening to adult birds, without any rewards or punishments. We also have seen those National Geographic television specials that show lion cubs learning to hunt by watching their mother. Apparently, some animals do learn by observation, and not always the animals we would expect. Research has shown that pigeons can learn from watching other pigeons (Zentall, Sutton, & Sherburne, 1996), but apes (orangutans) sometimes cannot learn from watching other apes (Call & Tomasello, 1995). A distinctive aspect of humans is that we learn nearly everything by observation.

Bandura provided a classic demonstration of how this process can work with his "Bobo doll" studies (see Figure 15.6). A Bobo doll is a large plastic clown on a round weighted base that bounces back when it is hit. In a series of studies, Bandura showed that a child who watches an adult hit the doll is likely to later hit the doll as well, especially if the child sees the adult rewarded for the aggressive behavior (Bandura, Ross, & Ross, 1963). The implications for the probable effects of television seem obvious. A person— particularly a child—who day after day watches violence glamorized and rewarded may become more likely to engage in such behavior.

Observational learning also can be used for positive purposes. A positive role model can provide useful and desirable behaviors for a young per-

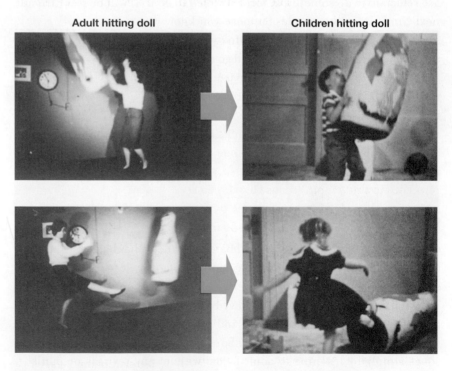

Adult hitting doll   **Children hitting doll**

Figure 15.6 **The Bobo Doll Study** In this classic study, children were more likely to beat up a Bobo doll if they had seen adults do so.

son to emulate. More specifically in the psychotherapeutic context, Bandura showed that one way to persuade a snake phobic to handle the feared reptile is to let him watch a research assistant handling a snake first. This kind of vicarious experience, or modeling, can make the next step—handling the snake himself—easier.

RECIPROCAL DETERMINISM

A third innovation in Bandura's social learning theory is **reciprocal determinism**, which is an analysis of how people shape their environments (Bandura, 1978, 1989). Classic versions of behaviorism, and even Rotter's refinement, tend to view reinforcements and the environments that contain them as influences inflicted on people; the people themselves remain basically passive. Bandura's analysis points out that this view is an oversimplification (see Figure 15.7). You are not just placed into the environments in your life, the way that a rat is placed into a Skinner box. In many circumstances, you choose the environments that influence you. If you go to college, all sorts of reinforcement contingencies kick in that cause you to study, attend class, read books, and do other things you might not do otherwise. But none of these contingencies takes effect until you voluntarily step on the campus (and pay your tuition). Similarly, if you join a gang or the army or a law firm, specific rules and contingencies immediately start to reshape your life. Do not underestimate their power; appreciate the implications of the social environments you choose.

A second aspect of reciprocal determinism is that the social situations in your life change, at least a little and perhaps importantly, because you are there. The party livens up or calms down when you arrive. The class discussion switches to a new topic because of your contribution. Your home environment is, to a large extent, a function of what you do there. In this sense, you control many of the environmental contingencies that in turn influence your behavior.

The third aspect of reciprocal determinism is perhaps the most important. Bandura's deepest departure from behaviorism is his claim that a "self system" develops that has its own effects on behavior, independent of the environment (see Chapter 17). Here

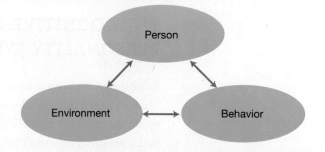

Figure 15.7 **Bandura's Model of Reciprocal Determinism** Persons, their environments, and their behaviors all affect each other in a constantly ongoing series of interactions.

Bandura forged a middle course between the phenomenologists considered in Chapter 13 and the behaviorists considered earlier in this chapter:

> Unidirectional environmental determinism is carried to its extreme in the more radical forms of behaviorism . . . [but] humanists and existentialists, who stress the human capacity for conscious judgment and intentional action, contend that individuals determine what they become by their own free choices. Most psychologists find conceptions of human behavior in terms of unidirectional personal determinism as unsatisfying as those espousing unidirectional environmental determinism. To contend that mind creates reality fails to acknowledge that environmental influences partly determine what people attend to, perceive, and think. (Bandura, 1978, pp. 344–345)

Think of the self system in reciprocal determinism as a chicken-and-egg problem. You have the environment affecting the self, which affects the environment, which affects the self. . . . But which came first? Bandura's answer is quite clear and essentially behaviorist: the environment. Still, social learning theory, especially Bandura's version, brought behaviorism a long way. Watson and Skinner emphasized how the environment shapes behavior. Bandura described how behavior shapes the environment. Very little influences you that you do not also influence in turn. Therefore, the causes of what you do cannot lie solely in the world (as the behaviorists would have it) or in your mind (as the humanists would have it); they originate in the interaction between the two.

THE COGNITIVE-AFFECTIVE PERSONALITY SYSTEM

Building on the work of Bandura, the cognitive social learning theorist Walter Mischel noted that people do not just behave, observe, or even expect—they *think*. An important intellectual antecedent of his approach to personality is the personal construct theory of George Kelly (1955), described in Chapter 13. Recall that these constructs are the idiosyncratic ideas about the world that guide each individual's perceptions and thoughts. Kelly's theory was essentially cognitive. For example, as will be described in Chapter 16, personal constructs affect the way information is noticed, organized, and remembered. Kelly's career came before the explosion of cognitive research in the late 1960s, however, and he never tied his ideas about constructs very closely to cognitive psychology.

Nevertheless, Kelly's theory inspired one of his students to develop the most explicitly cognitive verson of social learning theory. This student was Walter Mischel—yes, the very same person who triggered the person-situation controversy by claiming that personality traits are not important and that situations are much more powerful determinants of behavior (see Chapter 4). Mischel's approach combines two important ideas. The first is the phenomenological—specifically the Kellyan—idea that the individual's interpretation, or construal, of the world is all-important. From a phenomenological perspective, to understand a person's thoughts is to understand the person completely. The second idea is a view of the cognitive system that describes thought as proceeding simultaneously on multiple tracks that occasionally intersect. The combination of these two ideas is Mischel's theory of the *cognitive-affective personality system (CAPS)* (Mischel, 1999).

Interactions Among Systems

Mischel theorizes that the most important aspect of the many systems of personality and cognition is their interaction. Personality, then, is "a stable system that mediates how the individual selects, construes, and processes social information and generates social behaviors" (Mischel & Shoda, 1995, p. 246). He offered the following example:

> Suppose that while waiting for the results of medical tests, an individual scans for and focuses on a specific configuration of features in the situation, which activate the encoding that this is a health threat to the self, and concurrently trigger anxiety, which activates further scanning of and for those features, and simultaneously feeds back to reactivate the encoded health threat. The perceived threat activates the belief that this situation is uncontrollable, which triggers further anxiety and also negative outcome expectations. Both the negative expectancies and the anxiety concurrently activate defensive plans and scripts that generate a pattern of multiple behaviors at varying levels of strength. These events occur concurrently, in parallel activation within the system. The behaviors ultimately gen-

erated depend both on the situational features and on the organization of the network of cognitions and affects that become involved.
(Mischel & Shoda, 1995, p. 255)

In other words, a lot of processes are happening at the same time, and they
have many different results. There is not a single output from a single, linear, serial process. How the person feels, what she thinks, and what she
ultimately does involve compromises between many different processes.
Sigmund Freud and Walter Mischel seem to agree about that.

Cognitive Person Variables

The original version of Mischel's (1973) theory—when he first proposed
it, it was called "cognitive social learning theory"—claimed that individual
differences in personality stem from four *person variables* that characterize
properties and activities of the cognitive system:

1. **Cognitive and Behavioral Construction Competencies:** These
   competencies comprise an individual's mental abilities and behavioral skills and so might include such properties as IQ, creativity,
   social skills, and occupational abilities.
2. **Encoding Strategies and Personal Constructs:** These aspects
   of personality include a person's ideas about how the world can be
   categorized (one's Kellyan personal construct system) and efficacy
   expectations, or beliefs about one's own capabilities (of the sort
   described by Bandura). They also might include other beliefs about
   oneself, such as "I am a shy person."
3. **Subjective Stimulus Values:** This idea resembles the notion of
   expectancies in Rotter's social learning theory—an individual's
   beliefs about the probabilities of attaining a goal if it is pursued. It
   also includes how much people value different rewarding outcomes;
   for one person, money is more important than prestige, for example,
   whereas another person's priorities might be just the reverse.
4. **Self-Regulatory Systems and Plans:** These are closely related to
   Bandura's theory of the self system, a set of procedures that control
   behavior, including self-reinforcement, selection of situations, and
   purposeful alteration of the situations selected. This is more or less
   what Mischel had in mind, but Mischel was also interested in how
   people directly control their own thoughts.

An example Mischel addressed many times in his research concerned a child trying to delay gratification. As described in Chapter 7, most experiments of this sort present a child with two rewards, such as marshmallows and pretzels. The child is told that he can have the less preferred reward immediately, but can have the better reward if able to wait for a few minutes. Mischel was interested in the strategies the child might use to get through the waiting period.

One strategy he suggested to the waiting children was to mentally transform the object that presumably was being so eagerly awaited. For example, if a child's preferred treat was the marshmallow, she might hardly be able to wait while imagining its "chewy, sweet, soft taste." If instead she thought about the marshmallow as a cloud, it became easy to wait much longer. If a child preferred the pretzel, tolerance for waiting would end quickly if the child concentrated on its "crunchy, salty taste." But thinking about the pretzel as a brown log made the waiting easier.

Mischel drew from this research not only some pointers on how to help children delay gratification, but also a deeper moral that fits right into the point of view of the phenomenologists:

> The results [of the research just described] clearly show that what is in the children's heads—not what is physically in front of them—determines their ability to delay. (Mischel, 1973, p. 260)

Twenty-two years after his pioneering effort, and after a good deal of progress both in cognitive psychology and in tying cognition to personality, Mischel (and his student Yuichi Shoda) issued an updated version of the theory. Instead of four person variables, the new version had five; the new variable was *affects*, or feelings and emotions. According to Mischel, they added this new variable because by 1995 research had made it "clear that affects and emotions profoundly influence social information processing and coping behavior" (Mischel & Shoda, 1995, p. 252; see also Mischel, 1999).

If and Then

The most important recent addition to Mischel's theory of personality is the idea of what he calls *if . . . then contingencies*. The personality variables summarized in the previous section combine in each individual to yield a repertoire of actions triggered by particular stimulus situations. For example, one person, when insulted, might simply walk away. Another, with a different *if . . . then* pattern, might respond with a punch in the nose (Shoda, 1999). Every individual's pattern of contingencies is unique, and comprises his *behavioral signature* (Mischel, 1999, p. 44). In one recent application of this idea, the psychologist Susan Andersen has proposed that the psychoanalytic idea of transference, discussed in Chapter 10, can be conceived of in *if . . . then* terms. *If* a person encounters someone who reminds her of her father, for example, *then* she might feel and behave similarly to the way she used to relate to her father (Andersen & Chen, 2002).

Mischel's goal is for *if . . . then* contingencies to replace personality traits—for which he still has no great love, even after all these years—as the essential units for understanding personality differences. The main advantage of the *if . . . then* idea is its specificity. A trait such as dominance, for example, provides only general guidance for predicting what a dominant person might do. Reconceptualizing the trait in *if . . . then* terms might allow the specific prediction that if a person joins a business meeting, then she will quickly take charge. The *if . . . then* idea is also more sensitive to the way people change their behavior across situations. Perhaps the same person who dominates a meeting relates very differently to her family. A trait notion of dominance, in contrast, assumes that a person who is dominant in one situation is likely to display the trait in other situations, as well. Research shows this to be generally true (see Chapter 4), but the *if . . . then* theory describes the exceptions, and focuses more specifically on discerning which situations would probably elicit dominant behavior.

Mischel's *if . . . then* contingencies have the potential to integrate trait conceptions of personality with social learning conceptions and cognitive conceptions, by redescribing traits as specific behavior patterns. For example, *if* a friendly person meets a stranger, *then* he will probably engage in conversation. *If* a shy person is at a social gathering, *then* he will probably be sensitive to any sign of rejection. And so on. For all their demonstrated usefulness, personality traits are sometimes too broad and vague to provide the most useful way to think about behavior. Integrating traits with the *if . . . then* idea could make both concepts richer and more useful.

> *If* a person encounters someone who reminds her of her father, *then* she might feel and behave similarly to the way she used to relate to her father.

THE CONTRIBUTIONS AND LIMITATIONS OF LEARNING APPROACHES TO PERSONALITY

The learning approaches to personality can boast three major achievements.

First, the learning theorists—from Watson and Skinner to Bandura and Mischel, and everyone in between—conducted admirable research that approached the goal of establishing psychology as an objective science that can take its place among the other sciences. Most of their work, especially that of the early behaviorists, is characterized by tight theoretical reasoning, careful experimental design, and a style of argument that backs up every statement with data. In this way, the learning theorists might serve as role models for other research psychologists.

Second, the learning theorists recognize—better than the adherents of any other approach—how people's behavior depends on the environment and even the specific, immediate situation. Trait theorists emphasize the average of many behaviors performed over time and across situations; biologists examine physiological and genetic processes within the body; psychoanalysts and humanists study ways people are influenced by what goes on in the hidden recesses of their minds. Learning theorists, even latter-day ones such as Bandura and Mischel, instead emphasize situations, showing how what we do depends on the rewards and punishments present at that moment or—just a little different—the rewards and punishments that we *think* are present.

Each basic approach to personality may serve to remind us of important influences on behavior that the other approaches forget or neglect. Thus, the trait approach reminds us of the importance of individual differences; the biological approach reminds us of the influences of anatomy, physiology, and genetics; the psychoanalytic approach reminds us of the power of the unconscious; the humanistic approach reminds us of the importance of consciousness. In this list of job descriptions, the task of the learning theorist is clear: to remind us that physical and social environments and specific situations also cause what we do and shape who we are.

Third, the learning approaches have contributed a technology of behavior change. Because the process of learning is all about changing behavior, it was a short step to apply learning concepts to the treatment of phobias, addictions, and other emotional and behavioral disorders. The evidence clearly shows that such techniques work well—in the short run, at least.

But what about the long run? Here, the record is less clear and brings us to the first of two important limitations of the learning approaches to personality. It is not clear that the effects of behavioral therapies on phobias, addictions, and other problems are generalizable and long-lasting (H. J. Eysenck & Beech, 1971; Kazdin & Bootzin, 1972). Consider one example. An acquaintance of mine was once the director of drug treatment services for a county in California. He worked with alcoholics, treating them with a substance called Antabuse (the brand name for *disulfiram*). Antabuse is a drug that causes nausea when a person drinks alcohol. In the clinic, the therapist could be sure that the patient took the Antabuse regularly. This removed all temptation to drink, and you would think, based on classical conditioning, that after a while the alcoholics would find the very idea of drinking repulsive.

So what happened? Time after time, as soon as a patient was released from the rehab clinic, he or she stopped the car at the first pullout and threw the Antabuse pills into the dumpster. From there, the patient drove to the nearest liquor store. It turns out that people are more complicated than simple theories such as classical conditioning sometimes acknowledge. These alcoholics had understanding, not just learning. Even though the Antabuse made drinking unpleasant, they knew that as soon as they stopped taking it, they could resume drinking (until they landed back in jail or the clinic).

This observation leads to the second and more important limitation of the learning approaches. While recent versions of social learning theory acknowledge that people think, these theories still tend to underappreciate the degree to which the characteristic ways people think can cause them to respond differently to the same situation.[4] Cognitive evaluations of rewards can be more important than the rewards themselves, as the social learning theorists understood. But there is much more. Fantasies can be more important than real experiences; memories can interfere with, or even determine, perceptions; and complex and individualized processes of comparison, evaluation, and decision making place important complications between behavior and the environment that learning theorists assume causes everything we do. As a result, people and their behavior are much harder to change than the learning theories suggest. People tend to remain who they are, inevitably and even stubbornly, in the face of the strongest pressures from the environment.

---

[4] Rotter's version of social learning theory, with its attention to individual differences in locus of control, is an exception in this regard.

BEHAVIORISM AND PERSONALITY

Engineers have a saying they call "KISS," which stands for "Keep it simple, stupid." They use this phrase to remind themselves that every superfluous feature added to a design makes the whole system more likely to fail. In psychology, nobody followed the KISS principle more faithfully than the original behaviorists. The classic theories of John Watson, and later of B. F. Skinner, began with the principle that all psychology needed was stimuli and responses, reinforcements and punishments. This approach clarified the core processes of learning, but over time it became increasingly apparent that the appealing simplicity of behaviorism was too simple. As Albert Einstein is reputed to have said, "Make everything as simple as possible, but not simpler." To account for the full range of human and even animal behavior, behavioristically inclined psychologists found it necessary to add concepts such as perceiving, thinking, and strategizing. The most recent and most cognitive of the social learning theorists, Walter Mischel, has worked hard to integrate research findings about the causes of behavior and about how people think, culminating in his *if . . . then* model of personality that we reviewed a few pages back.

But there is an irony in this development. Mischel's latest ideas circle back to some deep ancestral roots. Recall that John Watson's S-R theory described personality as a matter of stimulus and response. For every person (or "organism"), the individual pattern of S-R connections would be a function of her idiosyncratic learning history, and hence unique. In addition, the fact that an individual had learned one S-R connection, leading her to be dominant in meetings, say, would not necessarily have to do with any other S-R connections she might have learned, such as whether she is dominant with her family. In other words, Watson, like Mischel, was not a big believer in cross-situational consistency of the sort that was argued over during the person-situation debate summarized in Chapter 4.

Walter Mischel is not a Watsonian behaviorist. The list of cognitive social learning variables that he formulated over decades of theorizing is enough to disqualify him for membership in the League of Hard-core Behaviorists. Yet his recent reconceptualization of personality, which views it as an idiosyncratic repertoire of learned *if . . . then* responses that have no necessary connection to each other, resembles in some ways the S-R conceptualization Watson propounded almost a century ago. *If . . . then* and stimulus-response: Walter Mischel, meet John Watson. The fundamental tenets of behaviorism continue to influence modern-day personality psychology.

SUMMARY

Behaviorism

- Behaviorism's key tenet is that all of behavior stems from the rewards and punishments in past and present environments.

- The philosophical roots of behaviorism include empiricism, a belief that all knowledge comes from experience; associationism, a belief that paired stimuli will come to be experienced as one; hedonism, the belief that the goal of life is "gentle pleasure"; and utilitarianism, the belief that the best society is the one that creates the most happiness for the most people. In behaviorist terminology, learning is any change in behavior that results from experience.

- The basic principles of learning include habituation, classical conditioning, and operant conditioning. Classical conditioning affects emotions, feelings, and physiological responses; operant conditioning affects behavior and how one "operates" in one's environment.

- Punishment is a useful technique of operant conditioning if applied correctly, which it almost never is.

Social Learning Theory

- Dollard and Miller's social learning theory explains motivation as the result of primary and secondary drives, aggression as the result of frustration from blocked goals, and psychological conflict as the result of conflicting motivations to approach and avoid a goal.

- Rotter's social learning theory emphasizes how expectancies of reward can be more important determinants of behavior than reward itself.

- Bandura's social learning theory focuses on how individuals' expectancies about their own behavioral capacities affect what they will attempt to do. His theory also develops a detailed analysis of observational learning, in which a person learns by watching the behaviors and outcomes of others, and reciprocal determinism, which involves a self system in which an individual's actions are determined by, and also change, the environment, which in turn affects the self system.

The Cognitive-Affective Personality System

- Mischel's cognitive social learning theory describes distinctive person variables, including construction competencies, encoding strategies, subjective stimulus values, and self-regulatory systems. The theory culminates in an *if . . . then* model of personality that describes how a person responds distinctively to each situation he encounters.

The Contributions and Limitations of Learning Approaches to Personality

• Learning approaches to personality have epitomized objective research, drawn necessary attention to the influence of the environment on behavior, and yielded a useful technology of behavioral change. However, they may underestimate the importance of individual differences.

Behaviorism and Personality

• The history of the learning approaches has come full circle, in that aspects of John Watson's original S-R theory have reemerged in the *if . . . then* approach of Walter Mischel.

THINK ABOUT IT

1. Does what you do depend on rewards and punishments? What else does it depend on?

2. Would you give up freedom for the sake of happiness? As discussed in the chapter, the utilitarian answer to this question is yes, and the existential answer is no. So, consider another question: Would you give up freedom for safety? In what way is this question similar to, and different from, the first question? Does the answer to the first question have implications for government policy? What about the second?

3. Is punishment an effective tool for teaching children how to behave? In what situations is it most effective? In what situations, if any, should punishment *not* be used?

4. Theories by Dollard and Miller, Rotter, Bandura, and Mischel have all been called social learning theories. Are they really similar enough to merit the same label? What do these theories have in common, and how do they differ?

5. Is Mischel's *if . . . then* approach to personality a reinvention of Watson's S-R theory of personality, or is it distinctive? What is new about it?

6. What might psychology look like today if behaviorism had never been invented?

SUGGESTED READINGS

Bandura, A. (1977). *Social learning theory*. Englewood Cliffs, NJ: Prentice-Hall.

Miller, N. E., & Dollard, J. (1947). *Social learning and imitation*. New Haven, CT: Yale University Press.

Rotter, J. B. (1954). *Social learning and clinical psychology*. Englewood Cliffs, NJ: Prentice-Hall.

> *Although many people identify Bandura as the originator of social learning theory, his version is actually the third of three major versions, summarized in the books above. Of these three, Rotter's may be the most interesting to read because of its direct applications and clinical examples.*

Skinner, B. F. (1938). *The behavior of organisms: An experimental analysis*. New York: Macmillan.

> *Nearly every college library has a copy of this book (either the original 1938 version or one of the reprints), and it is worth looking at firsthand. It is still the best comprehensive survey of the thinking of this prominent behaviorist, and helps to explain why he became so famous; the book is clearly written and full of clever insights.*

EMEDIA

 Go to StudySpace, wwnorton.com/studyspace, to access additional review and enrichment materials.

16

PERSONALITY PROCESSES:
Perception, Thought, Motivation, and Emotion

ON JUNE 27, 1995, Hugh Grant, popular actor and frequent escort of supermodels, was arrested by the Los Angeles police. They had caught him engaged in unlawful activities in a parked car with a local prostitute named Divine Brown. The result was a sensational media outcry. Grant went into hiding for weeks. When he finally emerged to appear on *The Tonight Show*, host Jay Leno lost no time asking the question on everyone's mind: "What the hell were you *thinking?*"

This was a good first question, if one wants to understand why Grant did what he did. But in his case—and probably for most actions by most people—"thinking" is only part of the story. We would also need to understand what he wanted, how he felt, and his perspective on reality. In addition to thinking, in other words, desires, emotions, and perceptions are also important. These activities make people psychologically different from each other, and if we understand them we have gone a long way toward understanding an individual's personality. The **personality processes** of perception, thought, motivation, and emotion are major topics of current research, and the subjects of the present chapter.

THE HISTORICAL ROOTS OF RESEARCH INTO PERSONALITY PROCESSES

A good deal of current research on personality processes stems directly from the learning-based approaches considered in the previous chapter. As we saw, learning theorists sprang onto the scene early in the 20th century with the bold pronouncement that events inside the head either don't exist or don't matter, and that in either case psychology would be better off ignoring them. But after a few decades, psychologists came to view this approach as being too limited. This realization opened the door for the social learning theorists, notably Rotter and Bandura, and later Mischel, who focused on cognitive processes such as interpretation, evaluation, and decision making. You will recall that Rotter emphasized how beliefs about the environment can determine expectations about the results of different behaviors; these expectations in turn determine what an individual decides to do. Bandura's theory, subtly different, emphasized that beliefs about yourself set expectations of your own capabilities, which also influence what you attempt to do. Mischel added a list of person variables, which refer to the cognitive processes that determine the *if . . . then* patterns of people's responses to varying situations.

Another historical influence on current personality process research is the phenomenological approach considered in Chapter 13, particularly the ideas of George Kelly (1955). Like personality process theorists, Kelly emphasized the way an individual's concepts for thinking about the world—her personal constructs—shape personality and behavior. Yet another perhaps surprising connection can be drawn between personality process theories and psychoanalysis (Chapters 10 through 12). Some modern theories find counterparts in Freud's notions concerning levels of consciousness, especially the preconscious and the unconscious and his idea that, within each of us, competing psychological subsystems need to seek compromise. As biological research advances, it, too, increasingly contributes to ideas about personality processes. For example, studies of brain-damaged individuals hint at how representations of the self may be organized in the brain (see Chapter 17). Finally, the venerable and still-active trait approach (Chapters 4 through 7) has addressed personality processes from the very beginning (e.g., McCrae & Costa, 1995). People are different from each other—have different degrees of different traits—precisely because they think, feel, and desire differently. As Gordon Allport observed years ago:

> For some the world is a hostile place where men are evil and dangerous; for others it is a stage for fun and frolic. It may appear as a place to do one's duty grimly; or a pasture for cultivating friendship and love. (Allport, 1961, p. 266)

PERCEPTION

As Allport's quote implies, people are predisposed to perceive the world in different ways. The differences can be surprisingly basic. One recent study noted that "dominant individuals frequently think in terms of dominance hierarchies (e.g., 'upper' vs. 'lower' class)" (Moeller, Robinson, & Zabelina, 2008, p. 354). Surprisingly—at least to me—the researchers found that dominant people are more sensitive to visual probes on the vertical, up-down dimension than they are to probes on the horizontal, side-to-side dimension! Apparently, the up-down metaphor associated with dominance and submission makes its way into participants' perceptions of the physical world. Is this view the result, or the cause, of a dominant personality? For now, the answer is unknown. But the results of this study provide a vivid demonstration about how different people may perceive the world differently on a fundamental level.

differences in perception can be explained through priming. - eg, someone who just lost money may complain a lot high prices

Priming and Chronic Accessibility

Differences in perception can be explained, in part, by the cognitive mechanism of **priming**. Concepts that have been activated recently, perhaps cued by something that happened today, or that are consistently activated, perhaps due to an attribute of the individual's personality, come to mind quickly, even with little stimulus. The cognitive system of a shy person may include so many memories and feelings related to social rejection and humiliation that they are recalled by the slightest hint. Priming can also come from the outside. A person who has suffered a recent financial setback might suddenly find that the prices of objects in a store are much more salient than they used to be. The mass media can, and often does, prime concepts in the whole population. In early 2001, a few shark attacks on the Florida coast received so much publicity that people all over the country were afraid to go in the water, even in lakes! After September 11 of that year, shark mania cooled. Instead, people went on high alert for signs of terrorists—not just on airplanes, but also in parks and shopping malls—and people with beards and swarthy complexions found themselves gazed at with deep suspicion no matter what they did. Over time, this kind of situational priming fades, fortunately, but the concepts that are

> The cognitive system of a shy person may include so many memories and feelings related to social rejection and humiliation that they are recalled by the slightest hint.

constantly primed and reprimed because of their **chronic accessibility** in our cognitive systems become part of our personalities.

It is possible that some patterns of priming are genetically built into everybody for evolutionary reasons (see Chapter 9). For example, we may be predisposed to have the concept of gender primed; most people are quick to perceive whether others are male or female and to think about many concepts in terms of their masculinity or femininity.[1] Anthropologists also have speculated that we might be genetically primed to dislike snakes (Öhman & Mineka, 2003), and may even have inherited from our ape ancestors a tendency to be especially fearful of falling out of trees!

Other perceptions are more likely to be different from one person to the next. For example, individuals characteristically see other people in consistent ways, a phenomenon one social psychologist has called the "perceiver effect" (Kenny, 1994). As we saw in Chapter 6, people with generally positive views of others are, in general, more accurate in their person perceptions (Letzring & Funder, 2006).

Where do individual differences like these come from? One possible source is inborn patterns of individual temperament (see Chapter 8). For example, for a person with a tendency to experience positive emotions, as part of that pattern, happy thoughts may be more easily accessible to consciousness, whereas more disturbing possibilities come to mind more slowly. This person would quickly see the good in anyone and anything, and generally be optimistic about the future (Carver & Scheier, 1995). In the same way, a person with a temperamental tendency toward negative emotions may equally quickly notice other people's less desirable traits and have a more negative view of the future. The first person might say of a new acquaintance, "Well, he's friendly." The second person might reply, "I thought he seemed kind of fake." The interesting and important fact is that both perceptions may be based on observing exactly the same behavior. But distinct temperaments and associated patterns of priming cause these people to see and interpret the same reality in different ways. Their contrasting perceptions may have compensating patterns of advantage and disadvantage. The first person may have more friends. The second person is probably harder to fool. Which is better? Take your pick.[2]

---

[1] Many languages—including French, Spanish, and German (but not English)—denote nearly every noun as masculine or feminine.

[2] Actually, the study by Letzring & Funder (2006), as well as research summarized near the end of this chapter, suggest that the positive view is generally more adaptive.

↓ stubborn vs. persistent priming activity.

Despite the possibility that patterns of priming might be rooted in evolutionary history or a biologically determined temperament, most current theorists assume that these patterns result mostly from experience. The effect of experience on priming can be demonstrated experimentally. One study asked participants to read aloud while they held in memory either the word *stubborn* or the word *persistent* (Higgins, 1999). Then, they completed a seemingly unrelated comprehension task, which included passages such as the following:

> Once Donald made up his mind to do something, it was as good as done no matter how long it might take or how difficult the going might be. Only rarely did he change his mind, even when it might well have been better if he had. (Higgins, 1999, p. 70)

After reading this passage, participants were asked to categorize Donald's behavior—as either "stubborn" or "persistent." Those primed with the word *stubborn* were more likely to describe Donald with that term, though they did not realize why (Higgins, Rholes, & Jones, 1977). This phenomenon has been replicated many times. When you could characterize someone you meet in more than one way, you will tend to form an impression related to whatever has been primed recently (Bargh, Bond, Lombardi, & Tota, 1986; E. R. Smith & Branscombe, 1987; Srull & Wyer, 1980).

In daily life and throughout every child's development, some ideas are primed over and over again. For example, if a child's parents strongly value certain attributes of people, the child is likely to grow up hearing these attributes referred to frequently. Every day, one child might hear people described as "honest" or "dishonest." Another child, whose parents hold different values, might frequently hear people described as "fearless" or "cowardly." As a result, different constructs will become chronically accessible to these two children (Bargh, Lombardi, & Higgins, 1988). The first child will grow up to be alert to signs of honesty (or lack thereof) in someone she meets; the second will be quicker to judge fearlessness—and these differences in perception may also affect how they see themselves.

We saw in Chapter 14 that some individuals are bicultural; for example, they may be immigrants who were raised in one culture and now live in a second culture. If these two cultures have their own characteristic styles of thinking, which one will the individual use? One recent line of research suggests that the answer may depend on what has been primed recently! You may recall from Chapter 14 a study in which bicultural Asian Americans viewed pictures including iconic Asian symbols such as a dragon or American sym-

"You're really starting to bug me."

bols such as the Statue of Liberty. Then, after viewing a brief cartoon of fish chasing each other, the participants were asked to explain what was going on. Those primed with symbols such as dragons were more likely to interpret the cartoon the way Asians usually do—which, in this case, meant seeing one fish as being pursued by the other fish—while those participants primed with symbols such as the Statue of Liberty reacted more like typical Americans, interpreting the same fish as *leading* the group (Hong, Benet-Martínez, Chiu, & Morris, 2003; Hong, Morris, Chiu, & Benet-Martínez, 2000). This research suggests that bicultural individuals can switch frames of reference quickly, and may do so without noticing or knowing why.

In the short run, anything primed is more likely to come to mind, given the slightest hint of a relevant stimulus. If one has had a bad scare recently, the next situation one enters may not have to be very dangerous in order to trigger a fearful response. But if one has recently received extremely good news, then everyone seems nice, the weather feels perfect, and the world is beautiful. In the long run, different people have a predisposition to be primed for certain concepts. A person with a positive temperament is "built," perhaps at a level of brain architecture and hormonal responses, so that positive ideas are more readily primed; the reverse is true for someone with a negative temperament. People with positive and negative temperaments have different sets of chronically accessible ideas, leading to different views of the world and different behavior.

Rejection Sensitivity

According to one analysis, chronic accessibility can lead to the personality disposition of *rejection sensitivity* (Downey & Feldman, 1996; Downey, Freitas, Michaelis, & Khouri, 1997). When a person afflicted with this syndrome discusses a relationship problem with a romantic partner, anxious expectations stimulate him to scan for suggestions of impending rejection. Such a person will likely interpret any ambiguous signals as confirmation that his partner is about to walk out.

You can imagine the result. The slightest expression of irritation or disinterest by his partner leads this person to conclude that he is being rejected, leading to an anxious or even panicked response. Often, the partner then rejects the person (wouldn't you?). In this way, the attribute of rejection sensitivity can produce the very outcome the person fears most.[3]

Rejection sensitivity and other forms of chronic accessibility come into play only when relevant stimuli are present. For example, rejection sensitivity is triggered by any indication—even an ambiguous one—that rejection may be imminent. But in the absence of such indications (perhaps, early in a relationship, when both partners are still being nice all the time), the very same person may be exceptionally caring and supportive. Depending on the circumstances, then, the same person might be "hurtful and kind, caring and uncaring, abusive and gentle" (Mischel, 1999, p. 51).

This observation raises a question: Which person is "real"—the kind, caring, and gentle one the partner sees at the beginning of the relationship, or the hurtful, uncaring, and abusive one who appears later? According to Walter Mischel's CAPS (cognitive-affective personality system) approach, summarized in Chapter 15, both are real because these behavior patterns stem from the same underlying system, and though they might seem inconsistent, in fact they are meaningfully coherent. As we saw in Chapter 7, a similar line of reasoning was applied many years ago to the construct of authoritarianism, an attribute that leads a person to be respectful of those higher in the status hierarchy but contemptuous of anyone lower. In the case of rejection sensitivity, authoritarianism, and probably many more attributes of personality, patterns of behavior that seem contradictory may, under close analysis, prove to be manifestations of a single, meaningful underlying pattern.

Aggression

Hostility is another behavior pattern related to chronic accessibility (Zelli, Cervone, & Huesmann, 1996). The accessibility of ideas related to hostility

---

[3] Notice how this pattern resembles the behavior of the anxious-ambivalent person described in the discussion of attachment theory in Chapter 12. It is possible that the same mechanism of chronic accessibility underlies the readiness of the anxious-ambivalent person to anticipate rejection (see also Zhang & Hazan, 2002).

"He didn't actually threaten me, but I perceived him as a threat."

can cause some people to perceive an ambiguous situation as threatening (Dodge, 1993). In one study, aggressive and nonaggressive boys were told the same story about a disagreement between two children. The aggressive boys believed that the children in the story had hostile intentions, while the nonaggressive boys came to a more benign interpretation (Dodge & Frame, 1982).

Other research suggests that the memories of aggressive people may be organized around hostile themes. In one pair of studies, college students tried to memorize a set of sentences that could potentially refer to a hostile situation but were basically ambiguous (e.g., "The policeman pushes Dave out of the way"). Students who were generally hostile—they had reported frequent occasions in which they had punched, kicked, or threatened others—found these ambiguous sentences easier to remember in the presence of hostility recall cues such as hostile words or pictures of weapons. Nonhostile students, however, did not find the cues helpful in recalling the sentences. These findings were interpreted as showing that hostile people tend to remember things in hostile terms, while nonhostile people organize their memories in other ways (Zelli, Huesmann, & Cervone, 1995; Zelli et al., 1996).

Organizing one's thoughts and memories around a theme of hostility may come to guide a person's perceptions and actions. For example, aggressive children tend to respond to a stressful situation in ways that make the situation worse, such as escalating a small problem. However, if you give them time to think before they act, they can respond more constructively (Rabiner, Lenhart, & Lochman, 1990).

There is a message of hope in this last result. It implies that even if certain ideas come quickly to mind and cause problems, it still might be possible to avoid responding to situations in a programmed manner. Someone with rejection sensitivity or excessive hostility has a chance to override her habitual response by remembering to slow down and think.

[handwritten margin note: Memories of aggressive people may be organized around hostile themes]

[handwritten: system has the ability to screen off info that may make someone anxious/uncomfortable]

Perceptual Defense

The flip side of chronic accessibility is **perceptual defense**. The perceptual system appears to have the ability to screen out information that might make the individual anxious or uncomfortable. Recall from the discussion of the defense mechanisms in Chapter 11 that psychoanalytic theory claims the ego tries to prevent stimuli that the superego finds overly threatening from even entering awareness. Psychologists have attempted to test this hypothesis experimentally.

In one early experiment, words were presented extremely briefly to participants by use of a machine called a tachistoscope, which flashes them on a screen. Some words were neutral, such as *apple*, *child*, and *dance*. Others were sexually charged, such as *penis*, *rape*, and *whore*. Over successive trials, words of both types were presented for increasing durations, beginning with flashes so brief nobody could perceive them and continuing until the long exposures made the words obvious. Researchers measured participants' detection of the words in two ways. One was simply to ask, "Can you read that?" after each presentation. The minimum exposure time required to perceive each word was recorded. The second way was to measure the participants' sweat-gland activity; when they began to sweat in response to a word such as *rape*, participants were assumed to have detected it. *[handwritten: — reading dirty words experiment.]*

The interesting finding was that these two ways of measuring perception did not exactly coincide. In particular, when emotionally charged words were shown very briefly, participants might say, "I can't read that word," even while their sweat glands were reacting strongly. Apparently, an unconscious part of their mind *could* read the word at the same time that the conscious part could not (McGinnies, 1949).

Results like these suggest that something much like an ego defense mechanism, of the sort discussed in Chapter 11, may prevent certain embarrassing stimuli from entering consciousness even while other aspects of the mind are well aware of and responding to them. These results also suggest that we might be able to avoid conscious awareness of aspects of the world that feel threatening, even when they are right in front of us.

Although many investigators have obtained results more or less like those just described, interpretations of them have been controversial. One obvious possibility is that subjects can read the word *penis* just fine—they are just embarrassed to tell the investigator. It is difficult and perhaps impossible for researchers to be 100 percent sure. Taken as a whole, however, the evidence seems persuasive that the mind has mechanisms that not only selectively attend to certain stimuli, but also actively screen out other stimuli that could cause anxiety (Erdelyi, 1974, 1985; Weinberger & Davidson, 1994).

Vigilance and Defense

The examples just discussed raise a difficult question. On the one hand, it seems that an important hallmark of personality is that people with different traits have a readiness to perceive different stimuli, such as a shy person who is vigilant for signs of rejection. On the other hand, the mind seems able to filter out information that might be disturbing or threatening. Why, then, does a shy person, or someone with rejection sensitivity, tend to see exactly what he fears most?

One possible answer is suggested by the idea, discussed in Chapter 11, that defense mechanisms exist for a purpose. Although they can be overused, in general they are adaptive functions of the ego that protect the individual from excessive anxiety (Block, 2002). It may be that the defense mechanisms of shy people don't work well enough. Perhaps the only way to avoid becoming shy is to be what clinical psychologists sometimes call *well defended*, to ignore and even fail to perceive small social slights.

Another possible answer is that people vary in the degree to which they are perceptually vigilant versus defensive. Years ago, the psychologist Donn Byrne developed the *repression-sensitization scale* to measure the extent to which people are relatively defensive or sensitive in their perception of potentially threatening information; this scale has been used in many studies since (Byrne, 1961). A more recent study developed a scale to measure the "need for affect," a related construct that involves the degree to which a person seeks to magnify or minimize emotional experience (Maio & Esses, 2001). Participants who were high in this need tended to hold extreme attitudes, liked to watch emotional movies, and even had extreme reactions to the death of Princess Diana! In this conception, perhaps people with a high need for affect magnify their emotional responses to rejection so much that they become at risk for shyness. Rejection upsets them more than it would other people, so some of them develop a style of avoiding social contact altogether.

THOUGHT

Thinking is among any individual's most important activities because, as William James memorably observed, "thinking is for doing" (1890, p. 520).

The decisions reached by an individual's thought processes determine many—though perhaps not quite all—of her actions (Morsella, 2005). Personality psychology points out a couple of aspects of thinking that might not be so obvious. First, not all thinking is conscious—it's possible to have thoughts that you don't know about. Second, there may be two fundamentally different ways to think.

Consciousness 7, plus or minus two.

Consciousness comprises whatever an individual has in mind at the moment. It includes a person's ongoing construal of reality—that concept so important to the phenomenologists (discussed in Chapter 13)—and many important behavioral decisions. Cognitive psychologists have a relatively mundane label for the place consciousness is located; they call it **short-term memory (STM)**, and they have discovered some interesting things about it.

For one thing, the capacity of STM—which can be equated to the capacity of consciousness itself—is specifically limited. To demonstrate this limit in class, I sometimes read a list of numbers to my students, asking them to hold all of the numbers in mind simultaneously as I go. I tell them to raise their hands when their brains are full. (Try it with a friend; read slowly the numbers 4, 6, 2, 3, 7, 6, 2, 8, 7, ...) The results are highly consistent. Hands begin to go up after about five numbers, most are up by seven, and by nine I have everybody.

This experiment illustrates the capacity of STM, which has famously been described as "seven, plus or minus two" (G. A. Miller, 1956). The next question, of course, is seven *what*? The answer is that the capacity of STM is about seven **chunks** of information. A chunk is any piece of information that can be thought of as a unit. It can vary with learning and experience. Seven random numbers, for example, comprise seven chunks. But your own phone number, which also includes seven numbers, is just one chunk. It seems to be about as easy to hold in STM seven familiar phone numbers (or 49 digits in all) as seven random digits.

STM AND THINKING

Chunking can work with ideas, too. If you know what "water pressure" is, or "existential philosophy," or even "short-term memory," these complex ideas can constitute single chunks. This is important, because the limit to STM implies that you can only think about seven things at a time, and that all new ideas you have must come from the interaction of no more than seven things at once. The more rich and complex each idea in STM is, the more rich and complex your thinking can be.

This is the best argument I know for education. You learn complicated ideas and concepts one small piece at a time, often slowly and painfully. But when you've finally learned them, complicated patterns of information and thinking become single chunks that you can manipulate and contrast in your mind simultaneously with other such chunks. Once you learn the many ideas that make up "conservatism" and "liberalism," you can then compare the two philosophies. By now, you should be able to say something about the basic differences between psychoanalysis and behaviorism, whereas before you understood these ideas you might have been able to compare only one aspect of each at a time. And until you really understand what water pressure is and can use it as a single idea, you will never be able to fix your plumbing.

This is the logic behind **Funder's Fifth Law**: *The purpose of education is to assemble new chunks*. That is the only way to expand your ability to think.

CONSCIOUSNESS AND PSYCHOLOGICAL HEALTH

Inherent in the limited capacity of consciousness is the danger of filling it up with the wrong things. For example, a shy person, to use that example again, might try to interact with an attractive individual of the opposite sex while simultaneously thinking, "Do I look like an idiot?" and "I bet he'd rather be somewhere else," and, "Why does nobody like me?" and, "Argh!"—which leaves only a couple of chunks to actually carry on a conversation. As a result, the shy person may seem distracted and confused and either babble incoherently or be unable to say anything at all.

Unhappy people also often fill their heads with comparisons between themselves and others and ruminations about things that have gone wrong or could go wrong (Lyubomirsky, 2001). These sorts of people obsess about whether other people make more money, have a bigger office, or drive a nicer car than they do, and pointlessly relive unpleasant memories and recycle worries. It is much more adaptive to avoid filling one's consciousness with thoughts like these and instead to use a few chunks to notice and appreciate the good things in life, and save the rest for constructive planning. For example, research has found that older (and wiser) persons pay more attention to the positive aspects of their environment, and thereby can maintain a positive mood in the face of life's adversities (Carstensen & Mikels, 2005).

[handwritten margin note: unhappy people compare themselves to everyone]

CONSTRUCTS, CHUNKS, AND CONSCIOUSNESS

The way you think is different from the way anyone else thinks because your thinking is made up of comparisons and contrasts between chunks of information and philosophy collected from your edu-
cation and your unique experience. This conclusion is consistent with Kelly's personal construct theory (Chapter 13), which holds that the critical aspects of thinking are the constructs (perhaps another word for chunks) that make up your distinctive view of the world. These chunks, or constructs, are also substantially culturally determined (as noted in Chapter 14).
A Japanese parent mindful of her child's *amae* may experience family life differently than a British parent could ever imagine (Tseng, 2003).

> Consciousness in the moment can include no more than about seven things—a surprisingly exact upper limit to the capacity of human awareness.

The idea of STM as consciousness has interesting parallels in other basic approaches to personality. Freud believed that consciousness was by far the smallest part of the mind. In the models of the mind constructed by cognitive psychologists, too, STM is the smallest part—and the only part that has a specifically limited capacity. To phenomenologists, all that matters is what you are conscious of now. As we have already seen, research on STM suggests that this consciousness in the moment can include no more than about seven things—a surprisingly exact upper limit to the capacity of human awareness.

UNCONSCIOUS THOUGHTS

We saw in Chapter 12 that modern research influenced by psychoanalytic ideas has documented important aspects of thinking that appear to happen outside of conscious awareness; the research on perceptual defense (summarized in the preceding section of this chapter) is an example. But a psy-
chologist need not be a psychoanalyst to do research on what is sometimes called the *cognitive unconscious* (Kihlstrom, 1990). Many experiments have shown that people can do things without knowing why, and can know things without knowing they know. For example, people tend to prefer objects—
including meaningless words, photographs, and Chinese characters—that they have seen more often, even if they have seen them only in tachistoscope projections too brief to consciously notice (Zajonc, 1980).

A particularly dramatic—and for a time, controversial—demonstration of the effect of subliminal stimuli on the unconscious mind was a series of studies by the psychoanalytic psychologist Lloyd Silverman (1976; see Hardaway, 1990, for a review). Flashing the words too quickly to be consciously seen, Silverman showed some of his participants messages that, on psychoanalytic grounds, were expected to be comforting and reassuring. For example, one of the phrases (printed in capital letters) was "MOMMY AND I ARE ONE." Another phrase, aimed at Oedipal anxieties (see Chapter 10), was "BEATING DAD IS OK." Participants in the control conditions saw neutral phrases such as "PEOPLE ARE WALKING." The astonishing result was that people in the experimental conditions reported feeling better without knowing why! This basic finding has now been replicated several times, with the important recent caveat that it doesn't work for everybody. The effect of reading "Mommy and I are one" apparently depends on the relationship you have or had with your mother (Sohlberg & Birgegard, 2003).

Three final observations underline the importance of the unconscious sectors of the mind. First, it is obvious that many things that we do—such as digest food, contract our pupils in response to strong light, and jump when we hear a loud noise—happen without our needing, or even being able, to think about it (Morsella, 2005). Second, notice how small consciousness is: a mere seven chunks? Life is more complicated than that. Even with the ability to combine many pieces of information, it is clear that much more must go on mentally than consciousness could contain. Third, remember Freud's fundamental argument for the existence of the unconscious (Chapter 10), the one that clinched the issue for me the first time I heard it: We do things without knowing why, and have thoughts and feelings we do not understand. It's obvious that our own minds are doing things we don't know about.

Two Ways of Thinking

One way to resolve the paradox of conscious and unconscious mental processes existing simultaneously is to divvy up the important components of thinking into separate systems. Throughout psychology, and in cognitive psychology in particular, theorists have proposed *dual-process models* that contrast the roles of conscious and unconscious thought (Chaiken & Trope, 1999; E. R. Smith & Coster, 2000). The key difference in most of these models is that conscious thought is slower.

Personality psychology has seen the development of a number of dual-process models over the years, including Freud's theory, which, at its most basic level, is about the different between rational and irrational thought. Another, more recent model, by the German psychologists Fritz Strack and

Roland Deutsch, contrasts what they call reflective and impulsive determinants of behavior (Strack & Deutsch, 2004). *Reflective determinants* are slow and largely rational while *impulsive determinants* are fast, almost automatic, and sometimes irrational.

Most of the key distinctions that have been theorized to distinguish the two personality systems are captured by Seymour Epstein's *cognitive-experiential self-theory (CEST)*, which seeks to explain unconscious processing and the seemingly irrational, emotion-driven sectors of the mind (Epstein, 2003). According to CEST, people use two major psychological systems—at the same time—to adapt to the world (Epstein, 1973, 1994). The *rational system*, an evolutionarily recent innovation, includes language, logic, and systematized, factual knowledge. It resembles Freud's conception of secondary process thinking (see Chapter 10). The *experiential system* is evolutionarily older, tied closely to emotion, and assumed to be the way other animals think (and how our prehuman ancestors also thought). This system resembles Freud's conception of primary process thinking.

The two systems differ in many ways, some of which are summarized in Table 16.1. The rational system is analytic, in that it breaks a situation

Table 16.1

EPSTEIN'S DUAL-PROCESS MODEL

Rational System	Experiential System
Is analytic	Is holistic
Resembles Freud's "secondary process thinking"	Resembles Freud's "primary process thinking"
Is logical: driven by what is sensible	Is affective: driven by what feels good
Affects behavior through conscious appraisal of events	Drives behavior through "vibes" from past experience
Thinks in terms of abstract symbols, words, and numbers	Thinks in terms of vivid images, metaphors, and stories
Operates at a slower speed, designed for deliberate action	Operates at a very high speed, designed for immediate action
Can change rapidly, at the speed of logical thought	Is slow to change, needs repetitive or intense experiences for change
Is effortful and deliberate (e.g., sitting down to do some serious thinking)	Is effortless and automatic (e.g., being seized by one's emotions)
Requires justification via logic and evidence	Is self-evidently valid: "experiencing is believing"
Produces knowledge	Produces wisdom

Source: Adapted from Epstein (1994), p. 711.

into its constituent pieces so they can be carefully analyzed; the experiential system is holistic and tends to react to a whole situation all at once. Rational thought is slow and deliberate, whereas experiential thought is fast, sometimes almost instantaneous. Rational thought is effortful. It feels like work. Experiential thought is effortless. Indeed, sometimes it occurs when we don't want it to, such as when we "can't help but think that . . . "

The rational system includes everything we are aware of and can talk about. The experiential system, in contrast, operates outside of conscious awareness and is something we cannot talk about directly; evolutionarily speaking, it is older than language itself. When Jay Leno asked Hugh Grant to explain his behavior with Divine Brown, Grant replied:

> I think you know in life what's a good thing to do and what's a bad thing, and I did a bad thing. And there you have it.

In other words, nobody could understand his motivation, and he didn't have a clue either. In Epstein's terms, Grant's rational system—the one that had to decide what to say on television—did not have access to the workings of the experiential system that initiated the consequential encounter with Ms. Brown. (Or, if his rational system did, it wasn't telling.)

The experiential system is likely to dominate when you are under the sway of your emotions, and the rational system to dominate when you are calm. This is why people sometimes give advice such as "Get a grip on yourself. You're too emotional to think straight. Once you calm down, you will see things differently" (Epstein, 1994, p. 710). The two systems may generate different decisions. As mentioned way back in Chapter 1, it is possible to feel intensely attracted to someone you just know is bad news. It is as if one part of your mind—the emotion-based experiential system—has one opinion, and the other part of your mind—the more logical rational system—has another opinion. Which will win out? As we all know, the outcomes vary. Hugh Grant apparently knew that what he was doing was unwise, but he did it anyway.

The experiential system is more than just a source of trouble, however. According to Epstein, it also produces intuition, insight, and wisdom. The distinction is a bit like the difference between the styles of Captain Kirk and Mr. Spock on the original *Star Trek* series (as well as some subsequent movies). Kirk was dominated by his experiential system. He was emotional, intuitive, and often surprisingly creative. Mr. Spock was obviously much smarter—he had a more developed rational system—but in episode after episode he was shown to be less resourceful than his captain.

Epstein believes that the rational and experiential systems interact. Recall the cases of Phineas Gage and of "Elliott," recounted in Chapter 8. When they lost contact with their emotional experience, their ability to make good judgments fell apart. In Epstein's terms, they may have lost part of their experiential system, or the ability of the experiential system to communicate with the rational system. This loss damaged not just their emotional experience but their ability to make reasonable decisions.

An interesting experiment by Epstein showed how the two systems can work at the same time. The experiment followed up on an earlier study that asked participants to imagine the following scenario: Two people get stuck in traffic on the way to the airport, and arrive at the gate 30 minutes after their planes' scheduled departure. Person A is told, "Sorry, your flight left on time." Person B is told, "Sorry, your flight left 29 minutes late, but it's gone now." Who is more upset, A or B? People typically report that person B is much more upset, even though persons A and B experienced the same outcome for the same reason. The conclusion drawn from this research was that people are basically irrational (Tversky & Kahneman, 1983).

Epstein's wrinkle on this study was to ask research participants two questions. The first was the same as one in the original study: How would A and B feel? The second question was, how would A and B respond if they were being rational? Everybody agreed that B would be more upset than A, but also everybody seemed to realize that this reaction was irrational—their answer to the second question was that A and B should feel the same (Epstein, Lipson, Holstein, & Huh, 1992). This result suggests that the human cognitive system is not simply irrational, as the original investigators assumed; people have two cognitive systems, one that responds emotionally and another system that at the same time draws the logically appropriate conclusion. It is possible—and perhaps you have had this experience—to have a crazy thought and at the same time know it is crazy.

MOTIVATION

What do you want? And how will you try to get it? These are the key questions of motivation, one of the oldest topics in psychology. Most of the early personality theories characterized people as having overriding, general motivations. Freud's original theory of psychoanalysis was based on sexual motives, and later versions included aggressive motives as well (Chapter 10). Humanistic theorists such as Rogers and Maslow (Chapter 13) proposed that the driving force in human thought and behavior is the goal of self-actualization. Even behaviorism (Chapter 15) assumes that "organisms" want something, and that getting what they want reinforces their behavior.

Current research addresses motivation through the study of goals and strategies. **Goals** are the ends that one desires, and **strategies** are the means the individual uses to achieve his goals. This is how goals drive behavior. They influence what you attend to, think about, and do (H. Grant & Dweck, 1999). If you are hungry (and thereby have the goal of eating and the motivation of hunger), you will be primed to attend very closely to the slightest whiff of cooking, think about where there might be food, and seek groceries. If you desire a successful career, you will be alert for opportunities to advance, think about how to get ahead, and work hard. (These effects of motivation on perception and thought sometimes can be detected using projective tests, as discussed in Chapter 5.) By the same token, if a person is not alert to opportunities, does not think about how to get ahead, and does not work hard, there are reasons to doubt how much he really wants to succeed.

Do people always know what they want? According to some research, the answer may be no (Brunstein, Schultheiss, & Grässmann, 1998). Psychologists have distinguished between *explicit goals*, those people can talk about and willingly describe, and *implicit goals* that, while important, people may not realize they have. Explicit goals can be measured with a simple questionnaire. Implicit goals generally must be measured more indirectly. One method is to use a projective test, in which people tell stories about a picture. The study by Brunstein et al. (1998) used a questionnaire to measure explicit goals and a projective test to measure implicit goals. The results showed that people who were making progress toward achieving their implicit goals were happy, whereas those who were making progress toward only their explicit goals, but not their implicit goals, remained dissatisfied.

The esteemed clinical psychologist David Shapiro (1965, 2000) has written extensively about people who state particular goals, out loud, as being centrally important, but make

"What do you think . . . should we get started on that motivation research or not?"

little or no moves toward fulfilling them. He describes a woman who continuously complains about an unsatisfactory relationship that she never actually ends; a man who states emphatically that he doesn't "*want* to drink," but continues to be a heavy drinker; and another woman who claims she "really wants" to move to a new city, but never makes the slightest move toward finding an apartment, looking for a job, or calling movers (Shapiro, 2000, p. 75).

Self-contradictions like this are surprisingly common. Many people express desires to get better grades, be promoted, improve their social life, or even leave their spouses, and yet never make the first move toward initiating these events. To know what people want, Shapiro implies, it may not be very informative to listen to what they say. Instead, watch what they do.

Goals

Much of life—it could be argued, all of life—consists of efforts to achieve goals. A goal can take many different forms. It might be a specific project: I want to finish this paper by Thursday; I want to mow the lawn. Or, it can be more general: I want to be a better person; I want to help the environment; I want to contribute to world peace. Specific goals are usually, though not always, immediate—they represent something that is intended to be accomplished soon. General goals tend to be long-term, because it takes a long time to be a better person, help the environment, or contribute to world peace.

SHORT-TERM AND LONG-TERM GOALS

Goals can be arranged hierarchically. You might have the general goal of impressing your neighbors. To reach that long-term goal, you seek to have a beautiful yard. Toward that shorter-term goal, you mow your lawn. Or, perhaps you want to be financially secure. To reach that general goal, you must get a good job. Toward that goal, you must graduate from college. Toward that goal, you must pass this course. Toward *that* goal, you must finish this book. Toward that goal, you have to read all the way to the bottom of this page.

Keeping your eye on a general, long-term goal can help you to choose wisely and to organize more specific, short-term goals. You have probably heard the old story about the two medieval workers who were asked what they were doing. One said, "I'm laying bricks." The other said, "I am building a cathedral." (Of course, they were actually doing the same thing.) The first worker focused on his specific activity, while the second focused on the ultimate purpose of that activity. When one's goal structures are well organized, life can be lived fairly smoothly and with clear purpose. If you know your general goals, then everything you do on a daily basis can be organized to help reach them.

Many people are not so fortunate, however. When a person has few or no general, long-term goals, or spends time in activities that do not serve general, personally relevant goals, then life is chaotic and disorganized, and nothing important seems to get done. Moreover, if you lack general goals or any clear connection between your daily activities and your general goals, your life may seem to lack meaning and your general motivation may suffer. Indeed, you may become depressed.

But the relationship between general and specific goals must not be too one-sided. The potential disadvantage of a general, cathedral-type goal is that you might become too inflexible to accomplish important short-term goals, such as fixing the leaky roof on your hut. If your general goal is to promote world peace, you might forget to be kind to your friends. So, it is useful to be able to shift flexibly between long-term and short-term goals (Vallacher & Wegner, 1987).

It is also important to realize that the only way to achieve a long-term goal many years off is to focus on the short-term goals you can achieve every day. President John F. Kennedy liked to tell the story of the French Marshall Lyautey, who asked his gardener to plant a tree so he could have some shade. The gardener replied that the tree was so slow-growing that it wouldn't provide any shade for 100 years. The Marshall replied, "In that case, there is no time to lose; plant it this afternoon!" (United Nations Environment Programme, 2009).

IDIOGRAPHIC GOALS

Idiographic goals are those that are unique to the individuals who pursue them. Various researchers have conceptualized idiographic goals in somewhat different terms.

Current Concerns   The psychologist Eric Klinger (1987) proposed that daily life is characterized by what he called current concerns. A *current concern* is an ongoing motivation that persists in the mind until the goal is either attained or abandoned. Examples include visiting a friend, keeping a dental appointment, losing weight, saving money, and finding a job. At any given moment, you can probably list around half a dozen current concerns that frequently come to mind (Klinger, 1977). Some of these can make you emotionally aroused when you think about them consciously, and you will find many of them drifting into your daydreams (Gold & Reilly, 1985; Nikula, Klinger, & Larson-Gutman, 1993). According to one study, the more a current concern is valued, committed to, and under threat, the more frequently a person thinks about it (Klinger, Barta, & Maxeiner, 1981). Moreover, when words relating to a person's current concerns are briefly presented on a computer screen, her thought processes are momentarily disrupted (Young, 1988). Concerns range from narrow to broad, and a given concern may last from a few seconds to a lifetime. Once the concern is resolved—when that person finally calls you, or that problem is finally fixed—you typically forget it quickly.

GIFTS FROM THE HOUSE OF LOW GOALS

Personal Projects   Another kind of idiographic goal is the psychologist Brian Little's idea of the personal project (Little, 1989). Whereas a current concern is something people think about, *personal projects* are what people do. They are made up of the efforts people put into such goals as "going to the prom with Brad," "finding a part-time job," "shopping for the holidays," or, as you may recall from Chapter 14, "working on my quilt" (Little, 1983). This idea is similar to *life tasks*, conceptualized by Nancy Cantor and her colleagues as the organizing goals people pursue at particular times of their lives. For example, a college student who has recently moved away from home for the first time might be pursuing the life task of attaining independence (Cantor & Kihlstrom, 1987). Later in life, this task will cease to be so important, and others will rise to the fore.

Personal Strivings   A somewhat broader kind of idiographic goal is Robert Emmons's (1996) idea of *personal strivings*, which are long-term goals that can organize broad areas of a person's life. For example, a person may be "trying to appear attractive to the opposite sex," "trying to be a good listener to friends," or "trying to be better than others."

The personal strivings that a person reports can provide useful insights into what she is like. One of Emmons's research participants, who called herself "Crocodile Dundee,"[4] said that her personal strivings included "always appear cool," "always amuse others," "always keep physically fit," and "dress fashionably" (Emmons, 1989, p. 38). Another participant, who called herself "0372," expressed the personal strivings to "please others," "tell the truth," and "be productive in work." It turned out that Crocodile Dundee scored high on a test of the personality trait of narcissism, which measures the tendency to be self-centered and exploitative of others (see Chapter 17). The person called 0372, as her relatively modest nickname perhaps suggests, scored low on this dimension.

Strivings can also be a source of difficulty, as people commonly report two or more strivings that are inconsistent with each other. I mentioned in Chapter 7 that the goal to "get ahead" (of others) and the goal to "get along" (with others) are often in conflict. If you strive to rise to the top, it is difficult to have everyone—such as the people you defeat—continue to like you. On the other hand, if you focus only on making people like you, you are unlikely to get ahead. One study found that people whose strivings are in conflict tend to experience more psychological distress and even more physical illness than those whose strivings are compatible (Emmons & King, 1988).

Properties and Limitations of Idiographic Goals   All of these concepts—current concerns, personal projects, life tasks, and personal strivings—have several elements in common. First, idiographic goals are held consciously at least some of the time. Indeed, typically they are measured by asking participants to list their concerns, projects, tasks, or strivings. Second, they describe thoughts and behaviors aimed at fairly specific outcomes. Third, they are changeable over time—one day's important personal project might be forgotten and irrelevant a few weeks later. Finally, an individual's various concerns, projects, tasks, or goals are assumed to function independently: Having the goal to be better looking, for example, is not assumed to have implications for other goals you might also have.

This last-named limitation is important (H. Grant & Dweck, 1999). Concerns, projects, tasks, or goals (by whatever label) can organize thought and

---

[4] Emmons asked his participants to give themselves pseudonyms so that they could be anonymously identified for follow-up studies.

behavior, but they are not themselves theoretically organized. For example, people typically present their strivings in a simple, unordered list (e.g., Emmons, 1989). To some researchers, this seems an unsatisfactory state of affairs. Can the many different goals that people might pursue be categorized to refine our understanding of what people seek in life?

"*At this point, my privacy needs are interfering with my intimacy goals.*"

NOMOTHETIC GOALS

The attempt to answer this question leads researchers to seek *nomothetic goals*, which refer to the relatively small number of essential motivations that almost everyone pursues. Researchers in this area hope to bring order to the domain of goals, much as the Big Five organizes thousands of personality traits (see Chapter 7).

The Big Three, or Five, or Two   According to the psychologist David McClelland (1985) and his colleagues, three primary motivations drive human behavior: the need for achievement, the need for affiliation (or intimacy), and the need for power. Research into these motives usually assesses whether they emerge as themes in stories people tell in response to the pictures that comprise the Thematic Apperception Test (TAT; see Chapter 5).

Achievement motivation is a tendency to direct one's thoughts and behavior toward striving for excellence. People high in this motive set standards for themselves and then work hard to attain them. *Affiliation motivation* is the tendency to direct thoughts and behavior toward finding and maintaining close, warm emotional relationships. People high in affiliation motivation seek the close company of others for its own sake, not as a means to any end (McAdams, 1980). *Power motivation* is the tendency to direct thoughts and behavior toward feeling strong and influencing others. People high in power motivation put great efforts into seeking prestige and status, prefer friends low in power motivation (whom presumably they can dominate), and are relatively promiscuous in their sexual behavior (Winter & Stewart, 1978).

What proportion of the goals that people follow can be organized around themes of achievement, intimacy, and power? At present, research offers only a general answer. Many goals fall into one of these categories, but not all of them do. For example, according to one research survey, five—not three—categories of goals emerged repeatedly in a number of studies (Emmons, 1997): (1) enjoyment, (2) self-assertion, (3) esteem, (4) interpersonal success, and (5) avoidance of negative affect. You can see for yourself where these five goals overlap with McClelland's three. According to another analysis, many goals generated by a group of college students could be boiled down to two types: goals related to work (in this case, academic work) and those related to social interaction (e.g., friendships, romantic relationships) (Kaiser & Ozer, 1999). This last finding is particularly interesting because it is reminiscent of Freud's formulation of the complete life, which was "to love and to work" (see Chapter 10).

The Goals Circumplex   Another way to represent goals is in terms of their arrangement around a circle, or a *circumplex* model. One recent study asked participants from 15 countries, including both wealthy ones and poor ones, to list their goals (Grouzet et al., 2005). Their responses showed a remarkable consistency across cultures. Most of the goals listed could be arranged in terms of two dimensions. The investigators named one of the dimensions "self-transcendence versus physical self." Goals high on self-transcendence included spirituality and helping one's community. Goals oriented more toward the physical self included hedonism (self-pleasure) and safety. The other dimension they named "extrinsic versus intrinsic." Popularity and financial success are extrinsic goals, whereas self-acceptance and affiliation (making friends) were more intrinsic. The circumplex representation of their findings is shown in Figure 16.1. The value of this diagram is the way it vividly displays the similarities and differences between goals.

Judgment Goals and Development Goals   The psychologist Carol Dweck and her colleagues claim that two other kinds of goals are also important (see H. Grant & Dweck, 1999). One kind she calls *judgment goals*. Judgment, in this context, refers to seeking to judge or validate an attribute in oneself. For example, you might have the goal of convincing yourself that you are smart, beautiful, or popular. The other kind she calls *development goals*. A development goal is the desire to actually improve oneself, to become smarter, more beautiful, or more popular.

At first glance, these goals might seem highly similar. Don't people want both to see themselves as smart and to be smart, for example? Indeed, Dweck notes that both kinds of goals "are natural and important in our everyday lives" (H. Grant & Dweck, 1999, p. 350). But the balance between them dif-

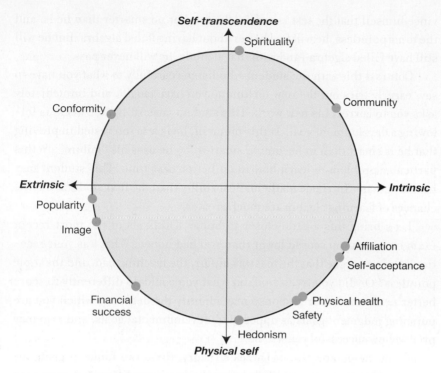

Figure 16.1 A Goals Circumplex This circumplex represents how goals were viewed as related to each other in 15 cultures.

Source: Grouzet, Kasser, Ahuvia, Dols, Kim, Lau, et al. (2005), p. 812.

fers from one person to another, and may even change within an individual from one situation to the next or across time. And, if you think about it for a moment, it is not difficult to find situations in which these two types of goals lead to different outcomes.

For example, consider the plight of a teacher trying to correct a student. Have you ever been in this situation? Let's say you are trying to help a high school student learn algebra. You look at his work, find a mistake, and point it out. You take a piece of paper and patiently begin to explain the right way to solve the problem. You are surprised when the student interrupts you. "This problem is unfair and too hard," he says, "and algebra is stupid. And what makes you so smart anyway?"

Why is the student responding so negatively? According to Dweck's perspective, he is pursuing a judgment goal instead of a development goal. He is anxious to demonstrate that he is smart and competent. He is so anxious to do this that when he makes a mistake, he belittles the test, the teacher, and perhaps the whole topic. This attitude has its uses, to be sure. If he can convince himself that the test is unfair, the teacher no smarter than he is, and the topic pointless, he will feel better about having failed algebra. But he will still have failed algebra—and with that attitude, he will never pass.

Contrast this with the student who listens carefully to what you have to say, eagerly tries out the new technique you have taught, and immediately asks you to correct his new work. This student, according to Dweck, is following a development goal. At this moment, he is less interested in proving that he is smart than in becoming smarter. So he uses his "failure" on this particular problem to learn how to do better next time. This student may have no greater intrinsic mathematical ability than the first student, but his chances of learning algebra are much greater.

Let's bring this a little closer to home. Think about the most recent exam on which you scored lower than you had hoped. What was your reaction? Did you argue that the test was unfair, the teaching bad, and the topic pointless? Or did you try to find out what you could do differently to score better next time? Your response may identify the degree to which you are pursuing judgment goals as opposed to developmental goals, and also may predict how successful you will be.[5]

From the perspective of Dweck's theory, these two kinds of goals are important in many areas of life because they produce different reactions to failure, and everybody fails sometimes. A person with a development goal will respond to failure with what Dweck calls a *mastery-oriented pattern*, in which she tries even harder the next time. The student might get a poor grade on her paper but be eager to learn from the experience how to do a better job on her next paper. In contrast, a person with a judgment goal responds to failure with what Dweck calls the *helpless pattern*: Rather than try harder, this individual simply concludes, "I can't do it," and gives up. Of course, that only guarantees more failure in the future.

Entity and Incremental Theories   Where do these dramatic differences in goals and behavior come from? Dweck believes they originate in different kinds of implicit theories about the nature of the world—personal constructs, if you will (see Chapter 13). Some people hold what Dweck calls **entity theories**, and believe that personal qualities such as intelligence and ability are unchangeable, leading them to respond helplessly to any indication that they do not have what it takes. Other people hold **incremental**

---

[5] Sometimes the test really *is* unfair, the teaching poor, and the topic pointless. Still, you can expect your situation to improve only if you focus on how to do better next time.

theories, believing that intelligence and ability can change with time and experience. Their goals, therefore, involve not only proving their competence but increasing it. Figure 16.2 diagrams these relationships. One young boy in Dweck's research, following a failure to solve an experimental puzzle, "pulled up his chair, rubbed his hands together, smacked his lips, and exclaimed, 'I love a challenge!'" (Dweck & Leggett, 1988, p. 258).

Research and Measurement   Most of the research on Dweck's theory has focused on academic goals or simulations of such goals. For example, the responses of children to their failure to solve word puzzles have been examined repeatedly. Dweck and her students have consistently found that children who are incremental theorists, as just described, do better in the face of failure than do entity theorists (e.g., C. I. Diener & Dweck, 1978; Goetz & Dweck, 1980).

How are these young "theorists" identified? In the time-honored method of trait psychology, they complete a self-report questionnaire (S data). For example, participants choose between options such as:

1. Smartness is something you can increase as much as you want to, or
2. You can learn new things, but how smart you are stays pretty much the same.

If you choose the first option, you are an incremental theorist; if you choose the second, you are an entity theorist (Dweck & Leggett, 1988, p. 263). Another method is to give subjects a questionnaire that describes a series of hypothetical social situations involving rejection. For example, a participant might be asked, "Suppose you move to a new neighborhood. A person you meet does not like you very much. Why would this happen to you?" If the participant responds that the likely reason is his own social incompetence, then the participant is assumed to be an entity theorist (Goetz & Dweck, 1980).

The goals that children pursue also can be manipulated experimentally. In one study, fourth- and fifth-grade children were asked to participate in a "pen-pal tryout" (Erdley et al., 1997). Each child wrote a letter to a potential pen pal, and were told that the letters would be rated to decide who could join the pen-pal club. Every child was initially told that the rater was "not sure whether to have

Figure 16.2 Dweck's Motivational Theory Dweck's theory describes the relationships between views of the world, goals, and behavioral responses.

you in the club" and was asked to write another letter. After that, all children were told they could join.

The experimental manipulation came before the children wrote the first letter. Half were told, "We'd like to see how good you are at making friends," which was intended to set up a judgment goal. The other half were told, "This is a chance to practice and improve how you make friends," to set up a development goal. The second letter (written after the initial failure) was then rated by independent coders, who found that letters written by children in the first (judgment) condition were shorter and of lesser quality than those written by children in the second (development) condition. Apparently, the first group of children came to believe they were socially inadequate and might as well give up; the second group saw a chance to improve.

This finding led to three conclusions. First, the kind of goal that a person pursues—judgment or development—can have important implications for how she responds to failure. (And, again, we all fail sometimes.) A judgment goal can lead to helplessness and withdrawal; a development goal can lead to renewed and improved effort. Second, this effect seems to occur in social as well as academic (and presumably work-related) realms. If a person fails an exam, or fails to close a deal at work, or fails to get a prospective date to say yes, she has two options. One—if the person pursues a judgment goal—is to decide she is inadequate, inept, or unattractive, and to simply give up. Another option—if the person pursues a development goal—is to try to learn from the failure and figure out what to do differently next time. The third implication is that the type of goal someone pursues can be determined from within or from without. Most of Dweck's research has assumed that people are either entity theorists or incremental theorists, and that they characteristically pursue judgment or development goals. But other research, including the pen-pal study by Erdley and colleagues, suggests that sometimes a person's goal can be determined by the way people around the person structure the task. This final point has obvious and important implications for teaching: Teachers should be sure that their students see class as a place to learn and improve, not merely a place to succeed or fail.

Goals Across the Life Span

The goals that matter most to an individual may depend on his stage in life (Carstensen & Mikels, 2005). When a person is young, and life seems as if it will go on forever, goals are focused on preparation for the future. On a broad level, they may include learning new things, exploring possibilities, and generally expanding one's horizons. More specific goals may include completing one's education, finding a spouse, and establishing a career. As old age approaches, priorities may change. As the end of life becomes a more salient concern, it may seem less important to start new relationships or to make that extra dollar. Instead, goals of older persons—defined in most research as those around age 70 and older—focus more on what they find emotionally meaningful, especially ties with family and long-time friends. They also—wisely, it would appear—work to regulate their emotional experience, by thinking more about the good things in life and less about things that trouble them. One advantage of old age is that one no longer must associate in the workplace or social settings with people whom one does not enjoy. Research by the gerontological psychologist Laura Carstensen and her colleagues indicates that older persons take advantage of this freedom. If being with someone is a hassle, they are pretty good at avoiding him or her (Carstensen, Isaacowitz, & Charles, 1999).

> One advantage of old age is that one no longer must associate in the workplace or social settings with people whom one does not enjoy.

This shift in goals is not an effect of age per se; rather, it appears to result from one's broader perspective about time. Young people with life-threatening illnesses also appear to shift their goals from exploration to emotional well-being (Carstensen & Fredrickson, 1998), and when older people are asked to imagine they will have at least 20 more years of healthy life than they expected, they exhibit a style of emotional attention otherwise more typical of the young (Fung & Carstensen, 2003). According to the research of Carstensen and her colleagues, the life goals that one sets depend on how much life one believes to have left.

Strategies

How do you get what you want? Let's say you are hungry and decide you want to get a hamburger at McDonald's.[6] Once there, you will follow what cognitive psychologists call the McDonald's script (e.g., Schank, 1996). Your knowledge of what to do at McDonald's is not based on any particular visit; it is an abstraction derived from the usual pattern. You follow this script without thinking about it. You won't sit down at a table and expect a waiter to take your order. You will stand in line, instead. The "how to get food at McDon-

---

[6] I do not mean to imply a position concerning the nutritional wisdom of this choice.

ald's" script can be thought of as a strategy. It is a sequence of activities that progress toward a goal, in this case to acquire food. However, it is not a very interesting strategy. From the perspective of personality psychology, the more important strategies are the broad ones that pursue important goals in life and organize a wide range of activities.

We have already seen a couple of examples of such broad strategies. Recall the discussion of rejection sensitivity, which can be viewed as a maladaptive strategy of automatically responding with fear and hostility to the slightest sign of disinterest from a significant other person. The strategy deploys in a wide variety of situations—triggered by the smallest threat of rejection—and with anybody important to the rejection-sensitive person. In a similar fashion, the authoritarian personality (Chapter 7) responds to situations involving authority relationships with a style of behavior that is obsequious to those of higher rank and contemptuous to those of lower rank.

STRATEGIES AND TRAITS

Many personality traits can be explained in terms of strategies. For example, the trait theorists Robert McCrae and Paul Costa (1995) developed a theory that describes how the Big Five personality traits, described in Chapter 7, produce *characteristic adaptations*, or generalized scripts. For example, the person high on the trait of agreeableness will typically follow a script that involves being warm, friendly, approachable, and slow to anger. This concept is similar to Mischel's notion of *if . . . then* patterns, described in Chapter 15. If a person is agreeable then he will probably not get angry in response to a mild insult. So far, however, few efforts have been made to explain personality traits in terms of characteristic scripts or *if . . . then* patterns, and vice versa. Integrating the two approaches offers an exciting, wide-open field for future research.

Such integration will be complicated, however. One reason is that a single strategy may produce a variety of behavior patterns (as we saw with rejection sensitivity and authoritarianism), while different strategies and goals may sometimes produce the same behaviors. For example, one person may work to make friends as part of a strategy to form a network of useful business associates, whereas another person may behave the same way in order to achieve a pleasant social life. Both people might appear sociable, but this similarity in behavioral style could mask a difference in their underlying goals and strategies.

DEFENSIVE PESSIMISM

At present, only a few strategies have received close attention in research. One of the most interesting is the strategic difference between optimists and pessimists. At a general level, the optimistic strategy is to assume that the best will happen. This assumption can produce a positive outlook and motivate goal-seeking behavior that is maintained by the cheerful assumption that if you do your part, all will be well. The pessimistic strategy assumes the reverse: The worst is likely to happen. This assumption produces a negative outlook on life but can also motivate goal-seeking behavior, driven by attempts to avoid almost certain doom.

The psychologist Julie Norem examined the difference between people who employ these contrasting strategies (Norem, 1989, 2002). One early study focused on the strategies college students use in dealing with their academic work. Optimistic students deal with anxiety about exams by expecting to do their best. Others expect the worst, so they can be pleasantly surprised when the worst does not happen—Norem calls these individuals *defensive pessimists*. Interestingly, Norem found that both kinds of student seem to succeed about equally in coping with anxiety and performing well on exams (although, admittedly, the optimists seem to enjoy life more). The two strategies represent different routes to a common goal. Indeed, if a researcher examined only the outcomes and not the strategies by which they are attained, the important difference between these two kinds of people would be masked.

Optimistic and pessimistic strategies also apply outside academic life. Several years ago, a friend of mine was waiting anxiously for his wife to have a baby. The pregnancy had been difficult, and the delivery was expected to be complicated. Many people would deal with this situation by hoping for the best, convincing themselves that the mother was a strong person who would do fine, that the doctors could take care of everything, and so on. My friend did just the reverse. An extremely defensive pessimist, he expected nothing but the worst from the very beginning. The night before the baby was born, he cornered the attending physician and demanded, "What is the worst that could possibly happen?" Understandably, the physician was taken aback, but under continued prodding he finally acknowledged that, well, the worst that could happen would be for the mother to die and for the baby to be born dead. My friend seemed strangely satisfied with this answer.

The next day, all did not go smoothly, but neither did the worst transpire. My friend seemed to maintain equilibrium through his constant awareness that things could be worse. And when, in the end, mother and baby came through fine, he seemed to have gotten through the trauma not much worse for the wear. Apparently, his insistence on focusing on the negative was just an exaggerated version of the strategy pursued by Norem's defensive pessimists. He reduced the anxiety that bad news might produce by imagining, in advance, the very worst possible news. Then, even as unpleasant news arrived, he could always compare it against this worst-case scenario and feel relieved. I am not sure that this is a wise strategy, but perhaps it works for some people.

Two important questions arise in connection with these different strategies. The first is, how general are optimistic and pessimistic strategies? Does someone who employs an optimistic strategy in the academic domain also act optimistically in social situations? Evidence suggests that the answer is yes, sort of. Correlations between the degree to which one uses an optimistic or pessimistic strategy in one context and the same strategy in another context range from about .30 to .40 (Norem & Chang, 2001). This means that these styles are generally consistent (see Chapters 3 and 4 on interpreting correlations). The friend whose reaction to his wife's childbirth I described earlier tends to evince gloomy and pessimistic attitudes about all aspects of his life—not just genuine crises. But a consistency correlation in the range of .30 to .40 leaves plenty of room for people to use an optimistic strategy in one domain and a pessimistic strategy in another. Some people are optimists in their personal relationships but pessimists in their academic life, for example.

The second question is, Which is better, optimism or pessimism? Cultural values in the United States certainly appear to value an optimistic outlook, and the research summarized near the end of this chapter suggests that happiness has many good consequences, but pessimism has its virtues too. An optimistic, self-enhancing style may help motivate individual achievement but interfere with emotional intimacy and interpersonal sensitivity. Pessimism may prove more adaptive than optimism in cultures that emphasize these more collectivist values (Norem, 2002; also, see Chapter 14). Furthermore, too much optimism can be dangerous, leading to carelessness and needless risk taking (Norem & Chang, 2002). Finally, the general fact—and it does seem to be a fact—that optimists are generally happier than pessimists does not necessarily mean that pessimists would be happier if they changed their strategy. Both optimists and defensive pessimists may have found viable strategies, and trying to change them is not necessarily a good idea. Indeed, Norem's research has shown that some people perform worse if they are forced to think optimistically because this deprives them of the negative thinking they use to manage anxiety.

EMOTION

Emotions lie close to the core of the experience of being alive, but they can be surprisingly difficult to describe. From the perspective of cognitive psychology, emotions can be considered a kind of **procedural knowledge**, similar to skills such as bike riding, singing, or shooting basketballs, which cannot be learned or fully expressed through words, but only through action and experience.[7] As is true about inner experience in general (see Chapter 13), you cannot fully understand emotions by reading about them, nor can you really describe emotions in words. But everybody knows what they are.

Consider anger. In the course of experiencing this emotion, a person's heart rate accelerates, and his blood pressure rises; he may get red in the face and clench his fist and jaw. His thoughts are taken over by the way the object of his anger mistreated or threatened him, and he makes plans to get even or lashes out without thinking. He may not recognize that everything he is doing is part of the emotion. That is, he will not necessarily say to himself, "Boy, am I angry." But that is what all of the other activities of his body and mind amount to.

Thus, an emotion is a set of mental and physical procedures. It is something you do, not merely a set of concepts or a passive experience (Ekman & Davidson, 1994), and therefore it qualifies as a personality process. Personality psychologists have attempted to describe emotional experience (despite the difficulty just noted), outlined relationships between different emotions, explored individual differences in emotional life, and studied the implications of the emotional experience of happiness.

Emotional Experience

The usual psychological account of emotional experience describes it as a series of stages (R. S. Miller, 1999). Above, I described the stages of experiencing anger. The very different emotion of joy follows the same steps. First, the person perceives that something great has happened—her lottery ticket number was just announced on TV! She might smile, laugh, and literally "jump for joy." Then she might begin to consider ways to expand on or share her happiness, such as calling her parents. The basic stages of emotion, then, are *appraisal*, when a stimulus is judged as emotionally relevant;

---

[7]The other kind, *declarative knowledge*, consists of the facts one can talk about, or "declare."

physical responses, such as changes in pulse, blood pressure, and bodily tension; *facial expressions*, such as smiles or snarls, paired with *nonverbal behaviors* such as jumping or fist clenching; and finally, the invocation of *motives* to spread one's joy or to harm someone.

This basic template is reasonable and seems to accurately describe many emotional experiences, but it can be slightly misleading: The stages do not have to happen separately or in a particular order. The psychologist Robert Zajonc suggested that appraisal does not have to come first; the physical and even behavioral changes associated with emotion can begin *before* the individual understands why (Zajonc, 1980). For example, a person might feel attraction to someone associated with a prior good experience, before explicitly recognizing that person. This is because, as Zajonc famously said, "preferences need no inferences" (1980, p. 151). The suggestion turned out to be controversial (see, e.g., Lazarus, 1984), and for several years psychologists vigorously debated whether emotion could occur prior to, or in the absence of, knowledge about the emotion's stimulus. The argument was never settled, but the discussions clarified that emotional experience does not happen in a clear-cut set of separate steps; the different aspects of emotion can occur out of order, simultaneously, or so close together in time that the sequence does not really matter. It is also clear that emotional experience is a complex mixture of thoughts, physical sensations, and motivations.

Another complication is that emotions can have at least three different sources. First, and most obviously, emotions can be triggered by immediate stimuli. Somebody does something obnoxious, and you become mad; someone does something kind, and you feel affection. Second, as discussed in Chapter 15, emotional experiences can be classically conditioned to almost anything. A house where you have had many happy experiences may feel pleasant to enter even when nobody is home. An office where you have had too many arguments may in a similar fashion become an unpleasant place to be. If properly conditioned, neutral stimuli such as ringing bells can make a human—or dog—feel nervous, happy or, as you may recall, hungry. A third source of emotions is a person's own memories or thoughts. A football player named Nobel Doss dropped an easy pass in a major game in the 1940s and reported more than 60 years later that he still felt shame about this every day (Leary, 2006). Humans can feel just about any emotion by thinking about past or potential events.[8]

---

[8] This aspect of emotional experience is probably unique to humans, though it's hard to be certain. (Who really knows what your dog is thinking?)

Varieties of Emotions

As far as I know, nobody has ever tried to count all the words in the dictionary that describe emotions, but it would not surprise me if there are almost as many as the 17,953 terms for personality traits mentioned in Chapter 7. But just as in the domains of traits and motives, it seems doubtful that all the terms for emotions are strictly necessary, and we can also ask whether one culture's terms for emotion mean the same thing—or mean anything at all—in a different culture (Chapter 14). The psychologist Paul Ekman (1992) has argued that a few core emotions have substantially the same meaning and means of expression in all cultures; these include happiness, sadness, anger, fear, surprise, and disgust. For example, when people anywhere in the world are happy, they generally pull the corners of their mouths upward and crinkle the skin around their eyes—in other words, they smile. A classic study by Ekman and his colleagues showed that natives of an isolated region of New Guinea could accurately identify the emotions portrayed in photographs of Americans' faces (Ekman, Sorenson, & Friesen, 1969).

Evolutionary theory (Chapter 9) suggests that some emotions may be universal because they are necessary for survival. It may be almost as important to be able to communicate and perceive these emotions accurately. For example, anger might be a response built in to protect us from those who would trespass on our land, steal our food, or abscond with our mates. Feeling the emotion can motivate a person to do something about these insults, but, even better, communicating anger might be enough to prevent them from happening in the first place. Shake your fist, and the trespasser might simply go away. On the other side of the transaction, realizing that one's actions are seriously angering someone else might also have important survival value.

Another way to categorize emotions is to try to find the essential words for emotions in a given language, much as the thousands of words in the trait lexicon were pared down to the Big Five (Chapter 7). One study began with a list of 590 emotional terms—not many by trait standards, but still quite a few—and a team of judges evaluated their similarity and overlap. The result was a "big three" of emotions: Almost all the terms were either negative, positive, or neutral. Analyses also yielded a tree of subcategories in which *bad-awful* emotions included pain and sadness, and *good-wonderful* emotions included happiness and joy (Storm & Storm, 1987; Averill, 1997).

Perhaps the differences among emotions are not as clear-cut or sharp as these categorical schemes suggest. The difference between happiness and joy might be just a matter of degree. Could the same thing be true of the difference between happiness and sadness? If so, then perhaps all emotions can be plotted and compared on a circumplex model like Figure 16.3. The model assumes that all emotions vary along two dimensions, from aroused to unaroused, and from negative to positive (Averill, 1997; J. A. Russell, 1983). Thus, "defiant" is both aroused and somewhat negative, while "envious" is more negative but less aroused. The model can also be rotated by 45 degrees, which does not change the relationships among the emotions but redefines the model's key dimensions as excited versus bored, and alarmed versus serene (D. Watson & Tellegen, 1985).

Circumplex models such as Figure 16.3 are more useful for comparing emotions to each other than they are for explaining particular emotions. For that, it seems necessary to examine emotions one at a time, to describe the bases and implications of each one in detail. For example, Table 16.2 summarizes a functional analysis of five basic emotions. For each one, it describes a typical stimulus for the emotion and its associated response, along with the emotion's possible adaptive function—what it's good for. For example, if you have harmed someone else in a way that violates the gen-

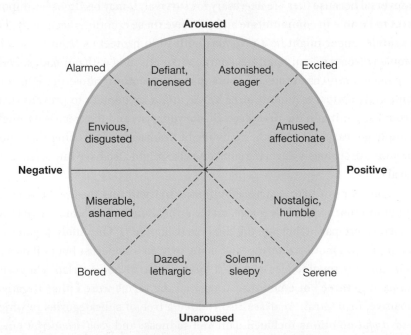

Figure 16.3 **An Emotions Circumplex** This circumplex arranges emotions in terms of whether they are positive or negative, and aroused or unaroused.
Source: Adapted from Averill (1997), p. 518.

Table 16.2

STIMULI, RESPONSES, AND FUNCTIONS
OF SOME BASIC EMOTIONS

Emotion	Typical Stimulus	Typical Responses	Adaptive Function
Anger	Threat, trespass	Threaten, attack	Protect territory, resources, or mates
Guilt	Harm to others that violates social code	Apologize, make amends	Obtain forgiveness from the offended party and reentry to the social group
Anxiety	Possibility of harm, danger	Worry, flee	Anticipate danger, escape harm
Sadness	Loss	Sad facial expressions, crying	Receive support from others, disengage from loss
Hope	Possibility of future gain	Continue effort, maintain commitment	Perseverance in the face of obstacles

Source: Adapted, in part, from Smith & Lazarus (1990), Table 23.2, p. 619.

erally accepted moral code, you might feel guilt, apologize, and receive for-
giveness from the wronged individual and reacceptance by the larger social
group (Keltner, 1995). Succeeding at this can literally be a matter of life and
death. In December 2005, convicted murderer Stanley "Tookie" Williams
appealed to the governor of California for clemency but died by lethal injection because, said the governor, Williams's attempts to show remorse were
not convincing enough.

Individual Differences in Emotional Life

General descriptions of emotions can be interesting and useful, but in the
end, emotional experience is personal. No two people ever have exactly the
same emotional experience, and individual differences in emotions are
core aspects of personality. People differ in terms of which emotions they
experience, how strongly they experience them, how frequently their emotions change, and how well they understand and control their emotions.

EMOTIONAL EXPERIENCE, INTENSITY, AND CHANGE

The fundamental trait of extraversion—the first and broadest of the Big Five
(Chapter 7)—appears to be based on a strong, consistent, and stable ten-

dency to experience positive and energizing emotions (D. Watson & Clark, 1997; Eaton & Funder, 2001). Extraverts feel good, and they are peppy. That's why they act they way they do. By contrast, one major study found that ill-tempered boys grew up to be grouchy men who held low-status jobs from which they were frequently fired. Their wives divorced them, too (Caspi, Elder, & Bem, 1987). Thus, individual differences in positive and negative emotions can affect behavior and have important consequences.

Separately from whether emotions are positive or negative, some people seem to experience them more strongly than others. People high in *affect intensity* (Larsen & Diener, 1987) experience both more intense joy and more powerful sadness. In some cases, they overreact. I once heard the psychologist Ed Diener, one of the originators of this construct, describe a young woman in one of his classes at the University of Illinois who had scored very high on the Affect Intensity Measure (AIM; Larsen & Diener, 1987). She missed the final exam in his course. When he inquired why, it turned out she had been reading one of the Chicago newspapers that morning and saw an ad for a really excellent sale at a department store. She jumped in the car to go shopping, so excited that she forgot that (1) Chicago is 130 miles from Champaign-Urbana and (2) her final exam started in 2 hours.

Not all the consequences of affect intensity are negative, but, in general, it does seem to be a risk factor for various bad outcomes. Women are generally higher than men in affect intensity, which may explain why they are more prone to depression (Fujita, Diener, & Sandvik, 1991). Even intense positive emotions can have costs (E. Diener, Colvin, Pavot, & Allman, 1991), including the possibility that experiencing one event as extremely positive can make other events seem less positive. If last night's party was the "best party ever," how good can tomorrow night's party possibly be? Another cost is that, paradoxically, people often perceive events as positive because they are rebounding from negative events. For example, one young woman in the study wrote that a strongly happy time in her life was the night she met her boyfriend. Just before that, she wrote, "It was a no win situation as far as guys went. Things were not working with me and the guys I was dating" (E. Diener et al., 1991, p. 498). In general, as Diener and his coauthors note, the price one pays for a strong positive experience might be a certain degree of suffering first. Recent evidence also suggests that, although positive emotions in general are good for one's health, emotions that are *extremely* positive may lead to physiological arousal that can harm the heart and the immune system (Pressman & Cohen, 2005).

Changing emotions rapidly can cause other problems. In one study, participants reported their emotions four times a day for 8 days. Those whose emotions showed the highest rate of change described themselves, and were described by people who knew them, as generally fearful and hostile (Eaton & Funder, 2001). Perhaps people like these lack a strong emotional core and as a result are buffeted more than most by the ever-changing circumstances of everyday life. Or, possibly, wide and frequent emotional swings cause stress for both the person who experiences them and the others who have to deal with the person. Probably, it's both.

EMOTIONAL INTELLIGENCE

I mentioned at the beginning of this section that emotions might be a kind of procedural knowledge. An increasing amount of research suggests that people vary in how much of this knowledge they have and can use, and that these differences are important. The construct of **emotional intelligence** includes accurately perceiving emotions in oneself and others, and controlling and regulating one's own emotions (Salovey, Hsee, & Mayer, 1993). At the low end of the emotional intelligence scale are people sometimes characterized as *alexithymic*, who have so little emotional awareness that they are virtually unable to think about or talk about their own feelings (Haviland & Reise, 1996; G. J. Taylor & Bagby, 2000). People high in emotional intelligence are more emotionally expressive, have better personal relationships, and tend to be optimistic (Goleman, 1995).

People high in emotional intelligence also can regulate their emotions with strategies such as focusing on the positive, planning ahead for big events, and remembering to take long, deep breaths and count to 10 to stave off the desire to scream at someone. Research is just beginning to identify the brain structures that make emotional self-control possible (Ochsner & Gross, 2005); people may vary in their ability to control their emotions because of differences in these biological structures.

Happiness

Everyone, except perhaps the most hard-core existentialist (Chapter 13), wants to be happy, and one of the key goals of the positive psychology movement summarized in Chapter 13 is to help people achieve happiness. The first step is to be clear about what happiness is. According to prominent researchers in the area, it has three components: (1) overall satisfaction with life, (2) satisfaction with how things are going in particular life domains (e.g., relationships, career) and, (3) generally high levels of positive emotion and low levels of negative emotion (Kesebir & Diener, 2008). Interestingly, these writers, along with some other happiness researchers, don't focus very much on the difference between hedonic well-being (pleasure seeking) and eudaimonic well-being (seeking a meaningful life) that was so important to the humanistically inclined psychologists discussed in Chapter 13. They write:

> Clearly, high subjective well-being and eudaimonic happiness are not necessarily interchangeable concepts, and it is easily imaginable that a person could feel subjectively happy without living a virtuous life. However, we believe . . . that subjective well-being and eudaimonic well-being are sufficiently close." (Kesibir & Diener, 2008, p. 119)

In other words, they (almost) say, happiness is happiness. They might be right. Another recent study looked for differences between people high in hedonic and eudaimonic well-being; they found very few, probably because people high in one tend to be high in the other (Nave, Sherman, & Funder, 2008). On reflection, this conclusion is not very surprising. All other things being equal, shouldn't living a meaningful life make a person feel good?

Current research suggests that overall happiness has three primary sources (see Figure 16.4). To a suprisingly large extent, one's happiness is determined by an individual *set point*, and so it is moderately stable over time (Fujita & Diener, 2005). This set point appears to be genetically influenced (Lykken & Tellegen, 1996) and based, in part, on the heritable traits of extraversion (which is good for happiness) and neuroticism (which is bad for it) (E. Diener & Lucas, 1999). When good or bad events happen, people temporarily feel better or worse, but over time have a way of drifting back to a seemingly built-in level of happiness. In part, this is because of the learning mechanism of habituation, described in Chapter 15. Something good feels less good with repetition, and the impact of bad things lessens over time too (Brickman et al., 1978).

Another, though apparently smaller, influence on happiness is one's objective life circumstances, including income, education, and marital status. Having more money, more education, and being married all have small detectable positive influences on happiness.

If we put these two influences—genetics and life circumstances—together, nearly half of the variability in individual happiness is still unexplained (Lykken & Tellegen, 1996; Lyubomirsky, Sheldon, et al., 2005). The implication of this finding is that a third factor is important: An individual's happiness is significantly influenced by what he does, such as "looking on the bright side," "making time for things that matter," and, "working on an important life goal" (Lyubomirsky, Sheldon, et al., 2005, p. 123; see also Carstensen & Mikels, 2005).

Another, surprising way to seek happiness is through one's political ideology. According to one study, thinking like a political conservative can lead a person to experience negative emotions less, whereas thinking like a liberal can lead a person to experience positive emotions more (Choma, Busseri, & Sadava, 2009). I don't have to reveal any bias here because you can take your pick—both approaches, apparently, will make you more happy in the end. People also seek happiness by protecting their health, working hard for occupational success, and building successful relationships.

But perhaps this last finding has things partially backward. According to an intriguing recent analysis, happiness may not be just a *result* of good health, occupational success, and supportive relationships, but a *cause* of all of these outcomes (Lyubomirsky, King, & Diener, 2005). The adaptive function of positive affect—happiness—is to signal to the individual "that life is going well, the person's goals are being met, and resources are adequate" (p. 804). According to psychologist Sonja Lyubomirsky and her colleagues, the results of feeling this way include becoming more confident, optimistic, likeable, sociable, and energetic. There is even evidence that happy feelings—if not too intense—improve immune function and overall physical health (Pressman & Cohen, 2005).

Happier people are more effective in a broad range of domains. They make better decisions, have higher levels of professional accomplishment, and even solve anagrams better (Kesebir & Diener, 2008). Resident advisors in dormitories who were higher in positive affect were rated by their residents as being more effective (DeLuga & Mason, 2000), and cricket players who were happier had higher batting averages (Totterdell, 2000)! Happy employees give better customer service (George, 1995), and happier farmers in Malaysia make more money (Howell, Howell, & Schwabe, 2006).

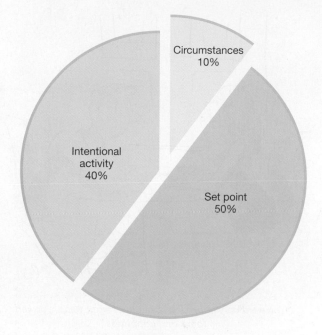

Figure 16.4 **Sources of Happiness** The three main contributors to happiness according to current research.
Source: Adapted from Lyubomirsky, Sheldon, & Schkade (2005), p. 116.

"You want only happiness, Douglas. I want wealth, power, fame, and happiness."

Happy people have more friends they can rely on (G. R. Lee & Ishii-Kuntz, 1987) and enjoy more social support (Pinquart & Sörenson, 2000). Not surprisingly, happiness is associated with less drug use. Happy people are also more likely to be cooperative, helpful, and creative.

The analysis of all these findings is complex because the causal arrow probably runs in both directions. For example, having more friends may make you happy, *and* happiness may help you to attract more friends. Overall, the analysis by Lyubomirsky and her colleagues convincingly shows that happiness promotes behaviors and problem-solving skills that in themselves can lead to good outcomes, which means that happiness can become a self-perpetuating cycle. The analysis also implies that happy times are useful occasions to "broaden and build" (Fredrickson, 2001). To unhappy people, something seems to be wrong, so they are motivated to undo the damage and protect themselves. Happy people, by contrast, can use their well-being as the foundation for creating and maintaining better life circumstances for themselves and others. In this light, happiness is not just an outcome. It's an opportunity.

PERSONALITY AS A VERB

The philosopher and architect R. Buckminster Fuller once wrote,

> . . . I don't know what I am. I know that I am not a category. I am not a thing—a noun. I seem to be a verb, an evolutionary process—an integral function of the universe. (Fuller, 1970, p. 1)

Fuller refers to being "a verb," but the psychological inner life he is discussing encompasses several verbs, including *perceive*, *think*, *want*, and *feel*. Anybody who is alive is doing all of these. The personality processes of perception, thought, motivation, and emotion that were the subjects of this chapter are also what the psychologist Nancy Cantor meant when she argued that personality is not something that an individual merely "has"; it is something a person "does" (Cantor, 1990). In that sense, "personality" is a verb.

SUMMARY

- The major personality processes include perception, thought, motivation, and emotion.

The Historical Roots of Research Into Personality Processes
- Modern research on personality processes has historical roots in the learning and phenomenological theories, but also includes elements of the psychodynamic and trait approaches.

Perception
- Concepts may readily come to mind because they have been primed through experience or because of one's temperament, personality, or biology.

- Patterns of priming are relevant to behavioral patterns such as rejection sensitivity and aggression, and to the flexible worldviews of bicultural individuals.

- Experimental demonstrations of perceptual defense indicate that people can screen potentially embarrassing or disturbing stimuli out of awareness.

- Some people, such as those who are shy, may be overly vigilant in certain domains of their lives because their systems of perceptual defense do not work well enough.

Thought
- Consciousness can be equated with short-term memory (STM), and has a capacity of seven chunks of information, plus or minus two.

- The limited capacity of consciousness implies that richer chunks will enhance thinking, that consciously attending to constructive thoughts is important, and that much of thinking occurs outside conscious awareness.

- Epstein's cognitive experiential self-theory (CEST) is a dual-process model that contrasts slow, deliberate, and rational conscious thought with fast, uncontrolled, and intuitive thought that may not be conscious. Each system has advantages and disadvantages; ideally, they work in coordination.

Motivation

- Motivation can be studied by examining goals and strategies.

- Goals can be specific and short-term, or general and long-term, and they can be arranged hierarchically. Ideally one should be able to shift flexibly between the two kinds of goals.

- Idiographic goals are unique to each individual and may include current concerns (Klinger), personal projects (Little), and personal strivings (Emmons).

- Nomothetic goals are common to all people; several studies have proposed different sets of these, including one with three primary goals (achievement, affiliation, and power), one with five goals (enjoyment, self-assertion, esteem, interpersonal success, and avoiding negative affect), and one supporting Freud's big two (love and work).

- Nomothetic goals can also be compared with each other on circumplex models such as one that describes the degree to which goals are extrinsic or intrinsic, and relate to the physical self or self-transcendence.

- Dweck's theory of motivation says that all people are theorists who hold differing views about the changeability of intelligence and ability. Entity theorists see intelligence and ability as unchanging while incremental theorists believe they can be improved. As a result, entity theorists pursue judgment goals and respond to failure with helplessness. Incremental theorists pursue development goals and respond to failure with mastery.

- Many and perhaps all personality traits can be conceptualized in terms of the strategies that people follow; for example, the agreeable person follows the strategy of avoiding arguments and being friendly to everyone.

- According to Norem, defensive pessimists follow the motivational strategy of imagining the worst outcomes and then seeking to avoid them.

Emotion

- Emotions are a form of procedural knowledge; everyone knows what they are, but they are difficult to put into words and can only be fully learned and expressed through action and experience.

- Emotional experience includes stages of appraisal, physical response, nonverbal behaviors, and motivation. These stages may occur nearly simultaneously or in various orders.

- A circumplex model of emotion contrasts the degrees to which emotions are aroused versus unaroused and negative versus positive; another widely used rotation of this model contrasts emotions on the dimensions of excited versus bored and alarmed versus serene.

- People differ in the degree to which they are prone to particular emotions; the intensity of their emotional experience; the frequency with which their emotions change; and their understanding of, and ability to control, their emotions (emotional intelligence).

- Happiness is determined by genetics, life circumstances, and intentional activities, and has positive effects on health, occupational success, and supportive relationships.

Personality as a Verb

- Personality is something an individual "does" as well as something the individual "has," so in that sense personality is a verb.

THINK ABOUT IT

1. Does the concept of *personality processes* constitute a "basic approach" like the trait, biological, psychodynamic, humanistic, and learning approaches considered in earlier chapters? Is it an amalgamation of these other approaches, or is it something else entirely?

2. If you have been cheated by someone recently—so that the idea of being cheated is primed—does this make you suspicious of *other* people? If so, is this good or bad? In general, when is priming a source of distortion, and when might it be helpful?

3. If subliminal presentations of the words MOMMY AND I ARE ONE and BEATING DAD IS OK make people feel better, what other phrases might have this effect?

4. If you had to choose, would you rather be influenced more by what Epstein calls the rational system or by what he calls the experiential system? Why?

5. Is your behavior generally part of a strategy to obtain a long-term goal? Would it be better if more of your behaviors were?

6. Do you think most college students have what Dweck would call judgment goals or development goals?

7. Can you really understand the emotions of another person? Do you ever find your own emotions difficult to understand?

8. Which would make you happier, (a) giving directions to a stranger who has gotten lost, helping him get to an important appointment on time; or (b) finding a $10 bill in the street? What if option b were a $100 bill?

9. When you are feeling down, what do you do to cheer yourself up? How well does it work? Can you think of other things you might do to improve your mood?

10. Research suggests that happiness has many good consequences, but other research describes the benefits of defensive pessimism. Do these two lines of research contradict each other, or could they both be right?

SUGGESTED READINGS

Lyubomirsky, S. (2008). *The how of happiness: A scientific approach to getting the life you want*. New York: Penguin Press.

> *A clear and succinct summary of the latest research on how to become a happier person.*

Norem, J. (2001). *The positive power of negative thinking: Using defensive pessimism to manage anxiety and perform at your peak*. New York: Basic Books.

> *A highly readable introduction to Julie Norem's defense of the benefits of a pessimistic outlook on life. The book summarizes current research and is full of useful advice.*

EMEDIA

 Go to StudySpace, wwnorton.com/studyspace, to access additional review and enrichment materials.

17

WHAT YOU KNOW ABOUT YOU: The Self

Tell me something about yourself.
—INTERVIEW QUESTION

A FEW YEARS AGO, I worked on a study that gathered a large amount of information on almost 200 undergraduate participants. The information included a life-history interview, which we videotaped. The very first question is quoted above, and the interviewer asked it straight out of the blue. How would you reply? Some participants simply told us their names, hometowns, and majors. Some described favorite activities or life goals. But the most common response by far was a quick look of panic and an answer along the lines of "um . . . er . . . well . . . " You might think we would know our "selves" better than we know anybody or anything else, but for most people this most basic question turns out to be surprisingly difficult.

As William James (1890) noted many years ago, "the self" can have two different meanings, which he called the *I* and the *me*. The *me* is a sort of object, which can be observed and described. The *I* is the somewhat mysterious entity that does the observing and describing. When you describe yourself as "friendly," you are describing your *me*. But when you try to describe how you feel deep down inside about knowing you are friendly, you are trying to talk about your *I*, which is not easy to do. To put this another way, the *me* is the collection of statements you could make about yourself ranging from

"I am friendly,"[1] to "I am 6 feet tall." The *I* is more like the little person in the head (sometimes called the *homunculus*), or even the soul, which experiences your life and makes your decisions. Although the theoretical distinction is important, in practice the *I* and the *me* are easily confused. As the eminent psychologist Ernest Hilgard once observed,

> the self-evident character of self-awareness is in fact most illusive. You presently find yourself as between the two mirrors of a barbershop, with each image viewing each other, so that as the self takes a look at itself taking a look at itself, it soon gets all confused as to the self that is doing the looking and the self which is being looked at. (Hilgard, 1949, p. 377)

The self that is doing the looking, as Hilgard said, is the *I*, and the self that is being looked at is the *me*. The existential-phenomenological psychologists discussed in Chapter 13 attempted to address the nature and mystery of the experience of the *I*. Beyond that, psychologists have not succeeded in saying very much that is useful or interesting about the *I*, though I will return to its implications at the end of this chapter. Recent research has more to say about the *me*, the part of the self that we and the people who know us can talk about, describe, and put into action. What you know about you, and what I know about me, is the topic of this chapter.

THE SELF ACROSS CULTURES

As we saw in Chapter 14, while individualistic cultures assume that the self has an independent and separate existence, collectivist cultures view it as embedded in a larger social context of obligations and relationships. This theme has played out in modern research in two ways. One approach, rooted in anthropological analysis, suspects that the self is a Western cultural artifact that has no meaning in other cultures. The second approach is less extreme, and addresses the way the self and its implications differ across cultural contexts.

---

[1] English grammar confuses the issue here, because in James's terms, we really should say, "Me am friendly" (which sounds like something Tarzan might say).

Is the Self a Cultural Artifact?

By studying the culture of Hindu India, the anthropologists Richard Shweder and Lyle Bourne (1982, 1984) concluded that its holistic outlook leads Indians to think of themselves in a fundamentally different way than do members of Western culture. (Some of their related work was described in Chapter 14.) The researchers performed a simple experiment: They asked American and Hindu Indian informants to describe people they knew. The groups' answers differed significantly. While an American might say, "She is friendly," an Indian would say, "She brings cakes to my family on festival days." An American might say, "He is cheap," while an Indian said, "He has trouble giving things to his family." And where an American might say, "He is kind," an Indian is more likely to say, "Whoever becomes his friend, he remembers him forever and will always help him out of his troubles" (Shweder & Bourne, 1984, p. 172). Overall, about 50 percent of the terms Americans used to describe their acquaintances were personality traits such as *friendly*, *cheap*, and *kind*, but only 20 percent of the terms Indians used were words like these. From this difference, Shweder and Bourne concluded that Americans and Hindu Indians think of people in fundamentally different ways, and assumed this included how they thought about themselves. They argued that the American-style sense of self is a distinctly Western idea not shared by members of other cultures such as Hindus in India.

If these researchers are right, then many ideas that have long been taken for granted should be discarded or revised. Personality psychology assumes that individuals have properties—whether conceived as traits, learning patterns, or mental structures—that belong to, or characterize, each of them. If they do not, then we need to fundamentally rethink concepts such as personality development, self-interest, morality, and personal responsibility, to name a few. Before we get started, however, a few points are worth considering.

First, reconsider the key experiment in which Indian and American subjects described people they knew, and in which Americans usually answered by naming traits while Indians more often used complex and contextualized phrases. As the social psychologist John Sabini (1995) pointed out, "It would be rash to impute a very different concept of the self on the basis of this kind of evidence" (p. 264). First of all, the finding that 20 percent of the Indians' descriptions of people were personality-trait terms shows that the idea of individual traits is not exactly foreign to them—if you know what I mean. Moreover, it is not clear that even the colorful phrases used by the Indian informants are fundamentally different from the Americans' descriptions. They may just be longer and more vivid ways of making the same points.

Sabini recalled the description offered by the former governor of Texas, Ann Richards, of the first President George Bush: "Poor George, he can't help it—he was born with a silver foot in his mouth." Ann Richards was nothing if not Western, and her comment is certainly a description—and a vivid one—of an aspect she perceived of Bush's personality.[2] There is nothing Eastern or contrary to the separateness of Bush's self about this description.

Now consider the Indian's description of his kind acquaintance as someone who "remembers [his friend] forever and will always help him out of his troubles." This description is positive, unlike Richards's, but it similarly provides a vivid description of the habitual behavioral style—the trait of kindness, in this case—of a person this informant knows well.

However, the difference between the 20-percent-Indian and the 50-percent-American usage of trait terms remains large enough to deserve attention. It seems that in India and some other Eastern cultures, trait terms are used less often than they are in North America, Europe, Australia, and New Zealand (Bond & Cheung, 1983; Cousins, 1989). As mentioned in Chapter 14, English appears to have several times more trait terms than does Chinese. Members of different cultures do vary in their ways of describing people. Traditions of Western and Asian philosophy seem related to these differences. But do Indians and other Asians lack a sense of self? The evidence on this point seems doubtful.

> Do Indians and other Asians lack a sense of self? The evidence on this point seems doubtful.

---

[2] In case a trait translation is necessary, Richards was calling Bush an inarticulate, overprivileged bumbler.

Individualist and Collectivist Selves

Rather than rejecting the idea of the self, a less extreme approach is to study how the nature of the self and its implications differ across cultures. Psychologists have conducted a large amount of this sort of research in the past few years, and based on the notions of individualism and collectivism, most of this research assumes that the Western self is a relatively separate entity while the Eastern self is more integrated into the social and cultural context. This idea has many implications, several of which were discussed in Chapter 14, such as the possibility that self-expression, as understood in Western culture, is more limited in Eastern culture.

SELF-REGARD

Another implication is that the individualist's need for positive self-regard may be felt less acutely by a member of a collectivist culture (Heine, Lehman, Markus, & Kitayama, 1999). Specifically, research has found that Japanese people may not have the pervasive need to think well of themselves that is so characteristic of North Americans, and the theoretical explanation is that they tie their individual well-being to that of a larger group. Consistent with this theory, studies have found Japanese and American students to respond differently to success, failure, and negative self-relevant information. For example, Canadian college students who heard they had failed a test of creativity quickly searched for ways to think well of themselves in other contexts, whereas Japanese students showed no sign of this response (Heine, Kitayama, & Lehman, 2001). In another study, Canadians who failed an experimental task persisted less on a second task and denigrated its importance. Japanese participants had the opposite reaction, working harder and viewing the task as something important they should strive to do better (Heine, Kitayama, Lehman, & Takata, 2001). Apparently, this is because they have learned the Confucian view that failure always opens an opportunity for learning.

CONSISTENCY

Another basic cross-cultural issue is the matter of *self-determination*. The individualist view of the self assumes that the cause of behavior lies within the person. As a result, an individual is expected to behave consistently from one situation to the next. Indeed, in American culture, behavioral consistency is associated with mental health (Donahue, Robins, Roberts, & John, 1993). The more socially embedded member of a collectivist culture, by contrast, might be expected to change his behavior more as a function of the particular immediate situation (Markus, Mullally, & Kitayama, 1997). As a result, a member of a collectivist culture might feel less pressure to behave consistently and less conflicted about inconsistent behavior. This difference is apparently the basis of the finding that, among Koreans, unlike among Americans, behavioral consistency is not associated with measures of mental health (Suh, 2002).

A small but increasing amount of evidence suggests that, compared to members of individualist cultures, the behavior and experience of members of collectivist cultures are less consistent from one situation to the next. For example, Koreans describe themselves as less consistent than Americans do, and different observers of a Korean tend to agree less in their descriptions of that person's personality than do observers of an American (Suh, 2002; see also Albright, Malloy, Dong, Kenny, & Fang, 1997). Emotional experience also seems to vary across situations more for Japanese persons than for Americans (Oishi, Diener, Scollon, & Biswas-Diener, 2004).

This last study adds an important qualification. Consistency can be conceptualized and analyzed in two ways. One way focuses on the degree to which an individual varies his behavior or experience from one situation to the next—absolute consistency. The other focuses on the degree to which an individual maintains his differences from other people across situations—relative consistency. For example, even a brave and confident person might be more nervous in a burning house than in a normal classroom (low absolute consistency), but still might be the most confident person present in both situations (high relative consistency; see also Funder & Colvin, 1991). The study by Oishi et al. (2004) found that Japanese had more inconsistent emotional experience than Americans in an absolute sense; their emotions changed more from one situation to the next. But they had equally consistent emotional experience in a relative sense, because a Japanese person who was happier than others in one situation also tended to be happier than most in other situations. This finding implies that while members of collectivist cultures may be more inconsistent in an absolute sense than members of individualistic cultures, individual differences and associated personality traits appear to be equally important in both contexts.

THE CONTENTS OF THE SELF

William James believed that our *me* includes everything we hold dear, and so includes not just our personality traits, but also our body, home, possessions, and even family members. He observed that if someone were to harm

Figure 17.1 Extensions of the Self The family along with the family's home and possessions may be part of the self, especially in collectivist cultures (left, Japan; right, Mali).

any of these, we would be upset and angry. Someone who hits your child might as well punch you in the face; your reaction will be the same, and we also do not take kindly to people who damage or even criticize our homes or stamp collections. The central aspect of the self, however, is surely our psychological self: our abilities and, especially, our personalities. If you see yourself as kind, this is important for several reasons. This self-image and your need to maintain it may influence your behavior (e.g., how you respond to a homeless person asking for spare change), and it organizes your vast array of memories about yourself, as well as your impressions and judgments of other people.

Self-knowledge can be divided into two types. **Declarative knowledge** about the self consists of the facts and impressions that we consciously know and can describe. It is self-knowledge we can "declare." For example, a person who knows that she is friendly can easily say so, and thus "friendliness" will be part of her declarative knowledge about herself. **Procedural knowledge**, as described in the previous chapter, is knowledge expressed through actions rather than words. For example, a shy person might habitually avoid other people and social interaction whenever possible, and this habit may be so ingrained that he does not consciously realize how characteristic this behavior is. Intriguingly, however, as we shall see later in this chapter, this shy person *might* be aware of his tendencies on some deeper, unconscious level. In both cases, these unconscious aspects of shyness would be considered part of his procedural self. Procedural self-knowledge includes patterns of social skills, styles of relating to others that comprise the *relational self*, and the unconscious self-knowledge that resides in the *implicit self*.

THE DECLARATIVE SELF

The **declarative self** comprises all of your (conscious) knowledge or opinions about your own personality traits. These opinions are of two sorts. First, there is your overall opinion about whether you are good or bad, worthy or unworthy, or somewhere in between. This opinion is called **self-esteem**. The second kind of opinion is more detailed and contains everything you know, or think you know, about your traits and abilities. Sometimes this supposed self-knowledge is correct, and sometimes it is wrong.

Self-Esteem

In one of its more famous acts, in 1987 the California legislature set up a task force to enhance the self-esteem of the state's residents. Perhaps this act was not as flaky as it sounds (though, decades later, the self-esteem of Californians has not noticeably improved). A large amount of research suggests that low self-esteem—feeling you are bad or unworthy—is correlated with outcomes such as dissatisfaction with life, hopelessness, and depression (Crocker & Wolfe, 2001; Orth, Robins, & Roberts, 2008), as well as loneliness (Cutrona, 1982) and delinquency (Donnellan, Trzesniewski, Robins, Moffitt, & Caspi, 2005; Trzesniewski et al., 2006). As we saw in Chapter 14, countries whose people have lower self-esteem, on average, also tend to have higher suicide rates (Chatard et al., 2009). This last finding is ironic, in a way, because research also shows that people with low self-esteem have a greater fear of death (Schmeichel et al., 2009). Psychologists have thought for a long time that low self-esteem is bad, and for good reason.

Indeed, low self-esteem might literally be a danger signal. According to psychologist Mark Leary's sociometer theory described in Chapter 9, your interest in maintaining high self-esteem may have evolutionary roots. Your self-esteem tends to suffer when you have failed in the eyes of your social group (Leary, 1999). If others have lost respect or liking for you, you are unlikely to feel good about yourself. This drop in self-esteem may warn you about possible rejection or even social ostracism—which, for our distant ancestors, could literally be fatal—and motivate you to restore your reputation. High self-esteem, by contrast, may indicate success and acceptance by one's social group.

Still, attempts to bolster self-esteem can backfire. Many self-help books urge people to chant phrases to themselves such as "I am a lovable person," "I'm powerful, I'm strong, and nothing in this world can stop me," and other so-called "affirmations" of the self. The early 20th-century French pharmacist Émile Coué told his patients to repeat "Every day, in every way, I am getting better and better."[3] The psychologist Joanne Wood and her colleagues argue that statements like these are potentially dangerous, because if the person who says them finds them to be too extreme to be plausible, a boomerang effect may actually cause the person to feel worse (J. V. Wood, Perunovic, & Lee, 2009). If you say "I am a lovable person," but you don't really believe it, repeating the phrase may make your (perceived) unlovability just that much more prominent in your mind.

Besides, it is not good for self-esteem to get *too* high. If a person fails to recognize the ways that other people dislike or have lost respect for her, she may feel better but also risk exploitation or social ostracism. People who *self-enhance*—who think they are better than the other people who know them think they are—run into problems in relations with others, mental health, and adjustment (Kurt & Paulhus, 2008; Kwan, John, Robins, & Kuang, 2008).[4] In terms of the sociometer analogy, if your gas gauge breaks you may happily think you don't need to fill your tank, but later you may find yourself stranded on the highway.

In other words, it is possible to love oneself too much. Overly high self-esteem can lead to behavior that is arrogant, abusive, and even criminal (Colvin, Block, & Funder, 1995; Baumeister, Smart, & Boden, 1996). As will be discussed in the next chapter, the trait of narcissism, if extreme, can

---

[3] Or, if you prefer the original French, *tous les jours à tous points de vue je vais de mieux en mieux.* This is a famous phrase, but I found the exact quote in Wikipedia (where else?): http://en.wikipedia .org/wiki/%C3%89mile_Cou%C3%A9#cite_note-britannica-0.

[4] The slightly awkward phrasing of this sentence is quite deliberate. People who describe themselves as better than *they* describe others are not necessarily maladjusted; sometimes—in fact, often—they really *are* better than others in certain respects. What turns out to cause problems is to see yourself as better than do other people who know you well. Or, on the flip side, the psychologist Virginia Kwan and her colleagues maintain that to see yourself as others see you is to exhibit *self-insight.* (See Kwan et al., 2008, and Kurt & Paulhus, 2008, for extended discussions.)

extend to a personality disorder that can harm both the affected individual and the people that he comes in contact with. A series of clever experiments showed that when narcissists with high self-esteem are provoked, they will retaliate in ways including blasting the offender with noise or giving him a grade that is lower than he deserves (Bushman et al., 2009). Narcissism is associated with high self-esteem that is brittle because it is unrealistic (Vazire & Funder, 2006; Zeigler-Hill, 2006), and unstable self-esteem may be worse than low self-esteem (Kernis, Lakey, & Heppner, 2008).

The bottom line is that promoting psychological health requires something more complex than simply trying to make everybody feel better about themselves (Swann, Chang-Schneider, & McClarty, 2007). The best way to raise self-esteem is through accomplishments that increase it legitimately (DuBois & Flay, 2004; P. Haney & Durlak, 1998). The most important aspect of your opinion of yourself is not whether your opinion is good or bad, but the degree to which it is accurate. Or, in the words of Socrates, "Know thyself." We will consider the accuracy of self-knowledge later in this chapter.

The Self-Schema

Some psychologists theorize that the declarative self resides in a cognitive structure called the **self-schema** (Markus, 1977), which includes all of one's ideas about the self, organized into a coherent system. When a trait psychologist asks someone to complete a personality questionnaire, the person presumably answers these questions by reaching into her memory system for the relevant information. This memory system is the self-schema, and the act of responding to the questionnaire amounts to reporting what the self-schema contains. That is why this kind of questionnaire is said to gather S data (Chapter 2); I hope you will recall that S stands for *self*-report. But there is more than one way to get at the self-schema.

The self-schema can be identified using S data, B data, or both (see Chapter 2). For example, one early study identified college students who were "schematic for" (had self-schemas pertaining to) the traits of dependence and sociability by simply asking them to rate themselves on a series of scales (Markus, 1977). If these S data indicated that a student rated himself as extremely sociable and that he also rated his sociability important, he was deemed schematic for that trait. Otherwise, he was deemed "aschematic." A later study employed the widely used California Psychological Inventory (CPI; Gough, 1968) to gather self-ratings on the traits of responsibility and sociability (Fuhrman & Funder, 1995). When these S data indicated an exceptionally high score on responsibility, the participant was deemed schematic for that trait.

Both of these studies also gathered B data. In this case, the B data were reaction times. Participants read words such as *friendly* or *responsible* on a computer screen, and then responded by pressing keys labeled "me" or "not me" as quickly as they could. Schematics responded to relevant traits more quickly than did aschematics, regardless of whether they were identified using Markus's rating scales or the CPI (Markus, 1977; Fuhrman & Funder, 1995).

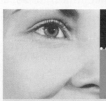

TRY FOR YOURSELF 17.1

Are You Schematic?

Instructions: Mark the point on each scale that best describes you:

| | Independent | 1 2 3 4 5 6 7 8 9 10 11 | Dependent |

How important to you is your description on this scale?

| | Unimportant | 1 2 3 4 5 6 7 8 9 10 11 | Important |

| | Individualist | 1 2 3 4 5 6 7 8 9 10 11 | Conformist |

How important to you is your description on this scale?

| | Unimportant | 1 2 3 4 5 6 7 8 9 10 11 | Important |

| | Leader | 1 2 3 4 5 6 7 8 9 10 11 | Follower |

How important to you is your description on this scale?

| | Unimportant | 1 2 3 4 5 6 7 8 9 10 11 | Important |

Interpreting Scores:
- If you rated yourself from points 1–4 on at least two of the three trait scales, and rated the same traits from points 8–11 on the importance scales, you are "schematic" for the trait of *independence*.
- If you rated yourself from points 8–11 on at least two of the three trait scales, and rated the same traits from points 8–11 on the importance scales, you are "schematic" for the trait of *dependence*.

Source: Markus (1977), p. 66.

This research has two important implications. A methodological implication is that the phenomena studied by cognitively oriented personality psychologists, of the sort discussed in this and the previous chapter, and those studied by the trait psychologists, of the sort discussed in Chapters 4 through 7, may not be as different as is sometimes presumed. Being assessed as schematic for a given trait and attaining a high score on that trait using a conventional personality inventory such as the CPI seem to have the same implications for response time and other indications of cognitive processing—and they may amount to much the same thing.

A second implication is that one's self-view—conceptualized as a schema or a trait, take your pick—may have important consequences for how one processes information. As the cognitive personality psychologist Nancy Cantor (1990) has pointed out, being schematic for a personality trait such as sociability, responsibility, or shyness amounts to being an "expert" about that trait. Research elsewhere in cognitive psychology has shown that experts in any domain—chess or mechanical engineering, for example— easily remember information relevant to their domain of expertise, tend to see the world in terms dictated by their expertise, and have a ready and almost automatic plan of action that can be invoked in relevant situations (Chase & Simon, 1973; Larkin, McDermott, Simon, & Simon, 1980). This kind of expertise has some obvious advantages—it can help a person to be a better chess player or engineer—but it also can limit that person's view of the world. An expert may view things too rigidly, or fail to test possibilities beyond the limits of her expertise. In the same way, your expertise about yourself can help you remember a lot of information about yourself and process this information quickly, but it also may keep you from seeing beyond the boundaries of your own self-image.

The self-schema embodies knowledge based on past experience, but not on any particular past experience. For example, perhaps you have behaved kindly many times and in many situations, and as a result have come to view yourself as a kind person. What would happen if you somehow forgot about all of the occasions on which you were kind, if they were literally erased from your memory? Would your self-view change?

This question might seem unanswerable, but it actually has been addressed by two remarkable case studies. In one case, a college student sustained a head injury that caused her temporarily to lose all memory of everything she had done during the past year (S. B. Klein, Loftus, & Kihlstrom, 1996). Yet she was able to describe her own personality almost perfectly, in a way that agreed with the perceptions of her parents and boyfriend. More remarkably, she could describe herself in ways that reflected how she had changed during the past year (which happened to be her first year of college), even without any memory of events that happened during the year.[5] A second case study was even more striking. As a result of a heart attack that cut off oxygen to his brain, a 78-year-old man lost almost all memory of specific events of his life. Yet he still had general knowledge of himself (e.g., "I usually try to be kind") that agreed with the impressions of others who knew him well (S. B. Klein, Rozendal, & Cosmides, 2002). These cases suggest that the answer to the question asked at the end of the preceding paragraph—would your self-view change if you lost memory of your past?—is *no*. Once formed, your impression of what you are like does not depend on your memory for specific things you have done, and these two bases of self-knowledge may exist independently in separate sectors of the brain (Lieberman et al., 2004). Your "self," in that sense, has a life of its own.

Self-Reference and Memory

Another indication of the deep roots of the self is its implications for memory. An old theory suggested that if you repeated something over and over in your mind, such *rehearsal* was sufficient to move the information into **long-term memory (LTM)**, or permanent memory storage. Later research showed that this idea is not quite correct. The best way to get information into LTM, it turns out, is not just to repeat it, but to really think about it (a process called *elaboration*). The longer and more complex the processing that a piece of information receives, the more likely it is to get transferred into LTM (Craik & Watkins, 1973; Craik & Tulving, 1975).

This principle of cognitive psychology yields some useful advice about how to study. A common strategy is rote repetition. Everyone has seen college students in the library with their yellow highlighters, marking passages in the textbook they think may pertain to the exam. To study, they reread everything highlighted; if they have time, they do it again and even again. This strategy usually fails dismally. A much better strategy is to take each of these highlighted passages, pause, and consider several questions. Do I agree with this statement? Why? Does this statement remind me of anything in my life? Is it useful? Does it contradict anything else I know from experience or have learned in this course? Answering these questions will make

---

[5] The case had a happy ending. Three weeks after the accident, the student recovered all of her memories except for a brief period immediately after her fall.

you much more likely to remember the statements you have read. Moreover, you might learn something.

A particularly good way to remember something, research has shown, is to think about some specific way that it relates to one's self (C. Symons & Johnson, 1997). For example, if you must memorize a long list of adjectives, it can be effective to ask yourself whether each of them describes you. The reason appears to be that the mental structure of self-knowledge, the self-schema, is rich, well developed, and often used. Any information tied to this schema in memory remains accessible for a long time. A good way to remember something, therefore, is to ask, "What does this have to do with me?" The answer doesn't really matter; the important part is to think about how the information *might* be self-relevant (even if it isn't). The enhancement of LTM that comes from thinking of how information relates to the self is called the **self-reference effect**, and recent evidence suggests that a particular area of the frontal cortex of the brain might be specialized to process this kind of information (Heatherton, Macrae, & Kelley, 2004).

The self-reference effect explains why your most personally meaningful memories stick with you the longest. These may include tragic events (such as the death of a loved one), major milestones (such as graduation day, your wedding day, and the day your child—especially your first child—is born), and other events that meant something special. Try this right now: Think of a memory from your early childhood. Why has this event stayed in your mind all of these years? It must mean something special to you—what?

We saw earlier in this chapter that the concept of the self appears to have different implications in collectivist cultures, such as China, than in individualist cultures, such as the United States. It is reasonable to suspect, therefore, that the self-reference effect might also work differently in different cultures. A recent study indicates that it does (Qi & Zhu, 2002). In Chinese culture, information thought about in terms of the self is indeed remembered better than most other kinds of information, but information thought about in terms of one's mother or father showed the same effect, leading the authors to conclude that "the self concept might include the concepts of father and mother in Chinese people, supporting the independent/dependent self-concept model in Eastern culture" (Qi & Zhu, 2002, p. 275).

Self-Efficacy

Because the (conscious) self-schema contains our ideas about our characteristics and capabilities (Markus & Nurius, 1986), it affects what we do. If we think we are sociable, we are more likely to seek out the company of others. If we think we are academically capable, we are more likely to go to college. Recall Bandura's ideas of self-efficacy from Chapter 15: Our opinions about our capabilities set the limits of what we will attempt. For example, perhaps you had a friend in high school who was just as smart and hardworking as you. For whatever reason, however, your friend thought that he couldn't possibly succeed in college. You might have tried to argue otherwise: "Of course you can do it—if I can, you can too!" But in the face of a negative self-attitude, such arguments are usually ineffective. So you went to college, and your friend did not. In a year or two, you will graduate, and your friend will still be pumping gas or flipping burgers.[6] The difference was not one of ability or drive—it was in the self. You believed you could do it, while your friend did not have such a positive self-view.

> Our opinions about our capabilities set the limits of what we will attempt.

This example shows how important and sometimes devastating one's self-concept can be. It also shows the dangers in persuading people that they cannot do certain things. For example, many young girls pick up the message from society that girls cannot—or should not—excel at math (Hilton & Berglund, 1974; Stipek & Gralinski, 1991). The result? Here's a personal example: I used to teach at a prestigious engineering college. More than 90 percent of the students were male—hardly a result of chance. Similarly, members of certain racial groups and economic classes are taught, usually implicitly but powerfully by the media and other sources, that "their kind" do not go to college or otherwise better themselves. So sometimes these individuals give up, or they find other ways—not necessarily constructive—to feel that they have succeeded. This is why people are not merely being sensitive when they object to stereotyped media portrayals of particular ethnic groups as lazy, unsuccessful, or even criminal, and why there was so much outrage a few years ago when a talking Barbie doll was sold that said, "Math class is tough!" These portrayals can have important consequences, especially for children.

Indeed, Carol Dweck, whose theory of entity and incremental self-views was surveyed in Chapter 16, believes that the beliefs that one develops about oneself form the basic foundations of personality (Dweck, 2008). We already saw how her theory describes the difference between people who think that ability is something that is an instrinic part of the self and cannot be changed,

---

[6] I am presuming that with your college education, you will find a better job than these two.

"Really, only you can tell yourself to giddyup."

and people who think it can be developed and grown. In a similar way, she theorizes that some people have self-views that lead them to anticipate being rejected by others, while other people anticipate acceptance. These beliefs have major consequences for how these people live their lives. Just as entity theorists give up in the face of adversity, "rejection theorists" enter social relationships acting as if they expect to be spurned—an expectation that often turns out to be self-fulfilling.

Dweck's optimistic message is that these beliefs can be changed. She reports some success in experimental attempts to change entity theorists into incremental theorists (in a school-based program called "Brainology"), which led to improved motivation to do well in their studies. A second program worked to change first-year college students' expectations from rejection to acceptance, and thereby improve their social lives (Walton & Cohen, 2007). Are other aspects of personality also based on changeable beliefs? Dweck believes so, but that point remains to be established in future research.

Possible Selves

The person that you are—is that the only person you could be? Probably not. For this reason, some psychologists have studied *possible selves*, the images we have, or can construct, of the other possible ways we might be. The possible self you envision for your future may affect your goals in life.

For example, David Buss (1989) showed that women, more than men, preferred mates who were older than themselves and had the ability to provide for them. As we saw in Chapter 9, Buss interpreted this result as indicating that women have evolved to seek mates who can protect and provide for them and their children, whereas men have other priorities for their ideal mates. A recent study questioned this interpretation, in an interesting way (Eagly, Eastwick, & Johannesen-Schmidt, 2009). Women *and* men were asked to imagine themselves—a possible future self—as a "married person with children who is either a homemaker or a provider" (2009, p. 403). Then they were asked what kind of mate would be best for them. People of either gender who imagined themselves as homemakers, compared with those who imagined themselves as providers, preferred a mate who was older and could provide for them! This finding implies that the different mate preferences of women and men might stem, to some degree, from the selves they expect to be possible in the future, which itself is a function of society—not necessarily from a built-in biological tendency.

Most work on possible selves has focused on our images of the people we wish we were. People report desiring future selves that fulfill their needs for self-esteem, competence, and meaning. But they don't want their future selves to change too much. Another desired attribute of the future self is *continuity*—maintaining the same identity over time (Vignoles, Manzi, Regalia, Scabini, & Jemmolo, 2008).

Self-Discrepancy Theory

According to *self-discrepancy theory*, you have not one but two kinds of desired selves, and the interactions between them and your actual self determines how you feel about life (Higgins, Bond, Klein, & Strauman, 1986; Higgins, Roney, Crowe, & Hymes, 1994). One desired self is the *ideal self*, which is your view of what you could be at your best. A second desired self is your *ought self*, which is your view of what you should—as opposed to what you would like—to be. Although they both represent hypothetical ideals, the ideal and ought selves often differ. For example, your ideal self might include an image of yourself as being so good-looking that people pause and stare as you walk by. Your ought self might include an image of yourself as somebody who never, ever tells a lie.

Both of these nonactual selves are probably unrealistic. Let's face facts: You are probably neither that good-looking nor that honest. But the discrepancies between the actual self and these two potential selves have different consequences, according to the theory. To the extent that you fail to attain your ideal self, you become depressed. To the extent that you fail to attain your ought self, you become anxious.[7]

Why do these reactions differ? According to the theorist Tory Higgins (1997), the two nonactual selves represent different foci to life. The ideal self

---

[7] The neo-Freudian theorist Karen Horney (see Chapter 12) also wrote extensively about the neurotic consequences of trying to live up to an unrealistic "ideal" self-image (see, e.g., Horney, 1950).

is reward based and resembles the Go system hypothesized by Jeffrey Gray (see Chapter 8). To some extent, you focus your life on the pursuit of pleasures and rewards. Your ideal self represents the goal state of that focus—the state where you finally attain all of the rewards you seek. The other focus is punishment based and resembles Gray's Stop system. It emphasizes avoiding punishments and other bad outcomes. Your ought self represents the goal state based on that focus—a state where no punishments or other bad events will occur.

Of course, everybody has both kinds of goals, just as in Gray's theory everybody has a Stop system and a Go system. And nobody achieves either final state described by the ideal or the ought self. But Higgins's point is that individuals balance these goals differently. If you primarily pursue reward—focused on the ideal self—failures to attain your goal will tend to depress you. If you primarily avoid punishment—focused on the ought self—failures to attain your goal will tend to make you anxious. In other words, the root of depression is disappointment. The root of anxiety is fear.

Accurate Self-Knowledge

As mentioned earlier, self-knowledge, like any other kind of declarative knowledge, might be right or wrong. You might think you are generous, but the people who know you well may be painfully aware that really you are cheap. Or you might, in the eyes of others, be more intelligent, kind, or attractive than you think you are. Accurate self-knowledge has long been considered a hallmark of mental health (e.g., Jahoda, 1958; Rogers, 1961) for two reasons. First, people who are healthy, secure, and wise enough to see the world as it is, without the need to distort anything, will tend to see themselves more accurately too. Second, a person with accurate self-knowledge is in a better position to make good decisions on important issues ranging from what occupation to pursue, to whom to marry (Vogt & Colvin, 2005). To choose the right major and the right occupation requires accurate knowledge of your own interests and abilities. To choose the right relationship partner, you need to know at least as much about yourself as you do about your partner.

The process for gaining accurate self-knowledge is outlined by the Realistic Accuracy Model (RAM; Funder, 1995, 2003). Recall from Chapter 6 that, according to RAM, one can gain accurate knowledge of anyone's personality through a four-stage process. First, the person must do something *relevant* to the trait being judged; second, the information must be *available* to the judge; third, the judge must *detect* this information; and fourth, the judge must *utilize* the information correctly. This model was developed to explain the accuracy of judgments of other people. In an important sense, though, you are just one of the people you happen to know, and to some degree you come to know yourself the same way you find out about anybody else—by observing what you do and trying to draw appropriate conclusions (Bem, 1972). Thus, if you are fully aware of what you do, and interpret your own actions appropriately, you come to accurately know yourself. But this is not necessarily easy.

"It's interesting—with each conviction I learn a little more about myself."

SELF-KNOWLEDGE VERSUS KNOWLEDGE OF OTHERS

Knowing yourself might in some respects be more difficult than figuring out someone else. Research indicates that, not surprisingly, we have better insight into our personal emotional experience than anyone else does (e.g., Spain et al., 2000). But when it comes to actual, overt behavior, the picture is somewhat different. In a study that obtained personality judgments from both the participants and their close acquaintances, the acquaintances' judgments more accurately predicted behavior than did the self-judgments in nearly every comparison (Kolar et al., 1996). For example, acquaintances' judgments of assertiveness correlated more highly with later assertive behavior observed in the laboratory than did self-judgments. The same was true for talkativeness, initiation of humor, feelings of being cheated and victimized by life, and several other characteristics of personality and behavior. A more recent study found similar results when self and others' judgments were used to predict behavior outside the laboratory, in normal daily life. Close acquaintances were as accurate as the self, and the average ratings of two or three acquaintances were sometimes even more accurate (Vazire & Mehl, 2008).

One reason for these surprising findings may be that attending to the self is actually rather difficult. From the inside you plan your next moves in response to the situations that confront you. All you see is what *you* decide to do, not what anybody else would do in the same situation. In terms of RAM, problems arise at both the relevance and detection stages. But when you view somebody else from the outside, you may be in a better position to compare what she does with what others do, and therefore be better able to evaluate her personality traits, which as you will recall from Chapter 4, are relative constructs. Their very essence entails comparing one person with another. If you can see two different people responding to the same situation, this is an ideal opportunity to judge differences in their personalities.

....

Attending to the self is actually rather difficult.

....

For example, imagine you are standing in a long line at an airline ticket counter, and, when it is finally your turn, the clerk is rushed and somewhat rude to you. You do your best to ignore the clerk's behavior, take your ticket, and leave. Whatever you learn about yourself from this episode is necessarily limited. Now imagine you get a chance to watch two other people who happen to be ahead of you in line. The first talks to the clerk, shrugs his shoulders, takes his ticket, and leaves. The second person begins to talk to the clerk and quickly becomes angry. He turns red in the face and is shaking a finger and raising his voice by the time they finish. Now you are in an excellent position to compare the personalities of these individuals who reacted very differently to the same stimulus.

One of the great misperceptions many people have about their own behavior is that it is the logical or natural response to the situation and is therefore what anyone would have done (Ross, Greene, & House, 1977). "What else could I do?" you may often hear people ask. Such explanations are somewhat like those of the alcoholic who, after a stressful argument, goes on a bender. The alcoholic might say, "The stress caused me to drink," but of course she forgets that nonalcoholics find other ways to respond to stress. You probably know people who are hostile, deceitful, or unpleasant, who similarly believe they are just responding normally to the situations at hand. The same thing tends to be true of people with personality disorders, who view their symptoms very differently than do the people around them (Thomas, Turkheimer, & Oltmanns, 2003; see Chapter 18). As an outside observer, you see their chronic patterns of behavior, not just the momentary pressures that impinge upon them, and you can also see that other people respond more constructively to similar situations (Kolar et al., 1996).

This phenomenon is probably not limited to negative behaviors, although the positive end of the effect has not yet been documented by research. You may know people who are consistently easygoing, kind, diligent, or brave. When asked about their behavior, they seem just as surprised as the alcoholic or hostile person just described: "What else would I do?" they respond. To them, acting in an easygoing, kind, diligent, or brave manner is simply the obvious response to the situations they experience, and they find it hard to imagine acting differently. It takes an outsider's perspective to recognize such behavior as consistent across situations, unusual, and even admirable. Perhaps the tendency to overestimate the influence of situations is more pronounced regarding negative traits such as alcoholism or personality disorders. But I suspect that individuals can be equally blind to their good qualities.[8]

In January 1982, an ice-covered airliner on takeoff plunged into the Potomac River in Washington, D.C., near the heavily traveled Fourteenth Street Bridge. Dozens of onlookers at the scene and thousands of television viewers watched as the handful of survivors clung to bits of floating wreckage amid the ice. Lenny Skutnik, a government clerk on his way home from work, saw one survivor begin to lose her grip and slip into the water; he immediately tore off his coat and plunged into the water, pulling the woman to safety. An instant hero, Skutnik was introduced to the nation later that month by President Reagan during the State of the Union address. But Skutnik was reluctant to take credit, saying that he had simply acted without thinking when he saw someone in need. The critical fact, obvious to everyone but him, was that he acted *differently* from the dozens of others standing on the shore.

Author James Brady, who has written about the World War II soldiers who raised the flag on Iwo Jima and other historical topics, has commented that

> it's the observer who sees a hero. . . . I've talked to Medal of Honor winners and everybody says the same thing: "I didn't do anything that anyone else wouldn't do." . . . [A solider who rescued a companion under fire] didn't see the bullets, he just saw a man that needed his help. It's the people on the outside who see the heroic stuff. It's all in the perspective. (Fisher, 2004)

---

[8] Social psychologists have researched in detail the *false consensus effect*, the tendency of people to see their own behavior as more common than it really is (see Ross et al., 1977). The present discussion can be compared to research on the *actor-observer effect* (e.g., Jones & Nisbett, 1971), which found that people typically see their own behavior as a response to momentary, situational pressures, whereas they see the behavior of others as consistent and as a product of their personality attributes. The present discussion differs from this research by not following the traditional assumption that the actor is correct in thinking his or her behavior is caused by the situation and the observer is wrong. I suspect that people more often tend to be blind to consistencies in their own behavior, which are better observed from an external perspective (see Funder, 1982; Kolar et al., 1996).

Figure 17.2 Just Doing What Anyone Would Do? Lenny Skutnik plunged into the frozen Potomac River and saved a passenger from a crashed jet, unlike dozens of bystanders at the scene. He was honored at President Reagan's State of the Union address in January 1982.

Occasionally, it might be possible to take an outsider's perspective on your own behavior. One such occasion might be when you use your memory to survey your past behaviors and see retrospectively how each of your actions fits into a pattern that may have been invisible to you at the time, and how your choices differed from those of others in the same situations. Perhaps Lenny Skutnik realized later how exceptional his behavior was; at the time, he was too focused on someone in need to wonder whether his action was typical, or to contrast his behavior with that of the other people at the scene. In a very different example, when an alcoholic explains the cause of a recent drinking relapse, he is likely to attribute it to a stressful day at work, a fight with a spouse, and so on. But as more time passes, he becomes more likely to view the relapse as part of his chronic pattern of alcoholism (McKay, O'Farrell, Maisto, Connors, & Funder, 1989). Time can give a person perspective.

The purpose of psychotherapy is often to try to gain a broad view of one's own behavior to discover where one's strengths and weaknesses lie. Therapists encourage the client to review past behavior and identify chronic patterns, rather than continuing to see maladaptive behaviors merely as responses to momentary pressures. The alcoholic, for example, must come to see his drinking as a chronic and characteristic behavior pattern, not a normal and inevitable response to situational stress. And then he must identify the inner strengths that can help overcome this problem.

IMPROVING SELF-KNOWLEDGE

In what ways can you improve how well you know yourself? There are three basic routes. First and perhap most obviously, you can use introspection to look into your own mind and understand who you are. Second, you can seek feedback from other people who—if they are honest and they trust you not to be offended—can be an important source of information about what you are really like, including aspects of yourself that might be obvious to everybody but you. Third, you can observe your own behavior, and try to draw conclusions from those observations much as anyone else, observing the same behaviors, would do (Bem, 1972).

In terms of RAM, introspection would be included at the fourth and final stage, utilization. The utilization stage emphasizes the importance of accurate memory for and honest evaluation of your behavior, which, as noted above, might become easier with the passage of time. The second and third stages, availability and detection, emphasize the information you might be able to get from other people about what you are like. They might simply tell you, thereby making the information obviously available. But you might also have to read subtle, nonverbal indicators of what other people think of you, which makes detection more of an issue.

Some of the most important implications of RAM for self-knowledge lie at the first stage: relevance. As with getting to know another person, you can evaluate yourself only on the basis of what you have observed yourself do, and this is limited by the situations you have experienced and even by restrictions you may have put on yourself. For example, some people test themselves with bungee jumping or mountain climbing, thus allowing themselves to demonstrate attributes they might not otherwise have known that they have. I am not really recommending that you go bungee jumping, but it might be worthwhile to consider how you could learn a lot about yourself by going to new places, meeting new people, and trying new things.

This may be difficult in some circumstances. If you live your whole life in a small town around the same few people, you may have no idea what you would do—what traits would emerge, what skills would develop—in a broader or different environment. During time I spent in New Zealand—an idyllic country on a set of small islands in the South Pacific—I was interested to see how many college students were desperate to travel. They live in a bit of paradise, but were eager to test themselves against some of the challenges in the wider, more crowded, and more dangerous worlds of Europe and North America.

Self-knowledge can also be limited by family or culture, rather than by geography. For example, some families (and some cultural traditions) curb the individual self-expression of young people to a significant degree (see Chapter 14). One's education, occupation, and even spouse may be chosen by others. More commonly, families may exert strong pressures on children to aim for certain educational objectives and follow certain career paths. My university—like many others—has many freshman premed students. Strangely, by senior year there are far fewer. In the most difficult kind of case, a student feels pressured by family expectations to be premed, and then in her junior year realizes that she lacks the skills, the interest, or both. It may feel to her as if she has only minutes to decide on a new major, a new occupation, and a new path in life. This will be even more difficult if she has not tried out alternatives—she may have very little basis for understanding her real talents and interests because she was never encouraged to find out what they were.

So regarding occupational choice, relationship formation, and many other areas, the best advice toward self-knowledge is probably to be yourself. It is not possible to avoid being influenced by the desires and expectations of friends, acquaintances, and family members. But you are most likely to find out about yourself by searching for your interests and testing your abilities. On the basis of self-knowledge, you are most likely to make wise choices about education, occupation, relationship partners, and everything else that matters.

THE PROCEDURAL SELF

We saw in the previous chapter that personality is not just something you have; it is also something you do. The unique aspects of what you do comprise the **procedural self**, and your knowledge of this self typically takes the form of procedural knowledge.

Procedural knowledge, as you recall, consists of ways of doing things, or procedures, which is why it is also called "knowing how." It is knowledge of a special sort—you are not conscious of the knowledge itself and generally cannot, if asked, explain it to anyone else very well. (In some cases, you may reply with a statement such as, "Here, let me show you.") Examples include the ability to read, to ride a bicycle, to close a business deal, to analyze a set of data, or to ask someone out on a date. For the most part—by which I mean about 98 percent of the time—you learn these skills by doing them and sometimes by watching them.

A classic example is bike riding. I can tell you how to ride a bike: Sit on the seat, grab the handlebars, pump the pedals around and around, and maintain balance so you will not fall off. I could say more, but it would never be sufficient for teaching you how to ride a bicycle, or even to let you know what bike riding is really like. You can learn how to ride a bicycle only by doing it and getting practice and feedback. Social skills are like this too. Despite the prevalence of books with titles like *How to Sell Anything to Anyone* or even *How to Pick Up Girls*, social skills must be acquired through practice.

> Despite the prevalence of books with titles like *How to Sell Anything to Anyone* or even *How to Pick Up Girls*, social skills must be acquired through practice.

The procedural self is made up of the behaviors through which you express who you think you are, generally without knowing you are doing so (Cantor, 1990; Langer, 1992, 1994). Like riding a bicycle, the working of the procedural self is automatic and not very accessible to conscious awareness.

Relational Selves

An aspect of the procedural self that has received particular research attention is the *relational self-schema*, said to be based on past experiences that direct how we relate with each of the important people in our lives (Baldwin, 1999).

As mentioned in Chapter 2, you have probably developed some specific patterns in the way you interact with your parents. You may even forget these patterns exist until you visit home after a long absence. Before you know it, you are falling into the same old, well-rehearsed childhood routine. This is rarely a pleasant experience, so a common response is to try to oppose old patterns by relating to the family as differently as possible from how you did before (Andersen & Chen, 2002). We all know what this can include: odd clothes, tattoos, body piercings, an unsuitable boyfriend or girlfriend, or maybe just a spectacularly bad attitude. All of these behaviors announce, "I'm not the child I used to be." This is only natural, but pause a moment, and have a kind thought for the baffled and dismayed parents.

Despite this example, most of our patterns of relating to other people are deeply ingrained and difficult to change. Even the multiply pierced adolescent may run to Mommy when feeling sick or after stubbing a toe. One reason these patterns persist is that their roots reach so deep. Attachment theory (e.g., Mikulincer & Shaver, 2003; Sroufe et al., 1993; see Chapter 12) and newer, relational self theory (Andersen & Chen, 2002) agree that many

scripts for relating to others are set early in life. Later, through transference (see Chapters 10 and 12), we may find ourselves responding to new people much like the people they seem to resemble from our past (Andersen & Baum, 1994; Zhang & Hazan, 2002). For example, if you were intimidated by your father and tried at all costs to avoid making him angry, you might find yourself treating your male boss the same way. Or, if your early romantic relationships did not turn out well, you might find yourself, in a self-perpetuating manner, approaching new relationships implicitly expecting betrayal and disappointment.

Implicit Selves

In many cases, these self-relevant behavioral patterns are not readily accessible to consciousness. Unlike the self-schema, which is generally assumed to be consciously accessible and which can be measured on straightforward questionnaires (i.e., S data; see Chapter 2), relational selves and other implicit aspects of the self-concept may work unconsciously and powerfully (Greenwald et al., 2002). In that case, how can they be measured? The psychologist Anthony Greenwald and his colleagues have invented an ingenious method called the IAT, or Implicit Association Test, which was mentioned in Chapter 5 (Greenwald et al., 1998).

The IAT is a measure of reaction time, in which participants are asked to push one of two buttons as quickly as possible, depending on which of four concepts is displayed to them. To understand how this works, imagine that, as a research participant, you are shown a series of playing cards and asked to push button A if a heart or diamond is displayed, or button B if a spade or club is displayed. This should be easy, because hearts and diamonds are both red, and spades and clubs are both black, and you can use either attribute to decide correctly. Now imagine being asked to push button A if a heart or spade is displayed, or button B if a club or diamond is displayed. For most people, this would be more difficult because color no longer helps.[9] The idea is that when two closely associated categories (e.g., heart–red) share the same button, responding will be easy and quick. If two categories that are less associated or that conflict with each other share the button (e.g., heart–black), then responding will be more difficult and slower. Greenwald creatively used this principle to measure the strength of associations in an individual's cognitive system of which the individual might not be conscious (Greenwald & Farnham, 2000).

SELF-ESTEEM

In a study of *implicit self-esteem*, the four concepts were "good," "bad," "me," and "not me." Before the study started, the experimenter obtained 18 self-descriptive words from each subject ("me") and 18 words each participant considered not self-descriptive ("not me"). The experimenter also assembled separate lists of pleasant ("good") words (e.g., diamond, health, sunrise) and unpleasant ("bad") words (agony, filth, poison). Now the study could begin. In the first part, the participant was asked to push button A if a "me" word or a "good" word is displayed, and B if a "not me" word or a "bad" word is displayed. In the second part, the pairings were switched. Now the participant pushed button A if a "me" word or "bad" word was displayed, and button B if a "not me" word or a "good" word was displayed.[10]

The logic is that, for someone with high self-esteem, reactions should be easier and quicker in the first part of the study than the second: See something self-relevant or good, push A—that's easy. But the second part should be harder, and slower: See something self-relevant or bad; that requires one to slow down and think a bit. The reason is that, for someone with high self-esteem, "good" and "me" are implicitly associated in the cognitive unconscious, as are "bad" and "not me." Now, what about someone with low self-esteem? For them, the me/good and not-me/bad associations might be weaker or even reversed. If this is true, then the difference in a participant's reaction time between the two parts of the experiment might measure that person's "implicit" self-esteem—someone with higher self-esteem should

---

[9] Greenwald and his colleagues point out that for an experienced bridge player, this might also be easy, because hearts and spades are the higher-ranking suits.

[10] The procedure also includes other kinds of counterbalancing to make sure, for example, that the A and B buttons are used equally for the various possible combinations of stimuli.

react more quickly in the first part relative to the second part; reaction times for someone with lower self-esteem should have a smaller difference, or even show the reverse effect.

It worked! It turned out implicit self-esteem—and other implicit attributes of the self such as stereotypes and attitudes—could be measured in this way. The measure was reliable, predicted responses to success and failure, and, perhaps most interesting of all, related only weakly to more traditional S-data measures of declarative self-esteem. Further research suggests that when one's implicit self-esteem is lower than one's declarative self-esteem, this can indicate the kind of fragile self-view associated with narcissism (Zeigler-Hill, 2006).

SHYNESS

On a conscious level, a person might be able to say, "I am shy," or "I am not shy," with some degree of validity. On a less conscious or even an unconscious level, a shy person might automatically tend to associate various ideas differently than a nonshy person would—a form of implicit knowledge of one's own shyness. These two kinds of self-knowledge are not quite equivalent, as was demonstrated in a study that assessed shyness using conventional self-reports along with the IAT, described earlier (Asendorpf et al., 2002). The first measure assessed the degree to which subjects explicitly, consciously knew and said they were shy. The second measure was designed to assess the degree to which they implicitly, unconsciously knew they were shy. The two measures correlated somewhat, but they predicted behavior differently. The S-data measure of shyness predicted what the authors called "controlled" behavior such as speech and gestures, while the IAT measure better predicted "spontaneous expressions of shyness" such as facial expressions, body movements, and tense body posture (Asendorpf et al., 2002, p. 386). The researchers concluded that some self-relevant behavior is under conscious control and some is not. To predict the first kind of behavior, S-data measures are sufficient, but to predict the second kind, B data seem to be necessary.

These findings show that we may have attitudes and feelings about many things, including ourselves, of which we are not entirely conscious, but which nonetheless can influence our emotions and behaviors, perhaps without our even knowing why. To the extent this is true—and it does seem to be true to some extent—then some of the cognitive patterns that guide our behavior are deeply embedded indeed.

Conscious and Unconscious Self-Consciousness

Another sense in which the self has a secret life is that its influence on behavior may not always be available to conscious awareness.

The traditional view of self-consciousness is that it amounts to awareness of who one is and what one is doing. A self-conscious person in a social interaction might spend so much cognitive capacity worrying about the impression she is making that little is left for actually holding a conversation, as we saw in Chapter 16. In a more positive light, it has also been suggested (and experimentally demonstrated) that people who are self-conscious in the sense that they know themselves well are more self-directed in their behavior (Carver, 1975). That is, their behavior is more likely to be guided by their general attitudes and values than by immediate situational pressures.

Another way self-consciousness might not be completely conscious is that some people may automatically tend to process information as relevant to their selves, even if it is not. A remarkable study that you may recall from Chapter 2 demonstrated this possibility (Hull et al., 2002). First, college-age subjects were measured as to their degree of self-consciousness using the Private Self-Consciousness Scale (Fenigstein, Scheier, & Buss, 1975). Then they were asked to unscramble sentences that, in the critical condition, included words relevant to stereotypes of the elderly: *gray*, *wise*, *bingo*, *forgetful*, *lonely*, *retired*, *wrinkle*, and (my favorite) *Florida*. After this, the subjects were excused and then covertly timed as they walked down the laboratory hallway (Hull et al., 2002, p. 408). It turns out that after this procedure, the highly self-conscious participants walked away more slowly—it took them about 2.2 seconds longer to walk a distance of 15.9 meters—whereas, the elderly-relevant words had no effect on the walking speed of participants low on self-consciousness. The investigators noted that the sentence task had no relevance to the participants' selves—but that highly self-conscious individuals apparently processed them as if they did, with the result that they subsequently walked more slowly. By contrast, the less self-conscious participants did not process the words as self-relevant, so the words had no

---

[11] The experiment also included a control condition in which participants worked with neutral words not relevant to stereotypes. In this condition, participants high and low in self-consciousness did not differ in walking speed.

effect on their behavior."¹¹ The moral of this story is that highly self-conscious people may tend to respond to everything as if it is personally relevant, and the effects of this tendency on their behavior may not even be conscious.

Acquiring and Changing Procedural Knowledge

Can the procedural self—or selves—be changed? The answer is yes, but implicit knowledge and associated behavioral patterns consist of procedural knowledge, not declarative knowledge, so changing them requires more than advice, lectures, or even well-meaning, conscious intentions to change. Procedural knowledge can be acquired or changed only by doing, specifically through practice and feedback.

Consider how one learns to think (assuming one ever does). A number of colleges now have courses on "How to Think," where instructors explain the rules of logic, describe tactics for organizing thinking, teach brainstorming methods, and so on. I am not a big fan of these courses because I believe all college courses ought to teach you how to think—by giving you something to think *about*. You then formulate ideas and get feedback on them (such as the instructor or a fellow student saying, "Good!" or "Very interesting!"). You learn to think with practice and feedback, the same way you learn how to do anything else.

Similarly, an athletic coach motivates practice and provides useful feedback. Teachers of singing, dancing, violin playing, and other forms of procedural knowledge play the same role as coaches. And, in some cases, a psychotherapist trying to help you change your behavior patterns may work the same way. First, the therapist must motivate his clients to practice their desired behavior change. (Don't contradict your mother every time she says something you disagree with; practice this restraint as often as possible.) Second, the therapist must provide feedback on how the clients are doing.

This teaching method points to a big difference between declarative and procedural knowledge. The first can be taught by reading or listening to lectures, the second only through practice and feedback. The first requires a teacher who is good at what is being taught; you cannot learn Russian history from somebody who does not know the topic. But you can learn to sing from somebody whose own voice is hoarse, or learn to bat from a middle-aged coach with slow reflexes and a beer gut. You might even get some help developing your personality from someone who has not yet worked out all of his own personal problems.

Which brings us back to how one acquires, and might be able to change, procedural knowledge about social behavior and the self. A style of responding to authority figures with fear, or of expecting and (mis)remembering repeated social rejection, has roots in bitter experience and was not created in a day. Undoing these learning experiences is not easy, therefore; verbal exhortation and even willpower are unlikely to be enough. The person, perhaps with help (professional or otherwise), must have the courage to change the relevant behavior and slowly but (hopefully) surely, begin to accumulate countervailing experiences that eventually generate a new behavioral style and outlook on life.

And, let us not forget that not all patterns of transference, or of characteristic perception and behavior, are maladaptive. A child fortunate enough to grow up in a supportive and encouraging environment may develop a resilient attitude that will help her to bounce back from defeat, rejection, or whatever other disappointments life might have in store. Whether it be explicit or implicit, a strong and consistent self-concept that is not easily changed is not necessarily a bad thing.

HOW MANY SELVES?

According to some theorists, you have not one declarative and procedural self, but many selves. For example, according to one theory, the particular subset of selves that is active in working memory and has conscious and unconscious effects on behavior at any given moment depends on where you are and who you are with (Markus & Kunda, 1986). In this way, your experience of yourself may shift from moment to moment. You might feel (and act) like a student, then like a parent, and then like a hard worker, as the situation and the people in it continue to change.

This view of the continuously changing self is called the *working self-concept* (Markus & Kunda, 1986). A particularly important influence on your working self-concept at a particular moment is the person you are with (Ogilvie & Ashmore, 1991; Andersen & Chen, 2002). You may have a different image of yourself—and act differently—when you are with your parents than when you are with your boyfriend or girlfriend. You may also find that, with some people, you become tense and irritable, and turn into someone you do not particularly like. With other people, you find yourself relaxed and charming, becoming someone you wish you could be all the time. (You should try to spend as much time as possible with this second kind of per-

"I know what I said ten minutes ago. That was the old me talking."

son.) The theory behind the working self-concept claims that you are characterized by not one but many selves. In different situations with different people, different selves come into play.

This view seems reasonable, but it has its problems. One major problem is that a unitary and coherent sense of self is generally viewed as a hallmark of mental health. Not knowing who you are, or feeling that your identity is constantly in flux, is a symptom of mental illnesses such as borderline personality disorder (see Chapter 18), and may result from traumatic experiences such as sexual abuse (Westen, 1992). People undergoing major transitions, such as the changes that occur during adolescence, suffer in part because they begin to lose their sense of having a single self that feels real in all the situations they encounter. By contrast, as was noted in Chapter 6, judgable people not only tend to present the same self in every situation, they are also judged by others as stable, well organized, and psychologically well adjusted (Colvin, 1993b).

The idea of multiple selves has also been criticized on philosophical grounds. One of the most important of the cognitive social-learning personality theorists discussed in Chapter 15, Albert Bandura (1999), argues that psychologists should reject "the fractionation of human agency into multiple selves" (p. 194) for two reasons. First, he notes, "a theory of personality cast in terms of multiple selves plunges one into deep philosophical waters" (p. 194). It seems to require one self that decides which self is appropriate for a given situation, and perhaps another self beyond that to decide which self should decide which self is currently relevant. Another difficulty with the idea of multiple selves is that it raises the following, perhaps unanswerable, question:

Once one starts fractionating the self, where does one stop? For example, an athletic self can be split into an envisioned tennis self and a golfing self. These separable selves would, in turn, have their subselves. Thus, a golfing self can be subdivided into different facets of the athletic ability to include a driving self, a fairway self, a

sand-trapped self, and a putting self. How does one decide where
to stop fractionating selves? (Bandura, 1999, p. 194)

Bandura's point is that there is no way to decide. Although we may seem like
different people in different situations or different company, each of us is,
in the end, one person. It is both more parsimonious and philosophically
coherent, he believes, to assume that one self interprets experience and
decides what to do next.

THE *REALLY* REAL SELF

As Bandura observed, beneath all of the real, ideal, ought, and relational
selves, it still seems that deep down, a single self must be running the whole
show. But how is this possible? All day long, and throughout our lives, we
move from situation to situation, from one relationship partner to another,
and through different stages of learning and aging. The fact that we inevitably
become different people as a function of these changes is the basis of the idea
that people have variable or even multiple selves. So what stays the same?

Years ago, my grandmother, then in her late 80s, told a little story that
has stuck with me ever since. She recalled being a teenager around the turn
of the (20th) century riding the El (elevated) train in Chicago. One day, she
watched an "old lady" (who was probably much younger than she was when
she told the story) shuffle slowly on board. "I remember wondering," she
said, "what must it feel like to be that *old*?"

"Well," she continued cheerfully, "now I know. It feels just the same.
Except, you're older."

I don't think my grandmother ever read anything by William James—
she never even went to high school—but I do think she and James had the
same view of the core, unchanging self. External appearances, attitudes, and
behaviors change across situations and over time, but the one who does the
experiencing is still in there someplace, watching (and perhaps directing)
everything. As James wrote, "the *I* is unaltered as the *me* is changed" (1890,
p. 378).

Is the "I" in this sense simply a passive bystander—an "epiphenome-
non," as the philosophers would call it—that seems to exist but cannot actually influence anything? Or is this inner, hidden, and unchanging observer
the *really* real self, perhaps even the "soul," and the basis of free will? This
question is probably too deep—and may be too unscientific—for a psychology book. But it is worth thinking about.

SUMMARY

- According to William James, the self includes the *me*, the object of self-knowledge, and the *I*, the mysterious entity that does the knowing. Psychology has much more to say about the *me* than the *I*.

The Self Across Cultures

- Some cross-cultural analyses have concluded that the idea of the "self" is a Western cultural artifact; other research has compared the ways the self is conceptualized in different cultures, including issues of self-regard and self-determination.

The Contents of the Self

- In terms of the *me*, the self comprises everything we know, or think we know, about what we are like, including both declarative and procedural self-knowledge.

The Declarative Self

- The declarative self includes self-esteem, one's opinion of one's own worth. Self-esteem can cause problems when it is too low *or* too high because, according to Leary's sociometer theory, it serves as a useful gauge of one's social standing.

- Psychologists theorize that the wide range of knowledge one has about one's psychological attributes is located in a cognitive structure called the *self-schema*. The self-schema can be assessed via S data (e.g., questionnaires, including traditional personality questionnaires such as the CPI) or B data (e.g., reaction-time studies).

- Case studies of brain-damaged individuals suggest that one's sense of self and personality can remain intact even when all the specific memories that created it are lost.

- A good way to remember something is to consider what it has to do with one's self; this effect on memory is called the self-reference effect.

- Your view of your own capabilities—your self-efficacy—influences what you will attempt to do.

- The psychologist Carol Dweck theorizes that beliefs about the self are a major foundation of personality, that they affect what a person will do in life, and that they can be changed.

- Discrepancies between one's real self and ideal self can lead to depression, whereas discrepancies between one's real self and ought self can lead to anxiety.

- The Realistic Accuracy Model (RAM) described in Chapter 6 can be used to explain the basis of self-knowledge, especially at the relevance, detection, and utilization stages.

The Procedural Self

- Aspects of the procedural self are not typically available to conscious awareness, but they can still drive behavior by means of deeply ingrained styles of thinking, feeling, and relating to others.

- One theory about the procedural self is the notion of relational selves, the habitual ways one interacts with different kinds of people.

- Implicit selves—notions of what we are like that affect our behavior but of which we may not consciously aware—can be measured through an instrument called the Implicit Association Test (IAT).

- Even self-consciousness may sometimes operate unconsciously, and some highly self-conscious people are especially likely to be affected by information that is potentially relevant to the self without realizing the effect. Implicit shyness affects different behaviors than the shyness of which we are consciously aware.

- The procedural self—or selves—can probably be changed slowly only, through practice and feedback, as with other procedural knowledge.

How Many Selves?

- While many theorists suggest that individuals have changing or even multiple selves, a constant sense of self is a hallmark of psychological health, and the social learning theorist Albert Bandura has pointed out that the idea of multiple selves raises philosophical difficulties.

The Really Real Self

- The inner observer that William James called the *I* appears to be the part of the self that remains constant across situations and throughout life.

THINK ABOUT IT

1. Is what William James called "the *I*" something that psychologists can study? How do we know whether it even exists?

2. Do you know anyone who has too little or too much self-esteem? How do you think this came about? Is it due to how this person was raised, to societal influences, or to some other factor?

3. How well do you think most people know themselves? What aspects of one-self are the hardest to know?

4. Do your beliefs about yourself affect what you do? Can these beliefs be changed? How?

5. The workings of the implicit self are described in this chapter in terms of relational selves, self-esteem, shyness, and self-consciousness. In what other areas do you think the implicit self might be important?

6. Can the self—its declarative part or its procedural part—be changed? Has your view of yourself ever changed? How did that come about? What kinds of experiences can change a person's self-image?

7. Is James's idea of the *I* the same as what psychologists now call the procedural self, or is the *I* something deeper?

SUGGESTED READING

Wilson, T. D. (2002). *Strangers to ourselves: Discovering the adaptive unconscious.* Cambridge, MA: Harvard University Press.

> *A lively survey of a wide range of research that explains why knowing ourselves is more difficult than we might think, and includes pointers on how to know yourself better.*

EMEDIA

 **Go to StudySpace, wwnorton.com/studyspace,** to access additional review and enrichment materials.

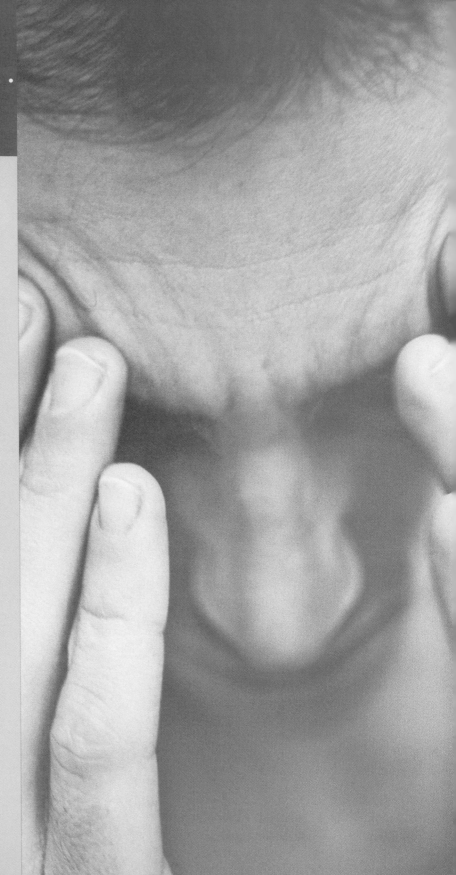

DISORDERS OF PERSONALITY

A neurosis simply emphasizes and throws into excessive relief the characteristic traits of a personality.

—CARL JUNG

IF THIS BOOK has a single, unifying theme, it is this: People are different. Every individual thinks, feels, and acts in distinctive ways. The entire field of personality psychology is an effort to specify how and explain why. The trait approach (Chapters 4 through 7) addresses individual differences more explicitly than any other, but as you have seen, biological research (Chapters 8 and 9), psychoanalytic approaches (Chapters 10 through 12), humanistic interpretations (Chapter 13), cultural psychology (Chapter 14), and even learning theories and descriptions of cognitive processes (Chapters 15 through 17)—all seek to outline the ways in which people are different from each other and to explain the causes of these differences.

It is good that people are different. Life would certainly be boring and even lose much of its meaning if everyone thought, felt, and acted the same. But it is also true that the variations in individual personality we celebrate sometimes go too far. For some people, aspects of their personality become so extreme as to cause problems for them or for others who must deal with them. When this happens, psychologists begin to speak of patterns of thought, feeling, and behavior beyond the normal range of psychological variation, patterns referred to as **personality disorders**.

In general, personality disorders manifest as configurations of traits considered "socially undesirable," meaning that most people don't like them. Patterns of behavior such as social awkwardness, suspiciousness, arrogance, whininess, and just plain strangeness, when taken to extremes, begin to shade into the range that might reasonably be characterized as a disorder. But it is difficult to specify the point beyond which a normal, if perhaps annoying or even self-defeating, degree of a personality trait becomes a full-fledged psychopathological symptom. In fact, finding an *exact* point may well be impossible. But this does not mean personality disorders are not real and important. Aspects of personality that cause severe problems for the affected individual or others who know that person can be identified, and it is rather likely that you could name a few people to whom this applies. Indeed, one recent survey estimates that about 15 percent of all adult Americans have at least one personality disorder (B. F. Grant et al., 2004), and there is no reason to think that the prevalence is much less elsewhere in the world.

THE *DIAGNOSTIC AND STATISTICAL MANUAL*

As long ago as the early 1800s, the pioneering French psychiatrist Philippe Pinel identified what he called *manie sans delire* (madness without distortion of reality), and for many years psychiatrists and psychologists discussed and sometimes attempted to treat people who, while not exactly insane, had unusual combinations of personality traits that got them into trouble. In 1952, the American Psychiatric Association imposed some order on this discussion by publishing the first edition of the *DSM*, the *Diagnostic and Statistical Manual*, which included a list and description of what were seen as the major disorders of personality. The most recent edition, the *DSM-IV-TR* (American Psychiatric Association, 2000), is considered the standard reference on the subject.[1] It lists the primary indicators for each disorder and specifies how many are required to make a diagnosis. For example, nine primary indicators or characteristics are listed for borderline personality

---

[1] The *DSM-IV-TR* (where TR stands for "text revision"), published in 2000, is a relatively minor update of the fourth edition of the *Diagnostic and Statistical Manual* (*DSM-IV*) issued in 1994. I will hereafter refer to the two editions together simply as the *DSM-IV*, and refer to the manual in general, across all editions, as the *DSM*. A similar system, the *International Statistical Classification of Diseases and Related Health Problems* (*ICD-10*), developed by the World Health Organization, is widely used in Europe and countries around the world. Revisions of both documents have attempted to make the two systems compatible so that every diagnosis has parallel categories in both (*DSM-IV-TR*, 2000).

disorder, and to receive the official diagnosis, an individual needs to exhibit any five.

The succeeding editions of the *DSM* have two purposes. The first is an effort to make psychological diagnosis more objective. Two clinical psychologists or psychiatrists cannot even talk about a patient, much less come to a mutual understanding, unless they have a common vocabulary for describing his problem. The hope of the *DSM* is that a precise list of criteria for diagnosis will make discussions and understanding clearer and more useful. This goal of objectivity is even more important for research. If a scientist believes that she has developed a promising treatment or a medication for a disorder, then there is no way to test the treatment or medication without a clear way to identify who has the disorder in the first place.

The second purpose for the *DSM* may sound trivial, but it is not. The *DSM* gives the psychiatrist or clinical psychologist something to write on the insurance billing form! Go ahead and chuckle, but I am not joking. Insurance providers will not reimburse for the care of something that is not specified. Your primary care physician is not permitted to write on your chart that you came in because you were "sick." Something a bit more descriptive is required. So, too, if psychological treatment is going to be paid for—which is the same as saying, if it is to be offered at all—then categories of psychological disorders must be specified. The *DSM* can be and has been criticized on many grounds, but lack of comprehensiveness is usually not among them. The 943 pages of the latest edition provide a label and a numerical code for a long list of things that could conceivably go wrong with a person, psychologically speaking.

The book is organized around five basic groups, or *axes* (see Figure 18.1). **Axis I disorders** include severe psychopathologies, such as schizophrenia, depression, and other major mental illnesses that can, in some cases, require hospitalization; a large section of the book discusses these disorders. **Axis II disorders** include the personality disorders. Axis III lists physical conditions that might be related to the patient's mental health, which can range from injuries and poisoning to brain diseases such as Alzheimer's that impair mental functioning. Axis IV includes stressors in the patient's social life such as unemployment, bereavement, or a recent divorce. Axis V is used to assess the patient's current ability to function self-sufficiently, including

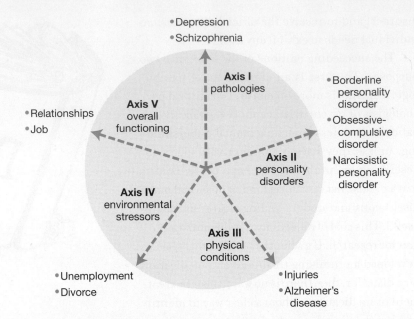

• Depression
• Schizophrenia

• Borderline
  personality
  disorder
• Obsessive-
  compulsive
  disorder
• Narcissistic
  personality
  disorder

• Relationships
• Job

Axis I
pathologies

Axis V
overall
functioning

Axis II
personality
disorders

Axis IV
environmental
stressors

Axis III
physical
conditions

• Unemployment
• Divorce

• Injuries
• Alzheimer's
  disease

Figure 18.1 Psychological Evaluation With the *DSM-IV* A complete evaluation of a client's psychological state is given in terms of five dimensions, or axes, which include assessments of psychopathology, personality disorder, physical health, environmental stressors, and the ability to function in daily life.

whether she can hold a job or maintain a relationship. A complete workup of a psychiatric patient in terms of the *DSM* includes ratings on all five axes.

Taken as a whole, the *DSM-IV* describes an amazing variety of patterns of thought, feeling, and behavior. These patterns include drug addiction, physical abuse, sexual deviations, and some specific (and, frankly, odd) categories such as *frotteurism* (the urge to seek erotic stimulation by rubbing up against people in crowded buses, billing code 302.89), *fugue state* (traveling abroad under an assumed identity, billing code 300.13), and even coffee nerves (billing code 305.90, the official term is *caffeine intoxication*). It is easy—maybe a little too easy—to make fun of some of the categories in the *DSM-IV*, and some writers have been unable to resist the temptation (see e.g., Davis, 1997, who wrote an amusing article that mocks the diagnoses I just cited). Examples such as these may be the price for attempting to be comprehensive, and even this long list apparently fails to capture everything. One of the most common diagnoses reached in clinical practice is PDNOS, or *personality disorder not otherwise specified*, which means a personality disorder that somehow fell between the cracks of all the ones that are actually listed (Verheul, Bartak, & Widiger, 2007). Still, and despite its shortcomings, the *DSM* stands as the indispensable reference for the practice of psychiatry and clinical psychology.

DEFINING PERSONALITY DISORDERS

Personality disorders have five general characteristics. All personality disorders are (1) unusual, and (2) by definition, tend to cause problems. In addition, most but not quite all personality disorders (3) affect social relations, and (4) are stable over time. Finally, (5) in some cases, the person who has a personality disorder may see it not as a disorder at all, but a basic part of who he or she is.

Unusually Extreme and Problematic

The two defining features of personality disorders were described by the pioneering psychiatrist Kurt Schneider (1923). The first is that a person exhibits an *unusually extreme* degree of one or more attributes of personality. It is important that the variation not only be extreme, but also unusual, especially considering the individual's cultural context. Thus, cutting somebody off in traffic on a Southern California freeway is an extreme behavior—it can be life-threatening for everyone involved—but it probably does not qualify as a symptom of personality disorder simply because it is (sadly) much too common. More seriously, clinical practice is just beginning to come to terms with the implications of cultural variations (see Chapter 14) for understanding abnormal psychology. For example, patterns of shy, self-effacing behavior or loud, aggressive behavior that otherwise could be viewed as symptoms of personality disorders might, in fact, be typical within certain cultures. Similarly, a normal child-rearing practice within one culture may seem harsh, and even draw the attention of the child protection authorities, if the neighbors notice it in a different cultural context. Recall the Danish mother, described in Chapter 14, who left her baby in a stroller parked outside a New York restaurant. Should she seek psychological treatment?

> Cutting somebody off in traffic on a Southern California freeway is an extreme behavior—it can be life-threatening for everyone involved—but it probably does not qualify as a symptom of a personality disorder simply because it is (sadly) much too common.

As we saw in Chapter 10, Freud firmly believed that the extremes on any dimension were pathological and that sanity always lies somewhere in the middle. This idea may offer a way to separate out what is extreme in a pathological way from something that is extreme only in relation to the practices of a particular culture. Extremism requires the denial of reality. We see this frequently in politics, where in order to occupy an extreme position it is necessary to deny any possibility that people who disagree with you could possibly be correct in any way. Similarly, extreme styles of behavior may stem from denying the reality that some people are trustworthy, that other people are worthy of respect, or even that oneself is actually, potentially loveable. So perhaps we can revise this first criterion a bit, to recognize that the extreme behavior is a sign of disorder if it stems, on some level, from a denial of reality.

The second fundamental criterion for a personality disorder is that the associated extreme behavioral pattern causes major problems for the person *or* for others. A personality disorder typically—not always—causes some degree of suffering for the person who has it, which may include anxiety, depression, and confusion. But in the case of several disorders, many and perhaps most of the associated problems are suffered not so much by the affected person, but by those—such as spouses, employers, and (former) friends—who must deal with the results (Heim & Westen, 2005; Yudofsky, 2005). For example, an acquaintance with antisocial personality disorder may blithely steal money from you, and while this is a problem for you, it is not really a problem for the acquaintance—unless he is caught.

Social, Stable, and Ego-Syntonic

Personality disorders have three other characteristics, which, while not as fundamental as the two criteria just discussed, are generally viewed as part of the pattern. First, personality disorders are *social*; they manifest in interactions with other people. Alone on a desert island, it would be difficult to do anything symptomatic of a personality disorder. After all, how can you be inflexible in your relations with a palm tree? How can you misperceive the intentions of a coconut? Other people are required for the full expression of many psychological symptoms.

Second, personality disorders are, by the usual definition, *stable*. They may first become visible in adolescence or even childhood and persist throughout life. Change can occur, but generally the time scale is years rather than weeks or months (Zanarini, 2008). Personality disorders are about as stable as personality itself (Durbin & Klein, 2006). This stability contrasts with the more severe Axis I disorders, which may come and go through acute phases and stages of remission much like medical conditions. Less extreme maladaptive patterns of thought, feeling, and behavior that turn out to be temporary—the familiar combination of anxiety and hostility sometimes exhibited in adolescence, for example—also are generally not considered personality disorders. Because personality disorders are stable, they are (of course) difficult to change through therapeutic intervention or any other means.

Third, and relatedly, personality disorders can be **ego-syntonic**, which means the people who have them do not think anything is wrong. People who suffer from Axis I disorders generally experience their symptoms of confusion, depression, or anxiety as **ego-dystonic** afflictions of which they would like to be cured. The same is true of at least some people with Axis II personality disorders, who may be distressed by the feelings associated with their disorder, or feel alienated from their own behavior—they may report that the way they act "isn't really me." For a surprising number of people with certain Axis II disorders, in contrast, their symptoms feel like normal and even valued aspects of their personalities. Individuals with the attributes of the paranoid, histrionic, antisocial, or narcissistic personality disorders, in particular, typically do not think they have a problem. They are more likely to see a disorder in the people who have problems with *them*. And the problems they cause others may be as serious, or even more serious, than the problems they cause themselves (Yudofsky, 2005).

This last characteristic implies, again, that therapists who treat personality disorders often have a tough hill to climb. My university operates an assistance program that is intended, among other purposes, to help employees who have psychological problems that interfere with their work. When I was chair of my department, I went to a presentation by the director of this program. He begged any supervisor making a referral to *please* call him first and let him know why. He was having difficulties because employees would suddenly appear at his office. He would ask them what the problem was, and they would reply, "I don't know; everything is fine." Individuals with personality disorders say things like that surprisingly often, even while causing havoc for themselves and the people around them.

THE MAJOR PERSONALITY DISORDERS

The *DSM-IV* lists 10 major disorders that describe patterns of personality so extreme that they can cause serious problems. These problems are of three main sorts. Personality disorders can make a person feel miserable, lead to patterns of behavior that cause trouble for the people who come into contact with the person with the disorder, and be associated with such a degree of confused thinking that the person risks losing contact with reality. While all personality disorders have all three of these characteristics to some degree, the most prominent aspect of each disorder can, I believe, be sorted into one of these three categories. The *dependent*, *avoidant*, and *obsessive-compulsive* personality disorders are associated with emotional upset, fear, and anxiety. The *paranoid*, *histrionic*, *antisocial*, and *narcissistic* personality disorders are associated with patterns of behavior that interfere with social relationships, and can make a person difficult to be around and in some cases even dangerous. The *schizotypal*, *schizoid*, and *borderline* personality disorders are serious mental problems characterized by severely confused thinking and lack of contact with reality.

In the sections that follow, I summarize how each of these 10 disorders is described and diagnosed, and discuss in detail one disorder from each of the three groupings: obsessive-compulsive (as an example of a disorder of unhappiness and anxiety), narcissistic (a disorder in relating to others), and borderline (a disorder of thinking and unreality). The chapter then explains how personality disorders are diagnosed and organized, and proceeds to a discussion of the meaning and implications of labeling people with personality disorders.

Disorders of Unhappiness and Anxiety

Three personality disorders are characterized by emotional and behavior patterns of insecurity, fear, anxiety, and general unhappiness.

DEPENDENT PERSONALITY DISORDER

Independence and decisiveness are generally viewed as desirable attributes, but not everybody can achieve them. Some people prefer to have their needs taken care of by others, and even for others to make their major (or minor) life decisions, ranging from what job to accept to which shirt to wear. When this pattern becomes extreme and causes problems, it may lead to a diagnosis of **dependent personality disorder**. People with this disorder typically rely heavily—too heavily—on a parent, sibling, or spouse to take care of everything, and this reliance goes beyond anything that might be reasonable due to age, illness, or physical handicap. Because of their utter dependence, they may exhibit a submissive interpersonal style. They are afraid to disagree with anybody about anything, because they fear having to think or even exist on their own. At the same time, a bitter, resentful edge to their behavior may be detectable just under the surface. They don't *really* agree with you, after all; they are just afraid to say that they don't, because then you might not take care of them. This conflict resembles the neurotic push and pull between love and hate described by Melanie Klein and the object relations theorists (Chapter 12).

As the *DSM-IV* notes, patterns of "passivity, politeness, and deferential treatment" are characteristic of some cultures, so such behaviors must be considered in context. If culturally normal, then such characteristics aren't signs of a disorder. The *DSM-IV* further notes that dependent personality disorder "is among the most frequently reported" (*DSM-IV-TR*, 2000, p. 723) on the list, but more recent data suggest that it is fairly rare, found in only one-half of 1 percent of the population (B. F. Grant et al., 2004). The disorder is diagnosed more frequently in women.

AVOIDANT PERSONALITY DISORDER

Everybody feels inadequate sometimes. Sometimes we do things we shouldn't, sometimes we fail at what we attempt, and sometimes we are rejected. Moreover, none of these experiences is pleasant, and everybody seeks to avoid them. Fear of failure or rejection can lead to patterns of behavior such as shyness, and in moderation such patterns are both common and normal. When taken to an extreme, the result may be **avoidant personality disorder**. The fundamental problem experienced by individuals with this disorder is that their fear of failure, criticism, or rejection may lead them to avoid normal activities of school, work, and interactions with others. They expect the absolute worst from others: criticism, contempt, and rejection. They cannot join a group activity or have a relationship without constant reassurance that they will be uncritically accepted, and they may actively inhibit any emotional expression toward others because they fear being mocked and rejected. As a result, others cannot get close to them, and their interpersonal world is constricted. It is safer to stay at home with the blinds pulled and the phone off the hook.

This is very sad because, according to clinical psychologists who have studied people with this disorder, they really have deep cravings for affection and social acceptance, and they may spend much of their solitary time fantasizing about how much fun it would be to have friends or a lover. They may have trouble in their careers as well, because they seek to avoid the meetings and social functions central to the business world.

A recent survey estimates that about 2.5 percent of the population suffer (and here the word *suffer* does seem appropriate) from this disorder, and its prevalence appears to be about the same in women and in men (B. F. Grant et al., 2004). In some people, the disorder may begin as severe shyness in childhood and gradually improve as they grow into later adulthood.

OBSESSIVE-COMPULSIVE PERSONALITY DISORDER

It can be nice when the world is orderly and structured, and everybody follows the rules. Some people feel this need for order and structure more strongly than others (just peek into some of your professors' offices if you want to see how widely this trait can range), and individual differences are both common and perfectly normal. The problematic extreme is called **obsessive-compulsive personality disorder (OCPD)**.[2] People with OCPD are bound by rituals and rules, may become "workaholics" who work for work's sake, rather than necessarily to get anything really done, and are often miserly and stubborn. The individual who has OCPD resembles, in many ways, the type of person that Freud called the anal character (Chapter 10). The *DSM-IV* lists eight characteristics of this disorder, and the official criterion for diagnosis is the manifestation at least four of them.

1. **Overconcern With Rules and Details:** Obsessive-compulsive disorder may be manifested by a deep reverence for rules, organization, and details, to the point where the person may forget the real point of what she is doing. She may follow a rule so inflexibly as to make cruel decisions, like refusing to help someone in great need because of the principle that people should be self-sufficient. She may be organized to the point of absurdity, like the characters in Anne Tyler's novel *The Accidental Tourist* who store everything in their kitchen in alphabetical order (the oranges next to the oregano, and so forth). The

---

[2] OCPD is an Axis II personality disorder. The similarly labeled *obsessive-compulsive disorder (OCD)* is a severe anxiety disorder characterized by compulsive behaviors that can range from repetitive hand-washing to bizarre rituals of speech or action (e.g., needing to touch every surface with which one comes into contact exactly 11 times before moving on). The personality disorder, in contrast, is in a sense less severe, because it generally does not include such specific compulsions, but can be more far-reaching because it may affect all areas of a person's life. Interestingly, OCD may actually be more treatable than OCPD (Foa, 2004).

obsessive-compulsive may seek to stay clean beyond any reasonable degree of neatness or sanitation. She may notice some small flaw in a large project, such as the construction of a house, and feel that everything is ruined. Above all else, the person with OCPD lacks a sense of proportion, the big picture that allows one to judge when rules fail to apply to given situation or when a particular detail just doesn't matter very much.

> The person with OCPD lacks a sense of proportion, the big picture that allows one to judge when rules fail to apply to a given situation or when a particular detail just doesn't matter very much.

Biological investigations of the personality disorders, including OCPD, are not far advanced, but it is interesting to note some similarities between this characteristic and Antonio Damasio's case of Elliott, described in Chapter 8. You may recall that Elliott had brain surgery that severed connections between the frontal lobes and the motivational centers in the limbic system. He suffered a serious loss of judgment, especially the ability to discern the difference between things that matter and things that don't. There is little direct evidence that persons with OCPD are brain damaged, but cases like Elliott's may provide some hints for future research about possible biological underpinnings of this disorder.

2. **Perfectionism:** There is nothing wrong with wanting to do things as well as possible, but people with OCPD take this inclination to the degree that it causes severe problems, because they think nothing is ever good enough. This characteristic makes them difficult to work with (you would not want someone with OCPD as your boss), and it also makes it very difficult for them to finish anything. I know a talented artist who will work for weeks on a painting and then, just before it is finished, have to stop, tear the whole thing up, and start over because it's not perfect. There are many other people who find it terribly difficult to ever finish an assignment,

"Is the Itsy Bitsy Spider obsessive-compulsive?"

a term paper, or even a home improvement project because it is never quite right, and there is always one more thing to do. I confess I sometimes have a bit of a problem along these lines when working on this book. I revise each chapter many times, and there is always more to do—I know it's not perfect—so it is difficult to know when to stop. So here is my rule of thumb: When I find that in the latest draft I changed two or more things back to the way they were in the previous draft, it's time to move on.

3. **Workaholism:** People with OCPD are often stereotypical workaholics. They cannot take a weekend or even an evening off because they "have so much to do." And yet, strangely, they seldom seem to get much done. It does seem that the amount of time people spend working correlates only loosely with how much they accomplish, and while people with OCPD may work long hours, they often don't have much to show for it.

4. **Inflexibility:** People with OCPD have set ways of thinking and behaving and are not open to change. They apply values, ethics, and principles mindlessly rather than with an appreciation for context, and even considering bending the rules can make them anxious and even more rigid. The *DSM-IV* warns that this criterion must be interpreted in cultural context, because some cultural and religious traditions are quite rigid, and it would be unwise to characterize all their followers as suffering from a personality disorder. For example, the more fundamentalist wings of many religions tend to be quite literal minded and severe with anyone who deviates even slightly from the established dogma. The *DSM-IV* cautions that this kind of rigidity is not diagnosable as a disorder. I am not sure it's a good idea to be too culturally sensitive here, however; the absolute and inflexible adherence to any rule or principle is a bad practice.

5. **Packrat Behavior:** People with OCPD may be compulsively unable to throw anything away, even things with no possible use or sentimental value. They become very anxious about discarding anything because they cannot escape feeling that they just might need it someday, no matter how absurd the prospect is. There are famous cases of people with OCPD collecting huge piles of newspapers that fill their homes, unable to throw away even the sports section from 11 years ago, because they haven't had a chance to read it yet.

This idea of the person with OCPD as a packrat is an interesting characteristic, in part because it seems to contradict some of the others, such as point 1, which involves being compulsively neat and clean. This is where Freud comes in, though not through the pages of the *DSM-IV*, which never mentions him. You may recall (from Chapter 10) that Freud believed opposites in character and behavior were always equivalent at a deep level, and the anal character is a good example. Anal characters might be compulsively neat *or* compulsively messy; the underlying dynamics in both cases are the same. The heaps of junk that fill the houses of some people with OCPD, and the sterile, bare, sparkling surfaces in the nearly empty houses of other people with OCPD may result from the same underlying psychological dynamics.

6. **Inability to Delegate:** The person with OCPD has to do everything for himself, because nobody else can possibly do things right. There is one and only one way to wash a dish, mow a lawn, paint a wall, or even make a decision. People who work for bosses with this characteristic of OCPD spend a lot of time waiting for authorization for the most basic actions, because the boss cannot trust anybody to get it right.

7. **Miserliness:** People with OCPD hoard pennies against unlikely future catastrophes, and they may live way below their means. When you read about someone who dies in a tiny, cold mountain shack with $100,000 hidden under the mattress, this might well be someone who had OCPD.

8. **Rigidity and Stubbornness:** People with OCPD like to do things the same way time after time, day after day. A change in the breakfast menu may cause a mild panic attack, and any kind of change in routine makes them anxious. Attempts to get them to alter their habits or to change their mind about anything are likely to fall on deaf ears—even the contemplation of a change upsets them.

OCPD is difficult to treat through psychotherapy. This may be, in part, because its basis could be biological. I mentioned earlier some hints that brain structures, particularly connections between the frontal cortex and the limbic system, may be involved. Other tentative evidence suggests that OCPD in children may sometimes result from streptococcal infection (strep throat), though the mechanism by which this may happen is not understood (Murphy et al., 2004; A. O'Connor, 2004).

A psychological barrier to treatment is that, although people with OCPD are compulsively driven and may suffer from extreme anxiety if things do not go exactly their way, in some cases OCPD may be ego-syntonic. It is true that people with this disorder are—relatively speaking—less impaired in their daily functioning than are people with some of the other personality disorders (Skodol et al., 2002). Indeed, strange as it may sound, some people with OCPD claim to *like* being that way, and to some degree the traits associated with OCPD may be useful. There is something to be said for a surgeon, an accountant, or a data analyst who checks everything several times, whether it is really necessary or not. Certain kinds of mistakes become less likely. On the other hand, some of the compulsions that often go with OCPD—such as obsessive worrying about things that don't really matter, needing to turn back several times after leaving home to check whether the gas stove was left on, and bodily tics and habits such as compulsively picking at one's scalp—are unpleasant symptoms from which most people would like to be free.

According to one major survey, OCPD is the most common of the personality disorders, characterizing about 8 percent of the U.S. population (B. F. Grant et al., 2004), and males and females appear to be equally at risk. Antidepressant drugs such as Prozac and other specific serotonin reuptake inhibitors (SSRIs) of the sort discussed in Chapter 8 can effectively treat OCPD (Piccinelli, Pini, Bellantuono, & Wilkinson, 1995). This finding hints at the nature of OCPD and the degree to which it may be fundamentally driven by anxiety, depression, and general unhappiness.

Disorders in Relating With Others

Four of the personality disorders cause as many (if not more) problems for the people who come into contact with the disordered person as for the person with the diagnosis. This is because the disorders are characterized by patterns of social interaction that may be annoying, exploitative, or even in some cases dangerous.

PARANOID PERSONALITY DISORDER

Nobody wants to be taken advantage of, and everybody needs to be wary of persons who might threaten their finances, relationships, or occupational success. When this vigilance rises to the level of an obsession and interferes with normal relationships, the diagnosis of **paranoid personality disorder** may be appropriate. People with this disorder characteristically assume the worst, and may be quite skilled in identifying patterns of events and behaviors of others that "prove" they are being plotted against. They watch everyone closely, alert for the slightest sign of betrayal. If they detect disloyalty or disrespect, they may maintain a grudge for a very long time. Not surprisingly, they are reluctant to trust or confide in anyone. While they may appear calm, rational, and analytic, more often they come off as angry, stubborn, and bitter. They frequently become embroiled in lawsuits! They can also be physically dangerous. One experienced therapist says that when dealing with people who have this disorder, the first priority should be to ensure your own safety (Yudofsky, 2005).

Paranoid personality disorder is surprisingly common, with a major survey estimating that it afflicts almost 5 percent of the population (B. F. Grant et al., 2004), and it appears to be more common in women than in men.

HISTRIONIC PERSONALITY DISORDER

Some people naturally attract attention by speaking or acting dramatically, dressing flamboyantly, or even acting in a sexually seductive manner to seemingly everyone they meet. As part of the great mix of humanity, these people help make life interesting. But when taken to an extreme, these behavior patterns may form part of the **histrionic personality disorder**. The goal of people with this disorder is to always be the center of attention, an end they may achieve through behavior, physical appearance, or dress, such as parading about in scanty swimwear or sporting outrageous tattoos. Such individuals may vehemently express strong opinions that turn out not to have much basis; when asked to defend their views, they may lack the slightest idea what they really think and give the impression of having expressed the opinion just for effect. Similarly, they may express strong emotions of happiness, sadness, liking, or disliking that suddenly change or disappear. They may describe even casual acquaintances as "dear, dear friends" (*DMV-IV-TR*, 2000, p. 712), and in general consider their relationships closer than they really are.

Not surprisingly, people who have this disorder may have trouble being taken seriously; they are difficult to get along with, and they experience serious difficulties in their personal relationships and occupational life without understanding why. They also create difficulties for the other people in life, especially those with whom they form serious relationships. For example, someone with this disorder, through very direct styles of flirtation, may seduce, form a relationship with, or even end up marrying someone, only to discard him or her once "won" in order to seek attention from others.

The *DSM-IV* estimates that the prevalence of histrionic personality disorder is about 2 to 3 percent in the general population, though another, more recent survey puts the figure a bit lower, at less than 2 percent (B. F. Grant et al., 2004). The effect of gender is somewhat surprising: The pattern might seem in many ways stereotypically (over)feminine; however, the evidence indicates it is about equally common in men and women, though they may manifest it differently. For example, a woman may draw attention to herself through revealing clothing, while a man may project a "macho," hypermasculine image and brag about his athletic abilities.

ANTISOCIAL PERSONALITY DISORDER

Some people are more honest than others, but when deceit and manipulation become core aspects of an individual's way of dealing with the world, he may be diagnosed with **antisocial personality disorder**. This dangerous pattern includes behaviors such as vandalism, harassment, theft, and a wide variety of illegal activities such as burglary and drug dealing. It is closely associated with the trait of psychopathy, which was mentioned in Chapter 9 (e.g., Mealey, 1995). People with this disorder are impulsive, and engage in risky behaviors such as reckless driving, drug abuse, and dangerous sexual practices. They typically are irritable, aggressive, and irresponsible. The damage they do to others bothers them not one whit; they rationalize (see Chapter 11) that life is unfair; the world is full of suckers; and if you don't take what you want whenever you can, then you are a sucker too. At first impression, they may appear articulate and charming, but watch out. Children unlucky enough to come under the care of someone with this disorder are at high risk for neglect or abuse. A wide variety of negative outcomes may accompany this disorder, including unemployment, divorce, drug addiction, imprisonment, murder, and suicide.

Indeed, people with antisocial personality disorder can be highly dangerous. The serial killer Ted Bundy used his clean-cut good looks and well-developed social skills, combined with a fake cast on his arm, to persuade young women near college campuses to help him load a sofa into his van. When his victim was all the way in the van he would slam the door shut and drive off to a secluded spot where he could abuse, torture, and eventually kill her. In general, people with this disorder have an eye for people who are "nonsuspicious, kindly, and generous" (Yudofsky, 2005, p. 219), and are ruthless about exploiting them. It can be difficult to protect oneself from people with antisocial personality disorder, but one experienced therapist recommends that you "pay attention to your feelings," especially feelings like "*At first I felt uncomfortable, but I couldn't quite figure out why*" (Yudofsky, 2005, p. 220, italics in original). In other words, listen to your gut.

Figure 18.2 Ted Bundy This sadistic killer was an extreme example of antisocial personality disorder. His "normal," unthreatening physical appearance helped him to lure his victims.

The *DSM-IV*'s summary includes an interesting discussion of the apparent association of this disorder with low economic status and urban settings—in other words, it's largely (but not solely) a disorder of the poor and criminal. This observation raises several questions. Is it possible that antisocial personality disorder describes a behavioral style that is adaptive or even necessary in certain settings? If so, should it still be considered a psychological disorder? Should a person with this disorder who commits a crime be considered not really a criminal but only ill? I will return to this issue near the end of the chapter, but this is a good time to begin thinking seriously about the disadvantages, as well as advantages, of having a psychological label for every pattern of socially undesirable behavior.

The estimated prevalence of this disorder is about 3.5 percent overall, being much more common in men than in women (B. F. Grant et al., 2004), and many clinical psychologists believe it tends to fade away as a person gets older. After about age 30, it appears, people who have exhibited this pattern of dangerous and criminal behavior may finally start to mellow. This might be because levels of testosterone, which as we saw in Chapter 8 are sometimes associated with aggressive behavior, gradually decline with age.

NARCISSISTIC PERSONALITY DISORDER

In an ancient Greek myth, a youth named Narcissus falls in love with his own beauty, and pines away while staring at his reflection in a pool. In modern days, the term *narcissism* is used to refer to excessive self-love, which at problematic extremes becomes **narcissistic personality disorder**. Narcissism in this clinical sense is not quite the same thing as the trait of narcissism as discussed in Chapter 17. The "normal" trait is associated with extraversion and (excessive) confidence, whereas the clinical syndrome is characterized more by emotional instability and an unpleasant emotional life (J. D. Miller & Campbell, 2008). While diagnoses of full-fledged narcissistic personality disorder are rare, each of its characteristics will, I suspect, describe familiar tendencies that are present to some degree in more than a few people you know. The *DSM-IV* lists nine characteristics; to earn an official diagnosis an individual needs to display at least five of them.

1. **Grandiose Sense of Self-Importance:** The narcissist believes, sometimes against all evidence, that he is a superior being, and expects recognition. This expectation is not based on real achievements, though the narcissist may indeed have some. The point is that the narcissist expects recognition with or without a specific reason, and is, therefore, genuinely surprised, even a bit bewildered, whenever this recognition is not forthcoming. He does not understand why other people fail to acknowledge such obvious superiority, and is forced to conclude that other people are unperceptive, unappreciative, or just plain jealous.

2. **Preoccupation With Fantasies of Ultimate Attainment:** The narcissist walks around much of the day with a head full of visions of unlimited wealth, absolute power, flawless beauty, or perfect love. Such visions are pleasant to contemplate, but may lead the narcissist to become detached from what is really going on, and unrealistic about the goals that she expects to achieve.

3. **Belief That He Should Associate Only With Others Who Are "Special":** The myth of Narcissus comes to mind, because the narcissist seems to see his self-image reflected in those he associates with. Thus, the narcissist may feel that it is important to hang out only with people who are wealthy, famous, brilliant, or physically attractive. Did you know anyone in high school who considered it to be social death to be seen standing next to anyone who wasn't good-looking, athletic, or otherwise part of the campus elite? If so, then you have seen an illustration of one aspect of narcissism. Similarly, narcissists may be inordinately attracted to elite institutions such as famous universities, exclusive neighborhoods (notice the term "exclusive" requires that those who are nonspecial be excluded), and even the kind of nightclub that has a velvet rope line, a bouncer dressed in black, and stringent standards for entrance (mostly hav-

ing to do with appearance, wealth, and fame). In each case, the basis of the institution's appeal is not really the quality of the education, the pleasantness of the lifestyle, or the excitement of the entertainment. Rather, the attraction is that *most people can't get in*, which is irresistible to the narcissist.

4. **Requirement for Excessive Admiration:** The narcissist does not just expect to be admired by others; she needs it. To go very long without receiving praise is tough for a narcissist to bear, so she may maneuver to evoke it. The tactics are not necessarily subtle. The narcissist may say things like, "Don't you love my dress?" or "How about my great new car?" or simply brag about her accomplishments, wealth, friends, or appearance. She does not seem to have a clue about how obvious these contrivances generally are, and happily accepts the most transparent kinds of flattery. Tell the narcissist that her clothes, car, accomplishments, or haircut are the greatest you have ever seen. She will agree; you will not be suspected of insincerity.

   This need for constant praise suggests that the narcissist's seemingly high self-esteem is actually very fragile, even brittle (Kernberg, 1984; Vazire & Funder, 2006). Since it is not based on real accomplishment, the narcissist's grandiose self-image is always in danger of destruction, which she may implicitly sense. The narcissist needs a constant stream of praise, sincere or otherwise, to prop her up.

5. **Sense of Entitlement:** The narcissist expects special treatment. Rules apply to other people, as does the need to stand in line, wait one's turn, or be judged by consistent standards. The narcissist is shocked when he isn't treated as exceptional, and concludes that the authority is unjust, the service is terrible, or the grading system is unfair. After all, in a perfect world, the narcissist would be allowed to do anything, be waited on instantly, and receive A's in every course regardless of what he actually does.[3] Moreover, there appears to be no upper limit to the entitlement. Any service, gift, praise, recognition, or award is at best a down payment on what the narcissist truly deserves.

6. **Exploitation of Others:** Because of this sense of entitlement, the narcissist feels justified in taking advantage of others whenever pos-

---

[3] A student once wrote on a course evaluation form that I was too tough on students who chat during class. "We paid our fees," the student wrote, "and should talk in class if we want to." This student, who I doubt has narcissistic personality disorder, does, however, seem to be on the way to showing one of its symptoms.

sible. After all, the purpose is merely to get what she deserves anyway. She may blithely lie, cheat, or simply leave the hard work to be done by other people. If a narcissist is your roommate, she will expect you to wash the dirty dishes. She has much more important things to do. You don't.

7. **Lack of Empathy:** This exploitation is accompanied by a lack of empathy for others. Empathy is not called for, from the narcissist's point of view, because he is the only person on earth who really matters. The narcissist assumes that everything about him must be of great interest, and may offer lengthy and inappropriately detailed monologues about his activities or feelings. At the same time, the narcissist can be shockingly inconsiderate of the feelings of others, happily telling a former lover that "I am now in the relationship of a lifetime!" or bragging about how healthy he is, in front of someone who is ill (*DSM-IV-TR*, 2000, p. 715).

8. **Enviousness:** A further clue to the brittleness of the narcissist's self-esteem is her proneness to envy. The narcissist is acutely aware of small differences in prestige, wealth, or attractiveness, and simultaneously gloats over those she views as lower in these attributes— while seething with envy over those perceived as superior.

In many workplaces, employees are assigned offices—or cubicles, as the case may be—more or less randomly, some bigger than others. Some employees will then obsessively envy those with slightly larger workspaces, while inwardly gloating about their superiority over those with slightly smaller ones. Similarly, I used to work at a state university where salaries were officially on the public record. This meant that one copy of a thick computer printout with everybody's salary was stored at the library reference desk and available on request. On July 1 of every year, one of my colleagues was always first in line, so he could find out exactly who was making even slightly more money than he was, and who was making even slightly less. For the next few weeks, he appeared to think about—and talk about—little else.

> Just about everybody would like to be better looking, have a bigger office, and make more money. The clue to narcissism is the peculiar structure of these desires.

Of course, just about everybody would like to be better looking, have a bigger office, and make more money. The clue to narcissism is the peculiar structure of these desires; the true narcissist would actually be perfectly happy with a small office as long as everyone else's were smaller. Similarly, the narcissist's obsession with wealth has much less to do with how much money she needs or wants to spend than with a need to feel superior to others.

9. **Arrogant Behavior and Attitudes:** Narcissists are not generally difficult to spot. Their arrogance gives them away. They belittle others and brag about themselves. They are rude to service people, seeming to revel in their small (and temporary) degree of social superiority over waiters and cashiers. They are boastful about small (or nonexistent) accomplishments, and sarcastic and condescending about the virtues or accomplishments of anybody else.

There is something pitiable about narcissists, but they can be highly dangerous. As one experienced therapist writes:

Sadly, the combination of burning ambition and a willingness to distort the truth in people with narcissistic personality disorder can lead them to acquire substantial power and high position. These individuals harm many innocent people along the route to their personal aggrandizement. (Yudofsky, 2005, p. 126)

A fascinating, recently declassified psychological study of Adolf Hitler, commissioned by the OSS (the precursor to the CIA) during World War II and written by the pioneering personality psychologist Henry Murray (mentioned in Chapters 4 and 7), describes him as a textbook case of narcissistic personality disorder (Murray, 1943). Interestingly, this study was written before the formal identification of this disorder in the first *DSM*. Apparently, being a narcissist is not a bar to becoming powerful, and other infamous figures such as Mussolini and Stalin have also been characterized by this syndrome. The sense of self-importance and lack of empathy, coupled with impressive political skills, seems to have made these individuals utterly ruthless—and successful—in their drive for power. The results were disastrous for everyone around them (and ultimately, in the cases of Hitler and Mussolini, for themselves).[4]

It is also important to realize that, as mentioned in Chapter 17, narcissism is a trait, and varying levels of it occur within the normal range of personality (e.g., Raskin, Novacek, & Hogan, 1991; Robins & John, 1997). Even at levels too low to diagnose as a full-blown personality disorder, narcissism can have important, negative consequences (Paulhus & Williams, 2002). While narcissists may appear superficially charming and make a good first impression, over time their characteristic arrogance typically becomes self-defeating (Paulhus, 1998; Robins & Beer, 2001). According to one widely accepted theoretical approach, narcissists follow an ill-advised strategy for dealing with life in which they seek to defend an unrealistically inflated self-concept through means such as bragging, which are ultimately unsuccessful (Morf & Rhodewalt, 2001). More recent theorizing has expanded this explanation to include the observation that narcissists may be poor at controlling their impulses and unable to delay gratification (Vazire & Funder, 2006). That is, they desperately crave feelings of power, prestige, success, and glory. Rather than take the slow and difficult route to enjoying these feelings—such as by working hard or being courageous—they take a shortcut, and express feelings of superiority whenever they experience the need, regardless of whether these feelings have any basis. The result, as is so often the case with impulsiveness, is short-term gain and long-term loss. They feel better at the moment, but they alienate others and ultimately prevent the very success and admiration they so desperately crave.

Narcissistic personality disorder is infamous among clinical psychologists for being difficult if not impossible to treat. One reason may be that

---

[4]All three caused the deaths of millions of people. Hitler committed suicide, and Mussolini was publicly hanged. But Stalin died peacefully in bed.

the disorder has surprisingly deep roots. Signs of future adult narcissism can be detected as early as preschool. In one study, small children who were described by their teachers as highly active, emotionally overexpressive, antagonistic, impulsive, and needing to be the center of attention were relatively likely to show narcissistic tendencies years later (Carlson & Gjerde, 2009).

Another reason why narcissism is difficult to treat is that, more than any other personality disorder, narcissism is ego-syntonic. Narcissists generally will not acknowledge having any sort of problem. Others may wish them to change; they have no desire to do so. Moreover, as already noted, narcissists may make a good first impression. According to one recent study, their self-assured manner, flashy dress, humorous conversation, and even straight posture make them attractive to others (Back, Schmukle, & Egloff, in press). When problems arise for narcissists, they tend to do so over time— a long time. Another recent study found that narcissists suffered a slow but steady decline in mental health over a 42-year period (Cramer & Jones, 2008). According to the authors of this last-mentioned study, the long-term problem for narcissisists is that their well-being depends too much on being admired by others, rather than being based on "independent growth and accomplishment" (Cramer & Jones, 2008, p. 1148).

The *DSM-IV* estimates that less 1 percent of the population can be characterized with this disorder. Does this seem like an underestimate to you? The *DSM-IV* also claims that between half and three quarters of people with this disorder are male.

Disorders of Thinking and Lack of Contact With Reality

The hallmark of three major personality disorders is poor contact between mental life and external reality. Thinking may be confused, delusional, or even self-destructive.

SCHIZOTYPAL PERSONALITY DISORDER

Some people are idiosyncratic; they experience odd thoughts, have seemingly strange ideas, and behave unconventionally. For example, they may have superstitious beliefs; they may actively avoid black cats or believe they have ESP or the ability to see the future. They may wear odd and unkempt clothing, and espouse unique ideologies or "theories of everything." They may also experience discomfort in relating to other people—their odd actions might be somewhat off-putting, for one thing—and have particular difficulty in close relationships. None of these characteristics is especially rare, and taken one at a time they may not pose serious problems. But when the pattern becomes extreme, the individual may be characterized as having **schizotypal personality disorder**.

This disorder is characterized by odd and eccentric beliefs and behaviors, interpersonal awkwardness to the point of strangeness, and a discomfort with social interaction that only gets worse as interactions progress. At its extreme, this disorder can dangerously approach *schizophrenia*, a serious Axis I condition characterized by major distortions of reality, jumbled thinking, and even hallucinations; indeed, some psychologists believe that schizotypal personality disorder should be grouped with it, rather than with the personality disorders.[5] According to the *DSM-IV*, shizotypal personality disorder has about a 3 percent prevalence rate in the general population, is slightly more common in males, and tends to be stable throughout life.

SCHIZOID PERSONALITY DISORDER

Some people are less interested in relationships than others are, and there is nothing necessarily wrong with being a loner, but extreme social disinterest may indicate **schizoid personality disorder**. Someone with this disorder is unable to take pleasure from any kind of social interaction, ranging from interesting conversation to sexual activity. At the same time, he is indifferent to others' opinions, rarely experiences strong feelings, and generally presents a bland façade to the world. An important event—such as a loss of a job, or even the death of a family member—may leave the individual literally at a loss as for how to react, and he may seem not to react at all. People with this disorder live solitary lives—they are unlikely to marry, for example—but can sometimes perform adequately in jobs that do not require interaction with others. They are unlikely to seek professional help. While the *DSM-IV* describes the disorder as rare, a more recent survey estimates its prevalence at over 3 percent (B. F. Grant et al., 2004), and to be about equally common in males and females.

---

[5] The film *A Beautiful Mind*, starring Russell Crowe, told the true story—with Hollywood's usual degree of poetic license—of the famous mathematician, John Nash, who suffered from full-blown Axis I schizophrenia, including complex hallucinations of an imaginary best friend and a top-secret relationship with a spy agency.

BORDERLINE PERSONALITY DISORDER

From day to day with different people, and over time with the same people, most individuals feel and act pretty consistently. This fundamental fact is discussed in detail (and debated, to some extent) in Chapter 4. This predictability makes it possible to deal with the people we know in a reasonable way, and gives each of us a sense of individual identity. But some people are less consistent than others, and have thoughts, emotions, and behaviors that are in flux and unpredictable even to them. When this pattern becomes extreme, a person may be diagnosed with **borderline personality disorder**, which is probably the most severe one on the list. It is characterized by unstable and confused behavior, a poor sense of identity (these people may literally not know who they are), and patterns of self-harm that may range from self-defeating behaviors to self-mutilation to suicide.

In general, the personality disorders on Axis II in the *DSM-IV* are considered less severe than the major psychopathologies described along Axis I, though some researchers question this distinction (Skodol et al., 2002). Borderline personality disorder (BPD) entails so many problems for the affected person that nobody doubts that it is, at the very least, on the "borderline" with severe psychopathology.[6] Its hallmark is emotional instability. The person's mood can change rapidly from one moment to the next, and he or she may seem on the verge of going to pieces (Gunderson, 1984). The foundation of the disorder, according to some writers, is a sort of "emotional hemophilia," in which a reaction, once stimulated, cannot be stanched—the individual emotionally "bleeds to death" (Kreisman & Straus, 1989, p. 8). Another prominent researcher writes that an individual with this disorder is "the psychological equivalent of [a] third-degree burn patient [with] . . . no emotional skin. Even the slightest touch or movement can cause immense suffering" (Linehan, 1993, p. 69).

The *DSM-IV* lists nine characteristics of borderline personality disorder, and the official diagnosis calls for the individual to manifest at least five of them.

1. **Rapid Mood Shifts:** Because of their emotional vulnerability, people with borderline personality disorder characteristically experience frequent shifts in mood, as often as every few hours or even less (Trull et al., 2008). They can swing from happiness to sadness and

---

[6] Some writers claim that this is why it's called "borderline," because it's in between the less serious *neuroses* and the more serious *psychoses*, but the actual origin of the term is obscure.

from anger to affection quickly with little or no apparent cause. A very small event—such as someone saying "thank you," or neglecting to say "thank you"—can send them into swoons of delight or "ruin their whole day." But shortly thereafter, the feeling will pass as if nothing ever happened.

2. **Uncontrollable Anger:** They may frequently experience anger that is inappropriate, intense, or out of control, with very little impetus or none (that anybody else can see) at all. But like other moods, this passes quickly.

3. **Self-Destructive Acts:** Borderline personality disorder is associated with a wide and dangerous range of self-destructive acts including suicide and self-mutilation. According to the *DSM-IV*, suicide attempts are common among people with BPD, and eventually 8 to 10 percent do kill themselves (*DSM-IV-TR*, 2000, p. 707). If this statistic is even close to correct, then BPD is a dangerous affliction indeed, comparable to the most threatening physical diseases. Even among nonsuicidal people with BPD, self-mutilation is common and may include compulsively "cutting"[7] (with fingernails or knives) parts of the body including the hands, arms, and even genitals. The reason for this is far from clear; possible explanations include the rather psychoanalytic-sounding speculation that the person feels guilty and is indulging in self-punishment, and the possibility that people with BPD are so emotionally disconnected that they must hurt themselves to know they are alive. Perhaps the most plausible explanation comes from the description of the inner life of someone with this disorder as characterized by "emotional cascades," which are "vicious cycles of intense rumination and negative affect" that lead to extreme suffering (Selby, Anestis, Bender, & Joiner, 2009, p. 375). Behaviors such as using fingernail clippers to pull off slices of skin (Cloud, 2008/2009) may interrupt the process.[8] Consider what this means: The emotions that would otherwise be experienced must hurt even worse.

4. **Self-Damaging Behaviors:** Other self-damaging behaviors of people with BPD are less directly physical but still harmful. These may

---

[7] I put this word in quotes because it's almost a technical term; tell a clinical psychologist that someone is "cutting" (or is a "cutter"), and the clinician will immediately understand what you are talking about.

[8] These authors suggest—seriously—that teaching these patients other means of distraction, such as Sodoku, might be helpful.

include drug abuse, compulsive gambling, eating disorders, shop-lifting, reckless driving, and the list goes on. A particular characteristic pattern appears to involve undermining oneself at (or just before) the moment of success. People with BPD may drop out of school just before graduation, break up a relationship when it starts to succeed, or quit working on and even destroy a major project (such as a book, painting, or construction job) when it is about to be finished. Some cases of "runaway brides" (and grooms) may fit this pattern—everything seems great until the moment just before completion. Then, panic.

5. **Identity Disturbance:** Many people with BPD literally do not know who they are. They may have great difficulty understanding how they appear to others, and be confused about their values, career goals, and even sexual identity. They do not understand their own actions—cutters, for example, can say almost nothing meaningful about why they do it—and those with BPD may try to be social chameleons, avoiding behavioral choices and fading into the background by doing what everybody else seems to be doing.

6. **Chronic Emptiness:** People with BPD may complain of feeling "empty" and bored all the time. To quote an overused expression, they desperately need to "get a life." They seem unable to find activities that are satisfying and enjoyable, or to establish personal relationships that might give their lives purpose and meaning.

7. **Unstable Relationships:** The interpersonal relationships of people with BPD are confusing, chaotic, noisy, unpredictable, and unstable. In part, this is because they are prone to *splitting*, a term you may recall from object relations theory (described in Chapter 12) that refers to the tendency to view other people as either all good or all bad. Thus, a new relationship may be perceived as perfect, the best ever. Then, the first disappointment leads the person to conclude that the new partner is hopelessly thoughtless and cruel. These two extreme views, as Freud would have noted, have the same underlying dynamic. In both cases, the person with BPD is unable to handle the complex reality that people have a mix of good and bad characteristics, so she oversimplifies by jumping to one extreme evaluation or the other.

8. **Fear of Abandonment:** A further problem in interpersonal relationships for many people with BPD is that they put a great deal of effort into frantically trying to fend off being abandoned. Sometimes these fears of abandonment are realistic; often they are not. In either

case, they find it difficult to be separated for any length of time from people who are important to them and may panic when someone is a few minutes late, when an appointment is canceled, or even when the therapist announces that the hour is almost up (*DSM-IV-TR*, 2000, p. 706). The self-destructive behaviors already noted might, in some cases, be attempts to seek the attention they desperately crave, and may be used to manipulate people into staying (e.g., "If you leave me, I'll kill myself!").

9. **Confusion and Feelings of Unreality:** This fear of abandonment sometimes leads to confused thinking and feelings of being disconnected from reality. This might include sudden, unrealistic, and paranoid fears, or even the inability to remember one's own name. In general, the person becomes so upset that he literally cannot think straight. The *DSM* observes that these symptoms may come and go; when the significant other person returns, the sufferer may return to reality (relatively speaking) for a while.

All of the personality disorders are rather mixed bags of symptoms, and BPD may be the most mixed of all. It is difficult to find a coherent, common thread among these nine characteristics, which may be why the label "borderline" is so descriptively unhelpful. Some psychologists, indeed, have suggested that this category is too diffuse to be useful. On the other hand, the confusing and mixed-up nature of the definition of BPD may be part of the point. The pattern of emotion and behavior of someone with this disorder is to have no pattern. The personality itself is confused and disorganized, and the results can be disastrous and even fatal.

A huge amount of research attention has been paid to BPD in recent years, and some progress has been made. The phenomena of cutting and other kinds of self-harm are better understood as ways to short-circuit the otherwise inexorable buildup of anxiety and other negative emotions (Selby et al., 2009). New theories have been proposed about the origins of the disorder. One promising suggestion is that it arises when a genetic risk factor combines with an early family environment that fails to teach children how to understand and regulate their emotions. Children are put at risk when their "expressions of emotion are . . . rejected by the family and life's problems are oversimplified" (Crowell, Beauchaine, & Linehan, 2009, p. 504).

The most encouraging development is in therapies that might actually help. A therapeutic technique called *dialectical behavioral therapy* (e.g., Linehan, 1993) teaches skills for emotional self-control. In individual and group sessions, the therapist and client closely examine past episodes of inappropriate emotional reactions and analyze how similar situations could be handled better next time. In a sense, it's basic training in how to deal with emotions—something people with this disorder somehow never learned.

The *DSM-IV* estimates that 2 percent of the population has this disorder, but a more recent survey puts the prevalence closer to 6 percent; it is equally common in women and in men (B. F. Grant et al., 2008). Considering how common this disorder is, and how much suffering it causes, it clearly deserves to be a priority for future research.

DIAGNOSIS AND THE PROTOTYPE MODEL

As we have seen, the *DSM* lists characteristics for each disorder, and for an official diagnosis, the individual needs to meet a specific, minimum number of them. This system means that that there are no clear-cut requirements for diagnosing a personality disorder, a fact that has a couple of important implications.

First, each of the disorders can be exhibited in many different ways. For example, because a person needs to show only five out of nine characteristics for a diagnosis of borderline personality disorder, 256 different patterns (of five or more characteristics) are consistent with a diagnosis. As a result, people with the same official diagnosis may be quite different from each other. This creates a certain amount of vagueness and confusion, as you might expect.

Second, it is highly possible for a given individual to exhibit characteristics of several different disorders at once. It is not difficult to imagine someone who has rapidly shifting moods, a preference for solitary activities, and a view of oneself as inferior, yet these are characteristics of three different disorders![9] In fact, it could be argued that one overarching fact is true about all of the personality disorders: There is something psychologically wrong with the person. A person with any of these disorders is not in complete contact with reality, and may have fundamental problems in thinking.

One recent study suggests that nearly all of the personality disorders are associated with an inability to hold thoughts in active, working memory (Coolidge, Segal, & Applequist, 2009). This inability prevents people from

---

[9] Borderline, schizoid, and avoidant personality disorder, respectively.

engaging in the "inner speech" (p. 359) that might allow them to find different ways to solve their problems relating to other people.

The confusion entailed by the overlap among the disorders can be alleviated, to some degree, by thinking about these categories in a different way. In cognitive psychology, researchers have concluded that most, perhaps all, natural categories are best thought of in terms of ideal exemplars, or **prototypes**, which real objects match more or less well, even while differing from each other and fitting more than one category (Rosch, 1973). The classic example is the category "bird." If you think in terms of exact rules that would qualify a creature as a bird, you will quickly find problems with this system. It might seem that for something to be a bird, for example, it needs to be able to fly. But penguins can't fly, and they are birds. Chickens can't really fly either, yet they are also birds (and very different from penguins). Robins and sparrows are "better" birds than penguins or chickens, in the sense that they more closely match our ideal mental picture of a bird. That ideal is the prototype of the bird category.

In the same way, each personality disorder is best thought of as a prototype. While no individual is likely to match any prototype perfectly, and while someone may resemble more than one prototype, it is still possible and meaningful to assess the degree to which she matches each one. This view goes a long way toward rescuing the system of categorizing and diagnosing personality disorders, because it acknowledges the complexity of diagnosis, the overlap of categories, and the heterogeneity within categories.[10] On the other hand, we should probably take a moment to remember that the psychiatrist or clinical psychologist will probably write just one billing code on the insurance form.

---

[10] The diagnosis of physical illness, sometimes portrayed as more cut-and-dried than psychological diagnosis, is fraught with many of the same ambiguities (Burnum, 1993), and it, too, may benefit from thinking of illnesses in terms of prototypes.

BASES FOR DIAGNOSIS

The diagnosis of a personality disorder may be based on several kinds of information, including a clinician's general impression, a self-report inventory, a structured interview, or informants' reports. As you might expect if you recall Funder's First Law (Chapter 1), each has both advantages and disadvantages.

Clinical Impressions

The most common basis for diagnosis is simply (or not so simply) the clinician's general impression, based on a professional encounter. The clinician usually conducts an unstructured interview, or series of interviews, with the individual and then comes to an overall diagnosis. This diagnosis may, and probably does, make reference to the characteristics and criteria specified by the *DSM-IV*, but in the end it is based on what the clinician was able to glean from talking to the individual and from using her clinical intuition and experience. This can be a good way to proceed because it is open and flexible; the clinician can adjust the formal criteria as seems necessary in a given case, and can add a dollop of common sense. But this flexibility entails some shortcomings, too. Not all clinicians are equally skilled or accurate, and even two expert clinicians might not conduct their interviews, apply the criteria, or diagnose a patient in the same way—the diagnosis of personality disorders is notoriously unreliable. A persistent goal of research, therefore, is to find methods of diagnosis other than clinical judgment.

> The diagnosis of personality disorders is notoriously unreliable.

Self-Report Scales

One alternative method is the self-report personality scale, of the sort discussed in Chapter 5. Many scales have been used for this purpose. Three particularly popular ones are the Minnesota Multiphasic Personality Inventory (MMPI), discussed in Chapter 5 (Morey, Waugh, & Blashfield, 1985); the Millon Clinical Multiaxial Inventory–II (MCMI-II; Millon, 1987), and the Personality Diagnostic Questionnaire–Revised (PDQ-R; Hyler & Rieder, 1987). Most of these inventories ask people whether they exhibit signs of the various disorders. For example, to assess narcissistic personality disorder, the MMPI items include (among many others), "I have no dread of going into a room by myself where other people have already gathered and are talking," the MCMI-II includes, "In the past, I've gotten involved sexually with many people who didn't matter much to me," and the PDQ-R includes, "I often find myself thinking about how great a person I am or will be."[11]

The advantages and disadvantages of measuring personality disorders through self-report are the same as those for S data in general, as discussed in detail in Chapter 2. The data are inexpensive, relatively easy to obtain, and yield scores that can be easily compared with other information. Indeed, evidence indicates that these scales have some degree of validity. The downside is that people may not always have insight into their own psychological symptoms or be willing to report them if they do. The *DSM-IV* explicitly mentions that antisocial personality disorder, in particular, probably should not be diagnosed (or dismissed as a possibility) on the basis of self-report, because deceit is a hallmark. But the same general principle may apply to most of the other personality disorders, which generally include misunderstandings of reality and confused self-concepts among their defining characteristics.

Structured Interviews

A third approach to diagnosis seeks to combine the advantages of the clinical encounter with the objectivity—or at least the numerical analyzability—of the self-report scale. Several **structured interviews** have been published for the major personality disorders (e.g., Structured Interview for DSM-IV Personality, also known as the SIDP-IV; Pfohl, Blum, & Zimmerman, 1997). These interviews comprise series of questions designed to maintain objectivity while zeroing in on the relevant characteristics. The interviewer is supposed to closely follow the script and thereby interview everybody in the same way, or almost the same way. For example, for borderline personality disorder the interviewer asks (among other questions), "Do you often have days when your mood is constantly changing—days when you shift back and forth from feeling your usual self, to feeling angry or depressed or anxious?" It goes on to ask (in the very next question), "Do you feel empty much of the

---

[11] Interestingly, each of the items just listed is biased in the sense that men answer True more often than women, which may cause narcissistic personality disorder to be overdiagnosed in men or underdiagnosed in women (Lindsay & Widiger, 1995).

time?" (Pfohl et al., 1997, p. 15). If you say yes to these questions, you are on your way to a diagnosis.

Structured interviews have several advantages. Diagnoses by two interviewers are much more likely to agree if both are based on scores from the same structured interview, than if the interviewers each use whatever methods they please and report an overall clinical impression. For this reason, the structured interview is often considered the gold standard for psychological diagnosis. Furthermore, an interviewer needs only minimal training, compared with that required of a psychiatrist or clinical psychologist. The authors of the SIDP-IV advise that an undergraduate degree in social science, plus some relevant experience, is all that is required.[12] What they don't mention, but which is clearly the implicit point, is that such individuals can be paid much less than fully trained psychiatrists or clinical psychologists.

Structured interviews have a couple of disadvantages, however. One is that their rigid structure may inhibit the client's ability to talk about the real problem. This issue may, of course, be remedied on subsequent visits, after the diagnosis is established. But it is difficult to look at a structured interview as anything other than a strange and stilted conversation. A second disadvantage is that the structured interview is, in format, surprisingly similar to the self-report instruments described above. This means that if the respondent does not have insight into her own condition, or is unwilling to be honest or forthcoming with the interviewer, we will be back to some of the same disadvantages that befall (much less expensive) S data.

Informant Reports

Another route for diagnosing a personality disorder is to ask knowledgeable informants, such as acquaintances, coworkers, or relatives, to describe the person's characteristics. In other words, gather I data of the sort discussed in Chapter 2. Research has shown that, in as little as 30 seconds, people can identify traits that are associated with personality disorders, if not the disorders themselves (J. N. W. Friedman, Oltmanns, & Turkheimer, 2007). For example, people watching brief videotapes rated individuals with traits related to schizoid and avoidant personality disorders as introverted, histrionic personality disorder as extraverted, and narcissistic personality disorder as "stuck up."

---

[12] Thus, they seem to be saying that a degree in political science or economics would be as useful as a BA in psychology. Do you agree?

"Now who's paranoid?"

Interestingly, the *SIDP-IV* includes questions (marked with an asterisk in the interview script) that could be appropriate for informant reports, though this usage is still relatively rare. In general, informant reports have all of the advantages and disadvantages of I data that you may recall from Chapter 2. An informant may have limited information about the person being described or give a biased description. On the other hand, recent research indicates that close acquaintances generally agree about whether an individual exhibits psychological symptoms in the *DSM-IV* (South, Oltmanns, & Turkheimer, 2005; see also De Los Reyes & Kazdin, 2005). And, not surprisingly, these judgments may not agree particularly well with the individual's self-report (Thomas et al., 2003; Oltmanns & Turkheimer, 2009).

When you think about it, it does seem surprising that so much research on personality disorders relies on self-report (Oltmanns & Turkheimer, 2009). There is good reason to think that self-report becomes most unreliable exactly when the personality disorder is most severe. In one study, the worse the pathology, the less participants' self-ratings agreed with the ratings of other people who knew them well (Furr, Dougherty, Marsh, & Mathias, 2007). I mentioned earlier that the *DSM-IV* recommends gathering opinions from acquaintances concerning the indicators of antisocial personality disorder; it probably would be a good idea to try this for the other personality disorders as well.

ORGANIZING THE PERSONALITY DISORDERS

The list of 10 personality disorders in the *DSM-IV* does not exhaust the ways that individual differences can become extreme and problematic. Psychologists have proposed many other disorders, and the canonical list is continuously being reorganized and rethought. For example, **passive-aggressive personality disorder** has gone on and off the list over succeeding editions (at the moment it is off, pending "further study," and has been tentatively renamed *negativistic personality disorder*). A major project for its next revision is to rethink how personality disorders are organized. Organization is an important issue, because some kind of structure is necessary for comparing the disorders with each other and for seeking psychological processes, causes, or cures that apply to more than one disorder.

The *DSM-IV* Clusters

The *DSM-IV* organizes the 10 personality disorders into three *clusters* that are named, not particularly helpfully, Clusters A, B, and C. These clusters are close to, but not quite the same as, the three groupings I used in summarizing the disorders earlier in this chapter. Cluster A in the *DSM-IV* contains disorders characterized by odd or eccentric patterns of thinking, including the schizotypal, schizoid, and paranoid personality disorders. Cluster B includes disorders characterized by impulsive and erratic patterns of behavior, including the histrionic, narcissistic, antisocial, and borderline personality disorders, and these are disorders that tend to be most stable—that change the least—over time (Durbin & Klein, 2006). Finally, Cluster C comprises disorders characterized by anxious and avoidant emotional styles, including the dependent, avoidant, and obsessive-compulsive personality disorders. Another way to describe them might be to note that Cluster A includes thinking disorders, Cluster B includes behavioral disorders, and Cluster C includes emotional disorders. But of course, this is much too simple, because all of the disorders are characterized by all three problems. Personally, I prefer to group disorders associated with unhappiness and anxiety (dependent, avoidant, and obsessive-compulsive; the same as the *DSM-IV*'s Cluster C), disorders that primarily cause problems for other people (paranoid, histrionic, antisocial, and narcissistic), and disorders associated with seriously distorted thinking (schizotypal, schizoid, and borderline), though my list has a similar (and perhaps inevitable) problem of category overlap. If you look at the research literature, you will find that the *DSM-IV*'s A, B, and C labels are used frequently, and clinical psychologists often discuss and write about disorders in these terms.

Dimensional Structures

Several psychologists have attempted to identify key dimensions that underlie the personality disorders. In some cases, their goal is similar to that of psychologists seeking to identify the essential traits of personality (see Chapter 7); they hope to identify a set of dimensions that can describe the entire range of personality, including both normal and abnormal patterns of behavior. For example, the prominent clinical psychologist Theodore Millon has offered a *biosocial learning model* that arranges the personality disorders according to the ways people focus on themselves or others, whether they are active or passive, and whether they primarily seek reward or avoidance of pain (Millon, 1996). This model is interesting, but empirical research has not consistently supported it (B. P. O'Connor & Dyce, 1998). Other theorists have proposed circumplex models, like those for goals and emotions shown in Chapter 16, in which the disorders and other attributes of personality are arranged around a circle that shows how they are related (e.g., Kiesler, 1986).

One of the best supported and most accepted ways of organizing the personality disorders is the Big Five set of personality traits (see Chapter 7; Widiger, Trull, Clarkin, Sanderson, & Costa, 1994, 2002). The Big Five basic traits, you may recall, are extraversion, neuroticism, agreeableness, conscientiousness, and openness to experience. Researchers studying the Big Five have proposed these traits as the foundation of most if not all of the variation in personality, with the idea that the 17,953 trait terms in the English language can be reduced to combinations of two or more of these five attributes.

Table 18.1 shows the hypothesized relationships between the Big Five and the 10 currently recognized personality disorders. Notice that all disorders but two (schizoid and obsessive-compulsive) are hypothesized to be associated with neuroticism, which makes sense, but this overlap also shows how the disorders resemble each other on a very basic level: They nearly all involve a certain amount of anxiety and unhappiness. Beyond neuroticism, the table suggests that schizotypal personality disorder, for example, can be viewed as a combination of low extraversion and high openness (Widiger et al., 1994, 2002), a description that has received a reasonable degree of empirical support (B. P. O'Connor & Dyce, 1998; Wright & Funder, 2007). Antisocial personality disorder, in contrast, is characterized by high extraversion, low agreeableness, and low conscientiousness. In general, the table provides a new way to compare personality disorders with each other, and so can be useful for that purpose. But it is also important to remember that personality disorders are defined as *extreme and troublesome* patterns of personality. So, for example, an individual who is moderately anxious (neurotic), introverted, and open probably does not have a personality disorder, but if these traits are all taken to extremes, he may start to have the problems of someone who would be usefully described as schizotypal.

Table 18.1

THE 10 PRINCIPAL PERSONALITY DISORDERS IN TERMS OF THE BIG FIVE TRAITS OF PERSONALITY

Personality Disorder	Neuroticism	Extraversion	Agreeableness	Conscientiousness	Openness to Experience
Schizotypal	High	Low			High
Schizoid		Low			Low
Paranoid	High		Low		
Histrionic	High	High	High		High
Narcissistic	High		Low	High	High
Antisocial	High	High	Low	Low	
Borderline	High		Low	Low	
Dependent	High		High		
Avoidant	High	Low			
Obsessive-compulsive		High	Low	High	Low

Note: Each of the 10 principal personality disorders can be described in terms of (extreme) positions on the Big Five factors of personality. A blank means that no association between that trait and the disorder is expected.

Source: Adapted from Widiger, Trull, Clarkin, Sanderson, & Costa (2002), Table 6.1, p. 90.

The Big Five is not the end of the story. Researchers have proposed that, to fully capture psychopathology, we may really need a Big Six, in which openness is distinguished from a sixth factor called *oddity* (D. Watson, Clark, & Chmielewski, 2008). Oddity is associated with characteristics such as perceiving things in unusual ways, feeling separated from one's own body and oneself, and experiencing detachment, mistrust, and "obliviousness" (Watson et al., p. 1561). We can describe many aspects of normal and abnormal personality using the same dimensions, it seems, but not quite all.

PERSONALITY AND DISORDER

Clinical psychology, psychiatry, and the successive editions of the *DSM* have displayed an increasing amount of insight and imagination formulating descriptions of many psychological disorders. The original edition, published in 1952, included 107 different diagnoses; the second edition had 180 diagnoses; the third edition had 226 diagnoses; and the latest edition, the

DSM-IV, includes descriptions of 365 different psychopathological conditions—one for each day of the year (Savodnik, 2006)! This very success and the resulting proliferation of diagnoses raise issues concerning the pitfalls of describing so many behaviors as pathological, the nature of mental health, the pros and cons of labeling in general, and the fine line between normal and abnormal personality.

Pathologizing

Personality disorders describe bad ways to be. Does this mean that bad people have personality disorders, by definition? For example, some psychologists have recently proposed that "pathological bias," such as extreme racism, homophobia, or other strong feelings about certain groups, should be defined as a personality disorder. One writer has noted that if this proposal succeeds, "perpetrators of hate crimes could become candidates for treatment, and physicians would become arbiters on how to distinguish 'ordinary prejudice' from pathological bias" (Vedantam, 2005, p. A01). Pathological bias has not yet been added to the *DSM*, but many of the *DSM*'s disorders include patterns of socially undesirable, illegal, or immoral behavior. For example, if certain people lie, cheat, steal, or even murder, should we refrain from punishing or perhaps even judging them, because they suffer from antisocial personality disorder, and therefore are not accountable for those actions?

If you think I am going to answer this question, you are in for a disappointment. The issue is an eternal conundrum in the foggy area where psychology meets moral reasoning, and has been a long-standing dilemma in philosophy, religion, and law. No resolution is in sight. Some people are sure that the answer to this question is yes, because it is absurd, pointless, and wrong to punish someone for having a psychological disorder. Others are sure the answer is no, because some behaviors should be punished regardless of their psychological (or even physical) cause. The truth, as always, lies somewhere in between—and, also as always, resists quick summary and easy understanding.

A further pitfall in pathologizing behaviors—describing them as the result of mental illness—is that it is entirely too easy. As mentioned near the beginning of this chapter, critics of the *DSM-IV* have enjoyed pointing out that it includes a label for everything from compulsive gambling to coffee nerves (Davis, 1997). It describes so many behavioral patterns as forms of mental illness that it threatens to

> If everything is a mental illness, then nothing is a mental illness.

undermine the meaning of the concept altogether. If everything is a mental illness, then nothing is a mental illness.

Mental Health

No matter how long and detailed a list of disorders might be, it does not tell us much about the nature of mental health.[13] Mental health certainly is more than not having any of the symptoms listed in the *DSM*—even if that were possible, which it is not; and critics have pointed out that, thorough as it is otherwise, the book says very little about psychological health. This is not merely a shortcoming of the *DSM*; psychology has a history of paying much more attention to defining and attempting to cure mental illness than to describing the ideal state that one might aspire to achieve. This omission is precisely what motivates the positive psychology movement discussed in Chapter 13. That movement aims to move beyond an exclusive focus on fixing what's wrong with people, and instead to promote meaningful and happy living. More generally, improving mental health requires an understanding of normal personality, not just mental illness and personality disorders.[14]

Labeling

The specific categories in the *DSM-IV* come in for a lot of criticism, and for good reason. No real person seems to exactly fit the criteria for any category, many people exhibit characteristics of several categories, and systems like the *DSM-IV*'s list of personality disorders are difficult to apply consistently and reliably. Thus, the labels in the *DSM-IV* are always a little bit misleading, sometimes seriously so. For example, it is important to avoid simply describing people we don't like as having personality disorders, tempting though that may be. Such a description is probably unfair. It can shut off rather than promote further understanding, because once we have labeled a person as mentally ill, we may no longer feel that we have to take seriously

---

[13] A colleague and I wrote an article that argues this point even more broadly: Psychology's many catalogs of human errors, shortcomings, and pathologies—and psychology has indeed developed many such catalogs—tell us surprisingly little about how people ought to think or behave. For this, a more positive approach is necessary (Krueger & Funder, 2004).

[14] This seemingly obvious point is sometimes a matter of political dispute. The National Institute of Mental Health in the United States has had directors (including the current one, as of this writing) who believe, despite the name of their institute, that the research it supports should focus solely on alleviating mental illness.

"Call it vanity, call it narcissism, call it egomania. I love you."

her feelings, outlook, and even rights, or to empathize with her point of view. A label is not an explanation, and the conclusion that someone has a personality disorder raises many more questions than it answers.

On the other hand, the labels *can* be useful. The syndromes described in the *DSM-IV*, while not as clear-cut as we would like, describe patterns that experienced clinicians have noticed over many years. So if you come across someone who exhibits one or more of the characteristics of a personality disorder, it might be worth your while to consider whether he or she might show some of the other symptoms as well. For example, if someone acts in a grandiose and arrogant manner (a sign of narcissistic personality disorder), it might pay to be wary of the possibility he could seek to take advantage of you. If somebody gives signs of being just a little too impressed by the rule book, and unable to adjust for the changing circumstances of real life (signs of obsessive-compulsive personality disorder), I would advise that you avoid at all costs putting her in charge of anything, or putting yourself in a position to take orders from her. And if someone you care about exhibits the emotional instability characteristic of borderline personality disorder, you might want to watch for indications that he might harm himself via drug addiction, eating disorders, cutting, or even suicide.

It might even be advisable to watch for signs of these disorders in yourself (although, as I discuss shortly, some of these attributes might sometimes be useful). If you find yourself treating people with arrogance, or following rules without thinking through their purpose, or even harming yourself, this could be a warning to prevent further movement in a potentially dangerous direction. Thus, no matter how uncomfortable we may be about labeling people, it is still worthwhile to learn the basic characteristics of the major personality disorders (Yudofsky, 2005).

Finally, it must be acknowledged that labels are absolutely necessary. There is simply no escaping them. When a psychiatrist or clinical psychologist records impressions of a patient, she must write *something*, so the more precise the labels, the better. Research, or even serious discussion, about mental illness would be completely impossible without words—labels—to refer to the different varieties that exist. Remember Funder's Second Law (Chapter 2), that something usually beats nothing: No matter how flawed they may be—and they are flawed—the labels in the *DSM-IV* will persist until something better comes along.

Normal and Abnormal

Although the issue used to be highly controversial, the modern research literature on personality disorders has come close to consensus about one conclusion: There is no sharp dividing line between psychopathology and normal variation (e.g., L. A. Clark & Watson, 1999a; Furr & Funder, 1998; Krueger & Tackett, 2003; B. P. O'Connor, 2002; Trull & Durrett, 2005). Indeed, the special personality tests designed to measure abnormal personality may do no better a job, for this purpose, than the instruments designed for the normal range, such as those surveyed in Chapter 7 (Walton, Roberts, Krueger, Blonigen, & Hicks, 2008). People show a wide range of normal variation in all kinds of attributes, and sometimes several traits at once become extreme enough to cause problems, as in the case of the personality disorders. But there is no exact point on the continuum for any trait that defines the boundary beyond which a person is mentally ill.

One implication of the continuum between normality and abnormality is that you may have recognized people you know, and even yourself, in parts of the descriptions of personality disorders. Your acquaintances, or even you, may indeed check the stove twice before leaving the house, experience deep hurt when other people don't recognize an accomplishment, or feel profoundly bored sometimes. But it is important to remember that having a mild degree of a few characteristics does *not* imply that someone has a personality disorder.

Moreover, as I have already mentioned, it is possible to think of each personality disorder as an exaggerated version of a trait that in the normal range can have some advantages (Oldham & Morris, 1995). For example, consider the person who is lovably unusual and idiosyncratic; has original, creative ideas; and generally marches to a different drummer. These fine tendencies overlap with elements of schizotypal personality disorder. An individual who is self-confident and proud has attributes that overlap with narcissistic personality, and so on. A list of some of the positive traits that might be paired with personality disorders appears in Table 18.2.

Table 18.2

ADAPTIVE TRAITS AND PERSONALITY DISORDERS

Positive Personality Trait	Related Personality Disorder
Idiosyncratic, original, "different drummer"	Schizotypal
Independent, self-sufficient, needs nobody	Schizoid
Vigilant, wary, a survivor	Paranoid
Dramatic, flamboyant, fun	Histrionic
Self-confident, proud	Narcissistic
Strong, willful, self-reliant	Antisocial
Mercurial, exciting, "fire and ice"	Borderline
Devoted, faithful, reliable mate	Dependent
Sensitive, quiet, a homebody	Avoidant
Conscientious, reliable, consistent	Obsessive-compulsive

Note: The personality disorders can be considered extreme variations of traits that may ordinarily be adaptive and desirable.
Source: Compiled from suggestions by Oldham and Morris (1995) and other writers.

An individual's personality is a complete package that cannot be separated tidily into good and bad parts. Indeed, elements of some of the personality disorders may be cherished aspects of yourself! Remember Funder's First Law (Chapter 1)—about great strengths often being great weaknesses, and vice versa? Perhaps your creative spark and original outlook are among the best things about you; it's just that occasionally this causes you to come off as a bit strange. Maybe you are valued for your perfectionism and attention to detail; only once in a while does this tendency go too far and annoy people. Your weaknesses may be part of your strengths; only when the characteristics are numerous, consistent, severe, and problematic should we speak about personality disorders.

Both normal people who have enjoyable quirks and people who have ego-syntonic personality disorders might use the descriptions in the left column of Table 18.2 to describe themselves. There may be a little—just a little—of the personality disorders in all of us, and even people suffering from severe personality disorders may have some sane, useful, and adaptive traits. This brings us back to the issue of normal behavioral variation and psychopathology. There is a difference, but the dividing line is neither sharp nor easy to find.

SUMMARY

- People are different from each other; when these differences consistently cause problems, they may amount to personality disorders.

The Diagnostic and Statistical Manual

- The *Diagnostic and Statistical Manual (DSM-IV)* of the American Psychiatric Association describes a wide variety of mental problems including personality disorders. The book is organized into groups, or axes, wherein Axis I includes severe psychopathologies such as schizophrenia, and Axis II includes the personality disorders.

- The *DSM-IV* attempts to make psychological diagnosis more objective and provides useful categories for various purposes including research and billing.

Defining Personality Disorders

- All personality disorders have two essential characteristics. (1) They are unusually extreme in a way that generally entails a distortion of reality, and (2) they cause problems for the self or others.

- Most, if not all, personality disorders are also social and stable. In addition, some disorders are ego-syntonic, which means they are not experienced as problems by the people diagnosed with the disorder.

The Major Personality Disorders

- The *DSM-IV* lists 10 major personality disorders. The dependent, avoidant, and obsessive-compulsive disorders are primarily associated with different kinds of emotional suffering. The paranoid, histrionic, antisocial, and narcissistic disorders involve problems relating to other people. And the schizotypal, schizoid, and borderline disorders are associated with serious distortions of thinking and a lack of stable contact with reality. However, all of the disorders include all three kinds of problems.

- Obsessive-compulsive personality disorder is a pattern of excessive devotion to rules, organization, and habits along with inflexibility or resistance to change.

- Narcissistic personality disorder is a pattern of excessive self-love that includes grandiose and arrogant behaviors, and exploitation of and lack of empathy for others. The trait of narcissism can also vary within the normal range.

- Borderline personality disorder is a serious affliction characterized by confused thinking, emotional vulnerability and instability, identity confusion, and dangerous patterns of self-harm.

Diagnosis and the Prototype Model

- For each disorder, the *DSM-IV* provides a list of characteristics and the minimum number that must be present to justify an official diagnosis. Thus, people with the same diagnosis may be quite different from each other, so each disorder should be thought of as a prototype rather than as a list of necessary and sufficient features.

Bases for Diagnosis

- Diagnosis of a personality disorder may be based on clinical impressions, self-report inventories, structured interviews, or informants' reports.

Organizing the Personality Disorders

- The *DSM-IV* organizes the 10 personality disorders into three clusters that describe patterns of thinking, behavior, and emotion. The Big Five list of essential traits is another widely used approach to organizing the disorders.

Personality and Disorder

- Personality disorders involve several key issues.

- One key issue is that pathologizing undesirable behavior can raise difficult moral issues, and also risks describing so many patterns as mental illnesses that the concept of illness begins to lose its meaning.

- A second key issue is that a list of psychological disorders does not imply a definition of mental health.

- A third key issue is that labeling disorders carries serious risks, but also has helpful applications and may be inevitable.

- And finally, the line between normal personality variation and personality disorder is fine and uncertain. Indeed, some personality disorders can be seen as exaggerations of traits that, in moderation, are desirable.

THINK ABOUT IT

1. It is generally good to be tolerant of individual differences and to accept people as they are. Is this wise in the case of someone with a personality disorder? Does the answer to this question depend on which disorder the person has? What else does the answer depend on?

2. Answer the following question in your own mind; if discussed out loud or in writing, be sure to protect the privacy of everyone involved: Do you know anyone who seems to have a personality disorder? What can be, or is being done, for this person? What is the best way for you to interact with this person?

3. Do any of the personality disorders entail characteristics that you think it might be good to watch out for—in oneself or others—even in people who are mentally healthy? Which characteristics in which disorders might be particularly important?

4. Experienced clinicians often report that, when dealing with someone with a personality disorder, they intuitively feel that something is "not quite right." Have you had this kind of intuition about a person? Did it turn out to be correct?

5. If someone with a personality disorder commits a crime, what is the right way for society to respond? Does the answer depend on whether the person has a *severe* mental illness? If so, how would you define a severe mental illness? Do any of the personality disorders qualify? If not, what does?

6. Are any of the personality disorders, or aspects of them, ever good to have?

7. What are the characteristics of a healthy personality? Put another way, how would you describe the most psychologically healthy person you know? What is he or she like?

SUGGESTED READINGS

American Psychiatric Association (2000). *Diagnostic and statistical manual of mental disorders: DSM-IV-TR.* (4th ed., text revision). Washington, DC: American Psychiatric Association.

> This standard reference book weighs several pounds and is organized around billing codes, but it is surprisingly readable and interesting. It describes more ways to go psychologically wrong than you would have thought possible, and includes detailed commentary and specific examples.

Murray, H. A. (1943). *Analysis of the personality of Adolf Hitler, with predictions of his future behavior and suggestions for dealing with him now and after Germany's surrender.* Washington, DC: Office of Strategic Services.

> During World War II, the U.S. Office of Strategic Services (now the CIA) commissioned the prominent personality psychologist Henry Murray to write an analysis of the personality of Adolf Hitler. The report has only recently become available. It is a fascinating mixture of insight and what at least one critic has called "psychobabble" (Carey, 2005), and includes the prediction—correct, as it turned out—that at the end of the war Hitler would retreat to his bunker and commit suicide. The report is available online at http://library.lawschool.cornell.edu/WhatWeHave/SpecialCollections/Donovan/Hitler/index.cfm.

Yudofsky, S. C. (2005). *Fatal flaws: Navigating destructive relationships with people with disorders of personality and character*. Washington, DC: American Psychiatric Publishing.

> *This well-written book, by an experienced and knowledgeable therapist, surveys the major personality disorders and provides sage—and potentially lifesaving—advice on how to deal with people who have them. He describes a large number of actual cases, carefully explains what therapy can and cannot do, and describes how people with these disorders affect everybody around them. It all makes for fascinating—and useful—reading.*

EMEDIA

 Go to StudySpace, wwnorton.com/studyspace, to access additional review and enrichment materials.

CONCLUSION:
Looking Back and Looking Ahead

PERSONALITY IS MY FAVORITE topic in psychology because it includes most of what makes the subject interesting. It is where all of the other strands of psychology come together—or should—into a complete account of what people think, how they feel, and what they do. This is the psychological triad I mentioned in Chapter 1, and we saw in the following 17 chapters that research attempting to get at these issues sometimes leads to theories that are deep and complex, and empirical methodologies that are sophisticated, complicated, and difficult. This complexity and rigor are all well and good, but they make it easy to forget why the research was done in the first place. After trekking through the deep thicket of a theoretical derivation or a set of research results, and coming out on the other side, it is important to remember to ask, "What do I now know about people that I didn't know before?"

Psychologists attempting to learn about personality have taken several approaches, each of which was the subject of a different part of this book. Here, in this final chapter, I will say a little more about why personality psychology has so many different approaches, and conclude by identifying some of the general lessons about personality that I want you to remember.

THE DIFFERENT APPROACHES

This book began with the observation that the field of personality involves the study of the whole person and everything that is important about an individual's psychology. A problem with this goal arises immediately, however: It is overwhelming—in fact, it is impossible. We cannot really account for everything at once; we must limit ourselves to a certain perspective and to the questions and variables that seem most important. The only alternative to such self-limitation is hopeless confusion.

For this reason, each basic approach to personality focuses on a limited number of key concerns and pretty much ignores everything else. The trait approach (Part II) focuses on individual differences, the personality traits that make every individual psychologically unique. The biological approach (Part III) concentrates on the architecture and function of the nervous system, and on the heritability and evolutionary history of behavioral patterns. The psychoanalytic approach (Part IV) focuses on the unconscious mind and the complicated effects of motivations and conflicts of which we are not even aware. The humanistic approach (Part V) focuses on moment-to-moment conscious awareness, and the way experiencing life one moment at a time might give us free will and the ability to choose how we see reality; this approach also leads to an appreciation of the way cultural differences create diverse construals of reality. The learning and cognitive approaches (Part VI) focus on how rewards and punishments in the environment shape behavior, and how behavior is in many ways a function of its situation. Modern cognitive research into personality emphasizes basic mental processes relevant to perception, memory, motivation, emotion, and the cluster of memories and attitudes called "the self."

Which One Is Right?

Anybody who has taught personality psychology has, after a semester of presenting these approaches in sequence, had a bright but confused student approach and ask, "Yes, but which one is right?" By now, you probably can predict that professors flounder around trying to answer this question, because it is not really answerable. To say which one is "right," the different approaches to personality psychology would have to give different answers to the same question. But they do not. Rather, they pose different questions. Each approach lives or dies not by being right or wrong—because in the end, all theories are wrong—but by usefully accounting for a limited set of known facts, for being useful in the real world, and for clarifying important facets of human nature.[1]

Thus, we cannot choose between the approaches to personality based on which one is right. A better criterion for evaluating a psychological approach is this: Does it offer a way to seek an answer to a question you feel is worthwhile? The trait approach asks about individual differences; the psychoanalytic approach asks about the unconscious; the biological approach asks about physical mechanisms; the humanistic approach asks about consciousness, free will, and individual and cultural construals of reality; the learning and cognitive approaches ask about behavioral change, along with the processes of thinking and feeling that underlie behavioral coherence. Which do you need or want to know about? The answer to this question tells you which approach to use. And, as we saw in the discussion of the personality disorders (Chapter 18), a full view of an important psychological topic sometimes requires *all* of the approaches.

The Order of Approaches

One interesting decision that any author of a book like this gets to make—amid much conflicting advice—is the order in which to present the chapters. This might seem like a trivial decision, but it can reveal much about the author's view of the field of personality.

One surprisingly common method is to begin with the author's least favorite approach and end by describing the author's most favorite approach. But such books leave the impression that the whole world was just marking time until the right approach came along. In the final chapter, the author can triumphantly announce that, at last, the truth has been discovered!

I have already explained why I am not a fan of such invidious comparisons. Portraying one approach as right and the others as wrong misses the point of why different approaches continue to exist and are important to learn about. So it should not be surprising that I did not choose this strategy of chapter arrangement.

> Portraying one approach as right and the others as wrong misses the point of why different approaches continue to exist and are important to learn about.

---

[1] The statistician G. E. P. Box once commented, "All models are wrong but some are useful" (Box, 1979, p. 202).

"It's dull now, but at the end they smash their instruments and set fire to the chairs."

A second common strategy is more evenhanded: The author arranges the chapters in more or less historical order. I say "more or less" because it is not an easy matter to settle the issue of which approaches are the older and which the newer. The philosophical tradition behind behaviorism is extremely old, but the research is comparatively new; the reverse could be said about psychoanalysis. One problem with this strategy is that a strict chronological ordering (assuming one can be determined) is not necessarily intellectually coherent. Another problem is that, much like the previous strategy, such a book tends to acquire the "psychology marches on" flavor that is somewhat misleading.

The final strategy I will mention—not coincidentally, the one I chose—is to arrange the approaches in the order in which they are most teachable. It is sometimes claimed that, unlike other sciences, psychology is not cumulative; its findings do not build on earlier work in an orderly manner as they do in physics, for example.[2] Psychology is cumulative in another way. The approaches branch off from, react to, and interact with each other in a way that suggests an order in which to present them.

So I began this book with a review of the data and research methods of personality psychology. This laid a base for everything that followed. Then I presented the trait approach first, because it raises a basic issue that logically precedes all others—does personality exist?—and because its focus on how people differ can be presented without much reference to the other approaches. The biological approaches that I considered next are direct outgrowths of the trait approach; they examine how neurostructure, bio-

---

[2] I think this claim simultaneously underestimates the cumulativeness of psychology and overestimates the cumulativeness of physics, but that is another story.

chemicals, genes, and evolutionary histories produce the broad patterns of behavior called personality traits.

By then, an attentive reader would suspect that these trait and biological approaches neglect some of the more mysterious aspects of the mind, such as the workings of the unconscious (you may recall, from Part IV's introductory comments, that this was Henry Murray's complaint about the trait approach). So I presented the psychoanalytic approach next. The psychoanalytic view of behavior as driven by irrational and mysterious impulses is countered in an interesting way by the humanistic approach, considered in the following part. The humanists believe people can (even must) consciously choose their construals of reality. We also saw that the essence of the psychological differences between cultures is a matter of members of different cultures construing reality differently.

The next set of chapters presented learning and cognitive approaches to personality. I first described classic behaviorism, then looked at the social learning theories that grew directly out of behaviorism, and finally considered the modern cognitive approaches that grew out of social learning. This included a survey of modern research on perception, motivation, emotion, and the self. Research on these four topics draws on all of the other approaches, including behaviorism, psychoanalysis, and even humanism. To appreciate the research fully, I think you need some familiarity with these other approaches. That is why this research was presented almost last. But the actual last chapter (until this one) was about the personality disorders, and applied the material from earlier chapters to real and pervasive psychological problems. One moral of the story of the personality disorders turns out to be that, although theoretical approaches gain intellectual coherence by enforcing boundaries on what they address, if you want to understand a complex psychological issue in the real world, you have to be willing to violate those boundaries.

No Single Approach Accounts for Everything

I have been saying this all along, and by now I hope you know what I mean. Einstein's theory of relativity unified physics. Darwin's theory of evolution unified biology. But psychology has no Darwin or Einstein—yet. The most comprehensive theory probably belongs to Freud, but you have already seen the problems there. As broad as Freud's theory is, it still does not address the key concerns of the other approaches, such as conscious experience, free will, or learning from experience. It also has not been particularly successful in generating empirical support, though that has begun to change in recent years.

The often-lamented lack of a single unifying perspective for psychology is an important source of the "physics envy" so often suffered by psychologists. So let me rock the boat a little: I think it's a good thing. I say this for two reasons.

The first reason is that any approach that tried to account for all of the key concerns of the current five basic approaches would almost inevitably be unwieldy, confusing, incoherent, and incomplete. The limitations that each basic approach imposes on observation and theorizing are not faults; they are the very purpose of these approaches. Such self-limitation helps to avoid becoming overwhelmed and confused. It also allows each basic approach to focus on providing a thorough account of, and useful knowledge about, the phenomena the approach is designed to address.

The second reason that having no single unifying perspective is good is that the existence of alternative viewpoints can keep us open-minded toward phenomena that any one view may fail to include. Intellectual competition is stimulating. It can prevent dogmatism and closed minds. No matter how emphatically a Freudian or a behaviorist or a biological psychologist believes that her approach accounts for everything, she also knows that a substantial number of her colleagues believe the approach to be dead wrong. That kind of knowledge is intellectually bracing.

I even fantasize, sometimes, that biology and physics might be better off if they had not settled so firmly, so soon, on a single unifying approach. What phenomena are scientists missing today because they do not happen to fit current views of evolutionary theory or relativity? Biologists and physicists might never find out what their theories and methods neglect because, as we have seen, adherence to one basic approach can blind you to things that are perfectly obvious from other perspectives. For my part, I enjoy personality psychology's lack of a single unifying approach. This lack leaves a lot of room for free thought and theorizing. Other sciences have always seemed a bit too closed for my taste. If you feel the same way, you might enjoy being a personality psychologist, too.

Choosing a Basic Approach

I believe that it is particularly important to learn each of the basic approaches to personality independently of each other, as they were presented in this book, so that you can get a sense of the full scope and flavor of each. And for most purposes—even the purpose of becoming a personality researcher—it is probably the most profitable as well as easiest course to choose a single paradigm to work within—the trait, biological, psychoanalytic, humanistic, behaviorist, or cognitive approach. As the cognitive scientist Howard Gardner (1987, p. 222) noted, "Even if, ultimately, everything turns out to be connected to everything else, a research program rooted in the realization might collapse of its own weight."

The choice of which approach to pursue cannot be based on which one is right or wrong, because all of them are right *and* wrong. Rather, the choice should be made on the basis of two (perhaps three) criteria. First, what do you want to understand—free will, individual differences, the unconscious mind, or the shaping of behavior? The second is even more personal: Which approach is the most interesting to you? If one of them really turns you on, maybe you should become a personality psychologist. And if you do, then a third criterion comes into play: Which basic approach offers you the best potential to do interesting work that can add to our knowledge?

My own choice has been the trait approach, mostly on the basis of this third criterion. As much as I admire psychoanalysis, for example, and even find it useful in daily life, I find it hard to imagine what kind of research can tell us more about it, since the case study method is, to me, unsatisfying. The trait approach, by contrast, has managed to keep me busy in a research career for the past three decades and will continue to do so, I hope, for many years to come.

Maintaining an Awareness of Alternative Approaches

Nevertheless, I try to take a vacation from my favored approach now and then. An occasion for such a trip is when I teach a personality course, or work on this book. I get the opportunity, for a time, to look once more at the psychological world through several different sets of fresh lenses. I think about questions I usually ignore—like, what is free will?—and entertain alternative visions of reality. I think this variation helps me keep an open mind; it is also fun.

No matter which basic approach you choose, there are five reasons why you should maintain an awareness and knowledge of the alternatives. The first is simply to avoid arrogance and to keep from thinking that you know it all. The second is to understand the proper basis for evaluating alternative approaches. Remember that each basic approach to personality, brilliant though it is, tends to look irrelevant and even foolish from the point of view of the other approaches. The third reason is to have a way of dealing with those psychological phenomena you will run across from time to time that do not fit into your favorite approach. I once heard the psychologist Ernest R. Hilgard say that we must not be in the position of the entomologist who found a bug he could not classify, so he stepped on it. The fourth reason is to give yourself the chance to change your mind later. If your interests or goals change, or if the phenomena you encounter refuse to fit your favorite approach, you will have someplace to go.

Finally, the fifth reason: At some point, it might make sense to integrate some of the different paradigms of personality psychology. To do this will require an understanding of each paradigm being integrated. In Chapter 1, I mentioned the dream of some psychologists to develop what I called the OBT (one big theory) that would explain absolutely everything. And recent years have seen increasing progress—some deliberate, some accidental—in combining the issues that traditionally have belonged to different approaches.

For example, the trait approach and the learning (especially cognitive and social learning) approaches seem to address many of the same phenomena from different (and not incompatible) angles. The cognitive social-learning approach itself has close ties to (and historical roots in) the humanistic and behaviorist approaches. It also is being applied to issues—such as the nature of unconscious thoughts about the self—that were long restricted to the psychoanalytic tradition. With each passing year, the biological approach, too, is having an increasing amount of influence on everybody. Evolutionary reasoning is used increasingly often to answer questions about why the mind works the way it does, and genetic, biochemical, and neurological knowledge is contributing to theories of how mental processes function and where they originate.

So, in the end, you may not have to choose. Out there, dimly glimmering on the horizon, is a hint of what an overall integrated theory of personality—the ultimate OBT—might look like, as the most important elements of the basic approaches gradually combine into a single overarching perspective. Look again into Chapters 16 and 17. That is probably where the beginnings of the OBT are hiding.

WHAT HAVE WE LEARNED?

One of my colleagues has a cartoon on his office door that depicts a student frantically cramming for exams. "It's not what you know," the caption reads, "it's when you know it." The implicit message is that most of what one learns in a college course, or reads in a 750-page book, is forgotten soon after finals week. That view is not cynical; it is realistic. What, then, will you retain from taking a personality course or reading this book? One lasting benefit may be that you became a little smarter. This is more likely to have happened if you thought about the material, whether you agreed or disagreed with my point of view, and received feedback from your instructor and fellow students. In particular, I hope you thought about how this material pertains to you because, as explained in Chapter 17, that is the most effective way to learn it—as well as the most interesting thing you can do with psychological knowledge.

"What does he know, and how long will he know it?"

Another realistic possibility after taking a course, and reading a long book such as this, is that past the final exam, you will retain not specific details of theories and experiments, surely, but knowledge about a few general themes that emerged again and again. Let's review a few of the major themes that are well worth remembering.

Cross-Situational Consistency and Aggregation

People remain who they are regardless of the situation. We have seen that psychologists still argue about this question of "behavioral consistency," but the evidence is clear and comes from all directions. Someone who dominates a business meeting will probably dominate a party; someone who is pessimistic about his career will probably also be pessimistic about the outcome of his wife's childbirth; and someone who has "issues" about her father is likely to bring them to bear in many of her other relationships with men. These examples come from three different basic approaches.

Research in the trait paradigm has demonstrated the consistency of dominance. Research in the cognitive paradigm has demonstrated the consistency of pessimism. And both the psychoanalytic and cognitive paradigms have demonstrated transference of consistent relationship patterns.

Let's consider consistency another way. If you were dropped off alone on a desert island, you would be in a unique situation with no expectations for your behavior from anybody else. You would nonetheless be who you are; whether you respond to this situation with fear, resourcefulness, loneliness, or joy at the peace and quiet depends on your personality. Personality is baggage you always have with you.

Still, consistency is limited in two ways. First, behavior surely changes from one situation to the next. I once did a two-session experiment in which I found that the participants were much less nervous in the second session than they were in the first session, an obvious effect of the familiarity of the setting (Funder & Colvin, 1991). But the people most nervous at the first session also tended to be the most nervous at the second session. To give another example, the most cheerful person at a party will surely become much less cheerful at a funeral. The consistency of his personality implies only that he will probably still be more cheerful than everybody else at the funeral, not that he will be equally cheerful in both situations (Oishi et al., 2004). Behavior and emotion change over time, but individuals maintain their differences. This idea is not obvious at first glance, and not even all psychologists quite grasp it, but it is important.

A second limitation is that behavioral consistency is not strong enough to predict a single action in a single situation with any great fidelity. Recall the personality correlation coefficient of around .30 to .40 (Chapter 4), which means a behavioral prediction is likely to be right about two times out of three. This is a useful level of accuracy, but it includes a lot of errors. Behavioral consistency only becomes truly worthy of the name when you predict the average or aggregate of several behaviors. Will your roommate greet you cheerfully when you come home next Tuesday at 4:30 P.M.? Who knows? But if she is a cheerful person, you can confidently predict that, in the 30 times you arrive home next month, her greeting will be more pleasant on average than that of your other, crabbier roommate.

The Biological Roots of Personality

As we saw in Chapters 8 and 9, biological research relevant to personality is progressing at a rapid and accelerating pace. Proponents of the other approaches (such as the learning and cognitive approaches) no longer try to deny that the consistent patterns of behavior manifesting as personality are rooted in anatomical structures such as the brain's frontal lobes and the amygdala, and in chemicals such as neurotransmitters and hormones, which in turn originate in the DNA people have inherited from their ancestors over the course of evolutionary history. These facts limit the possibilities for any individual. The philosopher John Locke thought that the human mind started out at birth like a blank slate, or tabula rasa. Nice idea, but he was wrong. The behaviorist John Watson thought he could take any baby and with the proper training produce a "doctor, lawyer, beggar man, or thief." Another nice idea, but he was wrong too.

> The philosopher John Locke thought that the human mind started out at birth like a blank slate, or tabula rasa. Nice idea, but he was wrong.

Biologically based research on psychology is technologically impressive. The sophisticated—and expensive!—equipment required to analyze hormonal levels or DNA structures, or to produce amazing color pictures that seem to show the brain in action, can be dazzling, even somewhat intimidating. It is important to remember, therefore, that this research is still near its beginning. What we don't know vastly exceeds what we know, and—as in all maturing fields of research—the growth of knowledge clarifies, above all else, just how complex everything is. Genetic structures, neurotransmitters, hormones, and regions of the brain all have important relationships with behavior and personality, but the connections are not simple because everything interacts with everything else. Genes interact with each other, the effect of one neurotransmitter or hormone depends on levels of others, and the densely interconnected regions of the brain act together in complex patterns all the time. And that is just the beginning. The whole neurological system constantly interacts with the external world, including all of the continually changing aspects of the environment and other people. The fact that psychology is beginning to appreciate this complexity more fully is an important sign of progress.

The Unconscious Mind

The unconscious is no longer an exotic, implausible idea kept alive by Freudian diehards. It has entered the mainstream. We saw evidence throughout this book that the unconscious part of the mind—the part we cannot describe or explain in words, and that can occasionally surprise or even mystify us—is important in many ways. Indeed, we saw in Chapter 16 that consciousness can only hold about seven (plus or minus two) ideas at a time anyway, so the idea that all of the mind's activities are conscious is implausible.

Recall just a few examples. Biological research has shown that the connections between the emotional and more rational areas of the brain can be damaged or severed to the point that people have thoughts that make no emotional sense, or emotions they cannot explain. Psychoanalytic theory provides many examples of how people fend off perceptions and thoughts they find too troublesome to experience immediately or directly. The cognitive approach to personality has demonstrated ways that perception, memory, and thought can be primed or unconsciously prompted. Indeed, in Chapter 17 we saw how even self-consciousness might be to some degree unconscious!

Free Will and Responsibility

Because psychology tries 99 percent of the time to behave like a "real," deterministic science, it tends to ignore the idea of free will and the related concept of responsibility. We saw theorists as diverse as Sigmund Freud and B. F. Skinner unite behind the idea that behavioral freedom is an illusion. The most valuable contribution of humanistic psychology (Chapter 13) has been a reasonable way to think about free will. Behavior is determined only up to a point, after which choices become possible. Kelly's theory of constructive alternativism implies that even a person who was abused as a child could reasonably conclude that either (1) "the world is a horrible place full of people who cannot be trusted," or (2) "I can survive anything, even abuse." Both conclusions are consistent with the individual's experience. The secret of psychological success may be recognizing the choice points in life and responsibly making the most of them.

The Nature of Happiness

Another contribution from the humanists and the related positive psychology movement is the reminder that happiness comes at least as much from the inside as from the outside. It matters less whether you are a millionaire, research shows, than how you choose to think about whatever you have (it helps to be grateful). Moreover, the goal of life is not to achieve a state of zero stress—a totally stress-free life would be boring and meaningless. A healthy life involves seeking out difficult but reasonable and meaningful challenges, and, when they are accomplished, seeking more. This kind of constant striving for growth is both a cause and a result of happiness. As I observed in Chapter 16, the experience of happiness is more than a passive end state. It is an opportunity to broaden and build the foundations for a better life for yourself and for others.

Behavioral Change

Rewarded behaviors become more likely, and punished behaviors become less likely (*duh*). This is true for creatures from amoebas to humans. The edifices of behaviorism and the social learning theories are based on this key idea, but the most important thing to remember is that rewards and punishments are not simply imposed. Often, you can choose which ones you will be subject to. Imagine a rat choosing his own Skinner box. Now think of someone choosing (or not) to enroll in medical school, or take a job with a law firm, or enlist in the military. What will be the consequences of the rewards and punishments in each of those environments? I mentioned choice points a moment ago. The most important choice points entail selecting an environment and its associated rewards and punishments. These choices include where to go to school, what career to enter, and whom to marry. Much of who you turn out to be will depend on these decisions.

And there is more. Once you enter an environment, it changes just because you are there, and what you do will cause further changes. If you ever find yourself in an unsatisfactory situation—a hostile work environment, an exploitative relationship—then ask yourself, "Is any aspect of this situation the result of something I am doing?" Maybe the answer is no. In that case, leave. But maybe the answer is yes. In that case, see if you can change things.

Culture and Personality

Psychologists have renewed their attention to psychological differences between cultures, and to the different ways people differ from each other *within* cultures. But very recent research also increasingly appreciates what we as humans have in common—not just our common mortal fate, as Sartre observed, but basic psychological processes, such as wanting to please our parents. Moreover, areas of the world often described as single "cultures"—including Asia, Europe, and the United States—have important diversity within them, and an individual can be a member of more than one culture at the same time. So it is important not to let a fascination with cross-cultural differences lead us back to into stereotyping—that would be ironic, wouldn't it.

Construals

It is not things that matter, but our opinions of things. This Talmudic insight not only is a theme of existential philosophy and humanistic psychology, but also lies at the core of the psychoanalytic, cross-cultural, and cognitive approaches to personality. Psychoanalysis emphasizes how unrealistic or fantasized views of reality can cause neurotic, self-defeating behavior. From a humanistic perspective, choosing a point of view is the core existential obligation. The only way to understand another person is to try to understand his personal and cultural perspective. The cognitive approach to personality does not often use the word *construal*, but almost all research in that approach intends to explain the origins and consequences of individuals' differing views of reality.

Indeed, it could be argued that all of psychology boils down to the moment of construal. All of your past experiences, biological processes, needs, ambitions, and perceptions combine to yield your view of reality, right now. Then, you decide what to do.

The Fine and Uncertain Line Between Normal and Abnormal

Personality psychology is in the business of understanding and even celebrating differences between people, but sometimes those differences go too far. A pattern of personality that is both unusual and problematic may be labeled a "personality disorder," and such labeling is at once useful, probably inevitable, and also dangerous. Terminology helps us to talk about and understand phenomena such as borderline, or avoidant, and other commonly recognized personality disorders, and there really is no way to avoid using labels to describe something so important. But labeling can also be dangerous, because it runs the risk of pathologizing so many undesirable patterns that the concept of mental illness begins to disappear. Furthermore, once a person is labeled, other people—even psychologists—may come to view the person only as the label and not as an individual. Another complication is that probably everybody has personality characteristics that, at their most extreme, would be labeled disorders, yet in the normal range, these aspects may be desirable—even essential—to a person's identity. As I said way back in Chapter 1, great strengths are often great weaknesses and vice versa. I'm not sure they should be separated. Plus, it doesn't matter what I think, because weakness and strengths *can't* be separated: Personality is a package deal.

THE QUEST FOR UNDERSTANDING

Remember S, I, L, and B data (Chapter 2)? To learn about a person we have no alternative but to watch what he or she does and listen to what he or she says. In the end, these behaviors form the basis of all our conclusions about personality, whether our approach is based on a trait, biological, psychoanalytic, behaviorist, cognitive, or even humanistic perspective. By the same token, the only way to find out whether we are right in thinking we understand an individual's personality is to try to explain (and sometimes predict) what the person does or says. Again, this is true no matter which basic approach we follow.

Our minds are forever sealed off from each other. We cannot directly know another person's thoughts or feelings; we can only watch what she does, or listen to what she says. From there, we can try to infer what is going on inside. And that inference, in turn, helps us begin to grasp the essence of each other's personality. So personality psychology is, in the final analysis, a quest for mutual understanding.

SUMMARY

The Different Approaches

• Each approach to personality explains some aspects of individuals well, while not explaining other aspects or ignoring them entirely. Thus, the choice between approaches depends not on which one is right, but on what we wish to know. We should try to stay open to alternatives.

What Have We Learned?

• It is unreasonable to expect to remember the details in a long book such as this, but certain recurring themes are important to retain. These include the nature of behavioral consistency; the biological roots of personality; the workings of the unconscious mind; the issues of free will and responsibility; the sources of behavioral change, especially the effects of choosing and changing one's environment; the nature of psychological differences within as well as across cultures; the importance of construals; and the inevitable connection between the difficult aspects of our personalities (especially at the extreme), and those aspects that make up the best and most important parts of our characters.

The Quest for Understanding

- In the final analysis, personality psychology attempts to turn our observations of ourselves and each other into mutual understanding.

THINK ABOUT IT

1. Is personality psychology really a science, and how can you tell? Is its scientific status important?
2. What is your favorite approach to personality among those covered in this book? What is your least favorite approach? Why?
3. Will the different approaches to personality someday be combined into one big, integrated approach? What would that approach look like?
4. How is personality psychology relevant to the following? (a) Your own daily life; (b) understanding and solving social problems; (c) understanding human nature.
5. Think about a course you took a year or two ago. What do you remember from it? If the answer is "not much," does that mean you did not benefit from the course?
6. What do you think you will remember, if anything, from this book and this course 20 years from now?
7. What do we know when we know a person?

SUGGESTED READINGS

John, O. P., Robins, R. W., & Pervin, L. A. (2008). *Handbook of personality: Theory and research* (3rd ed.). New York: Guilford Press.

> *This book is a collection of 32 state-of-the-art chapters written by active researchers (mostly Americans) on the many topics in personality psychology. It would be an excellent next step for a reader who, having finished this book, wants a more detailed and technical survey of the field. It could also be used as a graduate-level textbook.*

Corr, P. J., & Matthews, G. (2009). *The Cambridge handbook of personality psychology*. Cambridge University Press.

> *This book, with 46 chapters, has the same basic design as the handbook by John et al. (2008), but the chapters are shorter and more of the contributors are European. Comparing these two books provides an interesting glimpse of the somewhat different approaches to personality psychology in North America and Europe.*

EMEDIA

 Go to StudySpace, wwnorton.com/studyspace, to access additional review and enrichment materials.

CREDITS

REFERENCES

Abelson, R., Cohen, J., & Rosenthal, R. (Chairs). (1996). *Initial report of the task force on statistical inference*. Washington, DC: Board of Scientific Affairs, American Psychological Association.

Adams, C. (2001, Feb. 2). Are there nine Eskimo words for snow? *The Straight Dope*. Retrieved July 15, 2003, from www.straightdope.com/columns/010202.html

Adams, H. E., Wright, L. W., & Lohr, B. A. (1996). Is homophobia associated with homosexual arousal? *Journal of Abnormal Psychology, 105,* 440–445.

Ader, R., & Cohen, N. (1993). Psychoneuroimmunology: Conditioning and stress. *Annual Review of Psychology, 44,* 53–85.

Adler, A. (1939). *Social interest*. New York: Putnam.

Adler, J. (2006, March 27). Freud in our midst. *Newsweek, 197,* 42–49.

Adolphs, R. (2001). The neurobiology of social cognition. *Current Opinion in Neurobiology, 11,* 231–239.

Adorno, T. W. (1950). Politics and economics in the interview material. In T. W. Adorno, E. Frenkel-Brunswik, D. Levinson, & N. Sanford (Eds.), *The authoritarian personality* (pp. 654–726). New York: Harper & Row.

Adorno, T. W., Frenkel-Brunswik, E., Levinson, D., & Sanford, N. (1950). *The authoritarian personality*. New York: Harper & Row.

Ahadi, S., & Diener, E. (1989). Multiple determinants and effect size. *Journal of Personality and Social Psychology, 56,* 398–406.

Ainsworth, M. D. S., Blehar, M. C., Waters, E., & Wall, S. (1978). *Patterns of attachment: Assessed in the strange situation and at home*. Hillsdale, NJ: Erlbaum.

Albright, L., Kenny, D. A., & Malloy, T. E. (1988). Consensus in personality judgments at zero acquaintance. *Journal of Personality and Social Psychology, 55,* 387–395.

Albright, L., Malloy, T. E., Dong, Q., Kenny, D. A., & Fang, X. (1997). Cross-cultural consensus in personality judgments. *Journal of Personality and Social Psychology, 72,* 558–569.

Alley, T. R. (1988). Physiognomy and social perception. In T. R. Alley (Ed.), *Social and applied aspects of perceiving faces* (pp. 167–186). Hillsdale, NJ: Erlbaum.

Allport, G. W. (1937). *Personality: A psychological interpretation*. New York: Holt, Rinehart.

Allport, G. W. (1958). What units shall we employ? In G. Lindzey (Ed.), *Assessment of human motives* (pp. 239–260). New York: Holt, Rinehart.

Allport, G. W. (1961). *Pattern and growth in personality*. New York: Holt, Rinehart.

Allport, G. W. (1965). *Letters from Jenny*. New York: Harcourt, Brace.

Allport, G. W., & Odbert, H. S. (1936). Trait-names: A psycho-lexical study. *Psychological Monographs: General and Applied, 47*(1, Whole No. 211), 171–220.

Allport, G. W., & Vernon, P. E. (1933). *Studies in expressive movement*. New York: Macmillan.

Alonso-Zaldivar, R. (2002, December 11). Jet crash probe is concluded. *Los Angeles Times*, p. B1.

Alper, J., Beckwith, J., & Miller, L. G. (1978). Sociobiology is a political issue. In A. L. Caplan (Ed.), *The sociobiology debate: Readings on ethical and scientific issues* (pp. 476–488). New York: Harper & Row.

Altemeyer, B. (1981). *Right-wing authoritarianism*. Winnipeg: University of Manitoba Press.

Altemeyer, B. (1998). The other "authoritarian personality." *Advances in Experimental Social Psychology, 30,* 47–92.

Altemeyer, B. (2007). *The authoritarians*. Winnipeg, Manitoba, Canada: Altemeyer. Retrieved January 21, 2009, from http://home.cc.umanitoba.ca/~altemey/

Amabile, T. M., & Glazebrook, A. H. (1982). A negativity bias in interpersonal evaluation. *Journal of Experimental Social Psychology, 18,* 1–22.

Ambady, N., Hallahan, M., & Rosenthal, R. (1995). On judging and being judged accurately in zero-acquaintance situations. *Journal of Personality and Social Psychology, 69,* 518–529.

American Anthropological Association (1999). AAA statement on race. *American Anthropologist, 100,* 712–713.

American Psychiatric Association (1994). *Diagnostic and statistical manual of mental disorders: DSM-IV* (4th ed.). Washington, DC: American Psychiatric Association.

American Psychiatric Association (2000). *Diagnostic and statistical manual of mental disorders: DSM-IV-TR* (4th ed., text revision). Washington, DC: American Psychiatric Association.

American Psychological Assocation (2001). *Publication manual of the American Psychological Association* (5th ed). Washington, DC: American Psychological Association.

Anastasi, A. (1982). *Psychological testing.* New York: Macmillan.

Andersen, S. M. (1984). Self-knowledge and social inference: II. The diagnosticity of cognitive/affective and behavioral data. *Journal of Personality and Social Psychology, 46,* 294–307.

Andersen, S. M., & Baum, A. (1994). Transference in interpersonal relations: Inferences and affect based on significant-other representations. *Journal of Personality, 62,* 459–499.

Andersen, S. M., & Bem, S. L. (1981). Sex typing and androgyny in dyadic interaction: Individual differences in responsiveness to physical attractiveness. *Journal of Personality and Social Psychology, 41,* 74–86.

Andersen, S. M., & Berk, M. S. (1998). The social-cognitive model of transference: Experiencing past relationships in the present. *Current Directions in Psychological Science, 7,* 109–115.

Andersen, S. M., & Chen, S. (2002). The relational self: An interpersonal social-cognitive theory. *Psychological Review, 109,* 619–645.

Anderson, C., John, O. P., Keltner, D., & Kring, A. M. (2001). Who attains social status? Effects of personality and physical attractiveness in social groups. *Journal of Personality and Social Psychology, 81,* 116–132.

Anderson, C. A., Buckley, K. E., & Carnagey, N. L. (2008). Creating your own hostile environment: A laboratory examination of trait aggressiveness and the violence escalation cycle. *Personality and Social Psychology Bulletin, 34,* 462–473.

Anderson, E. (1994, May). The code of the streets. *Atlantic Monthly, 273,* 80–94.

Anderson, M. C., & Levy, B. (2002). Repression can (and should) be studied empirically. *Trends in Cognitive Science, 6,* 502–503.

Anderson, S. W., Bechara, A., Damasio, H., Tranel, D., & Damasio, A. R. (1999). Impairment of social and moral behavior related to early damage in the human prefrontal cortex. *Nature Neuroscience, 2,* 1032–1037.

Apter, M. J. (1992). *The dangerous edge: The psychology of excitement.* New York: Free Press.

Aronson, E. (1972). *The social animal.* San Francisco: Freeman.

Arsenian, J., & Arsenian, J. M. (1948). Tough and easy cultures: A conceptual analysis. *Psychiatry, 11,* 377–385.

Asendorpf, J. B. (2002). The puzzle of personality types [Editorial]. *European Journal of Personality, 16,* 51–55.

Asendorpf, J. B., Banse, R., & Mücke, D. (2002). Double dissociation between implicit and explicit personality self-concept: The case of shy behavior. *Journal of Personality and Social Psychology, 83,* 380–393.

Asendorpf, J. B., Borkenau, P., Ostendorf, F., & van Aken, M. A. G. (2001). Carving personality description at its joints: Confirmation of three replicable personality prototypes for both children and adults. *European Journal of Personality, 15,* 169–198.

Asendorpf, J. B., Denissen, J. J. A., & van Aken, M. A. G. (2008). Inhibited and aggressive preschool children at 23 years of age: Personality and social transitions into adulthood. *Developmental Psychology, 44,* 997–1011.

Asendorpf, J. B., & van Aken, M. A. G. (1991). Correlates of the temporal consistency of personality patterns in childhood. *Journal of Personality, 59,* 689–703.

Asendorpf, J. B., & van Aken, M. A. G. (1999). Resilient, overcontrolled, and undercontrolled personality prototypes in childhood: Replicability, predictive power, and the trait-type issue. *Journal of Personality and Social Psychology, 77*, 815–832.

Asendorpf, J. B., & Wipers, S. (1998). Personality effects on social relationships. *Journal of Personality and Social Psychology, 74*, 1531–1544.

Ashton, M. C., & Lee, K. (2005). Honesty-humility, the Big Five, and the Five-Factor Model. *Journal of Personality, 73*, 1321–1351.

Associated Press (1994, May 5). African emigrants spread practice. Retrieved online from Prodigy service.

Auyeung, B., Baron-Caron, S., Ashwin, E., Knickmeyer, R., Taylor, K., Hackett, G., et al. (2009). Fetal testosterone predicts sexually differentiated childhood behavior in girls and boys. *Psychological Science, 20*, 144–148.

Averill, J. R. (1997). The emotions: An integrative account. In R. Hogan, J. Johnson, & S. Briggs (Eds.), *Handbook of personality psychology* (pp. 513–541). San Diego: Academic Press.

Azrin, N. H., & Holz, W. C. (1966). Punishment. In W. K. Honig (Ed.), *Operant behavior: Areas of research and application* (pp. 380–447). New York: Appleton-Century-Crofts.

Bachrach, H. M., Galatzer-Levy, R., Skolnikoff, A., & Waldron, S. (1991). On the efficacy of psychoanalysis. *Journal of the American Psychoanalytic Association, 39*, 871–916.

Back, M. D., Schmukle, S. C., & Egloff, B. (in press). Why are narcissists so charming at first sight? Decoding the narcissism-popularity link at zero acquaintance. *Journal of Personality and Social Psychology*.

Bader, M. J. (1994). The tendency to neglect therapeutic aims in psychoanalysis. *Psychoanalytic Quarterly, 63*, 246–269.

Bailey, J. M., Dunne, M. P., & Martin, N. G. (2000). Genetic and environmental influences on sexual orientation and its correlates in an Australian twin sample. *Journal of Personality and Social Psychology, 78*, 524–536.

Bakan, D. (1966). *The duality of human existence*. Chicago: Rand McNally.

Balcetis, E., Dunning, D., & Miller, R. L. (2008). Do collectivists know themselves better than individualists? Cross-cultural studies of the holier-than-thou phenomenon. *Journal of Personality and Social Psychology, 95*, 1252–1267.

Baldwin, M. W. (1999). Relational schemas: Research into social-cognitive aspects of interpersonal experience. In D. Cervone & Y. Shoda (Eds.), *The coherence of personality: Social-cognitive bases of consistency, variability, and organization* (pp. 127–154). New York: Guilford Press.

Ball, J. D., Archer, R. P., & Imhof, E. A. (1994). Time requirements of psychological testing: A survey of practitioners. *Journal of Personality Assessment, 64*, 213–228.

Balter, M. (2002). What made humans modern? *Science, 295*, 1219.

Bandura, A. (1971). *Social learning theory*. New York: General Learning Press.

Bandura, A. (1977). *Social learning theory*. Englewood Cliffs, NJ: Prentice-Hall.

Bandura, A. (1978). The self system in reciprocal determinism. *American Psychologist, 33*, 344–358.

Bandura, A. (1989). Human agency in social cognitive theory. *American Psychologist, 44*, 1175–1184.

Bandura, A. (1999). Social cognitive theory of personality. In D. Cervone & Y. Shoda (Eds.), *The coherence of personality: Social-cognitive bases of consistency, variability, and organization* (pp. 185–241). New York: Guilford Press.

Bandura, A., Ross, D., & Ross, S. A. (1963). Imitation of film-mediated aggressive models. *Journal of Abnormal and Social Psychology, 66*, 3–11.

Bargh, J. A., Bond, R. N., Lombardi, W. J., & Tota, M. E. (1986). The additive nature of chronic and temporary sources of construct accessibility. *Journal of Personality and Social Psychology, 50*, 869–878.

Bargh, J. A., Lombardi, W. J., & Higgins, E. T. (1988). Automaticity of chronically accessible constructs in person × situation effects on person perception: It's just a matter of time. *Journal of Personality and Social Psychology, 55*, 599–605.

Barrett, L. F. (2006). Are emotions natural kinds? *Perspectives on Psychological Science, 1*, 28–58.

Barrett, L. F., & Wager, T. D. (2006). The structure of emotion: Evidence from neuroimaging studies. *Current Directions in Psychological Science, 15*, 79–83.

Barrick, M. R., & Mount, M. K. (1991). The Big Five personality dimensions and job performance: A meta-analysis. *Personnel Psychology, 44*, 1–26.

Bartholow, B. D., Sestir, M. A., & Davis, E. B. (2005). Correlates and consequences of exposure to video game violence: Hostile personality, empathy, and aggressive behavior. *Personality and Social Psychology Bulletin, 31*, 1573–1586.

Baumeister, R. F., Dale, K., & Sommer, K. L. (1998). Freudian defense mechanisms and empirical findings in modern social psychology: Reaction formation, projection, displacement, undoing, isolation, sublimation, and denial. *Journal of Personality, 66*, 1081–1124.

Baumeister, R. F., Smart, L., & Boden, J. M. (1996). Relation of threatened egotism to violence and aggression: The dark side of high self-esteem. *Psychological Review, 103*, 5–33.

Baumeister, R. F., & Tice, D. M. (1988). Metatraits. *Journal of Personality, 56*, 571–598.

Baumeister, R. F., & Vohs, K. D. (2002). The pursuit of meaningfulness in life. In C. R. Snyder & S. J. Lopez (Eds.), *Handbook of positive psychology* (pp. 608–618). London: Oxford University Press.

Baumrind, D. (1971). Current patterns of parental authority. *Developmental Psychology, 4*, 1–103.

Baumrind, D. (1985). Research using intentional deception: Ethical issues revisited. *American Psychologist, 40*, 165–174.

Baumrind, D. (1991). The influence of parenting style on adolescent competence and substance use. *Journal of Early Adolescence, 11*, 56–95.

Baumrind, D. (1993). The average expectable environment is not good enough: A response to Scarr. *Child Development, 64*, 1299–1317.

Bejjani, B.-P., Damier, P., Arnulf, I., Thivard, L., Bonnet, A-M., Dormonet, D., et al. (1999). Transient acute depression induced by high-frequency deep-brain stimulating. *New England Journal of Medicine, 340*, 1476–1480.

Bellamy, G. T. (1975). The Pygmalion effect: What teacher behaviors mediate it? *Psychology in the Schools, 12*, 454–461.

Belsky, J., Steinberg, L., & Draper, P. (1991). Childhood experience, interpersonal development, and reproductive strategy: An evolutionary theory of socialization. *Child Development, 62*, 647–670.

Bem, D. J. (1972). Self-perception theory. In L. Berkowitz (Ed.), *Advances in experimental social psychology* (Vol. 6, pp. 1–62). New York: Academic Press.

Bem, D. J. (1996). Exotic becomes erotic: A developmental theory of sexual orientation. *Psychological Review, 103*, 320–335.

Bem, D. J. (2001). Exotic becomes erotic: Integrating biological and experiential antecedents of sexual orientation. In A. R. D'Augelli & C. J. Patterson (Eds.), *Lesbian, gay, and bisexual identities and youth: Psychological perspectives* (pp. 52–68). London: Oxford University Press.

Bem, D. J., & Allen, A. (1974). On predicting some of the people some of the time: The search for cross-situational consistencies in behavior. *Psychological Review, 81*, 506–520.

Bem, D. J., & Funder, D. C. (1978). Predicting more of the people more of the time: Assessing the personality of situations. *Psychological Review, 85*, 485–501.

Benet-Martínez, V., & Haritatos, J. (2005). Bicultural identity integration (BII): Components and psychosocial antecedents. *Journal of Personality, 73*, 1015–1050.

Benet-Martínez, V., & John, O. P. (1998). Los Cinco Grandes across cultures and ethnic groups: Multitrait-multimethod analyses of the Big Five in Spanish and English. *Journal of Personality and Social Psychology, 75*, 729–750.

Benet-Martínez, V., & John, O. P. (2000). Toward the development of quasi-indigenous personality constructs: Measuring Los Cinco Grandes in Spain with indigenous Castilian markers. *American Behavioral Scientist, 44*, 141–157.

Benet-Martínez, V., Leu, J., Lee, F., & Morris, M. (2002). Negotiating biculturalism: Cultural frame switching in biculturals with oppositional versus compatible cultural identities. *Journal of Cross-Cultural Psychology, 35*, 492–516.

Benet-Martínez, V., & Waller, N. G. (1997). Further evidence for the cross-cultural generality of the Big Seven Factor model: Indigenous and imported Spanish personality constructs. *Journal of Personality, 65*, 567–598.

Benjamin, J., Li, L., Patterson, C., Greenberg, B. D., Murphy, D. L., & Hamer, D. H. (1996). Population and familial association between the D4 dopamine receptor gene and measures of novelty seeking. *Nature Genetics, 12*, 81–84.

Bentham, J. (1988). *The principles of morals and legislation*. Amherst, NY: Prometheus Books. (Originally published 1781)

Bergeman, C. S., Chipuer, H. M., Plomin, R., Pedersen, N. L., McClearn, G. E., Nesselroade, J. R., et al. (1993). Genetic and environmental effects on openness to experience, agreeableness, and conscientiousness: An adoption/twin study. *Journal of Personality, 61*, 159–179.

Berke, R. L. (1998, September 27). The good leader: In presidents, virtues can be flaws (and vice versa). *New York Times.*

Berkowitz, L. (1962). *Aggression: A social psychological analysis*. New York: McGraw-Hill.

Bernhardt, P. C., Dabbs, J. M., Jr., Fielden, J. A., & Lutter, C. D. (1998). Testosterone changes during vicarious experiences of winning and losing among fans at sporting events. *Physiology and Behavior, 65*, 59–62.

Bernstein, N. (2008, March 12). Foes of sex trade are stung by the fall of an ally [Electronic version]. *New York Times.* Retrieved March 17, 2009, from http://www.nytimes.com/2008/03/12/nyregion/12prostitute.html?_r=1

Berry, D. S., & Finch Wero, J. W. (1993). Accuracy in face perception: A view from ecological psychology. *Journal of Personality, 61*, 497–520.

Berry, D. S., & Pennebaker, J. W. (1993). Nonverbal and verbal emotional expression and health. *Psychotherapy and Psychosomatics, 59*, 11–19.

Berry, J. W. (1969). On cross-cultural comparability. *International Journal of Psychology, 4*, 119–128.

Betan, E., Heim, A. K., Conklin, C. Z., & Westen, D. (2005). Countertransference phenomena and personality psychology in clinical practice: An empirical investigation. *American Journal of Psychiatry, 162*, 890–898.

Bettelheim, B. (1943). Individual and mass behavior in extreme situations. *Journal of Abnormal and Social Psychology, 38*, 417–452.

Bettelheim, B. (1982). *Freud and man's soul*. New York: Vintage.

Bettelheim, B. (1988). *A good enough parent*. New York: Vintage.

Biernat, M. (1989). Motives and values to achieve: Different constructs with different effects. *Journal of Personality, 57*, 69–95.

Bigelow, H. J. (1850). Dr. Harlow's case of recovery from the passage of an iron bar through the head. *American Journal of Medical Sciences, 16*(39), 13–22.

Binswanger, L. (1958). The case of Ellen West. In R. May, E. Angel, & H. F. Ellenberger (Eds.), *Existence* (pp. 237–364). New York: Basic Books.

Binswanger, L. (1963). *Being-in-the-world: Selected papers of Ludwig Binswanger*. New York: Basic Books.

Birbaumer, N., Grodd, W., Diedrich, O., Klose, U., Erb, M., & Lotze, M. (1998). fMRI reveals amygdala activation to human faces in social phobics. *Neuroreport, 9*, 1223–1226.

Blackman, M. C. (2002a). The employment interview via the telephone: Are we sacrificing accurate personality judgments for cost efficiency? *Journal of Research in Personality, 36*, 208–223.

Blackman, M. C. (2002b). Personality judgment and the utility of the unstructured employment interview. *Basic and Applied Social Psychology, 24*, 241–250.

Blackman, M. C., & Funder, D. C. (1998). The effect of information on consensus and accuracy in personality judgment. *Journal of Experimental Social Psychology, 34*, 164–181.

Blanton, H., & Jaccard, J. (2006). Arbitrary metrics in psychology. *American Psychologist, 61*, 27–41.

Block, J. (1961). *The Q-sort method in psychological assessment and psychiatric research*. Springfield, IL: Thomas.

Block, J. (1971). *Lives through time*. Berkeley, CA: Bancroft Press.

Block, J. (1977). Advancing the science of psychology: Paradigmatic shift or improving the quality of research? In D. Magnusson & N. S. Endler (Eds.), *Personality at the crossroads: Current issues in interactional psychology* (pp. 37–64). Hillsdale, NJ: Erlbaum.

Block, J. (1978). *The Q-sort method in personality assessment and psychiatric research*. Palo Alto, CA: Consulting Psychologists Press. (Originally published 1961)

Block, J. (1989). Critique of the act frequency approach to personality. *Journal of Personality and Social Psychology, 56*, 234–245.

Block, J. (1993). Studying personality the long way. In D. C. Funder, R. D. Parke, C. Tomlinson-Keasey, & K. Widaman (Eds.), *Studying lives through time: Personality and development* (pp. 9–41). Washington, DC: American Psychological Association.

Block, J. (1995). A contrarian view of the five-factor approach to personality description. *Psychological Bulletin, 117,* 187–215.

Block, J. (2002). *Personality as an affect-processing system: Toward an integrative theory.* Mahwah, NJ: Erlbaum.

Block, J. (2008). *The Q-sort in character appraisal: Encoding subjective impressions of persons quantitatively.* Washington, DC: American Psychological Association.

Block, J., & Block, J. H. (2006a). Nursery school personality and political orientation two decades later. *Journal of Research in Personality, 40,* 734–749.

Block, J., & Block, J. H. (2006b). Venturing a 30-year longitudinal study. *American Psychologist, 61,* 315–327.

Block, J., Block, J. H., & Keyes, S. (1988). Longitudinally foretelling drug usage in adolescence: Early childhood personality and environmental precursors. *Child Development, 59,* 336–355.

Block, J., Block, J. H., Siegelman, E., & von der Lippe, A. (1971). Optimal psychological adjustment: Response to Miller's and Bronfenbrenner's discussions. *Journal of Consulting and Clinical Psychology, 36,* 325–328.

Block, J., Gjerde, P. F., & Block, J. H. (1991). Personality antecedents of depressive tendencies in 18-year-olds: A prospective study. *Journal of Personality and Social Psychology, 60,* 726–738.

Block, J. H. (1973). Conceptions of sex role: Some cross-cultural and longitudinal perspectives. *American Psychologist, 28,* 512–526.

Block, J. H., & Block, J. (1980). The role of ego-control and ego-resiliency in the organization of behavior. In W. A. Collins (Ed.), *Development of cognition, affect, and social relations: The Minnesota symposia on child psychology* (Vol. 13, pp. 40–101). Hillsdale, NJ: Erlbaum.

Blum, K., Cull, J. G., Braverman, E. R., & Comings, D. E. (1996). Reward deficiency syndrome. *American Scientist, 84,* 132–146.

Bogg, T., & Roberts, B. W. (2004). Conscientiousness and health-related behaviors: A meta-analysis of the leading behavioral contributors to mortality. *Psychological Bulletin, 130,* 887–919.

Bolger, N., & Zuckerman, A. (1995). A framework for studying personality in the stress process. *Journal of Personality and Social Psychology, 69,* 890–902.

Bond, M. H. (1979). Dimensions of personality used in perceiving peers: Cross-cultural comparisons of Hong Kong, Japanese, American, and Filipino university students. *International Journal of Psychology, 14,* 47–56.

Bond, M. H., & Cheung, T. (1983). College students' spontaneous self-concept: The effect of culture among respondents in Hong Kong, Japan, and the United States. *Journal of Cross-Cultural Psychology, 14,* 153–171.

Bond, M. H., Nakazato, H., & Shiraishi, D. (1975). Universality and distinctiveness in dimensions of Japanese person perception. *Journal of Cross-Cultural Psychology, 6,* 346–357.

Borkenau, P., & Liebler, A. (1993). Consensus and self-other agreement for trait inferences from minimal information. *Journal of Personality, 61,* 477–496.

Borkenau, P., Riemann, R., Angleitner, A., & Spinath, F. M. (2001). Genetic and environmental influences on observed personality: Evidence from the German observational study of adult twins. *Journal of Personality and Social Psychology, 80,* 655–668.

Borkenau, P., Riemann, R., Angleitner, A., & Spinath, F. M. (2002). Assessment issues in behavior-genetic research in personality. *Psychology: The Journal of the Hellenic Psychological Society, 9,* 212–225.

Borman, W. C., Hanson, W., & Hedge, J. (1997). Personnel selection. *Annual Review of Psychology, 48,* 299–337.

Borman, W. C., & Penner, L. A. (2001). Citizenship performance: Its nature, antecedents and motives. In B. W. Roberts & R. Hogan (Eds.), *Personality psychology in the workplace.* Washington, DC: American Psychological Association.

Born, J., Hitzler, V., Pietrowsky, R., Pairschinger, P., & Fehm, H. L. (1988). Influences of cortisol on auditory evoked potentials and mood in humans. *Neuropsychobiology, 20,* 145–151.

Bornstein, R. F. (1999a). Criterion validity of objective and projective dependency tests: A meta-analytic assessment of behavioral prediction. *Psychological Assessment, 11*, 48–57.

Bornstein, R. F. (1999b). Source amnesia, misattribution, and the power of unconscious perceptions and memories. *Psychoanalytic Psychology, 16*, 155–178.

Borsboom, D., Mellenbergh, G. J., & van Heerden, J. (2004). The concept of validity. *Psychological Review, 111*, 1061–1071.

Boss, M. (1963). *Psychoanalysis and daseinsanalysis.* New York: Basic Books.

Bower, G. H., & Hilgard, E. R. (1981). *Theories of learning* (5th ed.). Englewood Cliffs, NJ: Prentice-Hall.

Bowers, K. S. (1973). Situationism in psychology: An analysis and critique. *Psychological Review, 80*, 307–336.

Bowlby, J. (1982). *Attachment and loss: Vol. 1. Attachment* (2nd ed.). New York: Basic Books. (Originally published 1969)

Bowlby, J. (1988). *A secure base: Clinical applications of attachment theory.* London: Routledge.

Box, G. E. P. (1979). Robustness in the strategy of scientific model building. In R. Launer & G. Wilkinson (Eds.), *Robustness in statistics* (pp. 201–236). New York: Academic Press.

Brandt, V. S. (1974). Skiing cross-culturally. *Current Anthropology, 15*, 64–66.

Braun, C. (1976). Teacher expectation: Sociopsychological dynamics. *Review of Educational Research, 46*, 185–213.

Bremner, J. D. (2005). *Brain imaging handbook.* New York: Norton.

Brenner, C. (1974). *An elementary textbook of psychoanalysis.* Garden City, NY: Doubleday/Anchor.

Brenner, C. (1982). *The mind in conflict.* New York: International Universities Press.

Brickman, P., Coates, D., & Janoff-Bulman, R. (1978). Winners and accident victims: Is happiness relative? *Journal of Personality and Social Psychology, 36*, 917–927.

Brickner, R. M. (1936). *The intellectual functions of the frontal lobes.* New York: Macmillan.

Briggs, S. R., & Cheek, J. M. (1986). The role of factor analysis in the development and evaluation of personality scales. *Journal of Personality, 54*, 106–148.

Briggs, S. R., Cheek, J. M., & Buss, A. H. (1980). An analysis of the Self-Monitoring Scale. *Journal of Personality and Social Psychology, 38*, 679–686.

Brown, R. (1996). *Against my better judgment: An intimate memoir of an eminent gay psychologist.* New York: Harrington Park Press.

Brown, W. (1910). Some experimental results in the correlation of mental abilities. *British Journal of Psychology, 3*, 297–301.

Brunstein, J. C., & Maier, G. W. (2005). Implicit and self-attribute motives to achieve: Two separate but interacting needs. *Journal of Personality and Social Psychology, 89*, 205–222.

Brunstein, J. C., Schultheiss, O. C., & Grässmann, R. (1998). Personal goals and emotional well-being: The moderating role of motive dispositions. *Journal of Personality and Social Psychology, 75*, 494–508.

Brunswik, E. (1956). *Perception and the representative design of psychological experiments.* Berkeley: University of California Press.

Bryan, W. J. (1922/1999). *The menace of evolution.* Pamphlet retrieved June 6, 2009, from University of Missouri–Kansas City Law School, "Famous Trials" Web site (created by Doug Linder, Professor of Law, for "Seminar in Famous Trials"): http://www.law.umkc.edu/faculty/projects/ftrials/scopes/scopes.htm

Buck, R. (1999). The biological affects: A typology. *Psychological Review, 106*, 301–336.

Bullock, W. A., & Gilliland, K. (1993). Eysenck's arousal theory of introversion-extraversion: A converging measures investigation. *Journal of Personality and Social Psychology, 64*, 113–123.

Burnett, J. D. (1974). Parallel measurements and the Spearman-Brown formula. *Educational and Psychological Measurement, 34*, 785–788.

Burnum, J. F. (1993). Medical diagnosis through semiotics: Giving meaning to the sign. *Annals of Internal Medicine, 119*, 939–943.

Burwen, L. S., & Campbell, D. T. (1957). The generality of attitudes toward authority and nonauthority figures. *Journal of Abnormal and Social Psychology, 54*, 24–31.

Bushman, B. J. (2002). Does venting anger feed or extinguish the flame? Catharsis, rumination, distraction, anger and aggressive responding. *Personality and Social Psychology Bulletin, 28*, 724–731.

Bushman, B. J., & Anderson, C. A. (2009). Comfortably numb: Desensitizing effects of violent media on helping others. *Psychological Science, 20,* 273–277.

Bushman, B. J., Baumeister, R. F., Thomaes, S., Ryu, E., Begeer, S., & West, S. G. (2009). Looking again, and harder, for a link between low self-esteem and aggression. *Journal of Personality, 77,* 427–446.

Buss, A. R. (1979). The trait-situation controversy and the concept of interaction. *Personality and Social Psychology Bulletin, 5,* 191–195.

Buss, D. M. (1989). Sex differences in human mate preferences: Evolutionary hypotheses tested in 37 cultures. *Behavioral and Brain Sciences, 12,* 1–49.

Buss, D. M., & Barnes, M. F. (1986). Preferences in human mate selection. *Journal of Personality and Social Psychology, 50,* 559–570.

Buss, D. M., & Greiling, H. (1999). Adaptive individual differences. *Journal of Personality, 67,* 209–243.

Buss, D. M., Larsen, R. J., Westen, D., & Semmelroth, J. (1992). Sex differences in jealousy: Evolution, physiology and psychology. *Psychological Science, 3,* 251–255.

Butcher, J. N. (1999). *A beginner's guide to the MMPI-2.* Washington, DC: American Psychological Association.

Butler, J. M., & Haigh, G. V. (1954). Changes in the relation between self-concepts and ideal concepts consequent upon client-centered counseling. In C. R. Rogers & R. F. Dymond (Eds.), *Psychotherapy and personality change: Co-ordinated studies in the client-centered approach* (pp. 55–76). University of Chicago Press.

Bykov, K. M. (1957). *The cerebral cortex and the internal organs* (W. H. Gantt, Trans.). New York: Chemical Publishing.

Byrne, D. (1961). The repression-sensitization scale: Rationale, reliability, and validity. *Journal of Personality, 29,* 334–349.

Cabeza, R., & Nyberg, L. (2000). Imaging cognition II: An empirical review of 275 PET and fMRI studies. *Journal of Cognitive Neuroscience, 12,* 1–47.

Caldwell, D. F., & Burger, J. M. (1997). Personality and social influence strategies in the workplace. *Personality and Social Psychology Bulletin, 23,* 1003–1012.

Caldwell, D. F., & Burger, J. M. (1998). Personality characteristics of job applicants and success in screening interviews. *Personnel Psychology, 51,* 119–136.

Call, J., & Tomasello, M. (1995). The use of social information in the problem-solving of orangutans and human children. *Journal of Comparative Psychology, 109,* 301–320.

Camara, W. J., Nathan, J. S., & Puente, A. E. (2000). Psychological test usage: Implications in professional psychology. *Professional Psychology: Research and Practice, 31,* 141–154.

Campos, J. J., Barrett, K., Lamb, M. E., Goldsmith, H. H., & Stenberg, C. (1983). Socioemotional development. In M. M. Haith & J. J. Campos (Eds.), *Handbook of child psychology: Vol. 2. Infancy and developmental psychobiology* (pp. 783–916). New York: Wiley.

Canli, T. (2004). Function brain mapping of extraversion and neuroticism: Learning from individual differences in emotion processing. *Journal of Personality, 72,* 1105–1132.

Canli, T., Amin, Z., Haas, B., Omura, K., & Constable, R. T. (2004). A double dissociation between mood states and personality traits in the anterior cingulate. *Behavioral Neuroscience, 118,* 897–904.

Canli, T., & Lesch, K. (2007). Long story short: The serotonin transporter in emotion regulation and social cognition. *Nature Neuroscience, 10,* 1103–1109.

Canli, T., Silvers, H., Whitfield, S. L., Gotlib, I. H., & Gabrieli, J. D. (2002). Amygdala response to happy faces as a function of extraversion. *Science, 296,* 2191.

Cannon, W. B. (1932). *The wisdom of the body.* New York: Norton.

Cantor, N. (1990). From thought to behavior: "Having" and "doing" in the study of personality and cognition. *American Psychologist, 45,* 735–750.

Cantor, N., & Kihlstrom, J. F. (1987). *Personality and social intelligence.* Englewood Cliffs, NJ: Prentice-Hall.

Capgras, J., & Reboul-Lachaux, J. (1923). L'illusion des "sosies" dans un delire systematize chronique [The illusion of doubles as a chronically systematized delusion]. *Bulletin de la Societé Clinique de Medecine Mentale, 11,* 6–16.

Caplan, B. (2003). Stigler-Becker versus Myers-Briggs: Why preference-blind explanations are scientifically meaningful and empirically important. *Journal of Economic Behavior and Organization, 50*, 391–405.

Carlson, K. S., & Gjerde, P. F. (2009). Preschool personality antecedents of narcissism in adolescence and young adulthood: A 20-year longitudinal study. *Journal of Research in Personality, 43*, 570–578.

Carnahan, T., & McFarland, S. (2007). Revisiting the Stanford Prison Experiment: Could participant self-selection have led to the cruelty? *Personality and Social Psychology Bulletin, 33*, 603–614.

Carney, D. R., Colvin, C. R., & Hall, J. A. (2007). A thin slice perspective on the accuracy of first impressions. *Journal of Research in Personality, 41*, 1054–1072.

Carstensen, L. L., & Fredrickson, B. L. (1998). Influence of HIV status and age on cognitive representations of others. *Health Psychology, 17*, 494–503.

Carstensen, L. L., Isaacowitz, D. M., & Charles, S. T. (1999). Taking time seriously: A theory of socioemotional selectivity. *American Psychologist, 54*, 165–181.

Carstensen, L. L., & Mikels, J. A. (2005). At the intersection of emotion and cognition: Aging and the positivity effect. *Current Directions in Psychological Science, 14*, 117–121.

Carver, C. S. (1975). Physical aggression as a function of objective self-awareness and attitudes toward punishment. *Journal of Experimental Social Psychology, 11*, 510–519.

Carver, C. S., & Scheier, M. F. (1995). The role of optimism versus pessimism in the experience of the self. In A. Oosterwegel & R. A. Wicklund (Eds.), *The self in European and North American culture: Development and processes* (pp. 193–204). Dordrecht, Netherlands: Kluwer Academic Press.

Carver, C. S., & White, T. L. (1994). Behavioral inhibition, behavioral activation, and affective responses to impending reward and punishment: The BIS/BAS scales. *Journal of Personality and Social Psychology, 67*, 319–333.

Cases, W., Seif, I., Grimsby, J., Gaspar, P., Chen, K., Pournin, S., et al. (1995). Aggressive behavior and altered amounts of brain serotonin and norepinephrine in mice lacking MAOA. *Science, 268*, 1763–1766.

Caspi, A. (1998). Personality development across the life course. In N. Eisenberg (Ed.), *Handbook of child psychology: Vol. 3. Social, emotional, and personality development* (5th ed., pp. 311–388). New York: Wiley.

Caspi, A., Elder, G. H., & Bem, D. J. (1987). Moving against the world: Life course patterns of explosive children. *Developmental Psychology, 23*, 308–313.

Caspi, A., McClay, J., Moffitt, T. E., Mill, J., Martin, J., Craig, I., et al. (2002, August 2). Role of genotype in the cycle of violence in maltreated children. *Science, 297*, 851–854.

Caspi, A., Roberts, B. W., & Shiner, R. L. (2005). Personality development: Stability and change. *Annual Review of Psychology, 56*, 453–484.

Caspi, A., & Silva, P. A. (1995). Temperamental qualities at age 3 predict personality traits in young adulthood: Longitudinal evidence from a birth cohort. *Child Development, 66*, 486–498.

Caspi, A., Sugden, K., Moffitt, T. E., Taylor, A., Craig, I. W., Harrington, H., et al. (2003, July 18). Influence of life stress on depression: Moderation by a polymorphism in the 5-HTT gene. *Science, 301*, 386–389.

Cattell, R. B. (1950). *Personality: A systematic, theoretical and factual study*. New York: McGraw-Hill.

Cattell, R. B. (1952). *Factor analysis*. New York: Harper & Row.

Cattell, R. B. (1957). *Personality and motivation structure and measurement*. New York: World Book.

Cattell, R. B. (1965). *The scientific analysis of personality*. Baltimore: Penguin Books.

Cattell, R. B., & Eber, H. W. (1961). *The Sixteen Personality Factor Questionnaire* (3rd ed.). Champaign, IL: Institute for Personality and Ability Testing.

Cervone, D. (2005). Personality architecture: Within-person structures and processes. *Annual Review of Psychology, 56*, 423–452.

Chaiken, S., & Trope, Y. (Eds.). (1999). *Dual-process models in social psychology*. New York: Guilford Press.

Chao, R. (2001). Extending research on the consequences of parenting style for Chinese Americans and European Americans. *Child Development, 72*, 1832–1843.

Chaplin, W. F. (1991). The next generation of moderator research in personality psychology. *Journal of Personality, 59*, 143–178.

Chaplin, W. F., & Goldberg, L. R. (1985). A failure to replicate the Bem and Allen study of individual differences in cross-situational consistency. *Journal of Personality and Social Psychology, 47*, 1074–1090.

Chaplin, W. F., Phillips, J. B., Brown, J. D., Clanton, N. R., & Stein, J. L. (2000). Handshaking, gender, personality, and first impressions. *Journal of Personality and Social Psychology, 79*, 110–117.

Chase, W. G., & Simon, H. A. (1973). The mind's eye in chess. In W. G. Chase (Ed.), *Visual information processing* (pp. 215–281). New York: Academic Press.

Chatard, A., Selimbegović, L., & Konan, P. N. (2009). Self-esteem and suicide rates in 55 nations. *European Journal of Personality, 23*, 19–32.

Cheek, J. M. (1990). Shyness, self-esteem, and self-consciousness. In H. Leitenberg (Ed.), *Handbook of social and evaluation anxiety* (pp. 47–82). New York: Plenum Press.

Chen, D. W. (2001, July 31). Boy, 6, dies of skull injury during MRI. *New York Times*. Retrieved June 15, 2006, from http://query.nytimes.com/gst/fullpage.html?sec=health&res=9400EEDC1E3DF932A05754C0A9679C8B63

Cheung, F. M., Leung, K., Fan, R. M., Song, W. S., Zhang, J. X., & Zhang, J. P. (1996). Development of the Chinese Personality Assessment Inventory. *Journal of Cross-Cultural Psychology, 27*, 181–199.

Cheung, F. M., & Song, W. (1989). A review of the clinical applications of the Chinese MMPI. *Psychological Assessment, 1*, 230–237.

Chi, T. C., & Hinshaw, S. P. (2002). Mother-child relationships of children with ADHD: The role of maternal depressive symptoms and depression-related distortions. *Journal of Abnormal Child Psychology, 30*, 387–400.

Chiao, J. Y., & Ambady, N. (2007). Cultural neuroscience: Parsing universality and diversity across levels of analysis. In S. Kitayama & D. Cohen (Eds.), *Handbook of cultural psychology* (pp. 237–254). New York: Guilford Press.

Childs, R. A., & Eyde, L. D. (2002). Assessment training in clinical psychology doctoral programs: What should we teach? What do we teach? *Journal of Personality Assessment, 78*, 130–144.

Choma, B. L., Busseri, M. A., & Sadava, S. W. (2009). Liberal and conservative ideologies: Different routes to happiness? *Journal of Research in Personality, 43*, 502–505.

Church, A. T., Henderson-Harami, C. A., del Prado, A. M., Curtis, G. J., Tanaka-Matsumi, J., Medina, J. L. V., et al. (2008). Culture, cross-role consistency, and adjustment: Testing trait and cultural psychology perspectives. *Journal of Personality and Social Psychology, 95*, 739–755.

Church, A. T., Katigbak, M. S., Reyes, J. A. S., Salanga, M. G. C., Miramontez, L. A., & Adams, N. B. (2008). Prediction and cross-situational consistency across cultures: Testing trait and cultural perspectives. *Journal of Research in Personality, 42*, 1199–1215.

Clark, H. H., & Clark, E. V. (1977). *Psychology and language: An introduction to psycholinguistics*. New York: Harcourt, Brace.

Clark, J. M., & Paivio, A. (1989). Observational and theoretical terms in psychology: A cognitive perspective on scientific language. *American Psychologist, 44*, 500–512.

Clark, L. A., Livesley, W. J., & Morey, L. (1997). Personality disorder assessment: The challenge of construct validity. *Journal of Personality Disorders, 11*, 205–231.

Clark, L. A., & Watson, D. (1999a). Personality, disorder, and personality disorder: Toward a more rational conceptualization. *Journal of Personality Disorders, 13*, 142–151.

Clark, L. A., & Watson, D. (1999b). Temperament: A new paradigm for trait psychology. In L. A. Pervin & O. P. John (Eds.), *Handbook of personality: Theory and research* (2nd ed., pp. 399–423). New York: Guilford Press.

Cloud, J. (2008, January 8). The mystery of borderline personality disorder. *Time*. Retrieved January 24, 2009, from http://www.time.com/time/printout/0,8816,1870491,00.html

Cohen, A. (2004). *Special Report: The Abu Ghraib Supplementary Documents*. Washington, DC: Center for Public Integrity. Retrieved January 13, 2009, from http://www.publicintegrity.org/articles/entry/505/

Cohen, D., Nisbett, R. E., Bowdle, B. F., & Schwartz, N. (1996). Insult, aggression and the southern culture of honor: An "experimental ethnography." *Journal of Personality and Social Psychology, 70*, 945–960.

Cohen, J. (1994). The earth is round (*p* < .05). *American Psychologist, 49*, 997–1003.

Cokely, E. T., & Feltz, A. (2009). Individual differences, judgment biases, and theory-of-mind: Deconstructing the intentional action side effect asymmetry. *Journal of Research in Personality, 43*, 18–24.

Collins, W. A., Maccoby, E. E., Steinberg, L., Hetherington, E. M., & Bornstein, M. H. (2000). Contemporary research on parenting: The case for nature and nurture. *American Psychologist, 55*, 218–232.

Colvin, C. R. (1993a). Childhood antecedents of young-adult judgability. *Journal of Personality, 61*, 611–635.

Colvin, C. R. (1993b). "Judgable" people: Personality, behavior, and competing explanations. *Journal of Personality and Social Psychology, 64*, 861–873.

Colvin, C. R., & Block, J. (1994). Do positive illusions foster mental health? An examination of the Taylor and Brown formulation. *Psychological Bulletin, 116*, 3–20.

Colvin, C. R., Block, J., & Funder, D. C. (1995). Overly positive self-evaluations and personality: Negative implications for mental health. *Journal of Personality and Social Psychology, 68*, 1152–1162.

Colvin, C. R., & Bundick, M. J. (2001). In search of the good judge of personality: Some methodological and theoretical concerns. In J. A. Hall & F. J. Bernieri (Eds.), *Interpersonal sensitivity: Theory and measurement* (pp. 47–65). Mahwah, NJ: Erlbaum.

Colvin, C. R., & Funder, D. C. (1991). Predicting personality and behavior: A boundary on the acquaintanceship effect. *Journal of Personality and Social Psychology, 60*, 884–894.

Cook, T. D., & Campbell, D. T. (Eds.). (1979). *The design and analysis of quasi-experiments for field settings*. Chicago: Rand-McNally.

Coolidge, F. L., Segal, S. L., & Applequist, K. (2009). Working memory deficits in personality disorder traits: A preliminary investigation in a nonclinical sample. *Journal of Research in Personality, 43*, 355–361.

Corr, P. J., & Matthews, G. (Eds.). (2009). *The Cambridge handbook of personality psychology*. Cambridge University Press.

Corr, P. J., Pickering, A. D., & Gray, J. A. (1997). Personality, punishment and procedural learning: A test of J. A. Gray's anxiety theory. *Journal of Personality and Social Psychology, 73*, 337–344.

Costa, P. T., Jr. (1996). Work and personality: Use of the NEO-PI-R in industrial/organizational psychology. *Applied Psychology: An International Review, 45*, 225–241.

Costa, P. T., Jr., Herbst, J. H., McCrae, R. R., Samuels, J., & Ozer, D. J. (2002). The replicability and utility of three personality types. *European Journal of Personality, 16*, 573–588.

Costa, P. T., Jr., & McCrae, R. R. (1985). *The NEO Personality Inventory manual*. Odessa, FL: Psychological Assessment Resources.

Costa, P. T., Jr., & McCrae, R. R. (1994). Set like plaster? Evidence for the stability of adult personality. In T. Heatherton & J. Weinberger (Eds.), *Can personality change?* (pp. 21–40). Washington, DC: American Psychological Association.

Costa, P. T., Jr., & McCrae, R. R. (1997). Stability and change in personality assessment: The Revised NEO Personality Inventory in the year 2000. *Journal of Personality Assessment, 68*, 86–94.

Costa, P. T., Jr., & McCrae, R. R. (1998). Trait theories in personality. In D. F. Barone, M. Hersen, & V. B. Van Hasselt (Eds.), *Advanced personality* (pp. 103–121). New York: Plenum Press.

Costa, P. T., Terracciano, A., & McCrae, R. R. (2001). Gender differences in personality traits across cultures: Robust and surprising findings. *Journal of Personality and Social Psychology, 81*, 322–331.

Cousins, S. D. (1989). Culture and self-perception in Japan and the United States. *Journal of Personality and Social Psychology, 56*, 124–131.

Craik, F. I. M., & Tulving, E. (1975). Depth of processing and the retention of words in episodic memory. *Journal of Experimental Psychology: General, 104*, 268–294.

Craik, F. I. M., & Watkins, M. J. (1973). The role of rehearsal in short-term memory. *Journal of Verbal Learning and Verbal Behavior, 12*, 599–607.

Cramer, P. (1998). Defensiveness and defense mechanisms. *Journal of Personality, 66*, 879–894.

Cramer, P., & Davidson, K. (Eds.). (1998). Defense mechanisms in contemporary personality research [Special Issue]. *Journal of Personality, 66*(6).

Cramer, P., & Jones, C. J. (2008). Narcissism, identification, and longitudinal change in psychological health: Dynamic predictions. *Journal of Research in Personality, 42,* 1148–1159.

Crews, F. (1996). The verdict on Freud. *Psychological Science, 7,* 63–67.

Crews, F. (Ed.). (1998). *Unauthorized Freud: Doubters confront a legend.* New York: Viking Press.

Crocker, J., & Wolfe, C. T. (2001). Contingencies of self-worth. *Psychological Review, 108,* 593–623.

Cronbach, L. J. (1951). Coefficient alpha and the internal structure of tests. *Psychometrika, 16,* 297–334.

Cronbach, L. J. (1955). Processes affecting scores on "understanding of others" and "assumed similarity." *Psychological Bulletin, 52,* 177–193.

Cronbach, L. J., Gleser, G. C., Nanda, H., & Rajaratnam, N. (1972). *The dependability of behavioral measurements: Theory of generalizability for scores and profiles.* New York: Wiley.

Cronbach, L. J., & Meehl, P. E. (1955). Construct validity in psychological tests. *Psychological Bulletin, 52,* 281–302.

Crowell, S. E., Beauchaine, T. P., & Linehan, M. M. (2009). A biosocial developmental model of borderline personality: Elaborating and extending Linehan's theory. *Psychological Bulletin, 135,* 495–510.

Crowson, H. M., DeBacker, T. K., & Thoma, S. J. (2005). Does authoritarianism predict post-9/11 attitudes? *Personality and Individual Differences, 39,* 1273–1283.

Csikszentmihalyi, M., & Csikszentmihalyi, I. S. (Eds.). (1988). *Optimal experience: Psychological studies of flow in consciousness.* New York: Cambridge University Press.

Csikszentmihalyi, M., & Larson, R. (1992). Validity and reliability of the Experience Sampling Method. In M. V. deVries (Ed.), *The experience of psychopathology: Investigating mental disorders in their natural settings* (pp. 43–57). Cambridge University Press.

Cunningham, D. J. (1992). Assessing constructions and constructing assessments: A dialogue. In T. M. Duffy & D. H. Jonassen (Eds.), *Constructivism and the technology of instruction: A conversation* (pp. 34–44). Hillsdale, NJ: Erlbaum.

Cutler, A. G. (Ed.). (1976). *Stedman's medical dictionary.* Baltimore: Williams & Wilkins.

Cutrona, C. E. (1982). Transition to college: Loneliness and the process of social adjustment. In L. A. Peplau & D. Perlman (Eds.), *Loneliness: A sourcebook of current theory, research, and therapy* (pp. 291–309). New York: Wiley.

Dabbs, J. M., Jr. (1997). Testosterone, smiling, and facial appearance. *Journal of Nonverbal Behavior, 21,* 45–55.

Dabbs, J. M., Jr., Alford, E. C., & Fielden, J. A. (1998). Trial lawyers and testosterone: Blue-collar talent in a white-collar world. *Journal of Applied Psychology, 28,* 84–94.

Dabbs, J. M., Jr., & Morris, R. (1990). Testosterone, social class, and antisocial behavior in a sample of 4,462 men. *Psychological Science, 1,* 209–211.

Dabbs, J. M., Jr., Ruback, R. B., Frady, R. L., Hopper, C. H., & Sgoritas, D. S. (1988). Saliva testosterone and criminal violence among women. *Personality and Individual Differences, 9,* 269–275.

Dabbs, J. M., Jr., Strong, R., & Milun, R. (1997). Exploring the mind of testosterone: A beeper study. *Journal of Research in Personality, 31,* 577–587.

Dahlsgaard, K., Peterson, C., & Seligman, M. E. P. (2005). Shared virtue: The convergence of valued human strengths across culture and history. *Review of General Psychology, 9,* 203–213.

Dahlstrom, W. G., & Welsh, G. S. (1960). *An MMPI handbook: A guide to use in clinical practice and research.* Minneapolis: University of Minnesota Press.

Daly, M., & Wilson, M. (1988). Evolutionary social-psychology and family homicide. *Science, 242,* 519–524.

Damasio, A. R. (1994). *Descartes' error: Emotion, reason, and the human brain.* New York: Putnam.

Darley, J. M., & Batson, C. D. (1967). "From Jerusalem to Jericho": A study of situational and dispositional variables in helping behavior. *Journal of Personality and Social Psychology, 27,* 100–108.

Darley, J. M., & Fazio, R. (1980). Expectancy confirmation processes arising in the social interaction sequence. *American Psychologist, 35,* 867–881.

Darley, J. M., & Latané, B. (1968). Bystander intervention in emergencies: Diffusion of responsibility. *Journal of Personality and Social Psychology, 28,* 377–383.

Darwin, C. (1967). *On the origin of the species by means*

of natural selection, or the preservation of favoured races in the struggle for life. New York: Modern Library. (Originally published 1859)

Davidson, R. J. (1993). The neuropsychology of emotion and affective style. In M. Lewis & J. M. Haviland (Eds.), *Handbook of emotions* (pp. 143–154). New York: Guilford Press.

Davidson, R. J., Ekman, P., Saron, C. D., Senulis, J. A., & Frisesen, W. V. (1990). Approach/withdrawal and cerebral asymmetry: Emotional expression and brain physiology. *Journal of Personality and Social Psychology, 58,* 330–341.

Davis, L. J. (1997, February). The encyclopedia of insanity: A psychiatric handbook lists a madness for everyone. *Harper's,* pp. 61–66.

Dawkins, R. (1976). *The selfish gene.* New York: Oxford University Press.

Dawson, J. L. M. (1974). Ecology, social pressures toward conformity, and left-handedness: A biosocial psychological approach. In J. L. M. Dawson & K. W. J. Lonner (Eds.), *Readings in cross-cultural psychology* (pp. 124–149). University of Hong Kong Press.

Decety, J., Jackson, P. L., Sommerville, J. A., Chaminade, T., & Meltzoff, A. N. (2004). The neural bases of cooperation and competition: An fMRI investigation. *Neuroimage, 23,* 744–751.

De Los Reyes, A., & Kazdin, A. E. (2005). Informant discrepancies in the assessment of childhood psychopathology: A critical review, theoretical framework, and recommendations for further study. *Psychological Bulletin, 131,* 483–509.

DeLuga, R. J., & Mason, S. (2000). Relationship of resident assistant conscientiousness, extraversion and positive affect with rated performance. *Journal of Research in Personality, 34,* 225–235.

Denissen, J. J. A., & Penke, L. (2008). Neuroticism predicts reactions to cues of social inclusion. *European Journal of Personality, 22,* 497–517.

Dennett, D. C. (1994). Real consciousness. In A. Revonsuo & M. Kamppinen (Eds.), *Consciousness in philosophy and cognitive neuroscience.* Hillsdale, NJ: Erlbaum.

Dennett, D. C., & Weiner, P. (1991). *Consciousness explained.* Boston: Little, Brown.

DePaulo, B. M., Dull, W. R., Greenberg, J. M., & Swaim, G. W. (1989). Are shy people reluctant to ask for help? *Journal of Personality and Social Psychology, 56,* 834–844.

Depue, R. A., & Collins, P. F. (1999). Neurobiology of the structure of personality: Dopamine, facilitation of incentive motivation, and extraversion. *Behavioral and Brain Sciences, 22,* 491–569.

De Raad, B., & Peabody, D. (2005). Cross-culturally recurrent personality factors: Analyses of three factors. *European Journal of Personality, 19,* 451–474.

Derby, S. P. (1994, Nov. 2). Eskimo words for snow derby. *The AFU and Urban Legend Archive.* Retrieved July 15, 2003, from www.urbanlegends.com/language/eskimo_words_for_snow_derby.html

de Waal, F. B. M. (2002). Evolutionary psychology: The wheat and the chaff. *Current Directions in Psychological Science, 11,* 187–191.

Dewitte, M., & De Houwer, J. (2008). Adult attachment and attention to positive and negative emotional face expressions. *Journal of Research in Personality, 42,* 498–505.

DeYoung, C. G. (2006). Higher order factors of the Big Five in a multi-informant sample. *Journal of Personality and Social Psychology, 91,* 1138–1151.

Diamond, J. (1999). *Guns, germs and steel: The fates of human societies.* New York: Norton.

Diener, C. I., & Dweck, C. S. (1978). An analysis of learned helplessness: Continuous changes in performance, strategy and achievement cognitions following failure. *Journal of Personality and Social Psychology, 36,* 451–462.

Diener, E., Colvin, C. R., Pavot, W. G., & Allman, A. (1991). The psychic costs of intense positive affect. *Journal of Personality and Social Psychology, 61,* 492–503.

Diener, E., & Lucas, R. E. (1999). Personality and subjective well-being. In D. Kahneman, E. Diener, & N. Schwarz (Eds.), *Well-being: The foundations of hedonic psychology* (pp. 213–229). New York: Russell Sage.

Diener, E., Lucas, R. E., & Oishi, S. (2002). Subjective well-being: The science and happiness of life satisfaction. In C. L. M. Keyes & J. Haidt (Eds.), *Flourishing: Positive psychology and the life well-lived* (pp. 463–473). Washington, DC: American Psychological Association.

Digman, J. M. (1997). Higher-order factors of the Big

Five. *Journal of Personality and Social Psychology, 73,* 1246–1256.

Digman, J. M., & Takemoto-Chock, N. K. (1981). Factors in the natural language of personality: Reanalysis and comparison of six major studies. *Multivariate Behavioral Research, 16,* 149–170.

Dillehay, R. C. (1978). Authoritarianism. In H. London & J. E. Exner (Eds.), *Dimensions of personality* (pp. 85–127). New York: Wiley.

Dodge, K. A. (1993). Social-cognitive mechanisms in the development of conduct disorder and depression. *Annual Review of Psychology, 44,* 559–584.

Dodge, K. A., & Frame, C. L. (1982). Social cognitive biases and deficits in aggressive boys. *Child Development, 53,* 620–635.

Doi, T. (1973). Amae—A key concept for understanding Japanese personality structure. In R. J. Smith & R. K. Beardsley (Eds.), *Japanese culture: Its development and characteristics* (pp. 132–139). Chicago: Aldine.

Dollard, J., & Miller, N. E. (1950). *Personality and psychotherapy: An analysis in terms of learning, thinking, and culture.* New York: McGraw-Hill.

Donahue, E. M., Robins, R. W., Roberts, R. W., & John, O. P. (1993). The divided self: Concurrent and longitudinal effects of psychological adjustment and social roles on self-concept differentiation. *Journal of Personality and Social Psychology, 64,* 834–846.

Donnellan, M. B., Conger, R. D., & Burzette, B. G. (2005). Criterion-related validity, self-other agreement, and longitudinal analyses of the Iowa personality questionnaire: A short alternative to the MPQ. *Journal of Research in Personality, 39,* 458–485.

Donnellan, M. B., & Lucas, R. E. (2008). Age differences in the Big Five across the life span: Evidence from two national samples. *Psychology and Aging, 23,* 558–566.

Donnellan, M. B., Trzesniewski, K. H., Robins, R. W., Moffitt, T. E., & Caspi, A. (2005). Low self-esteem is related to aggression, antisocial behavior, and delinquency. *Psychological Science, 16,* 328–335.

Doran, J. M. (1990). The Capgras syndrome: Neurological/neuropsychological perspectives. *Neuropsychology, 4,* 29–42.

Downey, G., & Feldman, S. I. (1996). Implications of rejection sensitivity for intimate relationships. *Journal of Personality and Social Psychology, 70,* 1327–1343.

Downey, G., Freitas, A., Michaelis, B., & Khouri, H. (1997). The self-fulfilling prophecy in close relationships: Rejection sensitivity and rejection in romantic partners. *Journal of Personality and Social Psychology, 75,* 545–560.

Dozier, M., Stovall, K. C., & Albus, K. E. (1999). Attachment and psychopathology in adulthood. In J. Cassidy & P. R. Shaver (Eds.), *Handbook of attachment: Theory, research, and clinical applications* (pp. 497–519). New York: Guilford Press.

Drevets, W. C. (1999). Prefrontal cortical-amygdalar metabolism in major depression. *Annals of the New York Academy of Sciences, 877,* 614–637.

Druss, B. G., Marcus, S. C., Olfson, M., & Pincus, H. A. (2004). Listening to generic Prozac: Winners, losers and sideliners. *Health Affairs, 23,* 210–216.

Dubois, D. L., & Flay, B. R. (2004). The healthy pursuit of self-esteem: Comment on and alternative to the Crocker and Park (2004) formulation. *Psychological Bulletin, 130,* 415–420.

Durante, K. M, Li, N. P., & Haselton, M. G. (2008). Changes in women's choice of dress across the ovulatory cycle: Naturalistic and laboratory task-based evidence. *Personality and Social Psychology Bulletin, 34,* 1451–1460.

Durbin, C. E., & Klein, D. N. (2006). Ten-year stability of personality disorders among outpatients with mood disorders. *Journal of Abnormal Psychology, 115,* 75–84.

Dutton, D., & Aron, A. (1974). Some evidence for heightened sexual attraction under conditions of high anxiety. *Journal of Personality and Social Psychology, 30,* 510–517.

Dweck, C. S. (2008). Can personality be changed? The role of beliefs in personality and change. *Current Directions in Psychological Science, 17,* 391–394.

Dweck, C. S., & Leggett, E. L. (1988). A social-cognitive approach to personality and motivation. *Psychological Review, 95,* 256–273.

Dworkin, B. R. (1993). *Learning and physiological regulation.* University of Chicago Press.

Dyssegaard, E. K. (2004). The Danes call it fresh air. In D. C. Funder & D. J. Ozer (Eds.), *Pieces of the personality puzzle: Readings in theory and research* (3rd ed., pp. 369–370). New York: Norton. (Originally published May 17, 1997, in the *New York Times*)

Eagly, A. H., Eastwick, P. W., & Johannesen-Schmidt, M. C. (2009). Possible selves in marital roles: The impact of the anticipated division of labor on the mate preferences of women and men. *Personality and Social Psychology Bulletin, 35,* 403–414.

Eagly, A. H., & Wood, W. (1999). The origins of sex differences in human behavior: Evolved dispositions versus social roles. *American Psychologist, 54,* 408–423.

Eaton, L. G., & Funder, D. C. (2001). Emotional experience in daily life: Valence, variability and rate of change. *Emotion, 1,* 413–421.

Ebstein, R. P., Novick, O., Umansky, R., Priel, B., Osher, Y., Blaine, D., et al. (1996). Dopamine D4 receptor (D4DR) exon III polymorphism associated with the human personality trait of novelty seeking. *Nature Genetics, 12,* 78–80.

Edelstein, R. S., Ghetti, S., Quas, J. A., Goodman, G. S., Alexander, K. W., Redlich, A. D., et al. (2005). Individual differences in emotional memory: Adult attachment and long-term memory for child sexual abuse. *Personality and Social Psychology Bulletin, 31,* 1537–1548.

Eisenberg, N., Spinrad, T. L., & Cumberland, A. (1998). The socialization of emotion: Reply to commentaries. *Psychological Inquiry, 9,* 317–333.

Eisenberger, N. I., Lieberman, M. D., & Satpute, A. B. (2005). Personality from a controlled processing perspective: An fMRI study of neuroticism, extraversion, and self-consciousness. *Cognitive, Affective, and Behavioral Neuroscience, 5,* 169–181.

Ekman, P. (1992). Are there basic emotions? *Psychological Review, 99,* 550–553.

Ekman, P., & Davidson, R. J. (Eds.). (1994). *The nature of emotion: Fundamental questions.* New York: Oxford University Press.

Ekman, P., Sorenson, E. R., & Friesen, W. V. (1969). Pan-cultural elements in facial displays of emotion. *Science, 164,* 86–88.

Elder, G. (1974). *Children of the Great Depression.* University of Chicago Press.

Elms, A. C., & Milgram, S. (1966). Personality characteristics associated with obedience and defiance toward authoritative command. *Journal of Experimental Research in Personality, 1,* 282–289.

Emmons, R. A. (1989). Exploring the relations between motives and traits: The case of narcissism. In D. M. Buss & N. Cantor (Eds.), *Personality psychology: Recent trends and emerging directions* (pp. 32–44). New York: Springer-Verlag.

Emmons, R. A. (1996). Striving and feeling: Personal goals and subjective well-being. In P. M. Gollwitzer & J. A. Bargh (Eds.), *The psychology of action: Linking cognition and motivation to behavior* (pp. 313–337). New York: Guilford Press.

Emmons, R. A. (1997). Motives and life goals. In R. Hogan, J. Johnson, & S. Briggs (Eds.), *Handbook of personality psychology* (pp. 485–512). San Diego: Academic Press.

Emmons, R. A., & King, L. A. (1988). Conflict among personal strivings: Immediate and long-term implications for psychological and physical well-being. *Journal of Personality and Social Psychology, 54,* 1040–1048.

Emmons, R. A., & McAdams, D. P. (1991). Personal strivings and motive dispositions: Exploring the links. *Personality and Social Psychology Bulletin, 6,* 648–654.

Epstein, S. (1973). The self-concept revisited, or a theory of a theory. *American Psychologist, 28,* 404–416.

Epstein, S. (1979). The stability of behavior: I. On predicting most of the people much of the time. *Journal of Personality and Social Psychology, 37,* 1097–1126.

Epstein, S. (1980). The stability of behavior: II. Implications for psychological research. *American Psychologist, 35,* 790–806.

Epstein, S. (1994). Integration of the cognitive and the psychodynamic unconscious. *American Psychologist, 49,* 709–724.

Epstein, S. (2003). Cognitive-experiential self-theory of personality. In T. Millon & M. J. Lerner (Ed.), *Handbook of psychology: Personality and social psychology* (pp. 159–184). New York: Wiley.

Epstein, S., Lipson, A., Holstein, C., & Huh, E. (1992). Irrational reactions to negative outcomes: Evidence for two conceptual systems. *Journal of Personality and Social Psychology, 62,* 328–339.

Epstein, S., & Meier, P. (1989). Constructive thinking: A broad coping variable with specific components. *Journal of Personality and Social Psychology, 57,* 332–350.

Erdelyi, M. H. (1974). A "new look" at the New Look in perception. *Psychological Review, 81,* 1–25.

Erdelyi, M. H. (1985). *Psychoanalysis: Freud's cognitive psychology.* San Francisco: Freeman.

Erdelyi, M. H. (1994). Commentary: Integrating a dissociation-prone psychology. *Journal of Personality, 62,* 669–680.

Erdley, C. A., Cain, K. M., Loomis, C. C., Dumas-Hines, F., & Dweck, C. S. (1997). The relations among children's social goals, implicit personality theories, and responses to social failure. *Developmental Psychology, 33,* 263–272.

Erikson, E. (1963). *Childhood and society.* New York: Norton.

Erikson, E. (1968). *Identity: Youth and crisis.* New York: Norton.

Exner, J. E., Jr. (1993). *The Rorschach: A comprehensive system: Vol. 1. Basic foundations* (3rd ed.). New York: Wiley.

Eysenck, H. J. (1947). *Dimensions of personality.* London: Routledge.

Eysenck, H. J. (1967). *The biological basis of personality.* Springfield, IL: Thomas.

Eysenck, H. J. (1976). *Sex and personality.* Austin: University of Texas Press.

Eysenck, H. J. (1986). Models and paradigms in personality research. In A. Angleitner, A. Furhnam, & G. Van Heck (Eds.), *Personality psychology in Europe: Vol 2. Current trends and controversies* (pp. 213–223). Lisse, The Netherlands: Swets & Zeitlinger.

Eysenck, H. J. (1987). Arousal and personality: The origins of a theory. In J. Strelau & H. J. Eysenck (Eds.), *Personality dimensions and arousal* (pp. 1–13). New York: Plenum Press.

Eysenck, H. J., & Beech, H. R. (1971). Counter conditioning and related methods. In A. E. Bergin & S. Garfield (Eds.), *Handbook of psychotherapy and behavior change* (pp. 543–611). New York: Wiley.

Eysenck, H. J., & Eysenck, S. B. G. (1975). *Manual of the Eysenck Personality Questionniare.* San Diego: Testing Service.

Eysenck, H. J., & Gudjonsson, G. H. (1989). *The causes and cures of criminality.* New York: Plenum Press.

Eysenck, S. B. G., & Eysenck, H. J. (1967). Salivary response to lemon juice as a measure of introversion. *Perceptual and Motor Skills, 24,* 1047–1053.

Eysenck, S. B. G., & Long, F. Y. (1986). A cross-cultural comparison of personality in adults and children: Singapore and England. *Journal of Personality and Social Psychology, 58,* 281–291.

Fahrenberg, J., Myrtek, M., Pawlik, K., & Perrez, M. (2007). Ambulatory assessment: Monitoring behavior in daily life settings. *European Journal of Psychological Assessment, 23,* 206–213.

Fannin, N., & Dabbs, J. M., Jr. (2002). Testosterone and the work of firefighters: Fighting fires and delivering medical care. *Journal of Research in Personality, 37,* 107–115.

Farah, M. J. (2005). Neuroethics: The practical and the philosophical. *Trends in Cognitive Science, 9,* 34–40.

Fast, L. A., Reimer, H. M., & Funder, D. C. (2008). The social behavior and reputation of attributionally complex. *Journal of Research in Personality, 42,* 208–222.

Feldman-Barrett, L., & Barrett, D. J. (2001). An introduction to computerized experience sampling in psychology. *Social Science Computer Review, 19,* 175–185.

Feldman-Barrett, L., Williams, N. L., & Fong, G. T. (2002). Defensive verbal behavior assessment. *Personality and Social Psychology Bulletin, 28,* 776–788.

Fenigstein, A., Scheier, M. F., & Buss, A. H. (1975). Public and private self-consciousness: Assessment and theory. *Journal of Consulting and Clinical Psychology, 43,* 522–527.

Fenz, W. D., & Epstein, S. (1967). Gradients of physiological arousal of experienced and novice parachutists as a function of an approaching jump. *Psychosomatic Medicine, 29,* 33–51.

Ferdinand, R. F., van der Ende, J., & Verhulst, F. C. (2004). Parent-adolescent disagreement regarding psychopathology in adolescents from the general population as a risk factor for adverse outcome. *Journal of Abnormal Psychology, 113,* 198–206.

Ferguson, E. (2001). Personality and coping traits: A joint factor analysis. *British Journal of Health Psychology, 6,* 311–325.

Festinger, L., & Carlsmith, J. M. (1959). Cognitive consequences of forced compliance. *Journal of Abnormal and Social Psychology, 58,* 203–210.

Fischer, H., Tillfors, M., Furmark, T., & Fredrikson, M. (2001). Dispositional pessimism and amygdala activity: A PET study in healthy volunteers. *Neuroreport, 12,* 1635–1638.

Fishbein, M., & Ajzen, I. (1974). Attitudes toward objects as predictors of single and multiple behavioral criteria. *Psychological Review, 81,* 59–74.

Fisher, J. (2004). War, situations, opportunity can make heroic figures out of Eve. *Clarksburg Exponent Telegram.* Accessed December 22, 2005 from http://www.cpubco.com/cgibin/LiveIQue.acgi$rec=14128cbgCurrentLocalNews?cbgCurrentLocalNews

Fiske, D. W. (1949). Consistency of the factorial structures of personality ratings from different sources. *Journal of Abnormal and Social Psychology, 44,* 329–344.

Fitzgerald, P. B., Fountain, S., & Daskalakis, Z. J. (2006). A comprehensive review of the effects of rTMS on motor cortical excitability and inhibition. *Clinical Neurophysiology, 117,* 2584–2596.

Fleeson, W. (2001). Toward a structure- and process-integrated view of personality: Traits as density distributions of states. *Journal of Personality and Social Psychology, 80,* 1011–1027.

Fleeson, W. (2004). Moving personality beyond the person-situation debate: The challenge and the opportunity of within-person variability. *Current Directions in Psychological Science, 13,* 83–87.

Flint, A. (1995, October 25). Stone age weighs us down today. *Press-Enterprise* (Riverside, CA), p. D1.

Floody, O. R. (1983). Hormones and aggression in female mammals. In B. B. Svare (Ed.), *Hormones and aggressive behavior* (pp. 39–89). New York: Plenum Press.

Florida, R. (2008, May 4). Where do all the neurotics live? *Boston Globe.* Retrieved January 23, 2009, from http://www.boston.com/bostonglobe/ideas/articles/2008/05/04/where_do_all_the_neurotics_live/

Foa, E. B. (2004). *Mastery of obsessive-compulsive disorder: A cognitive-behavioral approach therapist guide.* New York: Oxford University Press.

Frank, L. K. (1939). Projective methods for the study of personality. *Journal of Psychology, 8,* 389–413.

Frankl, V. E. (1992). *Man's search for meaning: Foundations and applications of logotherapy.* Boston: Beacon Press. (Originally published 1959)

Frederick, D. A., Fessler, D. M. T., & Haselton, M. G. (2005). Do representations of male muscularity differ in men's and women's magazines? *Body Image, 2,* 81–86.

Frederick, D. A., & Haselton, M. G. (2007). Why is muscularity sexy? Tests of the fitness indicator hypothesis. *Personality and Social Psychology Bulletin, 33,* 1167–1183.

Fredrickson, B. L. (2001). The role of positive emotions in positive psychology: The broaden-and-build theory of positive emotions. *American Psychologist, 56,* 218–226.

Freeberg, N. E. (1969). Relevance of rater-ratee acquaintance in the validity and reliability of ratings. *Journal of Applied Psychology, 53,* 518–524.

Freeman, W., & Watts, J. W. (1950). *Psychosurgery: In the treatment of mental disorders and intractable pain* (2nd ed.). Springfield, IL: Thomas.

Freud, A. (1936). *The ego and the mechanisms of defense.* New York: Universities Press.

Freud, S. (1962). *Three essays on the theory of sexuality.* New York: Basic Books. (Originally published 1905)

Fridlund, A. J. (1994). *Human facial expression.* San Diego: Academic Press.

Friedman, H. S. (Ed.). (1991). *Hostility, coping, and health.* Washington, DC: American Psychological Association.

Friedman, H. S. (1992). Disease-prone and self-healing personalities. *Hospital and Community Psychiatry, 43,* 1177–1179.

Friedman, H. S., Tucker, J. S., Schwartz, J. E., Tomlinson-Keasey, C., Martin, L. R., Wingard, D. L., et al. (1995). Psychosocial and behavioral predictors of longevity. *American Psychologist, 50,* 69–78.

Friedman, H. S., Tucker, J. S., Tomlinson-Keasey, C., Schwartz, J. E., Wingard, D. L., & Criqui, M. H. (1993). Does childhood personality predict longevity? *Journal of Personality and Social Psychology, 65,* 176–185.

Friedman, I. (1955). Phenomenal, ideal, and projected conception of self. *Journal of Abnormal and Social Psychology, 51,* 611–614.

Friedman, J. N. W., Oltmanns, T. F., & Turkheimer, E. (2007). Interpersonal perception and personality disorders: Utilization of a thin slice approach. *Journal of Research in Personality, 41,* 667–688.

Fromm, E. (1941). *Escape from freedom.* New York: Holt, Rinehart.

Fuhrman, R. W., & Funder, D. C. (1995). Convergence between self and peer in the response-time processing of trait-relevant information. *Journal of Personality and Social Psychology, 69*, 961–974.

Fujita, F., & Diener, E. (2005). Life satisfaction set point: Stability and change. *Journal of Personality and Social Psychology, 88*, 158–164.

Fujita, F., Diener, E., & Sandvik, E. (1991). Gender differences in negative affect and well-being: The case for emotional intensity. *Journal of Personality and Social Psychology, 61*, 427–434.

Fuller, R. B. (1970). *I seem to be a verb*. New York: Bantam Books.

Funder, D. C. (1980). On seeing ourselves as others see us: Self-other agreement and discrepancy in personality ratings. *Journal of Personality, 48*, 473–493.

Funder, D. C. (1982). On the accuracy of dispositional versus situational attributions. *Social Cognition, 3*, 205–222.

Funder, D. C. (1983). Three issues in predicting more of the people: A reply to Mischel and Peake. *Psychological Review, 90*, 283–289.

Funder, D. C. (1987). Errors and mistakes: Evaluating the accuracy of social judgment. *Psychological Bulletin, 101*, 75–90.

Funder, D. C. (1991). Global traits: A neo-Allportian approach to personality. *Psychological Science, 2*, 31–39.

Funder, D. C. (1993). Judgments as data for personality and developmental psychology: Error vs. accuracy. In D. C. Funder, R. D. Parke, C. Tomlinson-Keasey, & K. Widaman (Eds.), *Studying lives through time: Personality and development* (pp. 121–146). Washington, DC: American Psychological Association.

Funder, D. C. (1995). On the accuracy of personality judgment: A realistic approach. *Psychological Review, 102*, 652–670.

Funder, D. C. (1998a). On the pros and cons of delay of gratification. *Psychological Inquiry, 9*, 211–212.

Funder, D. C. (1998b). Why does personality psychology exist? *Psychological Inquiry, 9*, 150–152.

Funder, D. C. (1999). *Personality judgment: A realistic approach to person perception*. San Diego: Academic Press.

Funder, D. C. (2001). Personality. *Annual Review of Psychology, 52*, 197–221.

Funder, D. C. (2003). Towards a social psychology of person judgments: Implications for person perception accuracy and self-knowledge. In J. Forgas, K. Williams, & W. von Hippel (Eds.), *Social judgments: Implicit and explicit processes. Sydney Symposium on Social Psychology* (pp. 115–133). New York: Cambridge University Press.

Funder, D. C. (2006). Towards a resolution of the personality triad: Persons, situations, and behaviors. *Journal of Research in Personality, 40*, 21–34.

Funder, D. C. (2008). Persons, situations and person-situation interactions. In O. P. John, R. Robins, & L. Pervin (Eds.), *Handbook of Personality* (3rd ed., pp. 568–580). New York: Guilford Press.

Funder, D. C., Block, J. H., & Block, J. (1983). Delay of gratification: Some longitudinal personality correlates. *Journal of Personality and Social Psychology, 44*, 1198–1213.

Funder, D. C., & Colvin, C. R. (1988). Friends and strangers: Acquaintanceship, agreement, and the accuracy of personality judgment. *Journal of Personality and Social Psychology, 55*, 149–158.

Funder, D. C., & Colvin, C. R. (1991). Explorations in behavioral consistency: Properties of persons, situations, and behaviors. *Journal of Personality and Social Psychology, 60*, 773–794.

Funder, D. C., & Dobroth, K. M. (1987). Differences between traits: Properties associated with interjudge agreement. *Journal of Personality and Social Psychology, 52*, 409–418.

Funder, D. C., Furr, R. M., & Colvin, C. R. (2000). The Riverside behavioral Q-sort: A tool for the description of social behavior. *Journal of Personality, 68*, 450–489.

Funder, D. C., & Harris, M. J. (1986). On the several facets of personality assessment: The case of social acuity. *Journal of Personality, 54*, 528–550.

Funder, D. C., & Ozer, D. J. (1983). Behavior as a function of the situation. *Journal of Personality and Social Psychology, 44*, 107–112.

Funder, D. C., & Ozer, D. J. (2010). *Pieces of the personality puzzle: Readings in theory and research* (5th ed.). New York: Norton.

Funder, D. C., Parke, R. D., Tomlinson-Keasey, C., & Widaman, K. (Eds.). (1993). *Studying lives through time: Personality and development*. Washington, DC: American Psychological Association.

Funder, D. C., & Sneed, C. D. (1993). Behavioral manifestations of personality: An ecological approach to judgmental accuracy. *Journal of Personality and Social Psychology, 64,* 479–490.

Funder, D. C., & West, S. G. (1993). Consensus, self-other agreement, and accuracy in personality judgment: An introduction. *Journal of Personality, 61,* 457–476.

Fung, H. H., & Carstensen, L. L. (2003). Sending memorable messages to the old: Age differences in preferences and memory for advertisements. *Journal of Personality and Social Psychology, 85,* 163–178.

Furmark, T., Tillfors, M., Garpenstrand, H., Maarteinsdottir, I., Långstrom, B., Oreland, L., et al. (2004). Serotonin transporter polymorphism related to amygdala excitability and symptom severity in patients with social phobia. *Neuroscience Letters, 362,* 189–192.

Furnham, A. (2001). Self-estimates of intelligence: Culture and gender differences in self and other estimates of both general (g) and multiple intelligences. *Personality and Individual Differences, 31,* 1381–1405.

Furr, R. M. (in press). Personality psychology as a truly behavioral science. *European Journal of Personality.*

Furr, R. M., Dougherty, D. M., Marsh, D. M., & Mathias, C. W. (2007). Personality judgment and personality pathology: Self-other agreement in adolescents with conduct disorder. *Journal of Personality, 75,* 629–662.

Furr, R. M., & Funder, D. C. (1998). A multi-modal analysis of personal negativity. *Journal of Personality and Social Psychology, 74,* 1580–1591.

Furr, R. M., & Funder, D. C. (2004). Situational similarity and behavioral consistency: Subjective, objective, variable-centered, and person-centered approaches. *Journal of Research in Personality, 38,* 421–447.

Furr, R. M., & Funder, D. C. (2007). Behavioral observation. In R. Robins, C. Fraley, & R. Krueger (Eds.), *Handbook of research methods in personality psychology* (pp. 273–291). New York: Guilford Press.

Gable, S. L., & Haidt, J. (2005). What (and why) is positive psychology? *Review of General Psychology, 9,* 103–110.

Gangestad, S. W. (1989). The evolutionary history of genetic variation: An emerging issue in the behav-ioral genetic study of personality. In D. Buss & N. Cantor (Eds.), *Personality psychology: Recent trends and emerging directions* (pp. 320–332). New York: Springer-Verlag.

Gangestad, S. W., & Buss, D. M. (1993). Pathogen preferences and human mate preferences. *Ethology and Sociobiology, 14,* 89–96.

Gangestad, S. W., & Simpson, J. A. (1990). Toward an evolutionary history of female sociosexual variation. *Journal of Personality, 58,* 69–96.

Gangestad, S. W., Simpson, J. A., DiGeronimo, K., & Biek, M. (1992). Differential accuracy in person perception across traits: Examination of a functional hypothesis. *Journal of Personality and Social Psychology, 62,* 688–698.

Gangestad, S. W., & Snyder, M. (1985). "To carve nature at its joints": On the existence of discrete classes in personality. *Psychological Review, 92,* 317–349.

Gangestad, S. W., & Snyder, M. (2000). Self-monitoring: Appraisal and reappraisal. *Psychological Bulletin, 126,* 530–555.

Garb, H. N. (2003). Incremental validity and the assessment of psychopathology in adults. *Psychological Assessment, 15,* 508–520.

Garb, H. N., Florio, C. M., & Grove, W. M. (1998). The validity of the Rorschach and the Minnesota Multiphasic Personality Inventory: Results from meta-analyses. *Psychological Science, 9,* 402–404.

Garb, H. N., Florio, C. M., & Grove, W. M. (1999). The Rorschach controversy: Reply to Parker, Hunsley, and Hanson. *Psychological Science, 10,* 293–294.

Garb, H. N., Wood, J. M., Nezworski, M. T., Grove, W. M., & Stejskal, W. J. (2001). Toward a resolution of the Rorschach controversy. *Psychological Asssessment, 13,* 433–448.

Gardner, H. (1987). *The mind's new science: A history of the cognitive revolution.* New York: Basic Books.

Gay, P. (1988). *Freud: A life for our time.* New York: Norton.

Gay, P. (Ed.). (1989). *The Freud reader.* New York: Norton.

Gazzaniga, M. S., & Heatherton, T. F. (2003). *Psychological science: Mind, brain, and behavior.* New York: Norton.

Gazzaniga, M. S., Ivry, R. B., & Mangun G. R. (1998). *Cognitive neuroscience: The biology of the mind.* New York: Norton.

Geen, R. G. (1984). Preferred stimulation levels in introverts and extraverts: Effects on arousal and performance. *Journal of Personality and Social Psychology, 46,* 1303–1312.

George, J. M. (1995). Leader positive mood and group performance: The case of customer service. *Journal of Applied Social Psychology, 25,* 778–795.

Gergen, K. (1973). Social psychology as history. *Journal of Personality and Social Psychology, 26,* 309–320.

Gettleman, J. (2002, December 1). A fall tradition: Rooting and rioting for the home team. *New York Times Week in Review,* p. 2.

Gigerenzer, G., Hoffrage, U., & Kleinbolting, H. (1991). Probabilistic mental models: A Brunswikian theory of confidence. *Psychological Review, 98,* 506–528.

Gilbert, D. T., & Malone, P. S. (1995). The correspondence bias. *Psychological Bulletin, 117,* 21–38.

Gillespie, N. A., Zhu, G., Evans, D. M., Medland, S. E., Wright, M. J., & Martin, N. G. (2008). A genome-wide scan for Eysenckian personality dimensions in adolescent twin sibships: Psychoticism, extraversion, neuroticism, and lie. *Journal of Personality, 76,* 1415–1445.

Gilmore, D. D. (1990). *Manhood in the making.* New Haven, CT: Yale University Press.

Gjerde, P. F. (2004). Culture, power, and experience: Toward a person-centered cultural psychology. *Human Development, 47,* 138–157.

Gleitman, H. (1995). *Psychology* (4th ed.). New York: Norton.

Glueck, S., & Glueck, E. (1956). *Physique and delinquency.* New York: Harper & Bros.

Goetz, T. E., & Dweck, C. S. (1980). Learned helplessness in social situation. *Journal of Personality and Social Psychology, 39,* 246–255.

Goffman, E. (1959). *The presentation of self in everyday life.* Garden City, NY: Doubleday/Anchor.

Gold, S. R., & Reilly, J. P. (1985). Daydreaming, current concerns and personality. *Imagination, Cognition and Personality, 5,* 117–125.

Goldberg, L. R. (1981). Language and individual differences: The search for universals in personality lexicons. In L. Wheeler (Ed.), *Review of personality and social psychology* (Vol. 2, pp. 141–165). Beverly Hills, CA: Sage.

Goldberg, L. R. (1990). An alternative "description of personality": The Big-Five factor structure. *Journal of Personality and Social Psychology, 59,* 1216–1229.

Goldberg, L. R. (1992). The social psychology of personality. *Psychological Inquiry, 3,* 89–94.

Goldman, W., & Lewis, P. (1977). Beautiful is good: Evidence that the physically attractive are more socially skillful. *Journal of Experimental Social Psychology, 13,* 125–130.

Goleman, D. (1995). *Emotional intelligence.* New York: Bantam Books.

Goodman-Delahunty, J. (Ed.). (2005). [Special issue]. *Psychology, Public Policy, and Law, 11*(2).

Gorer, G. (1943). Themes in Japanese culture. *New York Academy of Sciences, 5,* 106–124.

Gosling, S. D. (1998). Personality dimensions in spotted hyenas (*Crocuta crocuta*). *Journal of Comparative Psychology, 112,* 107–118.

Gosling, S. (2008a). Personality in non-human animals. *Personality and Social Psychology Compass, 2,* 985–1001.

Gosling, S. (2008b). *Snoop: What your stuff says about you.* New York: Basic Books.

Gosling, S. D. & John, O. P. (1999). Personality dimensions in nonhuman animals: A cross-species review. *Current Directions in Psychological Science, 8,* 69–75.

Gosling, S. D., John, O. P., Craik, K. H., & Robins, R. W. (1998). Do people know how they behave? Self-reported act frequencies compared with on-line codings by observers. *Journal of Personality and Social Psychology, 74,* 1337–1349.

Gosling, S. D., Ko, S. J., Mannarelli, T., & Morris, M. E. (2002). A room with a cue: Personality judgments based on offices and bedrooms. *Journal of Personality and Social Psychology, 82,* 379–398.

Gosling, S. D., & Vazire, S. (2002). Are we barking up the right tree? Evaluating a comparative approach to personality. *Journal of Research in Personality, 36,* 607–614.

Gosling, S. D., Vazire, S., Srivastava, S., & John, O. P. (2004). Should we trust Web-based studies? A comparative analysis of six preconceptions about internet questionnaires. *American Psychologist, 59,* 93–104.

Gough, H. G. (1968). An interpreter's syllabus for the

California Psychological Inventory. In P. McReynolds (Ed.), *Advances in psychological assessment* (Vol. 1, pp. 55–79). Palo Alto, CA: Science and Behavior Books.

Gough, H. G. (1995). Career assessment and the California Psychological Inventory. *Journal of Career Assessment, 3*, 101–122.

Gould, S. J. (2001, February 19). Humbled by the genome's mysteries. *New York Times*. Retrieved April 20, 2003, from http://www.nytimes.com/2001/02/19/opinion/19GOUL.html

Grant, B. F., Chou, P., Goldstein, R. B., Huang, B., Stinson, F. S., Saha, T. D., et al. (2008). Prevalence, correlates, disability, and comorbidity of DSM-IV Borderline Personality Disorder: Results from the Wave 2 National Epidemiologic Survey on Alcohol and Related Conditions. *Journal of Clinical Psychiatry, 69*, 533–545.

Grant, B. F., Hasin, D.S., Stinson, F. S., Dawson, D. A., Chou, S. P., Ruan, W. J., et al. (2004). Prevalence, correlates and disability of personality disorders in the United States: Results from the National Epidemiologic Survey on Alcohol and Related Conditions. *Journal of Clinical Psychiatry, 65*, 948–958.

Grant, H., & Dweck, C. S. (1999). A goal analysis of personality and personality coherence. In D. Cervone & Y. Shoda (Eds.), *The coherence of personality: Social-cognitive bases of consistency, variability, and organization* (pp. 345–371). New York: Guilford Press.

Gray, J. A. (1981). A critique of Eysenck's theory of personality. In H. J. Eysenck (Ed.), *A model for personality* (pp. 246–276). New York: Springer-Verlag.

Gray, J. A. (1987). *The psychology of fear and stress* (2nd ed.). Cambridge University Press.

Gray, J. R., & Braver, T. S. (2002). Personality predicts working-memory-related activation in the caudal anterior cingulate cortex. *Cognitive, Affective, and Behavioral Neuroscience, 2*, 64–75.

Gray, J. R., Burgess, G. C., Schaefer, A., Yarkoni, T., Larsen, R. J., & Braver, T. S. (2005). Affective personality differences in neural processing efficiency confirmed using fMRI. *Cognitive, Affective, and Behavioral Neuroscience, 5*, 182–190.

Graziano, W., & Bryant, W. H. (1998). Self-monitoring and the self-attribution of positive emotions. *Journal of Personality and Social Psychology, 74*, 250–261.

Graziano, W. G., & Eisenberg, N. (1997). Agreeableness: A dimension of personality. In R. Hogan, J. Johnson, & S. Briggs (Eds.), *Handbook of personality psychology* (pp. 795–824). San Diego: Academic Press.

Green, R. (2006, January 5). Tulsa pastor arrested on lewdness accusation. *Dallas Voice*. Retrieved September 9, 2009, from http://www.dallasvoice.com/artman/publish/article_324.php

Greenberg, J., & Folger, R. (1988). *Controversial issues in social research methods*. New York: Springer-Verlag.

Greenberg, J., Koole, S. L., & Pyszczynski, T. (Ed.). (2004). *Handbook of experimental existential psychology*. New York: Guilford Press.

Greenberg, J. R., & Mitchell, S. A. (1983). *Object relations in psychoanalytic theory*. Cambridge, MA: Harvard University Press.

Greenwald, A. G., Banaji, M. R., Rudman, L. A., Farnham, S. D., Nosek, B. A., & Mellott, D. S. (2002). A unified theory of implicit attitudes, stereotypes, self-esteem, and self-concept. *Psychological Review, 109*, 3–25.

Greenwald, A. G., & Farnham, S. D. (2000). Using the implicit association test to measure self-esteem and the self-concept. *Journal of Personality and Social Psychology, 79*, 1022–1028.

Greenwald, A. G., McGhee, D. E., & Schwartz, J. L. K. (1998). Measuring individual differences in implicit cognition. The implicit association test. *Journal of Personality and Social Psychology, 74*, 1464–1480.

Griffith, R. L., & Peterson, M. (Eds.). (2006). *A closer examination of applicant faking behavior*. Greenwich, CT: Information Age Publishing.

Grosjean, F. (1982). *Life with two languages*. Cambridge, MA: Harvard University Press.

Grouzet, F. M. E., Kasser, T., Ahuvia, A., Dols, J. M. F., Kim, Y., Lau, S., et al. (2005). The structure of goal contents across 15 cultures. *Journal of Personality and Social Psychology, 89*, 800–816.

Guarnaccia, V., Dill, C. A., Sabatino, S., & Southwick,

S. (2001). Scoring accuracy using the Comprehensive System for the Rorschach. *Journal of Personality Assessment, 77*, 464–474.

Guilford, J. P., & Zimmerman, W. S. (1956). Fourteen dimensions of temperament. *Psychological Monographs, 70*(10, Whole no. 417).

Gunderson, J. G. (1984). *Borderline personality disorder.* Washington, DC: American Psychiatric Association.

Gusnard, D. A., Ollinger, J. M., Schulman, G. L., Cloninger, C. R., Price, J. L., Van Essen, D. C., et al. (2003). Persistence and brain circuitry. *Proceedings of the National Academy of Sciences, 100*, 3479–3484.

Guthrie, G. M., & Bennett, A. B. (1971). Cultural differences in implicit personality theory. *International Journal of Psychology, 6*, 305–312.

Haas, B. W., Omura, K., Constable, R. T., & Canli, T. (2007). Emotional conflict and neuroticism: Personality-dependent activation in the amygdala and subgenual anterior cingulate. *Behavioral Neuroscience, 121*, 249–256.

Haidt, J. (2008, September 9) What makes people vote Republican? *Edge.* Retrieved January 23, 2009, from http://www.edge.org/3rd_culture/haidt08/haidt08_index.html

Haig, B. D. (2005). An abductive theory of scientific method. *Psychological Methods, 10*, 371–388.

Hamamura, T., Meijer, Z., Heine, S. J., Kamaya, K., & Hori, I. (2009). Approach-avoidance motivation and information processing: A cross-cultural analysis. *Personality and Social Psychology Bulletin, 35*, 454–462.

Hamann, S. B., Ely, T. D., Hoffman, J. M., & Kilts, C. D. (2002). Ecstasy and agony: Activation of the human amygdala in positive and negative emotion. *Psychological Sciences, 13*, 135–141.

Hamann, S. B., & Mao, H. (2002). Positive and negative emotional verbal stimuli elicit activity in the left amygdala. *Neuroreport, 13*, 15–19.

Hamer, D. (1997). The search for personality genes: Adventures of a molecular biologist. *Current Directions in Psychological Science, 6*, 111–113.

Hamer, D. H., & Copeland, P. (1994). *The science of desire: The search for the gay gene and the biology of behavior.* New York: Simon & Schuster.

Hammond, K. R. (1996). *Human judgment and social policy: Irreducible uncertainty, inevitable error, unavoidable injustice.* New York: Oxford University Press.

Hammond, K. R., & Stewart, T. R. (2001). *The essential Brunswik: Beginnings, explications, applications.* New York: Oxford University Press.

Han, S.-P., & Shavitt, S. (1994). Persuasion and culture: Advertising appeals in individualistic and collectivist societies. *Journal of Experimental Social Psychology, 81*, 869–885.

Haney, C., Banks, C., & Zimbardo, P. (1973). Interpersonal dynamics in a simulated prison. *International Journal of Criminology and Penology, 1*, 69–97.

Haney, P., & Durlak, J. A. (1998). Changing self-esteem in children and adolescents: A meta-analytic review. *Journal of Clinical Child Psychology, 27*, 423–433.

Hanson, F. A. (1993). *Testing testing: Social consequences of the examined life.* Berkeley: University of California Press.

Hardaway, R. A. (1990). Subliminally activated symbiotic fantasies: Facts and artifacts. *Psychological Bulletin, 107*, 177–195.

Hardyck, C., & Petrinovich, L. F. (1977). Left-handedness. *Psychological Bulletin, 84*, 385–404.

Hariri, A. R., Mattay, V. S., Tessitore, A., Kolachana, B., Fera, F., Goldman, D., et al. (2002). Serotonin transporter genetic variation and the response of the human amygdala. *Science, 297*, 400–403.

Haritatos, J., & Benet-Martínez, V. (2002). Bicultural identities: The interface of cultural, personality, and socio-cognitive processes. *Journal of Research in Personality, 36*, 598–606.

Harlow, J. M. (1849). Medical miscellany [Letter to the editor]. *Boston Medical and Surgical Journal, 39*, 506–507.

Harlow, J. M. (1868). Recovery from the passage of an iron bar though the head. *Publications of the Massachusetts Medical Society, 2*, 327–347.

Harlow, J. M. (1869). *Recovery from the passage of an iron bar through the head.* Boston: Clapp.

Harmon-Jones, E., & Allen, J. J. B. (1997). Behavioral activation sensitivity and resting frontal EEG asymmetry: Covariation of putative indicators related to risk for mood disorders. *Journal of Abnormal Psychology, 106*, 159–163.

Harris, C. R. (2000). Psychophysiological responses

to imagined infidelity: The specific innate modular view of jealousy reconsidered. *Journal of Personality and Social Psychology, 78*, 1082–1091.

Harris, J. R. (1995). Where is the child's environment? A group socialization theory of development. *Psychological Review, 102*, 458–489.

Harris, J. R. (1998). *The nurture assumption: Why children turn out the way they do*. New York: Free Press.

Harris, M. J., & Rosenthal, R. (1985). Mediation of interpersonal expectancy effects: 31 Meta-analyses. *Psychological Bulletin, 97*, 363–386.

Harris, R. J. (Ed.). (1997). Ban the significance test? [Special section]. *Psychological Science, 8*, 1–20.

Hartmann, H. (1964). *Essays on ego psychology: Selected problems in psychoanalytic theory*. New York: International Universities Press.

Haselton, M. G. (2002). The sexual overperception bias: Evidence of a systematic bias in men from a survey of naturally occurring events. *Journal of Research in Personality, 37*, 34–47.

Haselton, M. G., & Miller, G. F. (2006). Women's fertility across the cycle increases the short term attractiveness of creative intelligence. *Human Nature, 17*, 50–73.

Hassin, R., & Trope, Y. (2000). Facing faces: Studies on the cognitive aspects of physiognomy. *Journal of Personality and Social Psychology, 78*, 837–852.

Hastie, R., & Rasinski, K. A. (1988). The concept of accuracy in social judgment. In D. Bar-Tal & A. W. Kruglanski (Eds.), *The social psychology of knowledge* (pp. 193–208). Cambridge University Press.

Hastorf, A. H., & Cantril, H. (1954). They saw a game: A case study. *Journal of Abnormal and Social Psychology, 47*, 574–576.

Hathaway, S. R., & Meehl, P. E. (1951). *An atlas for the clinical use of the MMPI*. Minneapolis: University of Minnesota Press.

Haviland, M. G., & Reise, S. P. (1996). A California Q-set alexithymia prototype and its relationship to ego-control and ego-resiliency. *Journal of Psychosomatic Research, 41*, 597–607.

Hazan, C., & Shaver, P. (1987). Romantic love conceptualized as an attachment process. *Journal of Personality and Social Psychology, 52*, 511–524.

Hazan, C., & Shaver, P. (1990). Love and work: An attachment-theoretical perspective. *Journal of Personality and Social Psychology, 59*, 270–280.

Heatherton, T. F., Macrae, C. N., & Kelley, W. M. (2004). What the social brain sciences can tell us about the self. *Current Directions in Psychological Science, 13*, 190–193.

Heidegger, M. (1962). *Being and time*. New York: Harper & Row. (Originally published 1927)

Heim, A., & Westen, D. (2005). Theories of personality and personality disorders. In J. M. Oldham, A. E. Skodol, & D. S. Bender (Eds.), *The American Psychiatric Publishing textbook of personality disorders* (pp. 17–33). Arlington, VA: American Psychiatric Publishing.

Heine, S. J., Kitayama, S., & Lehman, D. R. (2001). Cultural differences in self-evaluation: Japanese readily accept negative self-relevant information. *Journal of Cross-Cultural Psychology, 32*, 434–443.

Heine, S. J., Kitayama, S., Lehman, D. R., Takata, T., Ide, E., Leung, C., et al. (2001). Divergent consequences of success and failure in Japan and North America: An investigation of self-improving motivations and malleable selves. *Journal of Personality and Social Psychology, 81*, 599–615.

Heine, S. J., Lehman, D. R., Markus, H. R., & Kitayama, S. (1999). Is there a universal need for positive self-regard? *Psychological Review, 106*, 766–794.

Heinz, A., Braus, D. F., Smolka, M. N., Wrase, J., Puls, I., Hermann, D., et al. (2005). Amygdala-prefrontal coupling depends on a genetic variation of the serotonin transporter. *Nature Neuroscience, 8*, 20–21.

Hemenway, D., Solnick, S., & Carter, J. (1994). Child-rearing violence. *Child Abuse and Neglect, 18*, 1011–1020.

Hetherington, E. M. (Ed.). (1983) *Socialization, personality, and social development*. New York: Wiley.

Hewig, J., Hagemann, D., Seifert, J., Naumann, E., & Bartussek, D. (2004). On the selective relation of frontal cortical asymmetry and anger-out versus anger-control. *Journal of Personality and Social Psychology, 87*, 926–939.

Higgins, E. T. (1997). Beyond pleasure and pain. *American Psychologist, 52*, 1280–1300.

Higgins, E. T. (1999). Persons and situations: Unique explanatory principles or variability in general principles? In D. Cervone & Y. Shoda (Eds.), *The coherence of personality: Social-cognitive bases of con-*

sistency, variability, and organization (pp. 61–93). New York: Guilford Press.

Higgins, E. T., Bond, R., Klein, R., & Strauman, T. J. (1986). Self-discrepancies and emotional vulnerability: How magnitude, accessibility, and type of discrepancy influence affect. *Journal of Personality and Social Psychology, 51*, 1–15.

Higgins, E. T., Rholes, W. S., & Jones, C. R. (1977). Category accessibility and impression formation. *Journal of Experimental Social Psychology, 13*, 141–154.

Higgins, E. T., Roney, C. J. R., Crowe, E., & Hymes, C. (1994). Ideal versus ought predilections for approach and avoidance: Distinct self-regulatory systems. *Journal of Personality and Social Psychology, 66*, 276–286.

Highfield, R. (2008, May 17). How a magnet turned off my speech. *The Telegraph*. Downloaded February 12, 2009 from http://www.telegraph.co.uk/scienceand technology/science/sciencenews/3342331/How-a-magnet-turned-off-my-speech.html

Highhouse, S. (2008). Stubborn reliance on intuition and subjectivity in employee selection. *Industrial and Organizational Psychology, 1*, 333–342.

Hilgard, E. R. (1949). Human motives and the concept of the self. *American Psychologist, 4*, 374–382.

Hiller, J. B., Rosenthal, R., Bornstein, R. F., Berry, D. T. R., & Brunell-Neuleib, S. (1999). A comparative meta-analysis of Rorschach and MMPI validity. *Psychological Asssessment, 11*, 278–296.

Hilton, T. L., & Berglund, G. W. (1974). Sex differences in mathematics achievement: A longitudinal study. *Journal of Educational Research, 67*, 231–237.

Hippocrates. (1923). *Works* (W. H. S. Jones, Trans.; Vol. 2). New York: Putnam.

Hoffman, D. L., & Novak, T. P. (2009). Flow online: Lessons learned and future prospects. *Journal of Interactive Marketing, 23*, 23–34.

Hofstede, G. (1984). The cultural relativity of the quality of life concept. *Academy of Management Review, 9*, 389–398.

Hofstee, W. K. B. (1994). Who should own the definition of personality? *European Journal of Personality, 8*, 149–162.

Hofstee, W. K. B., & Ten Berge, J. M. F. (2004). Personality in proportion: A bipolar proportional scale for personality assessments and its conse-

quences for trait structure. *Journal of Personality Assessment, 83*, 120–127.

Hogan, R. (1969). Development of an empathy scale. *Journal of Consulting and Clinical Psychology, 33*, 307–316.

Hogan, R. (1998). Reinventing personality. *Journal of Social and Clinical Psychology, 17*, 1–10.

Hogan, R., & Nicholson, R. A. (1988). The meaning of personality test scores. *American Psychologist, 43*, 621–626.

Hogan, R. T. (1983). A socioanalytic theory of personality. In M. Page (Ed.), *Nebraska Symposium on Motivation: Personality—Current theory and research* (pp. 58–89). Lincoln: University of Nebraska Press.

Holt, R. R. (1980). Loevinger's measure of ego development: Reliability and national norms for male and female short forms. *Journal of Personality and Social Psychology, 39*, 909–920.

Hong, Y., Benet-Martínez, V., Chiu, C., & Morris, M. W. (2003). Boundaries of cultural influence: Construct activation as a mechanism for cultural differences in social perception. *Journal of Cross-Cultural Psychology, 34*, 453–464.

Hong, Y., Morris, M., Chiu, C. Y., & Benet-Martínez, V. (2000). Multicultural minds: A dynamic constructivist approach to culture and cognition. *American Psychologist, 55*, 709–720.

Horner, K. L. (1998). Individuality in vulnerability: Influences on physical health. *Journal of Health Psychology, 3*, 71–85.

Horney, K. (1937). *The neurotic personality of our time.* New York: Norton.

Horney, K. (1942). *Self-analysis.* New York: Norton.

Horney, K. (1950). *Neurosis and human growth.* New York: Norton.

Howell, C. J., Howell, R. T., & Schwabe, K. A. (2006). Does wealth enhance life satisfaction for people who are materially deprived? Exploring the association among the Orang Asli of Peninsular Malaysia. *Social Indicators Research, 76*, 499–524.

Howell, R. T., & Howell, C. J. (2008). The relation of economic status to subjective well-being in developing countries: A meta-analysis. *Psychological Bulletin, 134*, 536–560.

Hughes, C. F., Uhlmann, C., & Pennebaker, J. W. (1994). The body's response to emotional trauma:

Linking verbal text with autonomic activity. *Journal of Personality, 62*, 565–586.

Hull, J. G., Slone, L. B., Meteyer, K. B., & Matthews, A. R. (2002). The nonconsciousness of self-consciousness. *Journal of Personality and Social Psychology, 83*, 406–424.

Hunsley, J., & Bailey, J. M. (1999). The clinical utility of the Rorschach: Unfulfilled promises and an uncertain future. *Psychological Assessment, 11*, 266–277.

Hunter, J. E. (1997). Needed: A ban on the significance test. *Psychological Science, 8*, 3–7.

Hyde, J. B. (2005). The gender similarities hypothesis. *American Psychologist, 60*, 581–592.

Hyler, S. E., & Rieder, R. O. (1987). *Personality Diagnostic Questionnaire—Revised*. New York: New York State Psychiatric Institute.

Isom, J., & Heller, W. (1999). Neurobiology of extraversion: Pieces of the puzzle still missing. *Behavorial and Brain Sciences, 22*, 524.

Iyengar, S. S., & Lepper, M. R. (1999). Rethinking the value of choice: A cultural perspective on intrinsic motivation. *Journal of Personality and Social Psychology, 76*, 349–366.

Jackson, D. C., Mueller, C. J., Dolski, I., Dalton, K. M., Nitschke, J. B., Urry, H. L., et al. (2003). Now you feel it, now you don't: Frontal brain electical asymmetry and individual differences in emotion regulation. *Psychological Science, 14*, 612–617.

Jackson, D. N. (1967). *Personality Research Form manual*. Goshen, NY: Research Psychologists Press.

Jackson, D. N. (1971). The dynamics of structured personality tests: 1971. *Psychological Review, 78*, 229–248.

Jahoda, M. (1958). *Current concepts of positive mental health*. New York: Basic Books.

James, W. (1890). *Principles of psychology* (Vol. 1). London: Macmillan.

Jensen-Campbell, L. A., Adams, R., Perry, D. G., Workman, K. A., Furdella, J. Q., & Egan, S. K. (2002). Agreeableness, extraversion, and peer relations in early adolescence: Winning friends and deflecting aggression. *Journal of Research in Personality, 36*, 224–251.

John, O. P. (1990). The "Big Five" factor taxonomy: Dimensions of personality in the natural language and in questionnaires. In L. Pervin (Ed.), *Handbook of personality: Theory and research* (pp. 66–100). New York: Guilford Press.

John, O. P., Donahue, E. M., & Kentle, R. L. (1991). *The Big Five Inventory*. University of California, Berkeley, Institute of Personality and Social Research.

John, O. P., & Robins, R. W. (1994). Accuracy and bias in self-perception: Individual differences in self-enhancement and narcissism. *Journal of Personality and Social Psychology, 66*, 206–219.

John, O. P., Robins, R. W., & Pervin, L. A. (2008). *Handbook of personality: Theory and research* (3rd ed.). New York: Guilford Press.

John, O. P., & Srivastava, S. (1999). The Big-Five trait taxonomy: History, measurement, and theoretical perspectives. In L. Pervin & O. John (Eds.), *Handbook of personality: Theory and research* (2nd ed., pp. 102–138). New York: Guilford Press.

Johnson, J. A. (1981). The "self-disclosure" and "self-presentation" views of item response dynamics and personality scale validity. *Journal of Personality and Social Psychology, 40*, 761–769.

Johnson, J. A. (2006). Ego-syntonicity in responses to items in the California Psychological Inventory. *Journal of Research in Personality, 40*, 73–83.

Johnson, W., Spinath, F., Krueger, R. F., Angleitner, A., & Riemann, R. (2008). Personality in Germany and Minnesota: An IRT-based comparison of MPQ self-reports. *Journal of Personality, 76*, 665–706.

Jonason, P. K., Li, N. P., Webster, G. D., & Schmitt, D. P. (2009). The Dark Triad: Facilitating a short-term mating strategy in men. *European Journal of Personality, 23*, 5–18.

Jones, E. E., & Nisbett, R. E. (1971). *The actor and the observer: Divergent perceptions of the causes of behavior*. Morristown, NJ: General Learning Press.

Jones, T. (2003, February 1). On eve of 800th win, Knight's antics still fan flames of debate. *Columbus Dispatch*, Sports, p. 6E.

Joseph, J. E., Liu, X., Jiang, Y., Lynam, D., & Kelly, T. H. (2009). Neural correlates of emotional reactivity in sensation seeking. *Psychological Science, 20*, 215–223.

Jost, J. T., Glaser, J., Kruglanski, A. W., & Sulloway, F. J. (2003). Political conservatism as motivated social cognition. *Psychological Review, 129*, 339–375.

Jost, J. T., Nosek, B. A., & Gosling, S. D. (2008). Ideology: Its resurgence in social, personality, and political psychology. *Perspectives on Psychological Science, 3,* 126–136.

Jourard, S. M. (1971). *Self-disclosure: An experimental analysis of the transparent self.* New York: Wiley.

Jung, C. G. (1971a). *The portable Jung* (J. Campbell, Ed.). New York: Viking.

Jung, C. G. (1971b). A psychological theory of types. In H. Read, M. Fordham, & G. Adler (Eds.), *Collected works of C. G. Jung* (Vol. 20, pp. 524–541). Princeton University Press. (Originally published 1931 in German)

Jussim, L. (1991). Social perception and social reality: A reflection-construction model. *Psychological Review, 98,* 54–73.

Jussim, L., & Eccles, J. (1992). Teacher expectations II: Construction and reflection of student achievement. *Journal of Personality and Social Psychology, 63,* 947–961.

Kagan, J. (1978). Sex differences in the human infant. In T. E. McGill, D. A. Dewsburg, & B. D. Sachs (Eds.), *Sex and behavior* (pp. 305–316). New York: Plenum Press.

Kagan, J. (1994). *Galen's prophecy: Temperament in human nature.* New York: Basic Books.

Kagan, J., Reznick, J. S., & Snidman, N. (1988). Biological bases of childhood shyness. *Science, 240,* 167–171.

Kaiser, R. T., & Ozer, D. J. (1999). *The structure of personal goals and their relation to personality traits.* Unpublished manuscript, University of California, Riverside.

Kasser, T., & Ryan, R. M. (1993). A dark side of the American dream: Correlates of financial success as a central life aspiration. *Journal of Personality and Social Psychology, 65,* 410–422.

Kasser, T., & Ryan, R. M. (1996). Further examining the American dream: Differential correlates of intrinsic and extrinsic goals. *Personality and Social Psychology Bulletin, 22,* 280–287.

Kazdin, A. E. (1994). Interventions for aggressive and antisocial children. In L. D. Eron, J. H. Gentry, & P. Schlegel (Eds.), *Reason to hope: A psychosocial perspective on violence and youth* (pp. 341–382). Washington, DC: American Psychological Association.

Kazdin, A. E., & Bootzin, R. R. (1972). The token economy: An evaluative review. *Journal of Applied Behavior Analysis, 5,* 343–372.

Keller, J., & Blomann, F. (2008). Locus of control and the flow experience: An experimental analysis. *European Journal of Personality, 22,* 589–607.

Keller, M. C., & Nesse, R. M. (2006). The evolutionary significance of depressive symptoms: Different adverse situations lead to different depressive symptom patterns. *Journal of Personality and Social Psychology, 91,* 316–330.

Kelly, G. A. (1955). *The psychology of personal constructs* (Vols. 1 and 2). New York: Norton.

Kelly, G. A. (1969). The autobiography of a theory. In B. Maher (Ed.), *Clinical psychology and personality: Selected papers of George Kelly* (pp. 46–65). New York: Wiley.

Keltner, D. (1995). Signs of appeasement: Evidence for the distinct displays of embarrassment, amusement, and shame. *Journal of Personality and Social Psychology, 68,* 441–454.

Kenny, D. A. (1991). A general model of consensus and accuracy in interpersonal perception. *Psychological Review, 98,* 155–163.

Kenny, D. A. (1994). *Interpersonal relations: A social relations analysis.* New York: Guilford Press.

Kenrick, D. T., & Funder, D. C. (1988). Profiting from controversy: Lessons from the person-situation debate. *American Psychologist, 43,* 23–34.

Kenrick, D. T., & Keefe, R. C. (1992). Age preferences in mates reflect sex differences in human reproductive strategies. *Behavioral and Brain Sciences, 15,* 75–91.

Kernberg, O. F. (1984). *Severe personality disorders.* New Haven, CT: Yale University Press.

Kernis, M. H., Lakey, C. E., & Heppner, W. L. (2008). Secure versus fragile high self-esteem as a predictor of verbal defensiveness: Converging findings across three different markers. *Journal of Personality, 76,* 477–512.

Kesebir, P., & Diener, E. (2008). In pursuit of happiness: Empirical answers to philosophical questions. *Perspectives on Psychological Science, 3,* 117–125.

Kesey, K. (1999). *One flew over the cuckoo's nest.* New York: Penguin Books. (Original work published 1962)

Keyes, C. L. M., & Haidt, J. (Eds.). (2003). *Flourishing: Positive psychology and the life well-lived.* Washington, DC: American Psychological Association.

Kiesler, D. J. (1986). The 1982 interpersonal circle: An analysis of *DSM-III* personality disorders. In T. Millon & G. Klerman (Eds.), *Contemporary directions in psychopathology: Toward DSM-IV* (pp. 571–597). New York: Guilford Press.

Kihlstrom, J. F. (1990). The psychological unconscious. In L. Pervin (Ed.), *Handbook of personality: Theory and research* (pp. 445–464). New York: Guilford Press.

Kihlstrom, J. F. (1994). Psychodynamics and social cognition: Notes on the fusion of psychoanalysis and psychology. *Journal of Personality, 62*, 681–696.

Kim, H. S. (2002). We talk, therefore we think? A cultural analysis of the effect of talking on thinking. *Journal of Personality and Social Psychology, 83*, 828–842.

Kim, H. S., & Markus, H. R. (1999). Deviance or uniqueness, harmony or conformity? A cultural analysis. *Journal of Personality and Social Psychology, 77*, 785–800.

King, J. E., & Figueredo, A. (1997). The five-factor model plus dominance in chimpanzee personality. *Journal of Research in Personality, 31*, 257–271.

King, L. A. (2001). The hard road to the good life: The happy, mature person. *Journal of Humanistic Psychology, 41*, 51–72.

King, L. A., & Napa, C. K. (1998). What makes a life good? *Journal of Personality and Social Psychology, 75*, 156–165.

King, M. G., & Husband, A. J. (1991). Altered immunity through behavioral conditioning. In J. G. Carlson & A. R. Seifert (Eds.), *International perspectives in behavioral psychophysiology and medicine* (pp. 197–204). New York: Plenum Press.

Kircher, P. (1985). *Vaulting ambition: Sociobiology and the quest for human nature.* Cambridge, MA: MIT Press.

Klein, G. S. (1970). *Perception, motives, and personality.* New York: Knopf.

Klein, M. (1964). *Contributions to psychoanalysis, 1921–1945.* New York: McGraw-Hill.

Klein, M. (1975). *Envy and gratitude and other works, 1946–1963.* New York: Delacorte Press.

Klein, M. (1986). The psycho-analytic play technique: Its history and significance. In J. Mitchell (Ed.), *The selected Melanie Klein* (pp. 35–54). New York: Free Press. (Originally published 1955)

Klein, S. B., & Kihlstrom, J. F. (1998). On bridging the gap between social-personality psychology and neuropsychology. *Personality and Social Psychology Bulletin, 2*, 228–242.

Klein, S. B., Loftus, J., & Kihlstrom, J. F. (1996). Self-knowledge of an amnesic patient: Toward a neuropsychology of personality and social psychology. *Journal of Experimental Psychology: General, 125*, 250–260.

Klein, S. B., Rozendal, K., & Cosmides, L. (2002). A social-cognitive neuroscience analysis of the self. *Social Cognition, 20*, 105–135.

Klinger, E. (1977). *Meaning and void: Inner experience and the incentives in people's lives.* Minneapolis: University of Minnesota Press.

Klinger, E. (1987). The interview questionnaire technique: Reliability and validity of a mixed idographic-nomothetic measure of motivation. In J. N. Butcher and C. D. Spielberger (Eds.), *Advances in personality assessment* (pp. 311–319). Hillsdale, NJ: Erlbaum.

Klinger, E., Barta, S. G., & Maxeiner, M. E. (1981). Current concerns: Assessing therapeutically relevant motivation. In P. C. Kendall & S. Hollon (Eds.), *Assessment strategies for cognitive-behavioral interventions* (pp. 161–195). New York: Academic Press.

Klohnen, E., & Block, J. (1995). [Correlates of ego resilience and ego control]. Unpublished data, University of California, Berkeley.

Klopfer, B., & Davidson, H. H. (1962). *The Rorschach technique: An introductory manual.* New York: Harcourt, Brace.

Kluckhohn, C., & Murray, H. A. (1961). Personality formation: The determinants. In C. Kluckhohn, H. A. Murray, & D. M. Schneider (Eds.), *Personality in nature, society, and culture* (2nd ed., pp. 53–67). New York: Knopf.

Knutson, B., Momenan, R., Rawlings, R. R., Fong, G. W., & Hommer, D. (2001). Negative association of neuroticism with brain volume ratio in healthy humans. *Biological Psychiatry, 50*, 685–690.

Knutson, B., Wolkowitz, O. M., Cole, S. W., Chan, T., Moore, E. A., Johnson, R. C., et al. (1998). Selective alteration of personality and social behavior by serotonergic intervention. *American Journal of Psychiatry, 155*, 373–379.

Köhler, W. (1925). *The mentality of apes* (E. Winter, Trans.). New York: Harcourt, Brace.

Kolar, D. W. (1996). *Individual differences in the ability to accurately judge the personality characteristics of others*. Unpublished doctoral dissertation, University of California, Riverside.

Kolar, D. W., Funder, D. C., & Colvin, C. R. (1996). Comparing the accuracy of personality judgments by the self and knowledgeable others. *Journal of Personality, 64*, 311–317.

Kramer, P. D. (1993). *Listening to Prozac*. New York: Viking.

Krauss, S., & Wassner, C. (2002, July). *How significance tests should be presented to avoid the typical misinterpretations*. Paper presented at the Sixth International Conference on Teaching Statistics, Cape Town, South Africa.

Krauss, S. W. (2002). Romanian authoritarianism 10 years after communism. *Personality and Social Psychology Bulletin, 28*, 1255–1264.

Kreisman, J., & Straus, H. (1989). *I hate you—don't leave me! Understanding the borderline personality*. New York: HarperCollins/Avon Books.

Krueger, J. I., & Funder, D. C. (2004). Towards a balanced social psychology: Causes, consequences, and cures for the problem-seeking approach to social behavior and cognition. *Behavioral and Brain Sciences, 27*, 313–327.

Krueger, R. F., & Johnson, W. (2008). Behavioral genetics and personality: A new look at the integration of nature and nurture. In O. P. John, R. W. Robins, & L. A. Pervin (Eds.), *Handbook of personality: Theory and research* (3rd ed.), pp. 287–310. New York: Guilford Press.

Krueger, R. F., & Tackett, J. L. (2003). Personality and psychopathology: Working toward the bigger picture. *Journal of Personality Disorders, 17*, 109–128.

Kruglanski, A. W. (1989). The psychology of being "right": The problem of accuracy in social perception and cognition. *Psychological Bulletin, 106*, 395–409.

Kübler-Ross, E. (1969). *On death and dying*. New York: Macmillan.

Kumakiri, C., Kodama, K., Shimizu, E., Yamanouchi, N., Okada, S., Noda, S., et al. (1999). Study of the association between the serotonin transporter gene regulatory region polymorphism and personality traits in a Japanese population. *Neuroscience Letters, 263*, 205–207.

Kurt, A., & Paulhus, D. L. (2008). Moderators of the adaptiveness of self-enhancement: Operationalization, motivational domain, adjustment facet, and evaluator. *Journal of Research in Personality, 42*, 839–853.

Kusserow, A. (1999). De-homogenizing American individualism: Socializing hard and soft individualism in Manhattan and Queens. *Ethos, 27*, 210–234.

Kwan, V. S. Y., Barrios, V., Ganis, G., Gorman, J., Lange, C., Kumar, M., et al. (2007). Assessing the neural correlates of self-enhancement bias: A transcranial magnetic stimulation study. *Experimental Brain Research, 182*, 379–385.

Kwan, V. S. Y., Bond, M. H., & Singelis, T. M. (1997). Pancultural explanations for life satisfaction: Adding relationship harmony to self-esteem. *Journal of Personality and Social Psychology, 73*, 1038–1051.

Kwan, V. S. Y., John, O. P., Robins, R. W., & Kuang, L. L. (2008). Conceptualizing and assessing self-enhancement bias: A componential approach. *Journal of Personality and Social Psychology, 94*, 1062–1077.

Laing, R. D. (1959). *The divided self*. Baltimore: Penguin Books.

Lally, S. J. (2001). Should human figure drawings be admitted into court? *Journal of Personality Assessment, 76*, 135–149.

Lam, A. (2003, June 15). Let the I's have it: Think for yourselves, a writer from Vietnam tells Asian American students. *Los Angeles Times*, p. M6.

Landy, F. J., & Guion, R. M. (1970). Development of scales for the measurement of work motivation. *Organizational Behavior and Human Performance, 5*, 93–103.

Langer, E. J. (1992). Matters of mind: Mindfulness/mindlessness in perspective. *Consciousness and Cognition, 1*, 289–305.

Langer, E. J. (1994). The illusion of calculated decisions. In R. C. Schank & E. Langer (Eds.), *Beliefs, reasoning, and decision making: Psycho-logic in honor of Bob Abelson* (pp. 33–53). Hillsdale, NJ: Erlbaum.

Larkin, J. H., McDermott, J., Simon, D. P., & Simon, H. A. (1980). Models of competence in solving physics problems. *Science, 200*, 1335–1342.

Larsen, R. J., and Diener, E. (1987) Affect intensity as an individual difference characteristic: A review. *Journal of Research in Personality, 2*, 1–39.

Lau, R. R. (1988). Beliefs about control and health behavior. In D. S. Gochman (Ed.), *Health behavior: Emerging research perspectives* (pp. 43–63). New York: Plenum Press.

Lazarus, R. S. (1984). On the primacy of cognition. *American Psychologist, 39*, 124–129.

Leary, M. R. (1999). Making sense of self-esteem. *Current Directions in Psychological Science, 8*, 32–35.

Leary, M. R. (2006, January). *How and why did the self get tangled up in emotion?* Paper presented at the SPSP Emotions Pre-Conference, Palm Springs, California.

Lee, G. R., & Ishii-Kuntz, M. (1987). Social interaction, loneliness, and emotional well-being. *Research on Aging, 9*, 459–482.

Lee, K., & Ashton, M. C. (2004). Psychometric properties of the HEXACO personality inventory. *Multivariate Behavioral Research, 39*, 329–358.

Lee, K., Ogunfowora, B., & Ashton, M. C. (2005). Personality traits beyond the Big Five: Are they within the HEXACO space? *Journal of Personality, 73*, 1437–1463.

Leichsenring, F., & Rabung, S. (2008). Effectiveness of long-term psychodynamic psychotherapy. *Journal of the American Medical Association, 300*, 1551–1565.

Letzring, T. D. (2008) The good judge of personality: Characteristics, behaviors, and observer accuracy. *Journal of Research in Personality, 42*, 914–932.

Letzring, T. D., Block, J., & Funder, D. C. (2005). Ego-control and ego-resiliency: Generalization of self-report scales based on personality descriptions from acquaintances, clinicians, and the self. *Journal of Research in Personality, 39*, 395–422.

Letzring, T. D., & Funder, D. C. (2006, January). *Relations between judge's personality and types of realistic accuracy.* Paper presented at the annual meetings of the Society for Personality and Social Psychology, Palm Springs, CA.

Letzring, T. D., Wells, S., and Funder, D. C. (2006). Quantity and quality of available information affect the realistic accuracy of personality judgment. *Journal of Personality and Social Psychology, 91*, 111–123.

Levine, M. (2006). *Humanism in psychology.* Unpublished manuscript, Kenyon College, Gambier, OH.

Levy, B. L., & Anderson, M.C. (2002). Inhibitory processes and the control of memory retrieval. *Trends in Cognitive Science, 6*, 299–305.

Li, J. (2003). The core of Confucian learning. *American Psychologist, 58*, 146–147.

Li, N. P., Bailey, J. M., Kenrick, D. T., & Linsenmeier, J. A. W. (2002). The necessities and luxuries of mate preferences: Testing the tradeoffs. *Journal of Personality and Social Psychology, 82*, 947–955.

Lieberman, M. D., Jarcho, J. M., & Satpute, A. B. (2004). Evidence-based and intuition-based self-knowledge: An fMRI study. *Journal of Personality and Social Psychology, 87*, 421–435.

Lilienfeld, S. O. (1999). Projective measures of personality and psychopathology: How well do they work? *Skeptical Inquirer, 23*(5), 32–39.

Lilienfeld, S. O, Wood, J. M., & Garb, H. N. (2000). The scientific status of projective techniques. *Psychological Science in the Public Interest, 1*, 27–66.

Lindsay, K. A., & Widiger, T. A. (1995). Sex and gender bias in self-report personality disorder inventories: Item analyses of the MCMI-II, MMPI, and PDQ-R. *Journal of Personality Disorders, 65*, 1–20.

Linehan, M. M. (1993). *Cognitive behavioral therapy of borderline personality disorder.* New York: Guilford Press.

Linville, P., & Jones, E. E. (1980). Polarized appraisals of out-group members. *Journal of Personality and Social Psychology, 38*, 689–703.

Lippa, R. A. (2002). Gender-related traits of heterosexual and homosexual men and women. *Archives of Sexual Behavior, 31*, 83–98.

Lippa, R. A. (2006). Sexual orientation and personality. *Annual Review of Sex Research, 16*, 119–153.

Little, B. R. (1983). Personal projects: A rationale and method for investigation. *Environment and Behavior, 15*, 273–309.

Little, B. R. (1989). Personal projects analysis: Trivial pursuits, magnificent obsessions, and the search for coherence. In D. M. Buss & N. Cantor (Eds.), *Personality psychology: Recent trends and emerging directions* (pp. 15–31). New York: Springer-Verlag.

Liu, T. T., & Brown, G. G. (2007). Measurement of cerebral perfusion with arterial spin labeling: Part

I. Methods. *Journal of the International Neurophysiological Society, 13*, 517–525.

Loehlin, J. C., Willerman, L., & Horn, J. M. (1985). Personality resemblances in adoptive families when the children are late-adolescent or adult. *Journal of Personality and Social Psychology, 48*, 376–392.

Loehlin, J. C., Willerman, L., & Horn, J. M. (1989). Personality resemblance in adoptive families: A 10-year follow-up. *Journal of Personality and Social Psychology, 53*, 961–969.

Loevinger, J. (1976). *Ego development: Conceptions and theories*. San Francisco: Jossey-Bass.

Loevinger, J. (1987). *Paradigms of personality*. New York: Freeman.

Loftus, G. R. (1996). Psychology will be a much better science when we change the way we analyze data. *Current Directions in Psychological Science, 5*, 161–170.

Lorenz, K. (1966). *On aggression*. New York: Harcourt, Brace.

Lorenzi-Cioldi, F. (1993). They all look alike, but so do we . . . sometimes: Perceptions of in-group and out-group homogeneity as a function of sex and context. *British Journal of Social Psychology, 32*, 111–124.

Lucas, R. E., Le, K., & Dyrenforth, P. S. (2008). Explaining the extraversion/positive affect relation: Sociability cannot account for extraverts' greater happiness. *Journal of Personality, 76*, 385–414.

Lykes, M. B. (1985). Gender and individualistic vs. collectivist bases for notions about the self. *Journal of Personality, 53*, 356–383.

Lykken, D., & Tellegen, A. (1996). Happiness is a stochastic phenomenon. *Psychological Science, 7*, 186–189.

Lyubomirsky, S. (2001). Why are some people happier than others? The role of cognitive and motivational processes in well-being. *American Psychologist, 56*, 239–249.

Lyubomirsky, S. (2008). *The how of happiness: A scientific approach to getting the life you want*. New York: Penguin Press.

Lyubomirsky, S., King, L., & Diener, E. (2005). The benefits of frequent positive affect: Does happiness lead to success? *Psychological Bulletin, 131*, 803–855.

Lyubomirsky, S., Sheldon, K. M., & Schkade, D. (2005). Pursuing happiness: The architecture of sustainable change. *Review of General Psychology, 9*, 111–131.

Maccoby, E. (1966). Sex differences in intellectual functioning. In E. Maccoby (Ed.), *The development of sex differences*. Stanford University Press.

Maccoby, E. E., & Jacklin, C. N. (1974). *The psychology of sex differences*. Stanford University Press.

Machover, K. (1949). *Personality projection in the drawing of the human figure*. Springfield, IL: Chas. C Thomas.

MacLean, P. D. (1982). On the origin and progressive evolution of the triune brain. In R. G. Grenell & S. Gabay (Eds.), *Biological foundations of psychiatry* (pp. 177–198). New York: Raven Press.

MacLean, P. D. (1990). *The triune brain in evolution: Role in paleocerebral functions*. New York: Plenum Press.

Maddi, S. R. (1985). Existential psychotherapy. In S. J. Lynn & J. P. Ganske (Eds.), *Contemporary psychotherapies: Models and methods* (pp. 191–219). Columbus, OH: Merrill.

Maddi, S. R. (2003). Hardiness: An operationalization of existential courage. *Journal of Humanistic Psychology, 44*, 279–298.

Maddi, S. R., & Costa, P. T. (1972). *Humanism in personology: Allport, Maslow, and Murphy*. Chicago: Aldine/Atherton.

Maddi, S. R., Khoshaba, D. M., Persico, M., Lu, J., Harvey, R., & Bleecker, F. (2002). The personality construct of hardiness: II. Relationships with comprehensive tests of personality and psychopathology. *Journal of Research in Personality, 36*, 72–85.

Maddux, W. W., & Galinsky, A. D. (2009). Cultural borders and mental barriers: The relationship between living abroad and creativity. *Journal of Personality and Social Psychology, 96*, 1047–1061.

Madon, S., Guyll, M., Spoth, R., & Willard, J. (2004). Self-fulfilling prophecies: The synergistic accumulative effect of parents' beliefs on children's drinking behavior. *Psychological Science, 15*, 837–845.

Madon, S., Willard, J., Guyll, M., Trudeau, L, & Spoth, R. (2006). Self-fulfilling prophecy effects of mothers' beliefs on children's alcohol use: Accumulation, dissipation, and stability over time. *Journal of Personality and Social Psychology, 90*, 911–926.

Mahbubani, K. (2002). *Can Asians think? Understanding the divide between East and West* (Rev. ed.: expanded for North America). S. Royalton, VT: Steerforth Press.

Maier, S. F., & Seligman, M. E. (1976). Learned helplessness: Theory and evidence. *Journal of Experimental Psychology: General, 105*, 3–46.

Main, M. (1990). Parental aversion to infant-initiated contact is correlated with the parent's own rejection during childhood: The effects of experience on signals of security with respect to attachment. In K. E. Barnard & T. B. Brazelton (Eds.), *Touch: The foundation of experience* (pp. 461–495). Madison, CT: International Universities Press.

Maio, G. R., & Esses, V. M. (2001). The need for affect: Individual differences in the motivation to approach or avoid emotions. *Journal of Personality, 69*, 583–615.

Mandler, G. (1997). *Human nature explored*. New York: Oxford University Press.

Markey, P. M., Markey, C. N., Tinsley, B. J., & Ericksen, A. J. (2002). A preliminary validation of preadolescents' self-reports using the five-factor model of personality. *Journal of Research in Personality, 36*, 173–181.

Markon, K. E., Krueger, R. F., Bouchard, T. J., Jr., & Gottesman, I. I. (2002). Normal and abnormal personality traits: Evidence for genetic and environmental relationships in the Minnesota study of twins reared apart. *Journal of Personality, 70*, 661–693.

Markus, H. R. (1977). Self-schemata and processing information about the self. *Journal of Personality and Social Psychology, 35*, 63–78.

Markus, H. R., & Kitayama, S. (1991). Culture and the self: Implications for cognition, emotion, and motivation. *Psychological Review, 98*, 224–253.

Markus, H. R., & Kitayama, S. (1998). The cultural psychology of personality. *Journal of Cross-Cultural Psychology, 29*, 63–87.

Markus, H., & Kunda, Z. (1986). Stability and malleability of the self-concept. *Journal of Personality and Social Psychology, 51*, 858–866.

Markus, H. R., Mullally, P. R., & Kitayama, S. (1997). Selfways: Diversity in modes of cultural participation. In U. Neisser & D. Jopling (Eds.), *The conceptual self in context: Culture, experience, self-understanding* (pp. 13–60). New York: Cambridge University Press.

Markus, H. R., & Nurius, P. (1986). Possible selves. *American Psychologist, 41*, 954–969.

Martin, R. (2006). *The psychology of humor: An integrative approach*. San Diego: Academic Press.

Mascaro, N., & Rosen, D. H. (2005). Existential meaning's role in the enhancement of hope and prevention of depressive symptoms. *Journal of Personality, 73*, 985–1013.

Maslow, A. H. (1987). *Motivation and personality* (3rd ed.). New York: Harper & Row.

Masson, J. M. (1984). *The assault on truth: Freud's suppression of the seduction theory*. New York: Farrar, Straus.

Masuda, T., & Nisbett, R. E. (2001). Attending holistically versus analytically: Comparing the context sensitivity of Japanese and Americans. *Journal of Personality and Social Psychology, 81*, 922–934.

Matsumoto, D. (2004). Paul Ekman and the legacy of universals. *Journal of Research in Personality, 38*, 45–51.

Matsumoto, D. (2006). Culture and cultural worldviews: Do verbal descriptions about culture reflect anything other than verbal descriptions of culture? *Culture and Psychology, 12*, 33–62.

Matsumoto, D., Nakagawa, S., & Estrada, A. (2009). The role of dispositional traits in accounting for country and ethnic differences in adjustment. *Journal of Personality, 77*, 177–211.

Mayer, J. D. (1998). A systems framework for the field of personality. *Psychological Inquiry, 9*, 118–144.

Mayer, J. D. (2005). A tale of two visions: Can a new view of personality help integrate psychology? *American Psychologist, 60*, 294–307.

McAdams, D. P. (1980). A thematic coding system for the intimacy motive. *Journal of Research in Personality, 14*, 413–432.

McAdams, D. P. (1984). Scoring manual for the intimacy motive. *Psychological Documents, 14*(Ms. no. 2613), 1.

McAdams, D. P. (1990). *The person*. San Diego, CA: Harcourt, Brace.

McAdams, D. P., Anyidoho, N. A., Brown, C., Huang, Y. T., Kaplan, B., & Machado, M. A. (2004). Traits and stories: Links between dispositional and narrative features of personality. *Journal of Personality, 72*, 761–784.

McCabe, D. P., & Castel, A. D. (2008). Seeing is believing: The effect of brain images on judgments of scientific reasoning. *Cognition, 107*, 343–352.

McCabe, K., Houser, D., Ryan, L., Smith, V., & Trourard, T. (2001). A functional imaging study of cooperation in two-person reciprocal exchange. *Proceedings of the National Academy of Sciences, 98*, 11832–11835.

McCann, S. J. (1990). Authoritarianism and preference for the presidential candidate perceived to be higher on the power motive. *Perceptual and Motor Skills, 70*, 577–578.

McCann, S. J. (1997). Threatening times, "strong" presidential popular vote winners, and the victory margin. *Journal of Personality and Social Psychology, 73*, 160–170.

McCarthy, M. M. (1995). Estrogen modulation of oxytocin and its relation to behavior. In R. Ivell & J. Russell (Eds.), *Oxytocin: Cellular and molecular approaches in medicine and research* (pp. 235–242). New York: Plenum Press.

McClelland, D. C. (1961). *The achieving society*. Princeton, NJ: Van Nostrand.

McClelland, D. C. (1972). Opinions reflect opinions: So what else is new? *Journal of Consulting and Clinical Psychology, 38*, 325–326.

McClelland, D. C. (1975, January). Love and power: The psychological signals of war. *Psychology Today, 8*, 44–48.

McClelland, D. C. (1984). *Motives, personality, and society*. New York: Praeger.

McClelland, D. C. (1985). How motives, skills, and values determine what people do. *American Psychologist, 40*, 812–825.

McClelland, D. C., & Boyatzis, R. E. (1982). Leadership motive pattern and long-term success in management. *Journal of Applied Psychology, 67*, 737–743.

McClelland, D. C., Koestner, R., & Weinberger, J. (1989). How do self-attributed and implicit motives differ? *Psychological Review, 96*, 690–702.

McCrae, R. R. (1982). Consensual validation of personality traits: Evidence from self-reports and ratings. *Journal of Personality and Social Psychology, 43*, 293–303.

McCrae, R. R. (1994). The counterpoint of personality assessment: Self-reports and observer ratings. *Assessment, 1*, 159–172.

McCrae, R. R. (2002). The maturation of personality psychology: Adult personality development and psychological well-being. *Journal of Research in Personality, 36*, 307–317.

McCrae, R. R. (2004). Human nature and culture: A trait perspective. *Journal of Research in Personality, 38*, 3–14.

McCrae, R. R., & Costa, P. T., Jr. (1987). Validation of the five-factor model of personality across instruments and observers. *Journal of Personality and Social Psychology, 52*, 81–90.

McCrae, R. R., & Costa, P. T., Jr. (1991). Adding Liebe und Arbeit: The full five-factor model and well-being. *Personality and Social Psychology Bulletin, 17*, 227–232.

McCrae, R. R., & Costa, P. T., Jr. (1995). Trait explanations in personality psychology. *European Journal of Personality, 9*, 231–252.

McCrae, R. R., & Costa, P. T., Jr. (1997). Conceptions and correlates of openness to experience. In R. Hogan, J. Johnson, & S. Briggs (Eds.), *Handbook of personality psychology* (pp. 825–847). San Diego: Academic Press.

McCrae, R. R., Costa, P. T., Jr., & Yik, M. S. M. (1996). Universal aspects of Chinese personality structure. In M. H. Bond (Ed.), *The handbook of Chinese psychology* (pp. 189–207). Hong Kong: Oxford University Press.

McCrae, R. R., Terracciano, A., & 78 members of the Personality Profiles of Cultures Project. (2005). Universal features of personality trait terms from the observer's perspective: Data from 50 cultures. *Journal of Personality and Social Psychology, 88*, 547–561.

McCrae, R. R., Terracciano, A., Costa, P. T., Jr., & Ozer, D. J. (2006). Person-factors in the California Adult Q-Set: Closing the door on personality trait types? *European Journal of Personality, 20*, 29–44.

McCrae, R. R., Yamagata, S., Jang, K. L., Riemann, R., Ando, J., Ono, Y., et al. (2008). Substance and artifact in the higher-order factors of the Big Five. *Journal of Personality and Social Psychology, 95*, 442–455.

McCrae, R. R., Yik, M. S. M., Trapnell, P. D., Bond, M.

H., & Paulhus, D. L. (1998). Interpreting personality profiles across cultures: Bilingual, acculturation, and peer rating studies of Chinese undergraduates. *Journal of Personality and Social Psychology, 74,* 1041–1055.

McGinnies, E. (1949). Emotionality and perceptual defense. *Psychological Review, 56,* 244–251.

McGue, M., & Lykken, D. T. (1992). Genetic influence on risk of divorce. *Psychological Science, 3,* 368–373.

McIntosh, A. R. (1998). Understanding neural interactions in learning and memory using functional neuroimaging. *Annals of the New York Academy of Sciences, 855,* 556–571.

McKay, J. R., O'Farrell, T. J., Maisto, S. A., Connors, G. J., & Funder, D. C. (1989). Biases in relapse attributions made by alcoholics and their wives. *Addictive Behaviors, 14,* 513–522.

Mealey, L. (1995). The sociobiology of sociopathy: An integrated evolutionary model. *Behavioral and Brain Sciences, 18,* 523–599.

Measelle, J. R., John, O. P., Ablow, J. C., Cowan, P. A., & Cowan, C. P. (2005). Can children provide coherent, stable, and valid self-reports on the Big Five dimensions? A longitudinal study from ages 5 to 7. *Journal of Personality and Social Psychology, 89,* 90–106.

Meewisse, M., Reitsma, J. B., De Vries, G.-J., Gersons, B. P. R., & Olff, M. (2007). Cortisol and post-traumatic stress disorder in adults: Systematic review and meta-analysis. *British Journal of Psychiatry, 191,* 367–392.

Megargee, E. I. (1966). Undercontrolled and overcontrolled personality types in extreme antisocial aggression. In E. I. Megargee & J. I. Moranson (Eds.), *Psychological monographs.* New York: Harper & Row.

Mehl, M. R., Pennebaker, J. W., Crow, D. M., Dabbs, J., & Price, J. H. (2001). The electronically activated recorder (EAR): A device for sampling naturalistic daily activities and conversations. *Behavior Research Methods, Instruments, and Computers, 33,* 517–523.

Mehra, A., Kilduff, M., & Brass, D. J. (2001). The social networks of high and low self-monitors: Implications for workplace performance. *Administrative Science Quarterly, 46,* 121–146.

Menand, L. (2002, November 25). What comes naturally: Does evolution explain who we are? *New Yorker,* pp. 96–101.

Mendelsohn, G. A., Weiss, D. S., & Feimer, N. R. (1982). Conceptual and empirical analysis of the typological implications of patterns of socialization and femininity. *Journal of Personality and Social Psychology, 42,* 1157–1170.

Mesquita, B. (2001). Emotions in collectivist and individualist contexts. *Journal of Personality and Social Psychology, 80,* 68–74.

Mesquita, B., & Karasawa, M. (2002). Different emotional lives. *Cognition and Emotion, 16,* 127–141.

Metzner, R. J. (1994, March 14). Prozac is medicine, not a miracle. *Los Angeles Times,* p. B7.

Meyer, G. J., Finn, S. E., Eyde, L. D., Kay, G. G., Moreland, K. L., Dies, R. R., et al. (2001). Psychological testing and psychological assessment: A review of evidence and issues. *American Psychologist, 56,* 128–165.

Michigan Department of Education (1989). *The Michigan employability survey.* Lansing, MI: Author.

Mikulincer, M., Gillath, O., & Shaver, P. R. (2002). Activation of the attachment system in adulthood: Threat-related primes increase the accessibility of mental representations of attachment figures. *Journal of Personality and Social Psychology, 83,* 881–895.

Mikulincer, M., & Shaver, P. R. (2003). The attachment behavioral system in adulthood: Activation, psychodynamics, and interpersonal processes. *Advances in Experimental Social Psychology, 35,* 53–152.

Miles, D. R., & Carey, G. (1997). Genetic and environmental architecture of human aggression. *Journal of Personality and Social Psychology, 72,* 207–217.

Milgram, S. (1975). *Obedience to authority.* New York: Harper & Row.

Miller, G. A. (1956). The magical number seven plus or minus two: Some limits on our capacity for processing information. *Psychological Review, 63,* 81–97.

Miller, J. D. (2009, January 11). American therapy [Letter to the editor]. *New York Times Book Review,* p. 6.

Miller, J. D., & Campbell, W. K. (2008). Comparing clinical and social-personality conceptualizations of narcissism. *Journal of Personality, 76,* 449–476.

Miller, J. G. (1999). Cultural psychology: Implications for basic psychological theory. *Psychological Science, 10,* 85–91.

Miller, J. G., & Bersoff, D. M. (1992). Culture and moral judgment: How are conflicts between justice and interpersonal responsibilities resolved? *Journal of Personality and Social Psychology, 62,* 541–554.

Miller, J. G., Bersoff, D. M., & Harwood, R. L. (1990). Perceptions of social responsibilities in India and in the United States: Moral imperatives or personal decisions? *Journal of Personality and Social Psychology, 58,* 33–47.

Miller, L. (1999). Stereotype legacy: Culture and person in Japanese/American business interactions. In Y.-T. Lee, C. R. McCauley, & J. G. Draguns (Eds.), *Personality and person perception across cultures* (pp. 213–232). Mahwah, NJ: Erlbaum.

Miller, N. E., & Dollard, J. (1947). *Social learning and imitation.* New Haven, CT: Yale University Press.

Miller, R. S. (1999). Emotion. In V. J. Derlaga, B. A., Winstead, & W. H. Jones (Eds.), *Personality: Contemporary theory and research* (pp. 405–431). Chicago: Nelson-Hall.

Miller, W. R., & Seligman, M. E. (1975). Depression and learned helplessness in man. *Journal of Abnormal Psychology, 84,* 228–238.

Millon, T. (1987). *Manual for the MCMI-II* (2nd ed.). Minneapolis: National Computer Systems.

Millon, T. (1996). *Disorders of personality: The DSM-IV and beyond.* New York: Wiley.

Mischel, W. (1968). *Personality and assessment.* New York: Wiley.

Mischel, W. (1973). Toward a cognitive social learning reconceptualization of personality. *Psychological Review, 80,* 252–283.

Mischel, W. (1999). Personality coherence and dispositions in a cognitive-affective personality system (CAPS) approach. In D. Cervone & Y. Shoda (Eds.), *The coherence of personality: Social-cognitive bases of consistency, variability, and organization* (pp. 37–60). New York: Guilford Press.

Mischel, W. (2009). From *Personality and Assessment* (1968) to personality science, 2009. *Journal of Research in Personality, 43,* 282–290.

Mischel, W., & Ebbesen, E. (1970). Attention in delay of gratification. *Journal of Personality and Social Psychology, 16,* 329–337.

Mischel, W., & Shoda, Y. (1995). A cognitive-affective system theory of personality: Reconceptualizing situations, dispositions, dynamics, and invariance in personality structure. *Psychological Review, 102,* 246–268.

Moeller, S. K., Robinson, M. D., & Zabelina, D. L. (2008). Personality dominance and preferential use of the vertical dimension of space. *Psychological Science, 19,* 355–361.

Moffitt, T. E. (1991). *An approach to organizing the task of selecting measures for longitudinal research* (Tech. Rep.). University of Wisconsin, Madison.

Moffitt, T. E. (2005). The new look of behavioral genetics in developmental psychopathology: Gene-environment interplay in antisocial behaviors. *Psychological Bulletin, 131,* 533–554.

Montag, I., & Levin, J. (1994). The five-factor personality model in applied settings. *European Journal of Personality, 8,* 1–11.

Moore, T. E., Griffiths, K., & Payne, B. (1987). Gender, attitudes towards women, and the appreciation of sexist humor. *Sex Roles, 16,* 521–531.

Morey, L. C., Waugh, M. H., & Blashfield, R. K. (1985). MMPI scales for *DSM-III* personality disorders: Their derivation and correlates. *Journal of Personality Assessment, 49,* 245–251.

Morf, C. C., & Rhodewalt, F. (2001). Unraveling the paradoxes of narcissism: A dynamic self-regulatory processing model. *Psychological Inquiry, 12,* 177–196.

Morgan, C. D., & Murray, H. A. (1935). A method for investigating fantasies: The Thematic Apperception Test. *Archives of Neurology and Psychiatry, 34,* 289–306.

Morokoff, P. J. (1985). Effects of sex guilt, repression, sexual "arousability," and sexual experience on female sexual arousal during erotica and fantasy. *Journal of Personality and Social Psychology, 49,* 177–187.

Morsella, E. (2005). The function of phenomenal states: Supramodular interaction theory. *Psychological Review, 112,* 1000–1021.

Mosig, Y. D. (1989). Wisdom and compassion: What the Buddha taught. *Theoretical and Philosophical Psychology, 9,* 27–36.

Mosig, Y. D. (1999). Zen Buddhism. In B. Engler, *Personality theories* (5th ed., pp. 451–474). Boston: Houghton Mifflin.

Mount, M. K, & Barrick, M. R. (1998). Five reasons why the "Big Five" article has been frequently cited. *Personnel Psychology, 51,* 849–857.

Munafó, M. R., Brown, S. M., & Hariri, A. R. (2008). Serotonin transporter (5-HTTLPR) genotype and amygdala activation: A meta-analysis. *Biological Psychiatry, 63,* 852–857.

Munafó, M. R., Yalcin, B., Willis-Owen, S. A., & Flint, J. (2008). Association of the dopamine D4 receptor (*DRD4*) gene and approach-related personality traits: Meta-analysis and new data. *Biological Psychiatry, 63,* 197–206.

Murphy, T. K., Sajid, M., Soto, O., Shapira, N., Edge, P., Yang, M., et al. (2004). Detecting pediatric autoimmune neuropsychiatric disorders associated with streptococcus in children with obsessive-compulsive disorder and tics. *Biological Psychiatry, 55,* 61–68.

Murray, H. A. (1938). *Explorations in personality*. New York: Oxford University Press.

Murray, H. A. (1943). *Analysis of the personality of Adolf Hitler, with predictions of his future behavior and suggestions for dealing with him now and after Germany's surrender*. Washington, DC: Office of Strategic Services.

Murray, H. A. (1943). *Thematic Apperception Test manual*. Cambridge, MA: Harvard University Press.

Myers, I. B. (1962). *The Myers-Briggs Type Indicator*. Princeton, NJ: Educational Testing Service.

Naroll, R. (1959). A tentative index of culture-stress. *International Journal of Social Psychiatry, 5,* 107–116.

Nave, C. S., Sherman, R. A., & Funder, D. C. (2008). Beyond self-report in the study of hedonic and eudaimonic well-being: Correlations with acquaintance reports, clinician judgments and directly observed social behavior. *Journal of Research in Personality, 42,* 643–659.

Neff, K. D. Pisitsungkagarn, K., & Hsieh, Y.-P. (2008). Self-compassion and self-construal in the United States, Thailand, and Taiwan. *Journal of Cross-Cultural Psychology, 39,* 267–285.

Nettle, D. (2006). The evolution of personality variation in humans and other animals. *American Psychologist, 61,* 622–631.

Newman, L. S., Duff, K., & Baumeister, R. F. (1997). A new look at defensive projection: Suppression, accessibility, and biased person perception. *Journal of Personality and Social Psychology, 72,* 980–1001.

Nikula, R., Klinger, E., & Larson-Gutman, M. K. (1993). Current concerns and electrodermal reactivity: Responses to words and thoughts. *Journal of Personality, 61,* 63–84.

Nisbett, R. E. (1980). The trait construct in lay and professional psychology. In L. Festinger (Ed.), *Retrospections on social psychology* (pp. 109–130). New York: Oxford University Press.

Nisbett, R. E., Peng, K., Choi, I., & Norenzayan, A. (2001). Culture and systems of thought: Holistic versus analytic cognition. *Psychological Review, 108,* 291–310.

Nisbett, R. E., & Wilson, T. D. (1977). Telling more than we can know: Verbal reports on mental processes. *Psychological Review, 84,* 231–259.

Norem, J. (2001). *The positive power of negative thinking: Using defensive pessimism to manage anxiety and perform at your peak*. New York: Basic Books.

Norem, J. K. (1989). Cognitive strategies as personality: Effectiveness, specificity, flexibility, and change. In D. M. Buss & N. Cantor (Eds.), *Personality psychology: Recent trends and emerging directions* (pp. 45–60). New York: Springer-Verlag.

Norem, J. K. (2002). Defensive self-deception and social adaptation among optimists. *Journal of Research in Personality, 36,* 549–555.

Norem, J. K., & Cantor, N. (1986). Defensive pessimism: "Harnessing" anxiety as motivation. *Journal of Personality and Social Psychology, 51,* 1208–1217.

Norem, J. K., & Chang, E. C. (2001). A very full glass: Adding complexity to our thinking about the implications and applications of optimism and pessimism research. In E. C. Chang (Ed.), *Optimism and pessimism: Implications for theory, research, and practice* (pp. 347–367). Washington DC: American Psychological Association.

Norem, J. K., & Chang, E. C. (2002). The positive psychology of negative thinking. *Journal of Clinical Psychology, 58,* 993–1001.

Norman, W. T. (1967). *2800 personality trait descriptors: Normative operating characteristics for a university population*. Ann Arbor, MI: University of Michigan.

O'Bannon, R. M., Goldinger, L. A., & Appleby, G. S. (1989). *Honesty and integrity testing*. Atlanta, GA: Applied Information Resources.

O'Connor, A. (2004, December 14). Can strep bring on anxiety disorder? *New York Times*. Retrieved September 9, 2009, from http://www.nytimes.com/2004/12/14/health/psychology/14ocd.html

O'Connor, B. P. (2002). The search for dimensional structure differences between normality and abnormality: A statistical reveiw of published data on personality and psychopathology. *Journal of Personality and Social Psychology, 83,* 962–982.

O'Connor, B. P., & Dyce, J. A. (1998). A test of models of personality disorder configuration. *Journal of Abnormal Psychology, 107,* 3–16.

Ochsner, K. N., & Gross, J. J. (2005). The cognitive control of emotion. *Trends in Cognitive Sciences, 9,* 242–249.

Ogilvie, D. M., & Ashmore, R. D. (1991). Self-with-other representation as a unit of analysis in self-concept research. In R. C. Curtis (Ed.), *The relational self* (pp. 282–314). New York: Guilford Press.

Öhman, A., & Mineka, S. (2001). Fears, phobias, and preparedness: Toward an evolved module of fear and fear learning. *Psychological Review, 108,* 483–522.

Öhman, A., & Mineka, S. (2003). The malicious serpent: Snakes as a prototypical stimulus for an evolved module of fear. *Current Directions in Psychological Science, 12,* 5–9.

Oishi, S. (2004). Personality in culture: A neo-Allportian view. *Journal of Research in Personality, 38,* 68–74.

Oishi, S. (2006). The concept of life satisfaction across cultures: An IRT analysis. *Journal of Research in Personality, 40,* 411–423.

Oishi, S., Diener, E., Lucas, R. E., & Suh, E. M. (1999). Cross-cultural variations in predictors of life satisfaction: Perspectives from needs and values. *Personality and Social Psychology Bulletin, 25,* 980–990.

Oishi, S., Diener, E., Scollon, C. N., & Biswas-Diener, R. (2004). Cross-situational consistency of affective experiences across cultures. *Journal of Personality and Social Psychology, 86,* 460–472.

Oishi, S., & Sullivan, H. W. (2005). The mediating role of parental expectations in culture and well-being. *Journal of Personality, 73,* 1267–1294.

Oldham, J. M, & Morris, L. B. (1995). *The new personality self-portrait*. New York: Bantam Books.

Oltmanns, T. F., & Turkheimer, E. (2009). Person perception and personality pathology. *Current Directions in Psychological Science, 18,* 32–36.

Ones, D. S., Viswesvaran, C., & Schmidt, F. L. (1993). Comprehensive meta-analysis of integrity test validities: Findings and implications for personnel selection and theories of job performance. *Journal of Applied Psychology, 78,* 679–703.

Ones, D. S., Viswesvaran, C., & Schmidt, F. L. (1995). Integrity tests: Overlooked facts, resolved issues, and remaining questions. *American Psychologist, 50,* 456–457.

Ones, D. S., Viswesvaran, C., & Schmidt, F. L. (2003). Personality and absenteeism: A meta-analysis of integrity tests. *European Journal of Personality, 17*(Suppl.: Personality and industrial, work, and organizational applications), S19–S38.

Ornstein, R. E. (1977). *The psychology of consciousness* (2nd ed.). New York: Harcourt, Brace.

Orth, U., Robins, R. W., & Roberts, B. W. (2008). Low self-esteem prospectively predicts depression in adolescence and young adulthood. *Journal of Personality and Social Psychology, 95,* 695–708.

Osborn, S. M., Feild, H. S., & Veres, J. G. (1998). Introversion-extraversion, self-monitoring and applicant performance in a situational panel interview: A field study. *Journal of Business and Psychology, 13,* 143–156.

Ostendorf, F., & Angleitner, A. (1994, July). *Psychometric properties of the German translation of the NEO Personality Inventory (NEO-PI-R)*. Paper presented at the Seventh Conference of the European Association for Personality Psychology, Madrid, Spain.

Oyserman, D., Coon, H. M., & Kemmelmeir, M. (2002). Rethinking individualism and collectivism: Evaluation of theoretical assumptions and meta-analysis. *Psychological Bulletin, 128,* 3–72.

Ozer, D. J. (1985). Correlation and the coefficient of determination. *Psychological Bulletin, 97,* 307–315.

Ozer, D. J., & Benet-Martínez, V. (2006). Personality and the prediction of consequential outcomes. *Annual Review of Psychology, 57,* 401–421.

Pagan, J. L., Eaton, N. R., Turkheimer, E., & Oltmanns, T. F. (2006). Peer-reported personality problems of research nonparticipants: Are our samples biased? *Personality and Individual Differences, 41,* 1131–1142.

Pakula, A. J. [Director], & Goldman, W. [Writer]. (1976). *All the president's men* [Motion picture]. United States: Warner Bros.

Park, B., & Rothbart, M. (1982). Perceptions of outgroup homogeneity and levels of social categorization: Memory for the subordinate attributes of in-group and out-group members. *Journal of Personality and Social Psychology, 42*, 1051–1068.

Park, G., Lubinski, D., & Benbow, C. P. (2007). Contrasting intellectual patterns predict creativity in the arts and sciences: Tracking intellectually precocious youth over 25 years. *Psychological Science, 18*, 948–952.

Parker, K. C. H., Hunsley, J., & Hanson, R. K. (1999). Old wine from old skins sometimes tastes like vinegar: A response to Garb, Florio, and Grove. *Psychological Science, 10*, 291–292.

Passini, F. T., & Norman, W. T. (1966). A universal conception of personality structure? *Journal of Personality and Social Psychology, 4*, 44–49.

Paulhus, D. L. (1998). Interpersonal and intrapsychic adaptiveness of trait self-enhancement: A mixed blessing? *Journal of Personality and Social Psychology, 74*, 1197–1208.

Paulhus, D. L., & Williams, K. M. (2002). The dark triad of personality: Narcissism, Machiavellianism, and psychopathy. *Journal of Research in Personality, 36*, 556–563.

Paunonen, S. V. (2003). Big Five factors of personality and replicated predictions of behavior. *Journal of Personality and Social Psychology, 84*, 411–422.

Paunonen, S. V. (2006). You are honest, therefore I like you and find you attractive. *Journal of Research in Personality, 40*, 237–249.

Paunonen, S. V., & Jackson, D. N. (2000). What is beyond the Big Five? *Journal of Personality, 68*, 821–835.

Pavlov, I. P. (1927). Conditioned reflexes: An investigation of the physiological activity of the cerebral cortex. *Classics in the history of psychology* (G. V. Anrep, Trans.). Retrieved July 16, 2003, from psychclassics.yorku.ca/Pavlov/lecture23 .htm

Penfield, W., & Perot, P. (1963). The brain's record of auditory and visual experience. *Brain, 86*, 595–596.

Pennebaker, J. W. (1992). Inhibition as the linchpin of health. In H. S. Friedman (Ed.), *Hostility, coping, and health* (pp. 127–139). Washington, DC: American Psychological Association.

Penton-Voak, I. S., Pound, N., Little, A. C., & Perrett, D. I. (2006). Personality judgments from natural and composite facial images: More evidence for a "kernel of truth" in social perception. *Social Cognition, 24*, 490–524.

Peterson, C., Maier, S. F., & Seligman, M. E. (1993). *Learned helplessness: A theory for the age of personal control*. London: Oxford University Press.

Peterson, C., & Seligman, M. E. P. (Eds.). (2004). *Character strengths and virtues: A handbook and classification*. Washington, DC: American Psychological Association.

Peterson, C., & Steen, T. A. (2002). Optimistic explanatory style. In C. R. Snyder & S. J. Lopez (Eds.), *Handbook of positive psychology* (pp. 244–256). London: Oxford University Press.

Pfohl, B., Blum, N., & Zimmerman, M. (1997). *Structured Interview of DSM-IV Personality (SIDP-IV)*. Washington, DC: American Psychiatric Press.

Piccinelli, M., Pini, S., Bellantuono, C., & Wilkinson, G. (1995). Efficacy of drug treatment in obsessive-compulsive disorder: A meta-analytic review. *British Journal of Psychiatry, 166*, 424–443.

Piedmont, R. L., & Chae, J. H. (1997). Cross-cultural generalizability of the five-factor model of personality. *Journal of Cross-Cultural Psychology, 28*, 131–155.

Pillsworth, E. G., & Haselton, M. G. (2006). Male sexual attractiveness predicts differential ovulatory shifts in female extra-pair attraction and male mate retention. *Evolution and Human Behavior, 27*, 247–258.

Pinker, S. (1997). *How the mind works*. New York: Norton.

Pinquart, M., & Sörensen, S. (2000). Influences of socioeconomic status, social network, and competence on subjective well-being in later life: A meta-analysis. *Psychology and Aging, 15*, 187–224.

Plomin, R., Chipuer, H. M., & Loehlin, J. C. (1990). Behavioral genetics and personality. In L. Pervin (Ed.), *Handbook of personality: Theory and research* (pp. 225–243). New York: Guilford Press.

Plomin, R., Corley, R., DeFries, J. C., & Fulker, D. W. (1990). Individual differences in television viewing in early childhood: Nature as well as nurture. *Psychological Science, 1*, 371–377.

Plomin, R., & Crabbe, J. (2000). DNA. *Psychological Bulletin, 126*, 806–828.

Pope, H. G., & Katz, D. L. (1994). Psychiatric and medical effects of anabolic-androgen steroid use: A controlled study of 160 athletes. *Archives of General Psychiatry, 51*, 375–382.

Pope, K. S., Tabachnick, B., & Keith-Spiegel, P. (1987). Ethics of practice: The beliefs and behaviors of psychologists as therapists. *American Psychologist, 42*, 993–1006.

Pressman, S. D., & Cohen, S. (2005). Does positive affect influence health? *Psychological Bulletin, 131*, 925–971.

Price, R. H., & Bouffard, D. L. (1974). Behavioral appropriateness and situational constraint as dimensions of social behavior. *Journal of Personality and Social Psychology, 30*, 579–586.

Public Health Service (1991). *Application for Public Health Service grant* (PHS 398; OMB Publication No. 0925-0001). Washington, DC: U.S. Government Printing Office.

Public Health Service (2001). *Mental health: Culture, race, and ethnicity. A supplement to mental health: A report of the Surgeon General.* Washington, DC: U.S. Government Printing Office.

Pulkkinen, L. (1995). *A person-centered approach to the analysis of personality.* Unpublished manuscript, University of Jyväskylä, Finland.

Pullum, G. K. (1991). *The great Eskimo vocabulary hoax, and other irreverent essays on the study of language.* University of Chicago Press.

Pyszczynski, T., Greenberg, J., & Solomon, S. (1997). Why do we need what we need? A terror management perspective on the roots of human social motivation. *Psychological Inquiry, 8*, 1–20.

Qi, J., & Zhu, Y. (2002). The self-reference effect of Chinese college students. *Psychological Science (China), 25*, 275–278.

Quartier, V., & Rossier, J. (2008). A study of personality in children aged 8-12 years: Comparing self- and parents' ratings. *European Journal of Personality, 22*, 575–588.

Rabiner, D. L., Lenhart, L., & Lochman, J. E. (1990). Automatic versus reflective social problem solv-

ing in relation to sociometric status. *Developmental Psychology, 26*, 1010–1016.

Rada, R. T., Laws, D. R., & Kellner, R. (1976). Plasma testosterone levels in the rapist. *Psychosomatic Medicine, 38*, 257–258.

Rahula, W. (1974). *What the Buddha taught.* New York: Grove Press.

Raine, A. (2008). From genes to brain to antisocial behavior. *Current Directions in Psychological Science, 17*, 323–328.

Raleigh, M. J. (1987). Differential behavioral effects of tryptophan and 5-hydroxy-tryptophan in vervet monkeys: Influences of catecholaminergic systems. *Psychopharmacology, 93*, 44–50.

Raleigh, M. J., McGuire, M. T., Brammer, G. L., Pollack, D. B., & Yuwiler, A. (1991). Serotonergic mechanisms promote dominance acquisition in adult male vervet monkeys. *Brain Research, 559*, 181–190.

Ramírez-Esparza, N., Gosling, S. D., Benet-Martínez, V., Potter, J. P., & Pennebaker, J. W. (2006). Do bilinguals have two personalities? A special case of cultural frame switching. *Journal of Research in Personality, 40*, 99–120.

Ramírez-Esparza, N., Mehl, M. R., & Álvarez-Bermúdez, J., & Pennebaker, J. W. (2008). Are Mexicans less sociable than Americans? Insights from a naturalistic observation study. *Journal of Research in Personality, 43*, 1–7.

Rapaport, D. (1960). *The structure of psychoanalytic theory: A systematizing attempt.* New York: International Universities.

Raskin, R., Novacek, J., & Hogan, R. (1991). Narcissistic self-esteem management. *Journal of Personality and Social Psychology, 60*, 911–918.

Reis, H. T., Capobianco, A., & Tsai, F. (2002). Finding the person in personality relationships. *Journal of Personality, 70*, 813–850.

Reise, S. (2006). *Notes on psychology lectures.* Unpublished manuscript, University of California, Los Angeles.

Rentfrow, P. J., & Gosling, S. D. (2003). The do re mi's of everyday life: The structure and personality correlates of music preferences. *Journal of Personality and Social Psychology, 84*, 1236–1256.

Rentfrow, P. J., & Gosling, S. D. (2006). Message in

a ballad: The role of music preferences in interpersonal perception. *Psychological Science, 17,* 236–242.

Rentfrow, P. J., Gosling, S. D., & Potter, J. (2008). A theory of the emergence, persistence, and expression of geographic variation in psychological characteristics. *Perspectives on Psychological Science, 3,* 339–369.

Revelle, W., Amaral, P., & Turriff, S. (1976). Introversion-extraversion, time stress, and caffeine: The effect on verbal performance. *Science, 192,* 149–150.

Revelle, W., Humphreys, M. S., Simon, L., & Gilliland, K. (1980). Interactive effect of personality, time of day, and caffeine: Test of the arousal model. *Journal of Experimental Psychology: General, 109,* 1–31.

Revelle, W., & Oehlberg, K. (2008). Integrating experimental and observational personality research: The contributions of Hans Eysenck. *Journal of Personality, 76,* 1387–1414.

Richard, F. D., Bond, C. F., Jr., & Stokes-Zoota, J. J. (2003). One hundred years of social psychology quantitatively described. *Review of General Psychology, 7,* 331–363.

Rickert, E. J. (1998). Authoritarianism and economic threat: Implications for political behavior. *Political Psychology, 19,* 707–720.

Ridley, M. (1999). *Genome: The autobiography of a species in 23 chapters.* New York: HarperCollins.

Riemann, R., Angleitner, A., & Strelau, J. (1997). Genetic and environmental influences on personality: A study of twins reared together using the self- and peer report NEO-FFI scales. *Journal of Personality, 65,* 449–475.

Rilling, J. K., Gutman, D. A., Zeh, T. R., Pagnoni, G., Berns, G. S., & Kilts, C. D. (2002). A neural basis for social cooperation. *Neuron, 35,* 395–405.

Roberts, B. W., Caspi, A., & Moffitt, T. (2001). The kids are alright: Growth and stability in personality development from adolescence to adulthood. *Journal of Personality and Social Psychology, 81,* 670–683.

Roberts, B. W., & DelVecchio, W. F. (2000). The rank-order consistency of personality traits from childhood to old age: A quantitative review of longitudinal studies. *Psychological Bulletin, 126,* 3–25.

Roberts, B. W., & Jackson, J. J. (2008). Sociogenomic personality psychology. *Journal of Personality, 76,* 1523–1544.

Roberts, B. W., & Pomerantz, E. M. (2004). On traits, situations and their integration: A developmental perspective. *Personality and Social Psychology Review, 8,* 402–416.

Roberts, B. W., Walton, K. E., & Viechtbauer, W. (2006). Patterns of mean-level change in personality traits across the life course: A meta-analysis of longitudinal studies. *Psychological Bulletin, 132,* 1–25.

Roberts, B. W., Wood, D., & Caspi, A. (2008). The development of personality traits in adulthood. In O. P. John, R. W. Robins, & L. A. Pervin (Eds.), *Handbook of personality: Theory and research* (3rd ed., pp. 375–398). New York: Guilford Press.

Robins, R. W., & Beer, J. S. (2001). Positive illusions about the self: Short-term benefits and long-term costs. *Journal of Personality and Social Psychology, 80,* 340–352.

Robins, R. W., Caspi, A., & Moffitt, T. (2002). It's not just who you're with, it's who you are: Personality and relationship experiences across multiple relationships. *Journal of Personality, 70,* 925–964.

Robins, R. W., & John, O. P. (1997). Effects of visual perspective and narcissism on self-perception: Is seeing believing? *Psychological Science, 8,* 37–42.

Robins, R. W., John, O. P., & Caspi, A. (1998). The typological approach to studying personality. In R. B. Cairns & L. R. Bergman (Eds.), *Methods and models for studying the individual* (pp. 135–160). Thousand Oaks, CA: Sage.

Robins, R. W., John, O. P., Caspi, A., Moffitt, T. E., & Stouthamer-Loeber, M. (1996). Resilient, overcontrolled, and undercontrolled boys: Three replicable personality types. *Journal of Personality and Social Psychology, 70,* 157–171.

Robinson, P. (1993). *Freud and his critics.* Berkeley: University of California Press.

Rogers, C. R. (1951). *Client-centered therapy: Its current practice, implications, and theory.* Boston: Houghton Mifflin.

Rogers, C. R. (1961). *On becoming a person.* Boston: Houghton Mifflin.

Rorer, L. G. (1990). Personality assessment: A conceptual survey. In L. Pervin (Ed.), *Handbook of personality: Theory and research*. New York: Guilford Press.

Rorschach, H. (1921). *Psychodiagnostik*. Bern, Switzerland: Huber.

Rosch, E. H. (1973). Natural categories. *Cognitive Psychology, 4*, 328–350.

Rosenthal, R. (1973a). Estimating effective reliabilities in studies that employ judges' ratings. *Journal of Clinical Psychology, 29*, 342–345.

Rosenthal, R. (1973b). The mediation of Pygmalion effects: A four-factor "theory." *Papua New Guinea Journal of Education, 9*, 1–12.

Rosenthal, R. (1973c). *On the social psychology of the self-fulfilling prophecy: Further evidence for Pygmalion effects and their mediating mechanisms* (Module No. 53). New York: MSS Modular Publications.

Rosenthal, R. (Ed.). (1980). *Quantitative analysis of research domains. New directions for methodology of social and behavioral science* (no. 5). San Francisco: Jossey-Bass.

Rosenthal, R., & DiMatteo, M. R. (2001). Meta-analysis: Recent developments in quantitative methods for literature reviews. *Annual Review of Psychology, 52*, 59–82.

Rosenthal, R., Hiller, J. B., Bornstein, R. F., Berry, D. T. R., & Brunell-Neuleib, S. (2001). Meta-analytic methods, the Rorschach, and the MMPI. *Psychological Asssessment, 13*, 449–451.

Rosenthal, R., & Jacobson, L. (1968). *Pygmalion in the classroom: Teacher expectation and pupils' intellectual development*. New York: Holt, Rinehart.

Rosenthal, R., & Rosnow, R. L. (1991). *Essentials of behavioral research: Methods and data analysis* (2nd ed.). New York: McGraw-Hill.

Rosenthal, R., & Rubin, D. B. (1978). Interpersonal expectancy effects: The first 345 studies. *Behavioral and Brain Sciences, 1*, 377–415.

Rosenthal, R., & Rubin, D. B. (1982). A simple, general purpose display of magnitude of experimental effect. *Journal of Educational Psychology, 74*, 166–169.

Rosolack, T. K., & Hampson, S. E. (1991). A new typology of health behaviors for personality-health predictions: The case of locus of control. *European Journal of Personality, 5*, 151–168.

Ross, L., Greene, D., & House, P. (1977). The false consensus phenomenon: An attributional bias in self-perception and social perception processes. *Journal of Experimental Social Psychology, 13*, 279–301.

Ross, L., Lepper, M. R., & Hubbard, M. (1975). Perseverance in self perception and social perception: Biased attribution processes in the debriefing paradigm. *Journal of Personality and Social Psychology, 32*, 880–892.

Ross, L., & Nisbett, R. E. (1991). *The person and the situation: Perspectives of social psychology*. New York: McGraw-Hill.

Rosse, J. G., Stecher, M. D., Miller, J. L., & Levin, R. A. (1998). The impact of response distortion on pre-employment personality testing and hiring decisions. *Journal of Applied Psychology, 83*, 634–644.

Rotter, J. B. (1954). *Social learning and clinical psychology*. Englewood Cliffs, NJ: Prentice-Hall.

Rotter, J. B. (1982). *The development and applications of social learning theory: Selected papers*. New York: Praeger.

Rowatt, W. C., Cunningham, M. R., & Druen, P. B. (1998). Deception to get a date. *Personality and Social Psychology Bulletin, 24*, 1228–1242.

Rowe, D. C. (1994). *The limits of family influence: Genes, experience, and behavior*. New York: Guilford Press.

Rowe, D. C., Rodgers, J. L., & Meseck-Bushey, S. (1992). Sibling delinquency and the family environment: Shared and unshared influences. *Child Development, 63*, 59–67.

Rozeboom, W. W. (1960). The fallacy of the null-hypothesis significance test. *Psychological Bulletin, 57*, 416–428.

Rozin, P. (1999). The process of moralization. *Psychological Science, 10*, 218–221.

Rozin, P., Markwith, M., & Stoess, C. (1997). Moralization and becoming a vegetarian: The transformation of preferences into values and the recruitment of disgust. *Psychological Science, 8*, 67–73.

Rozin, P., & Zellner, D. (1985). The role of Pavlovian conditioning in the acquisition of food likes and dislikes. *Annals of the New York Academy of Sciences, 443*, 189–202.

Rudikoff, E. C. (1954). A comparative study of the changes in the concepts of the self, the ordinary person, and the ideal in eight cases. In C. R. Rogers & R. F. Dymond (Eds.), *Psychotherapy and personality change: Co-ordinated studies in the client-centered approach* (pp. 85–98). University of Chicago Press.

Rule, N. O., & Ambady, N. (2008a). Brief exposures: Male sexual orientation is accurately perceived at 50 ms. *Journal of Experimental Social Psychology, 44*, 1100–1105.

Rule, N. O., & Ambady, N. (2008b). The face of success: Inferences from chief executive officers' appearance predict company profits. *Psychological Science, 19*, 109–111.

Rumelhart, D. E., McClelland, J. L., & The PDP Research Group (1986). *Parallel distributed processing: Explorations in the microstructure of cognition: Vol. 1. Foundations*. Cambridge, MA: MIT Press.

Russell, J. A. (1983). Pancultural aspects of the human conceptual organization of emotions. *Journal of Personality and Social Psychology, 45*, 1281–1288.

Russell, S. S., & Zickar, M. J. (2005). An examination of differential item and test functioning across personality judgments. *Journal of Research in Personality, 39*, 354–368.

Ryan, R. M., & Deci, E. L. (2000). Self-determination theory and the facilitation of intrinsic motivation, social development, and well-being. *American Psychologist, 55*, 68–78.

Ryan, R. M., Huta, V., & Deci, E. L. (2008). Living well: A self-determination theory perspective on eudaimonia. *Journal of Happiness Studies, 9*, 139–170.

Rychlak, J. F. (1988). *The psychology of rigorous humanism* (2nd ed.). New York University Press.

Ryff, C. D., & Singer, B. (2003). Flourishing under fire: Resilience as a prototype of challenged thriving. In C. L. M. Keyes & J. Haidt (Eds.), *Flourishing: Positive psychology and the life well-lived* (pp. 15–36). Washington, DC: American Psychological Association.

Sabini, J. (1995). *Social psychology* (2nd ed.). New York: Norton.

Sackett, P. R., Burris, L. R., & Callahan, C. (1989). Integrity testing for personnel selection: An update. *Personnel Psychology, 42*, 491–529.

Sacks, O. W. (1983). *Awakenings*. New York: Dutton.

Sahagun, L. (2005, November 28). Far more than creatures of habit. *Los Angeles Times*, p. B1.

Salovey, P., Hsee, C. K., & Mayer, J. D. (1993). Emotional intelligence and the self-regulation of affect. In D. M. Wegner & J. W. Pennebaker (Eds.), *Handbook of mental control* (pp. 258–277). Englewood Cliffs, NJ: Prentice-Hall.

Sartre, J. P. (1965). The humanism of existentialism. In W. Baskin (Ed.), *Essays in existentialism* (pp. 31–62). Secaucus, NJ: Citadel Press.

Saucier, G., & Goldberg, L. R. (1996). Evidence for the Big Five in analyses of familiar English personality adjectives. *European Journal of Personality, 10*, 61–77.

Saucier, G., & Goldberg, L. R. (1998). What is beyond the Big Five? *Journal of Personality, 66*, 495–524.

Saucier, G., & Goldberg, L. R. (2003). The structure of personality attributes. In M. R. Barrick & A. M. Ryan (Eds.), *Personality and work: Reconsidering the role of personality in organizations* (pp. 1–29). San Francisco: Jossey-Bass.

Sautter, S. W., Briscoe, L., & Farkas, K. (1991). A neuropsychological profile of Capgras syndrome. *Neuropsychology, 5*, 139–150.

Savodnik, I. (2006, January 1). Psychiatry's sick compulsion: Turning weaknesses into diseases. *Los Angeles Times*, pp. M1–M3.

Scarr, S., & McCartney, K. (1983). How people make their own environments: A theory of genotype-environment interactions. *Child Development, 54*, 424–435.

Schaller, M., & Murray, D. R. (2008). Pathogens, personality, and culture: Disease prevalence predicts worldwide variability in sociosexuality, extraversion, and openness to experience. *Journal of Personality and Social Psychology, 95*, 212–221.

Schank, R. C. (1996) Goal-based scenarios: Case-based reasoning meets learning by doing. In David Leake (Ed)., *Case-based reasoning: Experiences, lessons & future directions* (pp. 295–347). Cambridge, MA: AAAI Press/MIT Press.

Scherer, K. R. (1978). Personality inference from voice quality: The loud voice of extraversion. *European Journal of Social Psychology, 8*, 467–487.

Schlenker, B. R., Weigold, M. F., & Hallam, J. R. (1990). Self-serving attributions in social context: Effects of self-esteem and social pressure. *Journal of Personality and Social Psychology, 58*, 855–863.

Schmeichel, B.J., Gailliot, M. T., Filardo, E., McGregor, I., Gitter, S., & Baumeister, R. F. (2009). Terror management theory and self-esteem revisited: The roles of implicit and explicit self-esteem in mortality salience effects. *Journal of Personality and Social Psychology, 96*, 1077–1087.

Schmidt, D. B., Lubinski, D., & Benbow, C. P. (1998). Validity of assessing educational-vocational preference dimensions among intellectually talented 13-year-olds. *Journal of Counseling Psychology, 45,* 436–453.

Schmidt, F. L. (1996). Statistical significance testing and cumulative knowledge in psychology: Implications for training of researchers. *Psychological Methods, 1,* 115–129.

Schmidt, F. L., & Hunter, J. E. (1992). Development of causal models of processes determining job performance. *Current Directions in Psychological Science, 1,* 89–92.

Schmitt, D. P., & Buss, D. M. (2001). Human mate poaching: Tactics and temptations for infiltrating existing mateships. *Journal of Personality and Social Psychology, 80,* 894–917.

Schmitt, D. P., Realo, A., Voracek, M., & Allik, J. (2008). Why can't a man be more like a woman? Sex differences in Big Five personality traits across cultures. *Journal of Personality and Social Psychology, 94,* 168–182.

Schneider, K. (1923). *Die psychopathischen Persönlichkeiten* [Psychopathic Personalities]. Vienna: Deuticke.

Schuerger, J. M., Zarrella, K. L., & Hotz, A. S. (1989). Factors that influence the temporal stability of personality by questionnaire. *Journal of Personality and Social Psychology, 56,* 777–783.

Schultheiss, O. C. (2008). Implicit motives. In O. P. John, R. W. Robins, & L. A. Pervin (Eds.), *Handbook of personality* (3rd ed., pp. 603–633). New York: Guilford Press.

Schultheiss, O. C., Wirth, M. M., Torges, C. M., Pang, J.S., Vallacorta, M.A., & Welsh, K.M. (2005). Effects of implicit power motivation on men's and women's implicit learning and testosterone changes after social victory or defeat. *Journal of Personality and Social Psychology, 88,* 174–188.

Schwartz, B., Ward, A., Monterosso, J., Lyubomirsky, S., White, K., & Lehman, D. R. (2002). Maximizing versus satisficing: Happiness is a matter of choice. *Journal of Personality and Social Psychology, 83,* 1178–1197.

Schwartz, S. H., & Sagiv, L. (1995). Identifying culture-specifics in the content and structure of values. *Journal of Cross-Cultural Psychology, 26,* 92–116.

Schwarz, N. (1999). Self-reports: How questions frame the answers. *American Psychologist, 54,* 93–105.

Sears, D. O. (1986). College students in the laboratory: Influences of a narrow data base on social psychology's view of human nature. *Journal of Personality and Social Psychology, 51,* 515–530.

Sears, R. R. (1947). *Survey of objective studies of psychoanalytic concepts.* New York: Social Science Research Council.

Selby, E. A., Anestis, M. D., Bender, T. W., & Joiner, T. E., Jr. (2009). An exploration of the emotional cascade model in borderline personality disorder. *Journal of Abnormal Psychology, 118,* 375–387.

Seligman, M. E. P. (1968). Chronic fear produced by unpredictable electric shock. *Journal of Comparative and Physiological Psychology, 66,* 402–411.

Seligman, M. E. P., & Csikszentmihalyi, M. (2000). Positive psychology: An introduction. *American Psychologist, 55,* 5–14.

Selye, H. (1956). *The stress of life.* New York: McGraw-Hill.

Shanahan, J. (1995). Television viewing and adolescent authoritarianism. *Journal of Adolescence, 18,* 271–288.

Shapiro, D. (1965). *Neurotic styles.* New York: Basic Books.

Shapiro, D. (2000). *Dynamics of character: Self-regulation in psychopathology.* New York: Basic Books.

Sharpe, D., Adair, J. G., & Roese, N. J. (1992). Twenty years of deception research: A decline in subjects' trust? *Personality and Social Psychology Bulletin, 18,* 585–590.

Shaver, P. R., & Clark, C. L. (1994). The psychodynamics of adult romantic attachment. In J. M. Masling & R. F. Bornstein (Eds.), *Empirical perspectives on object relations theory* (pp. 105–156). Washington, DC: American Psychological Association.

Shaver, P. R., & Mikulincer, M. (2005). Attachment theory and research: Resurrection of the psychodynamic approach to personality. *Journal of Research in Personality, 39,* 22–45.

Shedler, J., & Block, J. (1990). Adolescent drug use and psychological health: A longitudinal inquiry. *American Psychologist, 45,* 612–630.

Shenk, J. W. (1999, May). America's altered states. *Harper's, 298,* 38–52.

Shoda, Y. (1999). Behavioral expressions of a personality system: Generation and perception of behavioral signatures. In D. Cervone and Y. Shoda (Eds.), *The coherence of personality: Social-cognitive bases of consistency, variability, and organization* (pp. 155–181). New York: Guilford Press.

Shweder, R. A., & Bourne, E. J. (1982). Does the concept of person vary cross-culturally? In A. J. Marsella & G. M. White (Eds.), *Cultural conceptions of mental health and therapy* (pp. 97–137). London: Reidel.

Shweder, R. A., & Bourne, E. J. (1984). Does the concept of person vary cross-culturally? In R. A. Shweder & R. LeVine (Eds.), *Culture theory* (pp. 158–199). Cambridge, UK: Cambridge University Press.

Shweder, R. A., Mahapatra, M., & Miller, J. G. (1990). Culture and moral development. In J. W. Stigler, R. A. Shweder, & G. Herdt (Eds.), *Cultural psychology* (pp. 130–204). New York: Cambridge University Press.

Shweder, R. A., & Sullivan, M. A. (1990). The semiotic subject of cultural psychology. In L. A. Pervin (Ed.), *Handbook of personality: Theory and research* (pp. 399–416). New York: Guilford Press.

Shweder, R. A., & Sullivan, M. A. (1993). Cultural psychology: Who needs it? *Annual Review of Psychology, 44,* 497–523.

Siegel, S. (1984). Pavlovian conditioning and heroin overdose: Reports by overdose victims. *Bulletin of the Psychonomic Society, 22,* 428–430.

Siegel, S., & Ellsworth, D. W. (1986). Pavlovian conditioning and death from apparent overdose of medically prescribed morphine: A case report. *Bulletin of the Psychonomic Society, 24,* 278–280.

Silverman, L. H. (1976). Psychoanalytic theory: The reports of my death are greatly exaggerated. *American Psychologist, 31,* 621–637.

Silverstein, S. (1993, July 10). Target to pay $2 million in testing case. *Los Angeles Times,* pp. D1–D2.

Simon, L., Greenberg, J., & Brehm, J. (1995). Trivialization: The forgotten mode of dissonance reduction. *Journal of Personality and Social Psychology, 68,* 247–260.

Simonton, D. K., & Baumeister, R. F. (2005). Positive psychology at the summit. *Review of General Psychology, 9,* 99–102.

Singh, D., Vidaurri, M., Zambarano, R. J., & Dabbs, J. M., Jr. (1999). Lesbian erotic role identification: Behavioral, morphological, and hormonal correlates. *Journal of Personality and Social Psychology, 76,* 1035–1049.

Sinn, D. L., Gosling, S. D., & Moltschaniwskyj, N. A. (2008). Development of shy/bold behavior in the squid: Context-specific phenotypes associated with developmental plasticity. *Animal Behaviour, 75,* 433–442.

Sirotin, Y. B., & Das, A. (2009). Anticipatory haemodynamic signals in sensory cortex not predicted by local neuronal activity. *Nature, 457,* 475–480.

Skinner, B. F. (1938). *The behavior of organisms: An experimental analysis.* New York: Macmillan.

Skinner, B. F. (1948). *Walden Two.* New York: Macmillan.

Skinner, B. F. (1971). *Beyond freedom and dignity.* New York: Knopf.

Skodol, A. E., Gunderson, J. G., McGlashan, T. H., Dyck, I. R., Stout, R. L., Bender, D. S., et al. (2002). Functional impairment in patients with schizotypal, borderline, avoidant, or obsessive-compulsive personality disorder. *American Journal of Psychiatry, 159,* 276–283.

Small, D. M., Gregory, M. D., Mak, Y. E., Gitelman, D., Mesulam, M. M., & Parrish, T. (2003). Dissociation of neural representation of intensity and affective valuation in human gestation. *Neuron, 39,* 701–711.

Smillie, L. D., Pickering, A. D., & Jackson, C. J. (2006). The new reinforcement sensitivity theory: Implications for personality measurement. *Personality and Social Psychology Review, 10,* 320–335.

Smith, C. A., & Lazarus, R. S. (1990). Emotion and adaptation. In L. A. Pervin (Ed.), *Handbook of personality: Theory and research* (pp. 609–637). New York: Guilford Press.

Smith, C. P. (Ed.). (1992). *Motivation and personality: Handbook of thematic content analysis.* New York: Cambridge University Press.

Smith, E. R., & Branscombe, N. R. (1987). Procedurally mediated social inferences: The case of category accessibility effects. *Journal of Experimental Social Psychology, 23,* 361–382.

Smith, E. R., & Coster, J. (2000). Dual-process models in social and cognitive psychology: Conceptual integration and links to underlying memory systems. *Personality and Social Psychology Review, 4,* 108–131.

Smith, S. S., & Richardson, D. (1983). Amelioration of deception and harm in psychological research: The important role of debriefing. *Journal of Personality and Social Psychology, 44,* 1075–1082.

Snyder, M. (1974). The self-monitoring of expressive behavior. *Journal of Personality and Social Psychology, 30,* 526–537.

Snyder, M. (1987). *Public appearances, private realities: The psychology of self-monitoring.* New York: Freeman.

Snyder, M., & Ickes, W. (1985). Personality and social behavior. In G. Lindzey & E. Aronson (Eds.), *Handbook of social psychology* (3rd ed., Vol. 2, pp. 883–948). Reading, MA: Addison-Wesley.

Snyder, M., & Monson, T. C. (1975). Persons, situations, and the control of social behavior. *Journal of Personality and Social Psychology, 32,* 637–644.

Snyder, M., & Swann, W. B. (1978). Confirmation in social interaction: From social perception to social reality. *Journal of Experimental Social Psychology, 14,* 148–162.

Snyder, M., Tanke, E. D., & Berscheid, E. (1977). Social perception and interpersonal behavior: On the self-fulfilling nature of social stereotypes. *Journal of Personality and Social Psychology, 44,* 510–517.

Sohlberg, S. & Birgegard, A. (2003). Persistent complex subliminal activation effects: First experimental observations. *Journal of Personality and Social Psychology, 85,* 302–316.

Somer, O., & Goldberg, L. R. (1999). The structure of Turkish trait-descriptive adjectives. *Journal of Personality and Social Psychology, 76,* 431–450.

South, S. C., Oltmanns, T., & Turkheimer, E. (2005). Interpersonal perception and pathological features: Consistency across peer groups. *Journal of Personality, 73,* 675–691.

Spain, J. (1994). *Personality and daily life experience: Evaluating the accuracy of personality judgments.* Unpublished doctoral dissertation, University of California, Riverside.

Spain, J., Eaton, L. G., & Funder, D. C. (2000). Perspectives on personality: The relative accuracy of self vs. others for the prediction of behavior and emotion. *Journal of Personality, 68,* 837–867.

Spearman, C. (1910). Correlation calculated from faulty data. *British Journal of Psychology, 3,* 271–295.

Spencer-Rogers, J., Boucher, H. C., Mori, S. C., Wang, L., & Peng, K. (2009). The dialectical self-concept: Contradiction, change, and holism in East Asian cultures. *Personality and Social Psychology Bulletin, 35,* 29–44.

Srivastava, S., John, O. P., Gosling, S. D., & Potter, J. (2003). Development of personality in early and middle adulthood: Set like plaster or persistent change? *Journal of Personality and Social Psychology, 84,* 1041–1053.

Sroufe, L. A., Carlson, E., & Shulman, S. (1993). Individuals in relationships: Development from infancy through adolescence. In D. C. Funder, R. D. Parke, C. Tomlinson-Keasey, & K. Widaman (Eds.), *Studying lives through time* (pp. 315–342). Washington, DC: American Psychological Association.

Sroufe, L. A., & Waters, E. (1977). Heart rate as a convergent measure in clinical and developmental research. *Merrill-Palmer Quarterly, 23,* 3–27.

Srull, T. K., & Wyer, R. S., Jr. (1980). Category accessibility and social perception: Some implications for the study of person memory and interpersonal judgments. *Journal of Personality and Social Psychology, 38,* 841–856.

Stanovich, K. E. (1991). Cognitive science meets beginning reading. *Psychological Science, 2,* 70–81.

Stelmack, R. M. (1990). Biological bases of extraversion: Psychophysiological evidence. *Journal of Personality, 58,* 293–311.

Sternberg, R. J. (1995). For whom the bell curve tolls. [Review of the book *The Bell Curve.*] *Psychological Science, 6,* 257–261.

Stipek, D. J., & Gralinski, J. H. (1991). Gender differences in children's achievement-related beliefs and emotional response to success and failure in mathematics. *Journal of Educational Psychology, 83,* 361–371.

Stoolmiller, M. (1999). Implications of the restricted range of family environments for estimates of heritability and nonshared environment in behavior-genetic adoption studies. *Psychological Bulletin, 125,* 392–409.

Storm, C. & Storm, T. (1987). A taxonomic study of the vocabulary of emotions. *Journal of Personality and Social Psychology, 53,* 805–816.

Strack, F., & Deutsch, R. (2004). Reflective and impulsive determinants of social behavior. *Personality and Social Psychology Review, 8*, 220–247.

Strong, E. K., Jr. (1959). *Strong Vocational Interest Blank*. Palo Alto, CA: Consulting Psychologists Press.

Stuss, D. T., & Levine, B. (2002). Adult clinical neuropsychology: Lessons from studies of the frontal lobes. *Annual Review of Psychology, 53*, 401–433.

Suh, E. M. (2002). Culture, identity consistency, and subjective well-being. *Journal of Personality and Social Psychology, 83*, 1378–1391.

Sullivan, A. (2000, May 21). The double-life crusade. *New York Times Magazine*, pp. 20–22.

Sulloway, F. J. (1979). *Freud: Biologist of the mind*. New York: Basic Books.

Suls, J., & Fletcher, B. (1985). The relative efficacy of avoidant and nonavoidant coping strategies: A meta-analysis. *Health Psychology, 4*, 249–288.

Sundberg, N. D. (1977). *The assessment of persons*. Englewood Cliffs, NJ: Prentice-Hall.

Swann, W. B., Jr., Chang-Schneider, C. C., & McClarty, K. L. (2007) Do our self-views matter? Self-concept and self-esteem in everyday life. *American Psychologist, 62*, 84–94.

Swann, W. B., & Ely, R. J. (1984). A battle of wills: Self-verification versus behavioral confirmation. *Journal of Personality and Social Psychology, 46*, 1287–1302.

Symons, C., & Johnson, B. T. (1997). The self-reference effect in memory: A meta-analysis. *Psychological Bulletin, 121*, 371–394.

Symons, D. (1979). *The evolution of human sexuality*. New York: Oxford University Press.

Szasz, T. S. (1960). The myth of mental illness. *American Psychologist, 15*, 113–118.

Szasz, T. S. (1974). *The myth of mental illness: Foundations of a theory of personal conduct* (Rev. ed.). New York: Harper & Row.

Taft, R. (1955). The ability to judge people. *Psychological Bulletin, 52*, 1–23.

Tanaka, J. W., & Farah, M. J. (1993). Parts and wholes in face recognition. *Quarterly Journal of Experimental Psychology A: Human Experimental Psychology, 46A*, 225–245.

Tansey, M. J. (1992). Countertransference theory, quantitative research, and the problem of therapist-patient sexual abuse. In J. W. Barron, M. N. Eagle, & D. L. Wolitzky (Eds.), *Interface of psychoanalysis and psychology* (pp. 539–557). Washington, DC: American Psychological Association.

Taylor, G. J., & Bagby, R. M. (2000). An overview of the alexithymia construct. In R. Bar-On & J. D. A. Parker (Eds.), *The handbook of emotional intelligence* (pp. 41–67). San Francisco: Jossey-Bass.

Taylor, S. E., & Brown, J. D. (1988). Illusion and well-being: A social psychological perspective on mental health. *Psychological Bulletin, 103*, 193–210.

Taylor, S. E., Klein, L. C., Lewis, B. P., Gruenewald, T. L., Gurung, R. A. R., & Updegraff, J. A. (2000). Biobehavioral responses to stress in females: Tend-and-befriend, not fight-or-flight. *Psychological Review, 107*, 411–429.

Tee, N., & Hegarty, P. (2006). Predicting opposition to the civil rights of trans persons in the United Kingdom. *Journal of Community and Applied Social Psychology, 16*, 70–80.

Tellegen, A. (1982). *Brief manual for the Multidimensional Personality Questionnaire*. Unpublished manuscript, University of Minnesota, Minneapolis.

Tellegen, A. (1985). Structures of mood and personality and their relevance to assessing anxiety, with an emphasis on self-report. In A. H. Tuma & J. D. Maser (Eds.), *Anxiety and the anxiety disorders* (pp. 681–706). Hillsdale, NJ: Erlbaum.

Tennen, H., Affleck, G., & Armeli, S. (Eds.). (2005). Advances in personality and daily experience [Special Issue]. *Journal of Personality, 73*, 1465–1774.

Thomas, C., Turkheimer, E., & Oltmanns, T. F. (2003). Factorial structure of pathological personality as evaluated by peers. *Journal of Abnormal Psychology, 112*, 81–91.

Thompson, C. (1995, July 19). Kennedy secretary writes of Rosemary. *Press-Enterprise*, p. A2.

Thorndike, E. L. (1911). *Animal intelligence*. New York: Macmillan.

Thornhill, R., & Palmer, C. T. (2000). *A natural history of rape: Biological bases of sexual coercion*. Cambridge, MA: MIT Press.

Todorov, A., Mandisodza, A. N., Goren, A., & Hall, C. C. (2005). Inferences of competence from faces predict election outcomes. *Science, 308*, 1623–1626.

Tomarken, A. J., Davidson, R. J., & Henriques, J. B. (1990). Resting frontal brain asymmetry predicts affective responses to films. *Journal of Personality and Social Psychology, 59,* 791–801.

Tomer, R., & Aharon-Peretz, J. (2004). Novelty seeking and harm avoidance in Parkinson's disease: Effects of asymmetric dopamine deficiency. *Journal of Neurology, Neurosurgery, and Psychiatry, 75,* 972–975.

Tooby, J., & Cosmides, L. (1990). On the universality of human nature and the uniqueness of the individual: The role of genetics and adaptation. *Journal of Personality, 58,* 17–67.

Tooke, W. S., & Ickes, W. (1988). A measure of adherence to conventional morality. *Journal of Social and Clinical Psychology, 6,* 310–334.

Totterdell, P. (2000). Catching moods and hitting runs: Mood linkage and subjective performance in professional sports teams. *Journal of Applied Psychology, 83,* 848–859.

Triandis, H. C. (1994). *Culture and social behavior.* New York: McGraw-Hill.

Triandis, H. C. (1997). Cross-cultural perspectives on personality. In R. Hogan, J. Johnson, & S. Briggs (Eds.), *Handbook of personality psychology* (pp. 440–464). San Diego: Academic Press.

Triandis, H. C., & Gelfand, M. J. (1998). Converging measurement of horizontal and vertical individualism and collectivism. *Journal of Personality and Social Psychology, 74,* 118–128.

Triesman, A. M. (1964). Selective attention in man. *British Medical Bulletin, 20,* 12–16.

Trivedi, N., & Sabini, J. (1998). Volunteer bias, sexuality, and personality. *Archives of Sexual Behavior, 27,* 181–195.

Trull, T. J., & Durrett, C. A. (2005). Categorical and dimensional models of personality disorder. *Annual Review of Clinical Psychology, 1,* 355–380.

Trull, T. J., Solhan, M. B., Tragesser, S. L., Jahng, S., Wood, P. K., Piasecki, T. M., et al. (2008). Affective instability: Measuring a core feature of borderline personality disorder with ecological momentary assessment. *Journal of Abnormal Psychology, 117,* 647–661.

Trzesniewski, K. H., Donnellan, M. B., Moffitt, T. E., Robins, R. W., Poulton, R., & Caspi, A. (2006). Low self-esteem during adolescence predicts poor health, criminal behavior, and limited economic prospects during adulthood. *Developmental Psychology, 42,* 381–390.

Tsai, J. L., Knutson, B., & Fung, H. H. (2006). Cultural variation in affect valuation. *Journal of Personality and Social Psychology, 90,* 288–307.

Tsai, J. L., & Chentsova-Dutton, Y. (2003). Variation among European Americans in emotional facial expression. *Journal of Cross-Cultural Psychology, 34,* 650–657.

Tseng, W.-S. (2003). *Clinician's guide to cultural psychiatry.* San Diego: Academic Press.

Tupes, E. C., & Christal, R. C. (1961). *Recurrent personality factors based on trait ratings* (Tech. Rep.). San Antonio, TX: USAF, Lackland Air Force Base.

Turkheimer, E. (1998). Heritability and biological explanation. *Psychological Review, 105,* 782–791.

Turkheimer, E., & Gottesman, I. I. (1991). Is $H_2 = 0$ a null hypothesis anymore? *Behavioral and Brain Sciences, 14,* 410–411.

Turkheimer, E., Haley, A., Waldron, M., D'Onofrio, B., & Gottesman, I. I. (2003). Socioeconomic status modifies heritability of IQ in young children. *Psychological Science, 14,* 623–628.

Turkheimer, E., & Waldron, M. (2000). Nonshared environment: A theoretical, methodological, and quantitative review. *Psychological Bulletin, 126,* 78–108.

Tversky, A., & Kahneman, D. (1973). Availability: A heuristic for judging frequency and probability. *Cognitive Psychology, 5,* 207–232.

Tversky, A., & Kahneman, D. (1983). Extensional versus intuitive reasoning: The conjunction fallacy in probability judgment. *Psychological Review, 90,* 1124–1131.

Tweed, R. G., & Lehman, D. R. (2002). Learning considered in a cultural context: Confucian and Socratic approaches. *American Psychologist, 57,* 89–99.

Twenge, J. M. (2006). *Generation me: Why today's young Americans are more confident, assertive, entitled—and more miserable than ever before.* New York: Free Press.

Twenge, J. M., Konrath, S., Foster, J. D., Campbell, W. K., & Bushman, B. J. (2008). Egos inflating over time: A cross-temporal meta-analysis of the Narcissistic Personality Inventory. *Journal of Personality, 76,* 875–902.

Twisk, J. W. R., Snel, J., Kemper, H. C. G., & van Mechelen, W. (1998). Relation between the longitudinal development of personality characteristics and biological and lifestyle risk factors for coronary heart disease. *Psychosomatic Medicine, 60,* 372–377.

United Nations Environment Programme (2009). *The billion tree campaign.* Retrieved July 30, 2009, from http://www.unep.org/billiontreecampaign/Treeandhumanity/index.asp

Uttal, W. R. (2002). Précis of *The New Phrenology: The Limits of Localizing Cognitive Processes in the Brain. Brain and Mind, 3,* 221–228.

Valenstein, E. S. (1986). *Great and desperate cure: The rise and decline of psychosurgery and other radical treatments for mental illness.* New York: Basic Books.

Vallacher, R., & Wegner, D. (1987). What do people think they're doing? Action identification and human behavior. *Psychological Review, 94,* 3–15.

Van Boven, L. (2005). Experientialism, materialism, and the pursuit of happiness. *Review of General Psychology, 9,* 132–142.

Van Hiel, A., & Kossowska, M. (2006). Having few positive emotions, or too many negative feelings? Emotions as moderating variables of authorianism effects on racism. *Personality and Individual Differences, 40,* 919–930.

Van Lieshout, C. F. M., & Haselager, G. J. T. (1994). The big five personality factors in Q sort descriptions of children and adolescents. In C. F. Halverson, Jr., G. A. Kohnstamm, & R. P. Martin (Eds.), *The developing structure of temperament and personality from infancy to adulthood* (pp. 293–318). Hillsdale, NJ: Erlbaum.

Vazire, S. (2006). Informant reports: A cheap, fast, and easy method of personality assessment. *Journal of Research in Personality, 40,* 472–481.

Vazire, S., & Funder, D. C. (2006). Impulsivity and the self-defeating behavior of narcissists. *Personality and Social Psychological Review, 10,* 154–165.

Vazire, S., & Mehl, M. R. (2008). Knowing me, knowing you: The accuracy and unique predictive validity of self-ratings and other-ratings of daily behavior. *Journal of Personality and Social Psychology, 95,* 1202–1216.

Vedantam, S. (2005, December 10). Psychiatry ponders whether extreme bias can be an illness [Electronic version]. *Washington Post,* p. A01. Retrieved December 10, 2005.

Verheul, R., Bartak, A., & Widiger, T. (2007). Prevalence and construct validity of personality disorder not otherwise specified (PDNOS). *Journal of Personality Disorders, 21,* 359–370.

Vignoles, V. L, Manzi, C., Regalia, C., Scabini, E., & Jemmolo, S. (2008). Identity motives underlying desired and feared possible future selves. *Journal of Personality, 76,* 1165–1200.

Virkkunen, M., Rawlings, R., Tokola, R., Poland, R. E., Guidotti, A., Nemeroff, C., et al. (1994). CSF biochemistries, glucose metabolism, and diurnal activity rhythms in alcoholics, violent offenders, fire setters, and healthy volunteers. *Archives of General Psychiatry, 51,* 20–27.

Vogt, D. S., & Colvin, C. R. (2003). Interpersonal orientation and the accuracy of personality judgment. *Journal of Personality, 71,* 267–295.

Vogt, D. S., & Colvin, C. R. (2005). Assessment of accurate self-knowledge. *Journal of Personality Assessment, 84,* 239–251.

von Hippel, W., Lakin, J. L., & Shakarchi, R. J. (2005). Individual differences in motivated social cognition: The case of self-serving information processing. *Personality and Social Psychology Bulletin, 31,* 1347–1357.

Vonnegut, K., Jr. (1963). *Cat's cradle.* New York: Holt, Rinehart.

Vonnegut, K., Jr. (1966). *Mother night.* New York: Delacorte Press.

Vul, E., Harris, C., Winkielman, P., & Pashler, H. (2009). Puzzlingly high correlations in fMRI studies of emotion, personality, and social cognition [formerly titled "Voodoo correlations in social neuroscience"]. *Perspectives on Psychological Science, 4,* 274–290.

Wagerman, S. A., & Funder, D. C. (2007). Acquaintance reports of personality and academic achievement: A case for conscientiousness. *Journal of Research in Personality, 41,* 221–229.

Wakefield, J. C. (1989). Levels of explanation in personality theory. In D. Buss & N. Cantor (Eds.), *Personality psychology: Recent trends and emerging directions* (pp. 333–346). New York: Springer-Verlag.

Waller, D. (1993, April 12). A tour through "hell week." *Newsweek*, p. 33.

Waller, N. G., & Shaver, P. R. (1994). The importance of nongenetic influences on romantic love styles: A twin-family study. *Psychological Science, 5*, 268–274.

Walton, G. M., & Cohen, G. L. (2007). A question of belonging: Race, fit, and achievement. *Journal of Personality and Social Psychology, 92*, 82–96.

Walton, K. E., & Roberts, B. W. (2004). On the relationship between substance use and personality traits: Abstainers are not maladjusted. *Journal of Research in Personality, 38*, 515–535.

Walton, K. E., Roberts, B. W., Krueger, R. F., Blonigen, D. M., & Hicks, B. M. (2008). Capturing abnormal personality with normal personality inventories: An item response theory approach. *Journal of Personality, 76*, 1623–1647.

Waters, E., Kondo-Ikemura, K., Posada, G., & Richters, J. E. (1991). Learning to love: Mechanisms and milestones. In M. R. Gunnar & L. A. Sroufe (Eds.), *Self processes and development* (pp. 217–255). Hillsdale, NJ: Erlbaum.

Watkins, C. E., Campbell, V. L., Nieberding, R., & Hallmark, R. (1995). Contemporary practice of psychological assessment by clinical psychologists. *Professional Psychology: Research and Practice, 26*, 54–60.

Watson, D. (1989). Strangers' ratings of five robust personality factors: Evidence of a surprising convergence with self-report. *Journal of Personality and Social Psychology, 57*, 120–128.

Watson, D., & Clark, L. A. (1984). Negative affectivity: The disposition to experience aversive emotional states. *Psychological Bulletin, 96*, 465–490.

Watson, D., & Clark, L. A. (1997). Extraversion and its positive emotional core. In R. Hogan, J. Johnson, & S. Briggs (Eds.), *Handbook of personality psychology* (pp. 767–793). San Diego: Academic Press.

Watson, D., Clark, L. A., & Chmielewski, M. (2008). Structures of personality and their relevance to psychopathology: II. Further articulation of a comprehensive unified trait structure. *Journal of Personality, 76*, 1545–1585.

Watson, D., & Tellegen, A. (1985). Toward a consensual structure of mood. *Psychological Bulletin, 98*, 219–235.

Watson, D. C. (2001). Procrastination and the five-factor model: A facet level analysis. *Personality and Individual Differences, 30*, 149–158.

Watson, J. B. (1930). *Behaviorism* (Rev. ed.). New York: Norton.

Weaver, I. C. G. (2007). Epigenetic programming by maternal behavior and pharmacological intervention—Nature vs. Nurture: Let's call the whole thing off. *Epigenetics, 2*, 22–28.

Weaver, I. C. G., Cervoni, N., Champagne, F. A., D'Alessio, A. C., Sharma, S., Seckl, J. R., et al. (2004). Epigenetic programming by maternal behavior. *Nature Neuroscience, 7*, 847–854.

Weinberg, R. S., Gould, D., & Jackson, A. (1979). Expectations and performance: An empirical test of Bandura's self-efficacy theory. *Journal of Sport Psychology, 1*, 320–331.

Weinberger, D. A., & Davidson, M. N. (1994). Styles of inhibiting emotional expression: Distinguishing repressive coping from impression management. *Journal of Personality, 62*, 587–614.

Weiss, J. M. (1970). Somatic effects of predictable and unpredictable shock. *Psychosomatic Medicine, 32*, 397–408.

Weiss, J. M. (1977). Psychological and behavioral influences on gastrointestinal lesions in animal models. In J. D. Maser & M. E. P. Seligman (Eds.), *Psychopathology: Experimental models* (pp. 232–269). San Francisco: Freeman.

Westen, D. (1990). Psychoanalytic approaches to personality. In L. Pervin (Ed.), *Handbook of personality: Theory and research* (pp. 21–65). New York: Guilford Press.

Westen, D. (1992). The cognitive self and the psychoanalytic self: Can we put ourselves together? *Psychological Inquiry, 3*, 1–13.

Westen, D. (1998). The scientific legacy of Sigmund Freud: Toward a psychodynamically informed psychological science. *Psychological Bulletin, 124*, 333–371.

Westen, D., Gabbard, G. O., & Ortigo, K. M. (2008). Psychoanalytic approaches to personality. In O. P. John, R. W. Robins, & L. A. Pervin (Eds.), *Handbook of personality: Theory and research* (3rd ed., pp. 61–113). New York: Guilford Press.

Westfeldt, A. (2008, March 10). NY Governor linked to prostitution ring. *Associated Press*.

Weston, M. J., & Whitlock, F. A. (1971). The Capgras syndrome following head injury. *British Journal of Psychiatry, 119*, 25–31.

Wheeler, L., Reise, H. T., & Bond, M. H. (1989). Collectivism-individualism in everyday social life: The Middle Kingdom and the melting pot. *Journal of Personality and Social Psychology, 57*, 79–86.

Wheeler, R. E., Davidson, R. J., & Tomarken, A. J. (1993). Front brain asymmetry and emotional reactivity: A biological substrate of affective style. *Psychophysiology, 30*, 82–89.

Whittle, S., Allen, N. B., Lubman, D. I., & Yücel, M. (2006). The neurobiological basis of temperament: Towards a better understanding of psychopathology. *Neuroscience and Biobehavioral Reviews, 30*, 511–525.

Whorf, B. L. (1956). Science and linguistics. In J. B. Carroll (Ed.), *Language, thought, and reality* (pp. 207–219). Cambridge, MA: MIT Press.

Widiger, T. A., Trull, T. J., Clarkin, J. F., Sanderson, C., & Costa, P. T., Jr. (1994). A description of the *DSM-III*-R and *DSM-IV* personality disorders with the five-factor model of personality. In P. T. Costa, Jr., & T. A. Widiger (Eds.), *Personality disorders and the five-factor model of personality* (pp. 41–56). Washington, DC: American Psychological Association.

Widiger, T. A., Trull, T. J., Clarkin, J. F., Sanderson, C., & Costa. P. T., Jr. (2002). A description of the *DSM-IV* personality disorders with the five-factor model of personality. In P. T. Costa, Jr., & T. A. Widiger (Eds.), *Personality disorders and the five-factor model of personality* (2nd ed., pp. 89–99). Washington, DC: American Psychological Association.

Widom, C. S. (1989). The cycle of violence. *Science, 244*, 160–166.

Wiggins, J. S. (1973). *Personality and prediction: Principles of personality assessment*. Reading, MA: Addison-Wesley.

Wiggins, J. S., & Trapnell, P. D. (1999). Personality structure: The return of the Big Five. In R. Hogan, J. Johnson, & S. Briggs (Eds.), *Handbook of personality psychology* (pp. 737–765). San Diego: Academic Press.

Wilkinson, L., & The Task Force on Statistical Inference, APA Board of Scientific Affairs (1999). Statistical methods in psychology journals. *American Psychologist, 54*, 594–604.

Wilson, E. O. (1975). *Sociobiology: The new synthesis*. Cambridge, MA: Harvard University Press.

Wilson, G. D. (1978). Introversion/extraversion. In H. London and J. E. Exner (Eds.), *Dimensions of personality*. New York: Wiley.

Wilson, T. D. (2002). *Strangers to ourselves: Discovering the adaptive unconscious*. Cambridge, MA: Harvard University Press.

Wilson, T. D., & Gilbert, D. T. (2005). Affecting forecasting: Knowing what to want. *Current Directions in Psychological Science, 14*, 131–134.

Winnicott, D. W. (1958). *Through paediatrics to psychoanalysis*. London: Hogarth Press.

Winnicott, D. W. (1965). *The maturational process and the facilitating environment*. New York: International Universities.

Winnicott, D. W. (1996). The niffle. In R. Shepherd, J. Johns, & H. T. Robinson (Eds.), *Thinking about children* (pp. 104–109). Reading, MA: Addison-Wesley.

Winter, D. G. (1991). Measuring personality at a distance: Development of an integrated system for scoring motives in running text. In D. J. Ozer, J. M. Healy, & A. J. Stewart (Eds.), *Perspectives in personality* (Vol. 3, pp. 59–89). London: Jennifer Kingsley.

Winter, D. G. (2002). The motivational dimensions of leadership: Power, achievement, and affiliation. In R. E. Riggio, S. E. Murphy, & F. J. Pirozzolo (Eds.), *Multiple intelligences and leadership* (pp. 119–138). Mahwah, NJ: Erlbaum.

Winter, D. G., John, O. P., Stewart, A. J., Klohnen, E. C., & Duncan, L. E. (1998). Traits and motives: Toward an integration of two traditions in personality research. *Psychological Review, 105*, 230–250.

Winter, D. G., & Stewart, A. J. (1978). The power motive. In H. London & J. E. Exner, Jr. (Eds.), *Dimensions of personality* (pp. 391–448). New York: Wiley.

Woike, B. A. (1995). Most-memorable experiences: Evidence for a link between implicit and explicit motives and social cognitive processes in everyday life. *Journal of Personality and Social Psychology, 68*, 1081–1091.

Woike, B. A., & Aronoff, J. (1992). Antecedents of complex social cognitions. *Journal of Personality and Social Psychology, 63*, 97–104.

Wood, J. M., Nezworski, M. T., & Garb, H. N. (2003). What's right with Rorschach? *Scientific Review of Mental Health Practice, 2*, 142–146.

Wood, J. V., Perunovic, E., & Lee, J. W. (2009). Positive self-statements: Power for some, peril for others. *Psychological Science, 20*, 860–866.

Wood, W., & Eagly, A. H. (2002). A cross-cultural analysis of the behavior of women and men: Implications for the origins of sex differences. *Psychological Bulletin, 128*, 699–727.

Woodworth, R. S. (1917). *Personal data sheet.* Chicago: Stoelting.

Wundt, W. (1894). *Lectures on human and animal psychology* (J. E. Creighton & E. B. Titchener, Trans.). New York: Macmillan.

Wylie, R. E. (1974). *The self concept* (Vols. 1 and 2). Lincoln: University of Nebraska Press.

Yang, K. S., & Bond, M. H. (1990). Exploring implicit personality theories with indigenous or imported constructs: The Chinese case. *Journal of Personality and Social Psychology, 58*, 1087–1095.

Yang, K. S., & Lee, P. H. (1971). Likeability, meaningfulness, and familiarity of 557 Chinese adjectives for personality trait description [in Chinese]. *Acta Psychologica Taiwanica, 13*, 36–37.

York, K. L., & John, O. P. (1992). The four faces of Eve: A typological analysis of women's personality at midlife. *Journal of Personality and Social Psychology, 63*, 494–508.

Young, J. (1988). *The role of selective attention in the attitude-behavior relationship.* Unpublished doctoral dissertation, University of Minnesota, Minneapolis.

Yudofsky, S. C. (2005). *Fatal flaws: Navigating destructive relationships with people with disorders of personality and character.* Washington, DC: American Psychiatric Publishing.

Zajonc, R. B. (1980). Feeling and thinking: Preferences need no inferences. *American Psychologist, 35*, 151–175.

Zald, D. H., & Curtis, C. (2006). Brain imaging and related methods. In M. Eid & E. Diener (Eds.), *Handbook of multimethod measurement in psychology* (pp. 173–188). Washington, DC: American Psychological Association.

Zald, D. H., Mattson, D. L., & Pardo, J. V. (2002). Brain activity in ventromedial prefrontal cortex correlates with individual differences in negative affect. *Proceedings of the National Academy of Sciences, 99*, 2450–2454.

Zanarini, M. C. (2008). Reasons for change in borderline personality disorder (and other Axis II disorders). *Psychiatric Clinics of North America, 31*, 505–515.

Zeigler-Hill, V. (2006). Discrepancies between implicit and explicit self-esteem: Implications for narcissism and self-esteem instability. *Journal of Personality, 74*, 119–143.

Zelli, A., Cervone, D., & Huesmann, L. R. (1996). Behavioral experience and social inference: Individual differences in aggressive experience and spontaneous versus deliberate trait inference. *Social Cognition, 14*, 165–190.

Zelli, A., Huesmann, L. R., & Cervone, D. (1995). Social inference and individual differences in aggression: Evidence for spontaneous judgments of hostility. *Aggressive Behavior, 21*, 405–417.

Zentall, T. R., Sutton, J. E., & Sherburne, L. M. (1996). True imitative learning in pigeons. *Psychological Science, 7*, 343–346.

Zernike, K. (2005, May 10). Behind failed Abu Ghraib plea, a tale of breakups and betrayal. *New York Times*, p. A1.

Zhang, F., & Hazan, C. (2002). Working models of attachment and person perception processes. *Personal Relationships, 9*, 225–235.

Zheng, Y., Xu, L., & Shen, Q. (1986). Styles of verbal expression of emotional and physical experience: A study of depressed patients and normal controls in China. *Culture, Medicine, and Psychiatry, 10*, 231–243.

Zhou, X., Saucier, G., Gao, D., & Liu, J. (2009). The factor structure of Chinese personality terms. *Journal of Personality, 77*, 363–400.

Zickar, M. J. (2001). Using personality inventories to identify thugs and agitators: Applied psychology's contribution to the war against labor. *Journal of Vocational Behavior, 59*, 149–164.

Zimbardo, P. (2004, May 9). Power turns good soldiers into "bad apples." *Boston Globe*, p. D11.

Zimbardo, P., Maslach, C., & Haney, C. (2000). Reflections on the Stanford prison experiment: Genesis, transformation, consequences. In T.

Blass (Ed.), *Obedience to authority: Current perspectives on the Milgram paradigm* (pp. 193–237). Mahwah, NJ: Erlbaum.

Zimbardo, P. G. (1977). *Shyness*. New York: Harcourt, Brace/Jove.

Zuckerman, M. (1979). Attribution of success and failure revisited; or, the motivational bias is alive and well in attribution theory. *Journal of Personality, 47*, 245–287.

Zuckerman, M. (1984). Sensation seeking: A comparative approach to a human trait. *Behavioral and Brain Sciences, 7*, 413–471.

Zuckerman, M. (1991). *Psychobiology of personality*. Cambridge University Press.

Zuckerman, M. (1998). Psychobiological theories of personality. In D. F. Barone, M. Hersen, & V. B. Van Hasselt (Eds.), *Advanced personality* (pp. 123–154). New York: Plenum Press.

Zuckerman, M., Koestner, R., DeBoy, T., Garcia, K. T., Maresca, B. C., & Sartoris, J. M. (1988). To predict some of the people some of the time: A reexamination of the moderator variable approach in personality theory. *Journal of Personality and Social Psychology, 54*, 1006–1019.

Zweigenhaft, R. L. (2008). A do re mi encore: A closer look at the personality correlates of music preferences. *Journal of Individual Differences, 29*, 45–55.

GLOSSARY

acculturation The process of social influence by which a person partially or fully acquires a new cultural outlook, either by having contact with, or by living in, a different culture from his or her culture of origin.

adrenal cortex The outer layer of the adrenal gland, atop the kidneys, that secretes several behaviorally important hormones.

aggregation The combining together of different measurements, such as by averaging them.

allele A particular variant, or form, of a gene; most genes have two or more alleles.

amygdala A structure located near the base of the brain that is believed to play a role in emotion, especially negative emotions such as anger and fear.

anal stage In psychoanalytic theory, the stage of psychosexual development, from about 18 months to 3½ or 4 years of age, in which the physical focus of the *libido* is located in the anus and associated eliminative organs.

anatta In Zen Buddhism, the fundamental idea of "nonself"—that the single, isolated self is an illusion.

Angst In existential philosophy, the anxiety that stems from doubts about the meaning and purpose of life. Also called existential anxiety.

anicca In Zen Buddhism, the recognition that all things are temporary and that, therefore, it is best to avoid attachments to them.

anima In Jung's version of psychoanalysis, the idea of the typical female as held in the mind of a male.

animus In Jung's version of psychoanalysis, the idea of the typical male as held in the mind of a female.

anterior cingulate The front part of the cingulate, a brain structure that runs from the front to the back of the brain in the middle, just above the *cor-pus callosum*. The anterior cingulate is believed to be important for the experience of normal emotion and self-control.

antisocial personality disorder An extreme pattern of deceitful, manipulative, and sometimes dangerous behavior.

approach-avoidance conflict In Dollard and Miller's social learning theory, the conflict induced by a stimulus that is at once attractive and aversive.

archetypes In Jung's version of psychoanalysis, the fundamental images of people that are contained in the *collective unconscious*, including (among others), "the earth mother," "the hero," "the devil," and "the supreme being."

ascending reticular activating system (ARAS) A part of the upper brain stem through which information flows into the brain and stimulates it.

associationism The idea that all complex ideas are combinations of two or more simple ideas.

association method In molecular behavioral genetics, the attempt to link genes to personality by comparing the DNA of people who score high and low on trait scales and behavioral measures.

attachment theory A theoretical perspective that draws on psychoanalytic thought to describe the development and importance of human attachments to emotionally significant other people.

authentic existence In existential philosophy, living with an awareness of the dilemmas concerning the meaning of life, mortality, and free will.

avoidant personality disorder An extreme pattern of feelings of inadequacy accompanied by fear of social contact.

Axis I disorders In the *DSM-IV*, patterns of severe mental illness.

Axis II disorders In the *DSM-IV*, the personality disorders.

basic approach (to personality) A theoretical view of personality that focuses on some phenomena and ignores others. The basic approaches are *trait*, *biological*, *psychoanalytic*, *phenomenological*, *learning*, and *cognitive* (the last two being closely related).

B data "Behavioral data," or direct observations of another's behavior that are translated directly or nearly directly into numerical form. B data can be gathered in natural or contrived (experimental) settings.

behavioral confirmation The "self-fulfilling prophecy" tendency for a person to become the kind of person others expect him or her to be. Also called the *expectancy effect*.

behavioral prediction The degree to which a judgment or measurement can predict the behavior of the person in question.

behaviorism (or behaviorist approach) The theoretical view of personality that focuses on overt behavior and the ways in which it can be affected by rewards and punishments in the environment. A modern variant is the social learning approach, which adds a concern with how behavior is affected by observation, self-evaluation, and social interaction. Also called the *learning approach*.

Binomial Effect Size Display (BESD) A method for displaying and understanding more clearly the magnitude of an effect reported as a correlation, by translating the value of r into a 2×2 table comparing predicted with obtained results.

biological approach The view of personality that focuses on the way behavior and personality are influenced by neuroanatomy, biochemistry, genetics, and evolution.

borderline personality disorder An extreme and sometimes dangerous pattern of emotional instability, emotional emptiness, confused identity, and tendencies toward self-harm.

California Q-Set A set of 100 descriptive items (e.g., "is critical, skeptical, not easily impressed") that comprehensively cover the personality domain.

case method Studying a particular phenomenon or individual in depth both to understand the particular case and in hopes of discovering general lessons or scientific laws.

central nervous system The brain and spinal cord.

chronic accessibility The tendency of an idea or concept to come easily to mind for a particular individual.

chunk Any piece of information that can be thought of as a unit. A chunk can vary with learning and experience. The capacity of short-term memory is 7 chunks, plus or minus 2.

classical conditioning The kind of learning in which an unconditioned response (such as salivating), that is naturally elicited by one stimulus (such as food), becomes elicited also by a new, "conditioned" stimulus (such as a bell).

cognitive Pertaining to basic mental processes of perception, memory, and thought.

cognitive approach The theoretical view that focuses on the ways in which basic processes of perception and cognition affect personality and behavior.

cognitive dissonance The unpleasant feeling that one is holding two conflicting attitudes at the same time. This feeling is held by some theorists to be an important mechanism underlying attitude change.

cohort effect The tendency for a research finding to be limited to one group, or "cohort," of people, such as people all living during a particular era or in a particular location.

collective unconscious In Jung's version of psychoanalysis, the proposition that all people share certain unconscious ideas because of the history of the human species.

compromise formation In modern psychoanalytic thought, the main job of the *ego*, which is to find a compromise among the different structures of the mind and the many different things the individual wants all at the same time. What the individual actually thinks and does is the result of this compromise.

condensation In psychoanalytic theory, the method of primary process thinking in which several ideas are compressed into one.

conscious mind That part of the mind's activities of which one is aware.

construal An individual's particular experience of the world or way of interpreting reality.

construct An idea about a psychological attribute that goes beyond what might be assessed through any particular method of assessment.

constructivism The philosophical view that reality, as a concrete entity, does not exist and that only ideas ("constructions") of reality exist.

construct validation The strategy of establishing the *validity* of a measure by comparing it to a wide range of other measures.

content validity The degree to which an assessment instrument, such as a questionnaire, includes content obviously relevant to what it is intended to predict.

convergent validation The process of assembling diverse pieces of information that converge on a common conclusion.

corpus callosum The thick bundle of nerve fibers connecting the right and left halves of the brain.

correlational method A research technique that establishes the relationship (not necessarily causal) between two variables, traditionally denoted x and y, by measuring both variables in a sample of participants.

correlation coefficient A number between −1 and +1 that reflects the degree to which one variable, traditionally called y, is a linear function of another, traditionally called x. A negative correlation means that as x goes up, y goes down; a positive correlation means that as x goes up, so does y; a zero correlation means that x and y are unrelated.

cortex The outside portion of an organ (see, e.g., *adrenal cortex*). In the context of this book, refers to the outer layers of the brain.

cortisol A collective term for the glucocorticoid *hormones*, which are released into the bloodstream by the *adrenal cortex* as a response to physical or psychological stress.

critical realism The philosophical view that the absence of perfect, infallible criteria for determining the truth does not imply that all interpretations of reality are equally valid; instead, one can use empirical evidence to determine which views of reality are more or less likely to be valid.

cross-cultural psychology Psychological research and theorizing that attempts to account for the psychological differences between and within different cultural groups.

declarative knowledge Information held in memory that is verbalizable; sometimes called "knowing that."

declarative self An individual's (conscious) opinions about his or her own personality traits and other relevant attributes.

deconstructionism A philosophy that argues reality does not exist apart from human perceptions, or "constructions," of it.

defense mechanisms In psychoanalytic theory, the mechanisms of the *ego* that serve to protect an individual from experiencing anxiety produced by conflicts with the *id*, *superego*, or reality.

denial In psychoanalytic theory, the *defense mechanism* that allows the mind to deny that a current source of anxiety exists.

dependent personality disorder An extreme pattern of relying on others to take care of one's needs and make decisions, combined with a bitter kind of agreeableness.

displacement In psychoanalytic theory, the *defense mechanism* that redirects an impulse from a dangerous target to a safe one.

doctrine of opposites In psychoanalytic theory, the idea that everything implies or contains its opposite.

dopamine A *neurotransmitter* in the brain that plays an important role in positive emotions and response to reward.

drive In learning theories, a state of psychological tension, the reduction of which feels good.

duck test If it looks like a duck, sounds like a duck, and acts like a duck, it probably *is* a duck.

effect size A number that reflects the degree to which one variable affects, or is related to, another variable.

efficacy expectation In Bandura's social learning theory, one's belief that one can perform a given goal-directed behavior.

ego In psychoanalytic theory, the relatively rational part of the mind that balances the competing claims of the id, the superego, and reality.

ego control In Jack Block's personality theory, the psychological tendency to inhibit the behavioral expression of motivation and emotional impulse. At the extremes, people may be either undercontrolled or overcontrolled.

ego-dystonic Refers to troubling thoughts, feelings, beliefs, or behaviors that one experiences as alien or foreign, and would like to be rid of.

ego psychology The modern school of psychoanalytic thought that believes the most important aspect of mental functioning is the way the ego mediates between, and formulates compromises among, the impulses of the id and the superego.

ego resiliency In Jack Block's personality theory, the ability to vary one's level of ego control in order to respond appropriately to opportunities and situational circumstances.

ego-syntonic Refers to thoughts, feelings, beliefs, or behaviors that one accepts as part of oneself and does not want to be "cured" of, even if others find them difficult to deal with.

Eigenwelt In Binswanger's phenomenological analysis, the experience of experience itself; the result of introspection.

electroencephalography (EEG) A technique for measuring the brain's electrical activity by placing electrode sensors on the outside of the skull.

emics The locally relevant components of an idea. In *cross-cultural psychology*, aspects of a phenomenon that are specific to a particular culture.

emotional intelligence The ability to perceive emotions accurately in oneself and others and to control and use one's own emotions constructively.

empiricism The idea that everything a person knows comes from experience.

enculturation The process of socialization through which an individual acquires his or her native culture, mainly early in life.

endorphins The body's own pain-killing chemicals, which operate by blocking the transmission of pain messages to the brain.

entity theory In Dweck's theory of motivation, an individual's belief that abilities are fixed and unchangeable.

epigenetics Nongenetic influences on a gene's expression, such as stress, nutrition, and so forth.

epinephrine A *neurotransmitter* in the brain and also a *hormone* that is released by the adrenal gland as part of the body's response to stress. Also called adrenaline.

essential-trait approach The research strategy that attempts to narrow the list of thousands of trait terms into a shorter list of the ones that really matter.

estrogen The female sex *hormone*.

etics The universal components of an idea. In *cross-cultural psychology*, aspects of a phenomenon that all cultures have in common.

eudaimonia Seeking happiness through developing one's full potential, helping others, and building community.

existentialism The approach to philosophy that focuses on conscious experience (phenomenology), free will, the meaning of life, and other basic questions of existence.

expectancy In Rotter's social learning theory, the degree to which an individual believes a behavior will probably attain its goal.

expectancy effect The tendency for someone to become the kind of person others expect him or her to be. Also known as a self-fulfilling prophecy and *behavioral confirmation*.

expectancy value theory Rotter's theory of how the value and perceived attainability of a goal combine to affect the probability of a goal-seeking behavior.

experimental method A research technique that establishes the causal relationship between an independent variable (x) and dependent variable (y) by randomly assigning participants to experimental groups characterized by differing levels of x, and measuring the average behavior (y) that results in each group.

face validity The degree to which an assessment instrument, such as a questionnaire, on its face appears to measure what it is intended to measure. For example, a face-valid measure of sociability might ask about attendance at parties.

factor analysis A statistical technique for finding clusters of related traits, tests, or items.

fixation In psychoanalytic theory, leaving a disproportionate share of one's libido behind at an earlier stage of development.

flow The totally absorbing experience of engaging

in an activity that is valuable for its own sake. In flow, mood is slightly elevated and time seems to pass quickly.

frontal cortex The front part of the *cortex* of the brain. Divided left and right into the two frontal lobes, this part of the brain is associated with cognitive functioning such as planning, foresight, and understanding.

frustration-aggression hypothesis In Dollard and Miller's social learning theory, the hypothesis that frustration automatically creates an impulse toward aggression.

functional analysis In behaviorism, a description of how a behavior is a function of the environment of the person or animal that performs it.

functional magnetic resonance imaging (fMRI) A technique for imaging brain activity by using a powerful magnet to help detect blood flow in the brain.

Funder's First Law Great strengths are usually great weaknesses, and surprisingly often the opposite is true as well.

Funder's Second Law There are no perfect indicators of personality; there are only clues, and clues are always ambiguous.

Funder's Third Law Something beats nothing, two times out of three.

Funder's Fourth Law There are only two kinds of data: Terrible Data and No Data.

Funder's Fifth Law The purpose of education is not to teach facts or even ideas. It is to assemble new *chunks*.

generalizability The degree to which a measurement can be found under diverse circumstances, such as time, context, participant population, and so on. In modern psychometrics, this term includes both *reliability* and *validity*.

genital stage In psychoanalytic theory, the final stage of psychosexual development, in which the physical focus of the libido is on the genitals, with an emphasis on heterosexual relationships. The stage begins at about puberty, but is only fully attained when and if the individual achieves psychological maturity.

goal In learning and cognitive approaches to personality, a desired end state that serves to direct perception, thought, and behavior.

gonads The glands, testes in men and ovaries in women, that (among other effects) produce the sex *hormones testosterone* and *estrogen*, respectively.

habit hierarchy In Dollard and Miller's social learning theory, all of the behaviors an individual might do, ranked in order from most to least probable.

habituation The decrease in response to a stimulus on repeated applications; this is the simplest kind of learning.

hedonia Seeking happiness through the pursuit of pleasure and comfort.

hedonism The idea that people are motivated to seek pleasure and avoid pain.

heritability coefficient A statistic that reflects the percentage of the variance of a trait that is controlled by genetic factors.

hippocampus A complex structure deep within the brain, behind the hypothalamus, that plays an important role in memory processes.

histrionic personality disorder An extreme pattern of attention-getting behavior and shallow but dramatically expressed emotions.

hormone A biological chemical that affects parts of the body some distance from where it is produced.

humanistic psychology The approach to personality that emphasizes aspects of psychology that are distinctly human. Closely related to the *phenomenological approach* and *existentialism*.

hypothalamus A complex structure near the lower center of the brain that has direct connections to many other parts of the brain and is involved in the production of psychologically important *hormones*; thought to be important for mood and motivation.

id In psychoanalytic theory, the repository of the drives, the emotions, and the primitive, unconscious part of the mind that wants everything *now*.

I data Informants' data, or judgments made by knowledgeable informants about general attributes of an individual's personality.

identification In psychoanalytic theory, taking on the values and worldview of another person (e.g., a parent).

incremental theory In Dweck's theory of motivation, an individual's belief that abilities can increase with experience and practice.

intellectualization In psychoanalytic theory, the *defense mechanism* by which thoughts that otherwise would cause anxiety are translated into cool, analytic, nonarousing terms.

interactionism The principle that aspects of personality and of situations work together to determine behavior; neither has an effect by itself, nor is one more important than the other.

interjudge agreement The degree to which two or more people making judgments about the same person provide the same description of that person's personality.

introspection The task of observing one's own mental processes.

judgeability The extent to which an individual's personality can be judged accurately by others.

judgments Data that derive, in the final analysis, from someone using his or her common sense and observations to rate personality or behavior.

L data "Life data," or more-or-less easily verifiable, concrete, real-life outcomes, which are of possible psychological significance.

learned helplessness A belief that nothing one does matters, derived from an experience of random or unpredictable reward and punishment, and theorized to be a basis of depression.

learning In behaviorism, a change in behavior as a result of experience.

learning approach The theoretical view that focuses on how behavior changes as a function of rewards and punishments. Also called *behaviorism*.

lexical hypothesis The idea that, if people find something is important, they will develop a word for it, and therefore the major personality traits will have synonymous terms in many different languages.

libido In psychoanalytic theory, the drive toward the creation, nurturing, and enhancement of life (including but not limited to sex), or the energy stemming from this drive. Also called *psychic energy*.

long-term memory (LTM) The final stage of information processing, in which a nearly unlimited amount of information can be permanently stored in an organized manner; this information may not always be accessible, however, depending on how it was stored and how it is looked for.

magnetoencephalography (MEG) A technique for using delicate magnetic sensors on the outside of the skull to detect brain activity.

many-trait approach The research strategy that focuses on a particular behavior and investigates its correlates with as many different personality traits as possible, in order to explain the basis of the behavior and to illuminate the workings of personality.

masculine protest In Adler's version of psychoanalysis, the idea that a particular urge in adulthood is an attempt to compensate for one's powerlessness felt in childhood.

mate selection What a person looks for in the opposite sex.

mating strategies How individuals handle heterosexual relationships.

measurement error The variation of a number around its true mean due to uncontrolled, essentially random influences. Also called error variance.

mental health According to Freud's definition, the ability to both love and work.

Minnesota Multiphasic Personality Inventory (MMPI) A widely used test derived through the empirical method. Originally designed for the diagnosis of psychopathology, it is used today to measure a wide range of personality attributes.

Mitwelt In Binswanger's phenomenological analysis, social experience, in particular, feelings and thoughts about others and oneself in relation to them.

moderator variable A variable that affects the relationship between two other variables.

narcissistic personality disorder An extreme pattern of arrogant, exploitative behavior combined with a notable lack of empathy.

neocortex The outer layer of the *cortex* of the brain, regarded as uniquely human.

neo-Freudian psychology A general term for the psychoanalytically oriented work of many theorists and researchers who are influenced by Freud's theory.

neuron A cell of the nervous system that receives and transmits information. Also called nerve cell.

neurotransmitters The chemicals that allow one neuron to affect, or communicate with, another.

nirvana In Zen Buddhism, the serene state of selfless being that is the result of having achieved enlightenment.

norepinephrine An important *neurotransmitter* in the brain that is associated with responses to stress. Also called noradrenaline.

objective test A personality test that consists of a list of questions to be answered by the subject as True or False, Yes or No, or along a numeric scale (e.g., 1 to 7).

object relations theory The psychoanalytic study of interpersonal relations, including the unconscious images and feelings associated with the important people ("objects") in a person's life.

observational learning Learning a behavior by watching someone else do it.

obsessive-compulsive personality disorder (OCPD) An extreme pattern of rigidly conscientious behavior, including an anxious and inflexible adherence to rules and rituals, perfectionism, and a stubborn resistance to change.

operant conditioning Skinner's term for the process of learning in which an organism's behavior is shaped by the effect of the behavior on the environment.

oral stage In psychoanalytic theory, the stage of psychosexual development, from birth to about 18 months of age, during which the physical focus of the libido is located in the mouth, lips, and tongue.

organ inferiority In Adler's version of psychoanalysis, the idea that people are motivated to succeed in adulthood in order to compensate for whatever they felt, in childhood, was their weakest aspect.

outgroup homogeneity bias The sociopsychological phenomenon by which members of a group to which one does not belong seem more alike than do members of a group to which one does belong.

oxytocin A *hormone* that may have specific effects in women of emotional attachment and calming.

paranoid personality disorder An extreme pattern of suspicion, hostility, and resentment.

parapraxis An unintentional utterance or action caused by a leakage from the unconscious parts of the mind. Also called "Freudian slip."

passive-aggressive personality disorder Not actually on the current *DSM-IV* list (though slated for further study), this is an extreme pattern of negative behavior that includes sullen and argumentative resistance to ordinary obligations of work and social life.

peripheral nervous system The system of nerves running throughout the body, not including the brain and spinal cord.

persona In Jung's version of psychoanalysis, the social mask one wears in public dealings.

personality An individual's characteristic patterns of thought, emotion, and behavior, together with the psychological mechanisms behind those patterns.

personality development Change in personality over time, including the development of adult personality from its origins in infancy and childhood, and changes in personality over the life span.

personality disorder A pattern of thought, feeling, and behavior that goes beyond the normal range and causes problems for the affected individual or for others. Ten personality disorders are recognized by the *DSM-IV-TR*.

personality processes The mental activities of personality, including perception, thought, motivation, and emotion.

phallic stage In psychoanalytic theory, the stage of psychosexual development from about 4 to 7 years of age in which the physical focus of the libido is the penis (for boys) and its lack (for girls).

phenomenological approach The theoretical view of personality that emphasizes experience, free will, and the meaning of life. Closely related to *humanistic psychology* and *existentialism*.

phenomenology The study of conscious experience. Often, conscious experience itself is referred to as an individual's "phenomenology."

p-**level** In statistical data analysis, the probability that the obtained correlation or difference between experimental conditions would be expected by chance.

positron emission tomography (PET) A technique for creating images of brain activity by injecting a radioactive tracer into the blood and then finding with a scanner where in the brain the blood is being metabolized.

preconscious Thoughts and ideas that temporarily reside just out of consciousness but which can be brought to mind quickly and easily.

predictive validity The degree to which one measure can be used to predict another.

primary drive In learning theories, a drive that is innate to an organism, such as the hunger drive.

primary process thinking In psychoanalytic theory, the term for the strange and primitive style of unconscious thinking manifested by the *id*.

priming Activation of a concept or idea by repeatedly perceiving it or thinking about it. The usual result is that this concept or idea comes to mind more quickly and easily in new situations.

procedural knowledge What a person knows but cannot really talk about. Sometimes called "knowing how."

procedural self Patterns of behavior that are characteristic of an individual.

projection In psychoanalytic theory, the *defense mechanism* of attributing to somebody else a thought or impulse one fears in oneself.

projective test A test that presents a participant with an ambiguous stimulus, such as a picture or inkblot, and asks the person to describe what he or she sees. Some psychologists believe that the answer reveals inner psychological states or motivations of which the participant may be unaware.

prototype An idealized, perfect example of a category; an object is considered a "better" or "worse" member of a category to the extent that it matches this example.

psychic conflict The phenomenon in which one part of the mind is at cross-purposes with another part of the mind.

psychic determinism The assumption that everything psychological has a cause that is, in principle, identifiable.

psychic energy In psychoanalytic theory, the energy that allows the psychological system to function. Also called *libido*.

psychoanalytic approach The theoretical view of personality, based on the writings of Sigmund Freud, that emphasizes the unconscious processes of the mind.

psychological triad The three essential topics of psychology: how people think, how they feel, and how they behave.

psychometrics The technology of psychological measurement.

punishment An aversive consequence that follows an act in order to stop the act and prevent its repetition.

rationalization In psychoanalytic theory, the *defense mechanism* that produces a seemingly logical rationale for an impulse or thought that otherwise would cause anxiety.

reaction formation In psychoanalytic theory, the *defense mechanism* that keeps an anxiety-producing impulse or thought in check by producing its opposite.

reciprocal determinism Bandura's term for the way people affect their environments even while their environments affect them.

regression In psychoanalytic theory, retreating to an earlier, more immature stage of psychosexual development, usually because of stress but sometimes in the service of play and creativity.

reinforcement In operant conditioning, a reward that, when applied following a behavior, increases the frequency of that behavior. In *classical conditioning*, refers to the pairing of an "unconditioned" stimulus (such as food) with a "conditioned" stimulus (such as a bell).

reliability In measurement, the tendency of an instrument to provide the same comparative information on repeated occasions.

repression In psychoanalytic theory, the *defense mechanism* that banishes the past from current awareness.

research Exploration of the unknown; finding out something that nobody knew before one discovered it.

respondent conditioning Skinner's term for *classical conditioning*.

response Anything a person or animal does as a result of a stimulus.

Rorschach test A projective test that asks subjects to interpret blots of ink.

scatter plot A diagram that shows the relationship between two variables by displaying points on a two-dimensional plot. Usually the two variables are denoted x and y, each point represents a pair of scores, and the x variable is plotted on the horizontal axis while the y variable is plotted on the vertical axis.

schizoid personality disorder An extreme pattern of seeming indifference to others and a cold, bland style of behavior.

schizotypal personality disorder An extreme pattern of odd beliefs and behaviors, and of difficulties relating to others.

S data Self-judgments, or ratings that people provide of their own personality attributes or behavior.

secondary drive In learning theories, a drive that is learned through its association with primary drives, and includes drives for love, prestige, money, power, and the avoidance of fear and of humiliation.

secondary process thinking In psychoanalytic theory, the term for rational and conscious processes of ordinary thought.

self-concept A person's knowledge and opinions about himself or herself.

self-efficacy One's beliefs about the degree to which one will be able to accomplish a goal, if one tries.

self-esteem The degree to which a person thinks he or she is good or bad, worthy or unworthy.

self-reference effect The enhancement of *long-term memory* that comes from thinking about how information being memorized relates to the self.

self-schema The cognitive structure hypothesized to contain a person's self-knowledge and to direct self-relevant thought.

self-verification The process by which people try to bring others to treat them in a manner that confirms their self-conceptions.

serotonin A neurotransmitter within the brain that plays an important role in the regulation of emotion and motivation.

short-term memory (STM) The stage of information processing in which the person is consciously aware of a small amount of information (about 7 *chunks*) as long as that information continues to be actively processed.

single-trait approach The research strategy of focusing on one particular trait of interest and learning as much as possible about its behavioral correlates, developmental antecedents, and life consequences.

situationism The belief, held by some psychologists, that behavior is primarily determined by the immediate situation and that personality traits are not very important.

sociality corollary In Kelly's personal construct theory, the principle that understanding another person requires understanding that person's unique view of reality.

somatic marker hypothesis Neurologist Antonio Damasio's idea that the bodily (somatic), emotional component of thought is a necessary part of problem solving and decision making.

Spearman-Brown formula In psychometrics, a mathematical formula that predicts the degree to which the *reliability* of a test can be improved by adding more items.

state A temporary psychological event, such as an emotion, thought, or perception.

stimulus Anything in the environment that impinges on the nervous system. (Plural: stimuli.)

strategy A sequence of activities directed toward a *goal*.

structured interview A clinical interview with a predetermined and consistent list of questions designed to produce objective ratings of *personality disorders*, personality traits, or other psychological attributes.

sublimation In psychoanalytic theory, the *defense mechanism* that turns otherwise dangerous or anxiety-producing impulses toward constructive ends.

superego In psychoanalytic theory, the part of the mind that consists of the conscience and the individual's system of internalized rules of conduct, or "morality."

symbolization In psychoanalytic theory, the process of *primary process thinking* in which one thing stands for another.

synapse The space between two *neurons* across which impulses are carried by *neurotransmitters*.

testosterone The male sex *hormone*.

Thanatos In psychoanalytic theory, another term for the *drive* toward death, destruction, and decay.

Thematic Apperception Test (TAT) A *projective test* that asks subjects to make up stories about pictures.

thrown-ness In Heidegger's existential analysis, the era, location, and situation into which a person happens to be born.

trait A relatively stable and long-lasting attribute of personality.

trait approach The theoretical view of personality that focuses on individual differences in personality and behavior, and the psychological processes behind them.

transference In psychoanalytic theory, the tendency to bring ways of thinking, feeling, and behavior that developed toward one important person into later relationships with different persons.

Type I error In research, the mistake of thinking that one variable has an effect on, or relationship with, another variable, when really it does not.

Type II error In research, the mistake of thinking that one variable does not have an effect on or relationship with another, when really it does.

typological approach The research strategy that focuses on identifying types of individuals. Each type is characterized by a particular pattern of traits.

Umwelt In Binswanger's phenomenological analysis, biological experience: the sensations a person feels of being a live animal.

unconscious (mind) Those areas and processes of the mind of which a person is not aware.

utilitarianism The idea that the best society is the one that creates the most happiness for the largest number of people.

validity The degree to which a measurement actually reflects what it is intended to measure.

NAME INDEX

SUBJECT INDEX

abandonment fear in borderline personality disorder, 719–720

abortion, moral issues in, 535

absenteeism from job, 223

absolute standards, 125–126

Abu Ghraib prison, 138–139, 140

abusive behavior
in Abu Ghraib prison, 138–139
in childhood bullying, 248
genetic factors in, 326
evolutionary theory on, 348–349, 351
humor and jokes on, 427
psychoanalytic theory on, 378
and punishment, 578, 579
in Stanford prison experiment, 137–138

The Accidental Tourist (Tyler), 702

acculturation, 511, 549

accuracy
of informant reports or I data, 39–40
of life outcome or L data, 43
of perceptions on others, 131
of personality judgments, 113, 131, 148, 189–209
based on facial appearance, 192–194, 195
characteristics of judges affecting, 196–198
in constructivism philosophy, 190
convergent validation of, 191
criteria on, 149, 190–191
in critical realism, 190
importance of, 208, 209

moderators of, 196–205, 208–209
on personality traits, 131, 148
quantity of information affecting, 201–203
realistic accuracy model on, 205–207, 209
in self-knowledge, 672–678
situations affecting, 204
by strangers and acquaintances, 201–202
and validity, 183, 191
and reliability of measurements, 68, 69
of self-knowledge, 664, 672–678
improvement of, 677–678
of self-reports or S data, 28–29

achievement
cross-cultural studies of, 518, 533
implicit need for, 158
measurement of need for, 158
as primary motivation, 629

acquaintances, accuracy of personality judgments by
compared to self-knowledge, 673
compared to strangers, 201–202
in personality disorders, 725, 726

acquaintanceship effect in personality judgments, 201–202

actor-observer effect, 675n

Adams, Cecil, 132n

adaptation
evolutionary theory on, 340, 347, 351
to situations, 140

Adler, Alfred, 377, 442–443, 466
case study method of, 80
on inferiority and compensation, 442–443
on social interest, 442

adopted siblings, personality traits in, 326, 359

adrenal hormones, 298, 308, 311, 313

adrenaline (epinephrine), 298, 308, 316

advertising, cross-cultural differences in, 524

affect
forecasting or prediction of, 566
intensity of, 644
need for, 616

Affect Intensity Measure (AIM), 644

afferent nerves, 271

affiliation
cross-cultural studies of, 518
need for, 159, 629
as primary motivation, 629

African Americans, aptitude test results for, 224

age
and consistency of behavior, 117
and delay of gratification, 233–235